EUROPEAN COMMUNITY LAW
AND
THE AUTOMOBILE INDUSTRY

EUROPEAN MONOGRAPHS

Editor-in-Chief Prof. Dr. K.J.M. Mortelmans

1. Lammy Betten (ed.) *The Future of European Social Policy* (second and revised edition 1991).
2. J.M.E. Loman, K.J.M. Mortelmans, H.H.G. Post, J.S. Watson, *Culture and Community Law: Before and after Maastricht* (1992).
3. Prof. Dr. J.A.E. Vervaele, *Fraud against the Community: The Need for European Fraud Legislation* (1992).
4. P. Raworth, *The Legislative Process in the European Community* (1993).
5. J. Stuyck, *Financial and Monetary Integration in the European Economic Community* (1993).
6. J.H.V. Stuyck, A. Vossestein (eds.) *State Entrepreneurship, National Monopolies and European Community Law* (1993).
7. J. Stuyck, A. Looijestijn-Claerie (eds.) *The European Economic Area EC-EFTA* (1994).
8. R.B. Bouterse, *Competition and Integration - What Goals Count?* (1994)
9. R. Barents, *The Agricultural Law of the EC* (1994).
10. Nicholas Emiliou, *The Principle of Proportionality in European Law: A Comparative Study* (1996).
11. Eivind Smith, *National Parliaments as Cornerstones of European Integration* (1996).
12. Jan H. Jans, *European Environmental Law* (1996).
13. Siofra O'Leary, *The Evolving Concept of Community Citizenship: From the Free Movement of Persons to Union Citizenship* (1996).
14. Laurence Gormley (ed.) *Current and Future Perspectives on EC Competition Law* (1997)
15. Simone White, *Protection of the Financial Interests of the European Communities: The Fight against Fraud and Corruption* (1998).
16. Morten P. Broberg, *The European Commission's Jurisdiction to Scrutinise Mergers* (1998).
17. Doris Hildebrand, *The Role of Economic Analysis in the EC Competition Rules* (1998).

European Community Law
and
The Automobile Industry

by

Christoforus Raymundus Albertus Swaak

KLUWER LAW
INTERNATIONAL
THE HAGUE · LONDON · BOSTON

Published by Kluwer Law International
P.O. Box 85889
2508 CN The Hague, The Netherlands

Sold and distributed in the USA and Canada by
Kluwer Law International
675 Massachusetts Avenue
Cambridge, MA 02139, USA

Sold and distributed in all other countries by
Kluwer Law International
Distribution Centre
P.O. Box 322
3300 AH Dordrecht, The Netherlands

Library of Congress Cataloging-in-Publication Data is available from the Library of Congress

Printed on acid-free paper

Cover design: Bert Arts bNO

ISBN 90 411 1140 9

Kluwer Law International incorporates the publishing programmes of Graham & Trotman Ltd, Kluwer Law and Taxation Publishers and Martinus Nijhoff Publishers.

TABLE OF CONTENTS

LIST OF ABBREVIATIONS xv

1. THEORETICAL FRAMEWORK
1.1 States, the Economy and the Industry 1
1.2 The Community, the Economy and the Industry 14
1.3 Subject of the Study 20
1.4 Outline of the Study 25

PART I - THE FACTUAL AND LEGAL CONTEXT OF THE CASE STUDY

2. THE AUTOMOBILE INDUSTRY
2.1 Introduction 29
2.2 The Development Towards Virtual Production 29
2.2.1 Craft Production 29
2.2.2 Mass Production 32
2.2.3 Lean Production 36
2.2.4 Virtual Production 42
2.3 The Development Towards a Real Global Market 45
2.4 The Socio-Economic Importance of the Automobile Industry 52
2.5 The Implications of the Socio-Economic Importance of the Automobile Industry 55
2.6 Concluding Remarks 63

3. THE EC TREATY
3.1 Introduction 65
3.2 The Preamble to the EC Treaty 65
3.3 The Task of the Community 68
3.4 The Means of the Community 70
3.4.1 Common Market 71
3.4.2 Economic and Monetary Union 72
3.4.3 Implementation of the Common Policies or Activities referred to in Articles 3 and 3a EC 75
3.4.3.1 Common Policies or Activities 75
3.4.3.2 Article 3 EC 77

3.4.3.3 Article 3a EC 78

3.5 Article 5 EC 78

3.6 GATT and the WTO Agreement 80

3.6.1 Position of the Member States and the Community under GATT 80

3.6.2 Position of the Member States and the Community under the WTO Agreement 86

3.6.3 The Impact of GATT and the WTO Agreement within the Legal System of the EC Treaty 88

3.6.3.1 Direct Effect 88

3.6.3.2 Indirect Effect 89

3.7 Concluding Remarks 91

PART II - THE CASE STUDY

4. THE ELIMINATION OF OBSTACLES TO INTRA-COMMUNITY TRADE AND THE AUTOMOBILE INDUSTRY

4.1 Introduction 95

4.2 Customs Union 97

4.2.1 Introduction 97

4.2.2 Elimination of Customs Duties and Charges having Equivalent Effect 102

4.2.3 Common Customs Tariff 104

4.3 Elimination of Quantitative Restrictions and Measures having Equivalent Effect 109

4.3.1 Introduction 109

4.3.2 Type Approval for Automobiles, Separate Technical Units, Systems and Components 116

4.3.3 Registration of Automobiles 133

4.3.4 Roadworthiness Tests for Automobiles 135

4.4 Internal Taxation 139

4.4.1 Introduction 139

4.4.2 Neutrality of Internal Taxation 142

4.4.2.1 Levy of Internal Taxation 142

4.4.2.2 Repayment of Internal Taxation 147
4.4.3 Harmonisation of Internal Taxation 147
4.4.3.1 Introductory Remarks 147
4.4.3.2 Indirect Taxation 148
4.4.3.3 Direct Taxation 154
4.5 Intellectual Property Rights 154
4.5.1 Introduction 154
4.5.2 Free Movement of Parts 156
4.5.3 Harmonisation of the Legal Protection of Designs 159
4.6 The Freedom of Establishment and the Free Movement of Capital 164
4.6.1 Introduction 164
4.6.2 Freedom of Establishment 165
4.6.3 Free Movement of Capital 167
4.6.4 1997 Communication on intra-EU investment 168
4.7 Concluding Remarks 170

5. COMMON COMMERCIAL POLICY AND THE AUTOMOBILE INDUSTRY

5.1 Introduction 173
5.2 Export 177
5.2.1 Common Rules on Exports 177
5.2.2 Access to Markets in Third Countries 178
5.3 Import 183
5.3.1 Common Rules on Imports 183
5.3.2 1991 "Consensus" between the Community and Japan . . . 187
5.3.2.1 Elements of Consensus 187
5.3.2.2 Scope 192
5.3.2.3 Legal Status under Community Law 195
5.3.2.4 Legal Status under the WTO Agreement 202
5.4 Concluding Remarks 202

6. UNDISTORTED COMPETITION AND THE AUTOMOBILE INDUSTRY

6.1 Introduction 205

6.2 Competition Policy . . . 205
6.3 Rules on Competition with relevance to the Automobile Industry . . . 210
6.3.1 Restrictive Agreements, Decisions or Practices . . . 210
6.3.2 Abuse of Dominant Position . . . 212
6.3.3 State Aids . . . 212
6.3.4 Merger Control . . . 213
6.4 Concluding Remarks . . . 214

7. DISTRIBUTION AND SERVICING IN THE AUTOMOBILE INDUSTRY
7.1 Introduction . . . 215
7.2 Distribution and Servicing of Automobiles and Spare Parts . . . 215
7.3 Article 85 EC . . . 217
7.3.1 The Early Days . . . 217
7.3.1.1 BMW Germany . . . 218
7.3.1.2 BMW Belgium . . . 222
7.3.1.3Ford . . . 223
7.3.1.4 Peugeot . . . 225
7.3.2 Regulation 123/85 . . . 227
7.3.2.1 Prelude . . . 227
7.3.2.2 Preamble . . . 229
7.3.2.3 The Core of Regulation 123/85 . . . 231
7.3.2.4 Possible Obligations on the Dealer . . . 235
7.3.2.5 Mandatory Obligations on Dealer and Supplier . . . 241
7.3.2.6 No Benefit of Block Exemption . . . 244
7.3.2.7 Legal Effect . . . 245
7.3.2.8 Review of Regulation 123/85 . . . 249
7.3.3 Regulation 1475/95 . . . 251
7.3.3.1 Prelude . . . 251
7.3.3.2 Preamble . . . 258
7.3.3.3 The Core of Regulation 1475/95 . . . 259
7.3.3.4 Possible Obligations on the Dealer . . . 260

7.3.3.5 Mandatory Obligations on Dealer and Supplier . . . 263
7.3.3.6 No Benefit of Exemption . . . 264
7.3.3.7 Legal Effect . . . 268
7.4 Article 86 EC . . . 270
7.4.1 General Remarks . . . 270
7.4.2 Type Approval . . . 271
7.4.3 Intellectual Property Rights . . . 273
7.5 Concluding Remarks . . . 275

8. STATE AID IN THE AUTOMOBILE INDUSTRY
8.1 Introduction . . . 277
8.2 Community Rules on State Aid . . . 278
8.2.1 General Remarks . . . 278
8.2.2 The Concept of State Aid . . . 282
8.2.3 Compatibility of State Aid with the Common Market . . . 285
8.2.3.1 General Rule: Article 92(1) EC . . . 285
8.2.3.2 Automatic Exceptions: Article 92(2) EC . . . 288
8.2.3.3 Other Exceptions: Article 92(3) EC . . . 290
8.2.3.4 Commission's Discretionary Power . . . 296
8.2.4 Review of State Aid . . . 298
8.2.5 Council Regulations . . . 301
8.3 1989 Framework on State Aid to the Motor Vehicle Industry . . . 302
8.3.1 Introductory Remarks . . . 302
8.3.2 Acceptance by Member States . . . 304
8.3.3 Legal Status . . . 308
8.3.4 Scope . . . 309
8.3.5 Notification and Annual Report . . . 311
8.3.6 Categories of Aid . . . 312
8.3.6.1 Introduction . . . 312
8.3.6.2 Rescue and Restructuring Aid . . . 313
8.3.6.3 Regional Aid . . . 316
8.3.6.4 Investment Aid for Innovation, Modernization or Rationalization . . . 320

8.3.6.5 Aid for Research and Development 321
8.3.6.6 Aid for Environmental and Energy Saving 323
8.3.6.7 Aid for Vocational Training linked to Investments 325
8.3.6.8 Operating Aid 326
8.4 1998 Framework for State Aid to the Motor Vehicle Industry 327
8.4.1 Introductory Remarks 327
8.4.2 Extended Scope 329
8.4.3 Notification and Annual Report 330
8.4.4 Monitoring 332
8.4.5 Categories of Aid 332
8.4.5.1 Introduction 332
8.4.5.2 Rescue and Restructuring Aid for Firms in Difficult 333
8.4.5.3 Regional Aid 333
8.4.5.4 Research and Development Aid 338
8.4.5.5 Investment Aid for Innovation 338
8.4.5.6 Aid for Environmental Protection and Energy Saving 339
8.4.5.7 Aid to Vocational Training 339
8.4.5.8 Aid for Modernization and Rationalization 339
8.4.5.9 Operating Aid 339
8.5 Concluding Remarks 340

9. CONCENTRATION AND CO-OPERATION IN THE AUTOMOBILE INDUSTRY
9.1 Introduction 343
9.2 Control of Concentrations with a Community Dimension in the Automobile Industry 346
9.2.1 General Remarks 346
9.2.2 The Scope of the Merger Regulation 347
9.2.3 One-Stop Shop 350
9.2.4 Compatibility with the Common Market 352
9.2.4.1 Appraisal 352

9.2.4.2 Relevant Market 354
9.2.4.3 Compatibility of the Creation or Strengthening of the Dominant Position with the Common Market 363
9.3 Control of Concentrations without a Community Dimension in the Automobile Industry 368
9.3.1 General Remarks 368
9.3.2 National Control 369
9.3.3 Dutch Clause 370
9.3.4 Application of the Principles of Articles 85 and 86 EC on the basis of Article 89 EC to Concentrations 371
9.3.4.1 Article 89 EC 371
9.3.4.2 Principles laid down in Articles 85 and 86 EC 372
9.4 Application of Articles 85 and 86 EC to Certain Cooperations in the Automobile Industry 374
9.4.1 General Remarks 374
9.4.2 Article 85 EC 375
9.4.2.1 Introductory Remarks 375
9.4.2.2 Horizontal Cooperation: Joint Venture "AutoEuropa" 377
9.4.2.3 Vertical Cooperation: ACEA-CLEPA Guidelines 386
9.4.3 Article 86 EC 390
9.4.3.1 Cooperation between Undertakings without a Dominant Position 390
9.4.3.2 Cooperation with an Undertaking in a Dominant Position 391
9.5 Concluding Remarks 392

10. STRENGTHENING OF THE COMPETITIVENESS OF COMMUNITY INDUSTRY AND THE AUTOMOBILE INDUSTRY

10.1 Introduction 395

10.2 Article 130 EC 395
10.3 Strengthening of the Competitiveness of the Automobile Industry 397
10.4 Concluding Remarks 408

11. PROMOTION OF RESEARCH AND TECHNOLOGICAL DEVELOPMENT AND THE AUTOMOBILE INDUSTRY
11.1 Introduction 411
11.2 Articles 130f to 130p EC 411
11.2.1 Objectives 412
11.2.2 Means 415
11.2.3 Report 415
11.3 Promotion of Research and Technological Development in the Automobile Industry 415
11.4 Concluding Remarks 420

12. EDUCATION AND VOCATIONAL TRAINING AND THE AUTOMOBILE INDUSTRY
12.1 Introduction 423
12.2 Articles 123 to 127 EC 423
12.2.1 The European Social Fund 423
12.2.2 Quality Education and Vocational Training 424
12.3 Community Measures on Education and Vocational Training and the Automobile Industry 426
12.4 Concluding Remarks 429

PART III - CONCLUSIONS

13. GENERAL CONCLUSIONS: EUROPEAN COMMUNITY LAW AND THE AUTOMOBILE INDUSTRY 433

SELECTIVE BIBLIOGRAPHY 441
TABLE OF CASES 457

INDEX 465
TRANSPOSITION TABLE - TREATY OF AMSTERDAM 477

LIST OF ABBREVIATIONS

ACEA	Association des Constructeurs Européens d'Automobile
ADAPT	Community initiative on adaptation of the workforce to industrial change
AG	Advocate General
AIT	Alliance Internationale de Tourisme
art.	article
arts.	articles
BCR	Community Bureau of Reference
BEUC	Bureau of European Consumers' Unions
BISD	GATT Basic Instruments and Selected Documents
BRITE	Basic Research in Industrial Technologies for Europe
CCT	Common Customs Tariff
CDE	Cahiers de Droit Européen
CEDEFOP	European Centre for the Development of Vocational Training
CESI	European Confederation of Independent Trade Unions
CFI	Court of First Instance of the European Communities
CLEPA	Comité de Liaison de la Construction d'Equipement et de Pièces d'Automobiles
CML Rev.	Common Market Law Review
COMETT	Community in Education and Training for Technology
Commission	Commission of the European Communities
Council	Council of the European Union
CRAFT	Cooperative Research Action for Technology
Dec	Decision
DG	Directorate General (of the Commission of the European Communities)
Dir	Directive
DRIVE	Dedicated Road Infrastructure for Vehicle safety in Europe
DVBl.	Deutsches Verwaltungsblatt
EAPA	European Automotive Panel Association
EC	European Community
EC Treaty	Treaty establishing the European Community (as

	amended by Title II of the Treaty on European Union)
ECAR	European Campaign for the Freedom of the Automotive Parts and Repair Market
ECE	Economic Commission for Europe (UN)
ECJ	Court of Justice of the European Communities
ECLR	European Competition Law Review
Ecosoc	Economic and Social Committee
ECSC Treaty	Treaty establishing the European Coal and Steel
EEA	European Economic Area
EEC	European Economic Community
EEC Treaty	Treaty establishing the European Economic Community
EEA	European Economic Area
EFTA	European Free Trade Association
ELRev	European Law Review
EMU	Economic and Monetary Union
EP	European Parliament
EPEFE	European Programme on Emissions, Fuels and Engine Technologies
EPL	European Public Law
ESB	Economisch Statistische Berichten
ESPRIT	European Strategic Programme for R&D in Information Technologies
ETSC	European Transport Safety Council
EU	European Union
EU Treaty	Treaty on European Union
EUCAR	European Council for Automotive R&D
EuR	Europarecht
EURAM	European Research in Advanced Materials
EURATEX	European Apparel and Textile Organisation
Euratom Treaty	Treaty establishing a European Atomic Energy Community
EUR-OP	Office for Official Publications of the European Communities
EUROSTAT	Statistical Office of the European Communities

LIST OF ABBREVIATIONS

EUROTECNET	Community action programme in the field of training and technological change
EuZW	Europäische Zeitschrift für Wirtschaftsrecht
FD	Het Financieele Dagblad
FIA	Fédération Internationale de l'Automobile
FORCE	Programme for the development of continuing vocational training
FT	Financial Times
GATT	General Agreement on Tariffs and Trade
HILJ	Harvard International Law Journal
IP	Commission Press Release
JAMA	Japanese Automobile Manufacturers' Association
JOULE	Joint Opportunities for Unconventional or Long-term Energy supply
J.W.T.	Journal of World Trade
LIEI	Legal Issues of European Integration
MERCOSUR	Southern Cone Common Market
NJB	Nederlands Juristenblad
NRC	NRC Handelsblad
NVER	Nederlandse Vereniging voor Europees Recht
OECD	Organisation for Economic Cooperation and Development
OJ	Official Journal
Pb	Publicatieblad
PETRA	Programme for the vocational training of young people and their preparation for adult and working life
QJE	Quarterly Journal of Economics
R.d.C.	Recueil des Cours
RMUE	Revue du Marché Unique Européen
RTD eur.	Revue trimestrielle de droit européen
SEW	Sociaal Economische Wetgeving; Tijdschrift voor Europees en economisch recht
SMMT	Society of Motor Manufacturers and Traders
UNICE	Union of Industrial and Employers' Confederations of Europe

LIST OF ABBREVIATIONS

VAT	Value Added Tax
WTO	World Trade Organization
WTO Agreement	Agreement establishing the World Trade Organization

1. THEORETICAL FRAMEWORK

1.1 States, the Economy and the Industry

The question whether the government of a sovereign state should intervene in the economic process, and if so, to what extent, has been the subject of research and public debate for many years. In this day and age there is little doubt that a government has a role to play. Over time, governments left their *laissez-faire* approach behind and went beyond the traditional "minimal" role that consisted of activities such as the implementation of a foreign policy, national defense, the enforcement of criminal law and the maintenance of a judicial system for the resolution of private law conflicts. This was stimulated by the introduction of universal suffrage and the undesirable consequences, both socially and economically, of the workings of the free market economy in its most extreme form, as manifested during the first and second Industrial Revolutions in so-called "minimal states" such as the United Kingdom and the U.S.A. Governments set out to develop and implement economic policies which led to public intervention in the economic process in an effort to correct market failures and meet social needs. Measures were taken to pursue what were considered to be public interests such as the protection and maintenance of a competitive market,[1] the improvement of health, safety and working conditions of employees[2] and the protection of consumers and the environment.[3]

The extent and degree to which a government ought to intervene in the economic process remains a popular topic of discussion and is closely related to

---

[1] See W.G. Shepherd and C. Wilcox, *Public policies towards business*, 6th edition, 1979, Richard D. Irwin, Homewood, at 84-89, for a short overview of the early history of competition law in the U.K. and the U.S.A.

[2] See P.J. Slot, *Technical and administrative obstacles to trade in the EEC*, 1975, A.W. Sijthoff, Leiden, at 31-32, for a short description of some aspects of the historical development of public intervention to safeguard the health and safety of citizens.

[3] For instance, the American government intervened in the automobile industry by setting standards on safety, emissions and fuel economy for new automobiles. See, for a description and analysis of (the (in)effectiveness of) these standards, R.W. Crandall, H.K. Gruenspecht, T.E. Keeler and L.B. Lave, *Regulating the automobile*, 1986, The Brookings Institution, Washington, D.C.

the (often political) choice for a particular economic system.[4] With the risk of over-simplifying economic reality, one could consider the "liberal" free market economy in which government intervention is minimal and mostly facilitative at one end of the spectrum with the collectivist system in which government intervention leads to the outright regulation of the economy at the other end.[5] Most, if not all states in the Western world find themselves between these two extremes in that after the Great Depression in the 1930's they developed so-called mixed economies which combine elements of a market economy with those of a collectivist system. The role of the government and the emphasis on collectivist measures is in some mixed economies stronger than in others.[6]

In a *free market economy*, the important economic decisions are not made by the government but instead by individuals who freely and separately pursue their own interests on the free market and, led by Adam Smith's invisible hand, promote the wealth of the nation.[7] Prices are set on the market where the market participants, buyers and sellers, meet and compete.[8] This leads, at least in theory, to an efficient allocation of resources. Competition finds itself close

---

[4] See, *inter alia*, *The Economist*, "State and market", 17 February 1996, at 66, and "Why governments should not be salesmen", 1-7 February 1997, at 15-16 and 23-25. See also R. Boyer, "State and market - A new engagement for the twenty-first century?" in *States against markets* (R. Boyer and D. Drache eds.), 1996, Routledge, London, at 84-114; *Marktwerking versus coördinatie*, Koninklijke Vereniging voor de Staatshuishoudkunde, Preadviezen 1996 (A. Nentjes ed.), 1996, Lemma, Utrecht; "The visible hand", *The Economist* (A survey of the world economy), 20 September 1997, at 17-56; R. Boot and A. Schmeits, "Overheidsingrijpen in de industriefinanciering", *ESB* 13-11-1996, at 928, and B. Nooteboom, "Makeling van clusters is een klus voor bedrijven", *ESB* 10-12-1997, at 947.

[5] See in this context W. Eucken, *Die Grundlagen der Nationalökonomie*, 1950, Springer, Berlin.

[6] See in this context E.S. Kirschen, F. Blackaby, L. Csapo, Z. Kamecki and P. Kestens, *Economic policies compared - West and East*, 1974, North-Holland Publishing Company, Amsterdam.

[7] According to A.E. Kahn, *The economics of regulation: Principles and institutions*, 1970, John Wiley & Sons, New York, Volume I, at 1, "[t]he competitive market guides and controls the self-seeking activities of each individual, so that, as Adam Smith stated in 1776, while 'he intends only his own gain, ... he is ... led by an invisible hand to promote an end which was no part of his intention" - that is, to maximize the wealth of the nation'".

[8] D.G. Goyder, *EC Competition Law*, 2nd edition, 1993, Clarendon Press, Oxford, at 8, describes "competition" as "the relationship that exists among any number of undertakings which find themselves selling goods or services of the same kind at the same time to an identifiable group of consumers".

to, if not at the very heart of the free market economy.[9] Goyder points out that according to economists, the presence of competition confers advantages such as

> (a) the part that it has played in allocating resources in the direction preferred by consumers ...; (b) the constant process of dynamic adjustment to the changes in consumer preferences ... and an incentive for producers to invest in research and development and to innovate; (c) the keeping of such producers, and all sellers in the market, under continual pressure to keep costs, and therefore prices, down for fear of losing custom to other sellers ...[10]

There is tension between the functioning of a free market economy and the existence of sovereign states with national boundaries, laws and other forms of public intervention that may form barriers to the efficient allocation of resources. In order to keep these barriers as low as possible, a liberal government tries to limit its policies and activities to the mere maintenance of the framework in which the economic process takes place.

Although in a free market economy the government's economic policy is directed towards the ordening rather than the regulation of the economy, it influences the functioning of the economy. However, as pointed out by Kahn, these influences "however pervasive, are intended to operate essentially at the periphery of the markets affected" and their role is "generally conceived as one of maintaining the institutions within whose framework the free market can continue to function, of enforcing, supplementing, and removing the

---

[9] See, *inter alia*, H.W. de Jong, "Competition and combination in the European market economy" in *Competition in Europe*, Essays in honour of Henk W. de Jong (P. de Wolf ed.), 1991, Kluwer Academic Publishers, Dordrecht, at 265-292; A. van Mourik, "The role of competition policy in a market economy" in *The competition policy of the European Community* (P. Nicolaides and A. van der Klugt eds.), 1994, EIPA, Maastricht, at 1-8, and R. Boyer and D. Drache, "Introduction" in *States against markets*, *supra* note 4, at 3.

[10] Goyder, *supra* note 8, at 9. See R. Whish, *Competition Law*, 3rd edition, 1993, Buttersworth, London, at 1-12, for a concise introduction to the theory of competition.

imperfections of competition - not supplanting it".[11] In a free market economy, goverments tend to limit themselves to dealing with macro-economic stabilization and redistribution of income. The efficient allocation of resources, or micro-economics, is mostly left to the forces of the competitive market which operate within the framework put in place and maintained by the government.[12]

The German economist Röpke, amongst others, was a fervent supporter of the free market economy. According to Röpke, the free market economy with the widest possible separation of the spheres of government and economy led in the second half of the nineteenth-century, the so-called liberal era, to the "depolitisation" of the economic sphere and made it possible "to reduce to a minimum the economic significance of the coexistence of sovereign states with their different legal orders, their frontiers, their systems of administration and separate citizenships".[13] As a result of the separation of the spheres of government and economy, the tension between the functioning of the free market and the existence of sovereign states was eased. Röpke stressed the advantages of the liberal economic system which facilitated in the liberal era an *ordre public international* that equipped international economic relations with the indispensable framework of an "As-If World Government" and, as a result of the separation of the political and economic spheres, reduced at the same time

[11] Kahn, *supra* note 7, at 2. See in a similar sense, *inter alia*, H.-J. Wagener, *Elementen van economische orde*, 1988, Wolters-Noordhoff, Groningen, at 27; A.I. Ogus, *Regulation - Legal form and economic theory*, 1994, Clarendon Press, Oxford, at 2, and De Jong, *Competition in Europe*, *supra* note 9, at 281, who emphasized that "... the market economy needs a framework, laid down in a constitutional charter and warranted by the (state) authorities. It is a dangerous illusion to think that such a framework is superfluous and that the market economy is a self-equilibrating system, producing optimal results".

[12] See in a similar sense T. Padoa-Schioppa and others, *Efficiency, stability, and equity*, 1987, Oxford University Press, Oxford, at 17-20, and basic economic handbooks such as P.A. Samuelson and W.D. Nordhaus, *Economics*, 12th edition, 1985, McGraw-Hill, Singapore, at 47-51, 699-702; R.A. Musgrave and P.B. Musgrave, *Public finance in theory and practice*, 5th edition, 1973, McGraw-Hill, New York, at 4-14, and P.R. Krugman and M. Obstfeld, *International Economics - Theory and Policy*, 3rd edition, 1994, Harper Collins College Publishers, New York, at 278.

[13] W. Röpke, "Economic order and international law" in *R.d.C.* 1954-II, at 224. See in this context also F.A. Hayek, *The road to serfdom*, 1944, University of Chicago Press, Chicago, and W. Eucken, *Grundsätze der Wirtschaftspolitik*, 1952, A. Francke AG. Verlag, Bern.

the dependency of international trade on that same framework.[14]

In a *collectivist system*, on the other hand, the government assumes a regulatory rather than a facilitative role as it intervenes to regulate the economic process by directing market behaviour with the aim of pursuing certain collective or public interest goals.[15] The allocation of resources in the economy is not determined by the forces of the free competitive market but by government regulation directing market behaviour. Political decisions instead of the market mechanism are decisive which leads to the "politisation" of the economic sphere and therefore to the end of the separation of the spheres of government and economy. In a collectivist system, the government's economic policy regulates the economy.[16] Soviet communism was an example of a collectivist system in which the government took a maximum role as it centrally planned the economy and owned the means of production.

Röpke warned against the dangers attached to an evolution from the predominantly liberal economic system with separation of the spheres of government and economy to the "pre-collectivist stage of the modern interventionist and Welfare State which works for a gradual dissolution of the liberal principle of separation".[17] According to Röpke, such an evolution would eventually lead to the complete politisation of the economy in which "the whole

---

[14] Röpke, *ibidem* note 13, at 227.

[15] See in this context, *inter alia*, M. Ellman, *Socialist planning*, 2nd edition, 1989, Cambridge University Press, Cambridge. See P. Hennipman, "Doeleinden en criteria der economische politiek", in *Theorie van de Economische Politiek*, 1962, H.E. Stenfert Kroese N.V., Leiden, for a description and analysis of the possible objectives of economic policy.

[16] According to Ogus, *supra* note 11, at 1, the term "regulation" is not a "term of art" and has acquired "a bewildering variety of meanings". See for literature on regulation, *inter alia*, G. Majone (and others), *Regulating Europe*, 1996, Routledge, London; *International regulatory competition and coordination* (J. McCahery, W.W. Bratton, S. Picciotto and C. Scott eds.), 1996, Clarendon Press, Oxford; Shepherd and Wilcox, *supra* note 1,; H.D. Jarass, "Regulation as an instrument of economic policy" and R.B. Stewart, "Regulation and the crisis of legislation in the United States" in *Law as an instrument of economic policy: Comparative and critical approaches* (T. Daintith ed.), 1988, Walter de Gruyter, Berlin, at 75-133; D.I. Bos, *Marktwerking en regulering*, 1995, Onderzoeksreeks Directie Marktwerking, Ministerie van Economische Zaken, and E.E.C. Van Damme, "Marktwerking en herregulering" in *Markt en wet* (R.A.J. van Gestel and Ph. Eijlander and others, eds.), 1996, W.E.J. Tjeenk Willink, Deventer, at 19-43.

[17] Röpke, *supra* note 13, at 233.

economic process - and not, as in the case of the interventionist Welfare State, only its conditions, its result and the distribution of this result - is being made one of the principal agenda of government, so that it is no longer the price mechanism but the authority which decides what use is to be made of the productive forces of the nation".[18] Röpke made the convincing argument that a trend towards collectivism is detrimental to international integration as a collectivist government is compelled to protect the national system of planning against all external disturbances which escape its control.

Most, if not all, states in Western Europe developed after the Great Depression of the 1930's into *mixed economies* that combine a free market economy with interventionist elements. The "visible hand" of the state became more prominent next to the "invisible hand" of the market mechanism.[19] Under the influence of economists like Schumpeter and Keynes,[20] it became generally accepted for governments to intervene in the economy through an active *economic policy* in order to improve and supplement the market mechanism in an effort to achieve a satisfactory economic order. An economic policy has an impact on all sectors of the national economy and can be considered as the common denominator of all deliberate state measures which intervene in the economy. It includes all purposeful governmental action whose primary objective is the improvement of the economic welfare of the whole population

---

[18] Röpke, *supra* note 13, at 236-237.

[19] See, *inter alia*, E.-J. Mestmäcker, *Die sichtbare Hand des Rechts*, 1978, Nomos Verlagsgesellschaft, Baden-Baden, and Wagener, *supra* note 11, at 29-32. See also "The visible hand", *The Economist* (A survey of the world economy), 20 September 1997, at 17-56.

[20] See, *inter alia*, J.M. Keynes, *The general theory of employment, interest and money*, 1936, Macmillan, London, and J.A. Schumpeter, *Capitalism, Socialism and Democracy*, 2nd edition, 1947, Harper, New York.

for which the government is responsible or of some segment of that population.[21]

The main *objectives* of an economic policy in a mixed economy are macro-economic stabilization, redistribution of income and an efficient allocation of resources.[22] In pursuing macro-economic stabilization, governments promote economic stability in order to keep inflation down, counter unemployment and promote economic growth. This is done through the implementation of policies such as monetary policy, budgetary policy and external exchange rate policy. For the purpose of redistribution of income, governments turn to measures such as progressive tax rates. In pursuit of the socially desirable allocation of resources (the micro-economic side of government policy), governments implement policies such as a competition policy to maintain effective competition and an industrial policy to encourage resources to move into particular sectors that the government views as important to future economic growth.[23] Whereas an economic policy is aimed at improving aggregate economic conditions, an industrial policy is directed towards the promotion of the efficiency of (particular sectors of) the national

---

[21] T. Daintith, "Law as a policy instrument: comparative perspective" in *Law as an instrument of economic policy: Comparative and critical approaches*, *supra* note 16, at 6. See in a similar sense: E.S. Kirschen and others, *Economic Policy in Our Time*, Volume I, 1964, North-Holland Publishing Company, Amsterdam, at 3; Hennipman, *supra* note 15, at 20-26; B. De Gaay Fortman, *Theory of Competition Policy*, 1966, North-Holland Publishing Company, Amsterdam, at 153-154, and P.J. Slot, "Sturing en Economisch Recht" in *Het Schip van Staat* (M.A.P. Bovens and W.J. Witteveen eds.), 1985, W.E.J. Tjeenk Willink, Zwolle, at 125-128.

[22] See Kirschen and others, *ibidem*, at 5-15, and Hennipman, *supra* note 15, at 32-55, for a more detailed classification.

[23] See Krugman and Obstfeld, *supra* note 12, at 278, and I. Harden, "The European Central Bank and the Role of National Central Banks in Economic and Monetary Union", in *Economic and Monetary Union: Implications for National Policy-Makers*, (K. Gretschmann ed.), 1993, Martinus Nijhoff Publishers, Dordrecht, at 150. See G.J. Wijers, *Industriepolitiek*, 1982, H.E. Stenfert Kroese, Leiden, on the development of the industrial policies of the Netherlands and England after World War II. See *Competition policies in Europe* (S. Martin ed.), 1998, North-Holland, Amsterdam, for an overview of the various national competition policies in Europe.

industry which may or may not eventually improve aggregate economic conditions.[24]

An economic policy comprises both ordering and process policies. *Ordering* policies alter the shape of the institutional and organisational framework in which the economic process takes place and tend to result in rule-making that lays down and specifies the competence of the public authorities to use economic instruments and governs the economic relations on the market. An example of an ordering policy is competition policy. *Process* policies, on the other hand, operate within this organisational framework in an effort to steer the economic process itself. Process policies tend to result in flexible measures that allow for adjustment to the ever-changing conditions of the economic process.[25] As pointed out by Kapteyn, the distinction between ordering and process policies runs to a certain extent parallel to that between rule-making and discretionary action.[26]

In an effort to achieve the objectives of these economic ordering or process policies, governments use policy instruments and take measures within

---

[24] In a similar sense: G. Hall, "Introduction", and A.B. Philip, "Europe's industrial policies", in *European industrial policy*, 1986, Croom Helm, London, at 1-20; P.J. Uitermark, "Industriepolitiek in Europa" SEW 6 (1992) June, at 504-508, and E. Nevin, *The economics of Europe*, 1990, St. Martin's Press, New York, at 132. See, however, D.B. Audretsch, *The market and the state*, 1989, Harvester Wheatsheaf, New York, at 10, who emphasizes that "[w]hatever form industrial policies ... take on, they have in common the goal of improving the efficiency of certain industries or sectors. In this sense not only can the 'traditional' and obvious forms of government intervention such as subsidies and tax advantages be viewed as industrial policies, but also antitrust and competition policies, as well as decisions to regulate or deregulate entire industries".

[25] See in this sense De Gaay Fortman, *supra* note 21, at 167-172; P.J.G. Kapteyn, "Outgrowing the Treaty of Rome: From market integration to policy integration" in *Mélanges Fernand Dehousse*, Volume 2, 1979, Fernand Nathan, Paris, at 45-46, and K.J.M. Mortelmans, "Short and long-term policy objectives and the choice of instruments and measures" in *Law as an instrument of economic policy: Comparative and critical approaches*, *supra* note 16, at 296-298.

[26] Kapteyn in *Mélanges Fernand Dehousse*, *supra* note 25, at 46. According to Kapteyn, "[g]overnment intervention in the economic process will mostly be based on the kind of ordering legislation that is confined to the creation of wide discretionary economic powers on behalf of public authorities, to procedural requirements, and to rules supporting the authorities in the exercise of those powers, such as civil or criminal sanctions in the case of violations by private persons of the decisions taken by the authorities".

the framework of a given legal system.[27] The economist Kirschen defines an *economic policy instrument* as something which the government itself can change in order to produce an economic effect. It is the legal or extra-legal means by which the objective is pursued within a given legal system. An instrument may therefore be an economic quantity like an interest rate, or it may be a part of the institutional framework, such as the rules which regulate the behaviour of undertakings.[28] Rule-making has become an important, if not the most important, instrument for governments to achieve objectives in the economic policy field.[29] In general, policy instruments become operational through measures. Kirschen defines a *measure* as the use of a particular instrument at a particular time in order to promote one or more objectives. For instance, the decision to raise an interest rate on a certain day is a measure.[30]

As rule-making became an important instrument for governments to achieve objectives in the economic policy field, the body of *national economic law* grew accordingly.[31] In addition, governments became increasingly protectionist in an effort to shield the domestic market from external disturbances which escaped their control.[32] This surge in protectionism lead to

---

[27] See in this sense Kirschen and others, *supra* note 21, who give an indepth analysis of the definition, interaction and relationship between economic policy aims, objectives, instruments and measures. See also J. Tinbergen, *Economic policy: Principles and design*, 1966, North-Holland Publishing Company, Amsterdam, and K.J.M. Mortelmans, *Ordenend en sturend beleid en economisch publiekrecht*, 1985, Kluwer, Deventer.

[28] Kirschen and others, *supra* note 21, at 15.

[29] See in this sense R. Mayntz, "Political intentions and legal measures: The determinants of policy decisions" in *Law as an instrument of economic policy: Comparative and critical approaches*, *supra* note 16, at 58.

[30] Kirschen and others, *supra* note 21, at 17-18.

[31] It should be emphasized, however, that economic law is not only instrumental or subservient to economic policy ("rechtsinstrumenten") but constitutes legal procedural and substantive quarantees to be adhered to ("rechtswaarborgen") as well. See K. Hellingman and K.J.M. Mortelmans, *Economisch publiekrecht*, 1989, Kluwer, Deventer, at 55.

[32] As pointed out by Ch. Joerges, "European economic law, the nation-state and the Maastricht Treaty" in *Europe after Maastricht - An ever closer Union?* (R. Dehousse ed.), 1994, LBE, München, at 36, "economic policy is bound to define national priorities and objectives. Economic law shares this in-built parochialism".

international negotiations to reduce protectionism and liberalize trade through agreement on rules of *international economic law* regulating the behaviour of governments that affected international economic transactions.[33] As pointed out by Blokker, "[t]he emergence of international economic law and international economic organizations can be considered ..., as an attempt to pursue an optimal allocation of the factors of production in an era of considerable government interference in the economy".[34]

Over the years, the instruments of protectionism changed and became more sophisticated[35] and so did the rules of international economic law promoting free trade. The role of rule-making as an instrument to counter protectionism and liberalize trade and thereby facilitate the economic process remains of utmost importance. One only has to compare the variety of the subjects covered by GATT and those dealt with in the WTO Agreement, to find evidence of the fact that the role of international economic law in providing a legal framework that facilitates trade, has grown considerably. In addition, various forms of regional economic integration such as the European Union, NAFTA, Mercosur and the Andean Group, became popular as a manner to remove both legal and extra-legal barriers to trade and to harmonize some areas of legislation in order to bring about regional integration which facilitates the functioning of the economic process.[36] These forms of regional economic integration are based on legal instruments of international economic law such as treaties.

---

[33] See on elaborate definitions of "international economic law", *inter alia*, Hellingman and Mortelmans, *supra* note 31, at 113-118; I. Seidl-Hohenveldern, *International economic law*, 1989, Martinus Nijhoff Publishers, Dordrecht, at 1-3 and D. Carreau, T. Flory and P. Juillard, *Manuel-Droit International Economique*, 3rd edition, 1990 Librairie Générale de droit et de jurisprudence Paris, at 45-46.

[34] N.M. Blokker, *International regulation of world trade in textiles*, 1989, Martinus Nijhoff Publishers, Dordrecht, at 29.

[35] For instance, subsidies and voluntary export restraints became popular instruments to protect domestic markets.

[36] See *World Investment Report 1994 - Transnational corporations, employment and the workplace*, UNCTAD, 1994, UN, New York, at 117-160, for a description and analysis of this development. See for an overview: P. Demaret, J.-F. Bellis and G.G. Jimenez, *Regionalism and multilateralism after the Uruguay Round*, 1997, EIP, Brussels. See also *FT*, "The World trade system at 50" (Survey), 18 May 1998.

After the implosion of the Soviet Union, the American model of what has been called "ruthlessly efficient capitalism" has been heralded "as the only road to success in an increasingly unforgiving global economy".[37] The interventionist elements in the mixed economies in Western Europe came under growing pressure from the forces of the market mechanism. Privatisations, deregulation and the ongoing removal of trade barriers lead to freer markets.[38] Technological developments make it feasible and relatively inexpensive for corporations to operate across national frontiers, foreign direct investment is growing and countries have to compete to attract industry. The costs of international trade decrease and multi-national corporations (have) acquire(d) a pivotal role in the world economy and continue to multiply.[39]

Nevertheless, national governments continue to play an important role in the operation of the market.[40] France is a good example of a mixed economy which continues to combine a market economy with strong interventionist elements such as an active economic policy which includes an industrial policy directed towards the needs of the domestic industry. The French government, according to Nevin, "[a]t the time of the drafting of the [EEC-] Treaty (and

---

[37] F. Hiatt, "Japanese Failure? No, Continued Success Looks More Likely", *International Herald Tribune*, 10 April 1997, at 8.

[38] Even France with its strong interventionist tradition, has made efforts to privatize and deregulate markets. See *FT*, "Privatisation issue comes to haunt the centre-right", 21 May 1997, at 4, for a concise overview of French companies on the 1993 privatisation list. It has been reported, however, that since the socialist Jospin took over from Juppé, further privatisations in France are in doubt. See, *inter alia*, *FT*, "Companies uneasy as Jospin victory casts pall over privatisation plans", 3 June 1997, at 2; "Jospin sets puzzle on privatisation", 14 July 1997, at 2, and "Chirac warning on hindering industry", 15 July 1997, at 1.

[39] *FT*, "New rivals rush to join the fray", 3 October 1997, at 10. It has been reported in "Banner day for Europe Inc.'s merger madness", *International Herald Tribune*, 14 October 1997, at 1, that according to bankers and executives "[i]ncreasing global competition combined with regulatory and technological developments put a tremendous premium on sheer corporate scale in a wide range of industries" and "[p]rovided they maintain a sharp industrial focus, big companies have the wherewithal to penetrate new markets and invest in new technology while enjoying economies of scale". See also *FT*, "Markets surge on corporate deals", 14 October 1997, at 1.

[40] See in this sense P. Dicken, *Global shift*, 2nd edition, 1992, PCP, London, at 148-188. According to "The visible hand", *The Economist* (A survey of the world economy), 20 September 1997, at 17-56, government in the advanced industrial economies has done nothing but grow if one looks at the share of national income spent by government.

indeed since) ... was inclined towards the concept of *l'economie concertée* - the need for government to guide and influence the development of industry, if not to centrally plan it in a socialist sense".[41] It is in line with this interventionist tradition that the French government induced the 1975 merger between the private companies Peugeot and Citroën and suggested in 1997 to regroup French and European automotive groups in order to face up to foreign competition. According to the French Prime Minister at the time, Juppé, it was up to the public authorities to consider which groups were essential to safeguard the European automobile industry.[42] There are indications that other Member States like Germany and Spain have followed the French example and have activated their national industrial policy in an effort to meet the needs of their domestic automobile industry.[43]

But as a result of the further internationalisation, and probably even globalisation, of economic activity and the growing role of the market mechanism, the ability of national governments to directly influence the domestic economy through the implementation of a national economic policy has

---

[41] See Nevin, *supra* note 24, at 133; Hall, *supra* note 24, "Introduction", and Dicken, *Global shift*, *ibidem* note 40, at 162-163.

[42] See "Mr Juppé asks French and European manufacturers to reflect upon possible regrouping in order to remain competitive", *Agence Europe*, 27 March 1997, at 14. See also *FT*, "When two is a crowd", 8 July 1997, at 13.

[43] With regard to *Germany*, *FT*, "Row clouds German car summit", 12-13 August 1995, at 2, and *International Herald Tribune*, "German carmakers cut a deal", 12-13 August 1995, at 9, reported on a summit between leading German politicians and German car industry chiefs (aimed at breathing new life into the German car sector) which lead to a deal under which the employers agreed to maintain certain levels of employment in Germany in return for "a clear political framework without further burdens on the car industry and motorists". With regard to *Spain*, P. Schwartz, "Spain's forgotten goal", *FT*, 15 August 1995, at 10, reported that Spain is evolving a new industrial policy with "[t]he intention ... to set up French-style partnerships between the state and the large national banks, to stop foreigners from controlling the economy". Incidents such as Suzuki's attempt to close down the loss-making car factory in Linares seem to have stimulated the Spanish government to develop a "Spanish hard-core" industrial strategy which prefers "the Frenchified policy of creating a core of tame Spanish shareholders within each basic industry".

come under pressure.[44] It has become more difficult for national governments to effectively intervene in their domestic economy by means of purely national legal and extra-legal policy instruments such as national economic law. Streeck pointed out that

> [i]n so far as the public power that served in the past to domesticate modern capitalism was vested in the sovereignty of national states, economic internationalization without corresponding internationalization of state soveignty results in *an integrated economy governed by fragmented sovereignty*. To the extent that this weakens the hold of politics over markets, the question poses itself whether state-like governance mechanisms can be devised above the nation-state that are capable of mobilizing the same kind of public power *vis-à-vis* the economy as was traditionally mobilized at the national level.[45]

[44] Several books have been written on the regionalisation, internationalisation or globalisation of economic activity. See, *inter alia*, R.B. Reich, *The work of nations*, 1991, Alfred A. Knopf, New York; J.M. Stopford, S. Strange and J.S. Henley, *Rival states, rival firms*, 1991, Cambridge University Press, Cambridge; B.R. Barber, *Jihad vs. McWorld*, 1995, Times Books, New York; R.J. Barnet and J. Cavanagh, *Global dreams: Imperial corporations and the new world order*, 1994, Simon & Schuster, New York; E.M. Graham, *Global corporations and national governments*, 1996, Institute for International Economics, Washington DC; J.-E. Nilsson, P. Dicken and J. Peck (eds.), *The internationalization process*, 1996, PCP, London; *States against markets*, *supra* note 4; Dicken, *Global shift*, *supra* note 40, and Demaret, Bellis and Jimenez, *supra* note 36.

[45] W. Streeck, "Public power beyond the nation-state - The case of the European Community" in *States against markets*, *supra* note 4, at 300-301. According to Streeck, "national governments refrain from imposing obligations on market participants, ..., either because of a general belief in the merits of withdrawal of public power from the market, or because international treaties and factual conditions have already *de facto* limited public intervention to the creation of incentives and the removal of deterrents for mobile investors. ... As both factual and international-legal constraints on national intervention in the economy become more stringent, national governments, ..., become dependent on the *voluntarism of the market-place*, having lost recourse to the 'hard law' that used to be the main tool of state interventionism in the past" (at 311).

In short, the role and impact of national economic law has changed and diminished and it seems up to international economic law to provide for a framework in which the internationalisation or even globalisation of economic activity can take place.[46]

1.2 The Community, the Economy and the Industry

There are strong indications that the EC Treaty provides for a Community based upon a *mixed economy* which combines a free market economy with (the legal basis for) a great variety of Community interventions.[47] Looking at the Community's task set out in Article 2 EC, and in particular the recognition of the limits to economic growth and its qualitative aspects, characterisations such

---

[46] See, for instance, the WTO Agreement, the discussions on the OECD Multilateral Investment Agreement, the call for a social dimension to globalisation and the proposals for global competition rules. For instance, see the Report of the Group of Experts "Competition policy in the new trade order: Strengthening international cooperation and rules", July 1995, European Commission, D.-G. IV/Competition; IP/96/523; *Agence Europe*, "Commission launches initiative aimed at setting international framework for competition rules within WTO", 20 June 1996, at 10; *FT*, "WTO urged to act on competition rules", 25 July 1997, at 4; "Group to bolster global anti-trust links", 25 November 1997, at 7; "Van Miert seeks global competition rules accord", 31 January-1 February 1998, at 4; "Clinton to hear union fears on globalisation", 9 June 1997, at 4; "Who's afraid of globalisation?", 8 January 1998, at 11; "No monopoly on antitrust" and "On the case of the big boys", 13 February 1998, at 22 and 23, and "Karel van Miert proposes the launch in 1999 of negotiations for a multilateral agreement on competition rules in trade", 23 April 1998, at 7. See also *Agence Europe*, "OECD ministers take six months for reflection before resuming negotiations on the multilateral agreement on investment", 29 April 1998, at 14; "Final communique of the OECD ministerial session and statement on multilateral agreement on investment (MAI)" (Europe Documents), 6 May 1998, and Written Question 3684/97 (Watts), OJ 1998, C174/98.

[47] See for both an elaborate analysis of the convincing arguments which lead to this conclusion and a reference to (mostly German) literature: R.-O. Schwemer, *Die Binding des Gemeinschaftsgesetzgebers an die Grundfreiheiten* (Schriften zum internationalen und zum öffentlichen Recht), 1995, Peter Lang, Frankfurt am Main. P. VerLoren van Themaat agrees with Schwemer's conclusion in his bookreview, 33 CML Rev. at 1089-1094. See in this context also W. Sauter, *Competition law and industrial policy in the EU*, 1997, Clarendon Press, Oxford, at 26-39; J. Mertens de Wilmars, "De economische opvattingen in de rechtspraak van het Hof van Justitie van de Europese Gemeenschappen", and G. Schrans, "The instrumentality and the morality of European economic law", *Miscellanea W.J. Ganshof van der Meersch*, Volume II, 1972, Bruylant, Brussels, at 287-306 and 402, and Kapteyn in *Mélanges Fernand Dehousse*, *supra* note 25, at 48.

as "market economics with a human face"[48] and "social market economy"[49] come to mind.[50] The text of the EC Treaty itself indicates that the Community is mainly *market-oriented*; the forces of the market mechanism (have to) play a central role in the economic process.[51] Some of these indications can be found amongst the "Principles" in Part One of the EC Treaty. For instance, the most explicit indication can be found in Article 3a EC which prescribes that economic and monetary policy has to be conducted in accordance with the principle of an open market economy with free competition. This obligation is repeated in Articles 102a and 105(1) EC which prescribe that the principle of an open market economy with free competition, favouring an efficient allocation of resources, has to be respected. Another indication can be found in Article 3(g) EC which provides that, for the purposes set out in Article 2 EC, the activities of the Community shall include a system ensuring that competition in the common market is not distorted. Keeping in mind that competition is close to, if not at the very heart of a market economy, it is important to emphasize that the ECJ held in *Metro I* that Articles 3 and 85 EC imply "the existence on the market of workable competition, that is to say the degree of competition necessary to ensure the observance of the basic requirements and the attainment of the objectives of the Treaty, in particular the creation of a single market achieving conditions similar to those of a domestic market".[52] References in the EC Treaty to open and competitive markets can for instance be found in Article

---

[48] R. Lane, "New Community competences under the Maastricht Treaty", 30 CML Rev. at 943.

[49] P. Buigues, A. Jacquemin and A. Sapir, "Introduction: Complementarities and conflicts in EC microeconomic policies", in *European policies on competition, trade and industry* (P. Buigues, A. Jacquemin and A. Sapir eds.), 1995, Edward Elgar, Aldershot, at xv.

[50] The Treaty of Amsterdam seems to further contribute to this "human face" by adding references to employment in several provisions and introducing a new title on employment in the EC Treaty.

[51] In this context, it is interesting to note that at the Summit of Copenhagen (June 1993), the European Council formulated as one of the conditions for membership of the European Union the existence of "a functioning market economy". See "Agenda 2000 - For a stronger and wider Union" (Volume I), COM(97) 2000 final, 15 July 1997, at 45.

[52] Case 26/76, *Metro SB-Grossmärkte* v *Commission (Metro I)*, [1977] ECR 1905, par. 20. See also Case 240/83, *Procureur de la République* v *Association de défense des brûleurs d'huiles usagées (ADBHU)*, [1985] ECR 531, and Case 229/83, *Association des Centres distributeurs E. Leclerc and others/Sàrl 'Au blé vert' and others*, [1985] ECR 1.

129b EC ("Trans-European Networks") and Article 130(1) EC ("Competitiveness of the Industry").[53]

Nevertheless, the EC Treaty provides the Community with the opportunity and competence to *intervene* in the economic process and (re)direct the free market forces in pursuit of the objectives set out in Article 2 EC.[54] The policies and activities listed in Article 3 EC give an impression of the manner in which the Community can have a direct impact on the functioning of the economy. For instance, the Community is competent to develop and implement a common commercial policy (Article 3(b) EC), a policy in the sphere of agriculture and fisheries (Article 3(e) EC), transport (Article 3(f) EC), competition (Article 3(g) EC), the strengthening of economic and social cohesion (Article 3(j) EC), environment (Article 3(k) EC), the strengthening of the Community industry's competitiveness (Articles 3(l) EC), promoting research and technological development (Article 3(m) EC), encouragement for the establishment and development of trans-European networks (Article 3(n) EC) and a policy contributing to education and training of quality (Article 3(p) EC).[55] Although some policies and activities provide the Community with more competences to intervene in the economic process than others, it is fair to conclude that in general the text of the EC Treaty keeps the door open for Community intervention in the economy.

VerLoren van Themaat is of the opinion that even after the entry into force of the Treaty of Maastricht, it follows from Articles 2, 3 and 3a EC and the third part of the Treaty that it is for the greater part up to the *political* organs, the European Council and the Community institutions, to determine the importance of the use of public measures that direct the functioning of the

---

[53] According to W. Devroe, "Privatizations and Community law: Neutrality versus policy", 34 CML Rev. at 299-300, "the principle of an open market economy with free competition, favouring an efficient allocation of sources" can be seen as "macroeconomic leitmotiv" indicating "*which* coherent macroeconomic policy should be pursued" by the Community.

[54] See Chapter 3, sections 3.2 to 3.4. As pointed out by Schrans in *Miscellanea W.J. Ganshof van der Meersch*, *supra* note 47, at 385-404, the Community legal order is used as an instrument to achieve the objectives set out in the EC Treaty.

[55] Upon the coming into force of the Treaty of Amsterdam, Article 3 EC will also include "the promotion of coordination between employment policies of the Member States with a view to enhancing their effectiveness by developing a coordinated strategy for employment".

economy. According to VerLoren van Themaat, these public measures can very well be substantially strengthened as long as they are to the benefit of the realization of the objectives set out in Article 2 EC, provided that the unity of the common market and sufficient effective competition are maintained. VerLoren van Themaat recognizes that pursuant to Article 3a EC (general) economic and monetary policy has to be conducted in accordance with the principle of an open market economy with free competition. According to VerLoren van Themaat, the extent to which measures directing the economy within the Community will be used, depends in practice on the efficiency of the composition, competence and (working-)methods of the Community institutions and will be further affected by Article 3b EC which prescribes subsidiarity and proportionality.[56]

The *manner* and the *extent* to which the Community intervenes in the economy within the legal system of the EC Treaty is to a large extent reflected in the implementation by the Community of the policies and activities referred to in Articles 3 and 3a EC. In general, Community intervention in pursuit of the objectives set out in Article 2 EC, is focused on the elimination of obstacles to trade between the Member States. This is done through the implementation of the free movement of goods, services and capital, the freedom of establishment and the competition rules ("negative" or "market" integration) and the coordination of national policies and the development and implementation of Community policies on a wide variety of subjects including the strengthening of the competitiveness of Community industry, the promotion of research and technological development and the contribution to education and training of quality ("positive" or "policy" integration).[57] Notwithstanding the fact that by

---

[56] See P. VerLoren van Themaat in P.J.G. Kapteyn and P. VerLoren van Themaat, *Inleiding tot het recht van de Europese Gemeenschappen - Na Maastricht*, 5th edition, 1995, Kluwer, Deventer, at 84-87.

[57] See J. Tinbergen, *International economic integration*, 2nd revised edition, 1965, Elsevier Publishing Company, Amsterdam, at 76-80; Schrans in *Miscellanea W.J. Ganshof van der Meersch*, *supra* note 47, at 387-401, and P.J.G. Kapteyn and P. VerLoren van Themaat, *Introduction to the law of the European Communities* (L.W. Gormley ed.), 2nd edition, 1989, Kluwer Law and Taxation Publishers, Deventer, at 587. See also N. Bernard, "The future of European economic law in the light of the principle of subsidiarity", 33 CML Rev. at 633-666. Mortelmans, *Ordenend en sturend beleid en economisch publiekrecht*, *supra* note 27, at 7-8, and Kapteyn, *Mélanges Fernand Dehousse*, *supra* note 25, at 45-54, relate negative integration to ordering policy and positive integration to process policy.

taking legal and extra-legal measures in the context of the policies and activities referred to in Articles 3 and 3a EC, the Community does not in principle supplant the market mechanism,[58] it influences the functioning of the economy to the extent that it creates and specifies the framework in which the economic process has to take place.[59] Together, the provisions of the EC Treaty and the various Community measures taken within the legal system of the EC Treaty make up the Community legal framework in which the economic process has to take place.

Industry has to operate within this legal framework as, with a few exceptions such as agriculture and transport, the policies and activities referred to in Articles 3 and 3a EC are not limited to nor focused on one particular sector.[60] In principle, the policy with regard to industry is based on Articles 3(l) and 130 EC. However, the explicit reference to "the strengthening of the competitiveness of Community industry" in Article 3(1) EC, seems to express the specific objective which the EC Treaty assigns to this particular policy.[61] In theory, the scope of the Community's activities under Articles 3(1) and 130 EC

---

[58] As pointed out by R. Barents in *Inleiding tot het recht van de Europese Gemeenschappen - Na Maastricht*, *supra* note 56, at 663, the Community only directs market behaviour when difficulties arise in the supply of certain products (Article 103a EC) and through the use of Structural Funds (Articles 130a to 130e EC). See in this context also G. Majone, "The European Community as a regulatory state" in *Collected courses of the Academy of European Law*, Volume V, Book I, 1994, Martinus Nijhoff Publishers, The Hague, at 321-419.

[59] De Jong emphasized in *Competition in Europe*, *supra* note 9, at 281, that "the market economy needs a framework, laid down in a constitutional charter and warranted by the (state) authorities" and adds that "[i]n the European Community, such a constitution is provided for by the Treaty, and the Commission, the Court of Justice, and the national states have an obligation to enforce its principles and the articles expressing these. Amongst others, these principles comprise stable money, free competition, ... Within our field, that entails the need for a competition policy, ... It also means the establishment of a regulatory network of rules meant to enforce the basic principles".

[60] See in this sense Barents, *supra* note 58, at 663. Barents emphasizes the negative effects of the implementation of the policies with regard to these sectors on both national and Community level.

[61] See in this sense, *inter alia*, J. Bourgeois and P. Demaret, "The working of EC policies on competition, industry and trade: a legal analysis" in *European policies on competition, trade and industry*, *supra* note 49, at 67.

is limited to the strengthening of the competitiveness of the industry.[62] The EC Treaty does not provide for a specific legal basis for a Community industrial policy as such.[63] It has been reported that this was the result of a difference of opinion between France and Germany on the extent to which a government can intervene in the economic process. As discussed above, France has a tradition in which the government actively intervenes in the operation of its industry, whereas the German tradition (at least at the time) placed more reliance on the forces of the competitive market.[64]

In reality, the Community's industrial policy can be considered a collection of the various measures directed towards and intended to effect in some way the industry, within the wider context of other Community policies and activities with a legal basis in the EC Treaty. The policy on industry's competitiveness is one of these policies and activies and can be seen as an important attempt to address the maximization of the benefits of other common policies such as the promotion of research and technological development and a contribution to education and training.[65] Policies and activities which generally touch all sectors of the economy like macroeconomic growth, unemployment,

---

[62] See Chapter 10. As pointed out by the Commission in its Communication to the Council, to the European Parliament, Economic and Social Committee and the Committee of the Regions "An industrial competitiveness policy for the European Union", COM(94)319 final, 14 September 1994, at 10-11, the Treaty on European Union introduced "the legal bases for implementing the industrial policy which, in line with the subsidiarity principle, is defined as a general obligation shared between the Community and the Member States for "the strengthening of the competitiveness of Community industry" (Article 3 of the Treaty) and to "ensure that the conditions necessary for the competitiveness of the Community's industry exist" (Article 130(1))".

[63] But some argue that an industrial policy could be based on open-ended provisions like Article 235 EC. See, for instance, Philip, *supra* note 24, at 3.

[64] Nevin, *supra* note 24, at 133, and Philip, *supra* note 24, at 11. See *Big business and the state* (R. Vernon ed.), 1974, MacMillan, London, at 45-141, for a description of (industrial) public policies in Italy (R. Prodi), Germany (G.H. Küster), United Kingdom (T. Smith), France (C.-A. Michalet) and Sweden (G. Ohlin). See *The European Union and national industrial policy* (H. Kassim and A. Menon eds.), 1996, Routledge, London, for an examination of the impact of European Union action on the industrial policies of the Member States. See also in this context *Industrial policy in the European Community: A necessary response to economic integration?* (P. Nicolaides ed.), 1993, Martinus Nijhoff Publishers, Dordrecht.

[65] See Lane, *supra* note 48, at 966. See Sauter, *supra* note 47, at 57-108, for a concise overview of the emergence of an industrial policy on Community level.

inflation and the like, are not included in this definition, as an industrial policy is primarily implemented to promote the efficiency of (particular sectors of) industry which may or may not eventually improve aggregate economic conditions.[66] This definition of the Community's industrial policy includes a great variety of policies and activities.[67]

1.3 Subject of the Study

In this study, an effort will be made to identify the manner and extent to which the Community intervenes in the automobile industry by implementing certain policies and activities referred to in Articles 3 and 3a EC. The focus will be on those provisions of the EC Treaty and the multiple Community legal measures that constitute the legal framework in which the automobile industry has to operate. This identification will be accomplished through a description and analysis of the substantive measures taken by the Community within the context of a selection of policies and activities referred to in Articles 3 and 3a EC with regard to the automobile industry. In other words, an effort is made to put the numerous pieces together. For the purpose of this study, the automobile industry is defined as the production of and trade in automobiles being motor vehicles for the carriage of passengers, intended for use on public roads and having at least four road wheels. Motor-cycles, trucks and automobiles for the carriage of ten

---

[66] See in a similar sense, *inter alia*, Hall, *supra* note 24, "Introduction"; Uitermark, *supra* note 24, at 504-508; Nevin, *supra* note 24, at 132, and Audretsch, *supra* note 24, at 10.

[67] See in this sense the Commission's first attempt to define an industrial policy, "Memorandum on Industrial Policy" to the Council of Ministers ("Colonna Report"), March 1970. See for a mostly historical overview Philip, *supra* note 24, at 1-20. See also Communication of the Commission to the Council and to the European Parliament "Industrial policy in an open and competitive environment - Guidelines for a Community approach", COM(90)556 final, 16 November 1990. In "Speech by Sir Leon Brittan at the European Parliament conference on the future of car industry in Europe - Brussels, 5 December 1991: "The Single market for cars", Brittan qualified "the creation of a sound competitive environment in Europe, and a genuine Single Market" as "the most far-reaching and adventurous industrial policy of all".

or more persons, including the driver, are excluded from the definition.[68] The terms "car", "vehicle" and "motor vehicle" will be used as synonyms of the term "automobile".

It would have been too ambitious, if not presumptuous, to set out on a mission to describe and examine all the features of the development, implementation and interaction of the Community policies and activities referred to in Articles 3 and 3a EC, that are in any way part of the Community framework in which the automobile industry has to operate. The scope of this study has therefore been restricted to the substantive provisions of the EC Treaty relevant to, and the substantive legal measures taken within the context of, (i) the elimination of obstacles to intra-Community trade (Article 3(a) and (c) EC), (ii) common commercial policy (Article 3(b) EC), and (iii) a system ensuring that competition is not distorted (Article 3(g) EC). The relevant measures taken within the sphere of the environment (Article 3(k) EC) will mainly be touched upon within the context of the elimination of obstacles to intra-Community trade in general, and the Community type approval procedure in particular. In addition, an impression will be given of the various policy measures taken with regard to the automobile industry within the context of, (i) the strengthening of the competitiveness of Community industry (Article 3(l) EC), (ii) the promotion of research and technological development (Article 3(m) EC) and (iii) a contribution to education and training of quality (Article 3(p) EC). As this delimitation is still not specific enough (entire books can be written on each of these policies and activities), the focus will be on those measures which are industry-specific and have a particular relevance to the automobile industry.

There are several reasons why the automobile industry was chosen for this study. *First* of all, the automobile industry is one of the most important industries in the Community. Its significance for the socio-economic well-being of the Community and the Member States is beyond any doubt. This gives

---

[68] See in this context Article 1 of Commission Regulation 1475/95 of 28 June 1995 on the application of Article 85(3) of the Treaty to certain categories of motor vehicle distribution and servicing agreements, OJ 1995, L145/25, and in particular the definition of Category M1 in Annex II of Council Directive 70/156 of 6 February 1970, on the approximation of the laws of the Member States relating to the type-approval of motor vehicles and their trailers, as amended by Council Directive 92/53 of 18 June 1992, OJ 1992, L225/1.

public authorities like the Community and the Member States a vested interest in the workings of the automobile industry.[69]

Secondly, it is an industry that is going through a sweeping restructuring and rationalization process which has been further accelerated by the succesful entry of mostly Japanese and Korean manufacturers on the global market for automobiles and their spare parts.[70] This process, which is closely related to the globalisation of the automobile industry, presents the Community and the Member States with the question of their respective roles in adapting the framework in which this important industry has to operate.[71] The interests of the main actors in the automobile industry vary and lead to both political and legal conflicts. There are even conflicts within and between Community institutions on the formulation and implementation of policies and activities. This makes the automobile industry of great interest to those who study the development, implementation and interaction of the Community policies and activities referred to in Articles 3 and 3a EC. The automobile industry provides for an interesting and relatively "unexploited territory" for legal research. One of the reasons for this may well be the remarkable lack of transparency of the workings of the automobile industry and the manner in which the Community deals with this industry. As it is difficult to lay hands on detailed information on the automobile industry, much of the factual information contained in this study is based on newspaper reports and statistics.

---

[69] See Chapter 2, sections 2.4 and 2.5.

[70] See Chapter 2. P. Dicken, "Europe 1992 and strategic change in the international automobile industry", *Environment and Planning A*, 1992, Volume 24, at 30, summarized in 1991 that the European automobile industry was in the process of immense change under the influence of "the Single European Market" but more importantly "the intensifying competitive pressures being exerted primarily by the Japanese manufacturers" which "is intensified by the revolutionary developments which are occurring in the technology and the organisation of automobile production".

[71] R. Vernon, "Enterprise and government in Western Europe" in *Big business and the state*, *supra* note 64, at 23, points out that "the time may well have passed when policies can any longer be made effectively at the European level without taking into account Europe's deep interdependencies with other parts of the world. The problem of interdependency is particularly evident in the mature oligopolistic industries. Any European regime that seeks to influence the competitive behavior of those industries ... will have to take into account the extensive entanglements of European firms with leaders headquartered outside of Europe. The costs and benefits of a European policy will always have to be weighed in terms of outside repercussions".

The *third* reason for choosing the automobile industry is that this industry has become an international and, according to many, even a global industry that is dominated by multi-national companies with plants in many countries on several continents, which sell their products all over the world.[72] Over the years, these multi-nationals have built up a strong position *vis-à-vis* national governments as they are in a position to shop around for the most favourable (business) conditions. Individual states have lost some of their grip on the domestic economy and, more particularly, on multi-nationals that seem to simply "pack their bags" if the public policy and socio-economic conditions in a state are not (anymore) to their liking. The automobile industry is increasingly in a position to exploit the differences in socio-economic conditions between states and move production sites to states with low wages.[73] This induces competition between states in various policy areas. The fact that national governments have lost some of their grip leads to the question whether this lost control *should* and, if so, *can* be regained by the Community within the legal system of the EC Treaty.[74] Furthermore, the globalisation of the

[72] See Chapter 2. See also "Table 2 - The 25 largest non-financial transnational undertakings", Opinion of the Economic and Social Committee on "Employment, Competitiveness and Economic Globalization", OJ 1997, C158/14, listing GM in 4th, Toyota in 6th, Ford in 7th and Nissan in 13th place. This listing is based on UNCTAD, World Investment Report 1995.

[73] The fact that "in a single-market Europe, multinational companies will ruthlessly exploit differences not just in wage costs, but employment laws" is illustrated by the fact that L. Schweitzer, chairman of Renault, motivated the abrupt closure of its profitable Belgian plant in Vilvoorde with the fact that "the cost of producing a vehicle at Vilvoorde was higher than in France or Spain because of salary costs". See *FT*, "Renault workers despair for Europe's job security", 6 March 1997, at 2, and "Van Miert threat to Renault", 7 March 1997, at 2. It was reported in *FT*, "Driving hard bargains with GM workforce", 8 April 1998, at 9, that in view of chronic overcapacity and increased access to cheap production sites in Eastern Europe, multinational carmakers like General Motors and Ford are in a position "to play off their plants -and sometimes governments- in different countries against each other". Barnet and Cavanagh, *supra* note 44, at 310-338, point at a similar development in the U.S.A.

[74] For instance, it was reported in *FT*, "Brussels looks at tightening rules on subsidies", 10 March 1997, at 1, that the Commission is preparing proposals to prevent companies "from "shopping around" for state or European Union aid". However, *Agence Europe*, 7 August 1997, at 4 ("CESI stance on Amsterdam summit, part time work and closure of Renault Vilvoorde"), reported that according to CESI, the closure of Renault Vilvoorde illustrates the "inadequacy of European and national legal provisions in the face of manoeuvres of multinationals". See in this context the Opinion of the Economic and Social Committee on "Employment, Competitiveness and Economic Globalization", OJ 1997, C158/14.

automobile industry makes it necessary to put the EC Treaty in a WTO-perspective. Although this study will first and foremost focus on the EC Treaty, the relationship between the Community and the WTO Agreement will be touched upon as the latter embodies a part of international economic law that places obligations on the Community, thereby limiting its freedom to develop and carry out its policies and activities referred to in Articles 3 and 3a EC.[75]

The manner in which the Community intervenes in the operation of the automobile industry has especially come into the spotlight as a result of the radical changes taking place in the automobile industry. Economic activity, and with it the automobile industry, has become more international, if not global. Studies confirm that manufacturers of automobiles and spare parts have to compete on a highly competitive global market with a structural overcapacity. The production of automobiles has dramatically changed character thereby redefining both the market and the relationships between the main actors in the industry. The production of automobiles was a craft, changed into mass production and developed into lean production. Some expect that the production will eventually be done by manufacturers that have the characteristics of so-called "virtual corporations" which will further change the relationship between car manufacturers, suppliers and other actors in the automobile industry. In an effort to remain competitive, manufacturers, suppliers and distributors are forced to further reorganize and rationalize their activities.

The Community evidently has a great socio-economic interest in the economic survival and well-being of the automobile industry within the Member States. Through the implementation of the policies and activities referred to in Articles 3 and 3a EC, the Community can intervene and play an important role in putting in place a legal framework that facilitates and possibly even pro-actively stimulates the adaptation of the automobile industry to the changes

---

[75] See Chapter 3, section 3.6. See for a description and an analysis of the "ins and outs" of the WTO Agreement, *inter alia*, J.H. Jackson, *The world trading system*, 2nd edition, 1997, The MIT Press, Cambridge Massachusetts. The ECJ confirmed in its judgment of 16 June 1998 in Case C-162/96, *Racke* (not yet reported), par. 45, that the Community "must respect international law in the exercise of its powers".

presently taking place in the global market-place.[76] This study gives a description and a legal analysis of the manner and the extent to which the Community has used a selection of these competences to intervene in the automobile industry.

1.4 Outline of the Study

The study is divided in three parts. **Part I** gives an introduction to the factual and legal context of the case study. It begins with an introduction to the automobile industry (*Chapter 2*). In order to facilitate a good understanding of this study, a concise description and analysis of the most relevant aspects of the EC Treaty, which constitutes the basic constitutional charter of the legal system in which the Community develops and implements its policies and activities, will then be given (*Chapter 3*). **Part II** consists of a case study on Community law and the automobile industry and includes developments through **1 August 1998**. To begin with, the provisions of the EC Treaty and the legal measures dealing with the elimination of obstacles to intra-Community trade (*Chapter 4*) and the common commercial policy (*Chapter 5*) will be examined. The focus will then shift to the maintenance of undistorted competition (*Chapter 6*), and in particular to distribution and servicing in the automobile industry (*Chapter 7*), state aid in the automobile industry (*Chapter 8*), and concentration and co-operation within the automobile industry (*Chapter 9*). Then, those measures will be looked at within the context of the strengthening of the competitiveness of Community industry (*Chapter 10*), the promotion of research and technological development (*Chapter 11*) and the contribution to education and training of quality (*Chapter 12*) that are of particular significance to the automobile industry. In **Part III**, some general conclusions will be drawn (*Chapter 13*).

[76] For instance, it was reported in "The Agreement on the transitional period has been formally accepted by both parties-Statements by Mr. Andriessen and Mr. Nakao, MITI minister-Link with EEC homologation of models", *Agence Europe*, 2 August 1991, at 6, that according to ACEA the necessary improvements of productivity in the automobile industry within the Community "will require the support of an efficient and comprehensive policy by the EC and national governments". ACEA expects that "such a policy will ensure an environment enabling change". *FT*, "French carmakers could cut thousands of jobs", 14 November 1996, at 16, and in particular "French Socialists attack cuts in car jobs", 4 June 1997, at 2, which reported that a former French (Socialist) European affairs minister stressed the need for "a special European strategy in the automotive sector".

PART I - THE FACTUAL AND LEGAL CONTEXT OF THE CASE STUDY

2. THE AUTOMOBILE INDUSTRY

2.1 Introduction

The purpose of this chapter is to facilitate a clear understanding of the factual context of the case study by giving an introduction to the automobile industry, which is, like an individual, part of all that it has met; it has a character, a structure and a system of habits of its own.[1] First, an overview will be given of the different stages in the development of production methods in the automobile industry (**2.2**) and the impact of the internationalisation, or even globalisation of the world economy that confronted the automobile industry with the need to compete on what seems to have become a global market (**2.3**). Then, the focus will be on the socio-economic importance of the automobile industry (**2.4**) and the implications of such importance (**2.5**). At the end of this chapter, some concluding remarks will be made (**2.6**).

2.2 The Development Towards Virtual Production

2.2.1 Craft Production

The early history of the automobile is closely related to the development of techniques for the production of the part that makes an automobile *auto mobile*: the engine. In the course of the 18th century, attempts were made to construct a moving vehicle with a steam-driven engine. Around 1765, Cugnot constructed a three-wheeled, steam-driven gun tractor which is considered to be the first vehicle capable of self-propulsion. Other attempts were made to construct moving vehicles with gas engines. These attempts with steam and gas engines were not very successful due to the weight and size of the engines and the inefficient use of fuel.[2] In 1882, Daimler established a company and designed, assisted by Maybach, a petrol engine which was built into a vehicle on two wheels. Daimler patented this motorcycle on 29 August 1885 and several test

---

[1] See in this sense W.H. Hamilton, *Price and Price Policies*, 1938, McGraw-Hill, New York, at 4, as referred to by A.E. Kahn, *The economics of regulation: Principles and institutions*, 1970, John Wiley & Sons, New York, Volume I, at 13, footnote 41.

[2] M. Matteucci, *History of the Motor Car*, 1970, New English Library, Turin, at 8 and 15; W. Roediger, *Hundert Jahre Automobil*, 3rd edition, 1990, Urania Verlag, Leipzig, at 8-9, and D.G. Rhys, *The motor industry: An economic survey*, 1972, Butterworths, London, at 1-5.

drives were made. Another German enterpreneur, Benz, also experimented with engines and patented in Germany on 29 January 1886 a "*Fahrzeug mit Gasmotorenbetrieb*" with three wheels. Benz contributed to a more practical and efficient use of engines in transportation vehicles and became one of the most innovative individuals in the early history of the automobile. Nevertheless, it was Daimler who built in the summer of 1886 one of his engines into a carriage with four wheels thereby creating what seems to have been the first ever motor vehicle on four wheels.[3]

The development of the automobile got a considerable impetus after the German technology became available in France through Daimler's Parisian contact Sarazin. After the death of her husband, Mrs. Sarazin encouraged Peugeot and the Parisian company Panhard & Levassor to design and further develop models for moving vehicles.[4] The French entrepreneurs were very successful in doing so. The first race for moving vehicles (without horses) in the world was held in France on 22 July 1894 between Paris and Rouen. The numbers one and two of the race were driving motor vehicles constructed by, respectively, Peugeot and Panhard & Levassor, and equiped with engines "*Système Daimler*".[5] This race together with a second race Paris-Bordeaux-Paris on 11 June 1895, put the motor vehicles in the centre of public attention which stimulated demand for this *nouveauté* and confirmed that the production of motor vehicles could become commercially attractive. This drew the attention of both investors and manufacturers who were active on other though related markets. The result was an influx of both capital and production facilities which stimulated the industrialization of the production of motor vehicles. The success of the German and French producers of automobiles encouraged entrepreneurs in several other European countries and the U.S.A (with support of German or French technology), to design and construct automobiles themselves. By the end of the 19th century, the basic technology needed for the production of automobiles had spread throughout Western Europe and the U.S.A.

The early history of the automobile was dominated by highly skilled European craftsmen with an interest in the construction and development of

---

[3] Roediger, *supra* note 2, at 14-18.

[4] Matteucci, *supra* note 2, at 33, and Roediger, *supra* note 2, at 22.

[5] Matteucci, *supra* note 2, at 37-38, and Roediger, *supra* note 2, at 25-26.

engines which could be used to propel vehicles. The first automobiles were assembled by hand and constructed in relatively small numbers. For instance, the leading manufacturer Panhard & Levassor could only build a few hunderd automobiles per year. Only wealthy individuals could purchase an automobile as the price was very high.[6] Many of the specific parts of the automobiles were constructed by independent craftsmen and subsequently supplied to the entrepreneur assembling the automobile. Each automobile was built in accordance with the specific needs and desires of the buyer. As none of the craftsmen used a standard gauging system, and the machine tools of that time could not cut hardened steel, the parts did not fit together precisely. As a result, no two automobiles were identical and both the reliability and durability left much to be desired.[7] The main drawbacks of craft production in the automobile industry were described as follows:

> Production costs were high and didn't drop with volume, ... In addition, because each car produced was, in effect, a prototype, consistency and reliability were elusive ...
> the system failed to provide product quality - in the form of reliability and durability rather than lots of leather or walnut - because of the lack of systematic testing.
> Also fatal to the age, however, was the inability of the small independent shops, where most of the production work took place, to develop new technologies. Individual craftsmen simply did not have the resources to pursue fundamental innovations; real technological advance would have required systematic research rather than just tinkering.[8]

These drawbacks paved the way for a new form of production which was to be named "Fordism" or mass production.

---

[6] Roediger, *supra* note 2, at 65.

[7] See J.P. Womack, D.T. Jones and D. Roos, *The machine that changed the world*, 1991, Harper Perennial, New York, at 21-26.

[8] Womack, Jones and Roos, *supra* note 7, at 25-26.

2.2.2 Mass Production

The presentation in 1893 of a Daimler automobile in Chicago was the "kick-off" for the development of the automobile industry in the U.S.A.[9] Soon after, several American entrepreneurs set out to design and construct automobiles with different objectives in mind.[10] Whereas Winton and the Packard-Brothers focused on the upper-end of the market by producing luxurious, expensive automobiles of a high quality, entrepreneurs like Olds and Ford wanted to construct cheap and practical automobiles which could also be bought by "the man in the street". Daimler aimed at the market-segment between these two extremes but was for various reasons not very successful in doing so.[11]

Ford triggered a revolution in the automobile industry with the introduction of his 1908 Model T which was designed in such a way as to facilitate its production.[12] In addition, the Model T was a practical automobile which was relatively easy to use and repair. By having his automobiles assembled on a moving line from parts which were completely and consistently interchangeable and easy to attach to each other, Ford created a system which he himself named "mass production" in a 1926 article for the *Encyclopedia Britannica*.[13] Ford divided labor, encouraged the use of a standard gauging system and acquired the most modern machine tools available to work on prehardened metals. Ford perfected his system of mass production in his 1913 Highland Park plant in Detroit thereby further increasing productivity and enhancing both the reliability and durability of the limited number of Ford

---

[9] See A.D. Chandler Jr., *Giant enterprise*, 1964, Harcourt, Brace & World Inc., New York, for a detailed description and analysis of the early development of the American automobile industry in general and Ford and GM in particular. See W. Lewchuk, *American technology and the British vehicle industry*, 1987, Cambridge University Press, Cambridge, at 33-65, for a concise description of the American automobile industry in the period 1889 to 1930.

[10] According to H. Simonian, *FT*, "Motor of the American dream", 27 December 1996, at 11, "[t]he US industry was born in 1896, when Frank and Charles Duryea, two brothers from Springfield, Illinois, built 13 similar cars from the same design".

[11] Roediger, *supra* note 2, at 40. See also L.R. Brown, C. Flavin and C. Norman, *Running on Empty - The Future of the Automobile in an Oil Short World*, 1979, W.W. Norton & Company, New York, at 10.

[12] Matteucci, *supra* note 2, at 153-166.

[13] Womack, Jones and Roos, *supra* note 7, at 26, footnote 4.

models under production.[14] As a result, the price of the Model T went down dramatically.[15] Until 1926, the Ford Model T (nicknamed "Thin Lizzie") was the best-selling automobile.[16] After having bought engines and chassis for years from independent entrepreneurs, Ford pursued a complete vertical integration and started producing a large number of parts in-house.[17] Other, mostly American, manufacturers followed Ford's example and some of them even improved mass production. General Motors, guided by Sloan, combined mass production with improved management and marketing techniques. Sloan reorganized and decentralized the management structure of General Motors and decided to offer consumers a greater variety of models.[18] As a result, General Motors was able to take over a substantial part of Ford's market share. Ford had to abandon the slogan "You can have any colour you like, so long as it's black" and was forced to bring more variety to his models.[19]

After the introduction of mass production, Ford, General Motors and Chrysler dominated the world market for automobiles. The automobile had become a means of mass transportation within the reach of millions of people. The remarkable success of the automobile industry in the U.S.A. stimulated the growth of and technological progress in other industries as large amounts of

---

[14] See K. Bhaskar, "Innovation in the EC automotive industry - An analysis from the perspective of state aid policy" (Commission of the European Communities), April 1988, at 9-11, for a concise description of the traditional Ford car manufacturing process.

[15] According to R.J. Barnet and J. Cavanagh, *Global dreams*, 1994, Simon & Schuster, New York, at 260, the price went down from $780 in 1910 to $360 in 1913. See also Matteucci, *supra* note 2, at 166, and Roediger, *supra* note 2, at 67.

[16] H. Brogan, *The Penguin History of the United States of America*, 1990, Penguin Books, London, at 509. See also Rhys, *supra* note 2, at 4-7.

[17] Womack, Jones and Roos, *supra* note 7, at 33-39.

[18] Womack, Jones and Roos, *supra* note 7, at 40-43. See also Brown, Flavin and Norman, *supra* note 11, at 10.

[19] Brogan, *supra* note 16, at 508. See A. Nevins and F.E. Hill, *Ford - Decline and rebirth*, 1962, Charles Scribner's Sons, New York, and M. Wilkins and F.E. Hill, *American business abroad - Ford on six continents*, 1964, Wayne State University Press, Detroit, for an extensive account of the history of Ford. See also *FT* (Survey - The Motor Industry), "Profile Ford - Stunning recovery from near ruin", 20 October 1988, at XII.

steel, glass, rubber and paint were needed.[20] Over the years, however, mass production ran into problems as workers found their jobs unrewarding. Workers organized themselves in unions and were successful in negotiating higher wages, reductions in the weekly hours of work and rules on job assignments. Mass production lost some of its efficiency and became increasingly stagnant.[21]

When craft production was replaced by mass production, Europe lost its dominance of the production of automobiles. This, notwithstanding the fact that already around 1920 several European companies, like Fiat and Citroën, experimented with mass production.[22] By 1955, the U.S.A. and Canada accounted for about 70% of the worldwide production of automobiles whereas Western Europe had about 25%.[23] But the European automobile industry adapted to the changes, adopted American mass production technology and managed to grow fast between 1955 and 1970.[24] This was facilitated by the rising demand for automobiles, relatively low wages, the rise of fuel prices and

---

[20] Roediger, *supra* note 2, at 72-73; Rhys, *supra* note 2, at 9-10, and Brogan, *supra* note 16, at 508-509.

[21] Womack, Jones and Roos, *supra* note 7, at 43-47 and 231-235. For instance, according to Barnet and Cavanagh, *supra* note 15, at 262, "[f]rom the sit-down strikes of the 1930s to the rising incidence of absenteeism and sloppy work of the 1970s, the human cog in the Fordist machine became an ever increasing problem for the company".

[22] Roediger, *supra* note 2, at 73-74.

[23] See Womack, Jones and Roos, *supra* note 7, at 44, Figure 2.2 on "Shares of World Motor Vehicle Production by Region, 1955 - 1989.

[24] See, for instance, Lewchuk, *supra* note 9, at 152-184, on the manner in which British manufacturers tried to adapt to mass-production. Rolls-Royce remained one of the very few craft car manufacturers. *FT*, "First production line for Rolls-Royce", 20 March 1997, at 25, reported that in order to improve productivity, Rolls-Royce eventually had to introduce a production line which will not do away, however, with the 77 craftsmen in the woodshop, nor the 90 skilled staff working on chrome "brightware". See in this context *FT*, "Rolls-Royce Motor to be sold", 27 October 1997, at 19; "Rolls-Royce enthusiasts plan $1bn bid", 9 January 1998, at 24, and "BMW wins Rolls-Royce auction with £300m bid", 30 March 1998, at 1.

the production of models which were different from the American automobiles.[25] New features like front-wheel drive and five-speed transmissions, were introduced and compact, economic and sporty models were produced. Whereas the situation of the European automobile industry in the fifties has been characterized as "the phase of peaceful coexistence", the sixties were referred to as the period of "rapid growth and increasing competition".[26] Although the production of automobiles in the Community between 1958 and 1968 increased from 2.6 to 6.3 million, the Community's 31% share of world-wide production of passenger cars in 1958, decreased to 29.7%. At the same time, Japan increased its share of about 0.6% to 9.7%.[27]

In the 1970s, and in particular after the oil crisis in 1973-1974 and 1979, a period of decline started for the automobile industry in the Community.[28] Economic growth stagnated and the competitive pressures were rising as the Japanese share of the world-wide production of passenger cars grew in 1970 to 14% and in 1980 to 24.1%.[29] Several manufacturers were not able to achieve the optimum production volume of that time; 200.000 automobiles per year.[30] The European automobile industry had to deal with

---

[25] According to H. Berg, "Motorcars: Between growth and protectionism" in *The structure of European industry* (H.W. de Jong ed.), 3rd revised edition, 1993, Kluwer Academic Publishers, Dordrecht, at 126, the automobile industry in the sixties and seventies was the "growth sector par excellence". For instance, Berg reports for instance that in W.-Germany the density of automobiles went from 53.8 automobiles for every 1000 inhabitants in 1958 via 182.2 in 1968 to 320.1 in 1978. See also H.W. de Jong and C.J.P. de Boer, *Competition and concentration in the passenger car market of the Netherlands*, Nr. 33, Evolution of concentration and competition series: Working papers, Commission of the European Communities, IV/458/81-EN, Figure 2 on the evolution of the market for new passenger cars in the Netherlands between 1955 and 1980.

[26] See Berg, *supra* note 25, at 125-135, for an analysis of the structure of the European automobile industry in the fifties and sixties. See Rhys, *supra* note 2, at 136-187, on the automobile industry in France, West-Germany, Italy and the Benelux.

[27] Berg, *supra* note 25, at 126 and 133.

[28] See, for instance, Lewchuk, *supra* note 9, at 185-220, on the collapse of the British system of mass production in the period 1930 to 1984. See P.J.S. Dunnett, *The decline of the British Motor Industry*, 1980, Croom Helm, London, and S. Wilks, *Industrial policy and the motor industry*, 1984, Manchester University Press, Manchester, on the role of government in the decline of the British automobile industry.

[29] Berg, *supra* note 25, at 139.

[30] See in this sense de Jong and de Boer, *supra* note 25, at 7, and Berg, *supra* note 25, at 127.

over-capacity and high costs. It suffered steady losses and declining international competitiveness.[31] Eventually, this crisis lead to several re-organizations, take-overs and cooperations between a number of manufacturers in the automobile industry.[32]

2.2.3 Lean Production

At the beginning of the 20th century, several Japanese manufacturers produced trial models for automobiles.[33] In 1920, Hakuyosha produced the "Otomogo" automobile which is considered to be the first successful Japanese automobile; 250 of these automobiles were constructed in 1923.[34] Toyoda was amongst the first Japanese producers of automobiles. Around 1935, Toyoda produced its first automobile after having sent one of its engineers to Packard in order to examine the production process.[35] It did so again in 1950 when Eiji Toyoda spent a few months in Ford's Rouge plant in Detroit. Back in Japan, Eiji Toyoda developed,

---

[31] K. Shimokawa, *The Japanese Automobile Industry - A Business History*, 1994, The Athlone Press, London, at 2.

[32] R. Linda, "Industrial and market concentration in Europe" in *Competition in Europe* (P. de Wolf ed.), Essays in honour of H.W. de Jong, 1991, Kluwer Academic Publishers, Dordrecht, at 99, gives a concise overview of the structural mutations in the automobile industry in the eighties. According to De Jong and de Boer, *supra* note 25, at 12, "[t]he most important mergers and take-overs until 1980 were those between Volkswagen-Audi-NSU, Peugeot-Citroën-Talbot, Volvo-DAF and Fiat-Autobianchi-Lancia".

[33] See (for references to further literature) on the Japanese automobile industry: Shimokawa, *supra* note 31; Rhys, *supra* note 2, at 188-204, and M.A. Cusumano, *The Japanese automobile industry*, 1985, The Harvard University Press, Cambridge Mass.

[34] Shimokawa, *supra* note 31, at 5.

[35] Roediger, *supra* note 2, at 110.

together with Taiichi Ohno, the Toyota Production System[36] which eventually became known as "lean production".[37]

In contrast to mass producers, Toyota did not have its employees perform only one or two very simple tasks. Instead, employees were grouped in teams and put in charge of several steps in the production process. Every team was encouraged to come up with suggestions to improve the process and was taught to solve the problems which arose. By doing so, Toyota redefined the participation of employees in the production process and made work at the moving line more interesting and at the same time more effective. Toyota did not make all parts in-house nor did it order the production of the necessary parts from independent companies on short-term contracts. On the contrary, Toyota established long-term relationships with its suppliers by taking part in their share capital and pursued an economic and flexible cooperation.[38] For instance, the just-in-time or *kanban* manufacturing system in which suppliers deliver parts to the assembly line at the moment that they are required in the manufacturing process, was introduced. Toyota further developed its production system and improved productivity, quality and its ability to adapt to the fragmentation of the market into a great number of product segments. Toyota also succeeded in creating a brand loyalty with its Japanese customers. The needs and desires of Toyota's customers had a direct impact on the product development processes.

---

[36] In 1936, the name "Toyoda" (meaning "abundant rice field" in Japanese) was changed into "Toyota" (without a specific meaning in Japanese) for marketing purposes. See Womack, Jones and Roos, *supra* note 7, at 48.

[37] Lean production is "lean" because it uses less of everything compared with mass production. See Womack, Jones and Roos, *supra* note 7, at 13. The term is now used world-wide. See, *inter alia*, Shimokawa, *supra* note 31, at 159 and Communication from the Commission to the Council and to the European Parliament on the "European Union Automobile Industry", 23 February 1994, COM(94)49 final ("1994 Communication"), at 2.

[38] See in this context A. Bongardt, "The automotive industry: Supply relations in context" in *The structure of European industry*, *supra* note 25, at 147-170.

By the early 1960s, Toyota had perfected its techniques for lean production.[39] Other Japanese companies adopted lean production thereby giving the Japanese automobile industry a competitive advantage over their American and European competitors. The Japanese automobile industry rapidly increased its share of world automobile production and exported large amounts of automobiles.[40]

According to observers, the European automobile industry initially set out to perfect mass production while the Japanese continued to perfect leanness.[41] A similar development took place in the U.S where Ford seemed the only company which took advantage of its financial crisis in the early 1980s to restructure its production line and implement (with help from Mazda) lean production methods.[42] General Motors got a first lesson in lean production through its cooperation with Toyota in the NUMMI joint venture.[43] As illustrated by the following listing, lean production methods spread slowly through the American and European automobile industry:

---

[39] See for a detailed description of the elements of lean production: Womack, Jones and Roos, *supra* note 7, at 71-222; Shimokawa, *supra* note 31, at 18-103, and J.P. Womack and D.T. Jones, *Lean Thinking*, 1996, Simon & Schuster, New York, at 10-98. See for a critical review of, and references to critical literature on lean production: L.U. de Sitter, *Synergetisch produceren*, 1994, Van Gorcum, Assen, at 282-285 and 407-408 ("Het Lean Production debat").

[40] Shimokawa, *supra* note 31, at 9, emphasizes that the Japanese automobile industry depended heavily on exports "sending abroad 51 per cent of its total output in 1977 and 54 per cent in 1980".

[41] See in this sense Womack, Jones and Roos, *supra* note 7, at 255. A.P. de Man, "Nieuwe organisatievormen en het industriebeleid", ESB 12 March 1997, at 214, notes that the slow introduction of new forms of organization (like lean production) may be to a large extent due to "institutions" such as legislation and trade unions.

[42] See Barnet and Cavanagh, *supra* note 15, at 267-268, 272-274 and 314-316.

[43] Shimokawa, *supra* note 31, at 149.

Introduction of "Just-in-time" or "kanban"[44]

1947	First experiments of Toyota which would lead to "Just-in-time"
End of fifties	Nissan starts the introduction of "Just-in-time"-like systems
1962	Introduction of "Just-in-time" at Toyota
End of sixties	Introduction of "Just-in-time" at Toyota subsidiairies
Mid seventies	Nissan starts the introduction of "Just-in-time" at suppliers
1982	First experiments of American companies with "Just-in-time"

A speedy transition from mass to lean production techniques turned out to be crucial for the economic survival of the European and American automobile industry.[45] Meanwhile, several studies have shown that the European and the American automobile industry have made considerable progress, with or without Japanese support,[46] in implementing lean production techniques that improved

[44] De Man, *supra* note 41, at 214, in which reference is made to "Source: M.A. Cusumano, "Manufacturing innovations: lessons from the Japanese auto industry", Sloan Management review, fall 1988, at 29-38" (translation by the author). See in this context also "The factory of the future" and "How solid models aid the designer", *The Economist*, 5 April 1986, at 83-84.

[45] Womack, Jones and Roos, *supra* note 7, at 227-255. Several studies including W. Lazonick, *Business organization and the myth of the market economy*, 1991, Cambridge University Press, Cambridge, confirm the importance of innovative management techniques and business organization.

[46] R.B. Reich, *The works of nations*, 1991, Alfred A. Knopf, New York, at 146-148 and 316, emphasizes that studies indicate that the Japanese management techniques are crucial to lean production. For instance, Reich reports that after Toyota took over the management of GM's factory in Fremont, California, in 1984, productivity soared by 50% over what it had been under GM's managers. Toyota was prepared to do this in exchange for a share of the resulting profits. See also Barnet and Cavanagh, *supra* note 15, at 271-274, on Ford's cooperation with Mazda.

efficiency and productivity.[47] Costs were brought down and the workforce was reduced.[48] But the over-capacity in the automobile industry still exists and will probably be even further expanded as new (mostly Asian)[49] competitors enter the highly-competitive market and car manufacturers further expand their activities.[50] Some estimates of the over-capacity in the automobile industry are higher than others. According to the chairman of Ford of Europe, Nasser, the manufacturing capacity within the Community is about 20% above annual demand.[51] The Commissioner for Industry, Bangemann, estimated the over-capacity at 5 to 10% but added that the situation varies considerably from one

---

[47] See in this context, *inter alia*, Bhaskar, *supra* note 14, at 11-33, and *FT*, "Eyes on the fast lane", 31 January 1995, at 18; "Opel beats Japanese at own game in Europe", 20 August 1996, at 2, and "Nissan UK plant tops productivity table", 27 August 1997, at 1. See also "The machine is getting leaner", *ACEA - The European Automakers*, January 1997, at 2-7. See P. Ingrassia and J.B. White, *Comeback - The fall and rise of the American automobile industry*, 1994, Simon & Schuster, New York, on the recovery of the American automobile industry in the late 1980s and early 1990s.

[48] For instance, *FT*, "Germany revs up", 27 March 1998, at 13, reported that since the early 1990s "every carmaker has negotiated efficiency improvements and job cuts with its unions" which raised productivity significantly. It was reported that output per employee at Audi rose by 45% between 1993 and 1996, while that at BMW, VW and Porsche has increased by more than a third.

[49] See *FT*, "S Korean motor industry attacks Samsung proposal" and "Tigers fill up their tanks", 10 June 1997, at 1 and 19, on the efforts of South Korea, Malaysia, Indonesia and Thailand to develop a domestic automobile industry.

[50] For instance, Toyota announced plans to increase its production. See *FT*, "Toyota set for $1.6bn car plant in France", 17 March 1997, at 1; "Toyota in the fast lane", 17 March 1997, at 17; "Toyota's odd French connection", 18 March 1997, at 2; "Swindon wins new Honda range", 27 October 1997, at 8; "Toyota assembly plant set to be built in France", 4 December 1997, at 1; "A steady drive around the world", 5 December 1997, at 16, and "Toyota seeks 5% sales rise despite weak markets", 8 January 1998, at 14. As reported in *FT*, "An aggressive driver", 8-9 March 1997, at 7, and "Renault in reverse", 8-9 March 1997, at 24, the closure Renault's plant in Vilvoorde, Belgium, will not reduce the capacity of the automobile industry within the Community if it is subsequently sold to a rival (Korean) car manufacturer. See also *FT*, "European motor groups fear flood of Asian imports", 5 December 1997, at 6; "Japan carmakers renew their European offensive", 15 January 1998, at 9, and "Japanese carmakers target Europe", 4 March 1998, at 16.

[51] *FT* (FT Auto), "Back on track for a bumper year", 6 March 1997, at VI. See also *FT*, "Rough ride for Renault", 6 March 1997, at 13, and "Europese autofabrikanten slanken permanent af", *Financieele Dagblad*, 8-10 March 1997, at 5. It was reported in *The single market review - Impact on manufacturing motor vehicles*, Subseries I: Volume 6, 1997, EUR-OP, Kogan Page/Earthscan, at 17, that "there appears to be an overall surplus of capacity of around 20% relative to average demand".

country to the next and from one enterprise to another.[52] In view of the considerable over-capacity, a further reduction in costs and a further improvement of productivity and innovation will be necessary.[53] Observers expect that in the end, a considerable reduction of capacity through mergers or a "shake-out" is unavoidable.[54]

Since 1991, the Japanese automobile industry has had difficulty maintaining its competitiveness and profitability due to factors such as a decrease in demand on the Japanese market, the appreciation of the yen and large investments made for the modernization of production plants. The growing diversification of model types and the ever-shortening lead times for new models resulted in a substantial increase in research and development costs

---

[52] *Agence Europe*, 12 March 1997, at 9 ("Mr Bangemann is willing to agree to Mr Donnelly's proposal for creation of a high-level panel of representatives of car makers and unions - The Renault case"). See for an analysis Commission Document "Examination of current and future excess capacity in the European automobile industry", EUR-OP, 1997.

[53] For instance, *FT*, "GM warns of more job cuts in European subsidiaries", 7 January 1998, at 1, reports on the fact that GM has warned its European subsidiaries further jobs might have to go to bring productivity and earnings to more competitive levels. See also *FT*, "Opel agrees job cuts package", 20 January 1998, at 17, and "GM comments sour Opel five-year job deal", 21 January 1998, at 21. At the same time, *FT*, "GM open to S Korean alliance", at 17, reports that GM is open to forming a joint production venture with a South Korean company to take advantage of the country's deflated currency and lower cost base. See in this context *FT*, "Kia looks at link-up with GM", 21 January 1998, at 22.

[54] See "Car crash ahead" and "The coming car crash - Global pile up", *The Economist*, 10 May 1997, at 11-12 and 19-21; *FT*, "Three-year slide in car sales forecast", 8 September 1997, at 2; "When two is a crowd", 8 July 1997, at 13; "Chicane of competition", 8 September 1997, at 2 and 17; (FT Auto) "Carmakers caught in twin vices", 9 September 1997, at I; "Korea car sector on rationalisation road", 9 December 1997, at 8; "Peugeot-Citroen set to pool costs", 19 January 1998, at 19; "Peugeot-Citroen unveils revamp", 22 January 1998, at 17; "Hyundai chairman calls for gradual decline of rival Kia", 19 January 1998, at 1; "Motor moves" (editorial), 28 January 1998, at 13; "Driving hard bargains with GM workforce", 8 April 1998, at 9; "Global automotive group consolidation tops $28bn", 11 May 1998, at 19; "Nissan's promises fail to dispel doubts", 21 May 1998, at 22; "Nissan shake-up after $107m loss", 21 May 1998, at 1; "Nissan posts loss of $102m as sales slip 14% in Japan", 28 May 1998, at 15; "Nissan gears up for better European integration", 28 May 1998, at 19, and "Mitsubishi Motors falls into the red", 19 May 1998, at 16. As pointed out in *FT*, "There's room for optimism" (Global business outlook"), 13 January 1998, at III, analysts argue that the turmoil in Asia and South America may represent "an essential break from the remorseless rise in the world's vehicle production capacity ... Investment decisions will be reconsidered in the light of the ... circumstances, prompting postponements and, occasionally, cancellations".

which could bring about "the self-destruction of the lean system".[55] In addition, the working relationship between the lean producers and their employees deteriorated.[56] However, the Japanese automobile industry has tried to further improve development and production efficiency, cost competitiveness and has focused increasingly on environmental and safety issues.[57] The Japanese automobile industry also tries to carve niches in a market which is already (over)crowded.[58] The system of lean production is in the process of being fine-tuned.[59]

2.2.4 Virtual Production

Several writers expect that automobiles will eventually become products delivering instant customer gratification in a cost-effective way which can be produced in diverse locations and offered in a great number of models; so-called "virtual products". In order to be able to produce these "virtual products", manufacturers will have to further reorganize and obtain the characteristics of

---

[55] Shimokawa, *supra* note 31, at 158-159.

[56] See D. Drache, "New work and employment relations" in *States against markets*, 1996, Routledge, London, at 227-249. For instance, Barnet and Cavanagh, *supra* note 15, at 315, reported that a 1990 survey of UAW workers at the Mazda assembly plant in Flat Rock, Michigan, indicated "that lean production, with its emphasis on eliminating wasted motion and filling idle time, meant that workers had to work faster and harder". Over 70% of the workers subscribed to the statement "If the present level of work intensity continues, I will likely be injured or worn out before I retire". See in this context also *FT*, "US car workers find the going hard", 12 June 1997, at 5, and Written Question 3198/95 (Ribeiro), OJ 1996, C109/32 and Written Question 382/97 (Ribeiro), OJ 1997, C217/168.

[57] See, *inter alia*, *FT*, "Mazda to speed up production cycle", 22 January 1997, at 15; "Nissan aims to reduce development times", 19 February 1997, at 20, and "Nissan in drive to tighten production methods", 28 January 1998, at 15.

[58] See "Fads on wheels", *The Economist*, 1-7 February 1997, at 80, on the importance of launching lots of models on the Japanese market for "carving niches in a crowded market". See also *FT*, "Honda expects record sales in home market", 11 February 1997, at 23, which illustrates the importance of the introduction of new models "recreational vehicles".

[59] T. Kojima, *Die zweite Lean Revolution: was kommt nach lean production?*, 1995, Verlag Moderne Industrie, Landsberg.

the so-called "virtual corporation".[60] Some manufacturers already try to "virtualize" the production of automobiles[61] in an effort to cut costs and production time so that automobiles can be produced to domestic order in just seventy-two hours. It has been pointed out that the building of virtual products will "require a company to utterly revise itself, control ever more sophisticated types of information, and master new organizational and production skills".[62] The future will tell whether manufacturers will turn into virtual corporations. If so, the relationships between the actors in the automobile industry will further change. Manufacturers will continue to outsource more of what they used to produce in-house to fewer suppliers and the latter will have to take on a bigger role in the development and global manufacturing of the automobile.[63] As a

---

[60] See, *inter alia*, W.H. Davidow and M.S. Malone, *The virtual corporation*, 1992, Harper Business, New York, and B.R. Barber, *Jihad vs. McWorld*, 1995, Times Books, New York, at 26-27. The political counterpart of the virtual corporation, the virtual state, has been examined by R. Rosecrance, "The rise of the virtual state", *Foreign Affairs*, July/August 1996, at 45-61.

[61] It has been reported in *FT*, "Ford's assembly lines will now be virtually foolproof", 14 April 1997, at 1, that Ford has made a breakthrough in developping a virtual assembly line which "will end trial and error in setting up production for new models and reduce the process by nine months - a third of the time needed to take a car from initial design to commercial production". The technology also appears to have major implications for Ford's large suppliers who are "increasingly being required to design and develop complex component assemblies for car makers, when it is introduced to them worldwide".

[62] See Davidow and Malone, *supra* note 60, at 4.

[63] See *FT*, "Alliances forged in the factory", 4 November 1996, at 10, on VW's new bus and truck plant in Resende, Brazil, which seems to resemble what has been described as a "virtual corporation" since it involves a high degree of co-operation with suppliers which even meet about 35% of the fixed costs. The plant will be managed by both VW and its suppliers under a profit-sharing "consortium". VW's main responsibilities will be quality control, sales and marketing. See also *FT*, "ZF joins forces with carmakers", 23 March 1994, and in particular "Brakes on at Toyota", 7 February 1997, at 8, on Toyota's "just-in-time" manufacturing system. *FT*, "Renault expands horizons", 2 January 1998, at 10, reported that in its drive to cutting costs Renault intends to move towards "Japanese-style long-term relationships with suppliers, with component companies expected to co-operate more closely in product planning and problem-solving". See also *FT*, "Carmakers are feeling uneasy" (FT Auto), 23 February 1998, at III. *FT*, "Steel gets tough with aluminium", 5 March 1998, at 23, reported that after the aluminium industry succesfully presented aluminium car bodies as as an attractive alternative to steel bodies, the steel industry recognized that car manufacturers are under increasingly severe pressures to produce lighter, more fuel efficient and less-polluting cars, and developed an ultra-light car body in high-strength steels.

result, car manufacturers will do even less work inhouse[64] and suppliers will have to compete fiercely for long-term orders and improve quality while intensifying their relationship with manufacturers.[65] In addition, manufacturers will tighten their grip on their distribution and servicing system in an effort to further reduce costs.[66] According to Davidow and Malone:

> It is not surprising then that profound changes are in store for both the company's distribution system and its internal organization as they evolve to become more customer driven and customer managed. On the upstream side of the firm, supplier networks will have to be integrated with those of customers often to the point where the customer will share its equipment, designs, trade secrets, and confidences with those suppliers. Obviously, suppliers will become very dependent upon their downstream customers; but by the same token the customers will be equally trapped by their suppliers. In the end, unlike its contemporary predecessors, the virtual corporation will appear less a discrete enterprise and more an ever-varying cluster of common activities in the midst of a vast fabric of relationships.[67]

The importance of new and innovative technology to manufacture automobiles

---

[64] According to R.B. Reich, *supra* note 46, at 94, by 1990, Chrysler directly produced only about 30% of the value of its cars and Ford about 50%. This leads to problems with the unions. See *FT*, "Ford union deal challenges GM", 18 September 1996, at 6; "Canadian car union makes headway", 19 September 1996, at 5, and "Dana looks beyond the auto sector for growth", 24 September 1996, at 19.

[65] See *FT*, "BMW to axe distribution contract with Unipart", 7 May 1998, at 24; "Volvo set to slash supplier base in cost-cutting drive", 18 May 1998, at 17; "Car component makers face consolidation", 21 May 1998, at 21; "Mercedes warns parts suppliers", 2 June 1998, at 10; "GM chief chides parts suppliers", 12 June 1998, at 9, and "Suppliers of car parts warned on cost and quality", 22 June 1998, at 6. Even suppliers who are still part of one car manufacturer take measures to raise sales to customers outside of their parent-company. See in this context *FT*, "GM prepares for components sell-off", 11 September 1997, at 18; "Ford to merge components divisions", 9 September 1997, at 1, and "Snell sees an opportunity in globalisation", 30 September 1997, at 24.

[66] *FT*, "Dealing with the car dealers", 4 March 1998, at 13, reports that after dramatically reducing the time to design and assemble a new model, cutting costs and improving quality in the assembly stage, car manufacturers are now trying to reduce the cost of selling a car which accounts for up to 30% of the total.

[67] Davidow and Malone, *supra* note 60, at 6-7.

in a cheaper and more efficient way, is illustrated by the bitter dispute between GM and VW which followed the decision by a leading exponent of a new way to make cars, José Ignacio López, to leave GM in order to join VW where he had allegedly succeeded in reducing the prices paid to suppliers and implemented his innovative views in several VW manufacturing plants. GM's accusations of industrial espionage lead to a criminal investigation and civil law suits. Eventually, a settlement was reached.[68]

2.3 The Development Towards a Real Global Market

From its early history, automobiles were produced both for the domestic market and for export to other countries.[69] Moreover, German and French technology necessary for the construction of automobiles was readily licenced to entrepreneurs in other countries so as to enable them to produce automobiles themselves or in cooperation with the licensor.[70] Although the international trade got a further impetus by the development of mass production in the U.S.A., many countries wanted to protect their domestic craft production of automobiles and barriers to the importation of (mostly mass-produced) automobiles were imposed.[71] As a result, the geography of automobile production was heavily influenced by national tariff-barriers.[72] Mass producers like Ford tried to adapt to these changes by producing parts for its automobiles in Detroit and assembling them not only in the U.S.A. but all over the world. But when it became clear that one standard product did not satisfy the local

---

[68] See *FT*, "Driven on the defensive" and "VW shares decline after US court ruling in row with GM", 28 November 1996, at 13 and 14; "$225.000 charity payment ends GM defector case", 28 July 1998, at 14, and *The Economist*, "Now for the market battle", 18 January 1997, at 67.

[69] Womack, Jones and Roos, *supra* note 7, at 21-24.

[70] See, for instance, Roediger, *supra* note 2, at 37-40, on the cooperation in the U.S.A. between Daimler Motor Company and Steinway & Sons.

[71] See, *inter alia*, Shimokawa, *supra* note 31, at 5-7.

[72] According to *World Investment Report 1994 - Transnational corporations, employment and the workplace*, UNCTAD, 1994, UN, New York ("*World Investment Report 1994*"), at 150, "[t]he inheritance of this regulation-driven pattern has been a subsequent lengthy rationalization and restructuring of national operations to reposition firms in regional and global markets".

demands for a great(er) variety of models and, at the same time, trade restrictions on the importation of parts and automobiles became tougher, Ford established fully integrated production plants in other countries.[73] By 1914, Ford had become the biggest car manufacturer in the United Kingdom.[74] By 1926, Ford automobiles were assembled in more than thirty-six cities in the U.S.A. and in nineteen foreign countries.[75] Other American mass producers followed suite and tried to get a foothold in other countries by setting up local subsidiaries or by purchasing local companies. For instance, over the years, General Motors took participations in or simply bought foreign competitors[76] and moved manufacturing facilities abroad in order to take advantage of cheaper labor, to get closer to markets and to avoid dependency on fluctuations of the dollar.[77] Ford and Chrysler followed a similar strategy.

In order to facilitate the growth and development of its domestic automobile industry, Japan prohibited direct foreign investment in its automobile industry and imposed high tariff barriers. These protectionist measures were of great importance to the Japanese automobile industry in its early days as it gave them the chance to enter their "fortified" domestic market and "mature" without the competition of their powerful foreign competitors.[78] In particular between 1960 and 1980, the production of the Japanese automobile industry increased rapidly and Japanese exports to both the U.S.A. and Europe boomed.[79] This created enormous trade imbalances with the Western world

---

[73] According to Ford's president, P. Benton, Ford began as a global company, exporting the same cars everywhere and "became a multinational comany with separate operations overseas". See Barnet and Cavanagh, *supra* note 15, at 268-271, on Ford's efforts to integrate its global operations and produce a car (Mondeo) which would come close to a "world car"; at least 75% of the parts in the U.S.A. and European versions would be the same.

[74] Barnet and Cavanagh, *supra* note 15, at 261.

[75] Womack, Jones and Roos, *supra* note 7, at 34-35.

[76] GM owns, controls or participates in Opel, Saab and Isuzu.

[77] See R.B. Reich, *supra* note 46, at 126-127, and Barber, *supra* note 60, at 30, who reports that GM produces over 40% of its cars beyond American shores.

[78] Womack, Jones and Roos, *supra* note 7, at 50, and Shimokawa, *supra* note 31, at 5-7.

[79] Womack, Jones and Roos, *supra* note 7, at 68-69, Figure 3.1 which illustrates the remarkable rise of the "Japanese Share of World Motor Vehicle Production, 1955-1989".

which resulted in protectionist non-tariff barriers such as restrictive administrative practices and voluntary export restraints.[80] Much like the American mass-producers in their time, the Japanese automobile industry tried to circumvent these measures by importing the necessary parts and by assembling the automobiles within the U.S.A. or Europe in so-called "screw-driver plants".[81] In an effort to transform these plants into a national (value-adding) industry, the U.S.A. and several European countries like the United Kingdom proposed to set rules on local-content levels in order to force foreign automobile producers to develop and set up not only assembly plants but engine plants and local suppliers as well.[82] Over the years, Japanese automobile manufacturers like Nissan, Toyota and Honda

---

[80] R.B. Reich, *supra* note 46, at 72-73, pointed out that every time one industry in the U.S.A. gained protection, another industry, dependent on the first for material or components, found itself squeezed and subsequently in need of protection. For instance, once the American steel industry successfully warded off cheap foreign steel, the Big Three American automakers discovered that they had to pay 40% more for it than their global competitors. This put them at a competitive disadvantage and made them all the more needful of protection. Reich emphasized that the voluntary export restraints on Japanese automobiles that temporarily helped the Big Three maintain their profits through the 1980s cost American consumers about $1 billion a year more than they would have paid for automobiles had the American market been open.

[81] See T. Abo, "The Japanese production system" in *States against markets*, *supra* note 56, at 140-141, for an overview of the distribution of overseas production plants of Japanese and American motor firms, by country and company, 1989 and 1980. The same strategy is still used. It was reported in *FT*, "Kit cars worry Poland's foreign vehicle makers", 3 October 1997, at 4, that Poland's foreign car manufacturers worry about plans by Hyundai to set up low-cost local assembly operations in Poland aimed at avoiding high import tariffs on finished vehicles.

[82] See Womack, Jones and Roos, *supra* 7, at 254-255, and Shimokawa, *supra* note 31, at 15-17 and 148-154. R.B. Reich, *supra* note 46, reports that by 1992, Japanese-owned automakers planned to make or buy within the U.S.A. at least 75% of the content of their American cars which is a higher percentage than American-owned automakers.

have moved considerable manufacturing facilities abroad and made large investments in greenfield sites outside of Japan.[83]

Before the creation of the Community, the markets of the Member States were clearly separated from each other by trade barriers such as import tariffs and quotas. Whereas the export shares were already high,[84] import shares in the three Member States with an important domestic automobile industry were small. In addition, the production of automobiles in these countries was highly concentrated.[85] As soon as the barriers to intra-Community trade came down, trade in automobiles grew rapidly, product differentiation was stimulated and competition between producers (also from third countries) was intensified.[86] The removal of the barriers between the national markets within the Community did not go hand-in-hand with the removal of trade restrictions to imports from third countries. The Italian import quotum for Japanese automobiles and the British and French agreements with Japan on voluntary exports restraints, were (only) replaced in July 1991 by the so-called "understanding" on voluntary export restraints between Japan and the Community until the end of 1999. These trade barriers have not only forced the Japanese automobile industry to invest and build up more production plants within the Community but to develop strategies

[83] See for instance *FT*, "Yet another Japanese transplant threat", 16 September 1986, at 9; "Cash subsidy for Nissan", 11 September 1986, and (Survey - The Motor Industry), "Transplant production increases", 20 October 1988, at X. According to Barber, *supra* note 60, at 30, Toyota's extranational production is up to 20% of its total. It was reported in *FT*, "Toyota sets out global plan to outstrip Ford", 28 October 1997, at 20, that as part of its "drive towards globalisation, Toyota wants to raise the proportion of cars built abroad from about 29 percent last year to almost 42 percent by early next century". See also *FT*, "Honda's production tilts overseas", 21 December 1995, at 4, which reported that "Honda is set to become the first Japanese carmaker to produce more vehicles abroad than at home ... in a move highlighting the accelerating internationalisation of Japan's motor industry".

[84] Berg, *supra* note 25, at 126, reports that "in 1958, the export share of the German producers amounted to 50.4 per cent, that of the French ... 45.7 per cent and that of the Italian .. 43.0 per cent".

[85] According to Berg, *supra* note 25, at 126, "[t]he national markets were too small so as to allow an intensity of competition to a sufficient degree, a sufficiently differentiated supply and an optimal amount of production at the lowest possible costs". Berg reports that in the year 1958, "in the FRG the three biggest enterprises had 73.3 per cent, in France 79.6 per cent and in Italy even 99.1 per cent of total domestic output".

[86] See in this sense Berg, *supra* note 25, at 132-135.

to enter the profitable higher market segments as well.[87]

The production of automobiles is concentrated in the European Union (in particular Germany, France and the United Kingdom), the U.S.A., Japan, the Soviet Union and Eastern Europa, Latin America (in particular Brazil, Mexico and Argentina) and (South-)East Asia (in particular South Korea). Although about 96% of the world trade in automobiles takes place between the European Union, the U.S.A. and Japan,[88] these three markets are still very much dominated by their own automobile industries.[89] The Commission specified that in 1993, the traditional automobile manufacturers in the Community had a 84% market share in the Community while American manufacturers had 74% of the U.S.A. market. The Japanese manufacturers dominate their national market with a 97% market share.[90] Notwithstanding the fact that economists seem to disagree on the question whether the world economy is globalizing, internationalizing or regionalizing,[91] experts believe that at least the globalisation of the organisation of the automobile industry is taking

---

[87] Berg, *supra* note 25, at 143.

[88] See in this sense P. Dicken, *Global shift*, 2nd edition, 1992, Paul Chapman Publishing Ltd., London, at 272-277.

[89] See Shimokawa, *supra* note 31, at 19-22, for an analysis of the different competitive structures of the three main trading areas.

[90] 1994 Communication, *supra* note 37, at 2.

[91] See, *inter alia*, P. Krugman, *Pop internationalism*, 1996, MIT Press, Cambridge. See for discussion in the Netherlands: B. Nooteboom, "Innoveren, globaliseren", ESB, 9 October 1996, at 828-830; A. Kleinknecht and J. ter Wengel, "Feiten over globalisering", ESB, 9 October 1996, at 831-833; N. Mensink and P. van Bergeijk, "Globlablablah", ESB, 6 November 1996, at 914-916, and R.F.M. Lubbers, "Globalisering is meer dan handel", ESB, 6 November 1996, at 917.

place.[92] Moreover, many believe that internationalisation has become a condition for survival in the automobile industry.[93] Already in the early 1970s, Wells noted that the European-based automobile industry was increasingly able to operate beyond the reach of national economic policies as they could raise money outside the home country and shift production in response to wage changes or threatened labor strife. According to Wells, the industry was no longer European and the survival of a major firm in the automobile industry depended on coordinated activities that could not be responsive to European interests only.[94]

---

[92] Already in 1988, it was reported in *FT* (Survey - The Motor Industry), "The eye of the storm", 20 October 1988, at I, that "[t]he globalisation of the world automotive industry is entering a new era as the major producers seek to gain a competitive edge on their rivals by establishing a worldwide sourcing network for vehicles and components". See, *inter alia*, L.T. Wells Jr., "Automobiles" in *Big business and the state* (R. Vernon ed.), 1974, MacMillan, London, at 245-254, and Dicken, *supra* note 88, at 268, who emphasizes that "[o]rganizationally, the automobile industry is one of the most global of all manufacturing industries. It is an industry of giant corporations, many of which are increasingly organizing their activities on internationally integrated lines. ..., the world automobile industry is predominantly an industry of transnational corporations ... The ten leading automobile producers account for no less than 76 per cent of world production".

[93] It was reported in *World Investment Report 1994*, at 150, that "[a]lthough, in order to compete with the Japanese, United States and European companies have adopted measures to introduce more flexible and lean production methods to rationalize and restructure their production networks and have engaged in strategic alliances, the actual extent of their international operations and degree of global integration varies enormously. ... GM and Ford ... are unequivocally moving towards globally (and regionally) integrated companies. ... But among the leading European producers, only Volkswagen can be regarded as pursuing a genuinely internationally integrated strategy. The Japanese companies, despite their recent international expansion, are far less global in their operations than the leading United States companies". It was reported in *FT*, "Renault at staging post on long route", 4 March 1997, at 22, that analysts have pointed out that the performance of French parts suppliers is much better than that of French carmakers, as a result of the fact that the former have internationalised more succesfully. According to *FT*, "Japanese buy more car parts from abroad", 4 July 1997, at 4, Japanese carmakers buy more foreign-made car parts which "underlines the growing globalisation of Japanese car companies". See also *FT*, "Peugeot-Citroen to boost sales abroad", 26 January 1998, at 19, and "March launch for new Clio", 27 January 1998, at 25.

[94] Wells, *supra* note 92, at 254. It was reported in *FT*, "Lessons from the east", 21 May 1997, at 19, that according to an expert "It's no longer true to talk about the British motor industry, but the motor industry in Britain".

In view of the fierce competition, manufacturers tend to build production plants in those countries which offer the best conditions.[95] They have to contract with those domestic or foreign suppliers which offer the best quality for competitive prices. Furthermore, manufacturers have to sell their automobiles on a global market and are forced to compete for a piece of the market in emerging markets such as Eastern Europe, the former Soviet Union, South-America, India and China.[96] The internationalisation or globalisation of the automobile industry is further illustrated by the fact that in many cases it has become almost impossible to identify the nationality of a particular automobile as the different phases in the production process often take place in different countries by people of different nationalities and parts come from different

---

[95] See *FT*, "Valeo chief threatens to move production abroad", 17 July 1997, at 16, which reported on the French car components manufacturer Valeo's threat to move production abroad in view of French plans to reduce the working week from 39 hours to 35 hours, with no loss in pay. The fact that this is not only taking place in the Community is illustrated by *FT*, "Peso crisis turbo-charges revolution in motor trade", 11 June 1997, at 6, which reported that as a result of the 1994 North American Free Trade Agreement and the collaps of the peso, Mexico "has emerged as an export base for cars, trucks and parts more swiftly and dramatically than anyone imagined".

[96] See, for instance, *FT*, "Volvo seeks factory site in Russia", 21 April 1994; "Rising incomes driving up car sales in E Europe", 28 August 1997, at 4; "Daimler raises stake in Indian joint venture", 11 September 1997, at 15; "Daewoo links with Ukraine carmaker", 18 September 1997, at 1; "Fiat on verge of Russian deal", 24 September 1997, at 16; "Fiat agrees $800m venture with Russia's Gaz", 30 September 1997, at 22; "Why Russia's cars can still fend off foreign competition", 3 October 1997, at 4; "Daewoo starts Polish car production", 7 October 1997, at 20; "Peugeot poised to expand in Brazil", 8 October 1997, at 21; "Toyota to raise output in Brazil", 10 October 1997, at 22; "Skoda signs Indian pact", 23 October 1997, at 7; "Car ventures to grow in China", 23 October 1997, at 8; "Renault in $350m deal to set up in Moscow", 1-2 November 1997, at 24; "Peugeot to break Indian partnership", 24 November 1997, at 23; "China looks to Italians to develop car industry", 26 November 1997, at 6; "Volvo focuses on east Europe", 1 December 1997, at 21; "Land Rover to invest $150m in Brazil", 11 December 1997, at 14; "Ford plans Russian joint venture", 19 January 1998, at 19, and "Skoda overtakes Fiat in eastern Europe", 3 February 1998, at 19.

countries.[97] Therefore, it will come as no surprise that many car manufacturers make an effort to adopt global strategies in order to deal with globalisation.[98] During the presentation of a plan designed to make Ford a global corporation, its chairman, Trotman, pointed out that the automobile industry "is a worldwide business that requires the broadest thinking and execution".[99]

2.4 The Socio-Economic Importance of the Automobile Industry

The socio-economic importance of the automobile industry, the so-called "industry of industries",[100] for the Community and the Member States is beyond any doubt. In its very first edition of *Panorama of EC Industry*, the Commission introduced the chapter on "Motor vehicles" with the following words:

> Representing about 9% of the EC industrial value-added content, the automotive sector employs 1.7 million people directly (about 8% of the employment in the manufacturing industry), although it is estimated that one out of 10 jobs in the EC depends directly or indirectly on the automobile sector in the largest sense (from third-tier suppliers to

---

[97] See, *inter alia*, Barber, *supra* note 60, at 24-26; Barnet and Cavanagh, *supra* note 15, at 279-281, and R.B. Reich, *supra* note 46, at 113, emphasizes that when an American buys a Pontiac Le Mans for $20,000 from GM, about $6,000 goes to South Korea for routine labor and assembly operations; $3,500 to Japan for advanced components; $1,500 to (West-)Germany for styling and design engineering; $800 to Taiwan, Singapore and Japan for small components, and $500 to Britain for advertising and marketing services, and $100 to Ireland and Barbados for data processing. According to Reich, the rest, less than $8,000, goes to strategists in Detroit, lawyers and bankers in New York, lobbyists in Washington, insurance and health-care workers all over the U.S.A., and GM shareholders most of whom live in the U.S.A., but an increasing number of whom are foreign national.

[98] The Commission reported in *Panorama of EU Industry 1997* (on 1996), at 17-8, that Ford, Fiat, VW, GM, PSA, Renault, Mercedes Benz and BMW have adopted global strategies. Opel advertised with the slogan "A true 'World Car' may not exist. But the Opel Corsa comes close", *FT*, 4 December 1996, at 5. It was reported in *FT*, "Fiat chooses Poland to make new world car", 6 February 1996, at 5, and "Fiat looks to Brazilian unit to lead growth", 28 October 1996, at 21, that Fiat will introduce the Pallio "world car" and that by 2000 it would be producing 54% of its cars outside Italy.

[99] See *FT*, "Tomorrow, the world", 22 April 1994, at 15. See also *FT*, "Drive to customise structures", 15 October 1997, at 14.

[100] P. Drucker, *Concept of the corporation*, 1946, The John Day Company, New York, at 176.

> servicing and repair shops). Its importance to the Community economy is vital in terms of external trade (21.1 billion ECU of net positive balance or 29% of the total manufactured goods balance in 1986), industrial development and technological innovation. Although the market is not expected to grow by more than 1% - 2% per annum, it should continue to be the largest world market for passenger cars with scope for growth in terms of value as European consumers tend to move upmarket.[101]

The many statistics published over the years by the Commission confirm the importance of the automobile industry to the economy of the Community and the Member States.[102] These statistics show, for instance, that the automobile industry is still an important positive contributor to the trade balance of the Community, and that although the automobile industry can no longer be regarded as a sector of employment growth, it still is one of the most important employers in the Community and the Member States. In 1992 the Commission estimated that about 10% of all employment in the Community depended directly or indirectly on the production of automobiles.[103] Two years later, in 1994, the Commission shifted from a percentage to numbers when it reported that the automobile industry in the Community employed more than 1.8 million people in the supply and manufacturing chain. According to the Commission, another 1.8 million people were employed in the distribution and repair sector and the livelihood of many more citizens depended indirectly on the success of the automobile industry.[104] In 1996, the Commission estimated that direct employment in the automobile industry had decreased from 2.2 million in 1980

---

[101] *Panorama of EC Industry 1989*, Commission of the European Communities ("*Panorama 1989*"), at 14-1.

[102] The Commission published a *Panorama of EC Industry* on 1989, 1990, 1991-1992 (with an additional supplement on 1992) and 1993. Subsequently, the Commission published a *Panorama of EU Industry* on 1994, 1995-1996 and 1997.

[103] Communication from the Commission to the Council, the European Parliament and the Economic and Social Committee on "The European Motor Vehicle Industry: Situation, Issues at Stake, and Proposals for Action", 8 May 1992, COM(92)166 final ("1992 Communication"), at 2-3.

[104] 1994 Communication, *supra* note 37, at 2.

to 1.6 million in 1994 and emphasized that in view of the considerable competitive pressure on the industry to reduce costs, further reduction was to be expected. But at the same time, the Commission repeated that "[t]aking upstream, downstream and related activities into account, up to ten jobs in Europe are dependant on each job in the automotive industry".[105]

The strategic role of the automobile industry for the economy in general is directly related to the manner of production and distribution of automobiles. According to Shimokawa,

> [t]he strategic role of the automobile industry in any economy of an automobile producing country is due principally to the nature of automobile design, production, distribution and method of transport. The industry requires support from a myriad of parts and component suppliers, as well as general material suppliers. The automobile represents the latest in design, materials construction and machine and electronic technologies ...
> At the same time, the industry requires extensive distribution networks and support services for the sale and maintenance of automobiles.[106]

But the automobile industry is not only a "pace-setting industry" and a "focal point of industrial progress"[107] which can and has been used by governments as a tool to promote national economic interests such as the promotion of regional development and a positive trade balance. It is also considered to be a key

---

[105] Communication from the Commission to the Council, the European Parliament, the Economic and Social Committee and the Committee of the Regions on the "European Automobile Industry", 10 July 1996, COM(96)327 final ("1996 Communication"), at 9, footnote 26.

[106] Shimokawa, *supra* note 31, at 19. See Dicken, *supra* note 88, at 269-271, for a concise description of the basic automobile production system.

[107] See, *inter alia*, *Panorama 1989*, *supra* note 101, at 14-1, and *Panorama of EC Industry 1990*, Commission of the European Communities ("*Panorama 1990*"), at 13-6.

industry for military strength and national prestige. Several car manufacturers have acquired the status of "national champion" and are still treated as such.[108]

2.5 The Implications of the Socio-Economic Importance of the Automobile Industry

The socio-economic importance of the automobile industry has been a reason for many Member States to be actively and directly involved in the automobile industry.[109] Several Member States have taken significant *share-holdings* in (parts of) their domestic automobile industry. For instance, the United Kingdom was the main shareholder in British Leyland[110] and Alfa Romeo was a subsidiary of the Italian government holding IRI.[111] Renault used to be a fully state-owned *regie*. After Renault's privatisation, France still holds a 44% interest and

---

108 According to "How to put a ruler in the driver's seat: a national carmaker", *International Herald Tribune*, 18-19 October 1997, at 1, national cars are intoxicating for political leaders as they create a whole national industry with a local demand for labor and a wide variety of products; producing cars has become a matter of national ego and nationalistic politics. National governments are still prepared, even in the face of international protests and over-capacity in the automobile industry, "to subsidize and protect their pet projects" as "the lure of joining the ranks of car-producing nations is a lot stronger than the discipline of economic logic".

109 See Dicken, *supra* note 88, at 284-287; Wells, *supra* note 92, at 229-254, and S. Reich, "Roads to follow: Regulating direct foreign investment", *International Organization* 43, 4, Autumn 1989, at 553-568, for a detailed description of the public policies of the German, Italian, French and British governments with regard to their domestic automobile industry. See also "The effect of different state aid measures on intra-Community competition - Exemplified by the case of the automotive industry" (prepared by K. Bhaskar and the Motor industry research unit), Commission of the European Communities, March 1990.

110 See in this context K. George, "Public ownership versus privatisation" in *Competition in Europe*, *supra* note 32, at 176-178. British Leyland was created when British Motor Holdings and Leyland Motor Corporation merged. Eventually, it was turned into the Rover Group which was taken over by BMW.

111 The Commission reported in Decision 89/661 of 31 May 1989, OJ 1989, L394/11, that Alfa Romeo became part of IRI in 1933. Eventually, Alfa Romeo was taken over by Fiat.

appoints five out of 14 seats on its board of directors.[112] The Netherlands decided to participate in a joint-venture between Volvo and Mitsubishi[113] and the German state Lower Saxony holds 20% of the shares of Volkswagen while its premier is on VW's supervisory board.[114] These participations not only provide the Member States with a certain grip on the strategies and operations of the manufacturers concerned, they also tend to shield the latter from the full impact of competitive pressures.[115]

In view of the socio-economic importance of the automobile industry, governments develop and implement various policies with the specific needs of the domestic automobile industry in mind.[116] These policies tend to focus on the (i) degree of access granted by the state to the foreign automobile industry and (ii) the type of support provided by the state to the domestic automobile

[112] As pointed out in *FT*, "Renault appoints Carlos Chosn", 4 September 1996, at 12, the majority of the shares of Renault "are now back in private hands for the first time in more than half a century". See also *FT*, "Santer hits at Renault closure", 10 March 1997, at 2; "Carmakers hit by rejection of retirement plan", 27 February 1997, at 2; "Belgium attacks Renault's "brutal" shutdown", 1-2 March 1997, at 1; "Belgium set to sue Renault on factory closure", 4 March 1997, at 1; "Renault at staging post on long route", 4 March 1997, at 22; "Renault looks again at plant closure", 11 June 1997, at 2, and "France prepares to sell part of Renault stake", 20 February 1998, at 1.

[113] See on the early history of Dutch car production: de Jong and de Boer, *supra* note 25, at 5-8. See also *FT*, "Volvo keen to raise stake in NedCar to 50%", 10 July 1997, at 14.

[114] See, *inter alia*, *FT*, "VW executive faces charges over GM papers", 9-10 November 1996, at 24, and "Driven on to the defensive", 28 November 1996, at 13.

[115] See *FT*, "Rough ride for Renault", 6 March 1997, at 13.

[116] For instance, Wells, *supra* note 92, at 233, has pointed out that "it is difficult to determine, in much of the history of the Italian automobile policy, whether the government was responsive to a perceived national interest, or whether the policies were simply responses to the requests of the leading automobile manufacturer".

industry.[117] Several Member States have a long tradition in limiting the possibilities for foreign corporations to *access* the domestic market.[118] This was accomplished primarily through protectionist trade policy measures in an effort to protect the domestic automobile industry. Before the creation of the Community, national import quota's and tariffs were popular instruments to restrict the importation of foreign-made automobiles. For instance, on 1 January 1959, the import tariff on cars in Italy was 46.8%, in France 34.7%, in Belgium and Luxemburg 27.9%, in the Netherlands 25.9% and in W.-Germany 14.8%. As a result, import shares were very small; in France and Italy 2% and in W.-Germany about 5% of total registrations.[119] After the creation of the Community and more particular in the period 1958 to 1968, trade in automobiles within the Community grew and led to a remarkable increase of import shares of total registration of newly licensed automobiles.[120]

In the 1960s, quotas, import tariffs, economic incentives and the creation of the Community attracted important direct foreign investments from

[117] See in this context S. Reich, *supra* note 109, at 546 who seems to come to the conclusion, based on a comparison of different European experiences (France, the United Kingdom and West Germany), that the most effective policy may be the (German) policy to combine unlimited access to multi-national corporations with discriminatory government policies designed to aid local automobile producers. See, however, *FT*, "Nissan UK plant tops productivity table", 27 August 1997, at 1, which reports that a study of productivity among European car companies by the Economist Intelligence Unit "confirms the resurgence of motor manufacturing in Britain on the back of Japanese investment" and provides "ammunition for supporters of Britain as a manufacturing base for foreign investors, in spite of the sharp rise in sterling". See also *FT*, "French go into overdrive to win investors" and "Toyota picks France for new plant", 10 December 1997, at 7.

[118] See S. Reich, *supra* note 109, at 553-568, for an overview of the French, British and West-German policies on access granted to foreign firms.

[119] Berg, *supra* note 25, at 126.

[120] See Chapter 4. Berg, *supra* note 25, at 133-135, reported that during this period the lions share of intra-Community trade had a complementary rather than a substitutive character. According to Berg, the mushroom growth of the economies of the Member States in the sixties made the liberalization possible; "[t]ariff reductions are politically easy to achieve if they cause a welcome expansion of supply and hardly necessitate adjustments".

the American automobile industry.[121] This was considered by several Member States to be a serious threat to both their domestic automobile industry and national economy.[122] As a result, a number of Member States restricted foreign direct investment, blocked American take-overs of domestic car manufacturers and instituted "local content" rules. Similar measures were taken when it became evident that the automobile industry within the Community had difficulty in competing with the Japanese automobile industry. A number of Member States with a domestic automobile industry implemented (further) quantitative restrictions with regard to the importation of Japanese automobiles.[123] Italy, Portugal and Spain fixed official quantitative restrictions.[124] France restricted Japanese imports to 3% of domestic sales by means of restrictive administrative practices leading to long delays in type-approval procedures.[125] The United Kingdom followed suit by means of a SMMT/JAMA voluntary export restraint agreement which limited the share of

---

[121] It is interesting to note that according to R. Gilpin, *U.S. power and the multinational corporation*, 1975, Basic Books Inc., London, at 108, the creation of the Community was supported by the U.S.A. in exchange for an assurance that "an American-owned subsidiary would be treated equally with national firms of European countries".

[122] See in this sense J.-J. Servan-Schreiber, *The American Challenge*, 1969, Pelican Books, Middlesex.

[123] In *Panorama 1989*, *supra* note 101, at 14-2, the Commission considered it "not surprising" that governments intervened by means of trade protection in order to facilitate the restructuring of the automobile industry. See in a similar sense: *Panorama 1990*, *supra* note 107, at 13-10.

[124] See for instance Council Regulation 288/82 of 5 February 1982 on common rules for imports, Annex I ("List of products subject to national quantitative restriction on their entry into free circulation"), OJ 1982, L35/1. See for details on the Italian quantitative restrictions: Case 82/87R, *Autexpo* v *Commission*, [1987] ECR 2131. According to Berg, *supra* note 25, at 142-143, "Italy had fixed the annually allowed imports of Japanese cars to a mere 2,000(!) items already at the beginning of the sixties".

[125] See for details on the French restrictive administrative practices: Case C-72/90, *Asia Motor France* v *Commission (Asia Motor I)*, [1990] ECR I-2181; Case C-29/92, *Asia Motor France* v *Commission (Asia Motor II)*, [1992] ECR I-3936; Case T-28/90, *Asia Motor France* v *Commission (Asia Motor III)*, [1992] ECR II-2285; Case T-7/92, *Asia Motor France and others* v *Commission (Asia Motor IV)*, [1993] ECR II-669; Case T-387/94, *Asia Motor France and others* v *Commission (Asia Motor V)*, [1996] ECR II-965; Case C-386/92, *Monin Automobiles - Maison du Deux-Roues (Monin I)*, [1993] ECR I-2049, and Case C-428/93, *Monin Automobiles - Maison du Deux-Roues (Monin II)*, [1994] ECR I-1707.

Japanese cars to about 11% of the British market.[126] Other countries in Europe took similar measures.[127] As a result, Japanese automobiles became the subject of intra-Community restrictions based on Article 115 EC in order to control "indirect imports" of Japanese cars into the markets of those Member States which had national quantitative restrictions. When the Japanese automobile industry set up production plants within the Community, several Member States took the position that depending on the level of "local content", automobiles manufacturered by the Japanese automobile industry within the Community should be included in the import quota.[128] In July 1991, the Community and Japan reached an "understanding" on voluntary export restraints for Japanese automobiles. In addition, targets were set for the export of Japanese cars to France, Italy, the United Kingdom, Spain and Portugal. This "understanding" will remain in force until the end of 1999.[129]

Besides limiting access to the domestic market, most Member States tend to develop and implement policies in an effort to *support* their domestic automobile industry. Member States facilitate access to, and at times even provide funds to finance the massive investments necessary to improve the

---

[126] See with regard to the British voluntary export restraints agreement between SMMT and JAMA: Case T-37/92, *BEUC* v *Commission (BEUC)*, [1994] ECR II-285. See also D. Greenaway and B. Hindley, *What Britain pays for voluntary export restraints*, Thames Essay No. 43, 1985, Trade Policy Research Centre, London, at 1-28, 64-93; M.C.E.J. Bronckers, "A legal analysis of protectionist measures affecting Japanese imports into the European Community - Revisited" in *Protectionism and the European Community* (E.L.M. Völker ed.), 2nd edition, 1986, Kluwer, Deventer, at 79; H. Yamane, "Grey area measures, the Uruguay Round, and the EC/Japan commercial census on cars" in *The European Union and world trade law - After the GATT Uruguay Round* (N. Emiliou and D. O'Keeffe eds.), 1996, Wiley, Chichester, at 279-280; *Panorama of EC Industry 1991-1992*, Commission of the European Communities, at 13-13, and *Panorama of EC Industry of 1993*, Commission of the European Communities, at 11-14.

[127] See *FT* (Survey - The Motor Industry), "Fighting off the Japanese", 20 October 1988, at VIII, on the voluntary export restraint-agreement between Japan and Sweden. See Written Question 590/95 (Nussbaumer), OJ 1995, C202/22, on the arrangement between Austria and Japan on "compensatory orders".

[128] This led to problems. For instance, problems arose with regard to the Nissan Bluebirds which were assembled in the United Kingdom and consisted for 80% of European parts. See in this context, *inter alia*, R.B. Reich, *supra* note 46, at 118.

[129] See Chapter 5.

competitiveness of, their domestic automobile industry.[130] Tax-schemes and subsidies are used to support and, if necessary, restructure the automobile industry. For instance, in the 1920s, tax-schemes were used in Italy and France to obstruct the import and sale of American automobiles.[131] More recently, government-sponsored incentives for car replacement have been used by France, Spain, Germany and Italy to boost the recovery of their respective national car markets and thereby their economies. In practice, these incentives were mainly to the benefit of the domestic automobile industry.[132] It has been reported that a car manufacturer like Renault has benefited for years from favourable tax treatment and alleviations of social security payments.[133] For instance, in 1996, Renault and PSA requested financial support from the French government to fund plans to improve the competitiveness and productivity by cutting thousands of jobs in French plants and reducing the average age of

---

[130] The Commission noted in *Panorama 1989*, *supra* note 101, at 14-2, that this "government intervention" is "not surprising". See in a similar sense *Panorama 1990*, *supra* note 107, at 13-10.

[131] Wells, *supra* note 92, at 233-234. See Rhys, *supra* note 2, at 243-256, for an analysis of government influence on the use of and demand for automobiles in the United Kingdom.

[132] See, *inter alia*, *FT*, "Hard road to higher sales", 15 December 1995, at 12; "Incentives are a hard habit to kick", 13 September 1996, at 2; "French scramble to buy cars before incentives go", 26 September 1996, at 3; "French car plan discontinued", 27 September 1996, at 2; "France boosts European car sales", 16 October 1996, at 2; "Italy ponders incentives for car market", 21 November 1996, at 3; "Italians look to the motor industry to lift economy", 2 January 1997, at 2; "Fiat looks to state for orders boost in Italy", 31 January 1997, at 22; "Incentives give Europe's car sales a boost", 15 January 1997, at 2; "Italian car registrations soar", 11 March 1997, at 2; "European car sales distorted by incentives", 16 April 1997, at 2; "New car sales rise on national incentive plans", 15 May 1997, at 2; "Italy boosts new car sales", 16 July 1997, at 2; "Italy scheme keeps car sales afloat", 12 August 1997, at 2; "French car sales hit by end of incentives", 3-4 January 1998, at 24; "Europe's car sales well ahead of forecasts", 14 January 1998, at 2, and "European car sales increase by 9.2%", 16 March 1998, at 3. It was reported in *FT* (World Economy and Finance), "Car sales are driving the recovery", 19 September 1997, at IX, that the second quarter recovery was mainly due to an incentive scheme to trade in used cars; Fiat was the main beneficiary of the scheme. In its answer to Written Question 626/97 (Moretti), OJ 1997, C319/139, the Commission noted that the Italian incentives cannot be qualified as state aid within the meaning of Article 92(1) EC and emphasized the non-discriminatory nature of the incentives.

[133] S. Reich, *supra* note 109, at 556.

employees. Only one day after this request was denied,[134] Renault announced the abrupt closure of its profitable plant in Vilvoorde, Belgium.[135] At the same time, Renault tried (without success) to obtain Spanish state aid for additional investment at its plant in Valladolid, Spain.[136]

Subsidies are also used to attract foreign direct investment from car manufacturers, particularly in economically deprived regions. Subsidies have made it financially attractive for the automobile industry to invest and locate new greenfield sites in poor regions with a high unemployment rate.[137] At times, the competition for direct foreign investment turns into a subsidy race between governments and even between different regional development boards.[138] The

---

[134] *FT*, "Carmakers hit by rejection of retirement plan", 27 February 1997, at 2, reported that the French government rejected the request but was ready "to discuss more general ways for the companies to improve their competitive position". Already in 1996, it was reported in *FT*, "French carmakers could cut thousands of jobs", 14 November 1996, at 16, that a "working group" had been set up by the French government and PSA and Renault, in view of the fact that both companies wanted to cut thousands of jobs in order to "improve competitiveness and contain costs in the face of cut-throat competition from foreign manufacturers".

[135] The Belgian plant accounted for less than 10% of Renault's passenger car output. See, *inter alia*, *FT*, "Renault to close Belgian car plant", 28 February 1997, at 16; "Belgium attacks Renault's 'brutal' shutdown", 1-2 March 1997, at 1; "Renault at staging post on long route", 4 March 1997, at 22, and "Paris calls Renault chiefs to new talks on jobs cuts", 5 March 1997, at 14.

[136] See *FT*, "Van Miert threat to Renault", 7 March 1997, at 2. It was reported in *FT*, "Plant closure hits Renault hopes for aid from Spain", 8-9 March 1997, at 2, that Commission officials warned that the aid "would be carefully scrutinised to ensure Renault was not moving production from Belgium to Spain to take advantage of state subsidies". According to *FT*, "Brussels looks at tightening rules on subsidies", 10 March 1997, at 1, the Commission is examining ways of preventing companies from relocating from one Member State to receive subsidies in another, or "hopping" between zones that are eligible for aid and collecting subsidies several times. The Commission looks at ways to stop companies from benefiting from aid -at least at full levels- more than once within a certain timeframe. See also *Agence Europe*, "Developments in the Renault affair - Spain suspends request concerning aid to valladolid installations, The Commission is to study relocation to maximise aid", 8 March 1997, at 9.

[137] See in this context Written Question 478/95 (Miranda), OJ 1995, C196/32.

[138] See, *inter alia*, R.B. Reich, *supra* note 46, at 295-298, and *FT*, "Affording Ford", 22 January 1997, at 13; "Ford workers set for strike action", 7 February 1997, at 8, and "Ford chief confident of state subsidy", 5 March 1997, at 8, on Ford's determination to build the next generation Escort at its Halewood-plant (N-W England) only if productivity improved and government incentives were offered. Ford threatened the United Kingdom to concentrate production in Spain and Germany. See *FT*, "Curb state aid" (editorial), 8 January 1998, at 11, on inter-regional competition to attract inward investors.

following chart gives an impression of the incentives given by state and local governments in the Community and the U.S.A. to attract investment by the automobile industry:

Auction-house frenzy[139]

Location	**Year**	**Plant**	**$ per employee**
Portugal	1991	Auto Europa (Ford/VW)	254,000
Alabama	1993	Mercedes-Benz	167,000
South Carolina	1994	BMW	108,000
Birmingham	1995	Jaguar	129,000
Lorraine	1995	Mercedes-Benz (Swatch)	57,000

Through these and other national policy measures, Member States try to temper with or even re-direct the forces of the free market economy in an effort to win the race for direct foreign investment, maintain and create jobs, develop economically deprived regions and protect, restructure and modernize the domestic automobile industry.[140] According to Holmes and Smith, it is evident that on the whole, Member States have chosen to sustain a larger automobile industry than market forces might have promoted. Holmes and Smith point out that as the objective position and therefore the national interests of Member States vary considerably, there has not been a true common market in this sector and the automobile industry "in Europe has been one of the less integrated industries, with even multinational producers supplying markets locally, many firms relying very heavily on home sales (especially Fiat), and a

[139] This chart is taken from "Uncommercial travellers", *The Economist*, 1-7 February 1997, at 25. Reference is made to "Sources: UNCTAD; press reports".

[140] See "Europe's great car war", *The Economist*, 8 March 1997, at 69-70, on the confrontation and "the growing gulf between Europe's business people and its politicians" with regard to the restructuring of the automobile industry and (in particular) its socio-economic consequences. See for an example *FT*, "French Socialists attack cuts in car jobs", 4 June 1997, at 2, in which a senior Socialist spokesman stresses that "[w]e will not allow the carmakers to do away with jobs without referring the matter to the public authorities".

considerable emphasis on the role of national champions".[141] The fact that the national interests of the various Member States with a domestic automobile industry are not necessarily the same or even compatible,[142] tends to further complicate and at times even frustrates clear policy-making within the Community.

2.6 Concluding Remarks

The production process in the automobile industry has gone from mass to lean production and is expected to head for virtual production. In addition, the organisation of the automobile industry is further globalizing and manufacturers compete on a highly competitive global market with overcapacity. The leading car manufacturers have production plants all over the world, contract worldwide with those suppliers which offer the best quality and price, and compete worldwide for market share in emerging markets. Most multi-national car manufacturers are in a position to shop-around from one state to another in search for the most attractive environment for their production sites. These developments have intensified competition, forcing the automobile industry in the Community to engage in an ongoing process of reorganization in an effort to catch-up with its competitors. These developments brought to light the urgent need to enhance competitiveness through the adoption of lean production techniques and a radical improvement in development and production efficiency, cost competitiveness and innovation. Furthermore, the change to lean and virtual production techniques will further alter the relationship between the manufacturers, suppliers and other actors in the automobile industry. For

[141] P. Holmes and A. Smith, "Automobile industry" in *European Policies on Competition, Trade and Industry* (P. Buigues, A. Jacquemin and A. Sapir eds.), 1995, Edward Elgar, Aldershot, at 134. *FT*, "Rough ride for Renault", 6 March 1997, at 13, reported that subsidies "have distorted the industry for too long by keeping open inefficient factories".

[142] For instance, it was reported in *FT*, "Renault's cruel cut", 5 March 1997, at 14, that the abrupt closure of Renault's Belgian plant created the impression that Renault was "pursuing a nationalistic approach to job cuts" and was ducking a more radical restructuring by shutting a productive foreign plant rather than one of its high-cost French ones. "Europe's great car war", *The Economist*, 8 March 1997, at 69, underlined the fact that "[c]ompanies in Europe have traditionally begun rationalisation farthest from home, by lopping off their branch factories and repatriating production to save domestic jobs".

instance, manufacturers will continue to outsource more of what they formerly produced in-house to fewer suppliers who will have to become closely involved in the design, development and manufacturing process. It is expected that manufacturers will also try to rationalize their distribution networks.

Notwithstanding these developments, the socio-economic importance of the automobile industry for the Community and the Member States is beyond any doubt. The operations of the automobile industry have an important impact on the trade balance, employment, industrial innovation and the development of other sectors of industries in the Community. The automobile industry triggers nationalistic sentiments and is considered a key industry for national prestige. For these reasons, Member States have been actively and directly involved in their domestic automobile industry. Over the years, Member States have taken considerable share-holdings in the automobile industry and have implemented policies on the degree of access granted by the state to the foreign autombile industry and the type of support provided by the state to the domestic automobile industry. These various forms of state intervention shielded the protected domestic automobile industry from the full impact of international competitive pressures.

3. THE EC TREATY

3.1 Introduction

The purpose of this chapter is to facilitate an understanding of the legal context of the case study. This chapter gives an introduction to the EC Treaty, being the basic constitutional charter of the legal system in which the Community operates.[1] It also elaborates on the relevance of GATT and the WTO Agreement. First, the wording and legal significance of the preamble to the EC Treaty will be looked at (**3.2**). Then, the task referred to in Article 2 EC (**3.3**) and the Community's means to accomplish this task as set out in Articles 3 and 3a EC (**3.4**), will be elaborated upon. The significance of Article 5 EC will also be touched upon (**3.5**). Subsequently, the position of the Community and the Member States under GATT and the WTO Agreement will be addressed (**3.6**). Finally, some concluding remarks are offered (**3.7**).

3.2 The Preamble to the EC Treaty

The nine recitals of the preamble to the *EC Treaty* set out the motives and ideals of the six founding Member States which led them to create the Community.[2] These Member States were determined to lay the foundations of an ever closer union among the peoples of Europe[3] and affirmed as the essential objective of their efforts the constant improvement of the living and working conditions of their peoples.[4] The Member States were resolved to ensure the economic and social progress of their countries by common action to eliminate the barriers that divide Europe,[5] and were anxious to strengthen the unity of their economies and to ensure their harmonious development by reducing the differences existing between the various regions as well as the "backwardness" of the less favoured regions.[6] The Member States recognized that the removal of existing obstacles calls for concerted action in order to guarantee steady expansion,

---

[1] Case 294/83, *Les Verts* v *European Parliament*, [1986] ECR 1365, par. 23.

[2] Recital 9 of the EC Treaty.

[3] Recital 1 of the EC Treaty.

[4] Recital 3 of the EC Treaty.

[5] Recital 2 of the EC Treaty.

[6] Recital 5 of the EC Treaty.

balanced trade and fair competition. Furthermore, the Member States desired to contribute, by means of a common commercial policy, to the progressive abolition of restrictions on international trade[7] and they confirmed the solidarity which binds Europe and the overseas countries as well as the desire to ensure the development of their prosperity, in accordance with the principles of the Charter of the United Nations.[8] By thus pooling their resources, the Member States wanted to preserve and strengthen peace and liberty, and called upon the other peoples of Europe who share their ideal to join in their efforts.[9]

The twelve recitals of the preamble to the *EU Treaty*, which substantially amended the EC Treaty, point to a new stage in the process of European integration.[10] In addition, they identify several ideals and intentions, such as the resolution of the Member States to achieve the strengthening and the convergence of their economies and to establish an economic and monetary union including, in accordance with the provisions of the Treaty, a single and stable currency.[11] The Member States confirmed their determination to promote economic and social progress for their peoples, within the context of the creation of the internal market and of reinforced cohesion and environmental protection, and to implement policies ensuring that advances in economic integration be accompanied by parallel progress in other fields.[12] The Member States expressed their resolution to continue the process of creating "an ever closer union" among the peoples of Europe, in which decisions are taken as closely as possible to the citizen in accordance with the principle of subsidiarity.[13]

The wording of these rather political motives and ideals set out in the preamble to the *EC Treaty* is of considerable importance as it constitutes the context in which the provisions of the EC Treaty have to be read, interpreted

---

[7] Recital 6 of the EC Treaty.

[8] Recital 7 of the EC Treaty.

[9] Recital 8 of the EC Treaty.

[10] Recital 1 of the EU Treaty. See also the second paragraph of Article A of the EU Treaty.

[11] Recital 6 of the EU Treaty. See also Article B of the EU Treaty.

[12] Recital 7 of the EU Treaty. See also Article B of the EU Treaty.

[13] Recital 11 of the EU Treaty. See also the second paragraph of Article A of the EU Treaty.

and applied.[14] The legal significance of the preamble has been explicitly confirmed by the ECJ in several cases. For instance, the ECJ held that Article 85 EC, being an important element of the Community's system to ensure that competition in the internal market is not distorted,[15] "should be read in the context of the provisions of the preamble to the Treaty which clarify it and reference should particularly be made to those relating to 'the elimination of barriers' and to 'fair competition' both of which are necessary for bringing about a single market".[16] It is not entirely clear whether the preamble to the *EU Treaty* is of similar importance for the interpretation and application of the amendments to the EC Treaty laid down in Title II of the EU Treaty. First of all, Article L of the EU Treaty does not list the preamble as falling under the jurisdiction of the ECJ, which could mean that the ECJ is not competent to even consider the preamble as part of the context of the amendments to the EC Treaty. Moreover, Article M of the EU Treaty provides that nothing in that Treaty shall affect the EC Treaty other than "the provisions amending the Treaty establishing the European Economic Community with a view to establishing the European Community" and the final provisions (Articles L to S) of the EU Treaty. This does not include the text of the preamble.[17] Therefore, one could come to the conclusion that Articles L and M of the EU Treaty imply that the preamble to the EU Treaty cannot be taken into account while reading, interpretating and applying the amendments to the EC Treaty brought about by Title II of the EU Treaty. It is submitted, however, that such an interpretation of Articles L and M of the EU Treaty is not desirable as the recitals of the preamble to the EU Treaty are an inherent part of its context which clarify the meaning of the amendments concerned and should therefore be taken into account for the interpretation and

[14] See, *inter alia*, M. Zuleeg in H. Von Der Groeben, J. Thiesing and C.-D. Ehlermann, *Kommentar zum EWG-Vertrag*, 4th edition, 1991, Nomos Verlagsgesellschaft, Baden-Baden, at 54, par. 2.

[15] See Article 3(g) EC.

[16] Case 32/65, *Italy* v *Council and Commission*, [1966] ECR 405. See also, *inter alia*, Case 26/62, *Van Gend en Loos* v *Nederlandse Administratie der belastingen*, [1963] ECR 12; Joined Cases 56 and 58/64, *Consten and Grundig* v *Commission*, [1966] ECR 340 and Case 136/79, *National Panasonic* v *Commission*, [1980] ECR 2057, par. 20.

[17] See Zuleeg in Groeben, Thiesing and Ehlermann, *supra* note 14, at 54-55, par. 3, for a similar reasoning in the context of Articles 31 and 32 of the Single European Act.

application of the amendments to the EC Treaty brought about by Title II of the EU Treaty.

3.3 The Task of the Community

Article 2 EC provides that the Community shall have as its task, to promote throughout the Community:

- a harmonious and balanced development of economic activities,
- sustainable and non-inflationary growth respecting the environment,
- a high degree of convergence of economic performance,
- a high level of employment and of social protection,
- the raising of the standard of living and quality of life,
- economic and social cohesion and solidarity among Member States.[18]

The Community has to perform this task by establishing a common market and an economic and monetary union and by implementing the common policies or activities referred to in Articles 3 and 3a EC. The task of the Community is to *promote* throughout the Community the objectives listed in Article 2 EC. The verb "promote" implies that the Community has to take an active stand and is, in principle, not competent to go against the objectives set out in Article 2 EC.

Article 2 EC defines and thereby limits the activities of the Community to the accomplishment of a particular task, using specific means. As pointed out in Article 3b EC, the Community shall act within the limits of the *powers* conferred upon it by the EC Treaty and of the *objectives* assigned to it therein. It also specifies that in areas which do not fall within its exclusive competence, the Community shall take action, in accordance with the principle of subsidiarity, only if and in so far as the objectives of the proposed action cannot be sufficiently achieved by the Member States and can therefore, by reason of the

---

[18] After the entry into force of the Treaty of Amsterdam, the wording will be as follows: "promote throughout the Community a harmonious, balanced and sustainable development of economic activities, a high level of employment and of social protection, equality between men and women, sustainable and non-inflationary growth, a high degree of competitiveness and convergence of economic performance, a high level of protection and improvement of the quality of the environment, the raising of the standard of living and quality of life, and economic and social cohesion and solidarity among Member States".

scale or effects of the proposed action, be better achieved by the Community. In addition, the third paragraph of Article 3b EC provides that any action by the Community shall not go beyond what is necessary to achieve the objectives of the EC Treaty.[19] In other words, the Community must actively carry out its task as set out in Article 2 EC and further elaborated upon in Articles 3 and 3a EC, acting within the limits of the powers conferred upon it by the EC Treaty; nothing more and nothing less.

The aims set out in Articles 2 and 3 EC cannot have the effect of either imposing legal obligations on the Member States or conferring rights on individuals.[20] It should be emphasized, however, that, vague as the wording of Articles 2, 3 and 3a EC may seem, they are of great legal significance for the way in which the other provisions of the EC Treaty have to be interpreted and applied. For instance, the ECJ held in *Continental Can* that:

> Article 3 considers the pursuit of the objectives which it lays down to be indispensable for the achievement of the Community's tasks. As regards in particular the aim mentioned in (f) [undistorted competition], the Treaty in several provisions contains more detailed regulations for the interpretation of which this aim is decisive.[21]

The ECJ emphasized that:

> if Article 3(f) provides for the institution of a system ensuring that competition in the Common Market is not distorted, then it requires *a fortiori* that competition must not be eliminated. This requirement is so essential that without it numerous provisions of the Treaty would be pointless. Moreover, it corresponds to the precept of Article 2 of the Treaty according to which one of the tasks of the Community is "to promote throughout the Community a harmonious development of economic activities". Thus the restraints on competition which the

---

[19] See in this context the Protocol on the application of the principles of subsidiarity and proportionality, attached to the Treaty of Amsterdam.

[20] Case C-339/89, *Alsthom Atlantique* v *Sulzer*, [1991] ECR I-123, paras. 8-9.

[21] Case 6/72, *Continental Can* v *Commission (Continental Can)*, [1973] ECR 244, par. 23.

> Treaty allows under certain conditions because of the need to harmonize the various objectives of the Treaty, are limited by the requirements of Articles 2 and 3. Going beyond this limit involves the risk that the weakening of competition would conflict with the aims of the Common Market.[22]

As was the case with the text of the preamble to the EC Treaty (and probably the EU Treaty), Articles 2 and 3 EC form part of the legal context of the provisions of the EC Treaty and are, therefore, of great legal significance for their interpretation and application. It is submitted that the same is true for Article 3a EC as its contents are to be considered additions to the list of activities to be undertaken by the Community. Article 3a EC has the same function as Article 3 EC in relation to the other provisions of the EC Treaty.[23]

3.4 The Means of the Community

The wording of Article 2 EC implies that the Community has to carry out its task (literally) by establishing a common market *and* an economic and monetary union *and* by implementing the common policies or activities referred to in Articles 3 and 3a EC. It is submitted that this should be read as a listing of means which are cumulative but distinct, thereby leading to the conclusion that all three constitute separate means. One can therefore argue that the obligation on the Community to establish both a common market and an economic and monetary union implies that it can do so through policies or activities other than or in addition to those listed in Articles 3 and 3a EC. One could take the position that the Community's obligation to create a common market as such constitutes a sufficient legal basis to do so by means of the various competences set out in the EC Treaty including but not limited to the competences referred to in Articles 3 and 3a EC. In practice, however, these competences are used to abolish the obstacles to the free movement of goods, persons, services and capital *and* to create a system ensuring that competition in the internal market is not distorted

---

[22] *Ibidem*, par. 24. See also *Italy* v *Council and Commission*, *supra* note 16 and Case 270/80, *Polydor* v *Harlequin Record Shops*, [1982] ECR 348, par. 16.

[23] See R. Lane, "New Community competence under the Maastricht Treaty", 30 CML Rev. at 944.

and, thereby, contribute to the establishment of a common market. At the same time, one could argue that the activities listed in Articles 3 and 3a EC are not only means to establish a common market and an economic and monetary union but constitute objectives themselves which can be pursued as such for the purposes set out in Article 2 EC.[24]

3.4.1 Common Market

The establishment of a common market in accordance with Article 7 EC is one of the Community's means for carrying out its task within the context of the motives and ideals set out in the preamble to the EC Treaty[25] and for pursuing the objectives set out in Article 2 EC. At the same time, however, the creation of the common market has become a purpose in and of itself.[26] The EC Treaty does not provide for a definition of common market. The ECJ, however, identified several elements of what can be considered a common market. The ECJ specified that "[t]he concept of a common market as defined by the Court in a consistent line of decisions involves the elimination of all obstacles to intra-Community trade in order to merge the national markets into a single market bringing about conditions as close as possible to those of a genuine internal market".[27] It is submitted that this description implies that the common market is not identical to nor interchangeable with the internal market. A common market *aims* at bringing about conditions which are as close as possible to those of an

---

[24] See P. VerLoren van Themaat in P.J.G. Kapteyn and P. VerLoren van Themaat, *Inleiding tot het recht van de Europese Gemeenschappen - Na Maastricht*, 5th edition, 1995, Kluwer, Deventer, at 74.

[25] See P.J.G. Kapteyn and P. VerLoren van Themaat, *Introduction to the law of the European Communities* (L.W. Gormley ed.), 2nd edition, 1989, Kluwer Law and Taxation Publishers, Deventer, at 501, footnote 134.

[26] Zuleeg in Groeben, Thiesing and Ehlermann, *supra* note 14, at 103, par. 18, emphasized the instrumental function of the common market but adds: "*Dies schliesst nicht aus, im Mittel selbst wieder ein Ziel zu erblicken*". See also K. Mortelmans, "The common market, the internal market and the single market, what's in a market?", 35 CML Rev. at 101-136.

[27] Case 15/81, *Schul* v *Inspecteur der Invoerrechten en Accijnzen*, [1982] ECR 1431-1432, par. 33.

internal market.[28] Furthermore, the simple fact that both terms are used in the EC Treaty seems to imply that the two are not identical.[29] According to Article 7a(2) EC, the internal market comprises an area without internal frontiers in which the free movement of goods, persons, services and capital is ensured in accordance with the provisions of this Treaty. Leaving aside the question whether the common market includes more than the internal market or *vice versa*, it is generally accepted that, in addition to the four freedoms referred to in Article 7a(2) EC, undistorted competition and a common commercial policy are essential for the establishment and functioning of the common market.[30]

3.4.2 Economic and Monetary Union

Recital 6 of the preamble to the EU Treaty confirms the resolution of the Member States to establish an economic and monetary union including a single and stable currency. In Article B of the EU Treaty, the establishment of economic and monetary union is listed as one of the means to promote economic and social progress which is balanced and sustainable. Article 2 EC identifies the establishment of the economic and monetary union as one of the means for the Community to carry out its task.[31] However, as is the case with the common market, there is no definition of the economic and monetary union to be found

---

[28] For a different view see R. Barents, "Milieu en interne markt", SEW 1 (1993) at 21, who argues that the definition given in the case *Schul* illustrates the fact that in the case law of the ECJ, the two terms are interchangeable.

[29] See, *inter alia*, A.M.M. Schrauwen, "De interne markt na Maastricht", SEW 10 (1992) at 771-778, and D. Wyatt and A. Dashwood, *European Community Law*, 3rd edition, 1993, Sweet & Maxwell, London, at 357-358.

[30] See, *inter alia*, Barents, *supra* note 28, at 20; Kapteyn and VerLoren van Themaat, *supra* note 25, at 501, 503-504, 557; Wyatt and Dashwood, *ibidem* and K. Lenaerts and P. Van Nuffel, *Europees Recht in Hoofdlijnen*, 1995, MAKLU Uitgevers, Antwerpen, at 80-83.

[31] See, *inter alia*, J.-V. Louis, "L'Union Economique et Monetaire", 1992 CDE XXVIII (no 3-4), at 252-253; J. Pipkorn, "Legal Arrangements in the Treaty of Maastricht for the Effectiveness of the Economic and Monetary Union", 31 CML Rev. at 263; M. Herdegen, "Price stability and budgetary restraints in the Economic and Monetary Union: The law as guardian of economic wisdom", 35 CML Rev. at 9-32; J.-V. Louis, "A legal and institutional approach for building a Monetary Union", 35 CML Rev. at 33-76, and H. Hahn, "The Stability Pact for European Monetary Union: Compliance with deficit limit as a constant legal duty", 35 CML Rev. at 77-100.

anywhere in the EC Treaty. Although the ECJ has used the term "economic and monetary union" in its caselaw,[32] it has not yet had an opportunity to elaborate upon the meaning of this term in the context of Article 2 EC.

The economic and monetary union is a combination of an economic union and a monetary union.[33] Commentators turn to Article 3a(1) EC and, subsequently, to the Articles 102a to 104c EC, to identify the characteristics of the *economic union*, emphasizing that it does not imply a common economic policy but an economic policy which is based on the close co-ordination of Member States' economic policies.[34] The economic union has been described as the completed common market with free movement of goods, services, persons and capital, and free and undistorted competition, in which the economic policy is coordinated, and binding rules for the budgetary policy of the Member States are operative.[35] It is interesting to note, however, that such a wide description of economic union leads to an odd textual incongruity, as Article 2 EC provides that the Community has to carry out its task by means of establishing a common market *and* an economic and monetary union *and* by implementing the common policies or activities referred to in Articles 3 and 3a EC.[36] The enumeration of

---

[32] See, *inter alia*, Opinion 1/91, [1991] ECR I-6102, par. 17 and Case 9/73, *Schlüter* v *Hauptzollamt Lörrach (Schlüter)*, [1973] ECR 1160, paras. 38-40.

[33] Committee for the Study of Economic and Monetary Union ("Delors Committee"), *Report on Economic and Monetary Union in Europe ("Delors Report")*, 1989, at 18.

[34] See, *inter alia*, P.J. Slot, "The Institutional Provisions of the EMU", in *Institutional Dynamics of European Integration*, Essays in Honour of Henry G. Schermers - Volume II (D. Curtin and T. Heukels eds.) 1994, Martinus Nijhoff Publishers, Dordrecht, at 229-230; R. Smits, "De Monetaire Unie van Maastricht", SEW 8/9 (1992) at 710; Louis, *supra* note 31, at 252-255, and A. Italianer, "Mastering Maastricht: EMU Issues and How They Were Settled", in *Economic and Monetary Union: Implications for National Policy-Makers*, (K. Gretschmann ed.), 1993, Martinus Nijhoff Publishers, Dordrecht, at 73. The latter is of the opinion that Article 3a(1) EC defines what is understood by the "economic policy" of EMU, namely close coordination of national economic policies, the internal market and the definition of common objectives.

[35] L.A. Geelhoed in P.J.G. Kapteyn and P. VerLoren van Themaat, *supra* note 24, at 557. See in a similar sense the economist W. Molle, *The Economics of European Integration-Theory, Practice, Policy*, 2nd edition, 1994, Dartmouth, Aldershot, at 11, and the Delors Committee in the Delors Report, *supra* note 33, at 20.

[36] See Italianer, *supra* note 34, at 73, who notes that the establishment of EMU has been added *alongside* that of the common market.

the common market and the economic and monetary union would make little sense if the establishment of an economic and monetary union automatically implies the creation of the common market. Why list both if the economic and monetary union necessarily includes the common market? One could therefore argue that the wording of Article 2 EC constitutes an argument against a wide definition of economic union that includes the common market, and in favour of a more narrow definition that mainly focuses on the coordination of economic policy and the binding rules on budgetary policy.

In order to identify the main characteristics of the *monetary union*, commentators turn to Article 3a(2) EC and, subsequently, to the Articles 105 to 109 EC. The monetary union can be described as a currency area in which policies are managed jointly with a view to attaining common macro-economic objectives by assuring total and irreversible convertibility of currencies, liberalization of capital transactions and full integration of banking and other financial markets, and the elimination of margins of fluctuation and the irrevocable locking of exchange rate parities.[37] As the creation of the common market implies the convertibility of currencies and the liberalization of capital transactions and full integration of financial markets, the creation of a monetary union, and in particular the introduction of the Euro, contributes to the elimination of margins of fluctuation and the irrevocable locking of exchange rate parities. This will reduce transaction costs and, more importantly, eliminate currency risks within the Community as fluctuations of exchange rates of the currencies of Member States will disappear.[38]

---

[37] Delors Report, *supra* note 33, at 18-19.

[38] See, *inter alia*, Council Regulation 974/98 of 3 May 1998 on the introduction of the euro, OJ 1998, L139/1. *Agence Europe*, "European industry to ask for no extension, after 1999, of import restrictions on Japanese cars despite devaluation of the Yen - Importance of Single Market and Euro", 22 January 1998, at 15, reported that according to Pischetsrieder, chairman of both ACEA and BMW, "[c]ompletion of the internal market will be accelerated by a fruitful introduction of the single currency that will not only reduce company costs in financial transactions, but also allow for better planning, a clear comparison of prices and intense competition (...) The Euro will also deepen and enlarge the European financial market in competition with Tokyo or New York. Externally, it will also be more stable than the national currencies when it comes to irregular and unpredictable fluctuations of the dollar".

3.4.3 Implementation of the Common Policies or Activities referred to in Articles 3 and 3a EC

Another means for the Community to carry out the task set out in Article 2 EC is the implementation of the common policies or activities referred to in Articles 3 and 3a EC. Articles 3 and 3a(1) EC explicitly indicate that the respective activities and common policies are part of the Community's activities for the purposes set out in Article 2. Article 3a(2) EC links up "[c]oncurrently with the foregoing" i.e., Article 3a(1) EC. The singular purpose of the activities and policies listed in Articles 3 and 3a EC is to enable the Community to carry out its task. In principle, these activities and policies play an *instrumental* and therefore, at the same time, a restricted role, as they are to be interpreted and implemented with an eye on the objectives set out in Article 2 EC.[39] Nevertheless, as was the case with the creation of a common market, the activities and policies referred to in Articles 3 and 3a EC can, and indeed have become objectives in and of themselves.[40] Both Articles 3 and 3a EC prescribe that the activities of the Community and, in case of Article 3a EC, the Community and the Member States, shall include specific activities and policies. The term "shall" reflects an obligation, whereas the term "include" implies that the listed activities and policies are not necessarily the only possible way for the Community to accomplish the objectives set out in Article 2 EC. The Community, however, has to act within the legal system created by the EC Treaty and is bound by, and therefore limited to, the task, objectives and competences set out in the EC Treaty.

3.4.3.1 Common Policies or Activities

Articles 3 and 3a EC enunciate "policies" and "activities" while failing to define these terms. The Concise Oxford Dictionary of Current English defines "policy" as "a course or principle of action adopted or proposed by a government, party,

---

[39] See also *Continental Can*, *supra* note 21, paras. 23-24.

[40] For instance, in Case 299/86, *Rainer Drexl*, [1988] ECR 1235, par. 24, the ECJ used the words "the objectives of the Treaty as laid down in Articles 2 and 3" thereby confirming the "up-grading" of Article 3 EC from a listing of mere activities to a listing of objectives.

business, or individual etc".[41] A somewhat more elaborate definition along the same lines is given by De Gaay Fortman, who defines a "policy" as "the concrete plan of action consisting of ends and means which at the moment of its formulation is felt to be in accordance with the norms or ethos of the group".[42] Taking these definitions into consideration, one could simply define a "policy" as a plan of action.

The implementation of a policy within the meaning of Articles 3 and 3a EC will normally take place by means of activities (to be) undertaken by the Community and possibly Member States. The fact that these activities take place within the framework of a policy has a considerable legal significance, as a policy provides its subjects with some assurance as to how these activities will take place or decisions will be taken. In principle, the formulation of a policy creates certain legitimate expectations as to its implementation which can be relevant for possible judicial review of the activities or decisions concerned. Underlining the fact that a policy means that the power of government cannot be used arbitrarily, De Gaay Fortman quotes Dimock who observed that:

> [a] foremost objective of social intercourse is to build confidence, to give the other fellow a feeling of security by offering him a reliable pattern of policy and the assurance that action now and in the future will be guided by it.[43]

A policy consists of a plan of action which may result in activities to implement

---

[41] *The Concise Oxford Dictionary of Current English* (R.E. Allen ed.), 8th edition, 1990, Clarendon Press, Oxford, at 921. T. Daintith, "Law as a policy instrument: A comparative perspective" in *Law as an instrument of economic policy: Comparative and critical approaches*, 1988, Walter de Gruyter, Berlin, at 6, refers to the Oxford English Dictionary which gives as policy's chief sense "a course of action adopted as advantageous or expedient". According to Daintith, this definition implies "action guided by deliberation, purpose and choice" whereas "[t]here are common uses of the term 'policy' which imply no action (as when a government's statements about its objectives and the means it proposes to use for attaining them are referred to as its 'policy') or little deliberation (as when any sequence of government actions is retrospectively called its 'policy' in a given field)".

[42] B. de Gaay Fortman, *Theory of Competition Policy*, 1966, North-Holland Publishing Company, Amsterdam, at 138.

[43] *Ibidem*, at 137. Reference is made to M.E. Dimock, *The new American political economy; a synthesis of politics and economics*, 1962, New York, at 23.

the policy "according to plan". A policy creates a framework for activities and decisions and leads to a more or less predictable pattern of behaviour. An activity, on the other hand, simply consists of acts which can be, but are not necessarily, a part of the implementation of a policy or, in other words, a plan of action.

The use of both the terms "policies" and "activities" in Article 2 EC ("common policies or activities referred to in Articles 3 and 3a EC") seems to imply that Article 2 EC recognizes a difference between the two.[44] However, the term "activities" used in the first lines of Article 3 EC ("For the purposes set out in Article 2, the activities of the Community shall include") covers a listing of both activities and common policies, indicating that "activities" include policies. The term "common policies" in Article 2 EC is probably intended to relate to those activities referred to in Articles 3 and 3a EC as (common) policies,[45] whereas the term "activities" covers the rest of the activities listed in Articles 3 and 3a EC. In view of the above, one gets the impression that the use of the terms "policies" and "activities" in Articles 2, 3 and 3a EC is of no legal significance.

3.4.3.2 Article 3 EC

The nature of the activities of the Community listed in Article 3 EC is diverse and the wording used to describe these activities very vague indeed. However, as discussed above, Article 3 EC is part of the context of the provisions of the EC Treaty and has proven to be of considerable importance for the interpretation and application of the other provisions of the EC Treaty. More specifics on the policies and activities listed in Article 3 EC can be found throughout the EC Treaty. In this study, the following policies and activities will be examined: (i) the elimination of obstacles to intra-Community trade (Article 3(a) and (c) EC), (ii) common commercial policy (Article 3(b) EC), (iii) a system ensuring that competition is not distorted (Article 3(g) EC), (iv) the strengthening of the competitiveness of Community industry (Article 3(l) EC), (v) the promotion of

---

44 The French text of the EC Treaty uses the words "*par la mise en oeuvre des politiques ou des actions communes visées aux articles 3 et 3 A*".

45 See, for instance, Article 3 (b), (e) and (f) EC.

research and technological development (Article 3(m) EC) and (vi) a contribution to education and training of quality (Article 3(p) EC). The relevant measures taken against the backdrop of the Community's environmental policy (Article 3(k) EC) will be touched upon in the context of the elimination of obstacles to intra-Community trade.

3.4.3.3 Article 3a EC

Article 3a EC provides for certain obligations of the Member States and the Community with regard to both their economic and monetary policy. The first paragraph of Article 3a EC concerns economic policy, the second focuses on monetary policy and the third lists four guiding principles to be complied with by the Member States and the Community. Articles 102a to 109m EC provide further details on the establishment of the economic and monetary union.

3.5 Article 5 EC

Pursuant to Article 5 EC, the Member States shall: (i) take all appropriate measures, whether general or particular, to ensure fulfilment of the obligations arising out of the EC Treaty or resulting from action taken by the institutions of the Community; (ii) facilitate the achievement of the Community's tasks; and (iii) abstain from any measure which could jeopardise the attainment of the objectives of the EC Treaty. Article 5 EC is one of the fundamental provisions of the EC Treaty, as it stands for the fact that solidarity is at the basis of the whole of the Community system.[46] In its extensive case law on Article 5 EC, the ECJ has confirmed that Article 5 EC puts both general and specific duties on the Member States as well as on the Community institutions. They are bound by mutual duties of genuine cooperation and assistance.[47] The "actual tenor" of the general duties of the Member States "depends in each individual case on the

---

[46] See Joined Cases 6 and 11/69, *Commission* v *France*, [1969] ECR 540, par. 16.

[47] See, *inter alia*, Case 32/79, *Commission* v *United Kingdom*, [1980] ECR 2432, par. 10; Case 804/79, *Commission* v *United Kingdom*, [1981] ECR 1075, par. 28; Case 44/84, *Hurd* v *Jones*, [1986] ECR 81, par. 38; Case 52/84, *Commission* v *Belgium*, [1986] ECR 105, par. 16; Case 186/85, *Commission* v *Belgium*, [1987] ECR 2057, par. 39; Case 235/87, *Matteucci*, [1988] ECR 5611, par. 19 and Case 94/87, *Commission* v *Germany*, [1989] ECR 192, par. 9.

provisions of the Treaty or on the rules derived from its general scheme".[48] For instance, the ECJ held in the context of the conservation of biological resources of the sea, that a particular resolution:

> makes specific the duties of co-operation which the Member States assumed under Article 5 of the EEC-Treaty when they acceded to the Community. Performance of these duties is particularly necessary in a situation in which it has appeared impossible, by reason of divergences of interest which it has not yet been possible to resolve, to establish a common policy and in a field such as that of the conservation of the biological resources of the sea in which worthwhile results can only be attained thanks to the co-operation of all the Member States.[49]

Article 5 EC puts duties on the Member States to both actively and passively contribute and cooperate in good faith whilst fully observing the provisions of the EC Treaty.[50]

3.6 GATT and the WTO Agreement

3.6.1 Position of the Member States and the Community under GATT

Article I GATT provides for a most-favoured-nation treatment obligation which implies that no discriminatory measures can be applied in the trade in goods. Contracting Parties are prohibited from discriminating between national and foreign goods and are obliged to apply favourable treatment given to a particular

---

[48] See Case 78/70, *Deutsche Grammophon* v *Metro*, [1971] ECR 499, par. 5.

[49] Case 141/78, *France* v *United Kingdom*, [1979] ECR 2942, par. 8.

[50] See, on the duties of Member States and Community institutions under Article 5 EC, *inter alia*, A. Bleckmann, "Art. 5 EWG-Vertrag und die Gemeinschaftstreue", DVBl. 1 July 1976, at 483-487; V. Constantinesco, "L'article 5 CEE, de la bonne foi à la loyauté communautaire" in *Du droit international au droit de l'intégration*, Liber Amicorum Pierre Pescatore (Capotorti and others, eds.), 1987, Nomos Verlagsgesellschaft, Baden Baden, at 97-114; J. Temple Lang, "Community Constitutional Law: Article 5 EEC Treaty", 27 CML Rev. at 645-681; W. Van Gerven and H. Gilliams, "Gemeenschapstrouw: goede trouw in EG-verband", Rechtskundig Weekblad 1989-1990, nr 33, at 1158-1169 and O. Due, "Artikel 5 van het EEG- Verdrag - Een bepaling met een federaal karakter?, SEW 1992, at 355-366.

foreign product, to all trade in such products with Contracting Parties. Article I GATT applies to all tariffs and other rules and formalities applying to imports and exports. As a result, Article I GATT in principle makes further integration in the form of a customs union or a free trade area not including all Contracting Parties, impossible. However, Article XXIV GATT provides, under specific conditions, for an exception by sanctioning the formation of customs unions and free trade areas as defined in Article XXIV GATT.

The six "Founding Fathers" of the Community were Contracting Parties to GATT before they signed the Treaty of Rome on 25 March 1957.[51] The other nine Member States were Contracting Parties before their accession to the Community.[52] From the very beginning, the six "Founding Fathers" indicated that they considered themselves bound by their obligations under GATT and that they would "submit for consideration by the Contracting Parties, in accordance with paragraph 7(a) of Article XXIV, any scheme decided upon before it was submitted to their respective parliaments for ratification".[53] The text of the Treaty of Rome was submitted at the end of March 1957 and the firm assurance was given "that as long as the Six would remain contracting parties to the General Agreement they would scrupulously observe their obligations under this

---

[51] Belgium, Luxemburg, France and the Netherlands undertook to apply GATT provisionally as from 1 January 1948 by signing the Protocol of Provisional Application of GATT dated 30 October 1947 (see BISD Volume I, at 77-78). Italy agreed to apply GATT provisionally upon entry into force of the Annecy Protocol of Terms of Accession to the GATT, dated 10 October 1949. The latter was signed by Italy on 30 April 1950 and entered into force on 30 May 1950. Germany undertook to apply GATT provisionally upon entry into force of the Torquay Protocol to the GATT, dated 21 April 1951. On 1 September 1951, Germany signed the Torquay Protocol which subsequently entered into force on 1 October 1951 (see BISD Volume I, at 79 and 86).

[52] The United Kingdom (GATT 1 January 1948 - EC 1 January 1973), Denmark (GATT 28 May 1950 - EC 1 January 1973), Greece (GATT 1 March 1950 - EC 1 January 1981), Portugal (GATT 6 May 1962 - EC 1 January 1986), Spain (GATT 29 August 1963 - EC 1 January 1986), Ireland (GATT 22 December 1967 - EC 1 January 1973), Austria (GATT 19 October 1951 - EC 1 January 1995), Sweden (GATT 30 April 1950 - EC 1 January 1995) and Finland (GATT 25 May 1950 - EC 1 January 1995). See GATT, *Analytical Index: Guide to GATT Law and Practice*, 6th Edition (1994), at 1046 and Pb 1972 L73/5 (not reproduced in OJ English Special Edition 1972), OJ 1979 L291/9, OJ 1985 L302/9 and OJ 1995 L1/1.

[53] As quoted by H. Steinberger, *GATT und regionale Wirtschaftszusammenschlüsse*, Max-Planck-Institut für Ausländisches Öffentliches Recht und Völkerrecht, 1963, Carl Heymanns Verlag, Köln, at 190, footnote 77 in which reference is made to PR GATT/319, at 8.

Agreement".[54] This intention was reflected in the text of the Treaty itself.[55] For instance, Article 229 EC instructs the Commission to ensure the maintenance of all appropriate relations with the organs of GATT and Article 234 EC provides that the rights and obligations arising from agreements concluded before the entry into force of the Treaty of Rome shall not be affected by the provisions of the Treaty.[56]

Upon receipt of the original text of the Treaty of Rome,[57] a GATT Committee was appointed to examine the text and sub-groups were established to examine questions regarding tariffs, the use of quantitative restrictions, trade in agricultural products and the association of overseas countries and territories with the common market.[58] As each sub-group submitted a report without any

---

[54] As quoted by E.U. Petersmann in "The EEC as a GATT Member - Legal conflicts between GATT law and European Community law" in *The European Community and GATT*, Studies in transnational economic law, Volume 4 (M. Hilf, F.G. Jacobs and E.U. Petersmann eds.), 1986, Kluwer, Deventer, at 34, footnote 27 in which reference is made to GATT doc. IC/SR, at 39. The ECJ refers to these declarations in Joined Cases 21 to 24/72, *International Fruit Co.* v *Produktschap voor Groenten en Fruit* (*International Fruit III*), [1972] ECR 1226, par. 12.

[55] See in this context E.-U. Petersmann, "Darf die EG das Völkerrecht ignorieren?", 11/1997 EuZW, at 325-331.

[56] The ECJ described the purpose of article 234 EC in Case 812/79, *Attorney General* v *Burgoa*, [1980] ECR 2802, par. 8, as "to lay down, in accordance with the principles of international law, that the application of the Treaty does not affect the duty of the Member State concerned to respect the rights of non-member countries under a prior agreement and to perform its obligations thereunder". See Case 10/61, *Commission* v *Italy*, [1962] ECR 1 and Case C-158/91, *Levy*, [1993] ECR I-4300. In its judgment of 10 March 1998 in Joined Cases C-364/95 and C-365/95, *T. Port*, not yet reported, the ECJ noted that the first paragraph of Article 234 EC must be interpreted as not applying to cases involving imports from a third country which is not a party to an international agreement concluded by Member States before the entry into force of the Treaty of Rome.

[57] Paragraph 7A of article XXIV GATT obliged any Contracting Party deciding to enter into a customs union or free-trade area, or an interim agreement leading to the formation of such a union or area, to promptly notify the Contracting Parties and make available to them such information regarding the proposed union or area as will enable them to make such reports and recommendations to Contracting Parties as they may deem appropriate. See in this context J.H. Jackson, *World Trade and the law of GATT*, 1969, The Michie Company Law Publishers, Charlottesville, at 575-623.

[58] BISD 6S/69 (1958). See also D. Lasok and W. Cairns, *The Customs Law of the European Economic Community*, 1983, Kluwer Law and Taxation Publishers, Deventer, at 14-15.

definite conclusions,[59] the Contracting Parties decided to have the GATT Intersessional Committee look at further questions regarding the compatibility of the Treaty of Rome with GATT.[60] Within a year, the Intersessional Committee came up with a report in which it took the position "that it would be more fruitful if attention could be directed to specific and practical problems, leaving aside for the time being questions of law and debates about the compatibility of the Rome Treaty with Article XXIV of the General Agreement".[61] The Committee suggested to use the consultation procedure of article XXII GATT for this purpose. But at their thirteenth session, the Contracting Parties noted that "because of the nature of the Rome Treaty there were a number of important matters on which there was not at this time sufficient information to enable the Contracting Parties to complete the examination of the Rome Treaty pursuant to paragraph 7 of Article XXIV" and the conclusion was reached that "this examination and the discussion of the legal questions involved in it could not usefully be pursued at the present time".[62] After establishing that this postponement did not prejudice the rights of the Contracting Parties under Article XXIV GATT, the Contracting Parties noted:

> that the other normal procedures of the General Agreement would also be available to contracting parties to call in question any measures taken by any of the six countries in the application of the provisions of the Rome Treaty, it being open of course to such country to invoke the

[59] BISD 6S/69 (1958).

[60] *Ibidem*. All Contracting Parties were represented in the Intersessional Committee as the EC Treaty was considered of considerable importance to all of them.

[61] BISD 7S/70 (1959).

[62] BISD 7S/71 (1959). See Jackson, *supra* note 57, at 622, for critical remarks on the refusal of the Community to provide information in a number of cases.

> benefit of Article XXIV insofar as it considered that this Article provided justification for any action which might otherwise be inconsistent with a provision or provisions of the General Agreement.[63]

Many questions regarding the interpretation and compatibility of the Treaty of Rome with GATT were dealt with during the Dillon and Kennedy Rounds of trade negotiations.[64] In 1970, the Community announced that it would stop submitting annual reports on the development of its customs union but emphasized that it was prepared to assume its obligations as a customs union and as an economic union in accordance with the letter and the spirit of GATT in the same way as all other Contracting Parties.[65] Officially speaking, the procedure under paragraph 7 of article XXIV GATT never came to an end.[66]

In practice, however, the Contracting Parties accepted the Community as both an active and passive participant in the GATT framework. Since the Dillon Round, the Commission participated like a Contracting Party in almost all GATT organs. Legal proceedings under GATT were instituted by and against

---

[63] *Ibidem*. The Japanese representative in the GATT Council noted in 1970 that "the fact that the Contracting Parties did not pursue the legal issue concerning the Community's status with regard to the requirements of Article XXIV did not prejudice any contracting party's rights and obligations under the General Agreement" (GATT doc. C/M/61, at 6).

[64] The Dillon Round took place from 1960 to 1961 and the Kennedy Round between 1964 and 1967. See in this context R.E. Hudec, *The GATT Legal System and World Trade Diplomacy*, 2nd edition, 1990, Buttersworth Legal Publishers, Salem, at 214, footnote 8 and Petersmann, *supra* note 54, at 35.

[65] See Petersmann, *supra* note 54, at 35-36 and especially footnote 32 on page 36 in which reference is made to GATT doc. C/M/61, at 6.

[66] See Petersmann, *supra* note 54, at 184-186; E.L.M. Völker, *Barriers to External and Internal Community Trade*, Ph.D. thesis (Amsterdam - 1993), at 36-37 and W.J. Davey, "An overview of the General Agreement on Tariffs and Trade" in *Handbook of GATT Dispute Settlement* (P. Pescatore, W.J. Davey and A. Lowenfeld eds.), 1991, Transnational Juris Publications, Kluwer Law and Taxation Publishers, Deventer, at 25-26. See for an analysis of the Community as a customs union in relation to article XXIV GATT: P. Demaret, "Le régime des échanges internes et externes de la Communauté à la lumière des notions d'union douanière et de zône de libre-échange" in *Du droit international au droit de l'intégration*, Liber Amicorum Pierre Pescatore (Capotorti and others, eds.), 1987, Nomos Verlagsgesellschaft, Baden Baden, at 139-165.

the Community.[67] The Commission represented the Community in the decision-making process in GATT organs and negotiated tariff and trade agreements in the framework of GATT. Although the Community never became nor was officially recognized as a Contracting Party,[68] it acted as such.[69] After establishing that the Community had assumed the functions inherent in the tariff and trade policy by virtue of Article 113 EC, the ECJ held that:

> [s]ince the entry into force of the EC Treaty and ..., since the setting up of the common external tariff, the transfer of powers which has occurred in the relations between Member States and the Community has been put into concrete form in different ways within the framework of the General Agreement and has been recognized by the other contracting parties.[70]

The ECJ noted that "in so far as under the EC Treaty the Community has assumed the powers previously exercised by Member States in the area governed by the General Agreement, the provisions of that agreement have the effect of binding the Community".[71] According to the ECJ, the Community had assumed the commitments of the Member States arising from GATT and was bound by them.[72] Moreover, the Community was obliged to ensure that the provisions of

---

[67] See R.E. Hudec, *Enforcing International Trade Law - The Evolution of the Modern GATT Legal System*, 1993, Buttersworth Legal Publishers, Salem, at 590-608, for a list of cases.

[68] This, notwithstanding the fact that Article XXXIII juncto XXIV(2) GATT provides for the possibility for customs unions to accede to GATT.

[69] See for an analysis of the legal position of the Community under GATT, *inter alia*, Petersmann, *supra* note 54, at 32-39, and G. Berrisch, *Der völkerrechtliche Status der Europäischen Wirtschaftsgemeinschaft im GATT*, 1992, Florentz. According to E.U. Petersmann, "Participation of the European Communities in the GATT: International Law and Community Law Aspects" in *Mixed Agreements* (D. O'Keeffe and H.G. Schermers eds.), 1983, Kluwer, Deventer, at 188, the legal status of the Community is "the sum of rights and obligations which the EC has gradually acquired under GATT and under international law over the past 25 years in regard to the GATT/MTN system".

[70] *International Fruit III*, *supra* note 54, at 1227, par. 16.

[71] *Ibidem*, par. 18.

[72] See also Case 38/75, *Nederlandse Spoorwegen* v *Inspecteur der invoerrechten en accijnzen (Nederlandse Spoorwegen)*, [1975] ECR 1450, par. 21.

GATT were observed in its relations with non-Member States which were Contracting Parties to GATT.[73] The latter could be considered binding on the Community in all areas governed by GATT where the powers previously exercised by Member States had been transferred to the Community. The ECJ held that "as regards the fulfilment of the commitments laid down in GATT the Community has been substituted for the Member States with effect from 1 July 1968, the date on which the Common Customs Tariff was brought into force".[74]

The ECJ has never explicitly declared GATT to be an integral part of Community law.[75] This, notwithstanding the fact that the ECJ has treated GATT in certain ways as an integral part of Community law by confirming, for instance, that it has jurisdiction to give preliminary rulings on the interpretation of provisions of GATT in order to ensure their uniform application throughout the Community.[76] Both the Community and the Member States were bound under Community law to ensure respect for commitments arising from GATT and agreements entered into by the Community.[77]

---

[73] Case 266/81, *SIOT* v *Ministerio delle Finanze and Others (SIOT)*, [1983] ECR 780, par. 28.

[74] Joined Cases 267 to 269/81, *Amministrazione delle Finanze dello Stato* v *Petrolifera (Petrolifera)*, [1983] ECR 829, par. 19. See also *International Fruit III*, *supra* note 54, at 1219 and Joined Cases 290 and 291/81, *Singer and Geigy* v *Amministrazione delle Finanze dello Stato (Singer)*, [1983] ECR 847.

[75] See, *inter alia*, E.L.M. Völker, "The Direct Effect of International Agreements in the Community's Legal Order", LIEI 1983/1, at 143.

[76] See Case 181/73, *Haegeman* v *Belgium*, [1974] ECR 459-460, par. 6. See also Case 104/81, *Hauptzollamt Mainz* v *Kupferberg (Kupferberg)*, [1982] ECR 3662, par. 14; *Petrolifera*, *supra* note 74, 14 and 15 and Joined Cases 267-269/81, *SPI and SAMI*, [1983] ECR 828, par. 15. It is interesting to note that the ECJ held in Case 130/73, *Vandeweghe* v *Berufsgenossenschaft für die chemische Industrie*, [1973] ECR 1333, par. 2 that it has no jurisdiction under Article 177 EC to give a ruling on the interpretation of provisions of international law which bind Member States *outside* the framework of Community law.

[77] According to E.U. Petersmann, "Application of GATT by the Court of Justice of the European Communities", 20 CML Rev. at 401, Community law must therefore be construed and applied in conformity with the GATT obligations of the Community.

3.6.2 Position of the Member States and the Community under the WTO Agreement

On 15 April 1994, the Uruquay Round trade negotiations came to an end in Marrakesh, Morocco, after more than seven years of negotiations between GATT Contracting Parties.[78] All participants, including the Community and the Member States, signed the Final Act embodying the results of the Uruguay Round multilateral trade negotiations and the WTO Agreement,[79] and agreed on the desirability of acceptance of the latter with a view to its entry into force as early as possible and not later than 1 July 1995.

The WTO Agreement has a confusing structure. Pursuant to its Article II(1), the WTO shall provide the common institutional framework for the conduct of trade relations among its Members in matters related to the agreements and associated legal instruments included in the following Annexes to the WTO Agreement:

- Annex 1A - Multilateral Agreements on Trade in Goods
- Annex 1B - General Agreement on Trade in Services (GATS)
- Annex 1C - Agreement on Trade-Related Aspects of Intellectual Property Rights, Including Trade in Counterfeit Goods (TRIPs)
- Annex 2 - Understanding on Rules and Procedures Governing the Settlement of Disputes
- Annex 3 - Trade Policy Review Mechanism
- Annex 4 - Plurilateral Trade Agreements

The Multilateral Agreements on Trade in Goods include the provisions of GATT as rectified, amended and modified by the terms of legal instruments which have entered into force before the date of entry into force of the WTO Agreement ("GATT 1994"). During the Uruguay Round trade negotiations, several

[78] The negotiations started officialy on 29 September 1986 in Punta del Este, Uruquay.

[79] Sir Leon Brittan qualified the Uruguay Round as "an unprecedented exercise in international economic rule-making" in a Guest Editorial in 31 CML Rev. at 229.

provisions of GATT and the most important GATT codes, were reviewed and the interpretation of certain provisions was agreed upon.[80]

As provided for in Article XIV(1) of the WTO Agreement, the Community became an original Member of the WTO together with the Member States. The competence to sign the WTO Agreement is shared by the Community and the Member States.[81] There can be no doubt whatsoever that the Community and the Member States are formally bound to comply with the obligations arising from the WTO Agreement.[82]

---

[80] For instance, the Subsidy Code was revised, a new Code on the interpretation of Article XIX GATT was negotiated and the participants agreed on the interpretation of provisions such as Articles XVII, XXIV, XXV, XXVIII and XXXV GATT.

[81] As pointed out in Opinion 1/94 of 15 November 1994, [1994] ECR I-5267, the Community has exclusive competence, pursuant to Article 113 EC, to conclude the Multilateral Agreements on Trade in Goods (par. 34). Only cross-frontier supplies of services are covered by Article 113 EC and international agreements in the field of transport are excluded from it (par. 53). On the other hand, however, apart from those of its provisions which concern the prohibition of the release into free circulation of counterfeit goods, TRIPs do not fall within the scope of the common commercial policy (par. 71). The Community and the Member States are jointly competent to conclude TRIPs (par. 105). Last but not least, the competence to conclude GATS is shared between the Community and the Member States (par. 98).

[82] By Council Decision 94/800 of 22 Decision 1994 concerning the conclusion on behalf of the European Community, as regards matters within its competence, of the agreements reached in the Uruguay Round multilateral negotiations (1986-1994), OJ 1994 L336/1, the Council gave its approval "on behalf of the European Community with regard to that portion ... which falls within the competence of the European Community". See in this context, *inter alia*, M.E. Footer, "Participation of the European Communities in the World Trade Organization" in *The legal regulation of the European Community's external relations after the completion of the internal market* (S.V. Konstadinidis ed.), 1996, Dartmouth, Aldershot, at 71-90.

3.6.3 The Impact of GATT and the WTO Agreement within the Legal System of the EC Treaty

3.6.3.1 Direct Effect

In view of the spirit, general scheme or terms of GATT, its provisions do not have direct effect.[83] In several instances, the ECJ has pointed out that GATT is not by itself capable of conferring on Community citizens rights which they can invoke before the courts, as:

> GATT, which is according to its preamble ... based on the principle of negotiations undertaken on "the basis of reciprocal and mutually advantageous arrangements", is characterized by the great flexibility of its provisions, in particular those conferring the possibility of derogation, the measures to be taken when confronted with exceptional difficulties and the settlement of conflicts between the contracting parties.[84]

But what about the provisions of the WTO Agreement and, more specifically, TRIPs, GATS and GATT 1994?

On the basis of an analysis of the spirit, general scheme and terms of *TRIPs*, Eeckhout comes to the conclusions that it is probable that provisions of TRIPs can have direct effect.[85] On the other hand, Eeckhout recognizes that direct effect of provisions of *GATS* is very unlikely in view of the fact that in the Introductory Note to the Schedule of Commitments under the GATS, the

---

[83] See, *inter alia*, *International Fruit III*, *supra* note 54, at 1227-1228, paras. 20-27; *Schlüter*, *supra* note 32; *Nederlandse Spoorwegen*, *supra* note 72; Case 112/80, *Dürbeck* v *Hauptzollamt Frankfurt*, [1981] ECR 1095; *SIOT*, *supra* note 73; *SPI and SAMI*, *supra* note 76; *Singer*, *supra* note 74, and Case C-280/93, *Germany* v *Council*, [1994] ECR I-4973.

[84] Case C-469/93, *Amministrazione delle Finanze dello Stato* v *Chiquita Italia*, [1995] ECR I-4565, par. 26.

[85] P. Eeckhout, "The domestic legal status of the WTO agreement: Interconnecting legal systems", 34 CML Rev. at 25-40. See also Conclusion Advocate-General Tesauro of 13 November 1997, Case C-53/96, *Hermès International* v *FHT Marketing Choice (Hermès)* (not yet reported). In its judgment of 16 June 1998 in *Hermès* (not yet reported), the ECJ did not address the issue of the direct effect of Article 50 TRIPs.

Community and the Member States have excluded direct effect, and the ECJ has held that "Community institutions which have power to negotiate and conclude an agreement with a non-member country are free to agree with that country what effect the provisions of the agreement are to have in the internal legal order of the contracting parties".[86] With regard to provisions of *GATT 1994*, Eeckhout emphasizes that the framework in which GATT 1994 (as well as TRIPs and GATS) has to be enforced, and in particular the dispute settlement mechanism,[87] has been improved and strengthened. According to Eeckhout, this has removed much of the flexibility which characterized GATT and it is therefore no longer possible to use the same argumentation to deny the provisions of GATT 1994 direct effect. Although the preamble to Council Decision 94/800 provides that "by its nature, the [WTO] Agreement ... is not susceptible to being directly invoked in Community or Member State courts",[88] it is unlikely that this statement in the preamble of this particular Community instrument will stand in the ECJ's way to declare provisions of the WTO Agreement to have direct effect.[89] The future will tell whether the ECJ will eventually grant direct effect to provisions of the WTO Agreement.[90]

3.6.3.2 Indirect Effect

GATT and WTO provisions can have an important effect on (the interpretation

---

[86] *Kupferberg*, *supra* note 76, par. 17.

[87] See on the WTO dispute settlement system: E.U. Petersmann, *The GATT/WTO dispute settlement system*, 1997, Kluwer Law International, London.

[88] Council Decision 94/800, *supra* note 82, at 2.

[89] See Tesauro, *supra* note 85, paras. 23-24.

[90] See for an analysis and further references to literature: Eeckhout, *supra* note 85, at 38-40; J.H.J. Bourgeois, "The Uruguay Round of GATT: Some general comments from an EC standpoint", and N.A.E.M. Neuwahl, "Individuals and the GATT: Direct effect and indirect effects of the General Agreement of Tariffs and Trade in Community Law", both in *The European Union and world trade law: After the GATT Uruguay Round* (N. Emiliou and D. O'Keeffe eds.), 1996, Wiley, Chicester, at 89-90 and 313-328; P.L.H. Van den Bossche, "The European Community and the Uruguay Round Agreements" in *Implementing the Uruguay Round* (J.H. Jackson and A. Sykes eds.), 1997, Clarendon Press, Oxford, at 92-95, and P. Manin, "A propos de l'accord instituant l'Organisation mondiale du commerce et de l'accord sur les marchés publics: la question de l'invocabilité des accords internationaux conclus par la Communauté européenne", RTD eur. 33(3) 1997, at 399-428.

of) Community law. In several judgments, the ECJ confirmed that GATT provisions can be relevant for the interpretation of Community instruments.[91] The same is true for the provisions of the WTO Agreement. In *Commission* v *Germany*, the ECJ again confirmed that "the primacy of international agreements concluded by the Community over provisions of secondary Community legislation means that such provisions must, so far as is possible, be interpreted in a manner that is consistent with those agreements".[92] Consequently, the provisions of the WTO Agreement may have a considerable impact on the interpretation and subsequent application of secondary Community law such as the common commercial policy instruments which were adopted after the Uruguay Round. Moreover, the case law of the ECJ has made it absolutely clear that GATT provisions can even be of great significance for the determination of the legality and therefore the validity of Community acts.[93] However, it should be kept in mind that according to the ECJ, "it is only if the Community intended to implement a particular obligation entered into within the framework of GATT, or if the Community act expressly refers to specific provisions of GATT, that the Court can review the lawfulness of the Community act in question from the point of view of the GATT rules".[94] The same is probably true for the WTO Agreement.[95]

---

[91] See, *inter alia*, Case 92/71, *Interfood* v *Hauptzollamt Hamburg*, [1972] ECR 231; Case C-79/89, *Brown Boveri*, [1991] ECR I-1853; Joined Cases T-163/94 and T-165/94, *NTN Corporation and Koyo Seiko* v *Council*, [1995] ECR II-1381; Case C-70/94, *Werner* v *Germany*, [1995] ECR I-3189, and Case C-83/94, *Leifer*, [1995] ECR I-3231.

[92] Case C-61/94, *Commission* v *Germany*, [1996] ECR I-4020, par. 52. Annotated by P. Eeckhout in 35 CML Rev. at 557-566, and confirmed in *Hermès*, *supra* note 85, par. 28.

[93] See in this context F. Castillo de la Torre, "The Status of GATT in EC Law, Revisited - The consequences of the judgment on the banana import regime for the enforcement of the Uruguay Round Agreements", 29 J.W.T. 1 at 53-68; M. Dony, "L'affaire des bananes", 1995 CDE XXXI (no 3-4), at 461-496, and Eeckhout, *supra* note 85, at 11-58.

[94] Case C-280/93, *Germany* v *Council*, [1994] ECR I-4973, par. 111. See also Case 70/87, *Fediol* v *Commission*, [1989] ECR 1781; Case C-69/89, *Nakajima* v *Council*, [1991] ECR I-2069; Case C-105/90, *Goldstar* v *Council*, [1992] ECR I-677; Case C-175/87, *Matsushita* v *Council*, [1992] ECR I-1409; Case C-188/88, *NMB* v *Commission*, [1992] ECR I-1689, and Case T-162/94, *NMB* v *Commission*, judgment of 5 June 1996 (not yet reported).

[95] See Eeckhout, *supra* note 85, at 46-48.

3.7 Concluding Remarks

The EC Treaty provides the Community with a particular task set out in Article 2 EC and certain means to perform this task being the establishment of a common market, an economic and monetary union and the implementation of the common policies or activities referred to in Articles 3 and 3a EC. These common policies and activities are further elaborated upon in provisions of the EC Treaty which have to be interpreted and applied in the light of the aims set out in the preamble to the EC Treaty and Articles 2, 3 and 3a EC.

In this study, the focus will be on (i) the elimination of obstacles to intra-Community trade (Article 3(a) and (c) EC), (ii) the common commercial policy (Article 3(b) EC), (iii) a system ensuring that competition is not distorted (Article 3(g) EC), (iv) the strengthening of the competitiveness of Community industry (Article 3(l) EC), (v) the promotion of research and technological development (Article 3(m) EC) and (vi) a contribution to education and training of quality (Article 3(p) EC). Relevant measures taken against the backdrop of the Community's environmental policy (Article 3(k) EC) will be touched upon in the context of the elimination of obstacles to intra-Community trade.

While implementing these policies and activities with regard to the automobile industry, Community institutions like the Commission have to remain and operate *within* the legal system created by the EC Treaty; they have to remain within the legal framework of the EC Treaty. In addition, these institutions have to respect the Community's obligations under the WTO Agreement. In theory, Community measures within the context of the various policies and activities set out in Articles 3 and 3a EC, have to comply with the EC Treaty and respect the Community's obligations set out in the WTO Agreement. The case study will show, however, that practice is often very different. In particular those measures designed to keep up with the American and Japanese automobile industry, and to facilitate and encourage the adaptation of the Community's automobile industry to the so-called whirlwind of international competition, tend to balance on, or even go over, the edge of the legal framework set out in the EC Treaty and the WTO Agreement.

PART II - THE CASE STUDY

4. THE ELIMINATION OF OBSTACLES TO INTRA-COMMUNITY TRADE AND THE AUTOMOBILE INDUSTRY

4.1 Introduction

One of the Community's means to carry out its task and pursue the objectives set out in Article 2 EC, is the establishment of a common market. This involves the elimination of all obstacles to intra-Community trade in order to merge the national markets into a single market bringing about conditions as close as possible to those of a genuine internal market.[1] It is therefore not surprising that the common policies or activities referred to in Articles 3 and 3a EC include (i) the elimination, as between Member States, of customs duties and quantitative restrictions on the import and export of goods, and of all other measures having equivalent effect (Article 3(a) EC), (ii) an internal market characterised by the abolition between Member States, of obstacles to the free movement of goods, persons, services and capital (Article 3(c) EC), and (iii) the approximation of the laws of Member States to the extent required for the functioning of the common market (Article 3(h) EC).

The provisions of the EC Treaty dealing with the abolition and prohibition of barriers to intra-Community trade and in particular the legal measures taken by the Community within this context, have (had) a considerable impact on the automobile industry. The elimination of obstacles to intra-Community trade makes it possible for the automobile industry to operate on a market which comes close(r) to being one single market instead of having to deal with a great many domestic markets separated by various technical, fiscal and physical trade barriers which tend to lead to a reduction of competitive

[1] See in this sense Case 15/81, *Schul* v *Inspecteur der Invoerrechten en Accijnzen (Schul I)*, [1982] ECR 1431-4132, par. 33.

pressures, higher costs, and a lower degree of efficiency and productivity.[2] In a study on the effect of the various single market programme measures on the automobile industry, the following "key conclusions" were drawn:

> The single market programme has contributed to the ongoing development of the EU motor vehicles sector at a time when it was undergoing important changes in terms of increased globalization, improved working methods and a deep recession. The single market is not making companies expand into new markets, but certainly helped this process by making it easier and cheaper for them to do so. The thrust of the single market measures was therefore in the right direction, but it did not radically alter business strategies.
>
> The single market programme has made it easier for new entrants to compete on equal terms with indigenous EU producers, and this has increased the levels of competition in the sector. This has provided further incentives for companies to decrease costs and increase product differentiation, placing downward pressure on prices and increasing customer service levels. Consumers, therefore, have benefited from the single market programme as a result of the increased choice of products available, increased safety and lower emissions.[3]

---

[2] See in this context *Research on the "cost of non-Europe", Basic findings - The EC 92 automobile sector ("Ludvigsen Report")*, Ludvigsen Associates, Volume 11, 1988, EUR-OP, for the identification and quantification of the economic benefits that would accrue to the EC automobile industry and to its customers through the removal of the fiscal, physical and technical internal barriers that divided the Community's Member States. It was reported in the *FT* (Survey - The Motor Industry", "Days of bilateral import restraints are numbered", 20 October 1988, at IV), that the Community had to deal with national barriers to the import of Japanese automobiles (for instance gentlemen's agreements with Japan limiting its market share to about 11% for the U.K. and 3% for France, and a voluntary export restraint limiting imports into Italy to less than 1%), and obstacles to intra-Community trade such as (i) a lack of a single EC-wide type-approval, (ii) different national emission standards and national equipment requirements, (iii) different taxation levels on for instance car sales and use, and (iv) border crossing documentary and inspection requirements.

[3] *The single market review - Impact on manufacturing motor vehicles*, Subseries I: Volume 6, 1997, EUR-OP, Kogan Page/Earthscan, at 4. See in this context also J. Pelkmans and L.A. Winters, *Europe's domestic market* (Chatham House Papers - 43), 1988, Routledge, London.

The purpose of this chapter is to describe and analyze both the provisions of the EC Treaty and the Community legal measures, be it general or industry-specific, which deal with the elimination of obstacles to intra-Community trade and obstacles to trade in automobiles and parts in particular. The focus will first be on the creation of the customs union through the abolition and prohibition of customs duties between Member States and charges having equivalent effect and the adoption of a Common Customs Tariff (**4.2**). Subsequently, the prohibition and abolition of quantitative restrictions between Member States and all measures having equivalent effect will be examined (**4.3**). The prohibition of internal taxation on products from other Member States in excess of that imposed on similar domestic products (**4.4**), the relevance of intellectual property rights (**4.5**) and the freedom of establishment and the free movement of capital (**4.6**) will then be looked at. Where necessary, the harmonisation of the laws of Member States will be elaborated upon. At the end of this chapter, some concluding remarks will be made (**4.7**).

4.2 Customs Union

4.2.1 Introduction

Article 9(1) EC provides that the Community shall be based upon a customs union which shall cover all trade in goods and shall involve the prohibition between Member States of customs duties on imports and exports and of all charges having equivalent effect, and the adoption of a common customs tariff in their relations with third countries. The term "goods" in the context of Article 9 EC, has been defined as "products which can be valued in money and which are capable, as such, of forming the subject of commercial transactions".[4] It is evident that automobiles and parts fall within the scope of this definition. However, pursuant to Article 9(2) EC, only two categories of goods can benefit from the customs union.[5]

---

[4] Case 7/68, *Commission* v *Italy*, [1968] ECR 423.

[5] Pursuant to Article 10(2) EC, it is up to the Commission to determine methods of administrative co-operation to be adopted for the purpose of applying Article 9(2) EC, taking into account the need to reduce as much as possible formalities imposed on trade.

The *first* category of goods consists of those originating in Member States. The Community has rules of origin that specify under what conditions goods can be considered to originate in Member States. These rules can be found in the Community Customs Code and the relevant implementation provisions drawn up by the Commission.[6] Article 23(1) of the Community Customs Code simply states that goods originating in a country shall be those wholly obtained or produced in that country. Article 24 provides that goods whose production involved more than one country shall be deemed to originate in the country where they underwent their last, substantial, economically justified processing or working in an undertaking equipped for that purpose and resulting in the manufacture of a new product or representing an important stage of manufacture. Over the years, the ECJ has been called upon to clarify (the predecessors of) these important but rather unsophisticated rules of origin.[7] With particular reference to the ECJ's judgments in the *Yoshida* cases,[8] Usher summarizes that "assembly operations which are economically justified, carried out in specially equipped premises and resulting in a new product or an important stage of manufacture, may well confer origin" and concludes that "[i]n the light of this, the enthusiasm of Japanese manufacturers to set up car assembly plants within the Community may be understood".[9]

The application of the Community rules of origin to automobiles in

---

[6] See Title II, Chapter 2 ("Origin of Goods") of Council Regulation 2913/92 of 12 October 1992 establishing the Community Customs Code, OJ 1992, L302/8, and Title IV ("Origin of Goods") of Commission Regulation 2454/93 of 2 July 1993 laying down provisions for the implementation of Council Regulation 2913/92 establishing the Community Customs Code, OJ 1993, L253/16. See in this context also the WTO Agreement on Rules of Origin, OJ 1994, L336/144.

[7] See I. Van Bael and J.-F. Bellis, *Anti-dumping and other trade protection laws of the EC*, 3rd edition, 1996, CCH Europe, Bicester, at 360-368, for a concise overview. See in this context also H.-J. Priess and R. Pethke, "The pan-European rules of origin: The beginning of a new era in European free trade", 34 CML Rev. at 773-809.

[8] Case 34/78, *Yoshida*, [1979] ECR 115, and Case 114/78, *Yoshida*, [1979] ECR 151.

[9] J. Usher, "Consequences of the Customs Union" in *The European Union and world trade law - After the Uruguay Round* (N. Emiliou and D. O'Keeffe eds.), 1996, Wiley, Chicester, at 122. Usher adds in footnote 76, that "before United Kingdom Accession, British Leyland established a plant in Belgium to assemble Minis for exactly the same reasons. It was closed after Accession".

general[10] and to Japanese automobiles assembled within the Community (so-called "transplants") in particular,[11] was highly disputed. The political sensitivity of rules of origin will come as no surprise as it is generally accepted that the determination of the origin of goods is almost invariably a function of the economic policy pursued.[12] Member States like France and Italy have urged the Commission to introduce a so-called "economic value-added test" or "local

---

[10] P. Eeckhout, *The European internal market and international trade: A legal analysis*, 1994, Clarendon Press, Oxford, at 225, points at the fact that "cars are an outstanding example of the ever increasing artificiality inherent in laying down rules determining the nationality of products". According to Eeckhout, "[t]he ... Community rules of origin are far too unsophisticated for delivering a satisfactory answer to the question of the origin of cars".

[11] This is illustrated by the politically sensitive dispute between France (and Italy), on the one hand, and the United Kingdom (and the Commission) on the other, with regard to the status of the Nissan "Blue Bird" which was assembled in the United Kingdom. A similar dispute arose with regard to the Toyota Hilux which was assembled in Germany by Volkswagen. See, *inter alia*, *Agence Europe*, "L'Italie importera 14.000 voitures Japonaises en libre pratique CEE (en plus du contingent direct)-Le cas des voitures Nissan montées au R.-U. demeure ouvert-Camionnettes Toyota assemblées en R.F.A.", 12 January 1989, at 7; "Compromis entre La France et le Royaume-Uni a propos des "Bluebird" de Nissan fabriquées au Royaume-Uni?", 4 February 1989, at 9; "Lettre de Lord Young a M. Bangemann sur l'affaire Nissan", 9 March 1989, at 13, and "L'Italie confirme sa position sur les Bluebirds Nissan fabriquées au Royaume-Uni et les autorités Britanniques sont satisfaites", 2-3 May 1989, at 8. See also R. Eccles, "When is a British car not a British car? - Issues raised by Nissan", 10 ECLR (1989), at 1-3, and P. Waer, "European Community rules of origin" in *Rules of origin in international trade* (E. Vermulst, P. Waer and J. Bourgeois eds.), 1994, The University of Michigan Press, Michigan, at 182-183.

[12] See in this sense D. Lasok and W. Cairns, *The Customs Law of the European Economic Community*, 1983, Kluwer Law and Taxation Publishers, Deventer, at 173. See also E. Vermulst and P. Waer, "European Community rules of origin as commercial policy instruments", 24 JWT (1990), at 55-99; E.I. Kingston, "The economics of rules of origin" and E.A. Vermulst, "Rules of origin as commercial policy instruments? - Revisited" in *Rules of origin in international trade*, *supra* note 11, at 9-10 and 433-483, and J.A. LaNasa III, "Rules of origin and the Uruguay Round's effectiveness in harmonizing and regulating them", 90 AJIL (1996), at 636-637.

content test" for the determination of the origin of automobiles.[13] Such a test is used for the determination of the origin of products like television receivers and photocopying apparatus.[14] Nevertheless, the Commission has refused to do so with regard to automobiles because "the Community is fundamentally in favour of direct foreign investment and is anxious to encourage better integration of such [transplant] production into its economy, while abiding by its international commitments and without resorting to compulsory local content formulas".[15] It is evident, however, that the value added to a product such as an automobile plays an important role in the determination under Article 24 of the Community Customs Code whether or not the product in question underwent its last, substantial, economically justified processing or working in that country thereby

---

[13] See, *inter alia*, "Les orientations de M. Bangemann concernant les relations avec le Japon rencontrent beaucoup de réserves et d'oppositions", *Agence Europe*, 1 July 1989, at 6. S. Reich, "Roads to follow: Regulating direct foreign investment", *International Organization* 43, 4, Autumn 1989, at 557, reported that "[a]s 1992 approaches, ..., the French are ... devising a series of policies to maintain trade barriers to American and Japanese automobile sales in the European market. The automobile markets of France and other EC countries will remain partially protected because of the stipulation that products sold in this enlarged European market should have a domestic content of 60 percent". According to Reich, the French initially insisted on 80% domestic content for cars to be sold in the Community. See P. Dicken, "Europe 1992 and strategic change in the international automobile industry", *Environment and Planning A*, 1992, Volume 24, at 27-28, for references to press reports in which Honda, Nissan and Toyota confirmed their commitment to reaching 80% local content.

[14] Article 39 of Regulation 2454/93, *supra* note 6. See in particular Annex 11.

[15] Commission Communication "A single Community Motor-vehicle market" SEC(89)2118 final, 18 January 1990 ("1990 Communication"), at 14. See also "L'Italie importera 14.000 voitures Japonaises en libre pratique CEE (en plus du contingent direct)-Le cas des voitures Nissan montées au R.-U. demeure ouvert-Camionnettes Toyota assemblées en R.F.A.", *Agence Europe*, 12 January 1989, at 7. Nevertheless, the Commission implicitly confirmed the importance of "local content" in its answer to Written Question 1818/88 (Ewing), OJ 1989, C255/13, on the definition of "domestically produced" cars; the Commission stressed that "[i]n order to take into account the technological realities of the sector in question and to add a technical element to the economic test, it is also necessary that not all the essential parts originate from outside the Community". It is interesting to note that *Agence Europe*, "Premier débat de la Commission sur la stratégie CEE", 1 June 1989, at 6, and "Industrie automobile: Positif sur les orientations génerales de la stratégie propose par M. Bangemann, les constructeurs Europeens restent cependant sceptiques quant à certaines modalites d'application", 5-6 June 1989, at 11, reported that "la grande majorité des constructeurs européens peuvent accepter la proposition de M. Bangemann, y inclus le rejet de règles obligatoires de contenu local, comme mode de régulation des investissement de pays tiers".

conferring origin.[16] Furthermore, several tariff and trade agreements concluded by the Community with third countries, include detailed rules of origin which tend to include a 60% economic value-added test for passenger cars.[17] Although the Commission has refused to introduce a compulsory value-added test or local content rules, this topic continually resurfaces in the context of the Community's drive to narrow the trade deficit with Japan.[18] Observers have noted that in reality, local content requirements are an important subject in negotiations between incoming car manufacturers and host states, rather than being the subject of official legislation.[19]

In order to prevent the abuse of the Community's rules on origin, Article 25 of the Community Customs Code provides that any processing or working in respect of which it is established, or in respect of which the facts as

---

[16] See in this sense Usher, *supra* note 9, at 122-123.

[17] An example was Annex II of Protocol 4 to the "interim" agreement between the Community and Poland (OJ 1992, L114/119) containing a "List of working or processing required to be carried out on non-originating materials in order that the product manufactured can obtain originating status" which specifies with regard to products under "HS Heading No: ex Chapter 87" which includes passenger cars, that the following working or processing has to be carried out on non-originating materials in order to confer originating status: "Manufacture in which the value of all the materials used does not exceed 40% of the ex works price of the product". Another example was Annex II of Protocol 3 to the "Free Trade" agreement between the Community and Austria (OJ Special English Edition 1972, L300/1, at 72), containing a "List of working or processing operations which result in a change of tariff heading without conferring the status of "originating" products on the product undergoing such operations, or conferring this status only subject to certain conditions", which specified with regard to products under "Customs Tariff heading No: ex Chapter 87" which includes passenger cars, that the following working or processing had to be carried out that confers the status of originating products: "Working, processing or assembly in which the value of the materials and parts used does not exceed 40% of the value of the finished product".

[18] For instance, it was reported in "Speech by Mr Andriessen at the world automotive forum - Dearborn, 23-24 February 1990: Latest EC thinking concerning external aspects of automotive trade and investment" (Speech/90/12), that according to Andriessen, there was "no reason to introduce specific rules of origin for motor vehicles". Andriessen emphasized that there was "no question of our imposing local content requirements, whether general ones or specific ones for the production of motor vehicles" but added that "the integration of Japanese investment into the local economy is desirable in itself" and welcomed "the announcement of Japanese producers of their intentions in this respect". See also *FT*, "Car parts groups argue their case", 7 March 1995, at 4.

[19] See in this sense A. Smith and A.J. Venables, "Automobiles" in *Europe 1992 - An American perspective* (G.C. Hufbauer ed.), 1990, The Brookings Institution, Washington D.C., at 150.

ascertained justify the presumption, that its sole object was to circumvent the provisions applicable in the Community to goods from specific countries shall under no circumstances be deemed to confer on the goods thus produced the origin of the country where it is carried out within the meaning of Article 24.[20]

The *second* category of goods which can benefit from the customs duty are those coming from a third country which are in free circulation in Member States. Article 10(1) EC provides that products coming from a third country shall be considered in free circulation in a Member State if the import formalities have been complied with and any customs duties or charges having equivalent effect which are payable have been levied in that Member State, and if they have not benefited from a total or partial drawback of such duties or charges.

4.2.2 Elimination of Customs Duties and Charges having Equivalent Effect

The customs union is *internally* characterized by the abolition and prohibition of customs duties and charges having equivalent effect on imports and exports. To this end, Article 12 EC obliges Member States to refrain from introducing between themselves any *new* customs duties on imports or exports or any charges having equivalent effect,[21] and from increasing those which they already apply in their trade with each other. The ECJ held that Article 12 EC has direct effect[22] and pointed out that "the prohibition of new customs duties, linked with the principles of the free movement of products, constitutes an essential rule and

[20] See in this context Article 13 of Council Regulation 384/96 of 22 December 1995 on protection against dumped imports from countries not members of the European Community, OJ 1996, L56/15.

[21] In Joined Cases 2 and 3/69, *Sociaal Fonds voor de Diamantarbeiders* v *Brachfeld and Chougol Diamond*, [1969] ECR 222, paras. 15-18, the ECJ defined charges having an equivalent effect within the meaning of Articles 9 and 12 EC, as "any pecuniary charge, however small and whatever its designation and mode of application, which is imposed unilaterally on domestic or foreign goods by reason of the fact that they cross a frontier, and which is not a customs duty in the strict sense, ..., even if it is not imposed for the benefit of the State, is not discriminatory or protective in effect or if the product on which the charge is imposed is not in competition with any domestic product".

[22] Case 26/62, *Van Gend en Loos* v *Nederlandse administratie der belastingen*, [1963] ECR 13.

that in consequence any exception, which moreover is to be narrowly interpreted, must be clearly stipulated".[23]

Article 13 EC obliges Member States to progressively abolish *existing* customs duties between themselves on imports and charges having an equivalent effect. In practice, customs duties were reduced and abolished under Articles 14 and 15 EC ahead of schedule; per 1 July 1968.[24] The obligation of Article 13(1) EC to abolish customs duties on imports is complemented by the obligation of Article 13(2) EC to abolish charges having equivalent effect.[25] The ECJ held that (from the end of the transitional period) Article 13(2) EC has direct effect.[26] Pursuant to Article 17(1) EC, the provisions of Articles 9 to 15(1) EC also apply to customs duties of a fiscal nature. In addition, Article 16 EC obliges Member States to abolish between themselves customs duties on exports and charges having equivalent effect.[27]

The provisions of the EC Treaty on customs duties and charges having an equivalent effect, have proven to be effective. The direct effect of most of these provisions makes it possible for private parties to take legal action against Member States violating their obligations. For instance, Ford Espana successfully invoked Articles 9 and 13 EC in legal proceedings against Spain with regard to the levy of a duty calculated as a proportion of the declared value of goods imported from other Member States. The duty was imposed where the operations relating to the customs clearance were carried out on premises or at places not open to the public. According to the ECJ, such a duty, which had to

[23] Joined Cases 2 and 3/62, *Commission* v *Luxembourg and Belgium*, [1962] ECR 432.

[24] See in this context Article 1 of the so-called Council Decision 66/532 of 26 July 1966 ("Acceleration Decision"), OJ 1966, 2971/66 (not reproduced in OJ English Special Edition). This, with the exception of products listed on Annex II to the EEC Treaty.

[25] The ECJ noted in Joined Cases 52 and 55/65, *Germany* v *Commission*, [1966] ECR 169, that "[t]he obligation placed on Member States by Article 13(2) to abolish progressively charges having an effect equivalent to customs duties is the logical and necessary complement of the obligation to abolish progressively customs duties on imports laid down in paragraph (1) of this Article".

[26] See, *inter alia*, Case 33/70, *SACE* v *Italian Ministry for Finance*, [1970] ECR 1222, par. 10 and Case 77/72, *Capolongo* v *Azienda Agricola Maya*, [1973] ECR 623, par. 11.

[27] The ECJ specified in Case 18/71, *Eunomia di Porro* v *Italian Ministry of Education*, [1971] ECR 816, paras. 6-7, that the prohibition of charges having equivalent effect to customs duties on exports has direct effect from 1 January 1962.

be regarded as a pecuniary charge imposed unilaterally on goods by reason of the fact that they cross a frontier, constituted a charge having equivalent effect in the meaning of Articles 9 and 13 EC. The ECJ held that even if the duty constituted remuneration for a service rendered to the importer or fell within the concept of costs which Council Directive 79/695[28] permitted to be charged to the declarant, its amount could not, as it was calculated on an *ad valorem* basis, be regarded as proportionate to that service or correspond to those costs.[29]

4.2.3 Common Customs Tariff

The customs union is *externally* characterized by the application of a Common Customs Tariff ("CCT") instead of national customs tariffs, on the importation of goods into the Community.[30] Following the procedure provided for in Articles 19 to 24 EC, Member States gradually adapted their national tariff systems to the CCT.[31] Since the coming into force of the CCT per 1 July 1968,[32] Member States are no longer competent to impose autonomous duties upon goods coming from third countries.[33] Measures were taken by the Community to

---

[28] Council Directive 79/695 of 24 July 1979 on the harmonization of procedures for the release of goods for free circulation, OJ 1979, L205/19, was repealed by Council Regulation 2913/92 of 12 October 1992 establishing the Community Customs Code, OJ 1992, L302/35.

[29] See Case 170/88, *Ford Espana* v *Spain*, [1989] ECR 2305-2308.

[30] Only the Benelux had already established a common external customs tariff in 1948.

[31] See P.J.G. Kapteyn and P. Verloren van Themaat, *Introduction to the Law of the European Communities* (L.W. Gormley ed.), 2nd edition, 1989, Kluwer Law and Taxation Publishers, Deventer, at 364-365; P.L. Kelley and I. Onkelinx, *EEC Customs Law*, 3rd Supplement, 1990 ECS Publishing Limited, Oxford, Part 1, at T-4, and Lasok and Cairns, *supra* note 12, at 143 to 148, for a concise history of the introduction of the CCT. See also N. Vaulont, *De douane-unie van de Europese Economische Gemeenschap*, 2nd edition, Bureau voor officiële publikaties der Europese Gemeenschappen, 1986.

[32] This, with the exception of products listed on Annex II to the EEC Treaty. See in this context Article 2 of the Acceleration Decision, *supra* note 24, and Council Regulation 950/68 of 28 June 1968 on the common customs tariff, OJ English Special Edition 1968-I, L172/1, at 275.

[33] See, *inter alia*, Joined Cases 37 and 38/73, *Sociaal Fonds voor de Diamantarbeiders* v *Indiamex en De Belder*, [1973] ECR 1622-1625.

ensure that the nomenclature of the CCT would be uniformly applied in all Member States.[34]

The CCT consists of the combined nomenclature, together with the rates of duty and other relevant charges, and the tariff measures included in the Taric or in other Community arrangements.[35] The *combined nomenclature*[36] is reproduced in Annex I to Regulation 2658/87.[37] Chapter 87 of Part II (entitled "Schedule of Customs Duties") of Annex I includes a schedule of customs duties for "Vehicles other than railway or tramway rolling-stock, and parts and accessories thereof". Heading 8703 regards "Motor cars and other motor vehicles principally designed for the transport of persons (other than those of heading No 8702),[38] including station wagons and racing cars" and headings 8706 to 8708 cover their spare-parts. The ECJ recognized that neither Article 28 EC nor Article 113 EC which provide for a common commercial policy based on uniform principles, expressly gives the Council power to establish a tariff nomenclature but held that as the establishment of a tariff nomenclature is indispensable to the application of customs duties, "the power given to the Council to make changes in rates necessarily implies, in the absence of express provision in the Treaty, power to establish and amend the nomenclature relating to the application of the Common Customs Tariff".[39]

The combined nomenclature constitutes the basis of the *Taric*, the so-

---

[34] See, for instance, Council Regulation 97/69 of 16 January 1969 on measures to be taken for uniform application of the nomenclature of the Common Customs Tariff, OJ English Special Edition 1969-I, L14/1, at 12.

[35] See Article 4(1) of Council Regulation 2658/87 of 23 July 1987 on the tariff and statistical nomenclature and on the Common Customs Tariff, OJ 1987 L256/1. Regulation 2658/87 has been amended several times.

[36] The combined nomenclature is based on the harmonized system nomenclature laid down in the International Convention on the Harmonized Commodity Description and Coding System. See Council Decision 87/369 of 7 April 1987 concerning the conclusion of the International Convention on the Harmonized Commodity Description and Coding System and of the Protocol of Amendment thereto, OJ 1987, L198/1.

[37] See in this context Regulation 1734/96 of 9 September 1996 amending Annex I to Regulation 2658/87 on the tariff and statistical nomenclature and on the Common Customs Tariff, OJ 1996, L238/1.

[38] Heading No 8702 is entitled "Motor vehicles for the transport of ten or more persons, including the driver".

[39] Case 165/87, *Commission* v *Council*, [1988] ECR 5560, paras. 7-8.

called integrated tariff of the European Communities. Article 5(1) of Regulation 2658/87 specifies that the Taric shall be used by the Commission and Member States for the application of Community measures concerning imports and, where necessary, exports and trade between Member States. The Commission is responsible for the management and publication of the Taric. Pursuant to Article 12 of Regulation 2658/87, the Commission has to adopt annually by means of a regulation a complete version of the combined nomenclature together with the corresponding autonomous and conventional rates of duty of the CCT, as it results from measures adopted by the Council or by the Commission.[40] Article 28 EC provides that any autonomous alteration or suspension of duties in the CCT shall be decided by the Council acting by a qualified majority on a proposal from the Commission.

It is up to the national customs authorities to apply the CCT.[41] As not every Community guideline on tariff classification is a very precise one, there is room for differences of interpretation by Member States. In order to avoid these differences and a subsequent deflection of trade, it is important that national customs authorities interpret and apply the CCT in the most uniform manner possible. Ideally, a specific good would get the same tariff classification in each Member State.[42] Therefore, Member States are precluded from issuing rules on the interpretation of (headings of) the nomenclature.[43] In order to facilitate uniform classifications, Part I (entitled "Preliminary Provisions") of Annex I to Regulation 2658/87 includes general rules for the interpretation of the combined

---

[40] See for the 1998 edition of Taric: OJ 1998, C115.

[41] See in this context Council Act of 18 December 1997 drawing up, on the basis of Article K.3 of the Treaty on European Union, the Convention on mutual assistance and cooperation between customs administrations, OJ 1998, C24/1.

[42] See, however, P. vander Schueren, "Customs Classification: One of the cornerstones of the single European market, but one which cannot be exhaustively regulated", 28 CML Rev. at 856, who pointed out that as tariff classification is in essence a matter of factual evaluation in view of the features and properties of the products to be classified, it is impossible to envisage all possible combinations of features and properties of products in an exhaustive list of ready-to-use tariff classification provisions.

[43] See, *inter alia*, Case 40/69, *Hauptzollamt Hamburg* v *Bollman*, [1970] ECR 69 and Case 74/69, *Hauptzollamt Bremen* v *Krohn*, [1970] ECR 451.

nomenclature.[44] The ECJ ensures the uniform application and interpretation of the CCT through preliminary rulings based on Article 177 EC. The ECJ held on numerous occasions that the decisive criterion for the customs classification of goods must be sought generally in their objective characteristics and qualities, as defined by the relevant heading of the CCT and in the notes to the sections or chapters.[45] In its judgment in *Tomatis and Fulchiron* which dealt with the French authorities' challenge of the Belgian tariff classification (subheading 87.02 B II a) 1 bb) CCT) of a particular type of Japanese automobile (Suzuki LJ 410) which was imported into Monaco via Belgium, the ECJ held that once goods from a non-member country have been imported into a Member State and released for free circulation on payment of the customs duty corresponding to the tariff classification decided on by the authorities in that Member State, the authorities in the other Member States no longer have any power to reclassify those goods under other headings of the CCT or to levy additional customs duty. The ECJ added, however, that the tariff classification given to a product by the authorities of a Member State may be challenged by the authorities of another Member State in connection with the classification of other examples of the same product or for the purposes of applying their national law. In this case, the French reclassification (subheading 87.02 A I b) CCT) would result in a higher national VAT-rate to be paid in France on the imported Japanese automobiles in question.[46]

On 1 January 1994, Regulation 2913/92 establishing the *Community*

---

[44] Vander Schueren, *supra* note 42, at 858-870, illustrates the fact that these rules for the interpretation of the nomenclature are "frequently far from being easy to apply in practice".

[45] Case C-228/89, *Farfalla Flemming und Partner* v *Hauptzollamt München*, [1990] ECR 3406, par. 13.

[46] See Case C-384/89, *Ministère public* v *Tomatis and Fulchiron*, [1991] ECR 1127-131 (Summary publication). The complete judgment is only available at the ECJ in French. The ECJ held that subheading 87.02 A of the CCT concerning motor vehicles for the transport of persons, including vehicles designed for the transport of both passengers and goods must be interpreted as including vehicles having, behind the driver's seat or bench, specially fitted spaces for fixed, folding or removable seats, and having side windows, a rear or side door or a tail-gate, and an interior finish similar to that of vehicles designed for the transport of passengers.

Customs Code entered into force.[47] The Community Customs Code assembles the provisions of customs legislation that were contained in a large number of Community regulations and directives and includes the general rules and procedures that ensure the implementation of the tariff and other measures introduced at Community level in connection with trade in goods between the Community and third countries.

There were worldwide fears that the Community would use the CCT to build a protectionist tariff wall around its single market creating a so-called "Fortress Europe". In order to counter these fears, the Member States explicitly confirmed in Article 18 EC, their readiness to contribute to the development of international trade and the lowering of barriers to trade by entering into agreements designed, on a basis of reciprocity and mutual advantage, to reduce customs duties below the general level of which they could avail themselves as a result of the establishment of a customs union between them. On the basis of Article 113 EC, the Community grants non-reciprocal *tariff preferences* in the form of customs duties reductions under the generalized system of preferences ("GSP"), to developing countries in order to stimulate their export.[48] The GSP-system is part of the Community's strategy to assist developing countries. As the preferential treatment is reserved for only those countries who really need it, GSP-treatment can be terminated for particular products originating from countries that, for the products in question, have become competitive. For instance, from 1 January 1996, the preferential treatment of cars originating

[47] Council Regulation 2913/92 of 12 October 1992 establishing the Community Customs Code, OJ 1992, L302/1. See also Regulation 2454/93, *supra* note 6. Over the years, amendments have been made. See, for instance, Commission Regulation 2193/94 of 8 September 1994, amending Regulation 2454/93 laying down provisions for the implementation of Council Regulation 2913/92 establishing the Community Customs Code, OJ 1994, L235/6. See also *Agence Europe*, "Aims and content of improvements to the customs code proposed by European Commission - Simplify, increase flexibility, combat fraud", 5 June 1998, at 14. See Commission Regulation (EC) No 1677/98 of 29 July 1998 amending Regulation (EEC) No 2454/93 laying down provisions for the implementation of Council Regulation (EEC) No 2913/92 establishing the Community Customs Code, OJ 1998, L212/18, and Commission Proposal for a European Parliament and Council Regulation (EC) amending Council Regulation (EEC) No 2913/92 establishing the Community Customs Code, OJ 1998, C228/8.

[48] See, *inter alia*, Council Regulation 3281/94 of 19 December 1994 applying a four-year scheme of generalized tariff preferences (1995 to 1998) in respect of certain industrial products originating in developing countries, OJ 1994, L348/1.

from South-Korea was terminated.[49] In addition, the Community concludes tariff and trade agreements with third countries that include detailed provisions on the reduction or even abolition of customs duties on imports and often set specific annual preferential tariff quota for particular "sensitive" products such as cars.[50]

4.3 Elimination of Quantitative Restrictions and Measures having Equivalent Effect

4.3.1 Introduction

The EC Treaty contains several provisions on the elimination of quantitative restrictions on imports and exports between Member States. In short, Article 30 EC prohibits quantitative restrictions between Member States on *imports* and all measures having equivalent effect. Articles 31 and 32 EC lay down so-called "standstill" obligations for Member States with regard to new quantitative restrictions, quotas and measures having equivalent effect. Article 32 EC provides that quotas have to be abolished by the end of the transitional period at the latest.[51] Furthermore, Article 34 EC prohibits quantitative restrictions between Member States on *exports* and all measures having equivalent effect, and obliges Member States to abolish by the end of the first stage at the latest, all quantitative restrictions on exports and any measures having equivalent effect. Last but not least, Article 36 EC provides that Articles 30 to 34 EC shall not preclude prohibitions or restrictions on imports, exports or goods in transit justified on a limited number of grounds which include public policy or public

---

[49] See Commission communication about a change of customs duties applicable under Council Regulation 3281/94 applying a four-year scheme of generalized tariff preferences (1995 to 1998) in respect of certain industrial products originating in developing countries, OJ 1995, C289/5.

[50] See, for instance, Article 4(2) and (3) of the Interim Agreement on trade and trade-related matters between the European Economic Community and the European Coal and Steel Community, of the one part, and the Republic of Poland, of the other part, OJ 1992, L114/2. See in particular Annex IVb which specified the tariff reduction and annual preferential tariff quota for the importation of certain types of cars originating in the Community into Poland.

[51] See in this context Article 3 of the Acceleration Decision, *supra* note 24, abolishing the quantitative restrictions on imports from other Member States (with the exception of products listed on Annex II of the EEC Treaty).

security, the protection of health and life of humans, animals or plants, and the protection of industrial and commercial property. Article 36 EC specifies that these prohibitions or restrictions shall not, however, constitute a means of arbitrary discrimination or a disguised restriction on trade between Member States.

As already indicated in the introduction to this Chapter, the application of these provisions has (had) an important impact on the automobile industry. After decades of using quantitative restrictions and measures having equivalent effect to limit the importation of foreign automobiles and parts, Member States have had to open up their markets for goods coming from other Member States. The impact of Article 30 EC in particular was and still is considerable. Article 30 EC has direct effect and creates individual rights which have to be protected by national courts.[52] All objects which are shipped across a frontier for the purpose of commercial transactions are subject to Article 30 EC, whatever the nature of those transactions.[53] It is evident that this includes trade between Member States in automobiles and parts.[54] Over the years, Article 30 EC became a popular instrument for traders to challenge national rules whose effect was to limit their commercial freedom even where such rules were not aimed at products from other Member States.[55] This led the ECJ in *Keck* to re-examine and clarify its case law on Article 30 EC. With reference to *Cassis de Dijon*,[56] the ECJ confirmed that:

> in the absence of harmonization of legislation, obstacles to free movement of goods which are the consequence of applying, to goods

---

[52] Case 74/76, *Iannelli & Volpi* v *Meroni*, [1977) ECR 575, par. 13.

[53] Case C-2/90, *Commission* v *Belgium*, [1992] ECR I-4478, par. 26. See in this context L. Hancher and H. Sevenster, 30 CML Rev. at 360.

[54] The ECJ held in Case C-55/93, *Van Schaik*, [1994] ECR I-4857, par. 14, that the servicing of a vehicle in another Member State which may involve a supply of goods (spare parts, oil etc.), does not fall within the scope of Article 30 EC as such a supply is not an end in itself, but incidental to the provision of services.

[55] Joined Cases C-267/91 and C-268/91, *Keck and Mithouard*, [1993] ECR I-6131, par. 14.

[56] Case 120/78, *Rewe-Zentrale* v *Bundesmonopolverwaltung für Branntwein (Cassis de Dijon)*, [1979] ECR 649.

> coming from other Member States where they are lawfully manufactured and marketed, rules that lay down requirements to be met by such goods (such as those relating to designation, form, size, weight, composition, presentation, labelling, packaging) constitute measures of equivalent effect prohibited by Article 30. This is so even if those rules apply without distinction to all products unless their application can be justified by a public-interest objective taking precedence over the free movement of goods.[57]

The ECJ held:

> By contrast, contrary to what has previously been decided, the application to products from other Member States of national provisions restricting or prohibiting certain selling arrangements is not such as to hinder directly or indirectly, actually or potentially, trade between Member States within the meaning of the *Dassonville* judgement ..., so long as those provisions apply to all relevant traders operating within the national territory and so long as they affect in the same manner, in law and in fact, the marketing of domestic products and of those from other Member States.
>
> Provided that those conditions are fulfilled, the application of such rules to the sale of products from another Member State meeting the requirements laid down by that State is not by nature such as to prevent their access to the market or to impede access any more than it impedes

---

[57] *Keck and Mithouard*, *supra* note 55, par. 15. In *Cassis de Dijon*, *ibidem*, par. 8, the ECJ held that "[i]n the absence of common rules relating to the production and marketing of alcohol ... it is for the Member States to regulate all matters relating to the production and marketing of alcohol and alcoholic beverages on thier own territory. Obstacles to movement within the Community resulting from disparities beween the national laws relating to the marketing of the products in question must be accepted in so far as those provisions may be recognized as being necessary in order to satisfy mandatory requirements relating in particular to the effectiveness of fiscal supervision, the protection of public health, the fairness of commercial transactions and the defence of the consumer".

the access of domestic products. Such rules therefore fall outside the scope of Article 30 of the Treaty.[58]

Articles 30 to 36 EC continue to play an important role as Member States keep coming up with ingenious schemes in an effort to protect the interests of their domestic automobile industry. This protectionist urge is illustrated by *Rémy Schmit* in which French rules on model-year dates for automobiles were held to be contrary to Article 30 EC as they had the effect of impeding imports.[59] Whereas most Member States employ the calendar year in which the automobile is sold or the date on which it is first registered, under French rules, automobiles sold between 1 July and 31 December in the year "n" were given the anticipated year date of the year "n + 1". The ECJ held that the French rules did not affect in the same way the marketing, on the one hand, of automobiles manufactured in France and intended for the home market or of automobiles imported by approved distributors and, on the other hand, of automobiles imported or reimported through parallel channels. Several French car manufacturers and official dealers advertised with the difference in treatment in order to encourage consumers to buy automobiles marketed by their sales network.[60] The ECJ noted that, in practice, the French rules had the effect that

---

[58] *Keck and Mithouard*, *supra* note 55, paras. 16-17. There is an abundance of literature on the application of Articles 30 to 36 EC. See, *inter alia*, P. Oliver, *Free movement of goods in the European Community*, 1996, Sweet & Maxwell, London, and S. Weatherill, "After *Keck*: Some thoughts on how to clarify the clarification", 33 CML Rev. at 885-906.

[59] Case C-240/95, *Rémy Schmit*, [1996] ECR I-3179. See for Dutch cases on the Dutch registration policy which negatively affected the value of imported automobiles: *De Bruin Auto's/Minister van Verkeer en Waterstaat* (Afdeling Rechtspraak RvS, 17-12-1993, No. R01.93.0856/Q01), SEW 1994, at 456-461, and *Directeur van de Dienst voor het Wegverkeer* v *Snellers Auto's* (Afdeling Bestuursrechtspraak RvS, 1-7-1997, No. K01.97.0053).

[60] *Rémy Schmit*, *supra* note 59, paras. 20-21. It was reported in "Paris High Court rules against Peugeot for false advertising", *Agence Europe*, 18 March 1995, at 11, that Peugeot was fined for false advertising along the Franco-Belgian border urging consumers to buy cars in France, with the slogan "There is only one meter between these two new Peugeots, but they are already separated by a year". In France, automobiles purchased after 1 July 1993, were considered to be 1994 vintage. It was reported that "[a]ccording to the Court, any car purchased in an EU Member State should benefit from the same advantages when it is resold in France, or the European market would ultimately be compartmentalized". See also "BEUC complains about Renault, Peugeot and Citroen for inciting to "Buy National" in breach of the common market to the detriment of consumers", *Agence Europe*, 22 September 1994, at 12.

parallel imports or re-imports had to be marketed under the model-year date applied in the Member State from which they were imported, which generally corresponds to the calendar year of sale or the date of first registration. Hence, the French rules were likely to discourage the sale of parallel imports or re-imports in so far as, although they were the same model as the others, they were presented as being of an earlier year and accordingly were at a discount on resale or compensation was payable in the event of a claim.[61] The ECJ noted that the rules were *not* appropriate to satisfy the requirements invoked by France relating to consumer protection or fairness of commercial transactions.[62] In its judment, the ECJ held that Article 30 EC precludes national legislation on model-year dates for automobiles which causes the administrative authorities and traders of the Member State in question (France) to consider that, where two automobiles of the same model and make are sold in that Member State after a particular date (30 June), only the automobile which was the subject of a parallel import would be prohibited from holding itself out as being of the following model year.[63]

Notwithstanding the effectiveness of Articles 30 to 36 EC, certain categories of obstacles to trade can best be eliminated through the *harmonisation* of national laws of the Member States.[64] Such a category is formed by technical barriers to trade that are the result of differences in national technical standards

---

[61] *Rémy Schmit*, *supra* note 59, paras. 17-19.

[62] *Rémy Schmit*, *supra* note 59, paras. 23-25.

[63] See also Written Question 103/97 (Kaklamanis), OJ 1997, C319/23, in which the Commission reported that it had initiated infringement proceedings under Articles 30 to 36 EC in respect of Greek regulations governing the importation of diesel-engined heavy goods vehicles and the use of diesel-engined private cars. Reference is also made to Petition 691/95 by Mr. G.G. (Greek).

[64] As pointed out by P.J. Slot, "Harmonisation", E.L.Rev. 1996, at 380, "the broader the interpretation given to the concept of "measures having equivalent effect" in Article 30, the smaller the sphere of application of harmonisation of law". Slot notes that "[a]lthough not even the most extensive interpretation will entirely do away with the need for harmonisation, Article 30 will only lead to negative integration, *i.e.* eliminate barriers for imported goods. It may therefore be necessary to have recourse to positive integration which would result in measures aligning product standards for both imported and nationally produced goods".

and regulations.[65] Already in the early days of the Community, Member States made an effort to prevent the creation of *new* technical barriers.[66] This resulted in the adoption of Directive 83/189 laying down a procedure for the provision of information in the field of technical standards and regulations, that aims, by preventive monitoring, at protecting the free movement of goods.[67] The ECJ confirmed that:

> [s]uch monitoring is necessary since technical regulations covered by the Directive are capable of hindering, directly or indirectly, actually or potentially, intra-Community trade in goods. Such hindrances may arise from the adoption of national technical regulations ... irrespective of the grounds on which they were adopted.[68]

---

[65] See in this context P.J. Slot, *Technical and administrative obstacles to trade in the EEC*, 1975, A.W. Sijthoff, Leiden.

[66] See, for instance, the Agreement of the Representatives of the Governments of the Member States meeting in Council of 28 May 1969 concerning standstill and information for the Commission, OJ 1969, C76/9.

[67] Council Directive 83/189 of 28 March 1983 laying down a procedure for the provision of information in the field of technical standards and regulations, OJ 1983, L109/8, as last amended by Directive 94/10 of the European Parliament and the Council of 23 March 1994 materially amending for the second time Directive 83/189 laying down a procedure for the provision of information in the field of technical standards and regulations, OJ 1994, L100/30. See in this context S. Weatherill, "Compulsory notification of draft technical regulations: The contribution of Directive 83/189 to the management of the internal market", (1996) 16 Yearbook of European Law, at 129-204. See also Commission Proposal for a European Parliament and Council Directive laying down a procedure for the provision of information in the field of technical standards and regulations (codified version), OJ 1997, C78/4; Amended Commission proposal for a European Parliament and Council directive amending for the third time Directive 83/189 laying down a procedure for the provision of information in the field of technical standards and regulations, OJ 1998, C65/12, and Council Common Position (EC) No 18/98 of 23 February 1998 with a view to adopting Directive 98/.../EC of the European Parliament and of the Council laying down a procedure for the provision of information in the field of technical standards and regulations, OJ 1998, C110/1. See "Progress on mutual recognition of national rules, difficulties for emergency interventions in case of obstacles to the free movement of goods", *Agence Europe*, 30-31 March 1998, at 8.

[68] See in this sense Case C-13/96, *Bic Benelux* v *Belgium*, [1997] ECR I-1776, par. 19. The ECJ emphasized that there is no basis in Directive 83/189 for an interpretation limiting its application to national measures capable of harmonisation only on the basis of Article 100a EC.

According to the Commission, non-compliance with the notification procedure would have the effect that the technical regulations concerned would not be binding on private parties.[69] The ECJ confirmed that the notification procedure set out in Directive 83/189 has direct effect.[70] Furthermore, a procedure was established for the exchange of information on national measures derogating from the principle of the free movement of goods within the Community. This procedure aimed at enhancing knowledge on the implementation of the free movement of goods in non-harmonized sectors and identifying the problems encountered with a view to finding appropriate solutions to them through harmonisation or the application of Article 30 EC.[71] In May 1998, the Member States also agreed upon the establishment of an intervention mechanism guaranteeing the free movement of goods in cases of sudden obstacles.[72]

Besides recognizing the need to prevent the creation of new technical

---

[69] Commission communication concerning the non-respect of certain provisions of Council Directive 83/189 of 28 March 1983 laying down a procedure for the provision of information in the field of technical standards and regulations, OJ 1986, C245/4. In its Fourteenth Annual Report on monitoring the application of Community law - 1996 ("14th Annual Report"), OJ 1997, C332/1, at 24, the Commission repeated that since 1989, it "has been monitoring compliance with the notification requirement by routinely scrutinizing the official gazettes of all the Member States".

[70] Case C-194/94, *CIA Security International* v *Signalson and Securitel*, [1996] ECR I-2201. See also the judgment of 16 June 1998 in Case C-226/97, *Lemmens* (not yet reported). See for a Dutch case on the question whether a particular change in the Dutch registration procedure for imported cars constitutes a technical regulation: *Algemeen Directeur van de Dienst voor het Wegverkeer* v *Snellers Auto's* (Afdeling Bestuursrechtspraak RvS, 1-7-1997, No. K01.97.0053 en 10-8-1998, No. H01.97.0519).

[71] See Decision 3052/95 of the European Parliament and of the Council of 13 December 1995 establishing a procedure for the exchange of information on national measures derogating from the principle of the free movement of goods within the Community, OJ 1995, L321/1.

[72] It was reported in "Tentative Council agreement on intervention mechanism for free movement of goods", *Agence Europe*, 18-19 May 1998, at 7, that a regulation was adopted establishing "an alert mechanism under which Member States are responsible for forwarding to their partners, via the Commission, all information at their disposal when faced with a hindrance to free movement". In addition, a resolution was adopted in which the Member States "agree to take all action ... to preserve free movement and to react rapidly to possible disturbances, and to ensure that any individual who suffers injury because of such a hindrance to free movement shall be guaranteed rapid and effective means of recourse". See also "Plan for rapid procedure against trade obstacles", *Agence Europe*, 19 November 1997, at 5, and Commission proposal for a Council Regulation (EC) creating a mechanism whereby the Commission can intervene in order to remove certain obstacles to trade, OJ 1998, C10/14.

barriers, the Council announced plans for the removal of *existing* technical barriers to trade in its General Programme of 28 May 1969 for the elimination of technical barriers to trade which result from disparaties between the provisions laid down by law, regulation or administrative action in Member States. The Council explicitly confirmed the need to remove the technical barriers to trade in automobiles through full harmonisation by means of directives. The General Programme announced harmonisation on the type-approval of automobiles and the mandatory technical requirements to be met by certain parts or components such as liquid fuel tanks and rear protective devices, audible warning devices, permissible sound level and the exhaust system.[73] In its efforts to eliminate quantitative restrictions and measures having equivalent effect, on trade in automobiles and parts, the Community focused on barriers caused by national type-approval procedures (**4.3.2**), registration procedures (**4.3.3**) and roadworthiness tests (**4.3.4**).

4.3.2 Type-Approval for Automobiles, Separate Technical Units, Systems and Components

In each Member State, automobiles may only be put on the market if they comply with a long list of mandatory technical requirements which are set to protect public interests such as road safety and the environment. It was practice in Member States to check per vehicle type whether these technical requirements were met. Manufacturers would subsequently issue a certificate of conformity for each automobile which conformed to the approved type. Initially, the mandatory technical requirements differed considerably from one Member State to another. This disparity constituted an important obstacle to trade within the Community. It could very well happen that a vehicle type which was admitted in one Member State was not allowed on the roads of another Member State.[74]

[73] OJ 1969, C76/1. Although a new approach towards technical harmonisation and standards was introduced in 1985 by means of Council Resolution of 7 May 1985 on a new approach to technical harmonisation and standards, OJ 1985, C136/1, the removal of technical barriers to trade in automobiles by means of full and detailed harmonisation was continued.

[74] For instance, G.C. Hufbauer, "An overview" in *Europe 1992 - An American perspective*, *supra* note 19, at 6, reported that even up to the mid-1980's, a German who wanted to register his car in France had to first change headlights, wiring, and windshield.

In order to reduce and eventually even eliminate these hindrances to the establishment and proper functioning of the common market, the Commission came up with a proposal for the approximation of the national laws of the Member States which required mutual recognition by the Member States of type-approval checks carried out by another Member State. The Commission's proposal led to the adoption of Council Directive 70/156 of 6 February 1970 on the approximation of the laws of the Member States relating to the type-approval of motor vehicles and their trailers[75] which introduced the *framework* for a Community type-approval procedure. Separate Community Directives were to specify the harmonised *technical requirements* applicable to individual parts such as fuel tanks and rear protective devices,[76] steering equipment,[77] doors[78] and audible warning devices,[79] and *characteristics* like permissible sound level, the exhaust system,[80] measures to be taken against air pollution by gases from positive-ignition engines[81] and space for mounting and fixing of rear registration

---

[75] OJ English Special Edition 1970, L42/1, at 96. See the most recent edition of the *Directory of Community legislation in force and other acts of the Community institutions*, Volume I, subheading 13.30.10 Motor Vehicle, Official Journal of the European Communities, for an overview of the amendments to Directive 70/156.

[76] Council Directive 70/221 of 20 March 1970 on the approximation of the laws of the Member States relating to liquid fuel tanks and rear protective devices for motor vehicles and their trailers, OJ English Special Edition 1970, L76/23, at 192.

[77] Council Directive 70/311 of 8 June 1970 on the approximation of the laws of the Member States relating to the steering equipment for motor vehicles and their trailers, OJ English Special Edition 1970, L133/10, at 375.

[78] Council Directive 70/387 of 27 July 1970 on the approximation of the laws of the Member States relating to the doors of motor vehicles and their trailers, OJ English Special Edition 1970, L176/5, at 564.

[79] Council Directive 70/388 of 27 July 1970 on the approximation of the laws of the Member States relating to audible warning devices for motor vehicles, OJ English Special Edition 1970, L176/12, at 571.

[80] Council Directive 70/157 of 6 February 1970 on the approximation of the laws of the Member States relating to the permissible sound level and the exhaust system of motor vehicles, OJ English Special Edition 1970, L42/16, at 111.

[81] Council Directive 70/220 of 20 March 1970 on the approximation of the laws of the Member States relating to measures to be taken against air pollution by gases from positive-ignition engines of motor vehicles, OJ English Special Edition 1970, L76/1, at 171.

plates.[82] These technical directives employed optional harmonisation[83] and were the first of what was to become a very long list of directives specifying harmonized technical requirements applicable to individual parts and characteristics of vehicles.[84]

The framework Directive 70/156 describes the *Community type-approval procedure* as the procedure whereby a Member State certifies that a vehicle type satifies both the technical requirements of the separate Community directives, and the checks listed in the Community type-approval certificate (Article 2(b)). Directive 70/156 does not apply to used vehicles.[85] An application for a Community type-approval must be submitted by or on behalf of the manufacturer, to no more than one Member State. It has to be accompagnied by a Community information document and the documents referred to therein (Article 3). A Member State has to approve all vehicle types which conform to the particulars in the Community information document and satisfy the checks listed in the Community type-approval certificate (Article 4(1)). The checking Member State is not only bound to take the necessary measures to verify through spot checks that production models conform to the approved prototype (Article 4(2)), it must also provide the other Member States with a copy of the Community information document and the Community approval certificate for each vehicle type which it approved or refused to approve (Article 5(1)). The manufacturer has to complete a Community certificate of conformity for each

---

[82] Council Directive 70/222 of 20 March 1970 on the approximation of the laws of the Member States relating to the space for mounting and the fixing of rear registration plates on motor vehicles and their trailers, OJ English Special Edition 1970, L76/25, at 194.

[83] See, *inter alia*, Economic and Social Committee on the Commission's proposal for Directive 70/156, *Pb*. 1969, C48/14, par. 1. In the Commission Notice on procedures for the type-approval and registration of vehicles previously registered in another Member State ("1988 Notice on Type-approval"), OJ 1988, C281/10, under III-A, the Commission noted that the "optional nature" meant "that the Member States are able to maintain or adopt national requirements in addition to the harmonized requirements and in some cases enables manufacturers to decide whether they wish to base their models on the harmonized requirements or the national requirements".

[84] See the most recent edition of the *Directory of Community legislation in force and other acts of the Community institutions*, Volume I, subheading 13.30.10 Motor Vehicle, Official Journal of the European Communities, for an overview of all the (many amendments to the) directives.

[85] See Written Question 2011/97 (Gallagher), OJ 1998, C60/77.

vehicle manufactured in conformity with the approved prototype (Article 5(2)). For the purpose of taxation or registration of a vehicle, Member States can ask for additional particulars to be provided on the Community certificate of conformity, provided that the particulars concerned are explicitly stated on the Community information document or can be derived therefrom by a straightforward calculation (Article 5(3)).

In principle, no Member State may refuse to register or prohibit the sale, entry into service, or use of any new vehicle on grounds relating to its construction or functioning, where that vehicle was accompagnied by a certificate of conformity (Article 7(1)). Nevertheless, Member States can take measures with regard to vehicles which do not conform to the approved type (Article 7(2)) or constitute a hazard to road safety (Article 9). In order to facilitate the adaptation to technical progress of (the three annexes to) Directive 70/156 and the separate Community directives, a special procedure is provided for in which the Commission and the Member States co-operate closely within the so-called Committee on the Adaptation to Technical Progress of the Directives on the Removal of Technical Barriers to Trade in the Motor Vehicle Sector (Articles 11-13).

The legal significance of the technical Community directives within the framework of Directive 70/156 is beyond any doubt. For instance, the ECJ confirmed the exhaustive nature of the list of technical devices in Directive 76/756 of 27 July 1976 on the approximation of the laws of the Member States relating to the installation of lighting and light-signalling devices on motor vehicles and their trailers.[86] The ECJ held that this particular list had to be interpreted in a manner which is consistent with the purpose of Directive 70/156 being to reduce, and even eliminate, hindrances to trade within the Community resulting from the fact that mandatory technical requirements differ from one Member State to another. According to the ECJ, that objective was reflected in the context of Directive 76/756, in the obligation imposed on the Member States to adopt the same requirements either in addition to or in place of their existing rules. The ECJ confirmed the importance of the separate Community directives which are envisaged by, and have a crucial function within, the framework put in place by Directive 70/156, and held that:

[86] OJ 1976, L262/1.

> the Member States cannot unilaterally require manufacturers who have complied with the harmonized technical requirements set out in Directive 76/756/EEC to comply with a requirement which is not imposed by that directive, since motor vehicles complying with the technical requirements laid down therein must be able to move freely within the common market.[87]

Nevertheless, the ECJ pointed out in *Gofette*, that Directive 70/156 did not at the time provide for a sufficient degree of harmonisation to permit national approval procedures to be entirely replaced by a Community approval procedure for each type of vehicle.[88] National requirements remained applicable in respect of parts and characteristics which were not yet covered by separate Community directives. As at the time certain technical requirements and characteristics still had to be dealt with in separate Community directives, Directive 70/156 provided for a *transitional system* under which a manufacturer could request a national type approval based on the harmonised technical requirements instead of on the corresponding national requirements.[89] On application by the manufacturer and on submission of the Community information document, the Member State concerned had to complete the Community type-approval certificate and provide the manufacturer with a copy. The copy of the Community type-approval certificate had to be accepted by other Member States to which application was made for national type-approval for the same type of vehicle, as proof that the requisite checks had been carried out (Article 10(1)).

---

[87] See in this sense Case 60/86, *Commission* v *U.K. and Northern Ireland*, [1988] ECR 3934, paras. 11-12.

[88] Case 406/85, *Procureur de la République* v *Gofette and Gilliard (Gofette)*, [1987] ECR 2542, par. 8.

[89] It should be pointed out that in drawing up the technical Community directives, the Community had to take into consideration the work of the Economic Committee for Europe of the United Nations in this field. See the 1958 Agreement concerning the adoption of uniform conditions of approval and reciprocal recognition of approval for motor vehicle equipment and parts, United Nations Treaty Series, Volume 335, 1959, at 212. See also Council Decision of 27 November 1997 with a view to accession by the European Community to the Agreement of the United Nations Economic Commission for Europe concerning the adoption of uniform technical prescriptions for wheeled vehicles, equipment and parts which can be fitted to and/or be used on wheeled vehicles and the conditions for reciprocal recognition of approvals granted on the basis of these prescriptions ("Revised 1958 Agreement"), OJ 1997, L346/78.

The transitional system was to be revoked once all the requirements necessary for the granting of Community type-approval were applicable (Article 10(2)).

In practice, the national procedures with which Member States check(ed) the conformity of imported vehicles with an approved type, led to a variety of problems. The ECJ explicitly confirmed in *Gofette* that Articles 30 and 36 EC are relevant for national procedures related to type-approval such as those in which Member States check the conformity of imported vehicles with an approved type. Imported vehicles which had previously been registered in another Member State were often subjected to these national procedures. According to the ECJ, the existence of these procedures could be in accordance with the requirements of Article 36 EC if it was not possible for the objective pursued to be realized as effectively by measures which did not restrict intra-Community trade to such an extent. The ECJ pointed out that consequently the control procedure must not entail unreasonable cost or delay. Furthermore, the authorities of the Member States are not entitled to require checks to be carried out if they have already been carried out in another Member State and the results are available to those authorities or may at their request be placed at their disposal. The ECJ held that the importing Member State must provide for the alternative of substituting the production by the importer of documents drawn up in the exporting Member State for the checks for the approval of the vehicle in so far as those documents contain the necessary information.[90]

In 1988, the Commission published a Notice on Type-approval in which it elaborated upon the implications of the ECJ's case law on Articles 30 and 36 EC for the type-approval and registration of vehicles previously registered in another Member State. The Commission noted that in the absence of full harmonisation at Community level, Member States were entitled to invoke Article 36 EC in order to guarantee road safety, but underlined at the same time that they could only do so in compliance with the conditions laid down in Article 36 EC. The Commission subsequently gave its opinion on the manner in which to interpret and apply the ECJ's case law to procedures in Member States to check the conformity of imported vehicles with an approved type, and focused in particular on the technical requirements to be satisfied by the imported vehicle and the documents relating to the technical characteristics of

[90] *Gofette*, *supra* note 88, paras. 10-11.

the vehicle.[91] Several cases have shown the manner in which these procedures have been (ab)used by the French authorities as a manner to counter the parallel importation of Asian cars which were first brought on the market in other Member States. For instance, in *Monin II*, a *Juge-Commissaire* who described Monin as "a company which specialized in the distribution of makes of Asian vehicles which were not accredited in the 'voluntary restraint' system, under which a ceiling of 3% of annual registrations was placed on the entry into France of vehicles of Japanese origin", established that this company was forced to have recourse to parallel imports. With regard to the French administrative practices, the *Juge-Commissaire* noted that:

> [s]ince the vehicles imported from other Member States had already been registered, they were regarded as second-hand vehicles and therefore had to be approved on an individual basis. The French administrative authorities did not carry out such approvals within a reasonable time, so that motorists who had been unable to have their vehicles registered within the statutory two-month period were prosecuted by the police. Faced with a large number of requests by purchasers for rescission of the sale contract, refund of the money paid and damages, Monin was faced to cease trading.[92]

---

[91] 1988 Notice on Type-approval, *supra* note 83, under III.A.

[92] Case C-428/93, *Monin Automobiles - Maison du Deux-Roues (Monin II)*, [1994] ECR I-1711, par. 3. See in this context also Case C-386/92, *Monin Automobiles - Maison du Deux-Roues (Monin I)*, [1993] ECR I-2049.

The impression is that commercial policy interests withheld the Community from investigating, let alone taking legal action against, these French practices.[93]

Over the years, important *amendments* were made to the text of Directive 70/156.[94] For instance, Community type-approval for separate technical units was made possible in 1977[95] and for components in 1987.[96] The most sweeping amendment, however, was made in 1992 through the adoption of Directive 92/53[97] which entailed the replacement of the various national type-approval systems by a Community type-approval procedure.[98] The amended text provides for a type-approval of motor vehicles[99] and their trailers built in one or

---

[93] See also Case C-72/90, *Asia Motor France* v *Commission (Asia Motor I)*, [1990] ECR I-2181; Case C-29/92, *Asia Motor France* v *Commission (Asia Motor II)*, [1992] ECR I-3936; Case T-28/90, *Asia Motor France* v *Commission (Asia Motor III)*, [1992] ECR II-2285; Case T-7/92, *Asia Motor France and others* v *Commission (Asia Motor IV)*, [1993] ECR II-669, and Case T-387/94, *Asia Motor France and others* v *Commission (Asia Motor V)*, [1996] ECR II-965. In paras. 68-69 of its jugdment in *Asia Motor III*, the CFI explicitly pointed at *Gofette* "as regards the conformity with Article 30 ... of the French system of 'individual' approval" and emphasized that "the authorization system laid down by the applicable national legislation does not concern the right to import but simply the question whether the approval of imported vehicles, which is a necessary precondition for allowing a vehicles on to public roads, is granted by type or in accordance with the so-called 'individual' procedure".

[94] See for an overview of the amendments the most recent edition of the *Directory of Community legislation in force and other acts of the Community institutions*, Volume I, subheading 13.30.10 Motor Vehicle, OJ. See, for instance, Commission Directive 98/14/EC of 6 February 1998 adapting to technical progress Council Directive 70/156/EEC on the approximation of the laws of the Member States relating to the type-approval of motor vehicles and their trailers, OJ 1998, L91/1.

[95] Council Directive 78/315 of 21 December 1977, OJ 1978, L81/1.

[96] Council Directive 87/358 of 25 June 1987, OJ 1987, L192/51.

[97] Council Directive 92/53 of 18 June 1992, OJ 1992, L225/1.

[98] 3rd Whereas of Directive 92/53. The Commission, however, pointed out in its interpretative communication on procedures for the type-approval and registration of vehicles previously registered in another Member State ("1996 Communication on Type-approval"), OJ 1996, C143/4, that Directive 92/53 entails the *gradual* replacement of the national schemes by a Community type-approval procedure.

[99] Article 2 of Directive 70/156, as amended by Directive 92/53, defines "vehicle" as any motor vehicle intended for use on the road, being complete or incomplete, having at least four wheels and a maximum design speed exceeding 25km/h, and its trailers, with the exception of vehicles which run on rails and of agricultural and forestry tractors and all mobile machinery.

more stages, of systems,[100] components[101] and separate technical units[102] intended for use on such vehicles and trailers (Article 1). The term "type-approval" is defined as the procedure whereby a Member State certifies that a type of vehicle, system, component or separate technical unit satisfies the relevant technical requirements set out in the exhaustive list of Annex IV ("List of requirements for the purposes of vehicle type-approval") or XI ("Nature of and provisions for special-purpose vehicles") (Article 2). Each Member State is obliged to grant vehicle type-approval to vehicle types that conform to the particulars in a given information folder and which meet the technical requirements of all the relevant separate Directives.[103] A similar obligation is provided for with regard to multi-stage type-approval, system type-approval and component or separate technical unit type-approval (Article 3(1)). A Member State may refuse to grant type-approval on the basis of a serious risk to road safety (Article 3(2)). The checking Member State has several administrative duties to perform which range from completing the type-approval certificate and the vehicle approval certificate to providing the approval authorities of the other Member States with a copy of the vehicle type-approval certificate for each vehicle type which it has approved or refused to approve or withdrawn (Article 4(3) to (6)).

---

[100] Article 2 of Directive 70/156, as amended by Directive 92/53 defines "system" as any vehicle system such as brakes, emission control equipment, interior fittings, etc. which is subject to the requirements in any of the separate Directives.

[101] Article 2 of Directive 70/156, as amended by Directive 92/53 defines "component" as a device, such as a lamp, subject to the requirements of a separate Directive, intended to be part of a vehicle, which may be type-approved independently of a vehicle where the separate Directive makes express provisions for so doing.

[102] Article 2 of Directive 70/156, as amended by Directive 92/53 defines "separate technical unit" as a device, such as a rear protective device, subject to the requirements of a separate Directive, intended to be part of a vehicle, which may be type-approved separately but only in relation to one or more specified types of vehicle, where the separate Directive makes express provisions for so doing.

[103] The importance of these separate Community directives is confirmed in Article 2(5) of Directive 92/53 which provides that subject to Article 8(2)(a) and (b) of Directive 70/156 as amended by this Directive, paragraphs 3 and 4 shall *not* permit Member States to derogate from any provisions of a separate Directive which lays down requirements based on total harmonisation in respect of the type-approval and initial entry into service of a vehicle, component or separate technical unit.

Furthermore, the amended text of Directive 70/156 includes provisions dealing with the application for type-approval (Article 3), amendments to approvals (Article 5), the certificate of conformity (Article 6) and registration and entry into service (Article 7).[104] The ECJ confirmed in *VAG Sverige* that, save in the highly specific circumstances regarding road safety, Directive 70/156 does not provide for any possibility for a Member State to refuse the registration of new vehicles covered by a valid Community type-approval certificate.[105] The amended text also includes provisions on exemptions and alternative procedures (Article 8), acceptance of equivalent approvals (Article 9), conformity of production arrangements (Article 10), nonconformity with the approved type (Article 11), notification of decisions and remedies available (Article 12), adaptation of the Annexes (Article 13) and notification of approval authorities and technical services (Article 14).

Member States were bound to implement Directive 92/53 on or before 31 December 1992 and had to apply its provisions as from 1 January 1993.[106] As far as vehicle type-approval is concerned, Member States are only obliged to apply the Directive for *vehicles of category M1* equipped with an internal combustion engine, pending an amendment of the Annexes that will include those vehicles of category M1 powered by engines other than internal combustion engines and other vehicle categories. The transitional system

---

[104] Article 2(4) of Directive 92/53 provides that until 31 December 1997 for complete vehicles and until 31 December 1999 for completed vehicles following multi-stage type-approval, *Article 7(1) and (2)* of Directive 70/156, as amended by this Directive, shall not apply to vehicles, components and separate technical units belonging to a type for which a national type-approval has been granted before 1 January 1996 or 1 January 1998 or to a type which a Member State has registered, permitted the sale or entry into service of before 1 January 1996 or 1 January 1998. Approvals forming part of the national type-approval procedure referred to above which have been granted pursuant to the separate Directives shall remain in force after 31 December 1997 for complete vehicles, and after 31 December 1999 for vehicles completed following multi-stage type-approval, unless one of the conditions laid down in the second subparagraph of Article 5(3) of Directive 70/156 as amended by this Directive should apply. See in this context also Article 2(5) of Directive 92/53.

[105] Case C-329/95, *VAG Sverige*, judgment of 29 May 1997, paras. 18-19, not yet reported. The national rules in question (on protection of the environment) did not satisfy the conditions governing derogation laid down in Article 7(3) of Directive 70/156 (on road safety).

[106] Article 2(1) of Directive 92/53.

discussed above,[107] is applicable to vehicle type-approval of the other vehicle categories.[108] The Commission summarized that the Directive provides for application by the Member States on an *optional* basis, over a transitional period, from 1 January 1993 to 31 December 1995, and for *mandatory* application from 1 January 1996 concerning new vehicle types, and from 1 January 1998 for all new vehicles registered, sold or entering service in the Community.[109] In April 1998, it was announced that the Commission had opened the LISTIC-web site (http://www.listec.lu/) providing information on type-approval of motor vehicles.[110]

In 1996, the Commission published a Communication on Type-approval which replaced the 1988 Notice on Type-approval.[111] In this Communication, the Commission defines category M1 vehicles (with an explicite reference to Annex II of Directive 70/156), as motor vehicles for the transport of up to eight persons including the driver. This definition is probably incorrect as M1 vehicles are defined in Annex II of Directive 70/156 as vehicles used for the carriage of passengers and comprising no more than eight seats *in addition to* the driver's seat,[112] which makes a maximum of nine instead of eight persons in total. In the 1996 Communication, the Commission clarifies that with regard to

---

[107] See in this context Article 10 of Directive 70/156 as amended by Directive 87/403, OJ 1987, L220/44.

[108] Article 2(2) of Directive 92/53.

[109] Written Question 2098/93 (Desmond), OJ 1994, C46/43. See also 1996 Communication on Type-approval, *supra* note 98, at 5, in which the Commission emphasized that the Community type-approval system "became obligatory from 1 January 1996 for new makes of passenger cars". In accordance with Article 3 of Directive 92/53, the Commission drew up a technical report on the application of the European type-approval procedures which was entitled "Report on the EC Workshop 94 on the application of European type-approval procedures to motor vehicles (cars)" (Brussels 22 November 1994), Brussels, 14/2/95, III/E/5, FR. The Commission reported in its 14th Annual Report, *supra* note 69, at 26, that "[t]he transposal of directives, so vital against a background of total harmonization, is going smoothly ... Given the detailed, technical nature ..., many Member States routinely refer in thier national legislation to the text published in the Official Journal"; see Table 2.2.2.8. "Progress in implementing Directives applicable to motor vehicles, tractors and motorcycles".

[110] See "Web site on type approval", *Agence Europe*, 1 April 1998, at 14.

[111] 1996 Communication on Type-approval, *supra* note 98.

[112] 1996 Communication on Type-approval, *supra* note 98, at 34.

used vehicles[113] with a certificate of conformity corresponding to a vehicle type for which Community type-approval has been granted, the carrying out of checks by the authorities of the Member State of destination on registration of the vehicle, is no longer justified since the vehicle is registered on the basis of Community type-approval, which is valid in all Member States.[114] The Commission recognizes that national type-approval will continue for vehicles other than category M1 vehicles in the absence of a comprehensive system of Community type-approval.[115] The Commission refers to *Gofette* and repeats that the introduction by a Member State of a procedure for the type-approval of vehicles imported from another Member State where they have already undergone type-approval, is not in itself incompatible with Articles 30 and 36 EC, provided that certain conditions are met. The Commission subsequently gives its opinion on how to interpret and apply the ECJ's case law to these national procedures and focuses in particular on the technical requirements to be satisfied by a vehicle previously registered in another Member State and on the documents relating to the technical characteristics of the vehicle.[116] The Commission keeps a close eye on the compatibility of the various national procedures with Articles 30 and 36 EC.[117]

---

[113] With the term "used vehicles" the Commission probably means "category M1 vehicles previously registered in another Member State regardless of whether they are new or used". See 1996 Communication on Type-approval, *supra* note 98, at 5 under 2.

[114] See 1996 Communication on Type-approval, *supra* note 98, at 9 under 1.2.

[115] See, however, Commission proposal for a European Parliament and Council Directive relating to special provisions for vehicles used for the carriage of passengers comprising more than eight seats in addition to the driver's seat and amending Council Directive 70/156, OJ 1998, C17/1.

[116] 1996 Communication on Type-approval, *supra* note 98, at 7 under 1.1. See also Written Question 2351/82 (Hume), OJ 1983, C189/24.

[117] For instance, the Commission announced in *Single Market News* (Newsletter of DG XV - Internal Market and Financial Services), No 9, October 1997, at 11, that it had decided to take action against Spain with regard to Spanish law and administrative practices concerning type-approval and registration of vehicles bought and/or previously registered in another Member State which constitute a barrier to the free movement of goods within the Single Market. Furthermore, the Commission reported in its 14th Annual Report, *supra* note 69, at 22, that after meetings with the national authorities "the Danish authorities ... adopted a circular on automobile parts, recognizing the certificates of conformity for tyres and wheels issued by other Union or EFTA Member States". See also Written Question 2011/97 (Gallagher), OJ 1998, C60/77, on national checks on imported used vehicles and Articles 30 to 36 EC.

Through amendments to the technical separate Community directives, the Community develops and implements a *policy* in pursuit of particular public interests such as the protection of the environment, road safety (including pedestrian safety) and the strengthening of the competitiveness of the automobile industry.[118] The fact that the Commission is eager to protect this policy instrument is illustrated by the Commission's action against the Swedish system of environmental classification of automobiles used to determine the fiscal incentives applicable in the Member States, as soon as it found out that the Swedish system was based in part on American and not Community emission standards. The Commission considered the Swedish system not to be consistent with Community rules. It stressed that the Community policy towards the granting of fiscal incentives by Member States to encourage the early marketing of clean vehicles is set down in successive Community directives on vehicle emissions.[119]

The contents of amendments to the separate technical Community directives is often the result of political haggling between all interested parties in the automobile industry. This is in particular the case with regard to the considerable number of measures that are part of the Community's

---

[118] In its 1990 Communication, *supra* note 15, at 5 and 8-9, the Commission confirmed the direct link between its policy on protecting the environment and the competitiveness of the automobile industry. The Commission announced that it would "propose setting for all motor-vehicles emission levels which protect the environment as far as available technology allows" and confirmed that "[o]ne of the major factors affecting the competitiveness of the motor industry in Europe and in the world at large is the use of technologies to reduce the adverse environmental effects of road traffic (pollution, noise, energy consumption, etc.)". See also Communication from the Commission to the Council, the European Parliament and the Economic and Social Committee on "The European motor vehicle industry: Situation, issues at state, and proposals for action", COM(92)166 final, 8 May 1992, at 7.

[119] Written Question 3435/96 (Gahrton), OJ 1997, C91/84.

environmental policy.[120] A good example is the manner in which the Community tries to control *air pollution* by amending on the basis of Article 100a EC, the original text of, (i) Directive 70/157 on measures relating to the permissible sound level and the exhaust system of motor vehicles;[121] (ii) Directive 70/220 on measures to be taken against air pollution by gases from positive-ignition engines of motor vehicles;[122] (iii) Directive 72/306 relating to measures to be taken against the emission of pollutants from diesel engines for use in vehicles;[123] (iv) Directive 80/1268 relating to the fuel consumption of motor

---

[120] As reported in *Agence Europe*, "Commission adopts communication on integrating environment in all union policies", 28 May 1998, at 9, the Community favours the integration of environmental requirements into all of its policies. See in this context Article 3(k) EC, Article G(38) TEU, Articles 130r to 130t EC and the five Community programmes of policy and action in relation to the environment and sustainable development: OJ 1973, C112/1; OJ 1977, C139/1; OJ 1983, C46/1; OJ 1987, C328/1, and OJ 1993, C138/1. See also Case C-300/89, *Commission* v *Council (Titanium Dioxide)*, [1991] ECR I-2869, in which the ECJ elaborates on the distinct role of Article 100a EC and Article 130s EC as a legal basis for environmental measures. See for an extensive analysis of the Community's environmental policy until 1 September 1993: H.G. Sevenster, *Milieubeleid en gemeenschapsrecht*, 1992, Kluwer, Deventer.

[121] Council Directive 70/157 of 6 February 1970 on the approximation of the laws of the Member States relating to the permissible sound level and the exhaust system of motor vehicles, OJ English Special Edition 1970, L42/16, at 111.

[122] Council Directive 70/220 of 20 March 1970 on the approximation of the laws of the Member States relating to measures to be taken against air pollution by gases from positive-ignition engines of motor vehicles, OJ English Special Edition 1970, L76/1, at 171. A "new approach" was set out in Article 4 of Directive 94/12 of the European Parliament and the Council of 23 March 1994 relating to measures to be taken against air pollution by emissions from motor vehicles and amending Directive 70/220, OJ 1994, L100/42. See also Proposal for a European Parliament and Council Directive relating to measures to be taken against air pollution by emissions from motor vehicles and amending Council Directives 70/156 and 70/220, OJ 1997, C77/8; Common Position (EC) No 40/97 adopted by the Council on 7 October 1997 with a view to adopting Directive 97/.../EC of the European Parliament and of the Council relating to measures to be taken against air pollution by emissions from motor vehicles and amending Council Directive 70/220/EEC, OJ 1997, C351/13, and Common Position (EC) No 27/98 adopted by the Council on 23 March 1998 with a view to adopting Directive 98/.../EC of the European Parliament of ... and of the Council relating to measures to be taken against air pollution by emissions from motor vehicles and amending Directive 70/220/EEC with regard to light commercial vehicles, OJ 1998, C161/45.

[123] Council Directive 72/306 of 2 August 1972 on the approximation of the laws of the Member States relating to the measures to be taken against the emission of pollutants from diesel engines for use in vehicles, OJ 1972, L190/1 (rectification OJ 1974, L215/20).

vehicles,[124] and (v) Directive 88/77 relating to the measures to be taken against the emission of gaseous pollutants from diesel engines for use in vehicles.[125]

Some of these amendments should be seen against the backdrop of the European "Auto/Oil I Programme" on air quality, road traffic emissions, fuels and engines technologies, which encourages technical collaboration between the Commission and the car and oil industries in order to facilitate the further reduction of emission levels and improve the quality of petrol and diesel fuels.[126] Research is done on the relationship between engine technology, fuel quality and emissions within the context of the European Programme on Engines, Fuels and Emissions, and efforts are made to develop so-called on-board diagnostics in order to permit an immediate detection of failure of anti-pollution vehicle equipment.[127] The Commission set up a Task Force on the "Car of Tomorrow" in order to better focus research and development initiatives.[128]

Further legislative measures can be expected on the basis of Article 100a EC, with regard to the further improvement of the quality of petrol and

---

[124] Council Directive of 16 December 1980 on the approximation of the laws of the Member States relating to the fuel consumption of motor vehicles, OJ 1980, L375/36.

[125] Council Directive 88/77 of 3 December 1987 on the approximation of the laws of the Member States relating to the measures to be taken against the emission of gaseous pollutants from diesel engines for use in vehicles, OJ 1988, L36/33. See also Written Question 2231/94 (Pollack), OJ 1995, C75/27.

[126] See the Commission Communication to the European Parliament and the Council on a future strategy for the control of atmospheric emissions from road transport taking into account the results from the Auto/Oil Programme, 18 June 1996, COM(96)248 final. This Communication includes a proposal for a directive relating to the quality of petrol and diesel fuels (amending Directive 93/12), and a directive relating to measures to be taken against air pollution by emissions from motor vehicles (amending Directives 70/156 and 70/220). See also Written Question 2943/97 (Hautala and others), OJ 1998, C158/22; *FT*, "Clean air costs will fall on oil industry as well as carmakers", 20 August 1998, at 2, and "Novel car oil", 27 August 1998, at 16. The setting up of an "Auto/Oil II Programme" is under discussion.

[127] See Written Question 1246/95 (Crawley), OJ 1995, C213/43; Written Questions 3014/95 (Bloch von Blottnitz) and 3294/95 (Lange), OJ 1996, C112/13, and Written Question 380/97 (Daskalaki), OJ 1997, C319/63.

[128] See Chapter 11. See also *FT*, "Cold start for electric car sales in California", 2 January 1998, at 3.

diesel fuels.[129] In addition, proposals have been published for the introduction, on the basis of Article 130s(1) EC, of a recycling scheme for vehicles in order to counter the eight to nine million tonnes of waste per year in the Community that is the result of discarded vehicles,[130] and a scheme to monitor the average specific emissions of carbon dioxide from new passenger cars.[131] All these legislative measures have been the subject of a long and heated debate both within Community institutions, and between the Community and interested parties such as the oil and automobile industry, consumer organizations and environmental groups. It will come as no surprise that most, if not all, consumer organizations and environmental groups advocate stricter standards whereas the oil and automobile industry object to the costs attached to meeting stricter

---

[129] See Council Directive 85/210 of 20 March 1985 on the approximation of the laws of the Member States concerning the lead content of petrol, OJ 1985, L96/25, and Council Directive 93/12 of 23 March 1993 relating to the sulphur content of certain liquid fuels, OJ 1993, L74/81. See also Proposal for a European Parliament and Council Directive relating to the quality of petrol and diesel fuels and amending Council Directive 93/12, OJ 1997, C77/1. See "ACEA calls for limits on sulphur in fuels", ACEA Newsletter, November 1997, no. 47, at 11.

[130] Proposal for a Council Directive on end of life vehicles, OJ 1997, C337/3. See also COM(97)358 ("Proposal for a Council Directive on End of Life Vehicles"). See also "Ook auto's kunnen 'plantaardig' zijn", *NRC Handelsblad*, 29 October 1996, at 15; *FT*, "Brussels plans to force makers to recycle old cars", 4 December 1996, at 16; Written Question 1664/97 (Bowe), OJ 1998, C21/79; Written Question 3269/97 (Bolea), OJ 1998, C174/33, and "End of life vehicles: Commission proposal weakens Government/Industry consensus", ACEA Newsletter, September 1997, no. 45, at 3-8.

[131] Commission Proposal for a Council Decision establishing a scheme to monitor the average specific emissions of carbon dioxide from new passenger cars, OJ 1998, C231/6. See in this context also Commission Proposal for a Council Decision amending Decision 93/389/EEC for a monitoring mechanism of Community CO2 and other greenhouse gas emissions, OJ 1996, C314/11, and Amended Proposal for a Council Decision amending Decision 93/389/EEC for a monitoring mechanism of Community CO2 and other greenhouse gas emissions, OJ 1998, C120/22. See also IP/96/546 ("Commissioners Bjerregaard and Bangemann invite car industry to talks on reduction of CO2 emissions"); ACEA Press Release "The European automobile manufacturers commit to substantial CO2 emission reductions from new passenger cars", 29 July 1998, and *Agence Europe*, "European environmental bureau and European federation for transport and environment criticize Commission for having accepted ACEA's voluntary undertaking regarding CO2 emissions", 14 August 1998, at 4.

standards.[132] Several of these measures are the result of international environmental conferences.[133]

Another example of the sensitive nature of the separate technical directives regards *car safety*.[134] Both Directive 96/27 on the protection of

---

[132] See, *inter alia*, *Agence Europe*, "Les constructeurs de la CEE seraient (a une exception pres) favorables aux normes anti-pollution revisees de la Commission Europeenne", 8 June 1989, at 12; "L'industrie est prete a appliquer les normes CEE antipollution mais elles doivent rester stables pour cinq ans au moins, a declare M. Agnelli", 10 November 1989, at 16; "ACEA calls for comprehensive analysis of the "Auto-Oil-Programme" findings before the Commission adopts proposals on emission standards for the year 2000 - Other measures needed", 8 December 1995, at 15, and *FT*, "Airing the differences" and "Carmakers pay the price of progress", 26 June 1996, at 10; "The ACEA considers Commission proposals on vehicle emissions for the year 2000 and on fuel quality unacceptable", *Agence Europe*, 27 June 1996, at 11; *FT*, "Car pollution curbs attacked", 16 October 1996, at 2; "GM sees shift to alternative fuels", 9 January 1997, at 13; "One for the road", 17 February 1997, at 16; "MEPs take aim at car pollution", 10 April 1997, at 3; "'Clean' cars in the pipeline-but the price is high", 2 December 1997, at 4; "Ford raises stakes on emissions", 6 January 1998, at 13; "Carmakers pressed to reduce CO2 emissions", 2 March 1998, at 2, and "European carmakers offer CO2 emission cuts", 12 March 1998, at 2; *Agence Europe*, "The Council (in which three "green" ministers were sitting) set emission norms for cars and quality standards for fuels stricter than those proposed by Commission", 25 June 1997, at 10, and "According to oil industry, EP's vote on Auto-Oil proposals represents 'victory by extremists over reason'", 20 February 1998, at 15. See also *FT*, "Smile milestone", 12 December 1996, at 10; "Brussels backs emissions proposals", 30 July 1998, at 2; "The SmILE Concept - The technology", Greenpeace, August 1996, Hamburg; "The dirty track of the car industry - A Greenpeace Report", Greenpeace, July 1996, Amsterdam; "The first step towards a fossil fuel free future", August 1996, and "Is the climate changing as Kyoto approaches?", ACEA Newsletter, October 1997, no. 46, at 1-3.

[133] For instance, the Proposal for a Council Decision establishing a scheme to monitor the average specific emissions of carbon dioxide from new passenger cars, OJ 1998, C231/6, is the result of the Protocol agreed at the December 1997 Kyoto Conference of the Parties to the United Nations Framework Convention on Climate Change. See in this context also Council Decision of 15 December 1993 concerning the conclusion of the United Nations Framework Convention on Climate Change, OJ 1994, L33/11; Commission Proposal for a Council Decision concerning the Signature by the European Community of a Protocol to the United Nations Framework Convention on Climate Change, COM(98)96 final; *Agence Europe*, "Commission to sign Kyoto Protocol in New York on Wednesday, thereby definitively committing EU to reducing greenhouse gas emissions", 29 April 1998, at 11, and "Disagreement remains on distribution of efforts at reducing emissions of greenhouse gases", 17 June 1998, at 7. See for an extensive analysis of the Community's competence to conclude international environmental agreements: P.J. Leefmans, *Externe milieubevoegdheden*, 1997, Kluwer, Deventer.

[134] The Commission noted in answer to Written Question 2342/97 (Hughes), OJ 1998, C82/60, that warning triangles, fire extinguishers and sealed gallons of petrol and other matters governing the safety of vehicles are "currently entirely within the legal competence of Member States and not of the Community".

occupants of motor vehicles in the event of a side impact[135] and Directive 96/37 relating to the interior fittings of motor vehicles (strength of seats and of their anchorages)[136] were the outcome of a long debate.[137]

4.3.3 Registration of Automobiles

An automobile has to be registered in the Member State in which the owner has "normal residence".[138] As the taxation systems applicable to automobiles vary considerably from one Member State to another and registration is regarded as the chargeable event for taxes on automobiles,[139] the criterion of "normal residence" was chosen to avoid that citizens would register their automobiles in

---

[135] Directive 96/27 of the European Parliament and of the Council of 20 May 1996 on the protection of occupants of motor vehicles in the event of a side impact and amending Directive 70/156, OJ 1996, L169/1.

[136] Commission Directive 96/37 of 17 June 1996 adapting to technical progress Council Directive 74/408 relating to the interior fittings of motor vehicles (strength of seats and of their anchorages), OJ 1996, L186/28.

[137] See *Agence Europe*, "BEUC criticises Commission proposals on car safety - Call for immediate measures to counter lethal airbag/child seat combination on passenger side", 15 March 1995, at 15; *FT*, "EU urged to adopt tougher car safety tests", 20 March 1995, at 2; *Agence Europe*, "The two-stage approach proposed by the Commission to strengthen the resistance of vehicles to frontal and lateral collissions widely criticized at the EP's public hearing", 23 March 1995, at 12; "ACEA backs Commission proposals on shock resistance of cars in frontal and lateral collision", 24 March 1995, at 15; "ETSC welcomes adoption of Donnely reports on lateral and head-on collision resistance in cars", 12 August 1995, at 3, and "BEUC and ETSC urge Member States not to sacrifice user safety to the interests of the car industry", 13 April 1996, at 15. See Written Question 2722/94 (Pollack), OJ 1995, C103/30 and in particular Written Question 114/97 (Donnelly), OJ 1997, C186/227, in which the Commission confirmed the potential benefit of "new car assessment programmes" for the enhancement of safety awareness and the promotion of improvements in car design, but expressed concerns about the negative effect of the proliferation of such programmes on the functioning of the internal market in passenger cars and on the existing European type approval system. See also *International Herald Tribune*, "Japanese automakers pitch a whole new concept: safety", 23-24 November 1996, at 4.

[138] Article 7(1) of Council Directive 83/182 of 28 March 1983 on tax exemption within the Community for certain means of transport temporarily imported into one Member State from another, OJ 1983, L105/59, defines "normal residence" as the place where a person usually lives, that is for at least 185 days in each calendar year, because of personal and occupational ties, or, in the case of a person with no occupational ties because of personal ties which show close links between that person and the place where he is living.

[139] Written Question 1369/93 (Lafuente Lopez), OJ 1994, C140/50.

the Member State with the lowest relevant tax rates.[140] Thus, after having gone through a Community type-approval procedure, automobiles must be registered under the national registration procedure of the Member State in which the owner has "normal residence".[141]

The laws of the Member States on (the various forms of) registration of automobiles differ. Although national registration procedures can very well constitute obstacles to intra-Community trade in automobiles, there is no harmonisation of the various national registration procedures within the Community. In 1994, the Commission specified that it was not planning on harmonizing national legislation on registration[142] but that it would "take care to ensure that the procedures in force in Member States are in keeping with the rules on the freedom of movement of goods".[143] The Commission did so, for instance, by succesfully taking legal action against Italy with regard to the Italian procedure to register imported vehicles. In its judgment, the ECJ confirmed that the Italian "Circulars" in question made the registration of imported vehicles more complicated, longer and more costly, and were likely to hinder intra-Community trade in motor vehicles and constituted measures having an effect equivalent to quantitative restrictions of the type prohibited by Article 30 EC.[144]

---

[140] See in this sense 1996 Communication on Type-approval, *supra* note 98, at 12.

[141] In its 1996 Communication on Type-approval, *supra* note 98, at 4, the Commission defined the term "registered vehicles" as "those which bear a permanent number-plate issued by the competent authorities of a Member State and those bearing a provisional number-plate ('transit' or 'customs' plates) which, although issued to meet a particular situation, proves that tax and roadworthiness requirements have been fulfilled".

[142] This, notwithstanding the fact that manufacturers and registration authorities are in favour of harmonisation of registration procedures. See Report on the EC Workshop 94 on the application of European type-approval procedures to motor vehicles, *supra* note 109, at 4-5. In addition, it was pointed out that "Directive 92/53/EEC attempted to improve ... situation by including, both in the information documents and the certificate of conformity, information that could be used for registration purposes". Whereas "[s]ome registration authorities welcomed this initiative and had found ways of overcoming the attendant problems, others preferred their existing practices. Manufacturers were unanimous in finding that the new procedures were burdensome and did not improve on their present methods which they preferred".

[143] Written Question 1369/93 (Lafuente Lopez), OJ 1994, C140/50.

[144] See Case 154/85, *Commission* v *Italy*, [1987] ECR 2717.

In what seems to be a turn around, the Commission announced in 1996 that efforts would be made to harmonise registration procedures as they continued to act as an obstacle to the smooth functioning of the type approval system.[145] The Community type-approval procedure is important in the context of the registration of automobiles as Article 7(1) of Directive 70/156 provides that new vehicles shall be registered by Member States on grounds relating to their construction and functioning if, and only if, they are accompanied by a valid certificate of conformity. Pursuant to Article 7(3) of Directive 70/156, Member States may refuse to register a vehicle with a valid Community type-approval certificate only if it finds that the vehicle is a serious risk to road safety. This refusal may last no longer than six months and the Member State taking such a decision must forthwith notify the other Member States and the Commission. The ECJ confirmed in *VAG Sverige* that "[s]ave in those highly specific circumstances, Directive 70/156 does not provide for any possibility of refusing to register new vehicles covered by a valid Community type-approval certificate".[146]

4.3.4 Roadworthiness Tests for Automobiles

Member States arrange for periodic roadworthiness tests for automobiles in order to ensure road safety within their territory. Initially, both the standards and methods of testing varied considerably from one Member State to another. As these differences distorted competition between the various transport undertakings in the Member States, efforts were made to harmonize roadworthiness testing within the context of the common transport policy.

It was within the context of its common transport policy that the Council adopted Directive 77/143 on the approximation of the laws of the Member States relating to roadworthiness tests for motor vehicles and their

---

[145] Communication from the Commission to the Council, the European Parliament, the Economic and Social Committee and the Committee of the Regions, European Automobile Industry 1996 ("1996 Communication on the European Automobile Industry"), COM(96)327 final, at 16. See also Commission proposal for a Council Directive on registration documents for motor vehicles and their trailers, OJ 1997, C202/13.

[146] *VAG Sverige*, *supra* note 105, par. 19.

trailers.[147] Directive 77/143 laid down rules on the frequency of the tests and the items to be tested. Moreover, it specified the particular categories of road vehicles to be tested which included buses, coaches, heavy goods vehicles, trailers, taxis and ambulances, but did not include motor vehicles used for the road carriage of passengers and with not more than eight seats excluding the driver's seat. However, Directive 77/143 allowed Member States to extend the requirement of a periodic roadworthiness test to other categories of vehicles. In addition, Directive 77/143 made it possible for Member States to bring forward the date for the first compulsory roadworthiness tests and, where appropriate, submit the vehicle for testing prior to registration (Article 3). Directive 77/143 provided for mutual recognition as it obliged each Member State "on the same basis as if it had itself issued the proof" to recognize the proof issued in another Member State to the effect that a motor vehicle registered in that other State, together with its trailer or semi-trailer, have passed a roadworthiness test complying with at least the provisions of the Directive (Article 5).[148]

In practice, roadworthiness tests can create obstacles to the importation of automobiles. Several cases have shown that in particular the requirement in most Member States that imported vehicles be submitted to a roadworthiness test *prior* to their registration, is open to protectionist (ab)use. For instance, in its judgment in *Commission* v *Italy*, the ECJ held the Italian rule that "buses from outside Italy may not be tested with a view to registration, if their proven date of construction is more than seven years prior to the application for a roadworthiness test", to be contrary to Article 30 EC. Although the ECJ confirmed that "at the present stage of the development of Community law, it is the responsibility of Member States to ensure road safety within their territories

[147] On the basis of Article 75 EC, the Council adopted Directive 77/143 of 29 December 1976 on the approximation of the laws of the Member States relating to roadworthiness tests for motor vehicles and their trailers, OJ 1977, L47/47.

[148] See in this context Council Regulation 4060/89 of 21 December 1989 on the elimination of controls performed at the frontiers of Member States in the field of road and inland waterway transport, OJ 1989, L390/18, and Council Regulation 3356/91 of 7 November 1991 amending Regulation 4060/89 on the elimination of controls performed at the frontiers of Member States in the field of road and inland waterway transport, OJ 1991, L318/1. See also Council Regulation 3912/92 of 17 December 1992 on controls carried out within the Community in the field of road and inland waterway transport in respect of means of transport registered or put into circulation in a third country, OJ 1992, L395/6.

and to arrange for such roadworthiness tests as they consider necessary for that purpose", it added that "if such requirements are to justify restrictions on imports, they must be necessary in order to attain the objective in view". The ECJ held that "a total refusal to allow old buses to undergo the roadworthiness tests with a view to registration exceeds what is necessary to ensure road safety within the Italian territory".[149]

In *Schloh*, the ECJ further specified the conditions under which a national requirement to submit imported vehicles to a roadworthiness test prior to registration, is in conformity with Articles 30 and 36 EC. The ECJ noted in the context of Article 30 EC that "[r]oadworthiness testing is a formality which makes the registration of imported vehicles more difficult and more onerous and consequently is in the nature of a measure having an effect equivalent to a quantitative restriction".[150] The ECJ held that Article 36 EC may justify such a formality on grounds of the protection of human health and life, provided that the test is necessary for the attainment of that objective, and that it does not constitute a means of arbitrary discrimination or a disguised restriction on trade between Member States. According to the ECJ, "[r]oadworthiness testing required prior to the registration of an imported vehicle may, even though the vehicle carries a certificate of conformity to the vehicle types approved in the importing Member State, be regarded as necessary for the protection of human health and life where the vehicle in question has already been put on the road". The ECJ held that "[i]n such cases, roadworthiness testing ... makes it possible to check that the vehicle has not been damaged and is in a good state of repair". However, the ECJ noted that "such testing cannot be justified on those grounds where it relates to an imported vehicle carrying a certificate of conformity which has not been placed on the road before being registered in the importing Member State".[151] Last but not least, the ECJ emphasized that "roadworthiness testing of imported vehicles cannot ... be justified under ... Article 36 of the Treaty if it is established that such testing is not required in the case of vehicles

[149] Case 50/83, *Commission* v *Italy*, [1984] ECR 1642-1643, paras. 12 and 17-19.

[150] Case 50/85, *Schloh* v *Auto contrôle technique (Schloh)*, [1986] ECR 1867, par. 12. See also 1996 Communication on Type-approval, *supra* note 98, at 10.

[151] *Schloh*, *ibidem*, par. 14.

of national origin presented for registration in the same circumstances".[152] In *Schloh*, the ECJ specified that Article 36 EC does not provide justification for roadworthiness testing which purpose is to obtain from the owner of the imported vehicle a written declaration certifying that the use of the vehicle qualifies it for exemption from annual testing. The ECJ held that "[t]hat purpose may be achieved simply by requiring the owner to supply that written declaration, without its being necessary for the vehicle to be presented to an approved vehicle testing agency".[153]

In its judgment in another case on roadworthiness tests, *Van Schaik*, the ECJ upheld the Dutch regulations on the periodic testing of motor vehicles, trailers and semi-trailers (the so-called "APK-rules") under Community law, notwithstanding the fact that it is impossible for persons who operate undertakings established *outside* the Netherlands to obtain the authorization to issue APK-test certificates. The ECJ confirmed that the requirement that vehicles undergo a periodic test serves the interests of road safety and held that "[t]he effectiveness of those tests is assured, in particular, by various requirements relating to the solvency and professional competence of the authorized garages, and by supervision of the tests carried out, which can only be undertaken on Netherlands territory and by the Netherlands authorities".[154] According to the ECJ, this view is in line with the underlying Directive 77/143 which imposes a territorial limitation on periodic testing and does not oblige each Member State to recognize test certificates issued in other Member States in respect of vehicles registered on its own territory.[155]

Over the years, Directive 77/143 has been amended several times. An important amendment was made by means of Directive 91/328 which added "private cars" or "motor vehicles used for the road carriage of passengers and with not more than eight seats excluding the driver's seat" to the list of vehicles

---

[152] *Schloh, ibidem*, par. 15.

[153] *Schloh, ibidem*, at 1869, par. 19.

[154] *Van Schaik, supra* note 54, 4858, paras. 19-20.

[155] *Van Schaik, supra* note 54, 4859, paras. 21-22.

to be tested.[156] Eventually, Directive 77/143 was replaced by Directive 96/96 on the approximation of the laws of the Member States relating to roadworthiness tests for motor vehicles and their trailers.[157] Directive 96/96 basicly consists of the consolidated text of its predecessor together with some further amendments. The most important change is the introduction of minimum *Community* standards and methods to be used for testing the items. These Community standards and methods are (to be) defined in separate Directives (Article 7). It is pointed out in the preamble of Directive 96/96 that as a transitional measure, *national* standards remain applicable in respect of items not (yet) covered by one of these separate Directives.[158] The Commission is to submit a report to the Council no later than 31 December 1998, on the implementation of roadworthiness testing of private cars, accompanied by any proposal deemed necessary, with particular reference to the frequency and contents of tests (Article 9).

4.4 Internal Taxation

4.4.1 Introduction

Each Member State is in principle free to establish the system of internal taxation which it considers the most suitable in relation to each product.[159] A system of internal taxation is a general system of internal dues applied systematically to categories of products in accordance with objective criteria

---

[156] Article 1 of Council Directive 91/328 of 21 June 1991 amending Directive 77/143 on the approximation of the laws of the Member States relating to roadworthiness tests for motor vehicles and their trailers, OJ 1991, L178/29.

[157] Council Directive 96/96 of 20 December 1996 on the approximation of the laws of the Member States relating to roadworthiness tests for motor vehicles and their trailers, OJ 1997, L46/1.

[158] 8th Whereas of Directive 96/96.

[159] See in this sense Case 127/75, *Bobie* v *Hauptzollamt Aachen-Nord (Bobie)*, [1976] ECR 1087, par. 9.

irrespective of the origin of the products.[160] The different national systems of internal taxation lead to barriers to trade within the Community.[161]

Some of these barriers come into conflict with Articles 95 and 96 EC which provide that a national system of internal taxation has to be completely neutral as regards competition between domestic products and imported products (**4.4.2**).[162] Other barriers, however, can only be removed through the harmonisation of the different national taxation laws of the Member States. It will come as no surprise that the discussion on harmonisation in the area of taxation in general and with regard to car taxes in particular, is politically very sensitive. Member States consider their national systems of internal taxation applicable to cars as an important source of revenue.[163] In addition, national systems of taxation are used as instruments to pursue a wide variety of public interests such as the protection of public health and the environment.[164] Several Member States tend to use their system of internal taxation as an instrument to protect their domestic industry and stimulate domestic demand which can be to

---

[160] See in this sense Case 193/85, *Co-Frutta* v *Amministrazione delle Finanze dello Stato*, [1987] ECR 2108, par. 10. For instance, in its judgment in Case C-343/90, *Dias* v *Director da Alfandega do Porto*, [1992] ECR I-4717, paras. 53-55, the ECJ concluded that a Portuguese motor-vehicle tax, which was applied without distinction to vehicles assembled and manufactured in Portugal and to imported new and second-hand vehicles alike, was part of a general system of internal charges imposed on categories of products in accordance with an objective criterion, namely cubic capacity. Confirmed in Case C-345/93, *Fazenda Pùblica* v *Nunes Tadeu (Tadeu)*, [1995] ECR I-494, paras. 6-7.

[161] See, for instance, *Ludvigsen report*, *supra* note 2, at 52-53.

[162] See in this sense Case 252/86, *Bergandi* v *Directeur général des impôts (Bergandi)*, [1988] ECR 1374, par. 24.

[163] See R.S. Smith, "Motor vehicle tax harmonization" in *Tax coordination in the European Community* (S. Cnossen ed.), 1987, Kluwer Law and Taxation Publishers, Deventer, at 142, Table 5.1 on "Motor vehicle tax revenues as a percentage of total tax revenues, 1972 and 1982". It is illustrative that *FT*, "German tax cuts luxury car sales by 9.5%", 11 June 1996, at 2, reported that after protests the German government declared itself prepared to reconsider the details of the company car tax "as long as any new arrangement would bring in the same amount of revenues".

[164] In 1997, the Commission published a Communication on environmental taxes and charges in the single market, OJ 1997, C224/6, which aims to guide Member States in order to ensure that national initiatives on environmental levies and charges are compatible with the existing Community framework. Appendix gives an "Overview of environmentally-related taxes and charges in EU and EEA countries as of October 1996". See also Written Question 1328/97 (Dury), OJ 1997, C373/107.

the detriment of other Member States.[165] The negative effects of tax competition between Member States led to proposals for more coordination and harmonisation of national tax laws within the Community.[166] Some

---

[165] As pointed out by Smith, in *Tax coordination in the European Community*, *supra* note 163, at 160, "[t]axes levied on owners and users of cars can be, and have been, designed to favor the purchase of domestically produced cars with certain characteristics - size, weight, power, price, emissions, fuel consumption, and so forth. Even if the taxes are applied in the same fashion to cars produced in other Member States, differing systems result in a fragmentation of the EC market". According to Pelkmans and Winters, *Europe's domestic market*, *supra* note 3, at 43, "not only taxes at the point of sale but also road and petrol taxes can be used to influence car-buying habits". They point at data which "suggest somewhat higher tax burdens on motoring in countries not having significant production facilities - e.g. Ireland and Denmark". See also *FT*, "Car sales set to exceed forecasts", 16 September 1997, at 2, on the impact of incentive schemes and changes in vehicle excise taxes on car sales.

[166] See, *inter alia*, "Taxation in the European Union", Discussion paper for the informal meeting of ECOFIN Ministers (20 March 1996), Commission of the European Communities, SEC(96) 487 final; "Taxation in the European Union - Report on the development of tax systems" (22 October 1996), Commission of the European Communities, COM(96)546 final; *FT*, "Commission backs EU-wide tax regime", 23 October 1996, at 3; Written Question 945/96 (Muscardini), OJ 1996, C345/19; *FT*, "EU-wide tax code urged", 28 January 1997, at 1, and "EU ministers open fire on tax poachers", 31 January 1997, at 2; Written Question 456/97 (Van Dijk), OJ 1997, C217/193; *Agence Europe*, "Fifteen agree it is appropriate to abolish "damaging competition" between them in tax matters but definition is still to be reached - objective: a Code of Conduct", 12 March 1997, at 10, and "The fiscal policy group examines the envisaged "Code of Conduct"-project", 20 June 1997, at 11; *FT*, "The big catch", 29 July 1997, at 11; *Agence Europe*, "Mr Strauss-Kahn gives all-out support to proposal for tax code of conduct", 5 September 1997, at 9; "Agreement in principle within informal Ecofin Council on new strategy for fiscal coordination and on draft code of conduct", 15-16 September 1997, at 10; "Proposal for tax code of conduct to be finalised within next two weeks and presented to Ecofin Council on 13 October", 19 September 1997, at 6; "Third Monti paper on fiscal cooperation in the EU" (Europe Documents), 24 September 1997; "The new European fiscal strategy" (Europe Documents), 9 October 1997; "Agreement in principle in favour of the Monti plan, although numerous aspects still have to be spelled out and considerable divergences remain", 13-14 October 1997, at 6; "Final version of Monti memorandum contains revised code of conduct and the elements of a directive on taxation from income on savings", 6 November 1997, at 7, and "Council conclusions on fiscal package, comprising Code of Conduct on company taxation and common guidelines on tax on savings" (Europe Documents), 3 December 1997. See also "Taxation and competition policy in the single market", 28th report of the Select Committee on the European Communities of the House of Lords (Session 1997-98), HL Paper 117.

harmonisation of internal taxation on automobiles has already taken place (**4.4.3**).[167]

4.4.2 Neutrality of Internal Taxation

4.4.2.1 Levy of Internal Taxation

Article 95(1) EC provides that no Member State shall impose, directly or indirectly, on the products of other Member States any internal taxation of any kind in excess of that imposed directly or indirectly on similar domestic products. Article 95(2) EC obliges Member States not to impose on the products of other Member States any internal taxation of such a nature as to afford indirect protection to other products. With regard to existing discriminatory internal taxation, Article 95(3) EC provides that Member States shall, not later than at the beginning of the second stage, being 1 January 1962, repeal or amend any provisions existing when the Treaty entered into force which conflict with the preceding rules.

According to the ECJ, Article 95 EC seeks to fill in any loop-hole which certain taxation procedures might find in the prohibitions of Articles 9, 12 and 17 EC[168] and is aimed at ensuring free movement of goods between the Member States in normal conditions of competition by the elimination of all forms of protection which may result from the application of internal taxation that discriminates against products from other Member States.[169] Article 95 EC has direct effect[170] and applies only to goods imported from other Member States and to goods originating in non-member countries which are in free circulation

[167] The Commission reported in its 1996 Communication on the European Automobile Industry, *supra* note 145, at 17, that it had commenced a comprehensive review of the different types of taxation applied to vehicles in different Member States in order to examine whether there is need for further approximation of such taxes for internal market reasons. The fact that the Commission added that this review will also assess what other Community policies could be advanced by initiatives in this area, confirms that the approximation of national systems of taxation is considered by the Commission to be a possible policy instrument to pursue various Community interests.

[168] Joined Cases 2 and 3/62, *Commission* v *Luxembourg and Belgium*, [1962] ECR 431.

[169] *Bergandi*, *supra* note 162, par. 24.

[170] See, *inter alia*, Case 57/65, *Lütticke* v *Hauptzollamt Saarlouis*, [1966] ECR 211.

in a Member State.[171] The ECJ has confirmed that in order to apply Article 95 EC, not only the rate of direct and indirect internal taxation on domestic and imported products but also the basis of assessment and the detailed rules for levying the tax, must be taken into consideration.[172] The system of taxation chosen by each Member State in relation to a specific domestic product constitutes the point of reference for the purpose of determining whether the tax applied to the similar product of another Member State complies with Article 95(1) EC.[173]

There is a long line of cases in which national systems of internal taxation on cars have been scrutinized under Article 95 EC. It is worthwhile to elaborate on some of these cases as they illustrate the manner in which Member States try to use their system of internal taxation for protectionist purposes. Furthermore, these cases confirm the importance of the prohibition set out in Article 95 EC for the creation of the common market. The *French system of road tax* in particular has attracted much attention. The ECJ confirmed in *Humblot* that although Member States are at liberty to subject cars to a system of road tax which increases progressively in amount depending on an objective criterion, a system of domestic taxation is only compatible with Article 95 EC in so far as it is free from any discriminatory or protective effect. According to the ECJ, this was not true for the French system of road tax which manifestly exhibited discriminatory or protective features contrary to Article 95 EC since the power rating determining liability for the special tax in question was fixed at a level such that only imported cars, in particular from other Member States, were subject to the special tax, whereas all cars of domestic manufacture were liable to the distinctly more advantageous differential tax. The ECJ held that the special tax reduced the amount of competition to which cars of domestic manufacture were subject and was therefore contrary to the principle of

171 See Case C-284/96, *Tabouillot* v *Directeur des Services Fiscaux*, [1997] ECR I-7471.

172 Case 74/76, *Iannelli & Volpi* v *Meroni*, [1977] ECR 578, par. 21.

173 *Bobie*, *supra* note 159, at 1088, par. 9.

neutrality with which domestic taxation must comply.[174] About two years later, the succeeding French system of road tax was also held to be contrary to Article 95 EC. In *Feldain*, the ECJ concluded that the French method of calculating the differential tax was such that only cars imported from other Member States were placed in the most heavily taxed categories, without any justification based on an objective criterion. The ECJ held that since that situation caused the owners of such vehicles to bear higher costs, consumers were encouraged to purchase top-of-the-range cars manufactured in France rather than those imported from other Member States.[175] Finally, in 1995, the ECJ upheld the French differential tax on motor vehicles. In *Jacquier*, the ECJ emphasized that in order to answer the question whether Article 95 EC precludes the application of national rules on motor vehicle taxation, it had to be ascertained whether the system of progression in question was free from any discriminatory or protective effect. The ECJ examined whether the increase in the progression coefficient of the differential tax above the 18 CV (horsepower) threshold deterred consumers from purchasing vehicles with a fiscal horsepower of over 18 CV, which were all of foreign manufacture, to the benefit of vehicles of domestic manufacture. The ECJ concluded that in the French system, the increase in the progression coefficient did not appear to have the effect of favouring the sale of vehicles of domestic manufacture.[176]

---

[174] Case 112/84, *Humblot* v *Directeur des services fiscaux (Humblot)*, [1985] ECR 1378-1379, paras. 12-15. See also Case 240/87, *Deville* v *Administration des impôts*, [1988] ECR 3513, on the French procedural rules which alledgedly reduced the possibilities of bringing proceedings for the recovery of the special fixed tax, which was held by the ECJ in *Humblot* to be contrary to Article 95 EC.

[175] Case 433/85, *Feldain* v *Directeur des services fiscaux*, [1987] ECR 3540-3541, paras. 12-18. See also Joined Cases 76, 86 to 89 and 149/87, *Seguela and Lachkar and others* v *Administration des impôts*, [1988] ECR 2397. In Case C-132/88, *Commission* v *Greece*, [1990] ECR I-1588, the ECJ confirmed that a system of taxation cannot be regarded as discriminatory solely because only imported products come within the most heavily taxed category, and dismissed the action brought against the Greek system of internal taxation on the ground that the Commission had not shown how the system in question had the effect of favouring the sale of cars of Greek manufacture. See D. Wyatt and A. Dashwood, *European Community Law*, 3rd edition, 1993, Sweet & Maxwell, London, at 194, for a critical review of the ECJ's reasoning.

[176] Case C-113/94, *Jacquier* v *Directeur Général des Impôts*, [1995] ECR I-4220-4221, paras. 19-25. See also "French tax on cars is not discriminatory and may be maintained", *Agence Europe*, 7 December 1995, at 11. See also Case C-421/97, *Tarantik*, OJ 1998, C41/15, and Cases C-28/98 and C-29/98, *Charreire and Hirtsmann*, OJ 1998, C94/13.

In 1989, the ECJ had to examine the *Dutch consumption tax* charged on passenger cars at the time of supply by the manufacturer or at the time of importation. In its judgment, the ECJ held that Community law "as it now stands" did not contain any specific provision designed to exclude or limit the power of the Member States to introduce taxes other than turnover taxes and confirmed that Member States could introduce taxes which could not be characterized as turnover taxes even where charging them on a transaction which was already subject to value-added tax led to the double taxation of that transaction.[177] The ECJ held that the tax in question which was charged on imported cars and cars of domestic origin alike, did not give rise to any discriminatory or protective effect, and concluded that the Dutch consumption tax was not incompatible with Article 95 EC.[178]

The very high, according to many even excessive, *Danish registration duty* on new and imported used cars was scrutinized by the ECJ in 1990. In its judgment, the ECJ confirmed that Article 95 EC cannot be invoked against internal taxation imposed on imported products where there is no similar or competing domestic production. The ECJ held that Article 95 EC does not provide a basis for censuring the excessiveness of the level of taxation which a Member State may adopt for particular products, in the absence of any discriminatory or protective effect. As Denmark did not have any domestic production of cars or of other products liable to compete with cars, the ECJ concluded that the Danish registration duty on *new* cars did not infringe Article 95 EC.[179] However, the fact that there is no Danish production of cars does not

[177] Joined Cases 93/88 and 94/88, *Wisselink and others* v *Staatssecretaris van Financiën*, [1989] ECR 2705, paras. 13-14. The ECJ emphasized that the Dutch consumption tax was independent of value-added tax and formed a part of the taxable amount for value-added tax purposes.

[178] *Ibidem*, par. 24. See HR 23 August 1996, Nr. 30 888, *Vakstudie Nieuws*, 26 September 1996, at 3478, for a Dutch case in which the Dutch Supreme Court held that the tax on the registration of cars ("Belasting van Personenauto's en Motorrijwielen") was not discriminatory and therefore did not violate Article 95 EC. See in this context also "Verslag over het adres van M.J. de Vreugd te Hoofddorp, met betrekking tot een aanslag in de Belasting van Personenauto's en Motorrijwielen (BPM) ter zake van een buitenlandse huurauto", 9 September 1997, Eerste Kamer, vergaderjaar 1996-1997, nr. LIV.

[179] Case C-47/88, *Commission* v *Denmark*, [1990] ECR I-4533, paras. 10-11. The ECJ reminded the Commission in par. 13 that "the only possibility of appraising an adverse effect of that kind on the free movement of goods is by reference to the general rules contained in Article 30 et seq. of the Treaty".

signify that Denmark has no *used*-car market. A car becomes a domestic product as soon as it has been imported and placed on the market. Imported used cars and those bought locally constitute similar or at the very least competing products. The ECJ held that Article 95 EC applies to the registration duty charged on the importation of used cars and proceeded with examining the Danish registration duty on imported used cars. The ECJ came to the conclusion that Denmark violated Article 95 EC by imposing a registration duty on imported used cars based on an estimated value which was higher than the real value of the car with the result that imported used motor vehicles were taxed more heavily than used cars which were sold on the domestic market after being registered in Denmark.[180]

In 1992, the ECJ examined the *Greek special consumption tax* on private cars. According to the Commission, the application of two different methods for the calculation of the basis of assessment of the tax according to whether the cars are imported or assembled in Greece, favoured cars assembled in Greece at the expense of those imported from other Member States. In its judgment, the ECJ determined whether the Greek system for calculating the basis of assessment of the tax introduced by the contested legislation was such as to exclude any risk of discrimination, and concluded that Greece violated Article 95 EC by laying down different rules for calculating the basis of assessment of the tax according to whether cars were imported from the other Member States or were assembled in Greece.[181]

In 1993, the ECJ gave judgment on a *Portuguese car tax* which was only charged on second-hand cars imported from other Member States. The tax was not applicable to second-hand cars purchased on Portuguese territory. The

---

[180] *Ibidem*, paras. 15-22. See in this context also Written Question 1958/93 (McCartin), OJ 1994, C234/28, on the Irish system of internal taxation on cars.

[181] Case C-327/90, *Commission* v *Greece*, [1992] ECR I-3058, par. 25. In Case C-375/95, *Commission* v *Greece*, judgment of 23 October 1997, the ECJ had to examine the Greek rules on taxable value of *imported used cars* and concluded that Greece violated Article 95 EC (i) by determining, for the application of the special consumer tax and the flat-rate added special duty, the taxable value of imported used cars by reducing the price of equivalent new cars by 5% for each year of age of the vehicles concerned, with, as a rule, a maximum reduction of 20%, and (ii) by excluding anti-pollution technology imported used cars from the benefit of the reduced rates of the special consumer tax applicable to that type of vehicle. See also Written Question 103/97 (Kaklamanis), OJ 1997, C319/23.

ECJ held that it is incompatible with Article 95 EC for a Member State to charge on second-hand cars from other Member States a tax which, being calculated without taking the vehicle's actual depreciation into account, exceeds the residual tax incorporated in the value of similar second-hand motor vehicles already registered in the national territory.[182]

4.4.2.2 Repayment of Internal Taxation

Article 96 EC provides that where products are exported to the territory of a Member State, any repayment of internal taxation shall not exceed the internal taxation imposed on them whether directly or indirectly. A Member State can only repay internal taxation if the charges are imposed on the product itself and the repayment remains lower than or equal to the taxation concerned.[183] According to the ECJ, the expression "directly" must be understood to refer to taxation imposed on the finished product, whilst "indirectly" refers to taxation imposed during the various stages of production on the raw materials or semi-finished products used in the manufacture of the product. Charges imposed on the producer undertaking rather than on the products as such, do not qualify for repayment under Article 96 EC.[184]

4.4.3 Harmonisation of Internal Taxation

4.4.3.1 Introductory Remarks

The national laws on the taxation of cars have not been significantly harmonized at Community level.[185] This, notwithstanding the fact that the different systems

---

[182] *Tadeu*, *supra* note 160, paras. 11-20.

[183] See HR 23 August 1996, Nr. 30 888, *Vakstudie Nieuws*, 26 September 1996, at 3478, for an unsuccesfull attempt to have the lack of repayment of the Dutch car registration tax ("Belasting van Personenauto's en Motorrijwielen"), reviewed by the Dutch Supreme Court.

[184] Case 45/64, *Commission* v *Italy*, [1965] ECR 866. This case regarded the repayment of internal taxation on exported products of the engineering industry including motor vehicles.

[185] See Written Question 1858/94 (Ferri), OJ 1995, C24/42.

of car taxation lead to the fragmentation of the car market in the Community.[186] Some progress has been made towards the convergence of VAT-rates on new cars.[187] Nevertheless, Member States still levy different types of car taxes, impose different tax rates[188] and use diverging tax structures.[189] Studies indicate that these substantive differences lead to higher costs and put certain specialist manufacturers at a considerable disadvantage.[190]

4.4.3.2 Indirect Taxation

Article 99 EC provides the Community with the competence to adopt provisions

---

[186] According to Smith in *Tax coordination in the European Community*, *supra* note 163, at 160, "[e]ven if the taxes are applied in the same fashion to cars produced in other Member States, differing systems result in a fragmentation of the EC market".

[187] See in this context *The single market review - Impact on manufacturing motor vehicles*, *supra* note 3, at 172, Table D.1 on "VAT on new cars in EU Member States, 1987 and 1994".

[188] See Smith in *Tax coordination in the European Community*, *supra* note 163, at 160-166, Table 5.11 on tax per litre of gasoline 1980, Table 5.12 on car purchase taxes in the EC 1985, and Table 5.13 on annual registration taxes on cars in eight EC countries 1980. See also *The single market review - Impact on manufacturing motor vehicles*, *supra* note 3, at 171-174, for an overview of the various rates of "VAT on new cars in EU Member States, 1987 and 1994", "Taxes on acquisition", "Taxes on ownership" and "Taxes on motoring".

[189] For instance, it was reported in *The single market review - Impact on manufacturing motor vehicles*, *supra* note 3, at 151 and 173, that six Member States base their ownership tax on the cubic capacity of the engine, four on the weight, two on the levels of horsepower and two on the fuel type used.

[190] For instance, it was reported in *The single market review - Impact on manufacturing motor vehicles*, *supra* note 3, at 151, that Volvo who concentrates on the market for medium and large cars, is placed at a disadvantage in Member States like Italy which have strong financial disincentives against larger cars or engines. Another example is Ford which had to redesign the final drive ratio of its model Galaxy before putting it on the market in France, in order to ensure that it was taxed by the French authorities in the same class as the main competitor. According to A. Smith and A.J. Venables, "Automobiles" in *Europe 1992 - An American perspective*, *supra* note 19, at 130, tax differences give rise to the following two kinds of costs: (i) high taxes tend to make consumers buy cheaper cars and different tax rates affect the product range that firms offer to the market, not only raising prices but also distorting consumer choices, and (ii) tax differences lead to the administrative cost of border tax adjustments. See also "CLCA attracts attention to the consequences of extreme differences existing in motor vehicle taxation", *Agence Europe*, 7 June 1990, at 15, and Written Question 2711/93 (Maher), OJ 1994, C279/32.

for the harmonisation of legislation concerning turnover taxes, excise duties and other forms of indirect taxation to the extent that such harmonisation is necessary to ensure the establishment and the functioning of the internal market.

(i) Value-added tax

It was on the basis of Article 99 (and 100) EC that the Community took steps towards the harmonisation of the legislation of Member States concerning turnover taxes and obliged the Member States to adopt a system of value-added tax.[191] In principle, Member States remain free to maintain or introduce certain indirect taxes such as a registration tax on new cars, provided that they constitute independent taxes[192] and cannot be characterized as turnover taxes.[193]

As the Community only introduced a basic minimum VAT-rate of 15%, rates can still differ from one Member State to another.[194] Different VAT-rates lead to a fragmentation of the market. Initially, goods were taxed in the importing Member State ("state of destination") instead of in the exporting Member State ("state of origin") and importing Member States collected their

[191] See the First Council Directive 67/227 of 11 April 1967 on the harmonization of legislation of Member States concerning turnover taxes, OJ English Special Edition 1967, at 14, and the Sixth Council Directive 77/388 of 17 May 1977 on the harmonization of the laws of the Member States relating to turnover taxes - common system of value-added tax: uniform basis of assessment, OJ 1977, L145/1. See also Council Regulation 218/92 of 27 January 1992 on administrative cooperation in the field of indirect taxation (VAT), OJ 1992, L24/1.

[192] See in this context Case 324/82, *Commission* v *Belgium*, [1984] ECR 1861, and Case 391/85, *Commission* v *Belgium*, [1988] ECR 579.

[193] See Article 33 of the Sixth Council Directive, *supra* note 191. As confirmed by the ECJ in Joined Cases 93/88 and 94/88, *Wisselink and others* v *Staatssecretaris van Financiën*, [1989] ECR 2706, par. 17, this provision seeks to prevent the functioning of the common system of value-added tax from being compromised by fiscal measures of a Member State levied on the movement of goods and services and charged on commercial transactions in a way comparable to value-added tax.

[194] See Council Directive 96/95 of 20 December 1996 amending, with regard to the level of the standard rate of value-added tax, Directive 77/338 on the common system of value added tax, OJ 1996, L338/89 (period 1 January 1997 to 31 December 1998).

VAT on imported goods at their borders.[195] The imposition of tax on imports and the remission of tax on exports in trade between Member States tended to create fiscal trade barriers. In an effort to eliminate these barriers within the Community, a wide range of drastic transitional measures were taken on the basis of Article 99 EC.[196] These transitional measures were taken in order to facilitate the transition to the definitive system for the taxation of trade between Member States. They entered into force on 1 January 1993 and introduced the principle that VAT was to be paid in the state of origin. The definitive system for the taxation of trade is still in the wings. Various simplification measures with regard to VAT have already been taken[197] and proposals to further reform the common VAT-system are under discussion.[198]

The transitional measures, however, make an *exception* for the supply of "new means of transport" to individuals.[199] The supply of a new car is still

---

[195] The ECJ pointed out in *Schul I*, *supra* note 1, paras. 31-34, that "at the present stage of Community law the Member States are free, by virtue of Article 95, to charge the same amount on the importation of products as the value-added tax which they charge on similar domestic products". However, the ECJ added that "this compensation is justified only in so far as the imported products are not already burdened with value-added tax in the Member State of exportation since otherwise the tax on importation would in fact be an additional charge burdening imported products more heavily than similar domestic products". See in this context also Case 47/84, *Schul* v *Inspecteur der Invoerrechten en Accijnzen*, [1985] ECR 1491, and Case 134/83, *Abbink*, [1984] ECR 4097.

[196] Council Directive 91/680 of 16 December 1991 supplementing the common system of value added tax and amending Directive 77/388 with a view to the abolition of fiscal frontiers, OJ 1991, L376/1.

[197] See the most recent edition of the *Directory of Community legislation in force and other acts of the Community institutions*, Volume I, subheading 09.30.10 Indirect Taxation, Official Journal of the European Communities, for an overview of all the amendments and supplements to the Community legislation on VAT.

[198] See, *inter alia*, Written Questions 981-2/96 (Langenhagen), OJ 1996, C297/60; "The European Commission's working programme for passage to the definitive tax system on added value (VAT)", *Agence Europe* (Europe Documents), 17 July 1996; *FT* (FT Exporter), "Taxing in harmony", December 1997, at 17; "Commission proposes reform of VAT system in order to facilitate and accelerate its management by entrusting Commission itself with wider implementing powers", *Agence Europe*, 16 July 1997, at 5-6; Proposal for a Council Directive amending Directive 77/388 on the common system of Value Added Tax (the Value Added Tax Committee), COM(97)325 final, and Opinion of the Economic and Social Committee on "A common system of VAT - a programme for the Single Market", OJ 1997, C296/51.

[199] See Article 28a(2) of the Sixth Council Directive, *supra* note 191, (as introduced by Article 22 of Directive 91/680, *supra* note 196) for definitions of "means of transport" and "new".

taxed in the Member State of destination where the car will be used and at that Member State's rates and under its conditions, "in so far as such transactions would, in the absence of special provisions, be likely to cause significant distortions of competition between Member States".[200] As a result, the price-before-tax of a new car is paid in the Member State in which the car is purchased whereas the VAT and other purchase-related taxes have to be paid in the Member State where the new car is actually registered.[201] The Commission recognizes that this special arrangement for the sale of new cars is not desirable.[202]

(ii) Excise Duty

Article 99 EC was also used by the Community as the legal basis for Directive 92/12 which lays down the arrangements for products subject to excise duties and other indirect taxes which are levied directly or indirectly on the consumption of such products, except for value added tax and taxes established by the Community.[203] Article 3(3) of this Directive explicitly confirms that Member States retain the right to introduce or maintain taxes which are levied on products other than mineral oils, alcohol and alcoholic beverages and manufactured tobacco provided, however, that those taxes do not give rise to border-crossing formalities in trade between Member States. Several Member States have used this competence to charge car taxes such as registration taxes,

---

[200] 11th Whereas, Directive 91/680, *supra* note 196. See also 1996 Communication on Type-approval, *supra* note 96, at 12. See also Written Question 1214/97 (Titley), OJ 1997, C373/89.

[201] It was reported in *The single market review - Impact on manufacturing motor vehicles*, *supra* note 3, at 72, that this impedes "consumers to make full use of the single market in this sector". Denmark levies close to a 100% purchase tax on new cars which alledgedly places a downward pressure on the pre-tax prices set by manufacturers in order to retain sales in Denmark. The argument was made that this forces pre-tax prices across the whole of the EU down "so that manufacturers can retain an EU-wide pricing policy minimizing tendencies towards cross-border shopping". However, one could argue that this downward pressure on the prices is a positive development which in itself minimizes the need for cross-border shopping.

[202] See, for instance, "Internal Market in 1993 - Commission's Annual Report", *Agence Europe* (Europe Documents), 18 March 1994, at 9.

[203] Council Directive 92/12 of 25 February 1992 on the general arrangements for products subject to excise duty and on the holding, movement and monitoring of such products, OJ 1992, L76/1. Amended by Council Directive 92/108 of 14 December 1992, OJ 1992, L390/124.

at often widely varying levels.[204] As "the measures taken by Member States to safeguard their revenue from such sources of taxation may appear to be incompatible with the concept of the internal market",[205] the Commission tries to maintain the pressure to amend and simplify the Directive in an effort to smoothen the functioning of the internal market.[206]

In addition to the measures with regard to value-added tax and excise duty, the Community has taken steps on the basis of Article 99 EC, to eliminate obstacles to the establishment of an internal market resulting from the taxation arrangements applied to temporary and permanent importation of certain means of transport for private and business use.[207] First of all, Directive 83/182 sets out the conditions under which the *temporary* importation of cars into one Member State from another, is exempted from taxes such as turnover tax, excise duties and other consumption taxes.[208] The Commission recognizes that the arrangements under Directive 83/182 fall short of what is often expected of an

---

[204] Cuts in registration taxes are used as incentives to boost demand for new cars. For instance, *FT*, "Europe's car sales well ahead of forecasts", 14 January 1998, at 2, reported that Spain cut registration taxes to stimulate new car sales.

[205] Written Question 1732/95 (Zimmermann), OJ 1995, C277/22. See also Written Question 2592/93 (Kostopoulos), OJ 1994, C219/71, and Written Question 1886/93 (Kostopoulos), OJ 1994, C336/9.

[206] See, *inter alia*, Proposal for a Council Directive amending Directive 92/12 on the general arrangements for products subject to excise duty and on the holding, movement and monitoring of such products, OJ 1997, C267/58.

[207] See in this context Case C-9/92, *Commission* v *Greece*, [1993] ECR I-4494, par. 6. See also Written Question 190/97 (Kaklamanis), OJ 1997, C319/35.

[208] See Council Directive 83/182 of 28 March 1983 on tax exemptions within the Community for certain means of transport temporarily imported into one Member State from another, OJ 1983, L105/59. The ECJ repeated in Case C-389/95, *Klattner* v *Greece*, judgment of 29 May 1997, par. 25, not yet reported, that "the provisions of the Directive must be interpreted in the light of the fundamental aims of the endeavour to harmonize VAT, in particular the promotion of freedom of movement for persons and goods and the prevention of double taxation". See also Written Question 1214/97 (Titley), OJ 1997, C373/89.

internal market.[209] Secondly, Directive 83/183 specifies the conditions under which the personal property imported *permanently* into a Member State from another Member State by private individuals is exempted from turnover tax, excise duties[210] and other consumption taxes which normally apply to such property.[211] It should be emphasized, however, that Article 1(2) of Directive 83/183 provides that specific and periodical duties and taxes connected with the use of such property within the Member State, such as motor vehicle registration fees and road taxes, are not covered by the Directive. Proposals to improve the rules of both Directive 83/182 and Directive 83/183 are under discussion.[212]

---

[209] For instance, in answer to Written Question 190/97 (Kaklamanis), OJ 1997, C319/35, the Commission confirmed that it is "examining Community legislation ... to ascertain what changes, if any, might be appropriate in order to lessen the burden of proof on the citizen and to place a greater onus on the authorities of the Member States to consult each other in such cases". See also Written Question 1415/95 (Wijsenbeek), OJ 1995, C273/17.

[210] Pursuant to Article 23(3) of Directive 92/12, *supra* note 203, the provisions on excise duty laid down in Directive 83/183 ceased to apply on 31 December 1992.

[211] Council Directive 83/183 of 28 March 1983 on tax exemptions applicable to permanent imports from a Member State of the personal property of individuals, OJ 1983, L105/64.

[212] *Agence Europe*, "The Commission proposes improving and simplifying the tax system of vehicles transferred definitively or used temporarily in a Member State other than that in which they are registered", 14 February 1998, at 12, reported that the Commission proposes to replace Directive 83/182 and Directive 83/183 by a new Directive which will give individuals the right not to pay a second registration duty (or similar tax) when transferring their residence from one Member State to another, if they wish to keep the car registered in their own country. In addition, in the case of a temporary move to another Member State, they would have the right to use the car without paying supplementary taxes) for six months in any twelve-month period. See Proposal for a Council Directive governing the tax treatment of private motor vehicles moved permanently to another Member State in connection with a transfer of residence or used temporarily in a Member State other than that in which they are registered, OJ 1998, C108/75.

4.4.3.3 Direct Taxation

Article 100 EC provides the Community with the legal basis to harmonize national legislation on *direct* taxation on the basis of Article 100 EC. The Community has used this competence to harmonize certain aspects of corporation tax.[213]

4.5 Intellectual Property Rights

4.5.1 Introduction

In this time of costly marketing campaigns and massive investments in research and technological development, it is beyond any doubt that the existence of a legal system which guarantees both the existence and exercise of intellectual property rights like patent rights, copyrights, trademark rights and rights to designs, is essential for the automobile industry within the Community. Intellectual property rights facilitate return on investment and make innovation and technological development attractive.

At the same time, however, intellectual property rights complicate the elimination of obstacles to intra-Community trade as they are territorial in nature and can hinder trade. Intellectual property rights provide the holder with an exclusive right in a particular territory only; they create quasi-monopolies along national territorial lines. In addition, Member States have different legal systems dealing with intellectual property rights. By their very nature, intellectual property rights create barriers to trade which can fall within the scope of Articles 30 to 36 EC. The latter provisions, however, do not prohibit nor remove all intellectual property barriers to trade. The fact that harmonisation or "unification" of the different national laws of the Member States on intellectual property is another, if not the most important, means to remove barriers to trade within the Community, was already recognized in the early days of the Community. The ECJ held:

---

[213] See, *inter alia*, Council Directive 90/434 of 23 July 1990 on the common system of taxation applicable to mergers, divisions, transfers of assets and exchanges of shares concerning companies of different Member States, OJ 1990, L225/1, and Council Directive 90/435 of 23 July 1990 on the common system of taxation applicable in the case of parent companies and subsidiaries of different Member States, OJ 1990, L225/6.

> The national rules relating to the protection of industrial property have not yet been unified within the Community. In the absence of such unification, the national character of the protection of industrial property and the variations between the different legislative systems on this subject are capable of creating obstacles both to the free movement of the patented products and to competition within the Common Market.[214]

Over the years, various Community directives harmonizing the different national laws of the Member States on industrial property rights such as rental and lending rights,[215] copyrights[216] and rights to trademarks[217] have been adopted.

For the automobile industry, national copyrights and registered design rights to *car parts* are of particular economic interest. In Member States such as France, design rights to parts provide car manufacturers with an important measure of control on the after-sales market of replacement parts for the repair or servicing of cars. Copyrights and design rights to parts give car manufacturers a quasi-monopoly on this commercially attractive after-sales market for protected parts. So-called "captive markets" are created as consumers have no choice but to purchase the original part produced by or with the consent of the holder of the exclusive copyright or design right to the car part in

[214] Case 24/67, *Parke, Davis* v *Centrafarm*, [1968] ECR 71. See also Joined Cases C-92/92 and C-326/92, *Phil Collins*, [1993] ECR I-5179, par. 22, in which the ECJ noted that intellectual property rights are of such a nature as to affect trade in goods and services and also competitive relationships within the Community.

[215] See, *inter alia*, Council Directive 92/100 of 19 November 1992 on rental rights and lending rights and on certain rights related to copyright in the field of intellectual property, OJ 1992, L346/61.

[216] See, *inter alia*, Council Directive 93/98 of 29 October 1993 harmonizing the term of protection of copyright and certain related rights, OJ 1993, L290/9.

[217] See, *inter alia*, Council Directive 89/104 of 21 December 1988 to approximate the laws of the Member States relating to trade marks, OJ 1989, L40/1.

question. This lack of competition by independently manufactured parts leads to high(er) prices for protected car parts.[218]

In view of the above, it is clear that both the caselaw of the ECJ on the application of Articles 30 to 36 EC to copyrights and design rights on spare parts (**4.5.2**), and the manner in which the legal protection of designs will eventually be harmonized (**4.5.3**), has an important impact on car manufacturers' market power and their relationship with independent part manufacturers, independent dealers and consumers who eventually pay the bill.

4.5.2 Free Movement of Parts

In principle, the EC Treaty does not affect the existence of intellectual property rights recognized by the legislation of a Member State.[219] But the exercise of those rights may nevertheless, depending on the circumstances, be restricted by the prohibitions in the EC Treaty such as Articles 30 and 34 EC.[220] Article 36 EC sets out an exception to the free movement of goods as it provides that Articles 30 to 34 EC shall not preclude prohibitions or restrictions on imports, exports or goods in transit justified on a limited number of grounds which include the protection of industrial and commercial property. Such prohibitions or restrictions shall not, however, constitute a means of arbitrary discrimination or a disguised restriction on trade between Member States. According to the ECJ, "[i]nasmuch as it provides an exception to one of the fundamental

---

[218] For instance, *Ford Motor Company Limited: A report on the policy and practice of the Ford Motor Company Limited of not granting licences to manufacture or sell in the United Kingdom certain replacement body parts for Ford vehicles*, Cmnd 9437, February 1985, reported extensively on the very large differences in price between Ford and the independent suppliers. This case triggered a discussion in the United Kingdom which eventually lead to exceptions to the protection given to designs for any design features enabling an article to be functionally fitted to ("must-fit"), or aesthetically matched with ("must-match"), another. See in this context Monopolies and Mergers Commission, *Motor car parts - A report on the wholesale supply of motor car parts within the United Kingdom ("MMC Parts Report")*, February 1992, Cm 1818, HMSO, London, at 4-6.

[219] See in this context Article 222 EC which provides that the Treaty shall in no way prejudice the rules in Member States governing the system of property ownership.

[220] See in this sense, *inter alia*, Case 119/75, *Terrapin* v *Terranova*, [1976] ECR 1061, par. 5. See for an example: *Agence Europe*, "Commission asks France to put an end to seizure of spare parts in transit (made in Spain and considered in France as counterfeit)", 6-7 July 1998, at 12.

principles of the common market, Article 36 in fact admits exceptions to the free movement of goods only to the extent to which such exceptions are justified for the purpose of safeguarding rights which constitute the specific subject-matter of that property".[221] In its case law, the ECJ had to specify what constitutes the specific subject matter of the various intellectual property rights.

In *Maxicar*, the ECJ elaborated on what constitutes the specific subject-matter of design rights. In its judgment, the ECJ answered questions raised by an Italian court in proceedings instituted by independent manufacturers against Renault seeking, *inter alia*, a declaration that the protective rights in respect of ornamental designs of which Renault was the proprietor were void, in so far as they relate to spare parts for the bodywork of cars, such parts having no intrinsic aesthetic value of their own.[222] First of all, the ECJ confirmed with regard to the protection of designs and models that in the absence of Community harmonisation, the determination of the conditions and procedures under which such protection is granted is a matter for national legislation. The ECJ held that it is for the national legislature to determine which products qualify for protection, even if they form part of a unit already protected as such.[223] Subsequently, the ECJ noted:

> that the authority of a proprietor of a protective right in respect of an ornamental model to oppose the manufacture by third parties, for the purposes of sale on the internal market or exports, of products incorporating the design or to prevent the import of such products manufactured without its consent in other Member States constitutes the substance of his exclusive right. To prevent the application of the national legislation in such circumstances would therefore be tantamount to challenging the very existence of that right.[224]

---

[221] *Ibidem*.

[222] Case 53/87, *CICRA and Maxicar* v *Renault (Maxicar)*, [1987] ECR 6069, par. 3.

[223] *Ibidem*, par. 10.

[224] *Ibidem*, par. 11. This judgment and the manufacturers' arguments in favour of design rights on car parts have been heavily criticized. See for a compelling criticism: I. Govaere, *The use and abuse of intellectual property rights in E.C. law*, 1996, Sweet & Maxwell, London, at 195-228. Govaere submits on page 197 that the most important question posed to the ECJ in the spare parts cases was whether or not design

As a result, the holder of a design right to a car part can prevent the manufacture and importation of parts incorporating the design and manufactured without his consent in other Member States. Indeed, according to the ECJ, this constitutes the substance of the design right.

On the very same day and in an even shorter judgment in *Volvo* v *Veng*, the ECJ answered questions raised by a British court on the interpretation of Article 86 EC with a view to determining whether the refusal by the proprietor of a registered design in respect of body panels for motor vehicles to grant a licence for the import and sale of such panels may, in certain circumstances, be regarded as an abuse of a dominant position.[225] The ECJ repeated that in the absence of Community harmonisation, the determination of the conditions and procedures under which protection of designs and models is granted is a matter for national rules.[226] The ECJ held that "the right of the proprietor of a protected design to prevent third parties from manufacturing and selling or importing, without its consent, products incorporating the design constitutes the very subject-matter of his exclusive right".[227]

Both judgments clarify the ECJ's interpretation of what constitutes the substance or specific subject matter of a design right and clearly confirm the important role of the very different national systems of design protection in the Member States.[228]

---

protection on spare parts of cars comes within the scope of the exception of Article 36 EC to the rules on the free movement of goods. According to Govaere, the answer to this question was decisive for a potential approximation of national design laws concerning components of complex products, and it set the tone for the answers to be given in *Maxicar* and *Volvo* v *Veng* concerning the applicability of the competition rules to the alleged anti-competitive behaviour of the car manufacturers.

[225] Case 238/87, *Volvo* v *Veng*, [1987] ECR 6233, par. 1.

[226] *Ibidem*, par. 8.

[227] *Ibidem*, par. 8.

[228] See A. Firth, "Aspects of design protection in Europe", [1993] 2 EIPR, at 42-47, on the various systems of design protection in the Member States. See in this context also Case C-38/98, *Renault* v *Maxicar and Orazio Formento*, OJ 1998, C113/8. See more specifically: Chapter 7, section 7.4.3.

4.5.3 Harmonisation of the Legal Protection of Designs

In an effort to further the creation of the common market, the Community took the initiative to harmonize certain aspects of the different laws of the Member States on the legal protection of designs. Several sources indicate that in doing so, various other Community policies such as competition policy and industrial policy were taken into consideration.[229] After the publication in 1991 of the Green Paper on the Legal Protection of Industrial Designs[230] and public hearings, the Commission put forward a proposal for a Directive on the harmonisation of the national laws of the Member States with regard to the protection of designs[231] (on the basis of Article 100A EC) and a proposal for the introduction of a Community design on 3 December 1993[232] (initially on the basis of Article 100A EC but later Article 235 EC).[233] Under these proposals, only certain aspects of the national protection of designs were to be harmonized and a Community design was to be introduced which would coexist with the national systems on the protection of designs.

As expected, the contents of the proposals triggered a heated debate amongst all interested parties in the automobile industry. The discussion focused

---

[229] For instance, it was reported in "Mr Bangemann anticipates the highlights of the Commission report on the car industry and presents guidelines for a relaunch of the industry", *Agence Europe*, 13 November 1993, at 9, that according to Mr Bangemann, Commissioner for industrial policy, design is "one of our best weapons in the battle for market share". See also B. Posner, "The Community design. Purpose and scope of the Green Paper on the legal protection of industrial design" in *The Green Paper on the legal protection of industrial design* (F. Gotzen ed.), 1992, E. Story-Scientia, Brussels, at 10, par. 29, who pointed out that "it was quite clear to me from the outset that we would have to find a compromise solution which was coherent with Commission policies in other areas". Posner identified Article 8 of the Preliminary draft regulation on "interconnections" as "an expression of such policies".

[230] See *The Green Paper on the legal protection of industrial design, supra* note 229, Annexes, for both the text and an analysis of the draft European design law presented by the Max Planck Institute (1 August 1990) and the preliminary draft of a proposal for a Regulation on the Community design and a proposal for a Directive on the approximation of the legislations of the Member States on the legal protection of design.

[231] Proposal for a European Parliament and Council Directive on the legal protection of designs, OJ 1993, C345/14. See COM(93)344 final-COD 464.

[232] Proposal for a European Parliament and Council Regulation on Community design, OJ 1994, C29/20. See COM(93)342 final-COD 463.

[233] See in this context *Opinion 1/94*, [1994] ECR I-5405, par. 59.

in particular on the proposed exceptions to the design protection of parts. These exceptions must be seen against the background of the discussion with regard to the "must-fit" and "must-match" exceptions that had already taken place in the United Kingdom.[234] The "must-fit" exception regards the exception to the protection given to designs for any design features enabling an article to be functionally fitted to another. The "must-match" exception regards the exception for design features enabling an article to be aesthetically matched with another. First of all, the proposals provided that a right was not to subsist in a design to the extent that the realization of a technical function leaves no freedom as regards arbitrary features of appearance. An *interconnection-clause* was provided for; a design right was not to subsist in a design to the extent that it must necessarily be reproduced in its exact form and dimensions in order to permit the product in which the design is incorporated or to which it is applied to be mechanically assembled or connected with another product.[235] In order to avoid the creation of captive markets in certain spare parts,[236] the proposals included a *repair-clause* which provided that the rights conferred by a design right could not be exercised against third parties who, after three years from the first putting on the market of a product incorporating the design or to which the design is applied, use their exclusive design right, provided that:

> (a) the product incorporating the design or to which the design is applied is a part of a complex product upon whose appearance the protected design is dependent;

---

[234] See in this context *MMC Parts Report*, *supra* note 218, at 4-6.

[235] See Article 7(1) and (2) of the 1993 proposal for a Directive on the legal protection of designs, and Article 9(1) and (2) of the 1993 proposal for a Regulation on Community design. It should be stressed, however, that the third paragraph of both articles make an exception for a design serving the purpose of allowing simultaneous and infinite or multiple assembly or connection of identical or mutually interchangeable products within a modular system.

[236] COM(93)342 final, at 20. Govaere, *supra* note 224, at 292-293, criticizes the fact that the Commission presented the repair-clause as a compromise between respecting the legitimate claims of a design holder and the need to safeguard competition in the market for replacement parts. According to Govaere, the underlying rationale of the clause should have been explained in terms of the *function* of design protection; "[i]f a part has to have a certain shape to restore the car to its original appearance, then the design obviously does not confer an added value to the spare part so that it should not benefit from exclusive protection".

(b) the purpose of such a use is to permit the repair of the complex product so as to restore its original appearance; and
(c) the public is not misled as to the origin of the product used for the repair.[237]

On 12 October 1995, the European Parliament delivered its Opinion on the proposal for a Directive on the protection of designs, in which it suggested several amendments including proposals for textual changes to both the interconnection- and the repair-clause.[238]

In 1996, the Commission published an amended proposal[239] which again became the subject of public debate. A great variety of arguments were presented in this discussion.[240] For instance, car manufacturers maintained that design rights on parts are necessary to recoup the large investments in design and for consumer protection in order to guarantee the quality of car parts and the safety of consumers. These arguments must be seen against the backdrop of the car manufacturers' argument that they do not just offer a new car but instead a so-called "package" which allegedly consists of the new car together with pre- and after-sales services including repair-work. Car manufactures argue that prices for new cars can be relatively low and therefore competitive as part of the manufacturing costs of new cars are recouped on the long(er) term through the sales of car parts for repair and servicing purposes. According to car

---

[237] See Article 14 of the 1993 proposal for a Directive on the legal protection of designs, and Article 23 of the 1993 proposal for a Regulation on Community design.

[238] OJ 1995, C287/157.

[239] Amended proposal for a European Parliament and Council Directive on the legal protection of designs, OJ 1996, C142/7. See also COM(96)66 final-COD 464. See in this context *FT*, "Brussels firm on car parts market", 28 November 1996, at 3, and "Maintaining the current situation for spare parts for cars is unacceptable to the Commission as it is against citizens' interests", *Agence Europe*, 28 November 1996, at 6.

[240] See, for instance, the various conference papers on (i) "The vehicle manufacturer's case for design protection of spare parts" by M. Franzosi (Legal view) and J. Kroher (Economic and public policy), (ii) "The after market case against design protection of spare parts" by G. Riehle (Legal view) and R. Hughes (Public and legal policy-legislator's opinions) and (iii) "The consumer interest in a free market in spare parts" by S. Locke, IBC Legal Studies-Conference on "The Commission's amended proposal for a Directive on the legal protection of designs - The implications for the Automotive Industries and the Automotive After Market", 18 June 1996, Munich, Germany.

manufacturers, consumers take the cost of parts into consideration when they make their decision to purchase a particular new car. Independent manufacturers and consumer organisations, on the other hand, reject these arguments and take the position that design rights on parts are simply (ab)used to restrict competition and to keep prices for car parts (too) high.[241] All interested parties lobbied for their position.[242]

On 17 June 1997, the Council adopted Common Position 28/97 in which it accepted the great majority of the European Parliament's proposals for amendments.[243] As the Council's Common Position is of considerable importance to the automobile industry within the Community, the most relevant provisions on parts will be highlighted.[244] A *design* is defined in Article 1(a) of the Council's proposal, as the appearance of the whole or a part of a product resulting from the features of, in particular, the lines, contours, colours, shape, texture and/or materials of the product itself and/or its ornamentation. Pursuant to Article 3(2), a design shall be protected by a design right to the extent that it is *new* and has *individual character*. Article 3(3) provides that a design applied to or incorporated in a product which constitutes a *component part* of a complex product shall only be considered to be new and to have individual character (a) if the component part, notwithstanding its having been incorporated into the complex product, could reasonably be expected to remain visible during normal use of the latter, and (b) to the extent that those visible features of the component part fulfil in themselves the requirements as to novelty and individual character. Normal use is defined in Article 3(4) as any use other than maintenance, servicing or repair. As a result, those car parts such as oil filters,

---

[241] See Govaere, *supra* note 224, at 195-228, for a critical appraisal of these arguments.

[242] For instance, it was reported in "ECAR warns against danger of competition being eliminated from automotive parts market", *Agence Europe*, 12 March 1997, at 15, that the Member States were under considerable pressure from powerful car lobbies to drop the "repair-clause".

[243] Common Position 28/97 adopted by the Council on 17 June 1997 with a view to adopting Directive 97/.. of the European Parliament and of the Council on the legal protection of designs, OJ 1997, C237/1.

[244] See H.M.H. Speyart, "The Grand Design: An update on the EC design proposals", [1997] 10 EIPR 603-612, for a concise description and analysis of both the history and contents of the discussion of the Council's Common Position.

fan belts and other engine parts, which do not remain visible during normal use of the car are excluded from protection.[245]

Article 7(1) provides that a design right shall not subsist in features of appearance of a product which are solely dictated by its technical function. Article 7(2) contains an *interconnection-clause* which provides that a design right shall not subsist in features of appearance of a product which must necessarily be reproduced in their exact form and dimensions in order to permit the product in which the design is incorporated or to which it is applied to be mechanically connected to or placed in, around or against another product so that either product may perform its function. The Council failed to reach agreement on a *repair-clause*. Article 14 provides that until such time as amendments to this Directive are adopted upon proposal by the Commission, Member States may maintain in force or introduce any provisions affecting the use of a protected design for the purpose of permitting the repair of a complex product so as to restore its original appearance, where the product incorporating the design or to which the design is applied constitutes a component part of a complex product upon whose appearance the protected design is dependent. In its statement of reasons attached to its Common Position 28/97, the Council clarifies that it came up with this so-called "solution" as it was "[a]nxious that this issue, which concerns a specific sector of industry, should not delay approximation of other provisions on which agreement has been reached". The removal of the repair-clause from the proposed Directive has been heavily

---

[245] As pointed out by Speyart, *ibidem*, Article 3(3) is probably redundant "because almost all "under the bonnet" parts would be excluded from protection anyway because they are "must-fit" parts or because their design is solely dictated by its technical function .., while the wording "reasonably be expected to remain visible during normal use" is bound to cause difficulties of interpretation before the Courts".

criticized.[246] In October 1997, the Council's proposal was reversed by the European Parliament[247] and the lobbying has started again.[248]

It is expected that the proposed Regulation on a Community design will eventually be revised in accordance with the amendments to the proposed Directive on the protection on designs once the latter has been adopted.[249]

4.6 The Freedom of Establishment and the Free Movement of Capital

4.6.1 Introduction

The creation of the common market within the Community stimulated intra-Community investment and confirmed the need for freedom of establishment

---

[246] See in this context *FT*, "Ministers halt plan to open EU car spares market", 23-24 November 1996, at 1; IP/97/221; *FT*, "Brussels loses battle over car spare parts", 14 March 1997, at 2; *Agence Europe*, "ECAR challenges Council agreement on spare care parts-Unice welcomes it", 19 March 1997, at 14; "SMES criticise the attitudes of major companies on the spare car body parts market", 27 March 1997, at 14; "The Council publishes and explains its common position on the problem of repairs, noting its hope that the difference of views on this point will not delay adoption of the directive on legal protection of designs", 22 August 1997, at 4; "Automobile organisations rally to the campaign for free market of car spare parts", 1-2 September 1997, at 8, and "ECAR urges European Parliament to vote for saving open spare parts market", 17 October 1997, at 13. See also Written Question 891/97 (Campos), OJ 1997, C373/35, and Written Question 2468/97 (Muscardini), OJ 1998, C102/43.

[247] See *FT*, "Hopes boosted for cheaper car parts and repairs", 23 October 1997, at 2, and "ECAR considers the European Parliament vote on spare parts is a clear signal in favour of consumers and SMES", *Agence Europe*, 24 October 1997, at 14. It is expected that the joint legislative procedure ex Article 189b EC will eventually lead to a conciliation committee. See on the joint legislative procedure, *inter alia*, T.C. Hartley, *The foundations of European Community law*, 3th edition, 1994, Clarendon Press, London, at 44-48.

[248] See *Agence Europe*, "Automobile manufacturers consider the "repairs clause" would be unworkable in practice" and "Motoring organisations urge in favour of the "repairs clause" to keep the spare parts market open", 20-21 October 1997, at 13; "Parliament-Council conciliation procedure on car repairs, against a backdrop of divergences between manufacturers and independent shops", 29 May 1998, at 13; "A draft compromise from Van Miert on automobile repair does not enable differences between Parliament and Council to be overcome", 4 June 1998, at 12, and "EURATEX calls on automobile industry not to endanger new rules on designs and models-UNICE grows impatient", 15-16 June 1998, at 14. See also B. Posner, "Proposal for a Directive on the legal protection of designs", International Business Lawyer, February 1998, at 80-82.

[249] See in this sense IP/97/221.

and the free movement of capital. These two freedoms are essential for an efficient allocation of resources within the Community and go to the very heart of the common market. In view of the internationalisation or even globalisation of the automobile industry, the extent and the manner in which the freedom of establishment and the free movement of capital are guaranteed is of great importance to this sector of industry. Therefore, attention will be paid to the most relevant provisions of the EC Treaty dealing with the freedom of establishment (**4.6.2**) and the free movement of capital (**4.6.3**). In addition, a summary will be given of the Commission communication on those aspects of the freedom of establishment and the free movement of capital, which relate to intra-EU investment (**4.6.4**).

4.6.2 Freedom of Establishment

Article 6 EC, which forms part of the "principles" of the Community, provides that within the scope of application of the EC Treaty, and without prejudice to any special provisions contained therein, any discrimination on grounds of nationality shall be prohibited. Article 52 EC provides for the implementation of this general provision in the special sphere of the *right of establishment* and is capable of being directly invoked by nationals of all the other Member States.[250] Article 52 specifies that restrictions on the freedom of establishment of nationals of a Member State in the territory of another Member State have to be (progressively) abolished. This also applies to restrictions on the setting up of agencies, branches or subsidiaries by nationals of any Member State established in the territory of any Member State. Freedom of establishment includes for instance the right to set up and manage undertakings in a Member State, under the conditions laid down for its own nationals, subject to the provisions of the EC Treaty relating to capital. Article 53 EC contains a stand-still clause; Member States shall not introduce any new restrictions on the right of establishment in their territories of nationals of other Member States. There are several *exceptions* to these rules such as with regard to activities connected with the exercise of official authority (Article 55 EC) and national provisions providing for special treatment for foreign nationals on grounds of public policy,

---

250 See Case 2/74, *Reyners* v *Belgium*, [1974] ECR 650, paras. 15-25.

public security or public health (Article 56 EC). Objectives of an economic nature cannot constitute grounds of public policy.[251]

Pursuant to Article 58 EC, companies or firms formed in accordance with the law of a Member State and having their registered office, central administration or principal place of business within the Community have to be treated in the same way as natural persons who are nationals of Member States.[252] The ECJ confirmed that Article 52 EC is concerned with differences in treatment as between natural persons who are nationals of Member States and as between companies that are treated in the same way as such persons by virtue of Article 58 EC.[253] On the other hand, however, the ECJ recognized in its judgment in *The Queen* v *Daily Mail* that:

> unlike natural persons, companies are creatures of the law and, in the present state of Community law, creatures of national law. They exist only by virtue of the varying national legislation which determines their incorporation and functioning.[254]

The ECJ held that the national laws of the Member States vary widely in regard to both the factor providing a connection to the national territory required for the incorporation of a company and the question whether a company incorporated under the legislation of a Member State may subsequently modify that connecting factor. The ECJ pointed out that the EC Treaty has taken account of that variety in national legislation and stressed that none of the directives on the coordination of company law dealt with the differences in question; future legislation or conventions had to deal with these issues. The ECJ concluded that:

> [u]nder those circumstances, Articles 52 and 58 of the Treaty cannot be

---

[251] See in this sense Case 17/92, *Fedicine* v *Spain*, [1993] ECR I-2272, par. 16.

[252] Article 58 EC defines "companies or firms" as "companies or firms constituted under civil or commercial law, including cooperative societies, and other legal persons governed by public or private law, save for those which are non-profitmaking".

[253] See in this sense Case 246/89, *Commission* v *United Kingdom*, [1991] ECR I-4615, par. 29.

[254] Case 81/87, *The Queen* v *Daily Mail*, [1988] ECR 5511, at 19.

> interpreted as conferring on companies incorporated under the law of a Member State a right to transfer their central management and control and their central administration to another Member State while retaining their status as companies incorporated under the legislation of the first Member State.[255]

As pointed out by Lever, Article 58 EC seems to prohibit discrimination against foreign companies rather than granting the same rights or applying the same rules which are applicable to individuals in every respect.[256]

4.6.3 Free Movement of Capital

Since 1 January 1994, Articles 73b to 73g EC lay down the rules on the *free movement of capital* between Member States as well as between Member States and third countries.[257] It should be kept in mind, however, that these provisions are without prejudice to the application of restrictions on the right of establishment.[258] The rules on the free movement of capital cover a wide variety of transactions including for instance direct investments and the acquisition of domestic securities.[259]

Article 73b EC provides that all restrictions (i) on the movement of capital and (ii) on payments, between Member States and between Member States and third countries shall be prohibited. This prohibition is subject to several *exceptions* which tend to be related to the different policies pursued by the Member States within the Community. For instance, Article 73d(1)(a) EC provides that Member States can apply their tax law which distinguishes

---

255 *Ibidem*, par. 24.

256 See J. Lever in his case note in 26 CML Rev. at 334.

257 See Article G(15) of the EU Treaty. As pointed out in Article 73a EC, "[a]s from 1 January 1994, Articles 67 to 73 shall be replaced by Articles 73b, c, d, e, f and g".

258 Article 73d(2) EC provides that "[t]he provisions of this Chapter shall be without prejudice to the applicability of restrictions on the right of establishment which are compatible with this Treaty".

259 See in this context Council Directive 88/361 of 24 June 1988 for the implementation of Article 67 of the Treaty, OJ 1988, L178/5, which contained an extensive overview of capital movements. This directive was adopted before the introduction of Article 73b EC but is still used as a source for interpretation.

between tax-payers who are not in the same situation with regard to their place of residence or with regard to the place where their capital is invested.[260] Article 73d(1)(b) EC allows Member States to take all requisite measures to prevent infringements of national law and regulations, in particular in the field of taxation and the prudential supervision of financial institutions, or to lay down procedures for the declaration of capital movements for purposes of administrative or statistical information, or to take measures which are justified on grounds of public policy or public security. Pursuant to Article 73d(3) EC, the measures and procedures referred to in Article 73d(1) and (2) EC shall not constitute a means of arbitrary discrimination or a disguised restriction on the free movement of capital and payments as defined in Article 73b EC.

There are even more possibilities for the restriction of the movement of capital between Member States and third countries. For instance, Article 73c(1) EC allows the retention of any restrictions which existed on 31 December 1993 under national or Community law, adopted in respect of the movement of capital to or from third countries involving "direct investment - including in real estate - , establishment, the provision of financial services or the admission of securities to capital markets". Pursuant to Article 73c(2) EC, the Council can adopt measures in this respect "[w]hilst endeavouring to achieve the objective of free movement of capital between Member States and third countries to the greatest extent possible".

4.6.4 1997 Communication on Intra-EU investment

In view of the fact that some Member States felt it necessary to introduce measures in order to monitor, and in some cases even control, the increasing intra-Community investment, the Commission published a Communication on intra-EU investment, in which it gives an interpretation of the relevant

[260] See in this context the Declaration on Article 73d of the Treaty establishing the European Community as attached to the EU Treaty in which "[t]he Conference affirms that the right of Member States to apply the relevant provisions of their tax law as referred to in Article 73d(1)(a) of this Treaty will apply only with respect to the relevant provisions which exist at the end of 1993. However, this Declaration shall apply only to capital movements between Member States and to payments effected between Member States".

provisions on capital movements and the right of establishment.[261] In its Communication, the Commission first elaborates on the rules on the freedom of capital movements and the right of establishment. In doing so, the Commission emphasizes that nationals of other Member States should be free to acquire controlling stakes, exercise voting rights and manage domestic companies under the same conditions laid down in a given Member State for its own nationals.[262] Subsequently, the Commission addresses the exceptions to the freedom of capital movements and the right of establishment.

The Commission focuses in particular on two categories of restrictive measures introduced by some Member States. The *first* category consists of measures with a discriminatory character. An example is the prohibition on investors from another Member State acquiring more than a limited amount of voting shares in domestic companies and/or having to seek authorization for the acquisition of shares beyond a certain threshold. The Commission considers these measures to be contrary to Articles 73b and 52 EC, unless they are covered by one of the exceptions set out in the EC Treaty.

The *second* category concerns measures applied without distinction to all investors. These measures include general authorization procedures for investors who want to acquire a stake in a domestic company above a certain threshold. The Commission considers these general authorization procedures only to be compatible with Articles 73b and 52 EC "if they can be justified by imperative requirements in the general interest and are based on a set of objective criteria, stable over time and made public, without which they could be implemented in such a way that control of the firm in question remains in the hands of national operators".[263] Another example of measures applied without distinction to all investors, is rights given to national authorities (in derogation of company law) to veto certain major decisions to be taken by the company, as

---

[261] Communication of the Commission on certain legal aspects concerning intra-EU investment, OJ 1997, C220/15.

[262] *Ibidem*, par. 4.

[263] *Ibidem*, par. 8. The Commission added that "[a]s the Court has indicated as a general principle, the fundamental freedoms recognised by the Treaty cannot be rendered illusory and exercising these rights cannot be submitted to the discretion of the administrative authorities, which an authorization procedure would imply".

well as the imposition of a requirement for the nomination of some directors as a means of exercising the right of veto. According to the Commission, measures like the right of veto, which are liable to hinder or make less attractive the exercise of fundamental freedoms guaranteed by the EC Treaty must fulfil the following four conditions: (i) they must be applied in a non-discriminatory manner, (ii) they must be justified by imperative requirements in the general interest, (iii) they must be suitable for securing the attainment of the objective that they pursue, and (iv) they must not go beyond what is necessary in order to attain it.

Last but not least, the Commission pointed out that it cannot accept so-called "national interest" considerations "as a legal cover for the measures mentioned above". According to the Commission, these considerations do "not appear to be sufficiently transparent and could, thereby, introduce an element of discrimination against foreign investors as well as legal uncertainty" and "could encompass both economic and non-economic criteria" going beyond the exceptions recognized in the EC Treaty.

4.7 Concluding Remarks

The Community actively pursues the elimination of obstacles to intra-Community trade. These efforts facilitate intra-Community trade and thereby the working of the market mechanism in the automobile industry. The elimination of and prohibition on customs duties on imports and exports between Member States and of all charges having equivalent effect, and the adoption of a CCT, made all Member States break down the tariff walls that separated their domestic markets. These Member States opened up their markets for automobiles and parts originating in other Member States and those coming from a third country which are in free circulation in Member States. The Community has resisted French and Italian pressure to introduced an official general "economic value-added test" or "local content test" for the determination of the origin of automobiles in general and so-called "transplants" in particular. It has been reported, however, that the Community and certain Member States (have) pressure(d) incoming Japanese car manufacturers into integrating their investment into the local economy through political agreement on an informal local content requirement. Nevertheless, the Community does not use the CCT to build or maintain a "Fortress Europe". On the contrary, as customs duties have been reduced considerably, trade with third countries is facilitated and it has even been reported that the so-called single market programme has in fact made it easier for new entrants to compete on equal terms with the indigenous "national champions" of the Community's automobile industry.

The elimination and prohibition of quantitative restrictions on both imports and exports between Member States and of all measures having equivalent effect, further facilitates intra-Community trade and the working of the market mechanism in the automobile industry. In particular the directly effective prohibition on quantitative restrictions between Member States on imports and all measures having equivalent effect, proves to be crucial as Member States continue to come up with schemes to create trade barriers in an effort to protect the interests of their domestic automobile industry. In addition, holders of copyrights and design rights to car parts try to exercise these rights in a manner that goes beyond the subject-matter of these exclusive rights. The Community has taken various initiatives to prevent the creation of new obstacles to trade such as technical standards and regulations. The Community has introduced a notification procedure set out in Directive 83/189, leading to preventive monitoring in the field of technical standards and regulations, and a procedure set out in Decision 3052/95, for the exchange of information on national measures derogating from the principle of the free movement of goods within the Community.

The Community has also taken measures to remove existing obstacles to trade in automobiles and spare parts by taking steps to harmonize certain national laws of Member States. Efforts are made to harmonize registration procedures and roadworthiness test for automobiles. The Community put in place a Community type-approval procedure which not only facilitates trade but also provides the Community with the possibility of pursuing public interests such as environmental protection and safety. In the context of its type-approval procedure, the Community sets detailed technical requirements applicable to car parts and characteristics like permissible sound level and the exhaust system. The Community is thereby in a position to actively re-direct the production of cars. It is increasingly using this position to improve and protect the environment. In addition, the Community is trying to harmonize certain aspects of the legal protection of designs. It has been reported that in doing so, competition and industrial policy considerations were taken into consideration. Notwithstanding fierce opposition from the automobile industry, proposals have been drawn up to introduce an exception to the design protection of parts in order to make it possible for independent manufacturers to compete with the car manufacturers on the after-sales market of replacement parts for the repair and servicing of cars.

A remarkably long line of cases indicates that Member States continue their efforts to use their national system of internal taxation as an instrument to protect their domestic automobile industry. This, notwithstanding the fact that Member States are under an obligation to keep their national system of internal taxation completely neutral as regards competition between domestic and imported products. Although the different systems of car taxation lead to a fragmentation of the car market in the Community, national laws on car taxation have not yet been significantly harmonized at Community level. The Community has taken certain measures to harmonize the national laws of the Member States on VAT and excise duties, and steps up efforts to eliminate obstacles to the establishment of an internal market resulting from the taxation arrangements applied to temporary and permanent importation of certain means of transport for private and business use.

In order to guarantee an efficient allocation of resources, the Community guarantees the freedom of establishment and the free movement of capital. Efforts by Member States to monitor or even control intra-Community investment are closely scrutinized. The guarantee of the freedom of establishment and the free movement of capital goes to the very heart of the common market and facilitates the working of the market mechanism as it opens the market to mergers and joint ventures.

5. COMMON COMMERCIAL POLICY AND THE AUTOMOBILE INDUSTRY

5.1 Introduction

Article 3(b) EC provides that for the purposes set out in Article 2 EC, the activities of the Community shall include a common commercial policy. The relevant provisions on the common commercial policy, Articles 110, 112, 113 and 115 EC, can be found in a separate Title VII (entitled "Common Commercial Policy") in Part Three of the EC Treaty.[1] The common commercial policy complements the customs union. The ECJ held in *Donckerwolcke* that "[t]he assimilation to products originating within the Member States of goods in 'free circulation' may only take full effect if these goods are subject to the same conditions of importation both with regard to customs and commercial considerations, irrespective of the State in which they were put in free circulation" and confirmed that "[u]nder Article 113 of the Treaty this unification should have been achieved by the expiry of the transitional period and supplanted by the establishment of a common commercial policy based on uniform principles".[2]

Article 110 EC seems to put the Community under the obligation to take common commercial policy measures which contribute to, or are at least in line with the liberalization of world trade. Article 110(1) EC provides that by establishing a customs union between themselves Member States aim to

---

[1] There is an extensive literature on the common commercial policy. See, *inter alia*, I. Macleod, I.D. Hendry and S. Hyett, *The external relations of the European Communities*, 1996, Clarendon Press, Oxford, at 266-295; *The legal regulation of the European Community's external relations after the completion of the internal market* (S.V. Konstadinidis ed.), 1996, Dartmouth, Aldershot; N. Emiliou, "The death of exclusive competence?", (1996) 21 E.L.Rev., at 294-311; *The European Union and world trade law - After the GATT Uruguay Round* (N. Emiliou and D. O'Keeffe eds.), 1996, Wiley, Chichester, and P.L.H. Van den Bossche, "The European Community and the Uruguay Round Agreements" in *Implementing the Uruguay Round* (J.H. Jackson and A. Sykes eds.), 1997, Clarendon Press, Oxford, at 23-102. See, more specifically, P. Eeckhout, *The European internal market and international trade: A legal analysis*, 1994, Clarendon Press, Oxford, at 148-170, on the completion of the common commercial policy on tariff quotas, quantitative restrictions, safeguard measures and voluntary export restraints, and I. Van Bael and J.-F. Bellis, *Anti-dumping and other trade protection laws of the EC*, 3rd edition, 1996, CCH Europe, Bicester, on anti-dumping, anti-subsidy, safeguard measures and the Trade Barriers Regulation.

[2] Case 41/76, *Donckerwolcke* v *Procureur de la République ("Donckerwolcke")*, [1976] ECR 1936, paras. 25-26. See in this context also Council Decision on a programme of action in matters of common commercial policy, OJ English Special Edition 1959-1962, 2353/62, at 269.

contribute, in the common interest, to the harmonious development of world trade, the progressive abolition of restrictions on international trade and the lowering of customs barriers. Pursuant to Article 110(2) EC, the common commercial policy shall take into account the favourable effect which the abolition of customs duties between Member States may have on the increase in the competitive strength of undertakings in those States. However, the ECJ held in *Opinion 1/78* that "[a]lthough it may be thought that at the time when the Treaty was drafted liberalization of trade was the dominant idea, the Treaty ... does not form a barrier to the possibility of the Community's developing a commercial policy aiming at a regulation of the world market for certain products rather than at a mere liberalization of trade".[3] Thus, the Community has a certain degree of discretion when taking commercial policy measures.

The Community has exclusive competence in the field of the common commercial policy. The ECJ held in *Donckerwolcke* that the common commercial policy is conceived "in the context of the operation of the Common Market, for the defence of the common interests of the Community, within which the particular interests of the Member States must endeavour to adapt to each other" and that "[q]uite clearly, ..., this conception is incompatible with the freedom to which the Member States could lay claim by invoking a concurrent power, so as to ensure that their own interests were separately satisfied in external relations, at the risk of compromising the effective defence of the common interests of the Community". According to the ECJ, "any unilateral action on the part of the Member States would lead to disparities in the conditions ..., calculated to distort competition between undertakings of the various Member States".[4] Member States are no longer competent to act on their own in the field of commercial policy. Measures of commercial policy of a national character are in principle only permissible by virtue of specific authorization of the Community.[5]

The term "common commercial policy" is not defined in the EC

---

[3] *Opinion 1/78*, [1979] ECR 2913, par. 44. See also Case 112/80, *Dürbeck* v *Hauptzollamt Frankfurt-am-Main - Flughafen*, [1981] ECR 1119-1120, par. 44, in which the ECJ confirmed that Article 110 EC does not stand in the Community's way in taking measures against the risk of a serious market disturbance.

[4] *Opinion 1/75*, [1975] ECR 1363-1364.

[5] See in this sense *Donckerwolcke*, *supra* note 2, par. 32.

Treaty. Article 113(1) EC provides for a non-exhaustive[6] list of examples of matters which are covered by the common commercial policy such as "changes in tariff rates, the conclusion of tariff and trade agreements, the achievement of uniformity in measures of liberalisation, export policy and measures to protect trade such as those to be taken in case of dumping or subsidies". As discussed, the ECJ held in *Donckerwolcke* that the conditions of importation of goods into the Community fall within the scope of the common commercial policy. In pursuit of the establishment of a common commercial policy based on uniform principles, the Community put in place common rules for imports which include provisions on safeguard measures,[7] common rules for exports[8] and various trade protection instruments such as those on anti-dumping,[9] anti-subsidy[10] and the so-called Trade Barriers Regulation.[11] These common commercial policy instruments are mostly "defensive" in nature with the possible exception of the measures under the Trade Barriers Regulation which can be qualified as "offensive" commercial policy instruments. The Community's use of the WTO-dispute settlement system can be seen as an "offensive" commercial policy instrument since the decision to use this procedure is mostly politically driven

[6] *Opinion 1/78*, *supra* note 3, par. 45.

[7] See in particular Council Regulation 3285/94 of 22 December 1994 on the common rules for imports and repealing Regulation 518/94, OJ 1994, L349/53, and Council Regulation 519/94 of 7 March 1994 on common rules for imports from certain third countries (so-called "non-market economy countries") and repealing Regulations 1765/82, 1766/82 and 3420/83, OJ 1994, L67/89. See in the context of safeguard measures Article XIX GATT 1994 and the WTO Agreement on Safeguards, OJ 1994, L336/184.

[8] See Council Regulation 2603/69 of 20 December 1969 establishing common rules for exports, OJ English Special Edition 1969-II, L324/25, at 590. Amended by Council Regulation 3918/91 of 19 December 1991 amending Regulation 2603/69, establishing common rules for exports, OJ 1991, L372/31.

[9] See Council Regulation 384/96 of 22 December 1995 on protection against dumped imports from countries not members of the European Community, OJ 1996, L56/1. See in this context Article VI GATT 1994 and the WTO Agreement on Implementation of Article VI of GATT 1994, OJ 1994, L336/103.

[10] See Council Regulation 2026/97 of 6 October 1997 on protection against subsidized imports from countries not members of the European Community, OJ 1997, L288/1. See in this context Articles VI and XVI GATT 1994 and the WTO Agreement on subsidies and countervailing measures, OJ 1994, L336/156.

[11] See Council Regulation 3286/94 of 22 December 1994 laying down Community procedures in the field of the common commercial policy in order to ensure the exercise of the Community's rights under international trade rules, in particular those established under the auspices of the World Trade Organization, OJ 1994, L349/71.

by the interests of domestic export industries in getting access to markets in third countries.[12]

As explicitly provided for in Article 113 EC, the Community has concluded a number of mostly preferential "tariff and trade agreements" with third countries such as Tariff Agreements, Free Trade Agreements, Customs Union Agreements, the Agreement on the European Economic Area, and so-called "Interim" Agreements.[13] These different kinds of "tariff and trade agreements" have in common that they lay down trade rules between the Community and particular third countries and include detailed provisions on the reduction or even abolition of customs tariffs, rules for exports, rules for imports (for instance including rules on origin), and rules on the use of trade protection instruments. Often, these agreements provide for a special regime for "sensitive products" such as automobiles.[14] As such, these mostly bilateral agreements are an important part of the common commercial policy.

In this chapter, the focus will be on those aspects of the common commercial policy which are most relevant to the automobile industry. First,

---

[12] In this sense E.-U. Petersmann, "The GATT dispute settlement system as an instrument of the foreign trade policy of the EC" in *The European Union and world trade law - After the GATT Uruguay Round*, *supra* note 1, at 272. See also *FT* (Editorial), "National cars", 13 June 1996, at 11. It was noted in "How to put a ruler in the driver's seat: a national carmaker", *International Herald Tribune*, 18-19 October 1997, at 1, that "[t]he Cold War may be gone, but the car wars are just starting" as "[n]ations that have made cars for decades and have run out of new customers at home are growing increasingly testy about the huge tariffs and legal restrictions that are designed to keep them from going head-to-head with local carmakers" in emerging markets such as Malaysia, Brazil and Indonesia.

[13] See Macleod, Hendry and Hyett, *supra* note 1, at 283-293 and 367-385, for more specifics on the Community's "contractual commercial policy". It was reported in *FT*, "WTO gives EU a clean bill of health in trade matters", 26 July 1995, at 4, that WTO members expressed some unease at the pace at which the EU is concluding new preferential deals and insisted that the basic principles of WTO rules would be maintained. In addition, several members insisted that compensation negotiations for future enlargements of the EU should take place in advance and raised concerns about high tariffs for "sensitive" goods such as vehicles. See in this context "Brittan Memorandum on European Union preferential agreements", *Agence Europe* (Europe Documents), 27 February 1997.

[14] See P. Vigier, "La politique communautaire de l'automobile", 1992 Revue du Marché Unique Européen, Nr. 2, at 108-111. For instance, the Europe Agreement with Poland (OJ 1993, L348/1), which was preceeded by an "Interim" Agreement (OJ 1992, L114/1) includes rules of origin laying down a 60% added-value rule, as well as a special regime and schedule for the elimination of customs duties on imports applicable to cars originating in the Community.

the common rules on exports (**5.2.1**) and the various Community measures to facilitate access to car markets in third countries will be touched upon (**5.2.2**). The common rules on imports will be addressed (**5.3.1**) and the 1991 "Consensus" between the Community and Japan will be examined (**5.3.2**). Concluding remarks will then be made (**5.4**).

5.2 Export

5.2.1 Common Rules on Exports

Regulation 2603/69 establishing common rules for exports does not restrict the exportation of cars from the Community to third countries. Article 1 of Regulation 2603/69 provides that the exportation of products from the Community to third countries shall be free, that is to say, they shall not be subject to any quantitative restriction. There are certain exceptions to this principle of freedom of export. Article 10 refers to a list of products which do not benefit from the principle of freedom of export. Cars are not on this list. Furthermore, Article 11 provides that Member States remain competent to adopt or apply quantitative restrictions on exports on grounds of public morality, public policy or public security; the protection of health and life of humans, animals or plants; the protection of national treasures possessing artistic, historic or archaeological value, or the protection of industrial and commercial property. As the automobile industry is an important positive contributor to the balance of payment of the Community, it is evident that the export of automobiles will not easily be resticted even on these grounds.

5.2.2 Access to Markets in Third Countries

In an effort to keep up with other trading blocs such as the U.S.A. and Japan,[15] the Community actively encourages exports and direct investment by taking measures in order to facilitate access to markets in third countries.[16] The Community has taken various initiatives to enhance export opportunities. For instance, as trade in automobiles can be facilitated if the latter are produced according to internationally recognised product regulations, the Community actively supports the work undertaken at Working Party 29 of the United Nations Economic Commission for Europe ("UN-ECE"), which is the body responsible for the implementation of the 1958 Agreement concerning the adoption of uniform conditions of approval and reciprocal recognition of approval for motor vehicle equipment and parts.[17] In January 1996, the Commission proposed to the Council that the Community becomes a Member of

[15] The U.S.A. is a vigorous defender of its industries' commercial interests. For instance, after the U.S.A. threatened to put import duties up to 100% on certain Japanese cars, an agreement was reached with Japan on 28 June 1995, on (i) access and sales of foreign motor vehicles in Japan, (ii) expansion of purchases by Japanese companies of foreign auto parts (in the case of their operations in Japan) and of parts from new or non-affiliated suppliers (in the case of their operations in other countries), and (iii) deregulation of the Japanese market for replacement of auto parts (Japan-U.S.A. Automotive Agreement and Supporting Documents, 23 August 1995, 34 International Legal Materials 1482 (1995)). It was reported that the "European Union" and Australia "observed" the implementation of the agreement. See *FT*, "EU will help monitor accord on cars", 23 October 1995, at 4; "Commission participates in monitoring meeting between United States and Japan on August 1995 automobile agreement", *Agence Europe*, 18 September 1996, at 13, and "EU participates in US-Japan car talks", IP/96/833. See for another example *FT*, "US-Korea trade friction grows", 3 October 1997, at 4. It was reported in *FT*, "US-Japan trade deals 'often miss target'", 5 December 1996, at IV, that according to the American Chamber of Commerce in Japan, only 13 out of 45 US-Japan trade pacts negotiated between 1980-1996 have fully succeeded in opening the Japanese market to foreign goods.

[16] See "Commission guidelines aimed at making EU trade policy more of an instrument for entering third country markets", *Agence Europe* (Europe Documents), 21 February 1996. It was reported in "Speech by Sir Leon Brittan at the European Parliament conference on the future of car industry in Europe - Brussels, 5 December 1991: "The Single market for cars", Speech/91/132, that according to Brittan "[t]he Commission must do all in its power to ensure that European producers do not face obstacles in their efforts to export". An "EU official" was quoted in *FT*, "Brussels acts to prise open foreign markets", 13 February 1996, at 8, as having said that "[i]t is time for Europe to abandon its defensiveness and focus fully on opening those markets that remain closed to our products and investments". See also *FT* (Personal view by Leon Brittan), "New tactics for EU trade", 11 November 1996, at 16.

[17] United Nations Treaty Series, Volume 335, 1959, at 212.

the revised UN-ECE Agreement in order to solidify the close link that already exists between the Community type approval directives and the UN-ECE regulations. According to the Commission, this should be accomplished as quickly as possible in view of the fact that the Community type approval system is now mandatory for category M1-vehicles and certifications to UN-ECE Regulations are an alternative means of meeting the prescriptions of Community directives.[18] In 1997, the Council decided that the Community shall accede to the revised UN-ECE Agreement.[19] The Community actively encourages other automobile producing states such as the U.S.A., Korea, China and India to participate in this effort in view of the fact that the revised UN-ECE Agreement will further facilitate access to third-country markets.[20] In addition to these efforts in UN-ECE context, the Community tries to make progress during bilateral discussions with various third countries such as the U.S.A. and Japan, on technical standards and certification procedures for European vehicles.[21]

---

[18] Commission Proposal of 15 January 1996 for a Council Decision with a view to accession by the European Community to the 1958 Revised Agreement concerning the adoption of uniform conditions of approval and reciprocal recognition of approval for motor vehicle equipment and parts, COM(95) 723 final - 96/0006(AVC), OJ 1996, C69/4. See Council decision of 27 November 1997 with a view to accession by the European Community to the Agreement of the United Nations Economic Commission for Europe concerning the adoption of uniform technical prescriptions for wheeled vehicles, equipment and parts which can be fitted to and/or be used on wheeled vehicles and the conditions for reciprocal recognition of approvals granted on the basis of these prescriptions, OJ 1997, L346/78.

[19] Council Decision of 27 November 1997 with a view to accession by the European Community to the Agreement of the United Nations Economic Commission for Europe concerning the adoption of uniform technical prescriptions for wheeled vehicles, equipment and parts which can be fitted to and/or be used on wheeled vehicles and the conditions for reciprocal recognition of approvals granted on the basis of these prescriptions ("Revised 1958 Agreement"), OJ 1997, L346/78. See *Agence Europe*, "EU accedes to the UN/ECE agreement", 26 March 1998, at 9.

[20] It was reported in "Positive and encouraging results of Sir Leon Brittan's talks on cars in Japan - Deregulation of technical standards and certification", *Agence Europe*, 6-7 June 1995, at 9, that "Japan intends to adhere to the revised UN/ECE agreement on mutual recognition of technical rules relating to vehicles".

[21] It was reported in "Obstacles to access to the Japanese market, European Commission requests concerning deregulation", *Agence Europe*, 26 March 1997, at 9, that according to the Commission "Japan should reduce the number of vehicle types requiring certification and separate component certifications should be provided for under Japanese regulations". See also WTO Agreement on Technical Barriers to Trade, OJ 1994, L336/86.

Furthermore, the Community makes an effort to intensify cooperation with third countries like the U.S.A. and Canada on various matters like customs matters, mutual recognition for a number of products and competition law.[22]

[22] See on EU/U.S.A. cooperation on customs matters: Council Decision 97/541 of 21 May 1997 concerning the conclusion of the Agreement between the European Community and the United States of America on customs cooperation and mutual assistance in customs matters, OJ 1997, L222/16. See on EU/U.S.A. cooperation on competition law: Agreement between the government of the United States of America and the Commission of the European Communities regarding the application of their competition laws, OJ 1995, L95/47, and Agreement between the European Communities and the Government of the United States of America on the application of positive comity principles in the enforcement of their competition laws, OJ 1998, L173/28. See on the Commission's proposal for an EU/U.S.A. "Trans-Atlantic Free Trade Area": *FT*, "European Commission's transatlantic trade initiative clears first political hurdle" and Brussels agrees plan for EU-US free trade area", 12 March 1998, at 6 and 12; "France blocks bid for EU-US 'marketplace'", 28 April 1998, at 8, and *Agence Europe*, "European Commission defines its major guidelines for the 'Brittan Project' of a transatlantic single market - The initiative to be launched next week?", 5 March 1998, at 4; "France asks the Commission to act carefully", 9-10 March 1998, at 13; "European Commission launches the 'new transatlantic marketplace' project and hopes for a rapid reaction from Council to be able to discuss it at June's Euro-America summit - Goals and contents", 12 March 1998, at 6; "France rejects transatlantic free trade project and Washington calls for agriculture and audiovisual to be included", 13 March 1998, at 7; "Text of the 'Brittan plan' for the creation of a common market between the European Union and the United States" (Europe Documents), 25 March 1998; "France confirms to Council its rejection of Sir Leon Brittan's ideas on new transatlantic market", 30-31 March 1998, at 7; "Presentation of the Commission's ideas regarding the 'new transatlantic marketplace' confirms deadlocks in Council - Mr. Vedrine replies firmly to Sir Leon Brittan", 1 April 1998, at 6, and "Overall agreement on laws on Cuba, Iran and Libya, definition of economic partnership, signing of agreement on mutual recognition of industrial products", 18-19 May 1998, at 6. See on EU/Canada mutual recognition agreement: *Agence Europe*, "Content and import of mutual recognition agreement signed last week, other agreements expected to be signed shortly - overview of results of London Summit", 20 May 1998, at 11.

The Community keeps a close eye on other access barriers to markets in third countries in general[23] and car markets in particular.[24] The Commission reported in 1996 that an initial study on access barriers to car markets in third countries had shown that "the levels of government intervention and trade protection prevailing in the industry were significantly higher than those affecting other industrial sectors". The Commission specified that the study was enlarged from 15 to 23 countries and that "[t]his work has supported a bilateral dialogue on market access issues with a number of countries, including Japan, Korea, China, Brazil, Taiwan, India and the members of ASEAN".[25]

As of yet, there are no examples available of "offensive" measures under the Trade Barriers Regulation or its predecessor, for the purpose of facilitating access to car markets in third countries.[26] But there are a number of cases in which the Community turned to the multilateral GATT - and now WTO

---

[23] In its Resolution of 21 November 1994 on the strengthening of the competitiveness of Community industry, OJ 1994, C343/1, the Council invited the Commission to take measures to establish a database on the obstacles faced by European companies in third countries. The Commission has a so-called "Market Access Database" (http://mkaccdb.eu.int) which covers many countries and various sectors (including "Automotive"). In addition, the Commission publishes annual reports on barriers to trade and investment. For instance, the "Report on United States barriers to trade and investment", July 1997, European Commission, Brussels, at 14-15 and 20, identified the Luxury tax, the Gas Guzzler tax and the Corporate Average Fuel Economy requirements, as well as certain labelling requirements including those on the proportion of U.S.A. made parts and the final point of assembly, as non-tariff barriers to the U.S.A. carmarket. See also *Agence Europe*, "Guidelines adopted by Council for implementing 'Brittan strategy' for third country market access", 11 June 1998, at 13.

[24] Council Resolution of 16 May 1994 on the automobile industry, OJ 1994, C149/1, at II-7, the Commission is invited to draw up a list of the most important barriers impeding better market access for Union automobiles on third markets. Furthermore, on the basis of this list, a market opening plan should be drawn up together with a timetable for achieving results. It was announced in OJ 1996, C45/26 and 45/28, that the Community would have an analysis made of all possible trade barriers to the Community automobile industry on markets outside the Community and of the impact of "Buy American" legislation in the U.S.A.

[25] Communication from the Commission to the Council, the European Parliament, the Economic and Social Committee and the Committee of the Regions, European Automobile Industry 1996, COM(96) 327 final, at 14. See also *FT*, "Daewoo calls for Ukraine car duties", 22 January 1998, at 4, and "Clash with EU looming over cars", 21-22 February 1998, at 2.

[26] See in this context Van Bael and Bellis, *supra* note 1, at 679-680 ("Table VI - New Instrument of Commercial Policy for Protection Against Illicit Practices").

- dispute settlement system for this purpose instead of resorting to unilateral or bilateral measures.[27] For instance, in 1992, the Community took steps against the *U.S.A.* with regard to the Gas Guzzler tax, the Luxury tax and the Corporate Average Fuel Economy requirements on automobiles. The Community considered these three to be discriminatory as they put large expensive European automobiles under a treble tax exposure in the U.S.A. whereas competitive and substitutable American cars did not suffer from this treble tax exposure. However, a GATT Panel rejected the Community's complaints that the three taxes discriminated against automobiles made by Mercedes, BMW and other European luxury car manufacturers.[28] In 1997, a WTO complaint was made against *Indonesia* with regard to its national car policy which, by means of reductions in taxes and tariffs, strongly favours the joint venture between Kia Motors (South-Korea) and PT Timor Putra Nasional Company (Indonesia). In the same year, a WTO complaint was brought against *Brazil* with regard to its restrictive car policy which grants trade advantages, such as import tariff reductions up to 50%, to those manufacturers investing in manufacturing plants in Brazil and agreeing to incorporate a minimum proportion of locally

---

[27] It was reported in *FT*, "WTO gets a vote of confidence", 24 September 1997, at 6, that the WTO "received the 100th request for consultation under its dispute settlement system, handling in its 2,5-year life a third as many cases as GATT, ..., dealt with in nearly 50 years". According to this report, "the EU and the US have been by far the biggest users - and beneficiaries - of the system". The U.S.A. brought 35 cases while defending 20. The EU brought 21 cases while defending 14. See also *FT* (Personal view by Leon Brittan), "Rough with the smooth", 10 September 1997, at 16. See in this context T. Cottier, "Dispute settlement in the World Trade Organization: Characteristics and structural implications for the European Union", 35 CML Rev. at 325-378.

[28] GATT Dispute Settlement Panel Report on United States Taxes on Automobiles (11 October 1994 - Doc. DS 31/R), 33 International Legal Materials 1397 (1994). See for some critical remarks by the Community's agent in this case: P.J. Kuyper, "Booze and fast cars: Tax discrimination under GATT and the EC" in Legal Issues of European Integration 1996/1 (Special edition dedicated to R.H. Lauwaars), Kluwer, at 129-144. See for new legal action against the American tax system "European Commission takes United States to WTO over American tax system which it says subsidizes exports", *Agence Europe*, 19 November 1997, at 7.

manufactured components.[29] In 1998, the Community requested consultations under the WTO with regard to Canada's tariff on imported vehicles.[30]

5.3 Imports

5.3.1 Common Rules on Imports

Regulation 3285/94 on the common rules for imports does not restrict the importation of cars into the Community. Article 1(2) of Regulation 3285/94 provides that products other than certain textile products and certain products originating in particular third countries,[31] shall be freely imported into the Community and accordingly shall not be subject to any quantitative restrictions. The Community can use its "defensive" common commercial policy instruments

[29] See with regard to Indonesia: *FT*, "WTO gives ruling against preferential treatment", 27 March 1998, at 7, reported that according to Japanese sources, a WTO-panel has upheld complaints from the U.S.A., the European Union and Japan against Indonesia's "national car" programme. See also *FT*, "WTO rules against Indonesia car policy", 23 April 1998, at 15, and *Agence Europe*, "Report on Indonesian car programme is in favour of EU", 24 April 1998, at 9. See with regard to Brazil: "Consultations on cars in Brazil", *Agence Europe*, 9 August 1996, at 3; *FT*, "Indonesia's national car drives into trouble", 30 August 1996, at 3; *FT*, "Indonesia faces WTO battle on car policy", 3 October 1996, at 5; "EU lodges complaint with WTO against Indonesia's discriminatory car policy - ASEAN and MERCOSUR also criticized", *Agence Europe*, 4 October 1996, at 8; *FT*, "Worldwide solutions", 5 December 1996, at IV; *FT*, "Brazil warned of WTO probe into car tariffs", 7 April 1997, at 5; "EU asks WTO for consultations on Brazil's import arrangements and opening of panel against Indonesia", *Agence Europe*, 15 May 1997, at 11; *FT*, "Testing time at WTO for Indonesia's controversial national car venture", 23 May 1997, at 6; "WTO examines, on Friday, EU's panel request against Indonesian automobile import system", *Agence Europe*, 24 May 1997, at 10; *FT*, "WTO to probe Indonesian car", 13 June 1997, at 7; "The United States may soon join panel opened by EU and Japan for Indonesian car import regime", *Agence Europe*, 16-17 June 1997, at 9, and *FT*, "Offer to raise EU car quota", 18 July 1997, at 4, and "Indonesia car plan challenge", 31 July 1997, at 4.

[30] See *FT*, "EU acts over Canadian car duty", 21 August 1998, at 3.

[31] See Regulation 519/94 on common rules for imports from certain third countries and repealing Regulations 1765/82, 1766/82 and 3420/83, OJ 1994, L67/89, for common rules on import of products originating from Albania, Armenia, Azerbaijan, Belarus, People's Republic of China, Georgia, Kazakhstan, North Korea, Kyrgyzstan, Moldova, Mongolia, Russia, Tajikistan, Turkmenistan, Ukraine, Uzbekistan and Vietnam. Estonia, Latvia and Lithuania were on this list until the date of entry into force of their Free Trade Agreement with the Community. See in this context Council Regulation 839/95 of 10 April 1995 amending the list of countries mentioned in Annex 1 to Regulation 519/94, OJ 1995, L85/9.

in order to protect its industry against imports which constitute "unfair competition" from third countries. Under certain conditions, the Community can take safeguard measures, initiate anti-dumping proceedings or start anti-subsidy proceedings. Some of these measures have been taken with regard to the importation of car parts from third countries into the Community.[32] However, none have been taken with regard to the importation of cars.[33]

In reality, the principle of "free import without quantitative restrictions" does not apply to the importation of cars from third countries. While putting in place the common rules for imports, the Community had to address the various national non-tariff barriers to the importation of cars from third countries. The Community's efforts to abolish these national restrictions met with fierce resistance. Some Member States were not prepared to give up their national non-tariff barriers out of fear for foreign competition on their domestic market. In particular Japanese cars have been subjected to non-tariff barriers such as national import quotas (Italy, Spain and Portugal), voluntary export restraints (United Kingdom) and restrictive administrative practices (France). Whereas Member States were prepared to adapt their national tariffs to the common customs tariff, some Member States were not prepared to abolish these national non-tariff barriers. The legality of (the consequences of) these national non-tariff

---

[32] For instance, the Community reintroduced a 4,9% countervailing duty for F15 car gearboxes produced by General Motors Austria and imported from Austria into the Community, within the context of the Free Trade Agreement between the Community and Austria (OJ 1972, L300/1). See also Council Regulation 3697/93 of 20 December 1993 withdrawing tariff concessions in accordance with Article 23(2) and Article 27(3)(a) of the Free Trade Agreement between the Community and Austria (General Motors Austria), OJ 1993, L343/1, and Case T-115/94, *Opel Austria* v *Council*, [1997] ECR II-39. See for an example of the initiation of an anti-dumping proceeding: Notice of initiation of an anti-dumping proceeding concerning imports of certain laser optical reading systems or the main constituent elements thereof for use in motor vehicles originating in Japan, Korea, Malaysia, the People's Republic of China and Taiwan, OJ 1997, C324/2.

[33] See Van Bael and Bellis, *supra* note 1, at 603-678 ("Table I - EC Anti-Dumping Proceedings (including Court cases)", "Table II - EC Anti-Dumping Assembly Proceedings", "Table III - ECSC Anti-Dumping Proceedings", "Table IV - EC and ECSC Anti-Subsidy Proceedings (including Court cases)" and "Table V - Safeguard Proceedings under Regulation 288/82").

barriers to the importation of Japanese cars under both Community law and GATT has often been called into question.[34]

Most of these Member States obtained the Commission's authorisation on the basis of Article 115 EC, for border controls on intra-Community trade in order to control and restrict the so-called "indirect importation" of automobiles which were in free circulation in the Community but originated in third countries like Japan.[35] In *Donckerwolcke*, the ECJ recognized that "[t]he fact that at the expiry of the transitional period the Community commercial policy was not fully achieved is one of a number of circumstances calculated to maintain in being between the Member States differences in commercial policy capable of bringing about deflections of trade or of causing economic difficulties in certain Member States". The ECJ held that Article 115 EC provides the Commission with "the power to authorize Member States to take protective measures particularly in the form of derogation from the principle of free circulation within the Community of products which originated in third countries

---

[34] See in this context, *inter alia*, M.C.E.J. Bronckers, "A legal analysis of protectionist measures affecting Japanese imports into the European Community - Revisited" in *Protectionism and the European Community* (E.L.M. Völker), 2nd edition, 1986, Kluwer, Deventer, at 78-82, and N.M. Blokker, "GATT en vrijwillige exportbeperkingen; het panelrapport over Japanse halfgeleiders", SEW 2 (1989) February, at 90-104. See on the French restrictive practices: Case C-72/90, *Asia Motor France* v *Commission (Asia Motor I)*, [1990] ECR I-2181; Case C-29/92, *Asia Motor France* v *Commission (Asia Motor II)*, [1992] ECR I-3936; Case T-28/90, *Asia Motor France* v *Commission (Asia Motor III)*, [1992] ECR II-2285; Case T-7/92, *Asia Motor France and others* v *Commission (Asia Motor IV)*, [1993] ECR II-669; Case T-387/94, *Asia Motor France and others* v *Commission (Asia Motor V)*, [1996] ECR II-965; Judgment of 7 May 1998 in Case C-401/96P, *Somaco* (not yet reported); Case T-225/97, *Asia Motor France and others* v *Commission*, OJ 1997, C318/28 (OJ 1998, C41/24); Case C-386/92, *Monin Automobiles - Maison du Deux-Roues (Monin I)*, [1993] ECR I-2049, and Case C-428/93, *Monin Automobiles - Maison du Deux-Roues (Monin II)*, [1994] ECR I-1707. See on the British voluntary export restraints agreement between SMMT and JAMA: Case T-37/92, *BEUC* v *Commission ("BEUC")*, [1994] ECR II-285. See on the Italian quantitative restrictions: Case 82/87R, *Autexpo* v *Commission (Autexpo)*, [1987] ECR 2131.

[35] See in this context also Commission Decision 80/47 of 20 December 1979 on surveillance and protective measures which Member States may be authorized to take in respect of imports of certain products originating in third countries and put into free circulation in another Member State, OJ 1980, L16/14.

and which were put into free circulation in one of the Member States".[36] These Article 115 EC measures were the proverbial thorn in the Community's side as they were the result of an incomplete common commercial policy and sanctioned border controls on intra-Community trade which obstructed the completion of the internal market.[37] A situation was created in which the circulation of Japanese cars within the Community was restricted and competition between undertakings of the various Member States was distorted as only the industry established in the more liberal Member States experienced the full impact of the competitive force of the Japanese automobile industry.

Only after Japan threatened to bring the various restrictions to imports of its products before a GATT panel were negotiations initiated. In the end, the Community agreed to the gradual abolition of certain restrictions.[38] However, the import restrictions on Japanese cars were to be the subject of separate negotiations. The prospect of negotiations which could lead eventually to the abolition of all national restrictions on the import of Japanese cars triggered a debate between all interested parties within the Community. This debate focused initially on the relationship between the Community and Japan and touched upon a wide range of politically sensitive subjects such as the Community's large trade deficit with Japan, the lack of openness of the Japanese market with regard to Community products and the large Japanese investments within the

---

[36] *Donckerwolcke*, *supra* note 2, paras. 27-28. See in this context, *inter alia*, S.V. Konstadinidis, "The new face of the Community's external relations: Recent developments on certain controversial issues" in *The legal regulation of the European Community's external relations after the completion of the internal market*, *supra* note 1, at 31-39.

[37] F.G. Jacobs, "The completion of the internal market v the incomplete common commercial policy" in *The legal regulation of the European Community's external relations after the completion of the internal market*, *supra* note 1, at 14, noted that "[i]t is obvious that the abolition of national QRs on imports from third countries is a big step toward a truly common commercial policy, based on uniform rules which are indispensable for establishing a single market. It is nonetheless noteworthy that it took the Community until 1994 to realize this, whereas the Treaty provides that this should have been achieved by 1970 (the end of the transitional period)". See in this context Written Question 2133/90 (de Vries), OJ 1991, C85/28.

[38] See in this sense Eeckhout, *supra* note 1, at 156-157.

Community.[39] The debate made it absolutely clear that an arrangement with Japan leading to the gradual liberalization of the importation of Japanese cars into the Community, had to include a transitional period in which the automobile industry within the Community was given sufficient time to prepare for the impact of international competition.

5.3.2 1991 "Consensus" between the Community and Japan

5.3.2.1 Elements of Consensus

The negotiations between the Community and Japan started in 1990[40] and led in July 1991 to the so-called "elements of consensus" on the monitoring of exports

---

[39] See, *inter alia*, *Agence Europe*, "M. Andriessen préconise une négociation avec le Japon sur l'ouverture progressive du marché communautaire, la libération totale étant le point d'arrivée", 4 February 1989, at 9; "Les orientations de M. Bangemann concernant les relations avec le Japon rencontrent beaucoup de réserves et d'oppositions", 1 July 1989, at 6; "M. Bangemann confirme son opposition a toute restriction quantitative sur les automobiles Japonaises apres 1992 en soulignant que 'les tactiques dilatoires ne sont jamais payantes'", 7 July 1989, at 9; "L'Italie demande un débat au sein du conseil 'général' sur les relations avec le Japon, avant que la Commission Européenne ait défini sa stratégie", 16 September 1989, at 9; "Le problème des importations de voitures Japonaises reste au centre des réflexions de la Commission Européenne-Elements d'une solution fondée sur une periode transitoire au-dela de 1992", 20 October 1989, at 5; "La Commission Européenne a defini les orientations de la politique Communautaire et les mesures transitoires à convenir avec le Japon", 7 December 1989, at 6; "According to head of Peugeot, the Community should fix an import quota on Japanese cars for at least ten years", 8-9 January 1990, at 10; "France seems to have defined its position with regard to imports from Japan", 25 January 1990, at 12; "The terms and content of the transition period for imports of Japanese cars are the subject of considerable differences among the twelve", 5-6 February 1990, at 7; "Council plans to reach consensus in March on transitional system for Japanese auto imports", 7 February 1990, at 11; "Japanese cars are welcome, but ..." (editorial), 12-13 February 1990, at 1, and "According to sir Leon Brittan, the transition period for Japanese car imports should not go beyond 1996-For vigorous EEC action in support of the European industry", 14 February 1990, at 12.

[40] See *Agence Europe*, "Mr. Andriessen starts exploratory talks on the interim scheme that will apply to the car sector", 29 March 1990, at 7; "Japan indicates to Mr. Andriessen that it is willing to discuss cars 'immediately'", 31 March 1990, at 7; "European manufacturers reaffirm the need for a 10-year transition period to adapt to a market fully open to Japanese imports", 21 April 1990, at 10; "In the new climate, a compromise between the twelve might be achieved during the Council meeting of 18 June, according to Mr. Ruggiero", 1 June 1990, at 5, and "The European Commission is given green light by the twelve to informally debate a flexible and discrete arrangement with Tokyo", 20 June 1990, at 7.

of motor vehicles from Japan to the Community.[41] The contents of these "elements of consensus" are set out in a statement by Andriessen, Vice-President of the Commission, and Nakao, Japanese Minister of International Trade and Industry. On 31 July 1991, the following statements were issued:[42]

(i) *Statement by Andriessen*

The EC side expressed its commitment to take the following measures with respect to the motor vehicle sector upon the completion of market unification by the end of 1992. The EC side confirmed that with respect to vehicles imported from Japan, (i) it would cease to authorize recourse to Article 115 EC by the end of 1992 at the latest, and (ii) France, Italy, Spain and Portugal would immediately ease the levels of quantitative restrictions (including restrictions on registration) imposed upon vehicles imported from Japan and totally abolish them by the end of 1992 at the latest.

In addition, the EC side would achieve full Community acceptance of type approval for motor vehicles by the end of 1992.

In view of the fact that there were concerns on the part of the Community that unexpected circumstances might arise after 1 January 1993, the EC side requested the Japanese side to take cooperative measures with respect to motor vehicles exported from Japan, so as to avoid disruption in the Community market as a whole as well as in the markets of France, Italy, Spain, Portugal and the United Kingdom. The EC side emphasized that such measures would be

---

[41] It is interesting to note that already in 1983, the Community requested Japan to moderate the exportation of cars to the Community. See, *inter alia*, Written Question 1289/84 (Boot), OJ 1985, C197/2; Written Question 214/85 (Catherwood), OJ 1985, C341/5, and Written Question 2011/85 (MacSharry), OJ 1986, C150/7. According to A. Smith and A.J. Venables, "Automobiles" in *Europe 1992 - An American perspective* (G.C. Hufbauer ed.), 1990, The Brookings Institution, Washington D.C., at 125-126, it could very well be that since 1986 at the request of the Commission to monitor Japanese sales to the Community as a whole, "the Japanese moderate their German sales" to around 15% of the market.

[42] Both statements are published in "The Agreement on the transitional period has been formally accepted by both parties-Statements by Mr. Andriessen and Mr. Nakao, MITI minister-Link with EEC homologation of models", *Agence Europe*, 2 August 1991, at 6. According to a letter of Mr. Haitze J.L. Siemers, Commission of the European Communities, D.-G. I, Directorate F, dated 29 April 1994, marked 007532, "confidentiality was agreed between the Commission and the Japanese authorities concerning all texts that are part of the EU-Japan arrangement" (letter on file with author).

completely terminated at the end of 1999 and that no cooperative measures would be requested on 1 January 2000 and thereafter.

The EC side declared that the necessary measures would be taken to ensure that the operation of competition law would not constitute an obstacle to the operation of the cooperative measures on the Japanese side.

(ii) *Statement by Nakao*

The Japanese side welcomed (i) the liberalisation of motor vehicle imports from Japan into France, Italy, Spain and Portugal through the elimination of all existing quantitative restrictions (including restrictions on registration), (ii) the Community's decision to cease authorisation for recourse to Article 115 EC for motor vehicles, (iii) the full Community acceptance of type approval for motor vehicles, and (iv) the Community's commitment to impose no restrictions on Japanese investment or on the free circulation of its products in the Community.

Upon request from the EC side, the Japanese side confirmed that it would take the following cooperative measures after the measures stated above have been completed:

- The Japanese side will monitor, until the end of 1999, motor vehicle exports to the market of the Community as a whole and the markets of its specific Member States: i.e. France, Italy, Spain, Portugal and the United Kingdom.
- The Japanese side will monitor exports from Japan to the EC market as a whole in accordance with forecast level of exports in 1999: 1.23 million based on the assumption of demand in the EC (including the five new Bundesländer) in 1999: 15.1 million.
- The Japanese side will monitor exports from Japan to France, Italy, Spain, Portugal and the United Kingdom in accordance with forecast level of exports in 1999, and based on the assumption of demand in 1999, as specified in Nakao's statement.
- The Japanese side was prepared to hold consultations twice a year in order to asses market developments in the Community with respect to motor vehicles as well as trends of motor vehicle exports from Japan to the Community.

These statements indicate that in exchange for the gradual liberalization of the importation of Japanese cars into the Community, the Japanese side was prepared to accept a transitional period until the end of 1999, in which it would take cooperative measures which result in the monitoring of exports to the market of the Community as a whole and of France, Italy, Spain, Portugal and the United Kingdom. During periodic consultations, market developments are assessed and the parties make estimates of demand and try to reach agreement on forecasts for the exportation of cars from Japan to the Community and from Japan to France, Italy, Spain, Portugal and the United Kingdom. The instrument of monitoring and consultation is used as a means to control and restrict the export of Japanese cars.[43] Furthermore, it recognizes and maintains the separation of the markets of France, Italy, Spain, Portugal and the United Kingdom. The "elements of consensus" amount to a voluntary export restraint until the end of 1999, so as to avoid disruption in the Community market as a whole and in France, Italy, Spain, Portugal and the United Kingdom, in particular.[44] This, notwithstanding the fact that studies have shown that the

---

[43] The joint setting of the annual quota is always in two stages: an initial provisional estimate (in the spring), of the quota, based on total sales forecasts on the European automobile market, followed in the fall, by the setting of the definitive quota, taking account of real market developments in the first nine to ten months of the year. See, for instance, Written Question 1194/93 (de la Malene), OJ 1994, C32/18; *Agence Europe*, "First Euro-Japanese consultation meeting on 1995 imports to be held in February in Tokyo", 14 January 1995, at 14; "Consultations on automobile regime for 1995 begin on Thursday - Expectation of the Japanese position", 16 February 1995, at 8; "First consultation on cars in 1995 reveals differences on market prospects and on arrangements for three new Member States", 20-21 February 1995, at 7; "Agreement on imports of Japanese cars in 1995 - Markets of three new Member States considered non-restricted", 1 April 1995, at 7; "The 1995 ceiling on the direct import of Japanese cars has been downwardly revised", 7 October 1995, at 10; "Consultations on Japanese car imports", 25-26 March 1996, at 8; "Commission and Japanese MITI increase the quota for Japanese imports in 1996, as evolution of Community market has been more favourable than predicted (but the quota will not be exhausted)", 19 October 1996, at 8; "ACEA challenges Commission forecast of 1996 demand (and resulting concession to Japan), 24 October 1996, at 15, and "Commission and MITI decide to increase the number of Japanese cars allowed to be imported into EU to 1,114,000 for 1997", 25 October 1997, at 9.

[44] It was reported in "Agreement reached on monitoring of exports of motor vehicles from Japan to the European Union", EC News, EC Delegation in Japan (Press and Information Service), 19 March 1994, that a progressive increase in exports to the five Member States that previously restricted imports from Japan, would be allowed.

economic cost of voluntary export restraints is very high.[45] It is curious to see that whereas the initial position of the Member States clearly frustrated the establishment of a common market, the Japanese demands for the liberalization of the import regime and the full Community acceptance of type approval for motor vehicles,[46] contributed to the Community's objective of creating a common market.

The arrangement has several different policy aspects. First of all, it is a measure of common commercial policy which, at the end of the day, contributes to "the progressive and full liberalization of the EC import regime on motor vehicles". Secondly, the arrangement can be qualified as a measure of (anti-) competition policy as it brings about, or at least encourages, an arrangement which restricts the importation of Japanese cars to the Community and reinforces the separation of certain national markets, thereby distorting conditions of competition. In addition, the arrangement is a measure to facilitate the strengthening of the competitiveness of Community policy as it allows for the liberalization of the import regime "with avoidance of market disruption" and "through an appropriate transitional period" which facilitates "structural

[45] See J. Pelkmans, *European integration - Methods and economic analysis*, 1997, Longman (Netherlands Open University), Heerlen, at 214, "Case study 13.2 Volume restrictions of car imports", for a short reference to studies by A. Krijger and L. Mennes (1986), and A. Smith and A. Venables (1991), which indicate that voluntary export restraints are economically (more) costly (than the use of tariffs). See also J. Pelkmans and L.A. Winters (with H. Wallace), *Europe's domestic market* (Chatham House Papers/43), 1988, Routledge, London, "Box 2.2 Trade barriers are in the eye of the beholder", at 39-40; Written Question 1288/84 (Boot), OJ 1985, C113/4, and Written Question 1289/84 (Boot), OJ 1985, C197/2.

[46] According to Smith and Venables, *supra* note 41, at 129, the delay in finalizing the Community-wide whole vehicle type approval "appears to be the result of industry (particularly French industry) fears" that such a Community type approval "would increase external competition". The authors point at page 16 of the November 1988 Commission Progress Report on the implementation of the White Paper in which the Commission noted that "the introduction of Community type approval, which is essential to free movement depends on the formulation of a common commercial policy in this sector".

adjustments that may be required of EC manufacturers to achieve adequate levels of international competitiveness".[47]

5.3.2.2 Scope

The product covered by the arrangement between the Community and Japan is not defined in the statements. However, when the parties notified the arrangement to GATT, it was specified that "[t]he coverage of this monitoring is passenger cars, off-road vehicles, light commercial vehicles, light trucks (up to 5 tonnes), and the same vehicles in wholly knocked down form (CKD sets)".[48] This definition seems to imply that Japanese cars assembled within the Community, the so-called *transplants*, other than CKD sets, are not monitored, which would be in line with what has been qualified by the Japanese side as "the EC side's commitment to impose no restrictions on Japanese investment and on

---

[47] "EC/Japan - Trade in Motor Vehicles", Joint communication from the European Communities and Japan, GATT, L/6922, 16 October 1991. According to Calvet, President of PSA, the duration of the voluntary export restraints arrangement should be extended in view of the devaluation of the yen. See "Peugeot wil Europese markt dicht voor Azië", *NRC Handelsblad*, 19-21 April 1997, at 5. See also "Paris seeks to extend car quotas", *International Herald Tribune*, 12-13 March 1994, at 13, and "Relatively moderate attitude shown by the ACEA on the 'Japanese import' agreement, but head of Peugeot-Citroen calls for renegotiation of 1991 Framework Agreement", *Agence Europe*, 23 March 1994, at 15. It was reported in *FT*, "European motor groups fear flood of Asian imports", 5 December 1997, at 6, that Schweitzer, chairman of both ACEA and Renault, noted that extension of the "gentleman's agreement was unlikely" but welcomed as a replacement "a form of monitoring of developments in the Japanese and European markets". *Agence Europe*, "European industry to ask for no extension, after 1999, of import restrictions on Japanese cars despite devaluation of the Yen - Importance of Single Market and Euro", 22 January 1998, at 15, reported that Pischetsrieder, chairman of both ACEA and BMW, confirmed that "[t]he Agreement with Japan will not be extended beyond ... 31 December 1999, ..., even if some members of ACEA would like it to". See als Written Question 2580/97 (Lienemann), OJ 1998, C117/25.

[48] See "EC/Japan - Trade in Motor Vehicles", Joint communication from the European Communities and Japan, GATT, L/6922, 16 October 1991.

the free circulation of its products in the Community".[49] However, it should at least be mentioned that there were several indications that transplants were to be monitored under the arrangement.[50]

The two statements do not mention (the status of) the *British restrictions* on the importation of Japanese cars. The statements provide that all possible French, Italian, Spanish and Portuguese quantitative restrictions on the importation of Japanese cars have to be replaced by a uniform Community regime at the latest by 1 January 1993. The voluntary export restraint agreement between SMMT and JAMA restricting the export of Japanese cars to the United Kingdom to 11% of the total annual car sales in the United Kingdom, is not mentioned at all in the statements. In *BEUC*, the CFI examined the statements by Andriessen and Nakao, the joint notification of the consensus to GATT and even an extract from the report of a House of Commons debate on 17 July 1991 before it came to the conclusion that it had "not been established that the commercial consensus between the Community and Japan would necessarily cause the ... [SMMT-JAMA] agreement, ..., to come to an end before 1

[49] H. Yamane, "Grey area measures, the Uruguay Round, and the EC/Japan commercial census on cars" in *The European Union and world trade law - After the GATT Uruguay Round*, *supra* note 1, at 280, footnote 7, reported that Germany only gave its approval to the Community/Japan arrangement on several conditions which included that Japanese investment in the relevant areas would not be discriminated against. According to a letter of Mr. Jonathan Claridge, Commission of the European Communities, D.-G. I, dated 29 October 1997, marked 70.838, "transplant production, including the production of semi-knocked-down vehicles, is not in any way affected or covered by the Elements of Consensus. Only the production of complete built-up and complete knocked-down vehicles comes under its terms of reference" (letter on file with author).

[50] According to Smith and Venables, *supra* note 41, at 143, the Commission published an official statement on 6 December 1989, which includes "a transitional 'monitoring' of Japanese imports, which is to take account of the number of cars assembled by Japanese-owned transplants in Europe". Furthermore, it was reported in "The agreement on the transitional period has been formally accepted by both parties-Statements by Mr. Andriessen and Mr. Nakao, MITI minister-Link with EEC homologation of models", *Agence Europe*, 2 August 1991, at 7, that the problem of transplants was "the subject of a unilateral EC statement indicating that the Community expects a progressive increase in this production which could result, in 1999, in 1.2 million cars per year. Should this figure be exceeded (which seems hardly likely given the development programmes for production plants), it would have to be accounted for in the monitoring of imports". It was reported in "Speech by Mr Andriessen at the world automotive forum - Dearborn, 23-24 February 1990: Latest EC thinking concerning external aspects of automotive trade and investment" (Speech/90/12), that, according the Andriessen, the arrangement with Japan "[t]o be meaningful, ... has to take into account transplants in the Community".

January 1993".[51] With reference to additional circumstances, the CFI noted that the mere existence of the commercial consensus reached between the Community and Japan, could not be regarded as assurance for the termination of the SMMT-JAMA agreement.[52] This, notwithstanding the fact that SMMT and JAMA publicly announced that "in view of the implementation of the EC-MITI agreement from 1/1/93, both sides agreed that these would be the last SMMT/JAMA presidential talks concerned with JAMA's policy of prudent marketing in the UK".[53]

Furthermore, the statements are not clear as to whether the cooperative measures only concern the importation of Japanese cars *directly* from Japan, or whether they also include Japanese cars imported into the Community from third countries such as the U.S.A. Whereas the statement by Andriessen only speaks of "cooperative measures with respect to motor vehicles exported from Japan",[54] Nakao's statement confirms that the Japanese side will monitor "motor vehicle exports to the market of the Community" as well as "exports from Japan to the EC market". Moreover, the Japanese side confirmed that it is prepared to hold consultations twice a year in order to assess both "market developments in the Community with respect to motor vehicles" and "trends of motor vehicle exports from Japan to the Community market". This could imply that motor vehicle exports to the Community from third countries which are monitored as part of "motor vehicle exports to the market of the Community" play a role during the consultations. One could imagine that a particular assessment of "market developments in the Community with respect to motor vehicles" and "trends of motor vehicle exports from Japan to the Community market", could lead to a decision by the parties to reduce the quotum for imports of Japanese cars directly from Japan in case the importation of Japanese cars from third countries has increased. On the other hand, one could also imagine that with an

---

[51] *BEUC*, *supra* note 34, par. 57.

[52] *Ibidem*, par. 60.

[53] *Ibidem*, par. 58. It was reported in *FT*, "Commission censured over car agreement", 19 May 1994, that according to SMMT "[t]he agreement finished in 1992 and the Commission was duly informed of that".

[54] Yamane, *supra* note 49, at 280, footnote 7, reports that Germany only approved the arrangement between the Community and Japan on several conditions which included that car imports from third countries would remain unaffected.

eye on "market developments in the Community with respect to motor vehicles", the Japanese manufacturers keep imports from third countries low so as to safeguard direct imports from Japan.[55] It is more than likely that voluntary export restraints directed towards one particular market will have effects on exports to other markets as the market for cars is a global one.[56]

5.3.2.3 Legal Status under Community Law

The legal status of the "elements of consensus" under Community law is not at all clear. Was the Community competent under Community law to enter into the voluntary export restraints arrangement with Japan? If so, what is the legal status of the arrangement under Community law? Are the Community and the Member States bound by the arrangement?

One could argue that the Community was competent to enter into the arrangement as voluntary export restraints fall within the scope of the common commercial policy and can be considered necessary to protect industry within the Community against increasing import competition under the Community's import regime.[57] It is questionable, however, whether the Community was competent to enter into the arrangement with Japan without following the procedural route set out in the EC Treaty, leading to a formal agreement with Japan. The two statements cannot be qualified as a formal agreement in the sense of Articles 113 and 228 EC. There are no indications that the Council has

---

[55] According to G.C. Hufbauer, "An Overview" in *Europe 1992 - An American perspective*, *supra* note 41, at 38, the "whole approach, with the implied foundation of understandings between Japanese producers and the Community, could endanger the potential growth of U.S.A. automobile exports to Europe shipped from Japanese transplant firms in Ohio (Honda) and Tennessee (Nissan). In fact, the proposed EC monitoring program assumes that exports to Europe from Japanese transplant firms in the U.S.A. will remain small - a forecast that has the quality of self-fulfilling prophecy".

[56] The fact that the car market is a global one, is illustrated by *FT*, "Japan targets Europe in car export drive", 25 September 1997, at 4, which reported that "Japanese car manufacturers are boosting their exports to Europe because of a slum in the domestic market and growing friction over Japan's trade surplus with the US". See also *FT*, "Blow to Japan's carmakers as local sales drop", 24 March 1998, at 4.

[57] See in this sense Bronckers, *supra* note 34, at 70. See Yamane, *supra* note 49, at 287-288, on the ECJ's case law on this topic.

signed an official agreement with Japan. Instead, the Community resorted to a so-called "grey area" measure.

According to Eeckhout, it is doubtful under both Community and international law whether the arrangement is binding on the Community and the Member States. Eeckhout specifies that "[i]t could ... be argued that the Community is not entitled to conclude a voluntary restraint arrangement without observing the rules of the Treaty on concluding international agreements and that the arrangement, as a result, is unlawful".[58] The Commission's representative in *BEUC* specified that the arrangement between the Community and Japan "was not recorded in writing and ... was not an official agreement for the purpose of Article 113 ... but rather a political commitment".[59] The CFI seems to qualify the arrangement as "an unwritten commitment, purely political in import and not made within the context of the common commercial policy".[60] As there can be little or no doubt that the topics dealt with in voluntary export restraints fall within the scope of the common commercial policy, the CFI's statement that the unwritten commitment was "not made within the context of the common commercial policy" probably refers to the fact that the arrangement does not take the form of an official agreement for the purposes of Article 113 EC. In view of the Community's obligation to develop a common commercial policy which is based upon *uniform* principles, Eeckhout argues that the restrictions on the export of Japanese cars to the national markets of Italy, Portugal and Spain could be justified as "transitional exceptions" towards a full liberalization of the import regime, since these Member States already had official import restrictions in place before the common commercial policy became effective. Eeckhout has serious doubts, however, whether the Community was competent under Community law to enter into a voluntary export restraint arrangement with Japan with regard to the national markets of

---

[58] Eeckhout, *supra* note 1, at 202, 214-215. Macleod, Hendry and Hyett, *supra* note 1, at 121, seem to have a somewhat different opinion as they take the position with regard to "informal or non-binding arrangements" such as "the EC-Japan Declaration" (footnote 215) that although "[t]he Treaties make no provision for the conclusion of such arrangements by the Communities ... there is no reason in principle why the Communities could not make such commitments, and the practice bears this out".

[59] *BEUC*, *supra* note 34, par. 59.

[60] *Ibidem*, par. 59.

France and the United Kingdom since these Member States did not have official quotas which preceded the establishment of the common commercial policy. Therefore, it cannot be argued that these arrangements can be qualified as "transitional exceptions".[61]

It is important to note that in Andriessen's statement, the EC side declared that the necessary measures will be taken to ensure that the operation of *EC competition law* does not constitute an obstacle to the operation of the cooperative measures on the Japanese side. Eeckhout suggests that in the absence of official quotas and Article 115 EC measures, this declaration was probably necessary in order to sanction (i) possible arrangements between Japanese car manufacturers on sharing exports to the Community in the context of the voluntary export restraint[62] and (ii) possible measures taken by Japanese car manufacturers in the context of their distribution network to control the final destination of exported cars in order to avoid that more Japanese cars than agreed will end up in Italy, Portugal, Spain, France or the United Kingdom.[63] Was the EC side in a position to give such a declaration? Is the Community competent to take common commercial policy considerations into account in the context of its competition policy and if so, to what extent?

In 1972, the Commission published a notice on imports of Japanese products in view of the rising popularity of industry-to-industry voluntary

---

[61] Eeckhout, *supra* note 1, at 215-216. See in this context the Commission's answer to Written Question E-590/95 (Nussbaumer), OJ 1995, C202/22, in which the Commission confirmed that the Austrian agreement with Japan on compensation orders for the national automobile industry terminated upon Austrian accession to the Community. At the same time, however, the Commission confirmed that it had conveyed to the Ministry of trade and industry in Japan (MITI) Austrian concerns that a sudden discontinuation would entail the risk of disruption in the business activities of Austrian car parts and component manufacturers and that this should be avoided as far as possible. The Japanese automobile manufacturers confirmed that they would continue to purchase Austrian car parts and components in so far as they are competitive both in terms of quality and price.

[62] See, however, Yamane, *supra* note 49, at 289, who suggests that MITI has been "most careful not to encourage horizontal agreements between exporters" and "has dealt with each car manufacturer through administrative guidance, although the legal status of written administrative guidance in Japanese antitrust laws has not been very firmly established".

[63] Eeckhout, *supra* note 1, at 216-221.

export restraints.[64] In its notice, the Commission reminds "those concerned" of the existence of Article 85(1) EC and gives the recommendation to notify in good time "such agreements, decisions and practices" after which the Commission will determine "whether they can be deemed compatible with the Community provisions on competition". It is important to note that the Commission added that "[a]t the same time the Commission will closely follow the development of the sectors concerned, and if need be will propose the appropriate measures of commercial policy with a view to remedying the problems in question".[65] The notice indicates that the Commission recognized that the underlying problems were of a common commercial policy nature and were not to be solved by arrangements violating Article 85(1) EC. But as long as effective common commercial policy measures were not taken, voluntary export restraints violating Community provisions on competition basicly remained the only practical solution.

In *BEUC*, the CFI qualified the SMMT/JAMA agreement on voluntary export restraints as "a meeting of minds between groupings of economic operators operating on the market" which is liable to fall within the scope of Article 85(1) and 86 EC if it has as its object or effect to restrict imports into a Member State.[66] The CFI pointed out that the SMMT/JAMA arrangements are "by their very nature, liable to impair the functioning of the common market" and added that:

> [a]s measures restricting imports into the Community and affecting the entire territory of a Member State, they are liable to interfere with the natural movement of trade, thus affecting trade between Member States,

---

[64] Commission Notice of 21 October 1972 on imports of Japanese products, OJ 1972, C111/13 (not published in the English Special Edition).

[65] From 1983 onwards, the Community obtained "export moderation assurances" from the Japanese authorities. See, *inter alia*, Written Question 1289/84 (Boot), OJ 1985, C197/2; Written Question 214/85 (Catherwood), OJ 1985, C341/5, and Written Question 2011/85 (MacSharry), OJ 1986, C150/7.

[66] *BEUC*, *supra* note 34, par. 68.

> and to reinforce the compartmentalization of markets on a national basis, thereby holding up the economic interpenetration which the Treaty is intended to bring about.[67]

One could argue that the arrangement between the Community and Japan should be seen in a similar light.[68]

Nevertheless, there are strong indications that common commercial policy considerations play an important role, if not prevail, in the application of competition law to the automobile industry. For instance, the Commission admitted that common commercial policy considerations had an impact on the block exemption for the distribution of cars. The first block exemption for the distribution of cars, Regulation 123/85, was adopted several years before the Community entered into the arrangement with Japan but was nevertheless seen by the Commission as a help for the implementation of the arrangement between the Community and Japan. The Commission noted in its 1992 Communication on the European Motor Vehicle Industry:

> If the selective distribution system were employed to allow major price differences between the various national markets it would create the risk of a sizeable parallel market emerging. This could make it considerably more difficult to implement the EC-Japan agreement. At the same time, the Commission considers that the implementation of the EC-Japan agreement calls for a system over the transitional period to ensure that the objectives of the arrangement are not endangered by large-scale importations of vehicles built in Japan. Provided that it works in a

[67] *BEUC*, *supra* note 34, at 75.

[68] As pointed out by Smith and Venables, *supra* note 41, at 136, "a quantitative restriction on imports has an inherently anticompetitive nature".

> satisfactory and efficient way, selective distribution would help in the management of the transitional period.[69]

While preparing the text of the succeeding block exemption, Regulation 1475/95, the Commission explicitly recognized that it would take into account the contribution of the selective and exclusive distribution system (part of competition policy) to the efficient management of the arrangement between the Community and Japan (part of common commercial policy).[70] In other words, the Commission admitted that while drafting the new text of the block exemption it would not only take competition considerations into account, but commercial policy considerations as well.

Furthermore, it is likely that the contents of the Commission's Notice on Intermediaries has been influenced by considerations directly related to the implementation of the arrangement between the Community and Japan.[71] It is interesting to note in this context that Commissioner Brittan has pointed out that Japanese manufacturers themselves can reduce the attraction of intermediary operations (and thereby facilitate the implementation of the arrangement) by ensuring that price differentials do not develop between different Member States. According to Commissioner Brittan, "[t]he real point .. is that even if

---

[69] See in this sense Commission's Communication to the Council and European Parliament entitled "European Motor Vehicle Industry: Situation, Issues at Stake and Proposals for Actions", COM(92) 166 final, at 17. With reference to Joined Cases 25 and 26/84, *Ford* v *Commission*, [1985] ECR 2725. Yamane, *supra* note 49, at 290, argues that the Commission's suggestion to use the block exemption as a means of preventing the flow of Japanese cars in certain 'restricted' markets could possibly be considered as a misuse.

[70] Communication from the Commission to the Council and the European Parliament on the "European Union Automobile Industry", 23 February 1994, COM(94)49 final, at 4.

[71] Clarification of the activities of motor vehicle intermediaries, OJ 1991, C329/20. According to Eeckhout, *supra* note 1, at 217-221, "[t]here is a palpable fear among the Commission and the Member States that a substantial growth in the activities of ... intermediaries may endanger the implementation of the EC-Japan arrangement". Eeckhout notes that although it is impossible to define beyond mere conjecture the role played by the existence of the arrangement in drawing up the Notice, "[o]ne would assume, ..., that the arrangement - and especially its provision which states that competition law will not obstruct the operation of the arrangement - has militated in favour of limiting the scope for large-scale intermediary activities, whereas pure competition policy considerations would normally have tended to work in favour of strengthening parallel imports in order to combat unwarranted price differences between national markets".

there is some trade in imported Japanese cars between national markets, this can be taken account of in the monitoring process during the transitional period by adjusting the number direct imports into the affected Member State in the following period".[72]

The Community cannot, however, have common commercial policy considerations completely override competition. The ECJ held in *Continental Can* that if Article 3g EC provides "for the institution of a system ensuring that competition in the Common Market is not distorted, then it requires *a fortiori* that competition must not be eliminated". The ECJ added:

> This requirement is so essential that without it numerous provisions of the Treaty would be pointless. Moreover, it corresponds to the precept of Article 2 of the Treaty according to which one of the tasks of the Community is "to promote throughout the Community a harmonious development of economic activities". Thus the restraints on competition which the Treaty allows under certain conditions because of the need to harmonize the various objectives of the Treaty, are limited by the requirements of Articles 2 and 3. Going beyond this limit involves the risk that the weakening of competition would conflict with the aims of the Common Market.[73]

The facts underlying the judgments in *BEUC* and the *Asia Motor* cases reinforce the suggestion that the Community is at the very least reluctant (officially because of "lack of Community interest") to even investigate, let alone enforce, Community competition law with regard to restrictive arrangements put in place for commercial policy reasons.[74] The Commission has created the impression that it apparently considers the possible violation of the competition rules in the

---

[72] "Speech by Sir Leon Brittan at the European Parliament conference on the future of car industry in Europe - Brussels, 5 December 1991: "The Single market for cars", Speech/91/132.

[73] Case 6/72, *Europemballage and Continental Can* v *Commission*, [1973] ECR 244, par. 24.

[74] See *BEUC, supra* note 34, and *Asia Motor I to V, supra* note 34. It was reported in "The Commission should have initiated an enquiry into the inter-professional agreement limiting Japanese car exports onto the British market", *Agence Europe*, 19 May 1994, at 14, that BEUC director Murray, noted that "the Commission cannot continue to turn a blind eye".

Community's interest and therefore refuses to investigate officially because of "lack of Community interest".

5.3.2.4 Legal Status under the WTO Agreement

For a long time, the compatibility of the arrangement between the Community and Japan with *GATT* has been questioned. Several writers have come to the conclusion that the implementation of the arrangement between the Community and Japan violates Article XI(1) GATT and could not be justified as a safeguard measure under Article XIX GATT.[75] However, the conclusion of the Uruguay Round which led to the signing of the *WTO Agreement* changed this situation. Article 11(1)(b) of the Agreement on Safeguards obliges a Member not to seek, take or maintain any voluntary export restraints, orderly marketing arrangements or any other similar measures on the export or the import side. Article 11(2) of the Agreement provides that the phasing out of these measures has to be carried out "within a period not exceeding four years after the date of entry into force of the WTO Agreement, subject to not more than one specific measure per importing Member, the duration of which shall not extend beyond 31 December 1999". The Annex to the Agreement qualifies the arrangement between the Community and Japan as a measure which has been agreed as falling under this exception. In a footnote to Article 11(2) of the Agreement, the arrangement is qualified as "[t]he only ... exception to which the European Communities is entitled".[76] This official recognition provides the arrangement between the Community and Japan with a legitimation in WTO-context.

5.4 Concluding Remarks

The Community has exclusive competence in the field of common commercial

---

[75] See, *inter alia*, Eeckhout, *supra* note 1, at 204-214.

[76] See footnote 3 to Article 11(2) of the WTO Agreement on Safeguards, OJ 1994, L336/184. The Annex "Exception referred to in paragraph 2 of Article 11" describes the relevant product as "[p]assenger cars, off road vehicles, light commercial vehicles, light trucks (up to 5 tonnes), and the same vehicles in wholly knocked-down form (CKD sets)". According to Yamane, *supra* note 49, at 280-284, 292, "[g]iven the new safeguard rules which prohibit governments from taking 'grey area' measures, industries themselves may devise means of protection giving rise to more complicated competition problems".

policy which puts it in a position to facilitate and stimulate the Community's automobile industry to compete on the global market. The Community has established common rules on export which do not restrict the exportation of automobiles and parts. On the contrary, in view of the considerable contribution of the automobile industry to the balance of payment, Community institutions actively try to facilitate and improve access to markets in third countries. This is done by using the WTO-dispute settlement system, acceding to international agreements like the revised UN-ECE Agreement, and by negotiating bilateral agreements with third countries on customs matters, competition law, and the harmonisation of technical standards and certification procedures. In addition, the Community has adopted common rules on imports which in principle do not restrict the importation of automobiles and parts.

Looking at the Community measures within the common commercial policy field, one gets the impression that the Community institutions are trying to catch up with the public authorities in the U.S.A. and Japan in supporting the "domestic" industry. The Commission seems to have taken on the role of defender of the interests of the Community's industry. In principle, there is nothing wrong with looking after these interests. However, the Commission can go too far in doing so. For instance, the Commission agreed on a voluntary export restraint-arrangement with Japan in order to provide the Community's automobile industry with a period in which it could improve its competitiveness while the importation of cars from Japan into the Community would only be gradually liberalized. In this case, policy considerations to strengthen the competitiveness of the Community's automobile industry had an overriding impact on common commercial policy measures. Under the arrangement, the importation of cars from Japan are monitored and restricted until the end of 1999. The arrangement even had a direct impact on the Community's competition policy since it declared that measures would be taken to ensure that EC competition law does not constitute an obstacle to the operation of the Japanese cooperative measures. In addition, it is likely that the content of the Commission's Notice on Intermediaries has been influenced by consideration regarding the implementation of the arrangement. There are good grounds to argue that by entering into this arrangement, the Commission violated the EC Treaty and the Community's obligations under GATT. The arrangement is now listed in the WTO Agreement as the only exception to the prohibition on voluntary export restraints, to which the Community is entitled. This seems to legitimize the arrangement.

6. UNDISTORTED COMPETITION AND THE AUTOMOBILE INDUSTRY

6.1 Introduction

Article 3(g) EC prescribes that, for the purposes set out in Article 2 EC, the activities of the Community shall include a system that ensures that competition in the internal market is not distorted. The relevant provisions laying down the rules on competition can be found in Chapter I (entitled "Rules on Competition") of Title V in Part Three of the EC Treaty.[1] The purpose of this chapter is to provide the legal background of, and thereby facilitate an understanding of Chapter 7 on "Distribution and Servicing and the Automobile Industry", Chapter 8 on "State Aid in the Automobile Industry", and Chapter 9 on "Concentration and Cooperation in the Automobile Industry". In this chapter, the focus will first be on the Community's competition policy (**6.2**), after which the rules on competition that are of particular relevance to the automobile industry will be introduced (**6.3**). Some concluding remarks will then be made (**6.4**).

6.2 Competition Policy

Competition policy sets out the objectives to be pursued by means of the rules on competition. Competition policy reflects the objectives underlying the practical application of the rules on competition.[2] The Community's competition policy is of great importance to the application of the rules on competition as the latter leave a

---

[1] There is an abundance of literature on the various aspects of the Community's rules on competition. See, *inter alia*, C. Bellamy and G. Child, *Common Market Law of Competition* (V. Rose ed.), 4th edition, 1993, Sweet & Maxwell, London; D.G. Goyder, *EC Competition Law*, 2nd edition, 1993, Clarendon Press, London; R. Whish, *Competition Law*, 3rd edition, 1993, Butterworths, London-Edinburgh, at 28-29; L. Ritter, D. Braun, R. Rawlinson, *EEC Competition Law*, Compact Edition, 1993, Kluwer Law and Taxation Publishers, Deventer-Boston; I. Van Bael and J.-F. Bellis, *Competition Law of the European Community*, 3rd edition, 1994, CCH Europe, and W. van Gerven, L. Gyselen, M. Maresceau and J. Stuyck, *Kartelrecht II-Europese Gemeenschap*, 1997, W.E.J. Tjeenk Willink.

[2] See P.J. Slot, "Sturing en Economisch Recht" in *Het Schip van Staat* (M.A.P. Bovens & W.J. Witteveen eds.), 1985, W.E.J. Tjeenk Willink, Zwolle, at 125, who used a similar technique to describe the difference between "economic law" and "economic policy". See also P. Hennipman, *De taak van de mededingingspolitiek*, 1966, De Erven F. Bohn, Haarlem; H.W. de Jong, "European competition policy: Goals and achievements" in *The structure of European industry* (H.W. de Jong ed.), 3rd revised edition, 1993, Kluwer, Dordrecht, at 399-420; D.E. Rosenthal, "Competition policy" in Europe 1992 - An American perspective (G.C. Hufbauer ed.), 1990, The Brookings Institution, Washington D.C., at 294-298, and M. Furse, "The role of competition policy: A survey", [1996] 4 ECLR, at 250-258.

considerable margin of discretion to the Community in applying the rules. Looking at the text of Articles 2 and 3(g) EC, one can only but come to the conclusion that ensuring undistorted competition through the application of the rules on competition, constitutes one of the Community's means to accomplish its task laid down in Article 2 EC.[3] The primary objective of the Community's competition policy is to pursue the objectives set out in Article 2 EC by ensuring that competition in the internal market is not distorted which leads at least in theory to an effective allocation of resources within the Community.

In practice, however, the Community applies the rules on competition with a great variety of objectives in mind, such as "single market integration", which illustrates that competition policy can contribute or even be instrumental to the implementation of other Community policies.[4] According to the Commission, the "link between Community objectives and competition policy is a two-way process" and therefore it is "inconceivable that competition policy could be applied without reference to the priorities fixed by the Community".[5] In the context of the application of Articles 85 and 86 EC, the Commission confirmed the fundamental role of the competition rules as an instrument underpinning other Community policies[6] and explicitly recognized that competition policy is an instrument which complements the Community's other policies.[7] For instance, the Commission

---

[3] See Opinion 1/91, [1991] ECR I-6102, paras. 17-18. See also D. Wyatt, A. Dashwood, *European Community Law*, 3rd edition, 1993, Sweet & Maxwell, London, at 377; Whish, *supra* note 1, at 28-29; Ritter, Braun, Rawlinson, *supra* note 1, at 2, and Bellamy and Child, *supra* note 1, at 33.

[4] See Whish, *supra* note 1, at 29. Whish gives an interesting overview of the possible functions of competition law on pages 12-16. See in this context also Goyder, *supra* note 1, at 12-14; C.-D. Ehlermann, "The contribution of EC Competition Policy to the Single Market", 29 CML Rev. 1992, at 257-282; R.B. Bouterse, *Competition and Integration - What Goals Count?* (European Monographs No. 8), 1994, Kluwer Law and Taxation Publishers, Deventer, at 1-12; R. Wesseling, "Subsidiarity in Community antitrust law: Setting the right agenda", (1997) 22 E.L.Rev (Feb), at 38-39 and 43-47, and P. Nicolaides, "The role of competition policy in economic integration" in *The competition policy of the European Community* (P. Nicolaides and A. van der Klugt eds.), 1994, EIPA, Maastricht, at 9-17. See also Communication from the Commission to the Member States on the links between regional and competition policy, OJ 1998, C90/3.

[5] XXIIIrd Report on Competition Policy, at 13, par. 2.

[6] *Ibidem*, at 44, par. 74.

[7] *Ibidem*, at 87, par. 149.

qualified competition policy to be central to the Community's industrial policy.[8] The Commission has pointed out that one aim of competition policy is to improve the international competitiveness of Community industry.[9] The message seems to be loud and clear. The Commission considers competition policy of crucial instrumental importance to the implementation of other Community policies. But how far can the Community go in having considerations of other policies override competition?

With reference to Article 3(g) EC, the ECJ held in *Continental Can* that competition within the Community may not be eliminated as competition as such is so essential that without it numerous provisions of the EC Treaty would be pointless.[10] The ECJ did not specify what kind or degree of competition should be maintained. However, in *Metro I*, the ECJ clarified that:

> [t]he requirement contained in Articles 3 and 85 ... that competition shall not be distorted implies the existence on the market of workable competition, that is to say the degree of competition necessary to ensure the observance of the basic requirements and the attainment of the objectives of the Treaty, in particular the creation of a single market achieving conditions similar to those of a domestic market.
>
> In accordance with this requirement the nature and intensiveness of competition may vary to an extent dictated by the products or services in question and the economic structure of the relevant market sectors.[11]

In short, the ECJ held that the Community is under an obligation to maintain *workable competition* as an absolute minimum degree of competition so as to ensure the observance of the basic requirements and the attainment of the

---

[8] *Ibidem*, at 19, par. 19. See also Council Conclusions of 6-7 November 1995, 11172/95(Presse 307), at 29, in which the Council welcomed initiatives to strengthen the application of competition policy as an important component of industrial competitiveness policy.

[9] See Commission communication amending the Community framework for state aid for research and development, OJ 1998, C48/2, at par. 3.

[10] See Case 6/72, *Europemballage and Continental Can* v *Commission ("Continental Can")*, [1973] ECR 244, par. 24.

[11] Case 26/76, *Metro SB-Grossmärkte* v *Commission* (*Metro I*), [1977] ECR 1905, par. 20.

objectives set out in the EC Treaty.[12] It is evident that the Community's obligation to maintain workable competition limits the extent to which the Community can establish and execute other policies to the detriment of competition within the common market. As such, workable competition can be considered the absolute minimum degree of competition to be maintained by the Community while carrying out its task and pursuing its objectives. But what constitutes workable competition?

According to Whish, certain economists which recognize the limitations of perfect competition,[13] have settled for a theory of workable competition in which the competitive arrangement that is practically attainable is pursued.[14] For instance, the economist Sosnick describes the theory of workable competition as an attempt to formulate certain normative standards which are to indicate what practically attainable states of affairs are socially desirable in the condition of individual capitalistic markets; workable competition constitutes a situation in which certain norms are fulfilled.[15] The ECJ's description in *Metro I* of what constitutes workable competition, seems to imply that there is in every specific case a minimum degree of competition which is necessary to ensure the observance of the basic requirements and the attainment of the objectives of the EC Treaty.[16]

The ECJ has confirmed several times that Article 3(g) EC envisages the

---

[12] According to P.J.G. Kapteyn and P. Verloren van Themaat, *Introduction to the law of the European Communities* (L.W. Gormley ed.), 2nd edition, 1989, Kluwer Law and Taxation Publishers, Deventer, at 509, the requirement of workable competition in the market place as a minimum requirement must be satisfied in all cases.

[13] See on the notion of "perfect competition": Whish, *supra* note 1, at 1-12; Goyder, *supra* note 1, at 8-12 and, in particular, B. de Gaay Fortman, *Theory of Competition Policy*, 1966, North-Holland Publishing Company, Amsterdam, at 41-44 and 67-70.

[14] Whish, *supra* note 1, at 11. See also De Gaay Fortman, *ibidem*, at 83-90 and, for a general overview of the literature, P.J. Uitermark, *Economische Mededinging en Algemeen Belang*, 1990, Wolters-Noordhoff, Groningen, at 170-186.

[15] S.H. Sosnick, "A critique of concepts of workable competition", 72 (1958) QJE at 383. See J.M. Clark, *Toward a Concept of Workable Competition*, 30 American Economic Review, 1940, at 241-256.

[16] See in this context R. Van den Bergh, *Economische analyse van het mededingingsrecht*, 1993 Gouda Quint, Arnhem, at 37-39, and R. Barents in Kapteyn-VerLoren van Themaat, *Inleiding tot het recht van de Europese Gemeenschappen*, 5th revised edition, 1995, Kluwer, Deventer, at 490.

maintenance of an *effective competitive structure* within the common market.[17] This probably means a structure with effective competition. But what constitutes effective competition? Wyatt and Dashwood describe effective competition as "a level of challenge from other operators sufficient to make efficiency and innovation a condition of ultimate survival as a market participant".[18] Ritter, Braun and Rawlinson emphasize that competition will only function effectively if firms make autonomous business decisions.[19] Effective competition seems to be nothing more and nothing less than the existence in a specific case of forces which create a situation in which market participants have to react in a certain manner to the forces on the market place. Effective competition presumes a certain degree of actual or potential competition amongst market participants. It is submitted that the degree or intensity of effective competition can vary depending on the conditions on the market concerned.

In its case law, the ECJ has used the term "workable competition" for the degree of competition necessary in order to ensure the observance of the basic requirements and the attainment of the objectives of the EC Treaty. The ECJ used the term "effective competition" mainly, if not exclusively, in connection with one of these Community requirements and objectives, namely the requirement laid down in Article 3(g) EC. This could imply that the two terms are not synonyms. The Community can only meet the obligation to maintain workable competition if it fullfills the requirement under Article 3(g) EC to keep an effective competitive structure in place. Effective competition is the absolute minimum degree of competition to be guaranteed under Article 3(g) EC.[20] But as in theory Community requirements and objectives *other* than Article 3(g) EC require the maintenance of a degree of competition which is higher than is needed for an effective competitive

[17] See in this sense, *inter alia*, Case 85/76, *Hoffmann-La Roche* v *Commission (Hoffmann-La Roche)*, [1979] 553, par. 125 and *Continental Can*, *supra* note 10, par. 25. See also Written Question 2532/96 (Amadeo), OJ 1997, C11/103.

[18] Wyatt and Dashwood, *supra* 1, at 377.

[19] Ritter, Braun, Rawlinson, *supra* note 1, at 11.

[20] See, *inter alia*, *Hoffmann-LaRoche*, *supra* note 17, par. 38.

structure, workable competition and effective competition are not necessarily the same.[21]

6.3 Rules on Competition with relevance to the Automobile Industry

The Community's competition policy is implemented by means of its rules on competition. Articles 85 to 94 EC form the backbone of these rules and provide the Community with legal means to ensure effective competition. The EC Treaty provides for the following *primary* rules on competition with relevance to the automobile industry: (i) Articles 85 to 89 EC on restrictive agreements, decisions or practices (**6.3.1**) and abuse of a dominant position (**6.3.2**), and (ii) Articles 92 to 94 EC on state aids (**6.3.3**). It should be kept in mind that Article 5 EC, in conjunction with Articles 3(g), 85 and 86 EC, requires Member States not to introduce or maintain in force measures, even of a legislative nature, which may render ineffective the competition rules applicable to undertakings.[22] In addition to these primary rules, various *secondary* sources of rules on competition are of importance. For instance, on the basis of Articles 87 and 235 EC, a Regulation was adopted laying down rules for merger control (**6.3.4**).

6.3.1 Restrictive Agreements, Decisions or Practices

Article 85(1) EC lays down a directly effective prohibition of all agreements between undertakings, decisions by associations of undertakings and concerted practices which may affect trade between Member States and which have as their object or effect the prevention, restriction or distortion of competition within the common market. In its case law, the ECJ provided a basis for a so-called *de minimis* rule that, in short, implies that an arrangement falls outside the scope of the prohibition of Article 85(1) EC when it only has an insignificant effect on the market.[23]

Article 85(2) EC provides that any agreement or decision prohibited by

---

[21] Some legal commentators consider workable competition to be identical to effective competition. See, *inter alia*, Bouterse, *supra* note 4, at 24, footnote 50.

[22] See, *inter alia*, Case 267/86, *Van Eycke* v *ASPA*, [1988] ECR 4791, paras. 15-16.

[23] Case 5/69, *Völk* v *Vervaecke*, [1969] ECR 302, par. 7. See Notice on agreements of minor importance which do not fall within the meaning of Article 85(1) of the Treaty establishing the European Community, OJ 1997, C372/13.

Article 85(1) EC is automatically void. Only those provisions which constitute a violation of Article 85(1) EC and do not appear to be severable from the agreement itself, render the whole agreement void. It is up to the national courts to implement this rule.[24]

According to Article 85(3) EC, only those agreements, decisions and practices can be exempted from the prohibition laid down in Article 85(1) EC, which contribute to improving the production or distribution of goods or to promoting technical or economic progress, while allowing consumers a fair share of the resulting benefit, and which do not (i) impose on the undertakings concerned restrictions which are not indispensable to the attainment of these objectives, nor (ii) afford such undertakings the possibility of eliminating competition in respect of a substantial part of the products in question. The Commission has the exclusive competence to grant individual exemptions on the basis of Article 85(3) EC.[25] In addition, the Commission is competent to grant so-called block or group exemptions for certain categories of agreements, on the basis of Regulation 19/65.[26] The Commission can do so after it has gained sufficient experience in the light of individual decisions so that it has become possible to define categories in respect of which the conditions of Article 85(3) EC may be considered as being fulfilled.[27] For instance, the Commission adopted a block exemption for the distribution and servicing of automobiles and spare parts thereof.

Over the years, the Commission has used its competence to grant exemptions under Article 85(3) EC, to pursue various interests such as the implementation of common commercial policy interests, the strengthening of the competitiveness of Community industry and the promotion of research and technological development. Although the Community's discretionary power under Article 85(3) EC can be used to pursue various policy interests, it should be kept in mind that the ECJ held in *Metro I* that:

> [t]he powers conferred upon the Commission under Article 85(3) show

---

[24] See in this context Joined Cases 56 and 58/64, *Consten and Grundig* v *Commission*, [1966] ECR 299.

[25] See Article 9(1) of Council Regulation 17/62, OJ Special English Edition 1962, 204/62, at 87.

[26] Council Regulation 19/65 of 2 March 1965 on application of Article 85(3) EC to certain categories of agreements and concerted practices, OJ Special English Edition 1965-66, 35.

[27] *Ibidem*, fourth "Whereas". See also Goyder, *supra* note 1, at 64.

> that the requirements for the maintenance of workable competition may be reconciled with the safeguarding of objectives of a different nature and that to this end certain restrictions on competition are permissible, provided that they are essential to the attainment of those objectives and that they do not result in the elimination of competition for a substantial part of the Common Market.[28]

In short, Article 85(3) EC can be used as a policy instrument provided that the restrictions on competition are essential and do not eliminate competition for a substantial part of the Common Market.

6.3.2 Abuse of Dominant Position

Article 86 EC provides for a directly effective prohibition of any abuse by one or more undertakings of a dominant position within a substantial part of the common market in so far as it may affect trade between Member States. Article 86 EC does not provide for an exception to the prohibition.

6.3.3 State Aids

Articles 92 to 94 EC provide for rules on state aids. Pursuant to Article 92(1) EC, save as otherwise provided in the EC Treaty, any aid granted by a Member State or through State resources in any form whatsoever, which distorts or threatens to distort competition by favouring certain undertakings or the production of certain goods shall, in so far as it affects trade between Member States, be incompatible with the common market. Article 92(2) EC lists three specific types of state aid which *shall* be compatible with the common market, whereas Article 92(3) EC lists five types which *may* be considered compatible with the common market.

According to Article 93(1) EC, the Commission shall, in cooperation with Member States, keep under constant review all systems of aid existing in those States. Furthermore, it shall propose to the latter any appropriate measures required by the progressive development or by the functioning of the common market. The Commission decided to introduce "appropriate measures" with regard

---

[28] *Metro I*, *supra* note 11, par. 21. See also Case 75/84, *Metro SB-Grossmärkte* v *Commission*, [1986] ECR 3085, par. 42.

to the automobile industry and informed the Member States of its decision to implement the Community Framework on State Aid to the Motor Vehicle Industry. Article 93(3) EC provides that the Commission shall be informed, in sufficient time to enable it to submit its comments, of any plans to grant or alter aid. If the Commission considers that any such plan is not compatible with the common market having regard to Article 92 EC, it shall without delay initiate the procedure provided for in Article 93(2) EC. Only after this procedure has resulted in a final decision, the Member State concerned may put its proposed measures into effect.

If the Commission finds that a state aid is not compatible with the common market having regard to Article 92 EC, or that such aid is being misused, it shall decide, in accordance with Article 93(2) EC, that the State concerned shall abolish or alter such aid within a specific period of time. If the Member State concerned does not comply with this decision within the prescribed time, the Commission or any other interested State may refer the matter to the ECJ directly. However, on application by a Member State, the Council may decide that the aid which that Member State is granting or intends to grant shall be considered to be compatible with the common market, if such a decision is justified by exceptional circumstances.

Based on Article 94 EC, the Council may make any appropriate regulations for the application of Articles 92 and 93 EC and may in particular determine the conditions in which Article 93(3) EC shall apply and the categories of aid exempted from this procedure. In doing so, the Council has to act by a qualified majority on a proposal from the Commission and after consulting the European Parliament.

6.3.4 Merger Control

The Merger Regulation introduced a new regime for the control at Community level of concentrations with a Community dimension.[29] The Merger Regulation also covers restrictions directly related and necessary to the implementation of the concentration. Under the Merger Regulation the Commission has to establish whether notified concentrations falling within the scope of the Merger Regulation are compatible with the common market. In doing so, the Commission has to take

---

[29] Council Regulation 4064/89 of 21 December 1989 on the control of concentrations between undertakings, OJ 1989, L395/1. The corrected text was published in OJ 1990, L257/13. Amended by Council Regulation 1310/97 of 30 June 1997, OJ 1997, L180/1.

account of (a) the need to maintain and develop effective competition within the common market in view of, among other things, the structure of all the markets concerned and the actual or potential competition from undertakings located either within or outwith the Community, and (b) the market position of the undertakings concerned and their economic and financial power, the alternatives available to suppliers and users, their access to supplies or markets, any legal or other barriers to entry, supply and demand trends for the relevant goods and services, the interests of the intermediate and ultimate consumers, and the development of technical and economic progress provided that it is to consumers' advantage and does not form an obstacle to competition. The Commission has to examine whether a concentration creates or strengthens a dominant position as a result of which effective competition would be significantly impeded in the common market or in a substantial part thereof. If so, the concentration will be declared incompatible with the common market. If not, the concentration will be declared compatible with the common market.

6.4 Concluding Remarks

The Community's competition policy reflects the objectives underlying the practical application of the rules on competition. Article 3(g) EC puts the Community under an obligation to ensure that competition in the internal market is not distorted, and envisages the maintenance of an effective competitive market structure. Effective competition in the market is the absolute minimum degree of competition to be guaranteed under Article 3(g) EC. But Community requirements and objectives other than Article 3(g) EC can require the maintenance of "workable competition" which is a degree of competition that can be higher, but in any case cannot be lower, than is needed for the maintenance of effective competition. Although the Community uses its discretionary power under the rules on competition as an instrument to pursue a great variety of objectives such as common commercial policy interests, the strengthening of the competitiveness of Community industry and the promotion of research and technological development, it can never go so far as to eliminate an effective competitive market structure. The manner in which the Community deals with distribution and servicing, state aid, and concentration and cooperation in the automobile industry, will illustrate the use and abuse of the application of the Community's competition rules for the implementation of a variety of the Community's other policies.

7. DISTRIBUTION AND SERVICING AND THE AUTOMOBILE INDUSTRY

7.1 Introduction

This chapter will describe and analyze the manner in which the Community applies Articles 85 and 86 EC to the distribution and servicing of automobiles and parts within the framework of the EC Treaty. After a short introduction to distribution and servicing of automobiles and parts (**7.2**), a summary will be given of the four important Commission decisions that set the stage for the block exemption of Regulation 123/85 (**7.3.1**). Subsequently, the focus will be on the technical contents of Regulation 123/85 (**7.3.2**) and the various detailed amendments introduced by Regulation 1475/95 (**7.3.3**). The manner in which Article 86 EC is applied within the context of the distribution and servicing of automobiles and parts will then be examined (**7.4**). At the end of this chapter, concluding remarks will be made (**7.5**).

7.2 Distribution and Servicing of Automobiles and Spare Parts

The distribution and servicing of automobiles and parts takes place in a so-called pyramidal structure which includes various actors such as car manufacturers, importers, distributors, dealers and possibly sub-dealers. Whereas domestic manufacturers usually organize their own distribution system, foreign manufacturers tend to arrange distribution through (in)dependent importers or distributors. In most cases, the distributor at the top of the pyramid, usually the domestic car manufacturer or the (in)dependent importer or distributor, tends to keep a firm grip on the distribution pyramid with at the bottom the individual (sub)dealers at retail level.[1]

It has been reported that, although the many manufacturers within the Community had different marketing and distribution strategies, a common core of marketing philosophy developed over the years with commonly defined views as to the usefulness of selective distribution schemes and certain vertical restraints therein. Apparently, the purest and most sophisticated version of this strategy, the "package" or "single product" theory, was pursued by German

[1] See Commission Decision of 21 January 1992 (Inchcape/IEP), Case IV/M182, par. 8 (OJ 1992, C21/27).

manufacturers.[2] Under this theory, the sale of new cars can best be achieved by ensuring prospective buyers that a dense network of qualified workshops is in place to service their cars and that the full line of spare parts is readily available over a reasonably long period of time. In short, the manufacturer does not simply offer a car but a "package" which includes a new car. Over the years, this "package" theory encouraged manufacturers to build up one-make distribution networks including after-sales services, to closely cooperate with their authorized workshops and to offer buyers a well organized logistic for spare parts.[3] However, as the Commission did not accept this "package" theory, different systems were adopted for the sale of new cars and the sale of spare parts.[4]

In recent years, there is a tendency amongst manufacturers to further tighten control on their distribution system. Manufacturers have importers and distributors closely cooperate[5] and increasingly acquire control of importers and distributors in order to gain complete control over all aspects of marketing, sales and financial management, to improve coherence between headquarters and local or national priorities, to bring manufacturing and distribution margins

---

[2] See C. Joerges, E. Hiller, K. Holzscheck and H.-W. Micklitz, *Vertriebspraktiken im Automobilersatzteilsektor - Ihre Auswirkungen auf die Interessen der Verbraucher*, 1985, Verlag Peter Lang, Frankfurt am Main, at 361-362.

[3] *Ibidem*, at 362.

[4] *Ibidem*, at 364.

[5] For instance, manufacturers encourage dealers to computerize their operations which allows for activities such as central filing of customers and stock management. See Case T-574/93, *Nouveau Garage and Max Labat* v *Commission*, OJ 1994, C43/12, with regard to a complaint that VAG France encouraged dealers to take a licence of the Vaudis software which gave VAG France full knowledge of its dealers' customers and included an automatic management of stock which allegedly interfered with the dealers' freedom in obtaining supplies of spare parts (see OJ 1994, C161/15). See also Case T-32/90, *OEC Nederland* v *Commission*, OJ 1990, C288/10, on OEC Nederland's complaint that Mitsubishi dealers wishing to computerize their operations were compelled to do so with Nixdorf and to refrain from using the software developed by OEC Nederland (see OJ 1991, C67/7). See *O.E.C. Nederland B.V.* v *Hart Nibbrig & Greeve B.V.*, District Court of The Hague (Nr. 89/6365), 17 October 1990.

within the control of a single organization,[6] and to maintain a competitive global and strategic pricing policy.[7] It has been reported that as "the cost of selling a car accounts for up to 30% of the total", the distribution of cars is "ripe for efficiency gains".[8]

7.3 Article 85 EC

7.3.1 The Early Days

Initially, the creation of a common market was the primary concern of the Community in its dealings with motor vehicle distribution and servicing agreements under Article 85 EC. Commission decisions BMW Germany, BMW Belgium, Ford and Peugeot illustrate the manner in which barriers to intra-

inside

[6] Agreements between members of a group fall outside the scope of Article 85(1) EC. See Case 48/69, *ICI* v *Commission*, [1972] ECR 619, par. 134; Case T-102/92, *Viho Europe* v *Commission*, [1995] ECR II-17, and Case C-73/95P, *Viho Europe* v *Commission*, [1996] ECR I-5457. See in this context R. Treacy and T. Feaster, "When two into one will go: Intra-group agreements and Article 85(1)", (1997) 22 E.L.Rev., at 573-578.

[7] See Commission Decision of 21 May 1992 (Volvo/Lex UK), Case IV/M224, par. 7 (OJ 1992, C142/18), and Commission Decision of 3 September 1992 (Volvo/Lex Ir), Case IV/M261, par. 7. There are multiple examples of car manufacturers taking control of their main importers/distributors such as Commission Decision of 28 June 1991 (Nissan/R. Nissan), Case IV/M099 (OJ 1991, C181/21); Commission Decision of 4 February 1993 (Volkswagen/VAG UK), Case IV/M304 (OJ 1993, C38/12); Commission Decision of 1 July 1993 (Toyota Motor Corp./Walter Frey/Toyota France), Case IV/M326 (OJ 1993, C187/4); Commission Decision of 7 March 1994 (Ford/Hertz), Case IV/M397 (OJ 1994, C121/4), and "Mitsubishi neemt Nederlandse import zelf ter hand", *Het Financieele Dagblad*, 25 February 1997, at 3. See also Case IV/M1036, OJ 1997, C369/5 (Chrysler/Distributiors (BeNeLux and Germany)) and *Agence Europe*, "Chrysler may directly control the sale and distribution of its cars and jeeps in Germany and the Benelux", 22-23 December 1997, at 13. *The Economist*, "Limited mileage", 18 January 1997, at 67, reported that whereas in the late 1980s rental firms were the perfect partner for the automobile industry, later when the sales recovered the costs of rental firms soared. As a result, Ford sold its Budget Rent a Car group and Chrysler is trying to sell Thrifty Rent-A-Car System and Dollar System.

[8] *FT*, "Dealing with the car dealers", 4 March 1998, at 13; "Why maps are being redrawn" (FT Auto), 11 May 1998, at XI, and "Ford to open 'one-stop' shops", 15-16 August 1998, at 4.

Community trade and to parallel imports in particular, were removed.[9] These Commission decisions were to be the stepping-stone for the block-exemption for motor vehicle distribution and servicing agreements.

7.3.1.1 BMW Germany[10]

In 1963, BMW notified the Commission with its distribution agreements used in Germany for the sale and service of its products including automobiles. Only in March 1972, the Commission sent BMW a statement of objections which was primarily focused on an *export ban* that obliged dealers in Germany, not to deliver new BMW automobiles to countries other than their own. The Commission considered this export ban to violate Article 85(1) EC. With regard to Article 85(3) EC, the Commission noted that the export ban led to a form of territorial protection enabling different retail prices to be charged in the various Member States, which did not guarantee consumers a fair share of the benefits which might otherwise have resulted from the exclusive dealing agreements. The Commission noted that the export ban was not indispensable for the improvement of distribution and protection of the BMW products, and refused the request for an individual exemption under Article 85(3) EC.

Subsequently, BMW notified its revised distribution agreements; an agreement between BMW and its main dealers, and an agreement to be used when appointing retail dealers. These agreements were almost identical but did not include an export ban. In its decision, the Commission first described in great detail the various provisions of the agreements which included objective criteria and minimum requirements to be applied uniformly, for the selection of BMW dealers in Germany. Under the agreements, BMW kept the right to choose amongst those dealers which were prepared to comply with these criteria

---

[9] The ECJ held in Case C-373/90, *Criminal Proceedings against X*, [1992] ECR I-149, par. 12, that "parallel imports enjoy a certain amount of protection in Community law because they encourage trade and help reinforce competition". See also Ist Report on Competition Policy, at 55; IVth Report on Competition Policy, at 24, and XIVth Report on Competition Policy, at 64, par. 69.

[10] Commission Decision 75/73 of 13 December 1974 (IV/14.650 - Bayerische Motoren Werke AG), OJ 1975, L29/1. Joerges, Hiller, Holzscheck and Micklitz, *supra* note 2, at 364, footnote 51, noted that this decision indicates that the Commission did not subscribe to the "package" theory in view of the fact that differentiated safeguards were applied to the sale of new cars and the sale of spare parts.

and requirements. BMW assigned to each dealer a specific territory and obliged dealers not to sell goods to independent dealers with the exception of original BMW parts for repair purposes only. BMW restricted the dealers' freedom to sell competing products and to promote sales outside their territory, even in respect of customers and BMW dealers appointed in countries other than Germany.

According to the Commission, the following obligations undertaken by BMW dealers, if normally applied, did not infringe Article 85(1) EC:

- the obligation to follow BMW's instructions regarding advertising designed to draw attention to BMW products and their properties (not including advertising on prices and conditions of sale);
- the obligation to use BMW's trade marks in a specified manner;
- the obligation to supply BMW with information on their trading position, sales trends, the market situation, stocks and expected demand.

The Commission considered BMW's power to terminate the agreement for substantial breach, and to alter the territory or instal further dealers in the territory, not to have a restrictive effect on competition as long as such power did not amount to an economic sanction which could be used to impose more extensive restrictions on dealers than those apparent from the wording of the agreements.

The Commission took the position that other provisions of the agreements infringed Article 85(1) EC and examined whether BMW's selective distribution system could be exempted under Article 85(3) EC. First, the Commission recognized that the selective distribution system contributed both to *improving the production and distribution of goods* and to *promoting technical progress* as, by means of limiting the number of dealers to those meeting the selective criteria, BMW was in a position to ensure:

- receipt and storage of BMW models in technically perfect condition;
- delivery to customers after a BMW pre-delivery check;
- sufficient availability and adequate quality for the consumer of

maintenance, preparation and services under guarantee and extended free service;
- the carrying out of any necessary modifications of the automobiles;
- sufficient availability of plant, equipment and BMW-trained personnel for the services concerned;
- the storage of spare parts which is adequate in range and quality;
- rapid and full information of appointed dealers of technical problems as they arise.

The Commission accepted BMW's reservation of the right to make individual appointments of *main* dealers from those applicants satisfying the objective requirements for BMW dealers, on the basis of considerations for which there were no universally predictable and objective criteria. In addition, the Commission noted that BMW's restrictive influence on the selection of *retail* dealers by its main dealers, facilitated rationalization, as BMW also cooperated directly with these retail dealers in order to improve service. The Commission considered the cooperation between BMW and its dealers to be a major factor in justifying BMW's selective distribution system as the cooperation was also aimed at improving service which went beyond the mere marketing of the products. In short, the Commission considered the selective distribution system as a method to rationalize the sale and servicing of BMW products and, thereby, provide better service to the consumer than a system of free marketing to which cooperation regarding marketing and servicing, was not attached.

Only after having made these observations, the Commission focused on the *characteristics* of the product concerned and qualified automobiles as products of limited life, high cost and complex technology, which require regular maintenance by specially equipped garages or service depots, because their use can be dangerous to life, health and property and can have a harmful effect on the environment. Therefore, the Commission considered it of importance that those responsible for the maintenance were made aware of the latest technical knowledge that the manufacturer acquired while developing and constructing the automobile. The Commission stressed that the continual cooperation between BMW and its dealers could assist BMW in preparing maintenance instructions and training programmes, and could even lead to improvements in the design. The Commission exempted clauses under Article 85(3) EC which contained:

- an obligation on dealers not to deal in competing products without BMW's consent;
- restrictions on dealers from taking certain measures to promote sales outside their territory;
- obligation on BMW not to sell automobiles directly to consumers;
- obligation on BMW of prior notification and to provide an opportunity to comment, before changing the territory, setting up branches or appointing further dealers in the territory.

Subsequently, the Commission noted that *consumers* received a *fair share of the benefit* resulting from the improvements and progress achieved through BMW's agreements in the form of improved service and through adequate competition at the distribution level which guaranteed that there remained a pressure to pass on to consumers the benefits resulting from rationalization. According to the Commission, "adequate competition" would remain as consumers were free to purchase goods and request service wherever they wished within the common market, and BMW dealers were free to purchase BMW products from other BMW dealers anywhere in the common market. In addition, consumers were free to choose parts of other makes than BMW, unless they were of particular importance for the safety of BMW automobiles and did not satisfy the standards of quality of BMW parts.

The Commission qualified the restrictions imposed on the parties to the agreements as *indispensable* for the attainment of the improvements and technical progress and pointed out that in operating a selective distribution system, BMW was doing no more than ensuring that, in addition and parallel to servicing by independent third parties, there was a service network available to the consumer which could provide the kind of service which BMW considered necessary for the maintenance and safety of its automobiles. The Commission emphasized that since consumers had complete freedom in purchasing BMW products within the common market and could take delivery from any undertaking they wished to act on their behalf, the restrictions inherent in BMW's selective distribution system were in this respect limited to their essential content. According to the Commission, the agreements did not provide the parties with the *opportunity to eliminate competition* in respect of a substantial part of the goods concerned as the BMW automobiles competed with a range of other automobiles and such competition was maintained at the various levels of distribution within the BMW network.

7.3.1.2 BMW Belgium[11]

In 1975, BMW Belgium notified its distribution agreement which largely corresponded to the BMW Germany-agreements. As a result of Belgian price controls, the retail prices for new cars in Belgium were lower than in other Member States. Consumers in other Member States purchased BMW-cars directly from BMW dealers in Belgium or used the services of intermediairies to do so. Belgian BMW dealers sold new BMW-cars to recognized BMW dealers as well as to independent dealers from outside the BMW distribution network. The Head Office of BMW received complaints from BMW dealers in Member States other than Belgium about the fact that they were obliged to provide guarantee service on BMW-cars that they had not sold themselves. After BMW's Head Office informed BMW Belgium that under the notified distribution agreement no BMW dealer was allowed to sell to *un*authorized dealers, BMW Belgium sent out a circular to BMW dealers in Belgium with the request to confirm that no cars would be sold "outside Belgium or to firms who propose to export them". A large number of Belgian BMW dealers did so. A few months later, BMW Belgium sent out another circular stating that the previous circular should be regarded as null and void "in so far as it might be construed as an export prohibition".

After a complaint, the Commission took a formal decision in which it took the position that BMW Belgium and its dealers had infringed Article 85(1) EC. In its decision, the Commission noted that it would:

> exempt selective distribution systems in the motor industry under Article 85(3) .., regarding the restrictions of competition inherent

[11] Commission Decision 78/155 of 23 December 1977 (IV/29.146 - BMW Belgium NV and Belgian BMW dealers), OJ 1978, L46/33.

> therein as indispensable for that purpose, only if there is no other restriction on the freedom of consumers to buy new cars anywhere in the common market or to effect such purchases by agents. An exemption always requires an examination as to whether potential competition remains between all the selected dealers in the common market, so that they are compelled through competitive pressures to react to each other's price structures and to respond to low prices quoted by other dealers.[12]

BMW initiated proceedings in order to have the Commission's decision declared void but the ECJ confirmed the Commission decision.[13]

7.3.1.3 Ford

In 1976, Ford notified to the Commission a Main Dealer Agreement which formed the basis of its selective distribution system in Germany. The agreement provided for: (i) the selection of dealers on qualitative and quantitative grounds; (ii) the allocation of an agreed territory to selected dealers; (iii) a ban on the sale of competing products; (iv) a ban on the sale of Ford-cars to dealers outside the distribution system and (v) a ban on certain marketing activities outside the agreed territory. Several years later, in 1982, the Commission opened an investigation into Ford's decision to stop the distribution of right-hand drive ("RHD") automobiles on Continental Europe thereby restricting the parallel importation of these RHD-vehicles into the United Kingdom. Ford had taken this decision on request of Ford Britain so as to keep up price levels in the United Kingdom, and to encourage dealers to focus their sales promotion efforts

---

[12] *Ibidem*, par. 21. See also Commission Decision 83/361 of 13 July 1983 (IV/30.174 - Vimpolty), OJ 1983, L200/44; Commission Decision 85/79 of 14 December 1984 (IV/30.809 - John Deere), OJ 1985, L35/58; Commission Decision 85/617 of 16 December 1985 (IV/30.839 - Sperry New Holland), OJ 1985, L376/21 and Commission Decision 93/46 of 15 December 1992 (IV/31.400 - Ford Agricultural), OJ 1993, L20/1, regarding various measures to restrict parallel trading in farm equipment (including agricultural tractors). See also Commission Decision 79/68 of 12 December 1978 (IV/29.430 - Kawasaki), OJ 1979, L16/9, in which the Commission decided that the export prohibition of Kawasaki Motors (UK) Ltd on its dealers in the United Kingdom, violated Article 85(1) EC.

[13] Joined Cases 32/78 and 36 to 82/78, *BMW Belgium and others* v *Commission*, [1979] ECR 2435.

in their own marketing territory. In a circular, Ford recommended its German dealers, as from 1 May 1982, to refer customers who asked for a RHD-vehicle, to Ford Personal Import and Export in London. The latter, however, only supplied a very limited group of customers with RHD-vehicles.

Out of fear that other manufacturers would follow Ford's example and in reaction to the numerous complaints and publications in the press which qualified Ford's measures as a challenge to the whole scheme of competition upheld by the Communty and its institutions,[14] the Commission decided to take interim measures and ordered Ford to withdraw its circular and inform its dealers in Germany that RHD-vehicles were still part of the agreed delivery range.[15] Ford took legal action against the Commission's decision and initiated, at the same time, summary proceedings in order to have the operation of the Commission's decision suspended. Ford was partly successfull in having the operation of the decision suspended[16] and succeeded in having the ECJ declare the decision void in view of the fact that the Commission had not remained within the limits of its powers to take interim measures.[17]

On 16 November 1983, the Commission refused to exempt Ford's Main Dealer Agreement as operated since 1 May 1982, under Article 85(3) EC.[18] The Commission argued that the most important part of the Main Dealer Agreement violated Article 85(1) EC and noted that in applying Article 85(3) EC, agreements have to be looked at in the light of all relevant circumstances. The Commission stressed that "of all the factors that must be taken into account, priority must be given to the issue of whether a party has restricted competition by impeding parallel imports"[19] as this has an important impact on intra-brand

---

[14] Fiat and Alfa Romea did follow Ford's example in making it more difficult, if not impossible, to purchase RHD automobiles in Luxembourg and Belgium for use in the United Kingdom. See XIVth Report on Competition Policy, at 65, paras. 71-72.

[15] Commission Decision 82/628 of 18 August 1982 (IV/30.696 - Distribution system of Ford Werke AG), OJ 1982, L256/20.

[16] Joined Cases 229 and 228/82 R, *Ford* v *Commission*, [1982] ECR 3091.

[17] Joined Cases 228 and 229/82, *Ford* v *Commission*, [1984] ECR 1129.

[18] Commission Decision 83/560 of 16 November 1983 (IV/30.696 - Distribution system of Ford Werke AG), OJ 1983, L327/31.

[19] *Ibidem*, par. 36.

price competition and therefore on the benefits of the agreement to consumers throughout the Community, not just in one Member State. The Commission found that:

> [i]n balancing the improvement in distribution of cars resulting from the agreement - and the share in those advantages allowed to consumers - against the disadvantages in all the legal and economic circumstances, ... Ford Germany's distribution system as applied since 1 May 1982 does not allow adequate competition at the distribution level, because it is no longer possible to buy RHD Ford cars in Germany at the very significantly lower German prices .. and so, the competitive pressure in the United Kingdom is significantly reduced.[20]

The Commission considered Ford's refusal to supply dealers in Germany with RHD automobiles suitable for export, as an instrument to partition the common market artificially, and refused to grant an exemption under Article 85(3) EC. The Commission ordered Ford to bring the infringement of Article 85(1) EC to an end. Ford initiated legal action but the ECJ confirmed the Commission's decision.[21]

7.3.1.4 Peugeot[22]

In 1963, Peugeot notified to the Commission its distribution agreement for France. Upon receipt of Commission's objections, Peugeot brought the agreement in line with the principles formulated in the BMW Germany Decision and deleted certain clauses including an export ban. In 1971, Peugeot provided the Commission with a copy of its distribution agreement for the Benelux. This agreement included a provision in which Peugeot reserved the right to sell its products to certain categories of purchasers such as those under transit arrangements "direct or through a specialized company". For this purpose, Peugeot had incorporated Sodexa which handled the sale of Peugeot and Talbot-

---

[20] *Ibidem*, par. 43.

[21] Joined Cases 25 and 26/84, *Ford* v *Commission*, [1985] ECR 2725.

[22] Commission Decision 86/506 of 25 September 1986 (IV/31.143 - Peugeot), OJ 1986, L295/19.

cars to purchasers temporarily resident in France. Dealers in Member States other than the United Kingdom, Belgium and Luxembourg, were unable to purchase right-hand drive ("RHD") vehicles directly from Peugeot. Instead, they had to send an order to Sodexa, which subsequently exercised the direct selling right reserved by Peugeot.

In 1982 and 1983, the prices for Peugeot and Talbot-cars in the United Kingdom were substantially higher than those in the Benelux which led to an increased demand for RHD-vehicles by British customers in the Benelux. In May 1982, Peugeot put the brakes on the increased demand of British customers in the Benelux by effectively blocking parallel imports into the United Kingdom. The Commission initiated proceedings and came to the conclusion that Peugeot's distribution agreement violated Article 85(1) EC. According to the Commission, Peugeot's ban of parallel imports of RHD-vehicles into the United Kingdom, considerably magnified both the restrictive effects of the contractual provisions and the degree to which trade between Member States was affected.

The Commission refused to exempt the distribution agreement under Article 85(3) EC and repeated that agreements like Peugeot's standard distribution agreement for the Benelux could in theory be exempted but that such was *not* the case if dealers were unable to order new cars of the make in question to satisfy demand of nationals of another Member State where such makes were marketed as well. According to the Commission, a manufacturer who reduces the supply of cars and the opportunities for purchasing them, by making use of the differences in the specifications of specific models with a view to controlling their outlets, and who limits the availability of respectively RHD or LHD-vehicles from his dealers, creates a situation in which the favourable effects which can in theory flow from a selective and exclusive distribution system, are nullified. The Commission took the position that the measures taken by Peugeot led to a partitioning of the market and the obstacles placed in the way of the supply of cars to purchasers resident in the United Kingdom made the restrictions on competition attached to the Peugeot distribution system not to be exemptable under Article 85(3) EC.

7.3.2 Regulation 123/85

7.3.2.1 Prelude

The preamble to Council Regulation 19/65 that provides the Commission with the competence to declare that Article 85(1) shall not apply to certain categories of agreements, illustrates that the Council was aware of the fact that the Commission was faced with a bulk of notifications submitted under Regulation 17/62 for evaluation under Article 85 EC.[23] In the preamble, the Council first recognized that the Commission's task had to be facilitated by enabling it to declare by way of regulation that the provisions of article 85(1) EC do not apply to certain categories of agreements and concerted practices, and then specified that the Commission "may exercise such powers after sufficient experience has been gained in the light of individual decisions and it becomes possible to define categories of agreements and concerted practices in respect of which the conditions of article 85(3) may be considered as being fulfilled".[24]

It was to be expected that the Commission, faced with the task of evaluating the large amount of notified motor vehicle distribution agreements, would use its competence under Regulation 19/65 as soon as possible to relieve itself from the burden to examine all these agreements individually under Article 85(3) EC, and create at the same time some measure of legal certainty in the automobile industry. The Commission announced in its IXth Report on Competition Policy that the experience gained with the BMW Germany Decision, would be used to establish principles to reflect the so-called need of the automobile industry.[25] Although there is no block exemption for selective distribution agreements as such, the Commission considered the selective distribution of automobiles and parts to be of such a special nature that a block

---

[23] Council Regulation 19/65 of 2 March 1965, OJ Special English Edition 1965-66, 35. See Case 32/65, *Italy* v *Council and Commission*, [1966] ECR 404-409.

[24] *Ibidem*, Whereas (4).

[25] IXth Report on Competition Policy, at 57-59. In its XVIIth Report on Competition Policy, at 39, par. 34, the Commission confirmed that "[o]ne of the purposes of the block exemption Regulation, and of the enabling legislation, Council Regulation 19/65/EEC, on which it was based, was to relieve the Commission of the administrative burden of dealing with large numbers of notifications without it having to take individual decisions in each case".

exemption was justified.[26] On 24 June 1983, the Commission published its first official draft for a block exemption for motor vehicle distribution and servicing agreements.[27] According to Lukoff, this first draft "strongly bore the imprint of the consumer organizations".[28] The draft triggered a heated debate which not only took place behind closed doors but also in national newspapers such as *The Times* and the *Financial Times*.[29] This public interest was to be expected as there is probably no block exemption of a greater immediate interest to so many millions of consumers. For most consumers, purchasing an automobile is still the most expensive consumer purchase in their lives.[30] The heated debate led to some major amendments to the first draft. The fact that "industry positions on pricing differentials and the legitimacy of selective distribution in the car sector" were now taken into consideration led Lukoff to the conclusion: "The monster has been tamed".[31] The final text of Regulation 123/85 on the application of

---

[26] G. Rocca pointed out in "La politique communautaire de concurrence en matière de distribution" in "Proceedings of the Second Seminar on European Union/Japan Competition Policy" (Brussel, 16 September 1994), at 54, that "[p]endant longtemps, la distribution sélective a été essentiellement utilisée pour commercialiser soit des produits de haute technicité, soit des article de luxe. En raison de la spécificité des secteurs concernés, la Commission n'a pas estimé opportun d'adopter un règlement d'exemption de portée générale, mais elle a suivi une approche cas par cas. La seule exception à cette approche pragmatique est constituée par le secteur automobile qui, à cause de son importance économique et des caractéristiques 'techniques' de ses réseaux de distribution, a fait l'objet d'une réglementation ad hoc [le règlement (CEE) n 123/85] aujourd'hui en voie de révision".

[27] OJ 1983, C165/2. The block exemption was thoroughly examined in the Member States as illustrated by the 27th report, 1984, entitled "The distribution, servicing and pricing of motor vehicles", of the House of Lords Select Committee on the European Communities.

[28] F.L. Lukoff, "European Competition Law And Distribution In The Motor Vehicle Sector: Commission Regulation 123/85 of 12 December 1984", 23 CML Rev. 1986, at 865. P. Groves, "Motor Vehicle Distribution: The Block Exemption", [1987] ECLR at 86, pointed out on page 78 that "[t]he Regulation was designed from the first to create a common market in cars regardless of what happened in other sectors".

[29] See Groves, *ibidem*, at 77, footnote 3. See also the XIIIth Report on Competition Policy, at 42.

[30] According to J.P. Womack, D.T. Jones and D. Roos, *The Machine That Changed The World*, 1991, Harper Perennial, New York, at 180, "our homes, the other big-ticket item in our personal consumption, usually appreciate in value, while our cars depreciate over a decade or less to near worthlessness".

[31] Lukoff, *supra* note 28. However, M.N. Jovanovic, *European economic integration - Limits and prospects*, 1997, Routledge, London, at 149-150, qualifies the very existence of the block exemption as an example of the fact that "[m]anufacturers in the EU wield a strong lobbying influence on economic policy".

Article 85(3) EC to certain categories of motor vehicle distribution and servicing agreements, entered into force on 1 July 1985.[32] On request of "some of the commercial sectors involved", the Commission published a notice on the block exemption.[33]

7.3.2.2 Preamble

The preamble to Regulation 123/85 provides the context in which the rather technical provisions of the block exemption have to be read and interpreted.[34] The preamble specifies that in the light of *experience* since the BMW Germany Decision and the many motor vehicle distribution and servicing agreements which have been notified, the Commission is in a position to define a category of "agreements, for a definite or an indefinite period, by which the supplying party entrusts to the reselling party the task of promoting the distribution and servicing of certain products of the motor vehicle industry in a defined area and

[32] OJ 1985, L15/16. See on Regulation 123/85, *inter alia*, I. Van Bael, J.-F. Bellis, *Competition Law of the European Community*, 3rd edition, 1994, CCH Europe, at 168-182; Bellamy & Child, *Common Market Law of Competition* (V. Rose ed.), 4th edition, 1993, London, Sweet & Maxwell, at 441-450; L. Ritter, W.D. Braun, F. Rawlinson, *EEC Competition Law - A Practitioner's Guide* (Compact Ed.) 1993, Kluwer Law and Taxation Publishers, Deventer - Boston, at 229-235; D.G. Goyder, *EC Competition Law*, 2nd edition, 1993, Clarendon Press, Oxford, at 253-260; K. Stöver, *The EC Block Exemption Regulation for Motor Vehicule Distribution Agreements (EEC/123/85)*, a compilation of statements by Stöver until mid 1992, published by C.E.C.R.A., and Joerges, Hiller, Holzscheck and Micklitz, *supra* note 2, at 317-352 and 353-386.

[33] Commission notice concerning Regulation 123/85 of 12 December 1984 on the application of Article 85(3) of the Treaty to certain categories of motor vehicle distribution and servicing agreements ("Notice 123/85"), OJ 1985, C17/4.

[34] The ECJ confirmed in Joined Cases C-319/93, C-40/94 and C-224/94, *Dijkstra*, [1995] ECR I-4506, paras. 16-24, that for the purpose of interpreting a provision of a regulation, it is necessary to take into account its genesis and the reasons on which the regulation is based. These can be found, *inter alia*, in the preamble to the regulation concerned. See also Case 170/83, *Hydrotherm Geratebau* v *Compact*, [1984] ECR 3018-3019, paras. 18-21, and Case C-70/93, *BMW* v *ALD Auto-Leasing ("BMW-ALD")*, [1995] ECR I-3473, par. 36. However, the provisions of the block exemption cannot be interpreted widely nor be construed in such a way as to extend the effects of the regulation beyond what is necessary to protect the interests which it is intended to safeguard. See, *inter alia*, Case T-9/92, *Peugeot* v *Commission*, [1993] ECR II-509, par. 37; Case C-322/93 P, *Peugeot* v *Commission*, [1994] ECR I-2727, and Case C-266/93, *Bundeskartellamt* v *Volkswagen ("Bundeskartellamt-VW")*, [1995] ECR I-3520, par. 33.

by which the supplier undertakes to supply contract goods for resale only to the dealer, or only to a limited number of undertakings within the distribution network besides the dealer, within the contract territory".[35] However, in view of the very few formal decisions available, it was at the time at the very least questionable whether the Commission had indeed gained sufficient experience before dealing with this category of agreements in Regulation 123/85.[36]

In the preamble, the Commission emphasizes that the exclusive and selective distribution clauses can be regarded as indispensable measures of rationalization in the automobile industry as automobiles are consumer durables which at intervals require expert maintenance and repair, not always in the same place. The Commission specifies that, on grounds of capacity and efficiency alone, the cooperation between manufacturers and selected dealers and repairers in order to provide specialized servicing for automobiles, cannot be extended to an unlimited number of dealers and repairers, and that the linking of servicing and distribution is more efficient than a separation between a distribution organization for new automobiles, and a servicing organization which would also distribute spare parts on the other.[37]

Subsequently, the Commission elaborates in the preamble on the rationale of its opinion that certain measures are, and others are not, indispensable for an efficient selective distribution system[38] and describes both the conditions which have to be satisfied[39] and the restrictions or provisions which should not be contained in the agreements,[40] if the declaration of inapplicability of Article 85(1) EC is to take effect. The Commission specifies that distribution and servicing agreements can only benefit from the block exemption so long as they bring about "an improvement in distribution and servicing to the benefit of the consumer and effective competition exists, not

---

[35] Whereas (1).

[36] According to Lukoff, *supra* note 28, at 844-845, the European Motor Vehicle Manufacturing Industry argued that the Commission had not acquired "sufficient experience in the light of individual decisions".

[37] Whereas (4).

[38] Whereas (5)-(10).

[39] Whereas (11)-(20).

[40] Whereas (21)-(25).

only between manufacturers' distribution systems but also to a certain extent within each system within the common market". According to the Commission, "the conditions necessary for effective competition, including competition in trade between Member States, may be taken to exist at present, so that European consumers may be considered in general to take an equitable share in the benefit from the operation of such competition".[41]

7.3.2.3 The Core of Regulation 123/85

The distribution and servicing of automobiles and their spare parts as such is not exempted from the application of Article 85(1) EC.[42] Only agreements falling within a particular category are exempted. Under Regulation 123/85, this category is defined as agreements to which only two undertakings are party, in which one, the supplier, agrees to supply within a defined territory of the common market, for the purpose of resale, certain motor vehicles intended for use on public roads and having three or more road wheels, together with spare parts therefor, only to the other party, the dealer, or both to the other party and

---

[41] Whereas (25). The Commission made an explicit reference to the need for "effective competition" in its Decision 92/154 of 4 December 1991 (IV/33.157 - Eco System/Peugeot), OJ 1992, L66/8, par. 27(b). According to *The Economist*, "Restraints on trade?". 24 September 1994, at 80, "[w]hether or not car makers use their distribution systems to rip off consumers depends on how competitive the car market is" ... "suspicions remain that car manufacturers are using their distribution system to exploit customers. The best way to ensure that they sell cars in a way that benefits consumers as well as themselves is to expose them to more competition. If the European Commission is serious about improving competition in the car market, it could start by scrapping its limits on the import of cars from Japan".

[42] See Case T-23/90R, *Peugeot* v *Commission ("Peugeot-Measures I")*, [1990] ECR II-195, par. 21.

a specified number of other undertakings within the distribution system (Article 1).[43] The supplier can also be obliged neither to sell contract goods[44] to final consumers nor to provide them with servicing for contract goods in the contract territory[45] (Article 2). The block exemption regards the distribution and servicing of *new* motor vehicles intended for use on public roads and having three or more road wheels, together with spare parts therefor.[46] The ECJ has not (yet) given criteria which facilitate the differentiation between new and second-hand vehicles.[47] The block exemption only covers agreements for the combined

---

[43] Groves, *supra* note 28, at 78, argues that Article 1(1) of Regulation 19/65 does not provide for the possibility for the supplier to supply within a defined territory both to the other party and a specified number of other undertakings within the distribution system. According to I. Van Bael, "Discretionary powers of the Commission and their legal control in trade and antitrust matters" in *Discretionary powers of the Member States in the field of economic policies and their limits under the EEC Treaty* (J. Schwarze ed.), European University Institute in Florence, 1988, Nomos Verlagsgesellschaft, Baden-Baden, at 177, "[t]here are virtually no distribution agreements in the motor vehicle sector that contain 'exclusive supply clauses' as referred to in ... Regulation [19/65]. Nevertheless, the Commission tailored the block exemption in line with ... Regulation [19/65] to a situation, unlike industry practice, where the dealer is being allotted an exclusive sales territory. So far, this 'Procrustean' approach followed by the Commission has not been challenged in Court even though it presents all the ingredients of an act which was unconstitutional because 'ultra vires'". See also Lukoff, *supra* note 28, at 860.

[44] Pursuant to Article 13(4) of Regulation 123/85, "contract goods" are automobiles and spare parts therefor, which are the subject of an agreement within the meaning of Article 1 of the Regulation.

[45] Pursuant to Article 13(3) of Regulation 123/85, the "contract territory" is the defined territory of the common market to which the obligation of exclusive supply in the meaning of Article 1 of the Regulation applies.

[46] The ECJ pointed out in *BMW-ALD*, *supra* note 34, par. 29, that the block exemption is exclusively concerned with "resellers of new motor vehicles". According to L. Ritter, W.D. Braun, F. Rawlinson, *EEC Competition Law*, Compact edition, 1993, Kluwer Law and Taxation Publishers, Deventer-Boston, at 231, footnote 325, almost by definition, motor manufacturers' distribution agreements only cover *new* automobiles.

[47] See Case C-309/94, *Nissan France and others* v *Dupasquier and others ("Nissan France")*, [1996] ECR 677, and Case C-128/95, *Fontaine and others* v *Acqueducs Automobiles ("Fontaine")*, [1997] ECR I-967. However, in Case C-373/90, *Criminal Proceedings against X*, [1992] ECR I-150, par. 14, the ECJ specified in the context of misleading advertising that "[i]t is when a car is first driven on the public highway, and not when it is registered, that it loses its character as a new car".

distribution of new motor vehicles and spare parts therefor.[48] Agricultural machinery[49] and motorcycles[50] are not covered. Spare parts can be defined as parts which are to be installed in or upon an automobile so as to replace components of that automobile. They are to be distinguished from other parts and accessories according to customary usage in the trade (Article 13(6)).

The parties to the agreement are a *supplier* and a *dealer*. The supplier is defined as the undertaking which supplies the contract goods, whereas the dealer is the undertaking entrusted by the supplier with the distribution and servicing of the contract goods (Article 13(2)). In *BMW-ALD*, the ECJ held that Regulation 123/85 is exclusively concerned with "resellers of new motor vehicles" and specified that leasing companies which do not offer an option to purchase cannot be regarded as such so long as they confine themselves to purchasing vehicles in order to satisfy requests from their customers and do not build up stocks which they offer to customers attracted in that way.[51] The block exemption also applies in so far as the obligations referred to in Articles 1 to 4 apply to undertakings which are connected with a party to an agreement (Article 11).[52] These so-called *connected undertakings* are defined as (a) undertakings one of which directly or indirectly (i) holds more than half of the capital or business assets of the other, or (ii) has the power to exercise more than half the voting rights in the other, or (iii) has the power to appoint more than half the members of the supervisory

---

48 The Commission specified in Decision 88/84 of 22 December 1987 (IV/31.914 - ARG/Unipart), OJ 1988, L45/39, par. 35, that the block exemption "only covers agreements for the combined distribution of new motor vehicles and parts therefor". It was reported in *Agence Europe*, 25 February 1994, at 11 ("Following a Commission intervention, Fiat opens to competitors the market for spare parts for its cars"), that the Commission did not accept two distribution systems for Fiat spare parts: one combined with automobile, the other exlusively spare parts. Article 12 of Regulation 123/85 clarified that the Regulation did also apply to *concerted practices* of the types defined in Articles 1 to 4 of the Regulation.

49 See XXth Report on Competition Policy, at 45, par. 42, and IP/90/917 in which the Commission announced that it would *no longer* tolerate that exclusive and selective distribution of agricultural machinery is exempt, just like road vehicles, by virtue of Regulation 123/85. The Commission emphasized that although tractors are allowed to circulate on the highway, they are intended for use on the land and do not travel widely.

50 See, *inter alia*, *Honda*, XXIst Report on Competition Policy, at 91, par. 123.

51 *BMW-ALD*, *supra* note 34, par. 29. See also *Bundeskartellamt-VW*, *supra* note 34.

52 See Lukoff, *supra* note 28, at 843.

board, board of directors or bodies legally representing the other, or (iv) has the right to manage the affairs of the other; (b) undertakings in relation to which a third undertaking is able directly or indirectly to exercise such rights or powers as are mentioned in (a) above (Article 13(8)).

The ECJ held in *Magne* that the block exemption is limited to providing economic agents in the automobile industry with certain *possibilities* enabling them to remove their distribution and servicing agreements from the scope of the prohibition contained in Article 85(1) EC despite the inclusion of certain types of exclusivity and no-competition clauses. The ECJ specified that the provisions of Regulation 123/85 do not compel economic agents to make use of these possibilities nor do those provisions have the effect of amending the content of such an agreement or rendering it void where all the conditions laid down in the regulation are not satisfied. If an agreement falls within the scope of Article 85(1) EC, there is always the possibility to notify the agreement to the Commission with the request of an individual exemption.[53] According to the ECJ, it is for the national court to determine under national law the extent and consequences for the contractual relations as a whole, of the nullity of certain contractual provisions under Article 85(2) EC.[54] In *Nissan France* the ECJ repeated that Regulation 123/85 only concerns contractual relations between suppliers and their approved distributors. The ECJ specified that the block

---

53 For instance, Ford notified its standard agreement on service outlets which will provide maintenance, repair and warranty services for Ford customers without having to sell vehicles but with the possibility of doing so in the name and on behalf of their affiliated main dealer against a commission on each sale (see Case IV/36.101 - Ford (service outlet), OJ 1996, C227/11). Another example is the notification by MC Micro Compact Car (Mercedes/SMH) of the distribution agreement for the SMART-car which initially had some characteristics of a franchise agreement (see Case IV/35.906 - MC Micro Compact Car AG/various dealers). The Commission reported in IP/97/740, that after several amendments it considered the SMART-distribution agreement to fall under the block exemption of Regulation 1475/95. It considered Ford's service outlet agreement not to fall under the block exemption as there was no connection between the sale and servicing of Ford cars. According to the Commission, the agreement falls under Article 85(1) EC but can be individually exempted under Article 85(3) EC.

54 Case 10/86, *VAG* v *Magne ("Magne")*, [1986] ECR 4088, paras. 12-15. Confirmed in Case C-230/96, *Cabour and others* v *Arnor "Soco" ("Cabour")*, judgment of 30 April 1998, par. 47, not yet reported. It is interesting to note that according to P. Roseren, "The application of Community law by French courts from 1982 to 1993", 31 CML Rev. at 361, "the *Cour de Cassation* quashed .. judgment of .. Court of Appeals declaring void an exclusive car dealer agreement on the sole ground that it did not comply with the provisions of Regulation No. 123/85".

exemption is only concerned "with the content of agreements which parties tied to a distribution network for a specified product, may lawfully conclude having regard to the rules of the Treaty prohibiting restrictions affecting normal competition within the common market" and does not "serve to regulate the activities of ... third parties, who may operate in the market outside the framework of distribution agreements".[55] More specifically, the block exemption does not prohibit an independent trader outside an official distribution network, from acquiring new automobiles via parallel imports and independently carrying on the business of marketing such automobiles, and carrying on at the same time the business of authorized intermediary within the meaning of Article 3(11) of the Regulation.[56]

7.3.2.4 Possible Obligations on the Dealer

Articles 3 and 4 of the Regulation list the various additional obligations that can be put on the dealer by the supplier. Some of these obligations have been further clarified in legal proceedings.

(i) Article 3 of Regulation 123/85

To begin with, the dealer can be obliged not without the supplier's consent, to *modify* contract goods or corresponding goods[57], unless such modification is the subject of a contract with a final customer and concerns a particular automobile

---

[55] *Nissan France*, *supra* note 47, paras. 16-18. See also Case C-226/94, *Grand Garage Albigeois and others* v *Garage Massol*, [1996] ECR I-651; Case C-410/95, *Société des Grands Garages Méditerranéens and Nissan France* v *Société Nice Ouest*, OJ 1996, C46/12 (action withdrawn, OJ 1997, C40/14); *Fontaine*, *supra* note 47, and Case C-41/96, *VAG-Händlerbeirat* v *SYD-Consult*, [1997] ECR I-3123.

[56] See *Nissan France*, *supra* note 47, paras. 20-21. See also Case T-77/96, *Garage Massol* v *Commission*, OJ 1996, C210/23, with regard to the Commission's refusal to investigate the complaint that the network of concessionaires with the PSA group oppose collectively and in concert, the activities of resellers who are not accredited by the manufacturer, contending that the activities of independent resellers are illegal under Regulation 123/85.

[57] Pursuant to Article 13(11) of Regulation 123/85, "corresponding goods" are those which are similar in kind to those in the contract programme, are distributed by the manufacturer or with the manufacturer's consent, and are the subject of a distribution or servicing agreement with an undertaking within the distribution system.

within the contract programme[58] purchased by that final consumer (Article 3(1)).

The dealer can be forbidden to manufacture *competing products* (Article 3(2)), to sell new competing automobiles or to sell, at the premises used for the distribution of contract goods, new automobiles other than those offered for supply by the manufacturer[59] (Article 3(3)).[60] In addition, an obligation can be imposed on the dealer, neither to sell competing spare parts which do not match the quality of the contract goods nor to use them for repair or maintenance of contract goods or corresponding goods (Article 3(4)).[61] A supplier is not allowed to take measures which dissuade dealers from purchasing competing spare parts which do match the quality of the contract goods.[62]

The dealer can also be obliged not to conclude any *distribution or servicing agreement* with third parties for competing goods (Article 3(5)). Moreover, the dealer can be barred, without the supplier's consent, from concluding distribution or servicing agreements with undertakings operating in the contract territory for contract goods or corresponding goods nor can he alter or terminate such agreements (Article 3(6)). In addition, the dealer can be

---

[58] Pursuant to Article 13(5) of Regulation 123/85, the "contract programme" refers to the totality of the contract goods.

[59] Pursuant to Article 13(7) of Regulation 123/85, the "manufacturer" is the undertaking (a) which manufactures or procures the manufacture of the automobiles in the contract programme, or (b) which is connected with an undertaking described at (a).

[60] The ECJ held in *Cabour*, *supra* note 54, par. 31, that this exemption does not cover an obligation imposed on a dealer not to sell new vehicles other than those offered for supply by the manufacturer at commercial premises other than those at which the contract goods are offered for sale.

[61] In this context, it is interesting to note that according to Joerges, Hiller, Holzscheck and Micklitz, *supra* note , at 364, the fact that differentiated safeguards are applied to the sale of new cars and the sale of spare parts, indicates that the Commission does not subscribe to the "package" theory.

[62] See, *inter alia*, *Agence Europe*, "Following a Commission intervention, Fiat opens to competitors the market for spare parts for its cars", 25 February 1994, at 11, which reported that the Commission intervened after a complaint that by granting rebates to dealers for the purchase of spare parts, Fiat provided incentives for small distributors to only market Fiat-parts and dissuaded dealers in general from buying competitors' products. See on the use of (national) intellectual property rights to prevent independent manufacturers from manufacturing and selling competitively-priced replacement parts, *inter alia*, Case 238/87, *Volvo* v *Veng*, [1988] ECR 6211; Case 53/87, *Maxicar* v *Renault ("Maxicar")*, [1988] ECR 6039 and *Ford*, XVth Report on Competition, at 56, par. 49, IP/90/4, and Written Questions 2015-2017 (Seal), OJ 1983, C189/7.

obliged to impose upon undertakings with which the dealer has concluded agreements with the supplier's consent, obligations corresponding to those which the dealer has accepted in relation to the supplier and which are covered by Articles 1 to 4 and in conformity with Articles 5 and 6 of Regulation 123/85 (Article 3(7)).

Outside the *contract territory*, the dealer cannot only be forbidden to maintain branches or depots for the distribution of contract goods or corresponding goods (Article 3(8)(a)), but also to seek customers for contract goods or corresponding goods (Article 3(8)(b)). The dealer can be obliged not to entrust third parties with the distribution or servicing of contract goods or corresponding goods outside the contract territory (Article 3(9)).[63]

The rights of the dealer to supply contract goods or corresponding goods can be limited to *resellers* within the distribution system only (Article 3(10)(a)).[64] Dealers can also be obliged to supply spare parts within the contract programme to resellers only where they are for the purposes of repair of maintenance of an automobile by the reseller (Article 3(10)(b)).

Dealers can be bound to sell automobiles within the contract programme or corresponding goods to final consumers using the services of an *intermediary* only if that intermediary has prior written authorization to purchase a specified automobile and, as the case may be, to accept delivery thereof on their behalf (Article 3(11)).[65] This provision gave rise to what has been qualified by the CFI as "serious problems of interpretation, particularly regarding the concept of intermediary authorized in writing ... a concept of that kind is of

---

[63] In *BMW-ALD*, *supra* note 34, par. 34, the ECJ pointed out that "the supply of vehicles ... by dealers in the system to independent leasing companies whose potential customers are situated outside their contract territory does not constitute the maintenance of a depot for the distribution of contract goods outside the contract territory. Nor do the independent leasing companies constitute third parties which the dealer might entrust with the distribution of vehicles ... outside the contract territory. Such companies outside the ... system do not act for the account of a dealer outside the latter's contract territory but pursue their activities in their own name and for their own account, so that they must be regarded as final users".

[64] As discussed above, the ECJ held in *BMW-ALD*, *supra* note 34, that leasing companies which do not offer an option to purchase cannot be regarded as resellers of new motor vehicles, so long as they confine themselves to purchasing vehicles in order to satisfy requests from their customers and do not build up stocks which they offer to customers attracted in that way.

[65] See in this context P.J. Groves, "Intermediaries: Last chance saloon for selective distribution in the automobile sector?", [1993] 1 ECLR 21-25.

essential importance in safeguarding parallel imports and opening up national markets in the concept of a system for the distribution of motor vehicles covered by a block exemption".[66] In *Eco System I*, the CFI specified that "it is apparent from the structure of Article 3(11) ... that its objective is to preserve the possibility of the involvement of an intermediary provided that there is a direct contractual relationship between the dealer and the final consumer". But the CFI added that "to protect the distribution network from unlawful competition which may arise from some non-approved reseller, the existence of such relationship must be established by a prior written authority, given by the final user of the vehicle to the intermediary acting in his name and on his behalf, to buy a specified vehicle".[67] According to the CFI, the wording of Article 3(11) cannot allow the exclusion of a duly authorized intermediary on the sole ground that he is acting in a professional capacity. The CFI emphasized that the exclusion of intermediaries acting in a professional capacity would in fact "deprive Article 3(11) of its effectiveness and would result in impeding parallel imports and, consequently, partitioning national markets"; "such exclusion ... would be likely to frustrate the most fundamental aims of the Community, particularly the attainment of a single market".[68]

The dealer can be bound to observe the obligations referred to in Article 3(1) and Articles 3(6) to 3(11), for a maximum period of one year after termination or expiry of the agreement (Article 3(12)).

It should be kept in mind that the terms "distribute" and "sell" include other forms of supply such as leasing (Article 13(12)). However, the ECJ held

---

[66] Cases T-23/90 (92) and T-9/92 (92), *Peugeot* v *Commission ("Costs")*, [1995] ECR II-2068, par. 27.

[67] Case T-9/92, *Peugeot* v *Commission ("Eco System I")*, [1993] ECR II-510, par. 40. Confirmed by Case C-322/93P, *Peugeot* v *Commission*, [1994] ECR I-2727. See in this context also *Peugeot-Measures I, supra* note 42; Case T-23/90, *Peugeot* v *Commission*, [1991] ECR II-653; Commission Notice "Clarification of the activities of motor vehicle intermediaries" ("Intermediaries Notice"), OJ 1991, C329/20, and *Alfa Romeo*, XIVth Report on Competition Policy, at 65, par. 72.

[68] *Eco System I, supra* note 67, paras. 41-42. New complaints have been brought by intermediaries against Peugeot. See Case T-9/96, *Européenne Automobiles* v *Commission*, OJ 1996, C95/16; Case T-211/96, *Européenne Automobiles* v *Commission*, OJ 1997, C54/33, and Case T-123/96, *SGA* v *Commission*, OJ 1996, C318/13. See also *Agence Europe*, "French importer claims damages from the European Commission which, he believes, refuses to take action against Peugeot", 6 March 1997, at 12, and "Parallel importer of Peugeot and Citroen cars in France attacks European Commission", 7 November 1996, at 8.

in *BMW-ALD* that this definition relates exclusively to the relationship between the manufacturer and the dealer and "is intended to prevent the dealer from circumventing certain of its contractual obligations by resorting to leasing". According to the ECJ, the object of Article 13(12) is "to prevent the dealer from evading his obligations not to sell vehicles of a different mark (Article 3(3) ...) by leasing to customers vehicles of a competing mark" and "ensures compliance by the dealer with his obligation not actively to seek customers outside his allotted territory (Article 3(8) ...) by preventing him from leasing the contract goods to customers outside his territory".[69]

(ii) Article 4 of Regulation 123/85

Article 4(1)(1) allows the supplier to impose, for distribution and servicing, *minimum standards* on the dealer, which relate in particular to (a) the equipment of the business premises and of the technical facilities for servicing; (b) the specialized and technical training of staff; (c) advertising; (d) the collection, storage and delivery to customers of contract goods or corresponding goods and servicing relating to them; and (e) the repair and maintenance of contract goods and corresponding goods, particularly as concerns the safe and reliable functioning of automobiles. The Commission has been vigilant in taking action against measures by manufacturers which dissuaded dealers from using competing lubricants or oils which meet the quality standards necessary to preserve the safe and reliable functioning of automobiles.[70]

The dealer can be obliged to *order* contract goods from the supplier only at certain times or within certain periods, provided that the interval between ordering dates does not exceed three months (Article 4(1)(2)).

The dealer can also be bound to endeavour to sell, within the contract

---

[69] *BMW-ALD*, *supra* note 34, par. 30. See also *Bundeskartellamt-VW*, *supra* note 34.

[70] See also Article 3(4) of Regulation 123/85. The Commission reported in *Oliofiat*, XVIIth Report on Competition Policy, at 77, par. 84, that, after its intervention, Fiat sent a circular letter to all its authorized dealers and workshops confirming that when servicing automobiles, Fiat network members could use either Fiat lubricants *or* lubricants from other manufacturers subject *only* to the proviso that they met the quality standards and specifications necessary to preserve the correct performance of the automobiles. In a similar sense: Commission Decision 91/39 of 19 December 1990 (IV/32.595 - D'Ieteren motor oils), OJ 1991, L20/42, with respect to recommendations concerning motor oils, and *BMW Iberica* and *Volvo Truck*, XXIst Report on Competition Policy, at 91, par. 123.

territory and within a specified period, such *minimum quantity* of contract goods as may be determined by agreement between the parties or, in the absence of such agreement, by the supplier on the basis of estimates of the dealer's potential sales (Article 4(1)(3)). The word "endeavour" should be emphasized as a dealer may not be bound to achieve a minimum sales target. The ECJ emphasized in *Cabour* that Article 4(1)(3) allows manufacturers to require dealers to endeavour to sell a minimum quantity of contract goods within the contract territory. With an eye on Article 5(2) and 5(4), the ECJ took the position that "where a dealer has failed to meet the sales target set because it is in breach of its duty to use its best endeavours, Regulation No 123/85 does not prohibit penalties, which may extend to termination of the agreement"[71].

The dealer can be obliged not only to keep a particular quantity of contract goods in *stock* (Article 4(1)(4)) but also to keep (a) certain (number of) demonstration automobiles within the contract programme (Article 4(1)(5)). The particulars can be determined by agreement between the parties or, in the absence of such agreement, by the supplier on the basis of estimates of the dealer's potential sales.

Dealers can be obliged to perform guarantee *work*, free servicing and automobile recall work (Article 4(1)(6)). For these activities alone, the use of spare parts within the contract programme or corresponding goods can be prescribed (Article 4(1)(7)).

Last but not least, the dealer can be obliged to both inform customers, in a general manner, of the extent to which *spare parts* from other sources might be used for the repair or maintenance of contract goods or corresponding goods (Article 4(1)(8)) and inform customers whenever spare parts from other sources have been used for the repair or maintainance of contract goods or corresponding goods for which spare parts within the contract programme or corresponding goods, bearing a mark of the manufacturer, were also available (Article 4(1)(9)).

Article 4(2) of Regulation 123/85 confirms that the exemption also applies where the obligation referred to in Article 1 is combined with obligations referred to in Article 4(1) and such obligations fall in individual cases under Article 85(1) EC.

---

[71] *Cabour*, *supra* note 54, par. 37.

7.3.2.5 Mandatory Obligations on Dealer and Supplier

Article 5(1) of the Regulation specifies certain mandatory obligations which have to be undertaken by respectively the dealer and the supplier in order to have the agreement(s) fall under the block exemption. These mandatory obligations are considered to be to the consumer's benefit. The *dealer* is obliged in respect of automobiles within the contract programme or corresponding thereto which have been supplied in the common market by another undertaking within the distribution network, to honour guarantees and to perform free servicing and vehicle recall work.[72] However, these activities do not have to exceed those imposed upon the undertaking within the distribution system or accepted by the manufacturer when supplying such automobiles (Article 5(1)(1)(a)). The dealer is bound to impose a similar obligation upon the other undertakings operating within the contract territory with which the dealer has concluded distribution and servicing agreements[73] (Article 5(1)(1)(b)).

The *supplier*, on the other hand, is obliged not to withhold his consent for the dealer to conclude, alter or terminate agreements with undertakings operating in the contract territory for contract goods or corresponding goods (Article 5(1)(2)(b)). With regard to the dealer's obligations referred to in Article 4(1) of the Regulation, the supplier shall not apply minimum requirements or criteria for estimates such that the dealer is subject to discrimination without objectively valid reasons or is treated inequitably (Article 5(1)(2)(b)). The term

[72] Over the years, the Commission tried to ensure that guarantee schemes on new automobiles were not (ab)used to dissuade consumers from purchasing in Member States other than their country of residence or from parallel importers. See, *inter alia*, *Ford Garantie Deutschland*, XIIIth Report on Competition Policy, at 78, paras. 104-106; *Fiat*, XIVth Report on Competition Policy, at 65, par. 70; *Lada*, XXIst Report on Competition Policy, at 91, par. 123; XXIInd Report on Competition Policy, at 169, par. 291, and *Agence Europe*, 8 June 1994, at 9 ("Judgement of the Court of Justice concerning Cartier Watches cannot be transposed as such to the Automobile Sector - Explanation from the European Commission"). See also Case C-373/90, *Criminal Proceedings against X*, [1992] ECR I-150, paras. 17-19.

[73] Article 13(1) of the Regulation defines the term "distribution and servicing agreements" as framework agreements between two undertakings, for a definite or indefinite period, whereby the party supplying goods entrusts to the other the distribution and servicing of those goods.

"objectively valid reason" is not further elaborated upon in the block exemption.[74]

In any scheme for aggregating quantities or values of goods obtained by the dealer from the supplier and from connected undertakings within a specified period, the supplier shall for the purpose of calculating discounts, at least, distinguish between supplies of (i) automobiles within the contract programme, (ii) spare parts within the contract programme, for supplies of which the dealer is dependent on undertakings within the distribution network, and (iii) other goods (Article 5(1)(2)(c)).

The supplier is bound to supply to the dealer, for the purpose of performance of a contract of sale concluded between the dealer and a final customer in the common market, any passenger car which corresponds to a model within the contract programme[75] and which is marketed by the manufacturer or with the manufacturer's consent in the Member State in which the automobile was to be registered (Article 5(1)(2)(d)). Practice has shown that suppliers are hesitant to comply with this obligation.[76]

Article 5(2) of the Regulation provides that in so far as the dealer has (in accordance with Article 4(1)) assumed obligations for the improvement of distribution and servicing structures, three requirements have to be fulfilled in

---

[74] According to Groves, *supra* note 28, at 81, "the least it means is that the manufacturer must have regard to something more than just his own interests". See also Lukoff, *supra* note 28, at 853.

[75] Pursuant to Article 13(10) of Regulation 123/85, a "passenger car which corresponds to a model within the contract programme" is a passenger car manufactured or assembled in volume by the manufacturer, and identical as to body style, drive-line, chassis, and type of motor with a passenger car within the contract programme.

[76] See, *inter alia*, IP/89/638 in which the Commission reported that upon request, VW adapted its ordering and production processes in order to better meet orders for new right-hand-drive ("RHD") cars placed through VW/Audi dealers in Member States on the Continent where prices were lower. These orders had to be treated in the same way as an order which was received directly from a dealer in the RHD country. See for other reports on Commission intervention in cases of various measures which impeded on parallel imports, *inter alia*, XVIth Report on Competition Policy, at 40, par. 30, and *Ford*, *Volkswagen* and *Nissan*, XXIst Report on Competition Policy, at 91, par. 123. It was reported in "Decisions concernant le Royaume-Uni, L'Irlande et L'Espagne", *Agence Europe*, 25 August 1989, at 4, that "Volkswagen a adapté ses procédures de sorte que les acheteurs de voitures avec conduite à droite (au Royaume-Uni et en Irlande) puissent obtenir de tels véhicules dans un délai de livraison normal sur le continent". See Written Question 3298/97 (Watts), OJ 1998, C158/82.

order to have the exemption referred to in Articles 3(3) and (5) apply to the dealer's obligation not to sell new automobiles other than those within the contract programme nor to make them the subject of a distribution and servicing agreement. *First*, the parties have to agree that the dealer shall be released from the obligations set out in Articles 3(3) and 3(5), where the dealer shows that there are objectively valid reasons for doing so (Article 5(2)(1)(a)). In addition, the parties have to agree that the supplier reserves the right to conclude distribution and servicing agreements for contract goods with specified further undertakings operating within the contract territory or to alter the contract territory only where the supplier shows that there are objectively valid reasons for doing so (Article 5(2)(1)(b)). *Secondly*, the agreement is for a period of at least four years or if for an indefinite period, the period of notice for regular termination of the agreement is at least one year for both parties, unless (i) the supplier is obliged by law or by special agreement to pay appropriate compensation on termination of the agreement, or (ii) the dealer is a new entrant to the distribution system and the period of the agreement, or the period of notice for regular termination of the agreement, is the first agreed by that dealer (Article 5(2)(2)). The *third* and last condition is that each party undertakes to give the other at least six months' prior notice of intention not to renew an agreement concluded for a definite period (Article 5(2)(3)). The conditions for exemption do not affect the right of a party to terminate the agreement for cause (Article 5(4)).

As discussed, when asked whether Article 5(2) lays down mandatory provisions directly affecting the validity or content of the agreement as a whole or certain clauses thereof or obliges the parties to adapt the content of their agreement in order to bring it into conformity with Article 5(2), the ECJ held that the block exemption "is limited to providing economic agents in the motor vehicle industry with certain possibilities enabling them to remove their distribution and servicing agreements from the scope of the prohibition contained in Article 85(1) despite the inclusion in those agreements of certain types of exclusivity and no-competition clauses". The ECJ specified that "the provisions of Regulation No 123/85 do not compel economic agents to make use of these possibilities [n]or do those provisions have the effect of amending the content of such an agreement or rendering it void where all the conditions laid down in the regulation are not satisfied".[77]

A party can only invoke particular "objectively valid grounds" which have been exemplified in the agreement, if such grounds are applied without discrimination to undertakings within the distribution system[78] in comparable cases (Article 5(3)).[79]

7.3.2.6 No Benefit of Block Exemption

Article 6 of Regulation 123/85 specifies that Articles 1, 2, 3 and 4(2) shall *not apply* where (i) both parties to the agreement or their connected undertakings are automobile manufacturers (Article 6(1)); or (ii) an undertaking within the distribution system obliges the dealer not to resell contract goods or corresponding goods below stated prices[80] or not to exceed stated rates of trade discount (Article 6(2)); or (iii) the parties make agreements or engage in

[77] *Magne*, *supra* note 54, par. 12.

[78] Pursuant to Article 13(9) of Regulation 123/85, "undertakings within the distribution system" are, besides the parties to the agreement, the manufacturer and undertakings which are entrusted by the manufacturer or with the manufacturer's consent with the distribution or servicing of contract goods or corresponding goods.

[79] It should be kept in mind that in *Cabour*, *supra* note 54, par. 27, the ECJ noted that Article 5(2)(1)(a) and (b) "do no more than lay down the principle that the parties must state in the agreement that it is possible for them to be released from the obligation not to compete by advancing evidence of such objectively valid reasons, but the agreement need not necessarily contain an exhaustive list of the reasons which may be put forward". Furthermore, the ECJ held in par. 32, that "the possibility for a dealer to put forward objectively valid reasons merely permits dealers, where they can show good reason, to sell vehicles of a different make, but not competing with the contract goods, even at the premises where those are sold". According to the ECJ, "[i]t cannot, however, mean that it is necessary to adduce evidence of objectively valid reasons in order to be able to sell vehicles other than those offered for supply by the manufacturer at commercial premises other than those at which the contract goods are sold".

[80] The Commission reported in IP/89/639 that it had taken action in Spain against practices of fixing resale prices which were incompatible with both Article 85(1) EC and Regulation 123/85. The Commission contacted various automobile sales networks in Spain which agreed to send "special circulars to their dealers and agents, indicating that the list prices for the resale of vehicles and spare parts are to be considered as recommendations, and not binding on the dealers, who may thus charge lower prices to their private or trade customers". See in this context also "Decisions concernant le Royaume-Uni, L'Irlande et L'Espagne", *Agence Europe*, 25 August 1989, at 4. See also IP/93/993 on price discounts by Rover Group.

concerted practices concerning automobiles or spare parts therefor which are exempted from Article 85(1) EC under Regulation 1983/83 ("exclusive distribution agreements") or Regulation 1984/83 ("exclusive purchasing agreements") to an extent exceeding the scope of Regulation 123/85 (Article 6(3)). In its XXIst Report on Competition Policy, the Commission stressed that the presence in an agreement of *additional clauses*, which restrict competition and are not exempted by Regulation 123/85, does not imply that the block exemption becomes inapplicable to the whole agreement:

> Given that the Regulation and the accompanying Notice do not expressly state otherwise and that Regulation 123/85 contains no "opposition procedure", the Commission took the view that the Regulation remains applicable to the clauses expressly exempted. However, the additional restrictive clauses could give rise to fines by the Commission or to sanctions under national law.[81]

This statement was at the time quite remarkable as the Commission thereby made Regulation 123/85 the first and only block exemption which remained applicable notwithstanding the fact that some additional clauses in the agreement(s) were in violation with Article 85(1) EC.

7.3.2.7 Legal Effect

Soon after the entry into force of the block exemption, the Commission reported in its XVIIth Report on Competition Policy that all European motor manufacturers had confirmed that they had adapted their dealership agreements to the requirements of Regulation 123/85. After the adoption of Regulation 123/85, the Commission sent out letters to those automobile manufacturers and traders which had notified agreements, pointing out that:

> any agreement satisfying the conditions of Articles 1 to 6 of Regulation 123/85 was already exempt and so did not require individual exemption to give the parties legal security. Should parties nevertheless desire an

[81] XXIst Report on Competition Policy, at 92, par. 124.

individual exemption of an agreement because it contained restrictive clauses going beyond those exempted by the Regulation, they were asked to identify the clauses concerned and to explain why in their opinion they warranted exemption under Article 85(3).[82]

The Commission noted that as no manufacturer had requested exemption of clauses, it had been able to close the file on 125 notifications. However, the Commission received several complaints with regard to the operation of certain distribution systems.[83]

Articles 7 to 9 of Regulation 123/85 provides for rules on subjects with a *transitional* nature, and Article 10 specifies the Commission's competence to *withdraw* the benefit of the block exemption, where it finds that in an individual case an agreement which falls within the scope of the Regulation nevertheless has effects which are incompatible with the provisions of Article 85(3) EC.[84] Article 10 provides for four examples of situations in which the exemption can be withdrawn. *One example* is the case where, in a substantial part of the common market, contract goods or corresponding goods are not subject to competition from products considered by consumers as similar by reason of their characteristics, price and intended use (Article 10(1)). A *second example* is the situation in which, continuously or systematically, and by means not exempted by Regulation 123/85, the manufacturer or an undertaking within the distribution system makes it difficult for final consumers or other undertakings within the distribution system to obtain contract goods or corresponding goods, or to obtain servicing for such goods, within the common market (Article

[82] See XVIIth Report on Competition Policy, at 39, par. 34.

[83] See, for instance, XVIIth Report on Competition Policy, at 41, par. 34, and more in particular Case T-64/89, *Automec S.r.l.* v *Commission (Automec I)*, [1990] ECR II-367, and Case T-24/90, *Automec S.r.l.* v *Commission (Automec II)*, [1992] ECR II-2223.

[84] The Commission reported in its XVIth Report on Competition Policy, at 40, par. 30, that, so far, it had not withdrawn the exemption under Regulation 123/85 in any case as, in most cases, the cause for complaint was removed after the Commission's intervention. The Commission used the threat of the withdrawal of the benefit of the exemption, as an effective instrument to have infringements terminated. See, *inter alia*, the text of Article 3 of Commission Decision 92/154 of 4 December 1991 (IV/33.157 - Eco System/Peugeot), OJ 1992, L66/12.

10(2)).[85] A *third example* is the situation where, over a considerable period, prices or conditions of supply for contract goods or for corresponding goods are applied which differ substantially as between Member States, and such substantial differences are chiefly due to obligations exempted by Regulation 123/85 (Article 10(3)).[86] The Commission undertook several investigations on price differentials in order to check whether the block exemption should be withdrawn because of large-scale price differentials for models with the same specifications, between Member States.[87] An important investigation took place in 1992.[88] The Commission found substantial variations in car prices and decided to develop a "twofold strategy of practical action" in order to both reduce the considerable price differentials and increase public confidence that the selective distribution system was compatible with the single market. Basicly, the Commission requested manufacturers to send out a mailing to their distributors with confirmation that they were free to sell to other approved distributors in the Community as well as to end-users in other Member States, and to intermediaries representing them. The mailing was also to ensure that cars would in reality be made available to fulfil such demand. In addition, the

(combating price differences)

[85] See in this context, *Citroën*, XVIIIth Report on Competition Policy, at 68, par. 56, in which the Commission reported that after its intervention, Citroën terminated its practice to offer special terms for certain models for a short time, only to residents of Belgium and Luxembourg. This practice was liable to disqualify the distribution agreements concluded by the Belgian Citroën from the benefit of the block exemption as "Citroën distributors and agents in those countries were thus dissuaded from selling the models to nationals of other Community countries". See IP/88/778 for a somewhat more extensive report.

[86] See Groves, *supra* note 28, at 84, and Lukoff, *supra* note 28, at 862, for a concise summary of the legislative history of the text of this provision.

[87] See, *inter alia*, XVIIth Report on Competition Policy, at 40, par. 34, in which the Commission reported in connection with Written Question 964/87 (Muhlen), OJ 1988, C93/35, Written Question 2001/86 (Battersby), OJ 1987, C157/28, and Written Question 2225/85 (Martin), OJ 1986, C137/17, that "[d]uring 1987 the incentive to buy a car abroad generally became less marked, as suppliers tended to reduce extreme price differentials across their dealer networks".

[88] See XXIst Report on Competition Policy, at 89, par. 121 in which the Commission set out the results and noted that "even after adjusting for differences in equipment, discounts, and exchange rates, there remain substantial variations in car prices between different countries". P. Vigier, "La politique communautaire de l'automobile", RMUE 4/1992, at 89, reported extensively on studies on price differences done by Université Libre de Bruxelles (1988), BEUC (1990), Monopolies and Mergers Commission (1992) and MIRU (1992). The Commission compares car prices on a regular basis. See, for instance, IP/94/704 and Written Question 2499/95 (Amadeo), OJ 1995, C340/40.

manufacturers were asked to publish price lists every six months in order to enable consumers to compare prices between different Member States. At the time, it was reported that initially, competition commissioner Sir Leon Brittan, and the industry commissioner, Mr Martin Bangemann, did not agree upon measures to remove barriers to the importation of cheaper cars.[89] The Commission monitors car prices and (since 1993) brings out detailed reports on car prices within the Community every six months.[90] It should be kept in mind, however, that other factors such as currency fluctuations and divergent national tax rates seem to have an impact on car price differences within the Community.[91] A *fourth example* is the situation where, in agreements concerning the supply to the dealer of automobiles which correspond to a model within the contract programme, prices or conditions which are not objectively justifiable, are applied, with the object or the effect of partitioning the common market (Article 10(4)).

Regulation 123/85 entered into force on 1 July 1985 and would apply until 30 September 1995.[92]

---

89 "Brussels will force cuts in UK car prices", *The Sunday Times*, 26 April 1992, reported that Mr Martin Bangemann had the support of "the European car industry's powerful Brussels lobby". See also XXIInd Report on Competition Policy, at 168, par. 290.

90 See, for instance, "Car prices within the European Union on 1 May 1997" (IV/F2/0597), "Car prices within the European Union on 1 November 1997" (IV/F2/1197), and respectively IP/97/640 and IP/98/154. The reports are available on RAPID database (http://europa.eu.int/rapid/start/welcome.htm), at the European Consumer Information Centres and Commission Offices in different Member States.

91 According to A. Murfin, "Price discrimination and tax differences in the European motor industry" in *Tax coordination in the European Community* (S. Cnossen ed.), 1987, Kluwer Law and Taxation Publishers, Deventer, at 171-194, "tax differences are shown to explain only a small proportion of the variation in [car] price levels between countries". In a letter *FT*, "Carmakers behind cross-border price discrimination", 24-25 February 1996, at 8, A. Kirman points at the strategic choice by manufacturers to "price to market" and stresses that "[e]ven after tax harmonisation manufacturers will still have an incentive to charge different prices for the same product in different countries".

92 See Article 13 of Commission Regulation 1475/95 of 25 June 1995, OJ 1995, L145/34.

7.3.2.8 Review of Regulation 123/85

The Commission confirmed in February 1994 that it had begun reviewing the functioning of the block exemption in conjunction with all interested parties.[93] The Commission did not address the question whether the specific rules and regulations for the distribution and servicing of automobiles should remain in place at all. This, notwithstanding the fact that earlier, BEUC had strongly urged the Commission not to extend the block exemption. According to BEUC, it was:

> up to those defending a new exemption by category to prove that the exemption proposed will bring advantages to the consumers and that these advantages cannot be obtained through market forces alone ... There should be no presumption in favour of continuing category exemption.[94]

Nevertheless, the Commission was already examining what changes could be made to Regulation 123/85:

> with a view to ensuring that the most efficient form of distribution will prevail in the Union, taking account of the need for a balance between the interests of the various parties involved and the contribution of the selective and exclusive distribution system to the efficient management of the arrangement between Japan and the EU on trade in automobiles;

---

[93] See page 4 of the document (entitled "The Automobile Industry - Current Situation, Challenges, Strategy for the Future and Proposals for Action") attached to the Commission's Communication to the Council and the European Parliament on the European Union Automobile Industry of 23 February 1994, COM(94) 49 final.

[94] *Agence Europe*, 27 January 1994, at 10 ("BEUC says Commission should not renew exemption in favour of selective and exclusive distribution"). It was reported in *Agence Europe*, 29 January 1994, at 15 ("Manufacturers reaffirm advantages of existing distribution system and reject BEUC criticism"), that ACEA considered BEUC's criticism without foundation and stressed, *inter alia*, that by abolishing the selective distribution system, the Commission would act against its objective of reinforcing the competitiveness of the automobile industry in the Community. See also *Agence Europe*, 14-15 February 1994, at 10 ("AIT and FIA are in favour of renewing the regulation on selective distribution with two major amendments") and 12 May 1994, at 11 ("BEUC does not accept the arguments of the automobile industry justifying the prolongation of the Community exclusive distribution system beyond June 1995").

> the efficient management of this arrangement must not be weakened in any way.[95]

After emphasizing that the aim of Regulation 123/85 had been to establish a fair balance of interests between all actors in the distribution chain (manufacturers, distributors and parts producers) while ensuring that consumers benefit overall from the system, the Commission made clear that in its review of Regulation 123/85, it would take account of the following elements:

> - the extent to which the Regulation contributes to improving distribution and increasing inter and intra-brand competition;
> - the progress in the functioning of the internal market in the automotive sector and the impact of the Regulation in this regard;
> - the balance of interests between the different parties concerned (constructors/distributors; constructors/parts producers; consumers);
> - the need to foster close partnership relations between all elements of the distribution chain in order to improve industrial efficiency and competitiveness in the automotive sector as a whole and preserve employment notably in small and medium sized enterprises;
> - the contribution of the selective and exclusive distribution system to the efficient management of the arrangement between Japan and the EU on trade in automobiles; the efficient management of this arrangement must not be weakened in any way.[96]

These elements illustrate that interests *other* than competition policy interests like the common commercial policy and the strengthening of the competitiveness

[95] Commission's Communication to the Council and the European Parliament on the European Union Automobile Industry of 23 February 1994, COM(94) 49 final, at 32. See also Vigier, *supra* note 88, at 95.

[96] *Ibidem*.

of Community industry, were of importance during the review and evaluation of Regulation 123/85 and the drafting of its successor.[97]

7.3.3 Regulation 1475/95

7.3.3.1 Prelude

The Commission's review of Regulation 123/85 led to extensive discussions with all interested parties involved and heated up after part of an internal Commission document regarding the revision of the block exemption had been published in the French press. The internal document consisted of a draft for an Explanatory Note together with that of a comparison between the provisions of Regulation 123/85 and those of a possible successor. On 9 May 1994, a French weekly published the text of the proposed amendments.[98] One may assume that the draft text reflected at the very least the opinion of the Commission's experts

[97] It was reported in *Agence Europe*, 27 January 1994, at 10 ("Mr Bangemann in favour of prolonging authorisation for selective distribution beyond 1995 in the automobile sector"), that the Commissioner responsible for industrial policy, Bangemann, informally said that "the automobile industry would be greatly helped in its restructuring effort if it can base itself on the assumption that the selective distribution system will not be abolished in 1995". *Agence Europe*, 2 March 1994, at 7 ("Eliminating exclusive distribution will not benefit consumer, Mr Bangemann believes"), reported furthermore that Bangemann confirmed that in reviewing Regulation 123/85, the Commission would also take into account "the contribution that this system has made to the successful functioning of the agreement between the European Union and Japan on the automobile trade".

[98] *Le Journal de l'Automobile*, No 440, 9 May 1994, at 2. See also *Agence Europe*, 12 May 1994, at 11 ("The Commission's services consider important changes, along the lines desired by dealers, to the exclusive distribution ruling - reservations on the part of manufacturers") and 20 May 1994, at 7 ("Mr Van Miert defends the plan - now under discussion - to build flexibility into exclusive distribution arrangements") which reported that the Commissioner responsible for Competition Policy, K. Van Miert, basicly assumed responsibility for the contents of the document.

working on the revision of the block exemption.[99] It is interesting to note that with regard to Regulation 123/85, it was explicitly recognized under the heading "Point of departure" that:

> the experience acquired over the past ten years shows that the said Regulation did not in any noticeable way contribute neither to the opening up of the national markets nor to the development of flexible and efficient distribution structures for motor vehicles and the spare parts thereof. In order to meet those shortcomings and to stimulate competition, a revision of the Regulation which will take into account the demands of the Internal Market, appears to be necessary.
>
> Such an approach implies the establishment of a better equilibrium between the motor vehicle manufacturers and their distributors, between manufacturers and producers or distributors of spare parts and, finally, between distribution systems and consumers.[100]

It would have made the discussion on the extension and revision of the block exemption much more transparent if the Commission had actually specified and elaborated upon, what it considered to be and indeed referred to as its "experience acquired over the past ten years". Unfortunately, the Commission did not do so publicly. It is assumed that some of the Commission's experience

---

[99] Notwithstanding the fact that the various drafts of the new block exemption were considered very confidential indeed J. Creutzig, a practising attorney in Neunkirchen, Germany, was apparently in the position to write in his article "Die neue Gruppenfreistellungsverordnung für Vertriebs- und Kundendienstvereinbarungen im Kfz-Bereich", 21/1995 EuZW, at 723, footnote 10, that there were "zahlreiche - immer streng vertrauliche - Texte der GD IV, einmal auch der GD III, die (ein bemerkenswertes Novum) den betroffenen Wirtschaftskreisen bzw. -verbänden nicht von der Kommission zur Kenntnis gebracht worden sind; so z.B. die Texte v. 28.4., 3.8., 8.9., 30.9. und 21.10.1994."

[100] This quote is taken from an English translation of the draft "Explanatory Note" to the revised text of the block exemption published in the French press and is on file with author. Notwithstanding the fact that this internal document circulated at the time freely amongst interested parties, it has not been published. The complete internal Commission document was for "Interservices consultation" and was distributed by C.D. Ehlerman to the Legal Department (Mr. Dewost), DG III (Mr. Perissich), DG XXIII (Mr. von Moltke) and Department "Consumer Policy" (Mr. Prendergast), with the request to provide him with observations before 16 May 1994.

is based upon the cases which led to case law of the ECJ, formal Commission decisions, press releases or concise reports in the yearly Reports on Competition Policy. However, an important part of the Commission's experience must have been acquired during the handling of complaints and notifications which did not lead to a publication of any kind. In addition, the various drafts of the new block exemption and the related documents were, and still are, considered by the Commission as internal documents which are not externally available. As a result, not all interested parties were in an equal position to participate in full in the early stages of the discussions on the contents of the block exemption. Only those with a cooperative contact within the Commission were able to obtain a copy of the relevant drafts. It is evident that both the lack of transparency and the selective distribution of internal Commission documents puts the various interested parties on an unequal footing which negatively affects the legitimation of the block exemption.

Some of these internal Commission documents indicate that, in order to improve the conditions of competition and bring about a better equilibrium between the various interests at stake, the Commission initially proposed important changes to the block exemption. These proposals led to more discussion and made the revision of the block exemption even more politicaly sensitive.[101] Both the text of the draft for the Explanatory Memorandum (not "Note" anymore) and the new block exemption were further amended several times. With regard to the Explanatory Memorandum, it is worth mentioning that the paragraph quoted above, under the heading "Point of departure" was watered down to the following text:

Experience over the last ten years shows that the Regulation has only

[101] *Agence Europe*, 30/31 May 1994 ("Manufacturers vigorously criticise Van Miert's proposal on exclusive distribution - Mr Calvet participates"), reported that G. Garuzzo, chairman of ACEA, declared that "the internal Commission document, .. , aims at undermining the entire base for car distribution in Europe, submitting the industry to arbitrary experience without precedent, while our competitors overseas continue to benefit from stability on their national markets". See, on the other hand, *Agence Europe*, 20/21 June 1994, at 15 ("BEUC considers preliminary draft of new regulation on exclusive distribution is still too restrictive"), for BEUC's critisism. *FT*, 19 April 1995, at 3, reported that R. van de Ven, chairman of the Committee of European Car Dealers and Retailers for Market Liberalisation, qualified the system of Regulation 123/85 even as "medieval" as it illogically puts "the interests of car manufacturers above those of consumers and dealers" by allowing "one-brand-only" dealerships.

> partly achieved its main objectives, which were the opening-up of national markets and the development of flexible and efficient structures. The need to remedy these shortcomings and stimulate competition calls for a revision of the Regulation, taking account of the requirements of the internal market and the provisions of Article 129A of the EC Treaty as modified by the Treaty on European Union.
>
> Such an approach means establishing a better balance between vehicle manufacturers and their dealers, between vehicle manufacturers and spare-part manufacturers or distributors, and between distribution networks and consumers.[102]

Again, the "[e]xperience over the last ten years" as referred to above, was not further specified nor elaborated upon.

The amended draft was presented to all Commissioners during a regular Commissioner's Meeting held on 5 October 1994[103] and approved by the Commission with only one major change. The new block exemption was not approved for a duration of seven but ten years with the possibility of re-examination after five years.[104] The draft was published and the Commission initiated another round of formal consultation.[105] The Commission received 71 submissions emanating from a wide range of different interest groups which

---

[102] Explanatory Memorandum at page 1. The (unpublished) Memorandum is referred to by P.J. Groves, "Whatevershebringswesing: DG IV Rebukes the Car Industry", [1995] 2 ECLR at 100, footnote 10, and is on file with author.

[103] See *Agence Europe*, 19-20 September 1994, at 6 ("On Wednesday the Commission should approve the altered draft new regulation on the exclusive distribution of automobiles - A "Van Miert Compromise" between the ideas of the manufacturers and distributors") and 21 September 1994, at 7 ("Commission's deliberations on car distribution postponed to 5 October").

[104] *Agence Europe*, 6 October 1994, at 5 ("Commission approves Van Miert compromise which will extend clearance of exclusive car distribution agreement for ten years, with significant changes"). See also *Agence Europe*, 7 October 1994, at 13 ("Welcoming the renewal of authorisation for selective distribution, the ACEA maintains some of its criticism") and 12 October 1994, at 12 ("Committee representing car distributors and repair firms welcomes (with reservation) the European Commission's draft").

[105] The Commission published the (amended) draft and invited all interested parties to send in their comments. See OJ 1994, C379/16 and *Agence Europe*, 20 January 1995, at 7 ("The Commission begins the formal consultation procedure on the new draft regulation on car distribution").

confirmed that there was "a wide spectrum of opinion on the review of Regulation No 123/85".[106] The draft became the subject of another round of consultation and was subjected to further criticism.[107] The EFTA Surveillance Authority turned out to be yet another critic of the extension of the block exemption. The EFTA Surveillance Authority took the position that it had not been demonstrated that there were specific circumstances which would support the block exemption's restrictions of competition in the distribution and servicing of automobiles. On the contrary, it believed that the fact that the European market was divided along national lines with big price differences for the same type of car, was counter-productive and that there was a need to open up this market for effective competition. The EFTA Surveillance Authority would support an extension of certain parts of the block exemption for a transition period only, not exceeding five years in order to allow the automobile industry time to adapt to effective competition in this market.[108]

The discussions on the contents of the draft were not only held behind closed doors. Several newspapers and magazines had rather critical editorials, articles and reports on the subject.[109] Many, if not most, publications were quite negative about the very existence and application of the block exemption. Economists aired their serious doubts as to the need for the specific rules and regulations for the distribution and servicing of automobiles. For instance, according to Mercer, the existing distribution system no longer met the

---

[106] See a Memorandum from Mr Van Miert, entitled "Review of Regulation No 123/95 - Suggestions for a revised draft", at 2. Notwithstanding the fact that this Memorandum is on file with several organizations in the automobile industry, Van Miert's D.G. IV officialy refused to provide the author with a copy of this document.

[107] See, *inter alia*, *Agence Europe*, 10 March 1995, at 15 ("FIA and AIT call for changes in the draft regulation on car distribution"); Written Question 1159/95 (Cruellar), OJ 1995, C277/5; *FT*, "Car sale curbs condemned", 19 April 1995, at 3; *Agence Europe*, 20 April 1995, at 13 ("Dealers, independent traders and consumers appeal to the European Commission for a liberal car distribution system") and 24/25 April 1995, at 13 ("BEUC urges the Commission to further modify its draft regulation on car distribution").

[108] *Agence Europe*, 14/15 November 1994, at 9 ("EFTA Surveillance authority does not agree to extending approval of exclusive distribution agreements for cars, acceptable for 5 years at most").

[109] See, *inter alia*, *FT*, "Brussels' foot on the brake", 6 October 1994; "Europe's car scam", *The Economist*, 24 September 1994, at 15, and "De lange schaduw van de Japanse auto-industrie", *Financieel Dagblad*, 8-10 October 1994.

industry's economic needs and resulted in stress at all levels. Mercer pointed out that all participants (manufacturers, dealers and consumers) were unhappy in the existing distribution system[110] and even qualified the distribution system as obsolete and inefficient as it fails to meet consumers' needs. Mercer disputed the main arguments put forward by the European automobile industry in support of a block exemption for the distribution and servicing of automobiles.[111]

Notwithstanding these criticisms, the Commission maintained the main elements of the December 1994-draft.[112] In a press release, the Commission pointed out that the block exemption could remain in place, because:

> - motor vehicles are technical consumer durables whose maintenance and repair must be entrusted to specialists, wherever and whenever (sometimes unexpectedly) the need arises,
> - it makes greater economic sense to combine sales and servicing,
> - there is competition between the networks of the various makes of vehicle and reinforcement of competition between members of the same network,
> - the distribution system benefits consumers by providing a basis for their mobility throughout the Union.[113]

why another block exemption could be allowed.

[110] See G.A. Mercer, "Don't just optimize - unbundle", *The McKinsey Quarterly* 1994, No 3, at 103-116. Exhibit 6 on page 114 indicates that in 1985, the American consumer enjoyed a visit to the dentist/doctor more than a new car purchase or car repair at a dealer or independent shop! See also *FT*, "Europe's car cartel", 30 May 1995, at 13. As reported in *FT* (FT Auto), "City 'village' cuts the flab", 4 December 1997, at VIII, several manufacturers are experimenting with different ways to sell cars.

[111] *FT*, "EU's new car distribution 'archaic'", 10 November 1994, at 8.

[112] See, *inter alia*, *Agence Europe*, 20 April 1995, at 6 ("Commission drafts final text of new regulation on car distribution") and 27 April 1995, at 8 ("The Commission defines the new regulation on selective distribution, but does not decide whether its duration is to be seven or ten years - definitive adoption in June"); *FT*, "Brussels votes to keep protection for car sales", 27 April 1995, at 3, and *Agence Europe*, 4 May 1995, at 14 ("Reactions of EP Liberal group, dealers and independent garages to new Commission text on selective distribution").

[113] IP/95/420.

The duration of the revised block exemption was set at seven years.[114] At the very last moment, a new provision was inserted which excludes the application of the block exemption for franchising, Regulation 4087/88, with regard to the products and services referred to in Regulation 1475/95.[115] This alteration was only made after the consultation procedure had already come to an end.

On 21 June 1995, the Commission adopted the final text of Commission Regulation 1475/95 on the application of Article 85(3) of the Treaty to certain categories of motor vehicle distribution and servicing agreements.[116] The revised block exemption is basicly an adjustment of Regulation 123/85. The structure of the block exemption remained the same. Besides some alterations of a purely textual nature,[117] the contents of the block exemption have been altered in order to reflect the more liberal attitude the Commission was prepared to take towards

[114] In reaction to Written Question 1834/97 (Fontaine), OJ 1997, C391/138, the Commission noted that the period of seven years is a minimum to ensure legal certainty for the sector. The Commission decided for the green paper on vertical restraints in Community competition policy (COM(96) 721), not to cover the automobile sector. The Commission specified that on questions of a general nature on vertical restraints, the outcome of the public consultation on the green paper will be taken into account when considering the future of the structure of the distribution system in the automobile sector. See Green paper on vertical restraints in EC competition policy, 22 January 1997, COM(96)721 final. The Green paper triggered an avalange of publications. See, *inter alia*, H.H.P. Lugard, "Vertical restraints under EC competition law: A horizontal approach?", [1996] 3 ECLR, at 166-177, and F.M. Carlin, "Vertical restraints: Time for change?", [1996] 5 ECLR, at 283-288.

[115] See *Agence Europe*, 22 June 1995, at 9 ("The European Commission adopts the new regulation authorizing selective distribution in the automobile sector - comes into effect in July, seven years duration") and 24 August 1995, at 6 ("BEUC says implementation of new regulation on car distribution should be closely monitored").

[116] OJ 1995, L145/25. See in this context also the Opinion of the Economic and Social Committee, OJ 1995, C133/27; Resolution of the European Parliament, OJ 1995, C109/314, and Written Questions 1649/95, 1650/95 and 1779/95 (Amadeo), OJ 1995, C277/17. See on Regulation 1475/95, *inter alia*, W.B.J. van Overbeek, *Contacten & contracten* (RAI Vereniging, Afdeling Auto's), 1996, SPR Producties, Eemnes; *La distribution dans le secteur automobile* (RDC-dossier nr. 3), 1996, E. Story-Scientia, Diegem; C.T. Ebenroth, K.W. Lange, S.A. Mersch, *Die EG-Gruppenfreistellungs-verordnung für Vertriebs- und Kundendienstvereinbarungen über Kraftfahrzeuge*, 1995, Verlag Recht und Wirtschaft, Heidelberg, and A.C. Carreras, *La Distribucion de Automoviles en la Comunidad Europea*, 1997, Tirant lo Blanch, Valencia. See also Groves, *supra* note 102, at 98-103; F. Wijckmans and A. Vanderelst, "The EC Commission's draft regulation on motor vehicle distribution: Alea Iacta est?", [1995] 3 ECLR, at 225-236, and Creutzig, *supra* note 99.

[117] For instance, the term "contract programme" is replaced by "contract range".

the distribution and servicing of automobiles and their spare parts. Soon after publication of the new block exemption, a Commission brochure entitled "Distribution of Motor Vehicles - Explanatory Brochure" became available which is intended "as a legally non binding guide to the Regulation which is aimed particularly at distributors and consumers" and to "provide consumers with information as to how the Regulation guarantees the freedom to buy a car anywhere in the Community in accordance with the principles of the single market".[118] In its Explanatory Brochure, the Commission directs consumers to their national courts in case of a conflict on the application of the block exemption, and underlines the possibilities for national courts to take action in conflicts on the applicability of the block exemption. Practice has shown, however, that not all complainants readily accept the Commission's refusal to investigate due to a "choice of priorities owing to lack of resources".[119]

7.3.3.2 Preamble

The text of the preamble reflects the somewhat more liberal approach to the distribution and servicing of automobiles. The first part of the preamble

---

[118] Commission brochure "Distribution of Motor Vehicles - Explanatory Brochure" (IV/9509/95EN) ("Explanatory Brochure"). See J. Creutzig, "Vertrieb von Kraftfahrzeugen - Zum Leitfaden der Kommission vom Oktober 1995", 7/1996 EuZW, at 197-201.

[119] For instance, the following cases illustrate that dealers like Max Labat (Volkswagen/Audi) and Guérin (Volvo/Nissan) initiated legal action against the Commission's decision not to investigate their complaints with regard to contract clauses on subjects like sales objectives, discounts and premiums, delivery to agents, sale of other makes, activities outside contract area and restriction of catories of customers, in their distribution agreements: Case T-186/94, *Guérin* v *Commission ("Guérin-Volvo I")*, [1995] ECR II-1753; Case C-282/95P, *Guérin* v *Commission ("Guérin-Volvo II")*, [1997] ECR I-1531; Case T-226/97, *Guérin* v *Commission ("Guérin-Volvo III")*, OJ 1997, C318/28 (see OJ 1998, C7/29); Case T-276/97, *Guérin* v *Commission ("Guérin-Volvo IV")*, judgment of 13 februari 1998, not yet reported; Case T-195/95, *Guérin* v *Commission ("Guérin-Nissan I")*, [1996] ECR II-171; Case T-195/95, *Guérin* v *Commission ("Guérin-Nissan II")*, [1997] ECR II-679; Case T-38/96, *Guérin* v *Commission ("Guérin-Nissan III")*, [1997] ECR II-1223; Case T-275/97, *Guérin* v *Commission ("Guérin-Nissan IV")*, OJ 1998, C7/21 (see OJ 1998, C113/15); Case T-574/93, *Nouveau Garage and Max Labat* v *Commission*, OJ 1994, C43/12 (see OJ 1994, C161/15; Case T-185/96, *Max Labat and others* v *Commission*, OJ 1997, C54/24; Case T-189/96, *Garage des Quatre Vallées and others* v *Commission*, OJ 1997, C54/25; Case T-190/96, *Palma and others* v *Commission*, OJ 1997, C54/25; Case C-153/98 P, *Guérin* v *Commission*, OJ 1998, C234/12, and Case C-154/98 P, *Guérin* v *Commission*, OJ 1998, C258/13.

elaborates on the basic principles underlying the new block exemption.[120] Leaving aside some minor grammatical changes, the text of Whereas (1) to (6) of the block exemption remains basicly the same. The text of Whereas (7) to (10), however, describes some of the important changes with regard to the ban on dealing in competing products, the supply of spare parts, the dealer's activities outside his territory and the obligations which can be imposed on the dealer. The second part of the preamble focuses on the conditions which must be satisfied if the declaration of inapplicability is to take effect.[121] The third part of the preamble provides the background of the clauses which bar the exemption from taking effect, and the practices that result in the automatic loss of the benefit of the exemption when committed systematically and repeatedly.[122] The fourth part of the preamble points at the limited period of the block exemption, the appraisal by 31 December 2000, the possibility to notify in case of doubt and the relationship of Regulation 1474/95 with other block exemptions.[123]

7.3.3.3 The Core of Regulation 1475/95

Articles 1 and 2 did not change substantially. Article 1 provides that Article 85(1) shall not apply to agreements to which only two undertakings are party and in which one contracting party agrees to supply, within a defined territory of the common market only to the other party, or only to the other party and to a specified number of other undertakings within the distribution system, for the purpose of resale, certain *new* automobiles[124] and spare parts[125] therefor. The

[120] See Whereas (1)-(10) which elaborate on Articles 1 to 4 of Regulation 1475/95.

[121] See Whereas (11)- (19) which elaborate on Article 5 of Regulation 1475/95.

[122] See Whereas (20)-(31) which elaborate on Articles 6 to 8 of Regulation 1475/95.

[123] See Whereas (32)-(35) which elaborate on Articles 11 to 13 of Regulation 1475/95.

[124] According to the Commission, Explanatory Brochure, *supra* note 118, at 4, "[t]he dividing line between new and used motor vehicles has to be drawn in accordance with commercial usage in a manner which prevents any circumvention of the Regulation".

[125] The definition of "spare parts" in Article 13(6) of Regulation 123/85 remained basicly the same in Article 10(6) of Regulation 1475/95. The words "customary usage in the trade" were replaced by "trade usage".

term "new" is also added to the definition of "contract goods" in Article 10(4) of the Regulation. Besides a minor textual change, Article 2 remained the same.[126]

7.3.3.4 Possible Obligations on the Dealer

The revised block exemption is aimed at reinforcing the position of the dealer *vis-à-vis* the manufacturer thereby stimulating competition. As a result, the Articles 3 and 4 were amended substantially.

(i) Article 3 of Regulation 1475/95

Pursuant to the revised text, the dealer can *modify* contract goods or corresponding goods, without the supplier's consent, if such modification has been ordered by the final consumer and concerns a particular automobile within the range convered by the contract, purchased by that final consumer. The consumer's order is enough (Article 3(1)).

The dealer can still be obliged not to manufacture *competing products* (Article 3(2)). However, the dealer cannot merely be prohibited to sell competing new products. The dealer cannot be obliged to refrain from selling new automobiles offered by persons other than the manufacturer, on separate sales premises, under separate management, in the form of a distinct legal entity and in a manner which avoids confusion between makes (Article 3(3)).[127] The question arises whether the separate sales premises can be located in the same building or does the term "premises" point in the direction of separate buildings?[128] According to the Commission, the separate sales premises may be located in the same building and separate management means in principle keeping separate records, accounts and sales forces.[129] A dealer can be obliged not to permit a third party to benefit unduly, through any after-sales service

---

[126] The words "[t]he exemption under Article 85(3) of the Treaty shall also apply" were replaced by "[t]he exemption shall also apply".

[127] See in this sense *Cabour*, *supra* note 54, par. 40.

[128] Whereas the English text speaks of "in separate sales premises", the French text of the Regulation uses the words "dans les locaux de vente séparés". The English text seems to point at separate buildings whereas the French text implies different sales areas under one roof. See the author's letter entitled "Commission ambiguous on the car sales front", *FT*, 27 June 1995, at 14.

[129] Explanatory Brochure, *supra* note 118, at 12.

performed in a common workshop, from investments made by a supplier, notably in equipment or the training of personnel (Article 3(4)). The supplier can oblige the dealer neither to sell *spare parts* which compete with contract goods without matching them in quality nor to use them for repair or maintenance of contract goods or corresponding goods (Article 3(5)).

The supplier can oblige the dealer, without the supplier's consent, neither to conclude distribution or servicing *agreements* with undertakings operating in the contract territory for contract goods or corresponding goods nor to alter or terminate such agreements (Article 3(6)). In addition, the supplier can oblige the dealer to impose upon undertakings with which the dealer has concluded agreements in accordance with Article 3(6), obligations comparable but *not* corresponding, to those which the dealer has accepted in relation to the supplier and which are covered by Articles 1 to 4 and are in conformity with Articles 5 and 6 of the Regulation (Article 3(7)).

With regard to activities *outside* the dealer's *territory*, the dealer can be obliged not to maintain branches or depots for the distribution of contract goods or corresponding goods outside the contract territory (Article 3(8)(a)). However, where Regulation 123/85 gave the supplier the right to oblige the dealer not to seek customers for contract goods or corresponding goods outside the contract territory, the revised block exemption provides that the dealer can only be restrained from soliciting customers for contract goods or corresponding goods, by personalized advertising (Article 3(8)(b)). The rule that the dealer can be obliged not to entrust third parties with the distribution or servicing of contract goods or corresponding goods outside the contract territory, remains the same (Article 3(9)).

The dealer can still be obliged not to *supply* to a *reseller:* (a) contract goods or corresponding goods unless the reseller is an undertaking within the distribution system, or (b) spare parts within the contract range unless the reseller uses them for the repair or maintenance of an automobile (Article 3(10)).

The supplier keeps the possibility to oblige the dealer not to sell automobiles within the contract range or corresponding goods to final consumers using the services of an *intermediary* unless that intermediary has prior written

no intermediary allowed

authority from such consumers to purchase a specified automobile or where it is taken away by him, to collect it (Article 3(11)).[130]

It should be kept in mind that "distribute" and "sell" include other forms of supply by the dealer such as leasing (Article 10(13)). The revised block exemption specifies that the term "*resale*" includes all transactions by which a physical or legal person, the reseller, disposes of an automobile which is still in a new condition and which he had previously acquired in his own name and on his own behalf, irrespective of the legal description applied under civil law or the format of the transaction which effects such resale. In addition, it is specified that the term resale shall include all leasing contracts which provide for a transfer of ownership or an option to purchase prior to the expiry of the contract (Article 10(12)).

(ii) Article 4 of Regulation 1475/95

Most of the text of Article 4 has not been changed in substance. However, some interesting amendments have to be highlighted. A remarkable change is the introduction of an *expert third party* to be involved in case of disagreement between the supplier and his dealer with regard to the minimum number of contractual goods endeavoured to be sold annually by the dealer (Article 4(1)(3)),[131] the quantity of stock of contract goods (Article 4(1)(4)) or the demonstration automobiles within the contract range, or number thereof, to be kept by the dealer (Article 4(1)(5)). In performing his task, the expert third party has to take account of sales previously achieved in the territory and of forecast sales for the territory and at national level.

Another alteration can be found in the new text of Article 4(1)(9). The dealer can be obliged to inform customers whenever *spare parts* from other sources have been used for the repair or maintenance of contract goods or corresponding goods. The fact that this obligation was only triggered when

---

[130] The Commission pointed out in its Explanatory Brochure, *supra* note 118, at 9, that the "Intermediaries Notice", *supra* note 67, remains applicable under the new block exemption.

[131] In *Cabour*, *supra* note 54, paras. 43-44, the ECJ noted within the context of Article 4(1)(3) that "[i]f sales targets are to be covered by the provision, they must not only represent simply an obligation to use best endeavours, but must also be determined by common agreement between the parties or, where they disagree, by an expert third party". The ECJ emphasized that the manufacturer is *not* permited to fix sales targets unilaterally.

spare parts within the contract programme or corresponding goods, bearing a mark of the manufacturer, were also available, was deleted.

Last but not least, Article 4(2) of the new block exemption provides that the exemption shall also apply to the obligations referred to in Article 4(1) where such obligations fall in individual cases under the prohibition contained in Article 85(1) EC.

7.3.3.5 Mandatory Obligations on Dealer and Supplier

As regards Article 5(1), the only substantial amendment can be found in Article 5(1)(1)(a) which specifies that the *dealer* has to undertake in respect of automobiles within the contract range or corresponding thereto which have been supplied in the common market by another undertaking within the distribution network: (i) to honour guarantees and to perform free servicing and vehicle-recall work to an extent which corresponds to the dealer's obligation covered by Article 4(1)(6); and (ii) to carry out repair and maintenance work in accordance with Article 4(1)(1)(e).[132] The addition that this does not have to exceed that imposed upon the undertaking within the distribution system or accepted by the manufacturer when supplying such automobiles, is deleted.

Article 5(2) has been amended. It formulates three conditions which have to be fulfilled in order to have the exemption apply in a situation where the dealer has, in accordance with Article 4(1), assumed obligations for the improvement of distribution and servicing structures. The *first* condition is that the supplier releases the dealer from the obligations referred to in Article 3(3) where the dealer shows that there are objective reasons for doing so. The *second* condition is that the agreement is for a period of at least five years or, if for an indefinite period, the period of notice for regular termination of the agreement is at least two years for both parties. This period is reduced to at least one year where (i) the supplier is obliged by law or by special agreement to pay

[132] The Commission points out in its interpretative communication on procedures for the type-approval and registration of vehicles previously registered in another Member State, OJ 1996, C143/4, that "[e]ach manufacturer's distribution-network outlets provide the minimum level of guarantee, free service and service following a recall laid down by the manufacturer, whatever the place of purchase of the vehicle within the common market (see Regulation ... 1475/95) on presentation of the guarantee documents signed by a member of the official distribution network".

appropriate compensation on termination of the agreement, or (ii) the dealer is a new entrant to the distribution system and the period of the agreement, or the period of notice for regular termination of the agreement, is the first agreed by that dealer. The *third* condition remained the same and specifies that each party has to undertake to give the other at least six months' prior notice of intention not to renew an agreement concluded for a definite period.

Articles 5(3) and 5(4) of Regulation 123/85 have been replaced by a new Article 5(3) which provides that the conditions for exemption laid down in Articles 5(1) and (2) shall not affect (i) the supplier's right to terminate the agreement subject to at least one year's notice in a case where it is necessary to reorganize the whole or a substantial part of the network and (ii) the right of one party to terminate the agreement for cause where the other party fails to perform one of its basic obligations. It is interesting to note that Article 5(3) prescribes that in each case, the parties must, in the event of disagreement, accept a system for the quick resolution of the dispute, such as recourse to an expert third party or an arbitrator, without prejudice to the parties' right to apply to a competent court in conformity with the provisions of national law. The new block exemption does not provide for any further details on how this expert third party or arbitrator should be selected nor should resolve the disagreements.

7.3.3.6 No Benefit of Exemption

The new text of Article 6 includes a long "black list" of situations in which the block exemption does not apply. According to the Commission, this "black list" improves the possibilities for national courts in the Member States to determine infringements of the Community's competition rules in this area. The Commission expects that the "black list" will give consumers the opportunity to purchase an automobile in any Member State and call upon the national courts in cases of refusal. The Commission emphasized that it would continue to take all necessary measures if undertakings through anti-competitive practices or agreements, isolate national markets by limiting parallel trade.[133]

Three of the situations listed in Article 6 are identical to or clearly based upon the old version of Article 6. There is *first* the situation in which both

---

[133] IP/96/1095.

parties to the agreement or their connected undertakings are automobile manufacturers (Article 6(1)(1)). The *second* regards the situation where in respect of automobiles or spare parts therefor, the parties make agreements or engage in concerted practices which are exempted from Article 85(1) EC under Regulations 1983/83 (exclusive distribution) or 1984/83 (exclusive purchasing) to an extent exceeding the scope of Regulation 1475/95 (Article 6(1)(4)). In this context, it should be noted that, pursuant to Article 12 of the revised block exemption, Regulation 4087/88 (franchising) is not applicable to agreements concerning the products or services referred to in Regulation 1475/95. As discussed, this provision was included at the very last minute during the meeting in which the Commission adopted the final text.[134] The *third* situation focuses on the restriction by the manufacturer, the supplier or another undertaking, directly or indirectly, of the dealer's freedom to determine prices and discounts in reselling contract goods or corresponding goods (Article 6(1)(6)).

Article 6 lists various new situations in which the exemption shall not apply. Article 6(1)(2) concerns the situation where parties link their agreement to stipulations concerning products or services *other* than those referred to in the block exemption or apply their agreement to such products or services. Article 6(1)(3) regards the situation where in respect of automobiles, the parties agree restrictions of competition that are not expressly exempted by the block exemption. Pursuant to Article 6(1)(5), the exemption does not apply where parties agree that the supplier reserves the right to conclude distribution and servicing agreements for contract goods with specified further undertakings operating within the contract territory, or to alter the contract territory.

Article 6(1)(7) is of great importance for consumers as it describes the situation where the manufacturer, the supplier or another undertaking within the network directly or indirectly restricts the freedom of final consumers, authorized intermediaries or dealers to obtain from an undertaking belonging to

[134] This *after* the consultation prescribed by Article 6 of Regulation 19/65 had already come to an end. It is an interesting question whether the consultation can be deemed sufficient now that the provision on Regulation 4087/88 was not included in the drafts presented to the Advisory Committee. If the contents of the provision concerned can be considered an essential issue at stake in the block exemption, one could argue that Regulation 1475/95 should be annulled as an essential procedural requirement was infringed. See H.G. Schermers, D. Waelbroeck, *Judicial Protection in the European Communities*, 5th edition, 1992, Kluwer Law and Taxation Publishers, Deventer, The Netherlands, at 203-204.

the network of their choice within the common market contract goods or corresponding goods or to obtain servicing for such goods, or the freedom of final consumers to resell the contract goods or corresponding goods, when the sale is not effected for commercial purposes. The importance of this provision is illustrated by the remarkable results of the Commission's investigation into complaints by consumers that Volkswagen, Audi, Mercedes and Opel systematically restrict parallel imports.[135]

Article 6(1)(8) regards the situation where the supplier, without any objective reason, grants dealers remunerations calculated on the basis of the place of destination of the automobiles resold or the place of residence of the purchaser. Article 6(1)(9) lists the situation where the supplier directly or indirectly restricts the dealer's freedom under Article 3(5) to obtain from a third undertaking of his choice spare parts which compete with contract goods and which match their quality. Article 6(1)(10) regards the situation where the manufacturer directly or indirectly restricts the freedom of suppliers of spare-parts to supply such products to resellers of their choice, including those which are undertakings within the distribution system, provided that such parts match

---

[135] See *Agence Europe*, "Mr Van Miert on current procedures", 7 December 1995, at 12, and "Communication of grievances to Volkswagen and Audi which prevent sale of their cars on Italian market to foreign customers", 29 November 1996, at 8; *FT*, "Brussels ultimatum to VW", 29 November 1996, at 2, and "Mercedes and Opel raided in EU pricing inquiry", 15-16 February 1997, at 1; "At times considerable price gaps remain on different EU markets, but tend to be stabilizing or closing - Commission initiatives to defend parallel imports", *Agence Europe*, 15 February 1997, at 14; "German carmakers in dock", *International Herald Tribune*, 15-16 February 1997, at 11; *NRC Handelsblad*, "VW zet dealers onder druk", 7 January 1998, at 15; *FT*, "VW faces fine over sales bar", 8 January 1998, at 2; "VW faces heavy fine over Italian practices", 27 January 1998, at 2; "VW to appeal against fine", 29 January 1998, at 2; IP/98/94, and *Agence Europe*, "Volkswagen will be penalized for refusing car sales in Italy to Austrian and German customers", 8 January 1998, at 11, "Fine for Volkswagen for restrictions on certain intra-Community trade practices in cars of around DM 200 million", 28 January 1998, at 15; "Heavy fine imposed on Volkswagen as the infringement is serious, says Karel van Miert", 29 January 1998, at 14; "Commission gives proof Volkswagen was fully aware it was behaving illegally in acting in a way that compartmentalized the European automobile market", 30 January 1998, at 8; "BEUC welcomes Volkswagen fine but deems this individual measure insufficient - Commission should introduce close monitoring of entire automobile market" and "Volkswagen contests existence of "systematic" infringement of European law", 31 January 1998, at 14. See also *The Economist*, "The irritating commissioner", 31 January 1998, at 78. See Commission Decision of 28 January 1998 relating to a proceeding under Article 85 of the EC Treaty (Case IV/35.733 - VW), OJ 1998, L124/60, and *FT*, "VW challenges record fine by Brussels", 15 April 1998, at 2.

the quality of contract goods. Article 6(1)(11) also concerns spare parts as it lists the situation where the manufacturer directly or indirectly restricts the freedom of spare part manufacturers to place effectively and in an easily visible manner their trade mark or logo on parts supplied for the initial assembly or for the repair or maintenance of contract goods or corresponding goods.

Last but not least, Article 6(1)(12) describes the situation where the manufacturer refuses to make accessible, where appropriate upon payment, to repairers who are not undertakings within the distribution system, the technical information required for the repair or maintenance of the contractual or corresponding goods or for the implementing of environmental protection measures, provided that the information is not covered by an intellectual property right or does not constitute identified, substantial, secret know-how. In such case, the necessary technical information shall not be withheld improperly.

Article 6(2) provides that without prejudice to the consequences for the other provisions of the agreement, in the cases specified in paragraph 1(1) to (5), the exemption shall not be applicable to all the clauses restrictive of competition contained in the agreement concerned. In the cases specified in paragraph 1(6) to (12), it shall apply only to the clauses restrictive of competition agreed respectively on behalf of the manufacturer, the supplier or another undertaking within the network which is engaged in the practice complained of. On the other hand, Article 6(3) provides that, without prejudice to the consequences for the other provisions of the agreement, in the cases specified in paragraph 1(6) to (12), the exemption shall not be applicable to the clauses restrictive of competition agreed in favour of the manufacturer, the supplier or another undertaking within the network which appear in the distribution and servicing agreements concluded for a geographic area within the common market in which the objectionable practice distorts competition, and only for the duration of the practice complained of.

The Commission qualifies Article 6(1)(1) to (5) as *black clauses* which "lead to an automatic loss of the benefit of the group exemption, if incorporated into exclusive and selective distribution agreements".[136] The exemption is not only inapplicable with regard to the black clauses but also with regard to all other restrictions of competition which are included in the agreement. It is a

---

[136] Explanatory Brochure, *supra* note 118, at 6.

question of national law whether or not the non-restrictive clauses in the agreement in question remain valid in such a situation. The practices listed in Article 6(1)(6) to (12) are so-called *black practices* which "also lead to the automatic loss of the exemption, if committed systematically or repeatedly".[137] In case of black practices, all clauses in the agreement which are restrictive of competition and which benefit the company responsible are no longer covered by the block exemption. The consequences of the misconduct are limited to the contract territory where the distortion of competition takes place but if competition is distorted in a larger area, the exemption is no longer applicable for all the distribution contracts concluded for the area concerned.[138]

7.3.3.7 Legal Effect

Notwithstanding the fact that Regulation 1475/95 entered into force on 1 July 1995, it only became applicable on 1 October 1995. The regulation will apply for a period of seven years until 30 September 2002.

The text of Articles 7 to 9 of Regulation 123/85 was deleted. Article 7 of the new block exemption deals with the *transition* from the old to the new block exemption. It provides that the prohibition of Article 85(1) EC shall not apply during the period from 1 October 1995 to 30 September 1996 to agreements already in force on 1 October 1995 which satisfy the conditions for exemption under the old block exemption.

Article 8 elaborates on the Commission's competence to *withdraw* the benefit of the exemption where it finds that in an individual case an agreement which falls within the scope of the block exemption nevertheless has effects which are incompatible with the provisions of Article 85(3) EC.[139] The provision gives three examples which differ from the four listed in the old block exemption. The *first* example describes the situation where, in the common

---

[137] *Ibidem*, at 6-7. According to the Commission, the word "repeatedly" means that the practice must have been committed several times. An isolated practice is sufficient only where it is part of a plan, in which case it is considered to be committed "systematically".

[138] *Ibidem*, at 7-8.

[139] It should be repeated that the Commission pointed out in its Explanatory Brochure, *supra* note 118, at 9, that the Notice 123/85, *supra* note 33, remains applicable under the revised block exemption.

market or a substantial part thereof, contract goods or corresponding goods are not subject to competition from products considered by consumers as similar by reason of their characteristics, price and intended use (Article 8(1)). The *second* regards the situation where prices or conditions of supply for contract goods or for corresponding goods are continually being applied which differ substantially as between Member States, such substantial differences being chiefly due to obligations exempted by the block exemption (Article 8(2)).[140] The *third* example on the list is the situation where the manufacturer or an undertaking within the distribution system in supplying the distributors with contract goods or corresponding goods apply, unjustifiably, discriminatory prices or sales conditions (Article 8(3)).

The text of Article 11 of Regulation 123/85 was deleted. Article 12 became Article 9 and confirms that the latter applies *mutatis mutandis* to concerted practices falling within the categories covered by Regulation 1475/95.

The new text of Article 11(1) puts the Commission under an obligation to *evaluate* on a regular basis the application of the new block exemption, particularly as regards the impact of the exempted system of distribution on price differentials of contract goods between the different Member States and on the quality of service to final users. In doing so, the Commission will collate the opinions of associations and experts representing the various interested parties, particularly consumer organizations (Article 11(2)). The Commission will draw up a report on the evaluation of the block exemption on or before 31 December 2000, particularly taking into account the impact of the exempted system of

[140] On 16 February 1996, both *FT*, at 1, and *Agence Europe*, at 14, reported on the release of Commission figures dated 1 November 1995, which showed that in spite of continued wide differences there is an overall narrowing of price differentials across the EU. See also IP/96/145 and IV/9511/96bn. See, however, *Agence Europe*, "Differences in car prices for the same models between Member States have increased and the Commission upholds the right of citizens to purchase in the country which is least expensive", 14 February 1998, at 15, and "Differentials between car prices in the EU are caused by monetary instability and tax differences, says ACEA", 19 February 1998, at 14. See also Written Question 2999/97 (Mather), OJ 1998, C158/26, and *Agence Europe*, "Price differences from one Member State to the next for the same model remain high, Commission is awaiting the Euro to determine whether or not the argument of monetary fluctuations is valid", 11 July 1998, at 10.

distribution on price differentials of contract goods between the different Member States and on the quality of service to final users.[141]

7.4 Article 86 EC

7.4.1 General Remarks

The block exemption for motor vehicle distribution and servicing agreements does not interfer with the application of Article 86 EC.[142] There is no doubt that Article 86 EC provides individuals both within and outside the pyramidical distribution and servicing system of a particular manufacturer with a legal basis for action against any abuse of a dominant position. These individuals can invoke Article 86 EC in complaints to the Commission and in legal proceedings before national courts. It will depend upon the specific circumstances of the case in question whether a party within the distribution system such as the manufacturer, importer or dealer is in a dominant position, and, if so, has abused it thereby (potentially) affecting trade between Member States. The Commission or the national courts will have to determine on a case-by-case basis whether or not Article 86 EC has been violated.[143] The discussion of the impact of Article 86 EC against the backdrop of the distribution and servicing of cars will be limited to cases dealing with the issuance of (type-approval)

---

[141] In its answer to Written Question 237/96 (Whitehead), OJ 1996, C122/36, the Commission specified that the regular evaluation will be carried out within the context of the Commission's annual report on competition policy and its bi-annual survey of car price differentials. The Commission noted that in its report to be drawn up by 31 December 2000 at the latest, it will analyse whether the objectives of the Regulation, and in particular those relating to car price differentials and service quality, have been attained. In view of the long list of cases in which complainants initiate legal action against the Commission for refusal to investigate, it is interesting to note that the Commission added that it "will actively monitor observance of the provisions of the Regulation".

[142] 35th Whereas of Regulation 1475/95. The ECJ pointed out in Case 226/84, *British Leyland* v *Commission ("BL")*, [1986] ECR 3301, par. 16, that the fact that a (BL's) distribution system has been accepted by the Commission cannot justify an (BL's) abuse of (its) dominant position.

[143] For instance, in *O.E.C. Nederland B.V.* v *Hart Nibbrig & Greeve B.V.*, 17 October 1990 (Nr. 89/6365), the District Court in The Hague, the Netherlands, found that the Mitsubishi supplier in question was in a dominant position *vis-á-vis* its dealers. The plaintiff also filed a complaint with the Commission. See Case T-32/90, *OEC Nederland* v *Commission*, *supra* note 5.

certificates of conformity (**7.4.2**), and the exercise of copyrights and design rights (**7.4.3**).

7.4.2 Type Approval

Before the Community type approval procedure was put in place, type approval and the issuance of certificates of conformity was primarily governed by the national laws of the Member States. Certificates of conformity issued in a Member State did not have to be accepted as such in other Member States. However, in most, if not all Member States, automobiles were not allowed on the road without a (type approval) certificate of conformity. In many cases, manufacturers were given by law the responsibility of issuing the necessary certificates of conformity including those for parallel imported automobiles. This brought manufacturers in a position to make the parallel importation of their makes outside the authorized distribution network less attractive.

For instance, in 1974, the Commission established that *General Motors Continental* had infringed Article 86 EC by charging an excessive price for the issuance of the legally required certificates of conformity and type-shields for new Opel-automobiles which were imported into Belgium through other channels than through GM's authorized distribution system.[144] Under Belgian law, both the certificates and shields were to be issued after the automobiles concerned were checked on their conformity with the generally approved type and after their identification was determined. In its decision, the Commission established that by virtue of Belgian law and of the authorization granted to it by Opel, GM had a *dominant position* with regard to applications for general type approval and the issue of certificates of conformity and type-shields in Belgium, both for new Opel vehicles and those registered abroad for no longer than six months in a substantial part of the common market. The Commission pointed out that purchasers of these Opel vehicles were obliged to avail themselves of GM's services before using the vehicle on the public highways in Belgium if (i) the relevant model had not yet received type approval, or (ii) no certificate of conformity or typeshield had been issued for the relevant vehicle. The

[144] Commission Decision 75/75 of 19 December 1974 (IV/28.851 - General Motors Continental), OJ 1975, L29/14.

Commission came to the conclusion that whenever a consumer or dealer in Belgium decides to purchase an Opel vehicle outside Belgium, he became completely dependent on GM.[145] Subsequently, the Commission found an *abuse* of dominant position as a number of circumstances showed that GM charged "substantially excessive prices" to applicants for the issue of certificates of conformity and typeshields for new Opel vehicles. The Commission noted the "extraordinary disparity between actual costs incurred and prices actually charged" and added that the excessive price acted to the detriment and unfairly discriminated against, those dealers who imported, or were in a position to import, new Opel automobiles into Belgium as parallel imports and who were able to compete in Belgium with the authorized Opel-dealers.[146] According to the Commission, the abuse affected *trade between Member States* as the reciprocal economic interpenetration of markets sought under the EC Treaty by means of the free flow of goods, had been impeded by the abusive inspection charges. The Commission considered it likely that the excessive charges would deter consumers and independent dealers in other Member States from purchasing Opel automobiles or noticeably impede such sales.[147] But GM was succesfull in having the ECJ declare the Commission's decision void. The ECJ confirmed that the GM was in a dominant position but did not find an abuse in view of the fact that after several complaints, GM reduced the charges and refunded the excess to the parties concerned.[148]

A similar situation arose when *British Leyland* took measures to restrict the parallel importation of cheap Metro's into the United Kingdom. These measures regarded the issuance of certificates of conformity for Metro's which were imported into the United Kingdom otherwise than through the authorized BL distribution system. In 1984, the Commission decided that by taking these measures, BL violated Article 86 EC.[149] In an instructive judgment, the ECJ

---

[145] *Ibidem*, par. 7.

[146] *Ibidem*, par. 8.

[147] *Ibidem*, par. 9.

[148] Case 26/75, *General Motors Continental* v *Commission*, [1975] ECR 1367.

[149] Commission Decision 84/379 of 2 July 1984 (IV/30.615 - BL), OJ 1984, L207/11.

upheld the Commission's decision.[150] First, the ECJ confirmed that BL was in a *dominant position* and specified that the relevant market was not that of the sale of vehicles but instead a separate, ancillary market, namely that "of services which are in practice indispensable for dealers who wish to sell the vehicles manufactured by BL in a specific geographical area". The ECJ held that the British rules conferred on BL a form of administrative monopoly in the relevant market and, with regard to the issue of certificates of conformity, placed the dealers in a position of economic dependence which is characteristic of a dominant position.[151] The ECJ subsequently agreed with the Commission that BL had *abused* its dominant position, in short, (i) by deciding not to renew the British type approval certificate which enabled the issuance of certificates of conformity for the LHD-Metro's as a means of impeding re-importation of these Metro's into the United Kingdom from other Member States; (ii) by refusing for about ten months while the British type approval certificate was still in place, to cooperate and provide services leading to the issuance of certificates of conformity for these LHD-Metro's; and (iii) by charging a fee which was clearly disproportionate to the economic value of the service provided.[152]

7.4.3 Intellectual Property Rights

Although a legal system which guarantees both the existence and exercise of intellectual property rights is essential for the automobile industry within the Community, it complicates the creation of a single market within the Community as intellectual property rights are territorial in nature and provide the holder with an exclusive right in a particular territory only. Notwithstanding Community efforts to harmonize the national laws of the Member States on intellectual property rights, there are still considerable differences in the manner in which Member States deal with the various intellectual property rights.

Car manufacturers use national copyrights and design rights on parts to prevent independent manufacturers from producing, importing and selling parts

[150] *BL*, *supra* note 142, at 3263.

[151] *Ibidem*, paras. 5-9.

[152] *Ibidem*, paras. 12-32.

which are often of a quality similar to "original" parts but much cheaper.[153] As car manufacturers simply refuse independent manufacturers their consent for the production and sale of protected parts, a so-called "captive market" is created leaving consumers no choice but to purchase the more expensive "original" parts from the car manufacturer holding the intellectual property right in question. In *Volvo* v *Veng*, the question arose whether the refusal by the proprietor of a registered design on body panels for motor vehicles to grant a licence for the import and sale of such panels may, in certain circumstances, be regarded as an abuse of a dominant position within the meaning of the Article 86 EC.[154] Volvo was the holder of a registered design on a particular body panel. Veng imported and sold the same body panels, manufactured without Volvo's consent, in the United Kingdom. In its judgment of 5 October 1988, the ECJ first held that in the absence of Community harmonisation, the determination of the conditions and procedures under which protection of designs and models is granted, is a matter for national rules and that it is for the national legislature to determine which products are to benefit from protection, even where they form part of a unit which is already protected as such. Then, the ECJ held:

> It must also be emphasized that the right of the proprietor of a protected design to prevent third parties from manufacturing and selling or importing, without its consent, products incorporating the design constitutes the very subject-matter of his exclusive right. It follows that an obligation imposed upon the proprietor of a protected design to grant to third parties, even in return for a reasonable royalty, a licence for the supply of products incorporating the design would lead to the proprietor thereof being deprived of the substance of his exclusive right, and that a refusal to grant such a licence cannot in itself constitute an abuse of a dominant position.

---

[153] See for instance the report of the Monopolies and Mergers Commission on *Ford Motor Company Limited*, "A report on the policy and practice of the Ford Motor Company Limited of not granting licences to manufacture or sell in the United Kingdom certain replacement body parts for Ford vehicles", Cmnd. 9437, London, Her Majesty's Stationery Office. See also "The European Commission closes the proceeding against Ford in the case involving sales of body panels", *Agence Europe*, 11 January 1990, at 7.

[154] Case 238/87, *Volvo* v *Veng*, [1988] ECR 6211.

> It must however be noted that the exercise of an exclusive right by the proprietor of a registered design in respect of car body panels may be prohibited by Article 86 if it involves, on the part of an undertaking holding a dominant position, certain abusive conduct such as the arbitrary refusal to supply spare parts to independent repairers, the fixing of prices for spare parts at an unfair level or a decision no longer to produce spare parts for a particular model even though many cars of that model are still in circulation, provided that such conduct is liable to affect trade between Member States.[155]

Thus, in certain circumstances, the exercise of an intellectual property right including the refusal to grant a license, may constitute a violation of Article 86 EC.[156] However, the ECJ specified in *Maxicar* with regard to the considerable difference in prices between "original" parts sold by the manufacturer and those sold by the independent producers, that a higher price in itself does not necessarily constitute an abuse, since the proprietor of protective rights in respect of an ornamental design may lawfully call for a return on the amounts which he has invested in order to perfect the protected design.[157]

7.5 Concluding Remarks

The pyramidal distribution and servicing networks of car manufacturers bring cars and parts from the manufacturer through importers, distributors, dealers and/or sub-dealers to the consumer. Already in the early days, the Community took the position that the specific characteristics of the product "automobile" justifies a selective distribution system. In 1985, the highly technical block exemption regulation 123/85 was adopted. Unfortunately, the Commission did not specify its experiences underlying the contents of the block exemption. The block exemption provided the automobile industry with an important possibility

---

[155] *Ibidem*, paras. 8-9. See also *Maxicar*, *supra* note 62, paras. 15-17, and Case C-38/98, *Renault* v *Maxicar and Orazio*, OJ 1998, C113/8.

[156] See also Joined Cases C-241/91P and C-242/91P, *RTE and ITP* v *Commission*, [1995] ECR I-743 and Case T-504/93, *Tiercé Ladbroke* v *Commission*, [1997] ECR II-923.

[157] *Maxicar*, *supra* note 62, par. 17.

to remove distribution and servicing agreements from the scope of Article 85(1) EC despite the inclusion of certain types of exclusivity and no-competition clauses.

By adopting the block exemption, the Community directly interfered with the relationship between the car manufacturer and dealers. It made it very attractive to draw up distribution and servicing agreements that conformed to the block exemption. The block exemption only regarded the relationship between the supplier and the approved dealers. It was heavily criticized for a variety of reasons. For instance, the block exemption gave manufacturers a strong grip on dealers. It complicated the entry on the market of manufacturers from third countries which had difficulty finding dealers. Furthermore, it was pointed out that the block exemption kept prices at a higher level than necessary.

After a long and heated debate, the block exemption was amended and replaced by Regulation 1475/95. Due to a lack of transparency, not all interested parties were in an equal position to participate in the early stages of the discussions. Again, the Commission did not specify its experience that lead to the various amendments which were to stimulate competition and strengthen the position of dealers vis-à-vis suppliers. The Commission underlined its efforts to reduce the considerable differences in car prices between Member States that are not necessarily the result of fluctuations in currency exchange rates and differences between national systems on car tax. The introduction of the Euro will probably reduce the price differences. The Commission encourages consumers to purchase cars in the Member State with the lowest price, and keeps a close eye on any possible barriers to parallel imports.

In 1995, the Commission did not discuss the very existence of the block exemption. It explicitly confirmed that the block exemption is not only a competition policy instrument but also an instrument to pursue other Community policy interests such as the efficient management of the voluntary export restraint arrangement with Japan, and the strengthening of the competitiveness of the Community's automobile industry. The Commission seems unwilling to have competition policy considerations thwart the efficient management of the arrangement with Japan.

8. STATE AID IN THE AUTOMOBILE INDUSTRY

8.1 Introduction

State aid to the automobile industry is scrutinized by the Community within the framework of its competition policy. Such scrutiny takes place on the basis of Articles 92 to 94 EC, the Community rules on state aid.[1] However, as is the case with the distribution and servicing of automobiles and parts, Community policies and activities other than competition policy such as the creation of an internal market, common commercial policy interests and the strengthening of the competitiveness of Community industry, have a significant impact on the manner in which the Community scrutinizes aid measures. This has been recognized by the Commission in general policy statements[2] and decisions.[3]

A description and analysis of the manner in which the Commission deals with state aid in the automobile industry is complicated by the fact that it is very difficult, if not impossible, to obtain a complete picture of the facts and the Commission's arguments to (dis)allow particular aid measures. It is often simply the lack of information available to the public which is the most important barrier to an examination of the Commission's policy on state aids.[4] This lack of transparency makes the scrutiny of aid measures somewhat obscure and tends to

---

[1] See on the Community rules on state aid, *inter alia*, L. Hancher, T. Ottervanger and P.J. Slot, *EC State Aids*, 1993, Chancery Law Publishing, London; Bellamy and Child, *Common market law of competition* (V. Rose ed.), 1993, Sweet & Maxwell, London, at 908-953; *State aid: Community law and policy* (I. Harden ed.), 1993, Bundesanzeiger, Köln; T. Joris, *Nationale steunmaatregelen en het Europees gemeenschapsrecht*, 1994, MAKLU, Antwerpen, and A. Evans, *European Community law of state aid*, 1997, Clarendon Press, Oxford.

[2] For instance, in its XVIIth Report on Competition Policy, par. 219, at 165, the Commission pointed out that state aids in favour of particular firms "in some cases might also undermine in the long run efforts to increase European competitiveness *vis-à-vis* third countries".

[3] For instance, in State Aid N 497/88 (Netherlands/Volvo Car), OJ 1989, C281/5, the Commission confirmed that it expected that the creation of "a single EEC market by 1992" will "contribute further to the competitiveness of the EEC car industry at world-level". The Commission was convinced, however, "that, in order for the EEC car industry to benefit fully from the internal market, it is also necessary to create an economic environment of fair competition, of openess towards the rest of the world and of strict control on state aid". In Decision 89/661 of 31 May 1989 (Decision Alfa Romeo), OJ 1989, L394/17, the Commission recognized that in its appreciation of aid cases, the fact that "[a]s market integration progresses as part of the process of creating a single market without internal frontiers by 1992, distortions of competition caused by granting aid are felt more and more keenly by competitors not receiving any aid", must also be taken into account.

[4] See in this context Written Question 2532/97 (Carlsson), OJ 1998, C82/103.

undermine the credibility of the Commission's activity in this politicaly speaking, highly sensitive part of competition policy.[5] One would expect that the Commission has a clear interest in pursuing a public policy on state aid which is truely *public* thereby encouraging and facilitating its implementation. It is remarkable that the Commission does not provide more information on its decisions with regard to state aids.[6]

This chapter will describe and analyze the manner in which Articles 92 to 94 EC are applied to state aid in the automobile industry. After an introduction to the Community rules on state aid (**8.2**), the guidelines set out in the 1989 Community Framework on state aid to the motor vehicle industry will be examined (**8.3**). Subsequently, the amendments introduced by the 1998 Community Framework for state aid to the motor vehicle industry will be described (**8.4**). This chapter comes to an end with concluding remarks (**8.5**).

8.2 Community Rules on State Aid

8.2.1 General Remarks

In its very first Report on Competition Policy, the Commission elaborated on the interpretation and application of the Community rules on state aids and emphasized that experience had shown that "Member States cannot always be immediately and fully aware of the Community perspective in the matter, such perspective nevertheless guaranteeing effectiveness and a saving in national

---

[5] This lack of transparency and credibility is illustrated by the manner in which the Commission dealt with the Italian aid to Fiat in support of its 2nd Mezzogiorno Investment Plan. Whereas the Commission announced the opening of the Article 93(2) EC procedure in a rather detailed publication of more than four pages in which major concerns were listed, the decision to terminate the procedure was motivated with just eleven (!) lines in the XXIInd Report on Competition Policy, par. 411, at 235. See State Aid C 45/91 (ex N 255/91) Italy (Mezzogiorno II), OJ 1991, C299/4. See also XXIst Report on Competition Policy, par. 236, at 173.

[6] The Commission's lack of openness is illustrated by the fact that the Commission was not prepared to make available to the public a discussion paper on regional state aid which was in one way or another at the disposal of the press; the paper was quoted in *FT*, 28 February 1996, at 2. In answer to the author's request for a copy, the Information Officer of DG IV characterized the paper in a fax dated 18 March 1996, as "merely a working document" which "cannot be made available to the public". The fax is on file with the author.

initiatives".[7] Member States tend to use aid measures as instruments of national economic policy in an effort to pursue their own national economic and social objectives.[8] State aid is often granted to attract investment in certain regions, to finance the restructuring of "national champions" and to stimulate research and development strengthening the competitiveness of domestic industries.[9] The Commission is aware of the fact that in view of the importance of the automobile industry at a national level for strategic, economic, technical, employment and political reasons, "the tendency to spend large amounts of public funds on State aids to the motor vehicle industry is high".[10]

Articles 92 to 94 EC are part of the Community's rules on competition and have to be read in the context of Article 3g EC that puts the Community under an obligation to ensure that competition in the internal market is not distorted.[11] The focal point of the Community rules on state aid is not the national

---

[7] Ist Report on Competition Policy, par. 133, at 113.

[8] For instance, the ECJ recognized in Case 61/79, *Amministrazione delle Finanze dello Stato* v *Denkavit (Denkavit)*, [1980] ECR 1228, par. 31, that Article 92(1) EC "refers to the decisions of Member States by which the latter, in pursuit of their own economic and social objectives, give, by unilateral and autonomous decisions, undertakings or other persons resources or procure for them advantages intended to encourage the attainment of the economic and social objectives sought". *FT*, "Commissioner urges tighter state aid rules", 17 April 1997, at 3, reported that "member states -particularly the richest- have resorted to state aid to cushion the effects of economic downturns and global competition on domestic industry". See also *FT*, "Keeping state aids in check", 3 July 1996, at 11.

[9] For instance, the Commission noted in State Aid C 38/93 (NN 43/93 and NN 58/93) The Netherlands, OJ 1994, C31/10, with regard to restructuring aid to DAF that the Dutch authorities wanted "to retain an innovative, technologically high-value company for the Netherlands, at the centre of a cluster of suppliers and knowledge institutes". See also Written Question 2594/97 (Van Velzen), OJ 1998, C82/115.

[10] XVIIth Report on Competition Policy, par. 219, at 165. The Commission reported in its Framework for state aid to the motor vehicle industry, OJ 1997, C279/1, that between 1970 and 1980, several Member States injected massive amounts of aid into the modernization and development, or the survival, of their domestic car industry. In the period 1977 to 1987, state aid to the motor vehicle industry, essentially in the form of capital injections or extensive debt write-offs, is estimated at ECU 26 billion. See for an overview also "The effect of different state aid measures on intra-Community competition - Exemplified by the case of the automotive industry" (prepared by K. Bhaskar and the Motor industry research unit), EUR-OP, March 1990.

[11] See in this context the First (1981-1986), Second (1987-1988), Third (1989-1990), Fourth (1991-1992) and Fifth (1993-1994) Survey on state aids in the European Community in the manufacturing and certain other sectors, published by the Commission of the European Communities.

interest of a particular Member State but the compatibility of the aid measures with the common market as a whole. Basicly, industrial problems and unemployment should not be transferred from one Member State to another as the result of aid measures.[12] State aid to undertakings active in the automobile industry constitutes a serious threat of distortion of competition in this highly competitive industry.[13] It is evident that this makes the application of the

[12] As pointed out in *FT*, "Foolish aid" (Editorial), 8 July 1997, at 13, "[i]f each nation tries to prop up industries at the expense of neighbours, they will all be rewarded by high prices, poor service - and higher unemployment". According to *FT*, "The aidbusters' charter", 14 November 1996, at 15, "there is a danger of member states becoming involved in a subsidy war in the fight against unemployment" and such a war "could only distort the single market and further widen the gulf between rich and poor countries".

[13] It is interesting to note that the ECJ recognized in Case 30/59, *De Gezamenlijke Steenkolenmijnen in Limburg* v *High Authority (GSL)*, [1961] ECR 19, in the context of the ECSC Treaty, that aid "constitutes an obstacle to the most rational distribution of production at the highest possible level of productivity inasmuch as, .., it makes it possible to fix or maintain selling prices which are not directly related to production costs and thereby to establish, maintain and develop economic activity which does not represent the most rational distribution of production at the highest possible level of productivity". The ECJ concluded that aid measures "are incompatible with the common market because they constitute an obstacle to one of its essential aims".

Community rules on state aid politically very sensitive.[14] Some Member States tend to aggressively pursue their national economic policy objectives and do not

[14] *FT*, "In pursuit of a competitive edge", 30 August 1995, at 13, reported that the Bundeskartellamt advocates an independent competition authority as a way of depoliticising decisions on state aid. *FT*, "Brussels may curb state aid to industry", 26 May 1997, at 2, reported that the Commission has drawn up proposals to depoliticise the process by which the Commission scrutinizes state aids, making it harder for governments to influence the outcome of decisions. UNICE called for the reinforcement of third party rights under the Community state aid rules. According to UNICE, rival companies are often in the best position to assess the potential impact of aid in their sector and their opinion may help counter political pressure exerted by Member States concerned with having aid approved but on which the Commission has doubts. See UNICE Position Paper, "Greater transparency and improved enforcement of state aid rules", 28 June 1996. See also *FT*, "Keeping state aids in check" (Editorial) and "Brussels urged to boost challenge to illegal state aid", 3 July 1996, at 11 and 2, and *Agence Europe*, "UNICE calls for regulation and directive in order to ensure fairer and more effective state aid and to strengthen the role of competitive companies", 8-9 July 1996, at 15; "Commission proposes strengthening controls on aid, improving procedures and making them more transparent", 19 February 1998, at 8; "Debate on state aid reveals radical divergences between Commission and Member States, but a first step forward to reform is taken", 9 May 1998, at 4, and "Commission recognizes downward trend in seven states, but claims aid levels remain too high and plans to maintain pressure on governments to reduce aid - initiatives taken or announced", 27 June 1998, at 10.

hesitate to put pressure on both "their" Commissioners[15] and the Commission as a whole, to approve certain aid measures.[16]

8.2.2 The Concept of State Aid

The Community rules on state aid are only relevant to measures which qualify as "aid" within the meaning of Article 92(1) EC: "any aid granted by a Member State or through State resources in any form whatsoever". The concept of state aid is not further specified nor defined in the EC Treaty. In its case law, the ECJ indicated that the concept of aid is very wide[17] and specified that Article 92(1) EC refers to the decisions of Member States to give "undertakings or other persons resources or procure for them advantages intended to encourage the attainment of the [Member States'] economic and social objectives".[18] This wide concept of aid

---

[15] See, for instance, "Sir Leon Brittan accused in Rover case: British Labour MEP Alan Donnelly wants a debate in the EP", *Agence Europe*, 10 May 1990, at 11, which reported on Donnelly's accusations that Brittan "covered up for the British government" and acted like a British politician rather than a European Commissioner. It should be kept in mind, however, that the Commission noted in Written Question 1404/97 (Pasty), OJ 1997, C391/81, that "the Members of the Commission are politicians carrying out a political function, who, while honouring the obligations imposed by this function, remain free to express their personal opinions quite independently and on their own responsibility".

[16] A good example is the political conflict between the Commission and Volkswagen, Germany and Saxony on state aid to VW in Eastern Germany. See *FT*, "EU plan to trim car aid hits snag", 19 June 1996, at 2; "VW halts expansion in east as Brussels cuts aid", 27 June 1996, at 1; "Brussels warns VW over $60 m state aid", 19 August 1996, at 16; "Brussels pressed to clear VW aid", 20 August 1996, at 2; "Brussels talks set on VW aid", 21 August 1996, at 2; (Editorial) "Subsidies in Germany", 28 August 1996, at 11; "Saxony enters aid minefield", 2 September 1996, at 10; "Compromise likely on E German aid to VW", 3 September 1996, at 14; "Bonn and Brussels in deal over aid for VW", 5 September 1996, at 12; "VW aid fight part of wider battle", 6 September 1996, at 2; "Bonn and EU resort to court", 13 September 1996, at 2; "Volkswagen row nears end", 26-27 April 1997, at 4; "Bonn close to resolving VW row", 8 August 1997, at 2, and "Deal near on illegal aid to VW", 25-26 October 1997, at 2. *Agence Europe*, "Reimbursement by Volkswagen of excessive aid granted in Saxony has allowed Commission to clear another aid scheme to the same company", 19 November 1997, at 15, reported that the Commission settled its dispute with Saxony.

[17] See *GSL*, *supra* note 13, in which the ECJ clarified that "[t]he concept of an aid is .. wider than that of a subsidy because it embraces not only positive benefits, .., but also interventions which, in various forms, mitigate the charges which are normally included in the budget of an undertaking and which, without, therefore, being subsidies in the strict meaning of the word, are similar in character and have the same effect". A concise description of some relevant case law on the concept of state aid is provided by M.M. Slotboom, "State Aid in Community Law: A Broad or a Narrow Definition?", (1995) 20 ELRev, at 289-301.

[18] *Denkavit*, *supra* note 8, par. 31.

includes a great variety of different forms of advantages or benefits granted (in)directly from state resources.[19] Several efforts have been made to categorize aid measures. Geelhoed distinguishes regional aid, sectoral aid (general and specific sectoral policy), facet-aid (environment, research and development) and a "rest" category which includes for instance export-aid, aid to individual companies and restructuring-aid.[20] Hancher, Ottervanger and Slot, on the other hand, distinguish between sectoral aid and horizontal aid[21] and identify the following principal forms of aid: capital grants, capital injections, compensation for government-imposed financial burdens, debt conversion, direct subsidies, disposal of publicly-owned assets on preferential terms, foregoing of profits or other sums due, preferential tariffs, reductions in social charges, state guarantees, tax concessions and direct as well as indirect state participation in share capital.[22]

Over the years, Member States have awarded many different advantages to undertakings operating in the automobile industry which amounted to state aid. These aid measures varied from straightforward capital injections for the

[19] See Cases C-72/91 and C-73/91, *Sloman Neptun*, [1993] ECR I-887.

[20] L.A. Geelhoed in Kapteyn-VerLoren van Themaat, *Inleiding tot het recht van de Europese Gemeenschappen*, 5th revised edition, 1995, Kluwer, Deventer, at 478.

[21] Hancher, Ottervanger and Slot, *supra* note 1, at iv-vi, subdivide the category "sectoral aid" in textiles, chemical and pharmaceutical sector, motor vehicles, shipbuilding, transport, SME's and public sector aids. The category "horizontal aids" is subdivided in regional aids, energy, environmental aid and research & development aid.

[22] *Ibidem*, at 34.

repayment of financial debts,[23] the write off of debts[24] and interest subsidies on loans[25] to more covert advantages such as a reduced price for a site,[26] tax reductions[27] or unduly generous terms for the purchase of shareholdings.[28] The fact that several Member States are not only benefactors but also shareholders in undertakings active in the automobile industry, further complicates matters. In order to determine whether a financial advantage granted by a Member State constitutes state aid within the meaning of Article 92(1) EC, it is necessary to consider whether in similar circumstances a *private* investor of a size comparable to that of the public bodies concerned and operating under normal market economy conditions, would have taken the aid measures.[29] The conduct of the

---

[23] See, *inter alia*, Case C-305/89, *Italy* v *Commission (Alfa Romeo)*, [1991] ECR I-1640, paras. 21-23, and Commission Decision 89/58 of 13 July 1988 (Rover Group I), OJ 1989, L25/92.

[24] See, *inter alia*, IP/87/466, and Commission Decision 88/454 (Renault Group) of 29 March 1988, OJ 1988, L220/30. See also *Agence Europe*, "Le Gouvernement Francais s'est prévalu de la decision de Mars de la Commission Européenne pour annuler les dettes de Renault, apres avoir soumis la firme au droit commun des sociétes", 3-4 January 1989, at 8; "La divergence entre la Commission Européenne et le gouvernement Francais à propos des aides a Renault est loin d'etre aplanie", 3 June 1989, at 14; "La Commission Européenne demande au gouvernement Francais de récuperer 12 milliards de FF d'aides verses a Renault, sauf si un plan satisfaisant de restructuration est mis en oeuvre", 16 November 1989, at 10; "State aid to Renault: Sir Leon Brittan clarifies conclusions he is to submit to European Commission-Divergence from Bets confirmed", 14-15 May 1990, at 10; "Renault case: France says it respected its commitments", 18 May 1990, at 10; "Renault: European Commission decision (after agreement with the French government), 23 May 1990, at 9, and "Renault case: Satisfaction in Paris and Brussels on compromise-European Commission gives signal-Likely increase of Renault capital in 1991 (legal if the company is healthy), 24 May 1990, at 11.

[25] See, *inter alia*, Commission Decision 84/364 (Italian engine and tractor manufacturer) of 16 May 1984, OJ 1984, L192/35.

[26] See, *inter alia*, Commission Decision 92/11 of 31 July 1991 (Toyota Derbyshire), OJ 1992, L6/36; State Aid C 3/91 (ex NN 5/91) Germany, OJ 1991, C128/5, and Commission Decision 92/465 of 14 April 1992 (C 3/91 ex NN 5/91) (Daimler-Benz Berlin), OJ 1992, L263/15.

[27] See, *inter alia*, State Aid C 27/97 (ex NN 35/A/97) Italy, OJ 1997, C268/4. See also *Agence Europe*, "Mr Van Miert announces that the Commission is drafting fiscal aid guidelines - timetable", 8 July 1998, at 5.

[28] See, *inter alia*, State Aid C 3/92 (ex N 645/91) Netherlands-Volvo Car, OJ 1992, C105/16 and Commission Decision 94/1036 of 27 September 1994 (Decision NedCar) (C 3/92 ex N 645/91), OJ 1994, L384/1.

[29] See in this context G.B. Abbamonte, "Market economy investor principle: A legal analysis of an economic problem", [1996] 3 ECLR, at 258-268.

public body has to be compared to the conduct of a private holding company or a private group of undertakings pursuing a structural policy, whether general or sectorial, and guided by prospects of profitability in the longer term; aid measures which comply with the so-called "market economy investor principle" do not constitute aid within the meaning of Article 92(1) EC.[30]

The Commission can make its decision that certain measures do not constitute aid within the meaning of Article 92(1) EC subject to conditions which can be imposed upon the Member State and the recipient of the aid.[31]

8.2.3 Compatibility of State Aid with the Common Market

8.2.3.1 General Rule: Article 92(1) EC

Article 92(1) EC provides that state aid is incompatible with the common market, save as otherwise provided in the EC Treaty, if it distorts or threatens to distort competition by favouring certain undertakings or the production of certain goods, in so far as it affects trade between Member States. General measures which are taken by a Member State within the framework of its economic policy and benefit *all* undertakings within the Member State concerned, remain in principle outside the scope of Article 92(1) EC as these measures do not favour certain

---

[30] For instance, in Renault Group, *supra* note 24, the Commission underlined its position that state aid is involved where fresh capital is contributed in circumstances that would not be acceptable to a private investor operating under normal market-economy conditions. According to the Commission, this is the case where the financial position of a company, and particularly the structure and volume of its debt, is such that a normal return (in dividends or capital gains) cannot be expected within a reasonable time from the capital invested, or where, because of its inadequate cash-flow if for no other reason, the company would be unable to raise the funds needed for an investment programme on the capital market. See also Xth Report on Competition Policy, par. 209, at 144 (Volvo Car), Commission Decision 89/633 (Enasa) of 3 May 1989, OJ 1989, L367/66; State Aid C 32/89 (ex N 497/88) Netherlands-Volvo Car, OJ 1991, C143/6; *Alfa Romeo*, *supra* note 23, paras. 19-20; Commission Decision 97/17 of 30 July 1996 (Santana Motor), OJ 1997, L6/34; "Allocation of costs of NedCar automobile manufacturer (involving Dutch State) does not comprise aid", *Agence Europe*, 3 July 1997, at 10, and State Aid N 463/95 (Cost allocation rules of NedCar), OJ 1998, C25/11.

[31] See, for instance, Decision NedCar, *supra* note 28.

undertakings or the production of certain goods.[32]

The ECJ's case law shows that it is often very difficult to determine whether aid is granted to all undertakings or (covertly) only to certain undertakings in the Member State.[33] With regard to infrastructure, the Commission has taken the position that the construction by public authorities of infrastructure that is traditionally paid for out of public funds does not constitute aid in the meaning of Article 92(1) EC. But this can be different if the infrastructure is construed for the benefit of certain undertakings or the production of certain goods.[34] The Commission has pointed out that the provision of infrastructure does not entail state aid where infrastructure services like electricity are normally provided to users on a commercial basis and the

---

[32] For instance, in its answer to Written Question 626/97 (Moretti), OJ 1997, C319/139, the Commission noted that the Italian law introducing subsidies for those buying new cars in Italy, provides aid measures irrespective of the origin of the car. The law does not include any condition, for instance technical specifications, that would be more likely to be fulfilled by certain producers. According to the Commission, this case is parallel to the cases of incentives to consumers for the renewal of old cars or for the purchase of low-polluting cars which have been in force in other Member States, where because of the non-discriminatory nature of the incentive, the Commission was of the view that it did not favour certain car producers and thus did not infringe Article 92(1) EC.

[33] See for instance Case 173/73, *Italy* v *Commission*, [1974] ECR 709 and Case 203/82, *Commission* v *Italy*, [1983] ECR 2525. See also Hancher, Ottervanger and Slot, *supra* note 1, at 25-26.

[34] In response to Written Question 28 (Dehousse), JO 1967, at 2311, the Commission noted that "la construction par la puissance publique d'infrastructures qui sont traditionnellement à la charge des budgets de l'État ou de ses démembrements ne constitue pas une aide au sens de l'article 92 ... . Il en est autrement au cas où ces ouvrages seraient réalisés au bénéfice d'une ou de certaines entreprises ou productions déterminées". In the context of aid to Daimler-Benz for the plant at Rastatt, the Commission reported in its XVIIth Report on Competition Policy, par. 220, at 166, that it considered "site clearance and the usual connection costs (sewerage, energy and water supply, etc.) which will be paid for by the .. authorities" not to constitute aid "as Daimler-Benz AG will contribute towards them through local taxes".

public authorities have undertaken that this will continue to be the case with no modification or special conditions.[35]

According to the Commission, not all aid measures have an appreciable effect on trade and competition between Member States. In its *de minimis*-notice, the Commmission has taken the position that under certain conditions, Article 92(1) EC does not apply to (mostly small amounts of) state aid, so that the latter need no longer be notified in advance to the Commission under Article 93(3) EC.[36] First of all, it is still a matter of considerable debate whether the Commission is in a position to introduce a *de minimis* rule into the Community rules on state aid.[37] Secondly, it is submitted that most, if not all, state aid to an undertaking active in the highly competitive automobile industry constitutes an appreciable[38] advantage *vis-á-vis* competitors which distorts or threatens to distort competition and effects trade between Member States; there is an intensive trade between Member States in the automobile sector.[39] The ECJ noted with regard to capital injections to *Alfa Romeo* that:

> where an undertaking operates in a sector in which there is surplus production capacity and producers from various member states compete, any aid which it may receive from the public authorities is liable to affect trade between the member states and impair competition,

[35] See Summary of the Commission Decision not to raise objections to the aid which the Portuguese Government plans to grant to the joint-venture of Ford and Volkswagen to establish a multi-purpose vehicle plant in the Setubal peninsula (AutoEuropa), OJ 1991, C257/5. Confirmed by Case C-225/91, *Matra* v *Commission*, [1993] ECR I-3250. See also Case C-225/91 R, *Matra* v *Commission*, [1991] ECR 5823.

[36] Commission notice on the *de minimis* rule for State aid, OJ 1996, C68/9. This notice builds on point 3.2 of the Community guidelines on State aid for small and medium-sized enterprises (SMEs), OJ 1992, C213/2.

[37] See, *inter alia*, E.G. Stuart, "Recent developments in EU law and policy on state aids", [1996] 4 ECLR, at 229-231.

[38] See Case 248/84, *Germany* v *Commission*, [1987] ECR 4041, par. 18.

[39] In its decisions, the Commission often illustrates the "intensive intra-Community trade" by quoting trade figures. See, *inter alia*, Decision Alfa Romeo, *supra* note 3.

> inasmuch as its continuing presence on the market prevents competitors from increasing their market share and reduce their chances of increasing exports.[40]

Nevertheless, the Commission has taken the position that the *de minimis* rule for state aid is also applicable with regard to the automobile industry.[41] It is up to the Commission to substantiate that the aid measures concerned distort or threaten to distort competition and are likely to affect trade between Member States.[42]

Aid measures can escape the qualification "incompatible with the common market" by meeting the conditions set out in Article 92(2) or (3) EC.[43] In its case law, the ECJ explicitly confirmed that the prohibition of Article 92(1) EC "is neither absolute nor unconditional since Article 92(3) and Article 93(2) give the Commission a wide discretion and the Council extensive power to admit aids in derogation from the general prohibition in Article 92(1)".[44]

8.2.3.2 Automatic Exceptions: Article 92(2) EC

Article 92(2) EC lists the following three specific types of state aid which *shall* be compatible with the common market:

> (a) aid having a social character, granted to individual consumers, provided that such aid is granted without discrimination related to the origin of the products concerned;

---

[40] See *Alfa Romeo, supra* note 23, par. 26. In Case 102/87, *France* v *Commission*, [1988] ECR 4087, paras. 19-20, the ECJ held that "aid to an undertaking may be such as to affect trade between the Member States and distort competition where that undertaking competes with products coming from other Member States, even if it does not itself export its products. Such a situation may exist even if there is no over-capacity in the sector at issue". In addition, the ECJ seemed to imply that the condition of Article 92(1) EC that the aid "affects trade between Member States" is fullfilled if the aid is *likely* to affect trade between Member States.

[41] See in this sense Competition Policy Newsletter, Spring 1996, Vol. 2, Number 1, at 33.

[42] See Joined Cases 296 and 318/82, *The Netherlands and Leeuwarder Papierwarenfabriek* v *Commission*, [1985] ECR 824-826, paras. 22-30, and *Germany* v *Commission, supra* note 38, par. 18.

[43] In addition, aid measures can escape the prohibition of Article 92 EC *via* special provisions like Article 90(2) EC. See for instance Case C-387/92, *Banco Exterior de España*, [1994] ECR I-909, par. 21.

[44] Case 78/76, *Firma Steinike und Weinlig* v *Germany (Steinike)*, [1977] ECR 609, par. 8.

(b) aid to make good the damage caused by natural disasters or exceptional occurrences;
(c) aid granted to the economy of certain areas of the Federal Republic of Germany affected by the division of Germany, in so far as such aid is required in order to compensate for the economic disadvantages caused by that division.

These types of aid are of an exceptional nature and the use of the word "shall" in Article 92(2) EC seems to imply that the Commission has a very limited margin of discretion.[45] Over the years, the Commission has been very reluctant to apply the derogations set out in Article 92(2) EC.[46]

Since the German reunification in 1990, the Commission has taken the position that state aid to areas in the former Federal Republic of Germany would not be dealt with (anymore) under Article 92(2)(c) EC but under Article 92(3)(c) EC instead.[47] The Commission has pointed out that the exemption provided for in Article 92(2)(c) EC must be interpreted strictly and that the derogations provided for in Article 92(3)(a) and (c) EC and the Framework, allow it to deal with the problems which the new *Länder* are facing.[48]

---

[45] See, for instance, Case 730/79, *Philip Morris Holland* v *Commission (Philip Morris)*, [1980] ECR 2690, par. 17.

[46] However, in Daimler-Benz Berlin, *supra* note 26, L263/23, the Commission recognized that the German authorities "could grant State aid and that such State aid was necessary in order to offset the disadvantages created for D[aimler-]B[enz] by the circumstances surrounding the contract of sale at that time before the unification".

[47] See XXth Report on Competition Policy, par. 178.

[48] Commission Decision 94/1068 of 27 July 1994 (VW I), OJ 1994, L385/1, and Commission Decision 96/666 of 26 June 1996 (VW II), OJ 1996, L308/46. Several appeals have been filed: Case C-301/96, *Germany* v *Commission*, OJ 1996, C336/18; Case C-302/96, *Commission* v *Germany*, OJ 1996, C336/19; Case T-132/96, *Sachsen* v *Commission*, OJ 1996, C336/29, and Case T-143/96, *Volkswagen* v *Commission*, OJ 1996, C336/30. See also Commission Decision 97/13 of 26 June 1996 (Mercedes-Benz/Ludwigsfelde), OJ 1997, L5/30. See for critical remarks: B. Perry, "State aids to the former East Germany: A note on the VW/Saxony case", (1997) 22 E.L.Rev: Feb., at 86-88, and "Mr Berend criticises certain Commission tendencies aimed at ending the current regional status of Eastern Germany - Letter to Commissioner Van Miert", *Agence Europe*, 20 April 1996, at 14.

8.2.3.3 Other Exceptions: Article 92(3) EC

Article 92(3) EC lists five types of aid which *may* be considered compatible with the common market. These exceptions have to be construed *narrowly* and can only be applied when the free play of market forces alone, would not induce the prospective aid recipient to adopt a course of action contributing to attainment of one of these objectives.[49] Furthermore, the aid has to be both necessary for and justified by, the recipient's contribution to the attainment of one of the objectives set out in Article 92(3) EC.[50]

Whereas the exception of Article 92(3)(e) EC provides the Council with the competence to derogate from Article 92(1) EC, it is up to the Commission to examine and eventually decide whether aid measures qualify for one of the exceptions formulated in Article 92(3)(a) to (d) EC. In doing so, the Commission exercises a discretion involving economic and social assessments which must be made in a Community context instead of in the national context of a single Member State. The exceptions listed in Article 92(3) EC specify objectives in the Community interest transcending the interests of the aid recipient.[51]

Over the years, the Commission specified the conditions under which particular types of aid measures can qualify for an exception under Article 92(3) EC and may, therefore, be considered compatible with the common market. For

---

[49] See, *inter alia*, Italian engine and tractor manufacturer, *supra* note 25; Renault Group, *supra* note 24; Rover Group I, *supra* note 23; Decision Alfa Romeo, *supra* note 3; Enasa, *supra* note 30, and Toyota Derbyshire, *supra* note 26. Advocate-General Capotorti in *Philip Morris*, *supra* note 45, 2701, confirmed the strict interpretation of Article 92(3) EC. See for a somewhat similar restrictive approach in the context of Article 85(3) EC, *inter alia*, Case C-70/93, *BMW* v *ALD Auto-Leasing*, [1995] ECR I- 3471, par. 28.

[50] See, *inter alia*, Italian engine and tractor manufacturer, *supra* note 25. In its XIIth Report on Competition Policy, par. 160, at 110, the Commission specified that it would take into consideration whether (i) the aid promotes a development which is in the interest of the Community as a whole, (ii) the aid is necessary to bring about the development concerned and (iii) the modalities of the aid (for instance the intensity, duration and the degree of distortion of competition) are commensurate with the importance of the objective of the aid.

[51] See, *inter alia*, Case 310/85, *Deufil* v *Commission (Deufil)*, [1987] ECR 926, par. 18, and *Philip Morris*, *supra* note 45, par. 17. In its Decision 85/378 of 19 December 1984 (FIM), OJ 1985, L216/18, the Commission emphasized in the context of Article 92(3) EC that "[f]urtherance of the priority industrial interests of France, .., .. cannot be said to be sufficiently in the Community interest to justify application of one of the exceptions, for in significant cases the schemes are likely to affect trading conditions to an extent contrary to the common interest by strengthening the position of the aided firms *vis-à-vis* their competitors in the Community".

instance, in a communication of 24 January 1979, the Commission emphasized that rescue aid can only be regarded as compatible with the common market, if it fulfils the following conditions:

- it must consist of cash aid in the form of loan guarantees or loans bearing normal commercial interest rates,
- it must be paid only for the time needed, generally not exceeding six months, to draw up the necessary and feasible recovery measures,
- it must not have any adverse effects on the industrial situation in other Member States,
- it must be notified to the Commission in advance in significant individual cases.[52]

The Commission can make its decision under Article 92(3) EC that certain aid measures are compatible with the common market, subject to conditions imposed upon the Member State or the recipient of the aid.[53] If a Member State does not comply with these conditions, the Commission can institute proceedings under the second subparagraph of Article 93(2) EC. If the Commission finds that the Member State concerned has granted new aid measures which were no part of the procedure leading to its decision specifying the conditions, the Commission has to institute the special procedure provided for by the first subparagraph of Article 93(2) EC.[54]

The following four of the five types of aid listed in Article 92(3) EC are relevant to the automobile industry.

---

[52] VIIIth Report on Competition Policy, par. 228. See also Decision Alfa Romeo, *supra* note 3.

[53] See, for instance, Rover Group I, *supra* note 23, L25/99.

[54] Case C-294/90, *British Aerospace and Rover* v *Commission (BA Rover)*, [1992] ECR I-493, paras. 12-13. After the annulment of its decision State Aid C 8/88 (EX N 119/88) United Kingdom, OJ 1991, C21/2, the Commission first confirmed the illegal status of the new aid measures in State Aid C 5/92 (ex NN 23/92) United Kingdom, OJ 1992, C122/3, after which it took Commission Decision 93/349 of 9 March 1993 (Rover Group II), OJ 1993, L143/7, ordering the refund of the aid increased with interest. See also XXth Report on Competition Policy, par. 260, at 195; XXIInd Report on Competition Policy, par. 413, at 235, and XXIIIrd Report on Competition Policy, par. 515, at 298.

(i) Article 92(3)(a) and (c) EC

Article 92(3)(a) and (c) EC provide for two exceptions which are to the benefit of the development of particular *regions*. Pursuant to Article 92(3)(*a*) EC, aid may be considered compatible with the common market if it promotes the economic development of areas where the standard of living is abnormally low or where there is serious underemployment. The assessment whether this is the case should take place in relation to the Community level only.[55] In *Enasa*, the Commission specified that the concept of regional aid development to which the exception of Article 92(3)(a) EC is linked, is based essentially on the provision of aid for new investment or major expansions or conversions of undertakings involving investments of a physical nature and the costs associated with these.[56]

Pursuant to Article 92(3)(*c*) EC, aid may be considered compatible with the common market if it facilitates the development of certain economic areas, where such aid does not adversely affect trading conditions to an extent contrary to the common interest. Whether this is the case can be assessed in relation to the national level.[57] The Commission uses the guidelines developped with regard to regional aid schemes in order to determine whether aid measures qualify for the exception of Article 92(3)(c) EC.[58]

An important element in the Commission's assessment of aid measures under Article 92(3)(a) and (c) EG is the contribution of the aid measures to the

---

[55] See, *inter alia*, *Philip Morris*, *supra* note 45, 2691, par. 25.

[56] Enasa, *supra* note 30.

[57] The ECJ held in Case 248/85, *Germany* v *Commission*, [1987] ECR 4042, par. 19, that "the use of the words "abnormally" and "serious" in ... Article 92(3)(a) shows that it concerns only areas where the economic situation is extremely unfavourable in relation to the Community as a whole. The exemption in Article 92(3)(c), on the other hand, is wider in scope inasmuch as it permits the development of certain areas without being restricted by the economic conditions laid down in Article 92(3)(a), provided such aid "does not adversely affect trading conditions to an extent contrary to the common interest". That provision gives the Commission power to authorize aid intended to further the economic development of areas of a Member State which are disadvantaged in relation to the national average".

[58] See, *inter alia*, Renault Group, *supra* note 24, and Daimler-Benz Berlin, *supra* note 26, L263/24.

long-term economic development of the region involved.[59] In *Alfa Romeo*, the Commission underlined that the simple fact that some of Alfa Romeo's production plants were located in regional assisted areas, was not enough. Instead, the Commission pointed out, with reference to its Communication on the method for the application of Article 92(3)(a) and (c) to regional aid,[60] that the aid measures concerned constituted rescue aid "which caused serious distortion of competition in the Community car industry since they were not linked to a restructuring plan which would solve the structural problems of the company and restore its viability". The Commission concluded that the aid measures "cannot be considered to have contributed to the long-term economic development of the regions since they did not secure the long-term viability of employment and were not linked to the regional economy and thus do not qualify as acceptable regional aid".[61]

---

[59] See, for instance, Vth Report on Competition Policy, par. 118, at 85, in which the Commission reported that it had not objected to aid measures to encourage the creation of new activities in certain parts of Germany. The aid became necessary after Volkswagen dismissed workers which created employment problems.

[60] OJ 1988, C212/2.

[61] Decision Alfa Romeo, *supra* note 3. Confirmed in *Alfa Romeo, supra* note 23, paras. 34-37. See also Enasa, *supra* note 30, in which the Commission concluded that the aid measures could not benefit from the exceptions in Article 92(3)(a) and (c) EC. The Commission noted that although one of Enasa's production plants was located in a regional assisted area, the aid measures under consideration were not intended to specifically develop the region concerned but to restructure a company operating throughout the Member State concerned. Moreover the aid related to the financing of a very small amount of investment in such areas.

(ii) Article 92(3)(b) EC

Article 92(3)(b) EC provides that aid may be considered compatible with the common market if it promotes the execution of an important *project* of common European interest or the *remedy* of a serious disturbance in the economy of a Member State. This exception has been invoked several times with regard to aid to the automobile industry but so far with little success. The Commission has taken the position that aid measures do not promote the execution of an important project of common European interest if the recipient of the aid would be led to undertake the investment in any case by market forces.[62] Furthermore, the Commission has pointed out that an event which merely has negative effects on the economy of a Member State, is not as such sufficient to apply Article 92(3)(b) EC to an aid scheme. The recovery of the entire national economy should be concerned.[63]

(iii) Article 92(3)(c) EC

Pursuant to Article 92(3)(c) EC, aid may be compatible with the common market if it facilitates the development of certain economic *activities*, where such aid does not adversely affect trading conditions to an extent contrary to the common interest. Various types of aid can be brought under this exemption. In view of the fact that the automobile industry is highly competitive even within the Community, aid measures easily affect trading conditions between Member States to the detriment of the common interest. Aid to one undertaking in the automobile industry has almost automatically detrimental effects for competitors within the common market.

Article 92(3)(c) EC provides the Commission with the possibility to declare *rescue or restructuring* aid compatible with the common market[64] if the aid is necessary for the development of the sector from a Community standpoint,

---

[62] See, *inter alia*, Italian engine and tractor manufacturer, *supra* note 25.

[63] The Commission has pointed out that although it is true that German unification has had negative effects on the German economy, these alone are not sufficient to apply Article 92(3)(b) EC to Germany. See Notice State Aid C 60/91 (ex NN 73/91, NN 76/91) Germany (Opel Eisenach), OJ 1993, C43/18, and VW I, *supra* note 48.

[64] In VIIIth Report on Competition Policy, par. 176, the Commission confirmed that Article 92(3)(c) EC favours "aid to facilitate the development of restructuring aids to be compatible with the common market if a number of criteria are fulfilled".

and the aid does not alter trading conditions to an extent contrary to the common interest.[65] The intensity of the aid has to be proportionate to the problem it is designed to resolve so that distortions of competition are kept to a minimum. In certain circumstances and under strict conditions, restructuring aid may reduce the social and economic costs of change. However, the aid should not have as a result that industrial problems and unemployment are transferred from one Member State to another.[66] The aid measures have to be part of or at least clearly linked to a restructuring plan leading to the restoration of long-term viability. Unless granted over relatively short periods, aid has to be progressively reduced. In view of the constant danger of excess capacity in the automobile industry, a restructuring plan will nearly always have to include a reduction of capacity in the sector. If the aid leads (even if it is not its primary purpose[67]) to a net expansion of the recipient's production capacity, the chances are very small that the aid will qualify for an exception under Article 92(3)(c) EC.[68]

Furthermore, aid measures which benefit *environmental improvements*[69] or *genuine innovations* at Community level may also be considered compatible with the common market under Article 92(3)(c) EC.[70] The innovations have to be

---

[65] *Philip Morris*, *supra* note 45, par. 26.

[66] In its Vth Report on Competition Policy, par. 118, at 85, the Commission reported in the context of aid to Citroën, British Leyland and Chrysler U.K., that "aids .. may be justified is so far as it is likely that the recipients, after reorganization, will be commercially viable and able to compete succesfully, and if the measures taken do not aggravate existing problems at Community level or merely transfer these problems to other Member States". See also Xth Report on Competition Policy, par. 208, at 144 (British Leyland) and XIth Report on Competition Policy, par. 216, at 136.

[67] See, *inter alia*, Italian engine and tractor manufacturer, *supra* note 25.

[68] See for other examples of restructuring aid in the automobile industry: XVIIth Report on Competition Policy, par. 224, at 168 (Pai-Demm); XIXth Report on Competition Policy, par. 183, at 163 (Ford Lusitana); Renault Group, *supra* note 24; Rover Group I, *supra* note 23, L25/98; Decision Alfa Romeo, *supra* note 3, and Enasa, *supra* note 30.

[69] The Commission reported in its Xth Report on Competition Policy, par. 207, at 143, that it had authorized aid to a "car firm located in the Antwerp region" for environmental improvements, under the terms of the Community approach to State aids in environmental matters.

[70] See in this context K. Bhaskar, *Innovation in the EC automotive industry - An analysis from the perspective of state aid policy*, April 1988, Luxembourg, EUR-OP.

"genuine". Modernization and product rejuvenation as such are not sufficiently in the Community interest to justify application of Article 92(3)(c) EC.[71]

(iv) Article 92(3)(e) EC

Acting by a qualified majority on a proposal from the Commission, the Council can on the basis of Article 92(3)(e) EC, decide that categories of aid measures may be considered compatible with the common market.

8.2.3.4 Commission's Discretionary Power

The Commission has a wide margin of appreciation in its assessment of aid measures.[72] Over the years, the Commission has tried to develop policies with regard to the evaluation of the different categories of state aid. The principles underlying those policies were initially set out in the Commission's General Reports and from 1971 onwards in its Reports on Competition Policy.

Eventually, the Commission published so-called *horizontal* guidelines on particular categories of state aid, such as:

---

[71] See, *inter alia*, XIIIth Report on Competition Policy, par. 261, at 169; XVIth Report on Competition Policy, par. 226 (Pai-Demm), at 153; Decision FIM, *supra* note 51; Renault Group, *supra* note 24; Commission Decision 89/348 of 23 November 1988 (Valeo), OJ 1989, L143/47, and Commission Decision 89/305 of 21 December 1988 (Peugeot), OJ 1989, L123/52.

[72] Advocate-General Capotorti described the Commission discretionary power in *Philip Morris*, *supra* note 45, at 2701, as "a discretionary power implying an assessment of an economic, technical and policy nature". The ECJ confirmed that "Article 92(3), unlike Article 92(2), gives the Commission a discretion by providing that the aid which it specifies "may" be considered to be compatible with the common market" (par. 17) and that "the Commission has a discretion the exercise of which involves economic and social assessments which must be made in a Community context" (par. 24).

- Community Framework for state aid for research and development,[73]
- Community Guidelines on state aid for rescuing and restructuring firms in difficulty,[74]
- Community Guidelines on state aid for environmental protection,[75]
- Community Guidelines on state aid for small and medium-sized enterprises,[76]
- Commission Communication on national regional aid,[77]
- Commission Communication to the Member States regarding the application of Articles 92 and 93 EC and of Article 5 of Commission Directive 80/723 to public undertakings in the manufacturing sector,[78]
- Commission Communication on the cumulation of aids for different purposes,[79]
- Commission Communication on the elements of state aid in land sales by public authorities,[80] and
- Multisectoral framework on regional aid for large investment projects.[81]

In addition, the Commission published guidelines on certain *sectors* such as the

[73] OJ 1996, C45/5. See also Commission communication amending the Community framework for state aid for research and development, OJ 1998, C48/2.

[74] OJ 1997, C283/2. See also Commission communication concerning extension of the guidelines on state aid for rescuing and restructuring firms in difficulty, OJ 1998, C74/31.

[75] OJ 1994, C72/3.

[76] OJ 1996, C213/4.

[77] OJ 1998, C74/9.

[78] OJ 1993, C307/3. See Commission Directive of 25 June 1980 on the transparency of financial relations between Member States and public undertakings, OJ 1980, L195/35; Commission Directive 93/84 of 30 September 1993 amending Directive 80/723 on the transparency of financial relations between Member States and public undertakings, OJ 1993, L254/16.

[79] OJ 1985, C3/2.

[80] OJ 1997, C209/3.

[81] OJ 1998, C107/7. See also Commission Notice pursuant to Article 93(2) of the EC Treaty to other Member States and interested parties regarding Germany's refusal to accept the introduction of the multisectoral framework on regional aid for large investment projects, OJ 1998, C171/4.

Community Framework for state aid to the motor vehicle industry.[82] The Commission has expressed its intention to come up with a horizontal or multi-sectoral framework after the year 2000 which could eventually replace the various sectoral frameworks.[83]

It can very well happen that aid measures have to be notified and scrutinized under more than one set of guidelines.[84] However, the Commission has pointed out that in sectors where special Community rules exist such as in the motor vehicle industry, the horizontal guidelines apply only to the extent that they are consistent with those special rules.[85]

8.2.4 Review of State Aid

Article 93 EC provides the Commission with the task of reviewing existing aids and assessing whether plans to grant or alter aid are compatible with the common market.[86] Article 93(1) EC provides that the Commission shall, in cooperation with Member States, keep under constant review all systems of aid existing in

---

[82] OJ 1997, C279/1.

[83] See, for instance, Commission Decision 96/313 (Spanish aid schemes) of 20 December 1995, OJ 1996, L119/55, and State Aid C 66/97 (Sweden), OJ 1997, C326/3, par. 1. *FT*, "Brussels may curb state aid to industry", 26 May 1997, at 2, reported that the Commission is drawing up proposals for a "multi-sectoral" framework under which all state aid over ECU 50 million would be examined by the Commission.

[84] For instance, the Commission noted in State Aid C 38/93 (NN 43/93 and NN 58/93) (The Netherlands), OJ 1994, C31/12-13, with regard to aid by the Dutch authorities to DAF that the measures "had to be notified both under the framework on State aid to the motor vehicle industry as under the framework for State aids for research and development" and emphasized that since the public intervention concerned a company in difficulties operating in a sector which suffers excess capacity, it considered it inevitable "to assess the measures with respect to DAF in the light of the Articles 92 *et seq.* of the EC Treaty and more in particular the provisions of the Community framework on State aid in the motor vehicle industry and the application of State aid rules to public authorities' holdings". See also State Aid C 36/93 (NN 27/93) Belgium, OJ 1994, C31/6.

[85] Mercedes-Benz/Ludwigsfelde, *supra* note 48.

[86] The ECJ confirmed the central role of the Commission in the application of the Community rules on state aid, *inter alia*, in *Steinike*, *supra* note 44, at 609, par. 9, as it emphasized that "the intention of the Treaty, in providing through Article 93 for aid to be kept under constant review and supervised by the Commission, is that the finding that an aid may be incompatible with the common market is to be determined, subject to review by the Court, by means of an appropriate procedure which it is the Commission's responsibility to set in motion".

those States (so-called "*existing aid*").[87] Furthermore, it shall propose to the latter any appropriate measures required by the progressive development or by the functioning of the common market.

Pursuant to Article 93(3) EC the Commission has to be informed, in sufficient time to enable it to submit its comments, of any plans to grant or alter aid (so-called "*new aid*").[88] Article 93(3) EC obliges Member States to notify and obtain the Commission's prior approval before implementing aid measures.[89] If the Commission considers after a preliminary assessment that any of the aid measures are not compatible with the common market having regard to Article 92 EC, it shall without delay initiate the procedure under Article 93(2) EC. The Commission has to define its attitude under Article 93(3) EC within a period of two months.[90]

The Member State concerned is obliged not to put its proposed measures into effect until this procedure has resulted in a final decision.[91] This prohibition laid down in the last sentence of Article 93(3) EC has direct effect. It is up to the national courts to safeguard and preserve the rights which individuals enjoy as a result of the direct effect of this prohibition until the final decision of the Commission.[92] In view of the mandatory nature of the rules of procedure laid

---

[87] Existing aids are aid measures which were already granted before the EC Treaty entered into force for the Member State concerned and those aid measures which have been introduced via the procedure of Article 93(2) or (3) EC.

[88] In practice, Member States do not always notify aid measures nor provide the Commission with correct information on the aid measures concerned. See for instance Opel Eisenach, *supra* note 63, and State Aid C 8/88 (EX N 119/88) United Kingdom, OJ 1991, C21/2.

[89] See in this context the Commission Communication on Article 93(3) EC, OJ 1983, C318/3.

[90] See Case 120/73, *Lorenz* v *Germany (Lorenz)*, [1973] ECR 1471, par. 4.

[91] As the ECJ pointed out in, *inter alia*, Case 77/72, *Capolongo* v *Maya*, [1973] ECR 621, par. 6, "[w]hilst, for projects introducing new aids or altering existing ones, the last sentence of Article 93(3) establishes procedural criteria which the national court can appraise, the same does not hold true for existing systems of aid referred to in Article 93(1)". The ECJ noted in *Lorenz, supra* note 90, at 1481, par. 4, that "[t]he objective pursued by Article 93(3), .., implies that this prohibition is effective during the whole of the preliminary period".

[92] See Case C-354/90, *Fédération nationale du commerce extérieur des produits alimentaires and Syndicat national des négociants et transformateurs de saumon* v *France*, [1991] ECR I-5527, paras. 9-14, and Notice on cooperation between national courts and the Commission in the State aid field, OJ 1995, C312/8.

down in Article 93(3) EC, aid granted without prior notification is illegal[93] but not necessarily incompatible with the common market.[94] The illegal nature of the aid cannot be remedied *ex post*[95] and the Commission can require the Member State concerned to recover the illegal aid with interest, from the recipient.[96] The Commission has made ample use of this possibility.[97]

Article 93(2) EC sets out the procedure which has to be commenced *immediately*[98] after the Commission has come to the conclusion that the notified aid measures are not compatible with the common market. It should be stressed, however, that the procedure can also be initiated with regard to existing aid and (other) aid measures which have not been notified to the Commission under Article 93(3) EC.[99] The first subparagraph of Article 93(2) EC provides that if, after giving notice to the parties concerned to submit their comments,[100] the Commission finds that aid granted by a State or through State resources is not compatible with the common market having regard to Article 92 EC, or that such aid is being misused, it shall decide, that the State concerned shall abolish or alter such aid within a specific period of time. The second subparagraph of Article 93(2) EC specifies that if the Member State concerned does not comply with this decision within the prescribed time, the Commission or any other interested State

---

[93] See, *inter alia*, *Lorenz*, *supra* note 90, par. 4, and *Steinike*, *supra* note 44, par. 9.

[94] It is up to the Commission to decide on the compatibility of the aid measures concerned on the basis of a substantive assessment. See Case C-301/87, *France* v *Commission*, [1990] ECR I-354, paras. 9-24.

[95] See, for instance, Commission Decision 88/468 of 29 March 1988 (International Harvester/Tenneco), OJ 1988, L229/37.

[96] See, *inter alia*, Case 70/72, *Commission* v *Germany*, [1973] ECR 829, par. 13; Case 173/73, *Italy* v *Commission*. [1974] ECR 717, par. 9, and, more recently, with regard to the recovery of illegal aid from Alfa Romeo: Case C-348/93, *Commission* v *Italy*, [1995] ECR I-673.

[97] See, *inter alia*, Rover Group II, *supra* note 54; Peugeot, *supra* note 71; Decision Alfa Romeo, *supra* note 3; Toyota Derbyshire, *supra* note 26. For instance, the Commission reported in IP/89/452, that Peugeot repaid the state aid following its negative decision.

[98] See, *inter alia*, Case 84/82, *Germany* v *Commission*, [1984] ECR 1488, par. 12.

[99] See, *inter alia*, Case 173/73, *Italy* v *Commission*, [1974] ECR 716, paras. 7-9.

[100] As the term "interested parties" refers to all persons, undertakings or associations whose interests might be affected by the grant of the aid, a notice in the OJ was considered by the ECJ to be "an appropriate means of informing all the parties concerned that a procedure has been initiated". See Case 323/82, *Intermills* v *Commission*, [1984] ECR 3826, paras. 16-17.

may refer the matter to the ECJ directly.

However, pursuant to the third subparagraph of Article 93(2) EC, the *Council* may, on application by a Member State, acting unanimously, decide that aid which that State is granting or intends to grant shall be considered to be compatible with the common market, in derogation from the provisions of Article 92 or from the regulations provided for in Article 94, if such a decision is justified by exceptional circumstances. If, as regards the aid in question, the Commission has already initiated the procedure provided for in the first subparagraph of Article 93(2) EC, the fact that the State concerned has made its application to the Council shall have the effect of suspending that procedure until the Council has made its attitude known. According to the fourth subparagraph of Article 93(2) EC, the Commission shall give its decision on the case if the Council has not made its attitude known within three months of said application being made.

8.2.5 Council Regulations

Based on Article 94 EC, the Council may make any appropriate regulations for the application of Articles 92 and 93 EC and may in particular determine the conditions in which Article 93(3) EC shall apply and the categories of aid exempted from this procedure. In doing so, the Council has to act by a qualified majority on a proposal from the Commission and after consulting the European Parliament. The Council agreed upon a regulation based upon Article 94 EC, which will enable the Commission to define block exemptions for certain categories of horizontal aid. Aid measures falling under a block exemption do not have to be notified under Article 93(3) EC.[101]

---

[101] See Council Regulation 994/98 of 7 May 1998 on the application of Articles 92 and 93 of the Treaty establishing the European Community to certain categories of horizontal State aid, OJ 1998, L142/1. See also "Industry Council gives political agreement on draft regulation aimed at exempting certain categories of horizontal aid from the obligation to notify the Commission", *Agence Europe*, 14 November 1997, at 6. See also Proposal for a Council Regulation laying down detailed rules for the application of Article 93 of the EC Treaty, 18 February 1998, COM(1998)73 final.

8.3 1989 Framework on State Aid to the Motor Vehicle Industry

8.3.1 Introductory Remarks

Article 93(1) EC prescribes that the Commission shall, in cooperation with Member States, keep under constant review all systems of aid existing in those States. Furthermore, it obliges the Commission to propose to the latter any appropriate measures required by the progressive development or by the functioning of the common market. The Commission decided to introduce such "appropriate measures" with regard to the automobile industry and informed the Member States of its decision to implement the Community Framework on State Aid to the Motor Vehicle Industry.[102]

In view of the growing sensitivity of competition in the automobile industry,[103] the Commission proposed that the Member States notify as from 1 January 1989, in advance "significant cases of aid to the motor vehicle sector" in accordance with the rules laid down in the Framework.[104] The Commission emphasized the automobile industry's strategic industrial and employment importance to the Community and pointed out that the Framework was introduced with the *intention* to:

> establish full transparency of aid flows to the industry and impose at the same time a stricter discipline to the granting of aids in order to assure that the competitiveness of the Community industry is not distorted by

---

[102] OJ 1989, C123/3. In its XIth Report on Competition Policy, par. 215, at 136, the Commission had expressed "its intention of establishing an *a posteriori* monitoring system for national aids, which would cover both specific aids and the use of other schemes to assist the automobile industry". See also XIIth Report on Competition Policy, par. 191, at 131.

[103] Point 1, par. 4, of the Framework. The Commission noted in Netherlands/Volvo Car, *supra* note 3, that distortion of competition caused by the granting of aid to one Community car producer is more and more keenly felt by competitors not receiving aid, in particular when taking into account the process of creating a single market without internal frontiers by 1992. The fact that this had to be taken into account by the Commission in its appreciation of aid cases, was explicitly confirmed in Decision Alfa Romeo, *supra* note 3.

[104] Point 1, par. 6 of the Framework. Changed by Framework for State aid in the motor vehicle sector, OJ 1995, C284/3, into "Having completed its examination, the Commission decided to propose to the Member States under Article 93(1) of the EC Treaty that they notify in advance, in accordance with the rules set out below, significant cases of aid to the motor vehicle sector".

> unfair competition. The Commission can operate an effective policy only if it is able to take position on individual cases before the aid is paid.[105]

The Commission confirmed that interests other than purely competition policy interests are relevant to the application of Articles 92 to 94 EC to the automobile industry. The Commission noted that it can "contribute to the healthy development of the sector and ensure that the companies adapt and adjust in time to changing market circumstances"[106] but added that it "is not seeking to impose an industrial policy strategy on the sector" as "such decisions are best left to the industry and the market itself".[107] Nevertheless, the Commission announced that its aid policy was to "be geared to the process of creating a single market without internal frontiers by 1992"[108] and pointed out:

> As market integration progresses, distortions of competition caused by the granting of aid are felt more and more keenly by competitors not receiving any aid. All manufacturers are entitled to a consistent approach compatible with the Treaty. At the same time, the market integration process may provoke a growing tendency for Member States to provide aid to firms that are no longer able to stand up to fair competition. In this more efficient market, so as to ensure their survival. Furthermore, over-reliance on State aid to solve problems of industrial adjustment *vis-à-vis* third country producers undermines competitiveness of the Community car manufacturing by hindering the economically healthy influence of market forces.[109]

---

[105] Point 1, par. 4 of the Framework. See also Commission Communication "A single Community motor-vehicle market", SEC(89) 2118 final, par. 2.2.4.

[106] Point 1, par. 2 of the Framework.

[107] Point 3, par. 2 of the Framework.

[108] Point 1, par. 3 of the Framework. Changed by Framework for State aid in the motor vehicle sector, OJ 1995, C284/3, into "The Commission's future aid policy must be in line with the conditions of a single market without internal frontiers that has been in operation since end 1992".

[109] Point 1, par. 3 of the Framework.

The distortive effect of aid measures has put all actors within the automobile industry including the Commission and Member States on alert.[110]

8.3.2 Acceptance by Member States

A large majority of 10 Member States agreed from the outset with the application of the Framework. Spain and Germany, however, refused to do so for various, sometimes even conflicting, reasons. Whereas *Germany* formally rejected the Framework as it "is motivated by and pursues industrial policy objectives",[111] *Spain* was disposed to apply the Framework "provided that the framework forms part of a Community-wide industrial policy for the sector".[112] In reaction, the Commission initiated the procedure provided for by Article 93(2) EC with respect to all approved aid schemes which were at the time in operation in Germany and Spain and (potentially) benefited the automobile industry. In the end, the implementation of the Framework was delayed during the first six months of 1989 pending its acceptance by 10 Member States, until January 1990 for Spain and May 1990 for Germany.[113] It was reported that the very first case which was dealt with under the Framework, regarded aid by the Italian authorities to Ferrari for technological innovation.[114]

At the end of the Framework's first two years covering the period *1989-1990*, the Commission carried out a first review of the utility and scope of the

---

[110] For instance, the Commission reported in VW I, *supra* note 48, and VW II, *supra* note 48, that France would keep a close eye on the Commission's handling of the case. The active role of the Commission is illustrated by Decision 96/179 of 31 October 1995 (C 62/91 ex NN 75, 77, 78 and 79/91), OJ 1996, L53/50, in which the German Government was obliged to provide all documentation, information and data on the aid to the new investment projects of the Volkswagen Group in the new German Länder.

[111] See State Aid E 4/89 (Federal Republic of Germany), OJ 1989, C281/6, 8th par.

[112] See State Aid E 5/89 (Spain), OJ 1989, C281/8, 5th and 7th par.

[113] See XXth Report on Competition Policy, par. 249, at 157; 1st renewal of the Community Framework on State Aid to the Motor Vehicle Industry, OJ 1991, C81/4, footnote 2, and Commission Decision 90/381 of 21 February 1990 (German aid schemes), OJ 1990, L188/55.

[114] *Agence Europe*, 14 September 1989, at 14 ("Premiere application du Code des aides à l'automobile, la Commission approuve une aide à Ferrari (Italie)"). See also XIXth Report on Competition Policy, par. 189, at 166. Certain aid cases which started before the coming into force of the Framework were not dealt with under the Framework. See XXth Report on Competition, paras. 258-260, at 194-195.

Framework.[115] The Commission concluded in the first quarter of 1991 that it was necessary to renew the Framework for the period *1991-1992* and confirmed that a second review would take place at the end of this period.[116] On 8 December 1992, the second review took place during a multilateral meeting with the Member States. As a large majority of Member States was satisfied with the application of the Framework, the Commission decided on 23 December 1992 that the Framework would "remain valid until a next review to be organized by the Commission" thereby renewing the Framework for the period 1993 until the date of review.[117] Spain did not agree and initiated legal action against the Commission. One of the Spanish grievances was that by deciding to extend the validity of the Framework until a further review, the Commission altered the very nature of the Framework by making it valid for an indefinite period. Spain argued that by unilaterally changing the nature of the Framework in this way without first consulting the Member States and obtaining their consent, the Commission went beyond the limits of its competence under Article 93(1) EC. In its judgment of 29 June 1995, the ECJ first confirmed previous case law that:

> where the wording of secondary community law is open to more than one interpretation, preference should be given to the interpretation wich renders the provision consistent with the treaty rather than the interpretation which leads to its being incompatible with the Treaty.[118]

Subsequently, the ECJ recognized that the provision to the effect that the

---

[115] Point 2.5 of the Framework. In 1995, the first two sentences were changed by Framework for State aid in the motor vehicle sector, OJ 1995, C284/3, into "The appropriate measures shall enter into force when all Member States have signalled their agreement or at the latest by 1 January 1996. All aid projects, which have not yet received a final approval by the competent public authority by that date, shall be subject to prior notification".

[116] 1st renewal of the Community Framework on State Aid to the Motor Vehicle Industry, OJ 1991, C81/4. See also XXth Report on Competition Policy, paras. 250-251, at 189-190. The Commission extended the prior notification obligation for the Federal Republic of Germany to (West-)Berlin and the territory of the former GDR.

[117] 2nd renewal of the Community Framework for State Aid to the Motor Vehicle Industry, OJ 1993, C36/17. The Commission emphasized that, in December 1990, it "decided to renew the framework without setting a time limit on its application". However, it "undertook to review it after two years". See also XXIInd Report on Competition Policy, par. 405, at 232.

[118] Case C-135/93, *Spain* v *Commission*, [1995] ECR I-1683, par. 37.

Framework would "remain valid until a next review to be organized by the Commission" may appear ambiguous but added that looking at Article 93(1) EC, the Commission's decision of 23 December 1992 had to be interpreted "as having extended the framework only until its next review, which, like the previous ones, had to take place at the end of a further period of application of two years".[119] As a result, the Framework was only extended until 1 January 1995 covering the period *1993-1994*.[120] This created a legal vacuum for the monitoring under the Framework for the period starting on 1 January 1995.

In an effort to fill this vacuum, the Commission resorted to some unconventional measures which were discussed and agreed upon with the Member States in a multilateral meeting on 4 July 1995, and subsequently announced in a press-release.[121] The Commission decided to introduce interim measures to ensure the continued effective enforcement of State aid control and took the peculiar step of retroactively prolonging the Framework from 1 January 1995 until the re-introduction of the Framework. The Framework's maximum duration would be until 31 December 1995 (covering the period *1995*). In addition, the Commission decided to re-introduce the (slightly amended) Framework as from 1 January 1996 covering the period *1996-1997*.[122]

Again, Spain did not agree and initiated legal action. In its turn, the Commission started the procedure under Article 93(2) EC with regard to all

---

[119] *Ibidem*, par. 39.

[120] It was reported in *Agence Europe*, 1 July 1995, at 8 ("The Court of Justice notes that the guidelines for state aid for the car sector expired end-1994 thereby creating, according to Mr. Van Miert, a "dangerous situation"-Commission initiative"), that "[s]ome circles consider that this case could have a certain influence on on-going discussions over Spanish State aid for the SEAT car firm, subsidiary of Volkswagen". It was reported that the Commission had received notification, by the Spanish authorities, of the restructuring plan of SEAT which enabled the Commission to decide on aid under this plan.

[121] IP/95/698. See also Written Question 2227/95 (Méndez de Vigo), OJ 1996, C40/18, and *Agence Europe*, 6 July 1995, at 10 ("In order to fill the legal void left by the Court of Justice decision, the Commission extends for 1995 the Aid Framework to the Automobile sector and proposes a slightly modified regime for next year").

[122] The threshold of ECU 12 million was changed into ECU 17 million, taking into account inflation over the last 7 years. See 3rd renewal and re-introduction of (amended) Framework for State aid in the motor vehicle sector, OJ 1995, C284/3, and Corrigendum to "Framework for State aid in the motor vehicle sector", OJ 1995, C307/22. See also *Agence Europe*, 4 November 1995, at 9 ("Commission publishes decisions concerning aid framework").

approved aid schemes in operation in Spain under which aid could be awarded from 1 January 1996 to undertakings operating in the automobile industry,[123] and decided on 20 December 1995 that in the period 1996-1997, Spain had to notify under Article 93(3) EC, all aid measures granted in respect of projects costing more than ECU 17 million under any existing or approved aid schemes to undertakings operating in the automobile industry.[124] In its judgment of 15 April 1997, the ECJ annulled the Commission's decision as it accepted Spain's argument that the retroactive extension of the framework amounted to "its reintroduction, that is to say, the adoption of a new framework having the same content as that which had just expired, and that it ought therefore to have been decided on with the agreement of the Member States".[125] The ECJ held that:

> [w]ithout any prolongation, the framework ceases to exist on the date on which it is set to expire, so that a decision to prolong it, adopted, as in this case, after expiry of the period of validity of the decision which it prolongs constitutes a modification of the existing legal situation and must be adopted according to the same procedure as that required for the adoption of the decision which established the original framework or of a decision making modifications to it.[126]

In addition, the ECJ specified that the exceptional circumstances created by the judgment of 29 June 1995 (creating a legal vacuum) and having regard to "the overriding need to maintain undistorted competition in the motor vehicle sector and to avoid effects contrary to the common interest and irreversible for the structure of the market in the sector concerned" allowed the Commission "to justify giving retroactive effect to the contested decision" but "could not dispense

---

[123] State Aid C44/95 (E16/95) (Spain), OJ 1995, C304/14. See also IP/95/1007, IP/95/1442 and *Agence Europe*, 5 January 1996, at 11 ("The Spanish authorities must now notify aid measures for projects in the motor vehicle sector whose costs exceed ECU 17 Million").

[124] Commission Decision 96/313 (Spanish aid schemes) of 20 December 1995, OJ 1996, L119/51.

[125] Case C-292/95, *Spain* v *Commission*, [1997] ECR I-1957, paras. 28-29. See in this context N. Travers, "Retroactivity and the Commission's powers to implement state aid rules", (1998) 23 E.L.Rev., at 264-271.

[126] *Ibidem*, par. 30.

it from obtaining the Member States' agreement for the purposes of adopting that decision".[127]

8.3.3 Legal Status

The Framework is based on Article 93(1) EC and includes guidelines on the course of conduct that the Commission intends to follow with regard to state aid to the automobile sector.[128] These guidelines limit the Commission's margin of discretion[129] but do not and cannot derogate from Articles 92 and 93 EC.[130] Article 93(1) EC involves an obligation of regular, periodic cooperation on the part of the Commission and the Member States, from which neither the Commission nor a Member State can release itself for an indefinite period depending on the unilateral will of either of them. It is submitted that the Framework is an element of that obligation of regular, periodic cooperation from which neither the Commission nor a Member State can release itself. In view of the periodic consultations in what could be called a "spirit of cooperation" between the Commission and the Member States and the acceptence of the rules set out in the Framework by the Member States, one

[127] *Ibidem*, paras. 32-34.

[128] The Commission noted in Decision 91/254 of 28 November 1990 (VW Brussels), OJ 1991, L123/48, that it "explained how it will apply Article 92 ... to the automobile sector in its framework on State aid to the motor vehicle industry".

[129] The Commission pointed out in Decision 96/76 of 4 October 1995 (Daf Netherlands), OJ 1996, L15/43, that it "has for the motor vehicle industry adopted Community guidelines setting out the criteria for assessing the compatibility with the common market of State aid to this industry, thereby limiting the scope of discretion under point (c) of Article 92(3)". See also Decision 96/75 of 4 October 1995 (Daf Flanders), OJ 1996, L15/36; Decision 96/257 of 31 December 1995 (Seat Spain), OJ 1996, L88/16, and Santana Motor, *supra* note 30.

[130] See *Deufil*, *supra* note 51, par. 22. According to Bellamy and Child, *Common Market Law of Competition* (V. Rose ed.), 4th edition, 1993, London, Sweet & Maxwell, at 919 footnote 69, guidelines including those with regard to the motor vehicle industry, do not derogate from Articles 92 and 93 EC.

could argue that the Commission and the Member States have established a binding framework of cooperation from which neither can release itself.[131]

8.3.4 Scope

The Framework regards aid from the Member States to undertakings operating in the motor vehicle sector. Paragraph 2.1 of the Framework provides that the term *motor vehicle sector* stands for the manufacture and assembly of motor vehicles and the manufacture of motor vehicle engines.[132] The Commission has pointed out that, in general, a plant can be regarded as a manufacturing and/or assembly operation when vehicle bodies are constructed, painted, assembled or trimmed. If manufacturing and assembly are separated in two different plants at different geographical locations, each of these plants' activities falls under the definition of the motor vehicle industry.[133] The Framework specifies that the term *motor vehicle* includes passenger cars (volume, specialist and sports cars), vans, trucks, road tractors, buses, coaches and other commercial vehicles.[134] The term *motor vehicle engines* covers compression and spark engines for motor vehicles.

The Framework explicitly excludes all *parts and accessories* for both motor vehicles and motor vehicle engines.[135] It has been the Commission's constant practice to treat aid measures to the vehicle manufacturers' production of parts or components differently from aid measures to car and/or truck

---

[131] See in this context Case C-311/94, *IJssel-Vliet Combinatie* v *Minister van Economische Zaken ("IJssel-vliet")*, [1996] ECR I-5056, paras. 36-42. See also Case C-313/90, *CIRFS and others* v *Commission*, [1993] ECR I-1186, paras. 35-36.

[132] In Toyota Derbyshire, *supra* note 26, the Commission confirmed that car assembly is within the parameters of the Framework. See also State Aid NN 39/90 (United Kingdom), OJ 1990, C326/10.

[133] State Aid C 48/97 (ex NN 75/96, N 942/96) (Sweden/Volvo Umea), OJ 1997, C343/3.

[134] The Framework explicitly excludes from the definition: racing cars, non-traffic cars, motorcycles, trailers, agricultural and forestry tractors, caravans, special purpose lorries and vans, dumpers, work trucks and military vehicles.

[135] However, the Commission pointed out in State Aid N 933/95 (France/Smart), OJ 1996, C391/11, that the Framework had to be applied to the whole of the French aid notwithstanding the fact that, according to the French authorities, part of the aid would be received (directly or indirectly) by a number of equipment suppliers in proportion to their investments carried out and the number of jobs created by them ("system partner concept").

manufacture itself. The Commission justifies this different treatment by pointing at the fact that a component plant is normally in competition with independent suppliers and, consequently, exercising stricter control over component plants owned by vehicle manufacturers would discriminate in favour of independent suppliers.[136] In its decision on regional aid to Cadiz Electronica, a 100% subsidiairy of Ford that manufactures parts for motor vehicles (electronic modules for advanced braking systems), the Commission noted that in assessing the aid, it did not apply "the same strict discipline as it does to final vehicle assembly or engine production projects, since this would lead to unfair treatment by comparison with aid to projects being undertaken by independent component producers, which are not notifiable under the framework".[137]

The Commission tends to give a wide interpretation of the scope of the Framework. In *Daimler-Benz Berlin*, for instance, the German Government denied the applicability of the Framework with the argument that the Daimler-Benz subsidiary Debis that moved to the alledgedly subsidized site in question, was completely independent of Daimler-Benz's motor vehicle subsidiary. Nevertheless, the Commission argued that the Framework was applicable since the activities of Debis included the leasing agreements with Mercedes-Benz customers and the decision to move parts of Debis to Berlin was intended to strenghten its position in Eastern Europe.[138] In *Saab-Scania*, on the other hand, the Commission specified that the decentralisation of Scania's Paris-based activities essentially concerned only "commercial and retailing activities" that does not come under the motor vehicle industry within the meaning of the Framework.[139]

---

[136] Sweden/Volvo Umea, *supra* note 133. The Commission emphasized that a company cannot escape the control imposed by the Framework by outsourcing its production of completely finished truck cabs elsewhere. According to the Commission, the Volvo cabins manufactured in Umea did not qualify the plant as a component supplier but fell within the category of "manufacture" within the meaning of the Framework.

[137] XXIIIrd Report on Competition Policy, par. 512, at 296 (Ford Cadiz). See also XXIVth Report on Competition Policy, par. 367, at 178.

[138] Daimler-Benz Berlin, *supra* note 26, L263/20.

[139] State Aid C 5/96 (Saab-Scania), OJ 1998, C79/10.

8.3.5 Notification and Annual Report

Article 93(3) EC provides that the Commission shall be informed, in sufficient time to enable it to submit its comments, of any plans to grant or alter aid. The Framework specifies that all aid to be granted by public authorities *within* the scope of an approved aid scheme to (an) undertaking(s) operating in the motor vehicle sector, where the cost of the project to be aided exceeded 17 million ECU,[140] are subject to prior notification.[141] All aid to be granted *outside* the scope of an approved aid scheme, whatever its cost and aid intensity, is subject to the obligation of notification under Article 93(3) EC. Where aid is not directly linked to a particular project, all proposed aid must be notified, even if paid under schemes already approved by the Commission. If a motor vehicle manufacturer or its subsidiary obtains aid for the manufacture of parts or accessories, or if aid is granted for the manufacture of parts or accessories under licence or patents of a vehicle manufacturer, or of its subsidiary, such aid should also be notified.[142] Member States have to inform the Commission, in sufficient time to enable it to submit its comments, of any plan to grant or alter aid.[143] In addition, the Commission requests the Member States to provide it with an annual report on all aid payments under whatever form granted to all motor vehicle and motor vehicle engine producers during the year of reference. The annual report should reach the Commission at the end of the first quarter following the year reported on. Aid payments which do not fulfil the threshold of prior notification should also be included in the annual report.

---

140 In 1995, the threshold of 12 million ECU was changed into 17 million ECU. See Framework for State aid in the motor vehicle sector, OJ 1995, C284/3.

141 See 2.2. of the Framework.

142 Point 2.1, par. 6 of the Framework.

143 Pursuant to Point 2.4. of the Framework, the Commission will monitor all applications and approvals for assistance under Community instruments like the Structural Funds and the European Investment Bank, in order to ensure compliance with the provisions of the EC Treaty on state aid and coherence with the guidelines set out in the Framework.

8.3.6 Categories of Aid

8.3.6.1 Introduction

The Framework provides that notified state aids to the automobile industry will be evaluated by the Commission taking into account so-called general economic and industrial factors, sector and company specific considerations, and regional and social factors.[144] In addition, all aid has to be in proportion to the problems it seeks to solve and the criteria used by the Commission in the assessment of aid cases, vary according to the objectives pursued by the aid in question.[145] The Commission subdivides the possible objectives of aid measures in seven categories and formulates rather general guidelines for the assessment of the different categories of aid.[146] Most, if not all, guidelines reflect the Commission's practice in applying Article 92(2) and (3) EC before the Framework entered into force on 1 January 1989.[147] The guidelines on the respective categories of aid measures do not refer to the exceptions listed in Article 92 EC. This is somewhat surprising since the latter constitutes the actual legal basis for the Commission's competence to declare aid measures compatible with the common market.[148]

---

144 Point 3, par. 2 of the Framework.

145 Point 3, par. 3 of the Framework.

146 In Mezzogiorno II, *supra* note 5, the Commission called the guidelines "the common criteria for aid under the Community framework for State aid to the motor industry".

147 For instance, in German aid schemes, *supra* note 113, Re 7, the Commission counters the argument that the Framework might boost sectoral aid by pointing out that it is a mere continuation of established policy. According to the Commission: "Recent cases on sectoral aid demonstrate clearly the restrictive approach which the Commission has adopted (e.g. Alfa Romeo, Renault, Rover Group, Enasa). This approach has been applied in the framework's guidelines which allow for sectoral aids only under very exceptional circumstances and only if very restrictive conditions are fulfilled". Another example can be found in VW I, *supra* note 48, in which the Commission explicitly pointed out that its decision was "in line with the approach the Commission has taken in other cases of restructuring aid, such as the Renault, Rover and ENASA cases".

148 The Commission explicitly recognized in German aid schemes, *supra* note 113, Re 10, that its assessement of individual awards under existing regional and general aid schemes are always based on Articles 92 and 93 EC.

8.3.6.2 Rescue and Restructuring Aid

(i) Guidelines

The Commission takes a very strict attitude with regard to this type of aid which should only be approved in exceptional circumstances. The aid has to be linked to a satisfactory restructuring plan. Furthermore, it has to be demonstrated that the Community's interest is best served by keeping a manufacturer in business and by re-establishing its viability. The aid should not allow the beneficiary to increase its market share at the expense of its competitors which do not receive aid. The Commission indicates that it may require reductions in capacity in order to contribute to the overall recovery of the sector, in cases where certain companies still have excess capacity, like in the commercial vehicle sector.

(ii) Comments

Rescue and restructuring aid have different characteristics. Rescue aid is merely granted to keep an undertaking in business while the causes of its difficulties are discovered and a remedy worked out. Restructuring aid, on the other hand, is linked to a viable restructuring plan as part of a single "one-off" effort to restore the long term viability and recovery of the beneficiary.[149] The Commission tends to assess rescue and restructuring aid, under both the sectoral and general horizontal requirements set out in the guidelines of the Framework and the

[149] See State Aid C 1/95 (NN 144/94) Spain (Suzuki-Santana), OJ 1995, C144/13. The Commission looks at the characteristics of aid before qualifying it. In State Aid N 513/95 (Spain/Nissan Motor Iberica), OJ 1996, C391/9, the Commission dealt with a regional aid which contributed indirectly to the restructuring of the whole Nissan Motor Iberica company, under the category restructuring aid but considered that in view of the "limited scope of the aid", it did not have to apply the same strict discipline as it does to restructuring aid cases in which the keeping of a manufacturer in business is at stake. In addition, the Community guidelines on State aid for rescuing and restructuring firms in difficulty, establish that, when assessing restructuring projects in assisted areas eligible for regional aid, the severity of the regional problems affecting those areas has to be taken into account. In Mercedes-Benz/Ludwigsfelde, *supra* note 48, the Commission considered a regional aid and loss coverage as part of efforts to restore the long-term viability of the project in question and concluded that they had to be assessed as restructuring aid.

Community guidelines on state aid for rescuing and restructuring firms in difficulty.[150]

Before the Commission is in a position to assess whether a particular restructuring aid is compatible with the common market, it will examine the business plan(s) and the financial forecast(s) in order to determine whether they reflect a sound approach towards re-establishing the economic viability of the firm concerned within a reasonable period. These plans and forecasts have to be detailed. In addition, there has to be a true link between the proposed restructuring aid and the restructuring plan. If the aid is not linked to the restructuring plan, it will have to be assessed by the Commission under a different category of aid.[151] It can be in the Community's interest to keep the beneficiary in business if employment is maintained.[152] The Commission can approve aid under the condition that the restructuring plan is implemented in full.

The Commission will try to avoid undue distortion of competition through the aid in question. In market segments where there is (a risk of) overcapacity, irreversible capacity reductions which contribute to the overall recovery of the sector, are usually a condition for approval of aid measures under the Framework. There has to be a relationship between the aid and the reduction of capacity resulting from the restructuring.[153] The Commission will review a restructuring plan for a 100% subsidiary in the context of the overall capacity-strategy of the group. For instance, with regard to the restructuring aid to Seat, the Commission noted that since Seat is a 100% subsidiary of VW, the restructuring

---

[150] See Seat Spain, *supra* note 129; Suzuki-Santana, *ibidem*, and Santana Motor, *supra* note 30. See also Written Question P-3584/95 (Aramburu del Rio), OJ 1996, C112/49. However, in Mercedes-Benz/Ludwigsfelde, *supra* note 48, the Commission specified that since the criteria set out in the Framework do not differ from those set out in the Guidelines on State aid for rescuing and restructuring firms in difficulty, which nevertheless specify the procedure more clearly, its assessment would be based on those guidelines.

[151] For instance, in VW I, *supra* note 48, the Commission considered the aid up to and including 1993 as relating to "investments for the transformation of the plant into a modern car assembly facility which forms a necessary element of the restructuring plan" whereas it looked upon the aid in the period 1994 to 1997 as "not linked to the restructuring plan and ... to be assessed according to the Community framework on innovation, modernization and rationalization".

[152] See, *inter alia*, VW I, *supra* note 48, and Mercedes-Benz/Ludwigsfelde, *supra* note 48.

[153] See VW I, *supra* note 48; XXIVth Report on Competition Policy, par. 367, at 178; Mercedes-Benz/Ludwigsfelde, *supra* note 48, and Santana Motor, *supra* note 30.

operation had to be reviewed in the context of "the overall strategy of the VW group in the EU, on the basis of the interest of the Union as a whole and without merely transferring problems from one Member State to another".[154] In doing so, the Commission noted that the VW-group made a substantial contribution to the restructuring of the automobile industry in Europe, and made its approval of restructuring aid to Seat conditional upon the VW-group not offsetting the reduction of capacity at the end of 1997 with contributions that had not been notified to the Commission.[155]

Restructuring aid has to be in proportion to the problems it seeks to redress and the restructuring effort. This can be the case when the share of the aid in the total financial needs of the company during the restructuring plan is approximately equivalent to the share of capacity reduction undertaken as part of the restructuring process.[156] The Commission will verify that the measures on which the restructuring is based on for whose implementation the aid will be granted are necessary for the objectives pursued by the restructuring operation as a whole.[157]

The Commission takes a strict attitude towards rescue aid but recognizes that in certain circumstances, rescue aid has to be approved in order to guarantee interim financing so as to avoid that a potential beneficiary of state aid goes under, pending the Commission's final assesment of the proposed aid measures. For instance, the Commission approved rescue aid in the form of bank loan guarantees to secure the interim financing of Mosel I until the Commission's

---

[154] Commission Notice State Aid C34/95 (Notice Seat Spain), OJ 1995, C237/15.

[155] Seat Spain, *supra* note 129. The Commission obliged the VW-group to limit the group's technical capacity to 11 813 units a day. In VW II, *supra* note 48, the Commission obliged Germany to ensure that the capacity of the Mosel plants in 1997 does not exceed a level of 432 units per day. In Santana Motor, *supra* note 30, the Commission obliged the Spanish authorities to ensure that the idle paint shops which constituted potential capacity that could be utilized in the future without major new investment, were closed by September 1997.

[156] See Enasa, *supra* note 30; Rover Group I, *supra* note 23; Renault Group, *supra* note 24; VW I, *supra* note 48; Mercedes-Benz/Ludwigsfelde, *supra* note 48, and Santana Motor, *supra* note 30.

[157] Seat Spain, *supra* note 129.

decision on the proposed aid measures.[158] Serious social difficulties can also warrant rescue aid. This is especially the case if the undertaking concerned is a significant employer which is established in a region that is affected by a general lack of economic and social infrastructure.[159]

8.3.6.3 Regional Aid

(i) Guidelines

The Commission acknowledges the valuable contribution to regional development which can be made by the implantation of new motor vehicle and component production facilities or the expansion of such existing activities in disadvantaged regions and takes a generally positive attitude towards investment aid granted in order to help overcome structural handicaps in disadvantaged parts of the Community. The prior notification of this type of aid gives the Commission an opportunity to assess the regional development benefits (like the promotion of a lasting development of the region by creating viable jobs, linkages into local and Community economy) against possible adverse effects on the sector as a whole (such as the creation of important overcapacity). This assessment is to ensure that other aspects of Community interest such as the development of the Community's industry are also taken into account.

(ii) Comments

The Commission will examine whether regional aid can be granted at all by determining whether the region is eligible for assistance and whether the investment is mobile meaning that the investor has the option of locating the project at another location. In cases of investment aid for the expansion of

---

[158] See VW I, *supra* note 48. See also Aid N 313/93, OJ 1993, C214/9. The Commission reported in XXIIIrd Report on Competition Policy, par. 509, at 295 (Volkswagen SAB), that certain Treuhandanstalt guarantees constituted rescue aid to SAB/Mosel I which was made necessary as a result of the Article 93(2) EC procedure initiated in December 1991.

[159] Suzuki-Santana, *supra* note 149. The Commission was prepared to cooperate with the parties "in formulating a rescue plan compatible with the granting of State aid as regulated by the EC Treaty". See also European Parliament, Resolution on the planned closure of the Japanese company Santana Motor (Suzuki) in Linares (Spain), OJ 1994, C91/215.

existing plants in disadvantaged regions, the Commission policy is to have a positive attitude towards investments that involve changes in product and production processes that are so drastic that they can be qualified as mobile investment. In order to verify the mobility, the Commission requests evidence of cost-benefit studies for the alternative location examined by the company, which would prove that without regional aid the company in question would delocalize the production covered by the investment.[160] However, it should be kept in mind that, where appropriate, innovation aid may be granted for the non-mobile parts of a regional investment.[161]

The Commission makes a cost-benefit analysis in order to assess the benefits for regional development against possible adverse effects on the sector as a whole (such as the creation of overcapacity).[162] However, the Commission announced at the end of 1996, that it will no longer use the cost-benefit analysis in cases where a proposed aid intensity amounts to less than 10% of the regional aid ceiling, since all the areas eligible for regional aid possess a certain minimum degree of net incremental handicaps.[163] In making the cost-benefit analysis, the Commission will have external experts identify the region-specific handicaps facing the investor like additional investment costs and operating costs[164] over a particular period which tends to vary from a three year period for the expansion

---

[160] See in this sense State Aid N 396/94 (Sevel), OJ 1995, C298/10.

[161] See State Aid N 475/96 (Austria-BMW Steyr), OJ 1998, C12/11.

[162] The Commission pointed out in State Aid N 512/95 (France/Heuliez), OJ 1996, C391/7, that it is not "the purpose of the assessment to deny the essential contribution of regional aid to cohesion at Community level but rather to ensure that other factors in the Community interest, such as development of the sector at Community level are also taken into account".

[163] See "Motor vehicles industry: Cost-benefit analysis is no longer used in cases with low aid intensities", *Competition policy newsletter*, Volume 2, Number 3, Autumn/Winter 1996, at 49-50. The report regarded State Aid N 781/96 (UK/Ford Bridgend).

[164] See, *inter alia*, State Aid C 60/91 (NN 73/91 and 76/91) Germany, OJ 1992, C68/2; Opel Eisenach, *supra* note 63; State Aid C 61/91 (NN 74/91 and 80/91) Germany, OJ 1992, C68/8; State Aid C 62/91 (NN 75, 77, 78, 79/91) Germany, OJ 1992, C68/14; XXIIIrd Report on Competition Policy, par. 510, at 295, and par. 516, at 298; State Aid N 241/95 Belgium (Ford Genk), OJ 1996, C5/10, and State Aid C 5/96 (NN 138/95) France (Saab-Scania Angers), OJ 1996, C84/6.

of existing activities,[165] to a five year period for the implantation of a new greenfield site.[166] The Commission compares the costs for the investor of locating the project in that particular assisted area with those in a central, non-assisted region.

The Commission ensures that the aid is in proportion to the problem it seeks to resolve, so that it does not give rise to unwarranted distortions of competition. The Commission tries to avoid adverse effects on the sector as much as possible.[167] In determining the possible negative sectoral effects in general and the increase of overcapacity in particular,[168] the Commission determines the relevant market segment in order to examine the manufacturers' overall group

[165] A period of three years has been used in Sevel, *supra* note 160; State Aid 81/94 (UK/Jaguar X 100), IP/94/254 (OJ 1994, C201/4); State Aid N 511/95 (UK/Jaguar X 200), OJ 1996, C311/17; Ford Genk, *ibidem*; VW II, *supra* note 48, and State Aid N 452/96 (UK/Vauxhall), OJ 1997, C202/6. However, in Seat Pamplona, OJ 1993, C310/7, a period of five years was used for what seemed to have been an extension.

[166] A period of five years has been used in Opel Eisenach, *supra* note 63; AutoEuropa, *supra* note 35, and Fiat Mezzogiorno (OJ 1993, C37/15). The Commission pointed out in VW II, *supra* note 48, that the term "greenfield site" does not simply mean that the project is situated in a green field somewhere, but that, from the investor's point of view, the site is a new, as yet undeveloped one. As a result, the investor faces (i) lack of adequate infrastructure, (ii) lack of organized logistics, (iii) no trained workforce adapted to the needs of the company, and (iv) no established supplier structure. The Commission emphasized that if "these services can be provided by a nearby plant belonging to the same group, then the project is treated as an extension, even if it is located in a green field".

[167] In its XXth Report on Competition Policy, par. 255, at 161, the Commission noted with regard to aid to General Motors for the setting up of a new R&D centre in Luxemburg, that the aid concerned "would not have adverse effects on the industry sufficient to outweigh the regional benefits". See also par. 256, at 161, in which the Commission reported with regard to aid to Delco Remy that the aid "was considered to have a considerable impact on the economic development of this part of Portugal without adversely affecting the sector at Community level".

[168] In VW II, *supra* note 48, the Commission confirmed that the latest estimates suggest that the present serious overcapacity problems in the Community, where average capacity utilization in 1995 was reported to be only 70%, will persist during most of the decade unless the industry decides to close down excess capacities over the next few years. The Commission added that since, in industries suffering from large overcapacity, the distortive effect on competition caused by state aid granted to individual producers is particularly strong, it will be especially vigilant in assessing proposals for aid to projects which entail new car production capacity.

capacity in Western Europe.[169] The Commission will also take into account a possible growing demand in the Community car market[170] and the proportion of the output which is or will be exported outside the Community.[171]

The Commission only approves regional aid without looking at the effect on (over)capacity in the sector, if the aid is *less* or *equivalent* to the regional disadvantages resulting from the investment in the assisted region.[172] However, there are examples of cases in which the Commission did not object to the fact that the proposed regional aid *slightly exceeded* the net regional handicaps with the argument that in the absence of any negative sectoral effects, the difference of aid intensity between the intended regional aid and the additional costs associated with locating the investment in the region, constituted an additional incentive, ensuring that the investment would actually take place in the disadvantaged region concerned (so-called "top-up measures").[173]

---

[169] The Commission clarified in Seat Pamplona, *supra* note 165, that "[i]n order to evaluate whether an expansion project contributes to or aggravates overcapacity problems in the sector, the Commission must take in account all other capacity changes of the same manufacturer at group level within the relevant segment of the market". See also AutoEuropa, *supra* note 35; Opel Eisenach, *supra* note 63; Fasa-Renault, IP/94/982, and UK/Jaguar X 200, *supra* note 165. See also XXIIIrd Report on Competition Policy, par. 513, at 297.

[170] For instance, in "Commission approves aid for Ford Motor components plant in France", IP/91/832, the Commission reported that one of the reasons for approving French regional aid to Ford for the expansion and installation of new production lines at its motor components plant which was to facilitate the manufacture of air induction and fuel vapour storage systems, was that it will meet a growing demand for such systems in the Community car market.

[171] See "Commission approves regional aid for Daimler-Benz in Bremen", IP/88/304.

[172] See Seat Pamplona, *supra* note 165; Opel Eisenach, *supra* note 63; Ford Genk, *supra* note 164; Mezzogiorno II, *supra* note 5; State Aid N 851/95 (Spain/Mercedes Benz Espana), OJ 1996, C276/3; State Aid N 1025/95 (Germany/Smart Engines), OJ 1996, C324/4; VW II, *supra* note 48; State Aid N 126/96 (Portugal/GM-Opel), OJ 1996, C343/2; UK/Vauxhall, *supra* note 165, and Austria-BMW Steyr, *supra* note 161.

[173] See Sevel, *supra* note 160; XXIVth Report on Competition Policy, par. 367, at 178; Fasa-Renault, *supra* note 169; UK/Jaguar X 100, *supra* note 165; UK/Jaguar X 200, *supra* note 165, and VW II, *supra* note 48. In France/Smart, *supra* note 135, the Commission qualified SMART as a new type of car which forms a distinct market segment and is only partially substitutable for vehicles belonging to other segments. With reference to AutoEuropa, *supra* note 35, the Commission confirmed that in the case of state aid for projects whose expected impact on the sector is limited (i.e. no increase in production capacity or the development of a new market segment), it can allow a 3% top-up.

8.3.6.4 Investment Aid for Innovation, Modernization or Rationalization

(i) Guidelines

The Commission takes a strict attitude towards aid for modernization and innovation as these activities have to be undertaken by companies themselves and should be financed from their own resources or by commercial loans as part of their normal company operation in a competitive market environment. With regard to aid for fundamental rationalization, the Commission will carefully verify whether it brings about a necessary, radical change in the structure and organization of the company's activities and that the financing required goes beyond that which companies should normally be expected to finance from own resources. As concerns aid for innovation, the Commission will determine whether it really relates to the introduction of genuinely innovative products or processes at Community level.

(ii) Comments

Under strict conditions, aid for innovation, modernization or rationalization can be considered compatible with the common market under Article 92(3)(c) EC. The very first case which was dealt with under the Framework, regarded Italian aid to Ferrari for *innovation*. The Commission concluded that in view of the specific characteristics of the market for sports cars, the aid was compatible with the Framework's guidelines on aid for innovation, and aid for research and development. The Commission recognized that Ferrari's R&D program related to the introduction of genuinely innovative products and processes at Community level.[174] Aid for innovation can only satisfy the criteria set out in the Framework if it relates to the introduction of genuinely innovative products or processes at Community level.[175] In *Sevel*, the Commission considered aid to innovation compatible with the guidelines after its motor expert had established

---

[174] Ferrari, *supra* note 114.

[175] VW Brussels, *supra* note 128. In its decision, the Commission explicitly linked up with Renault Group, *supra* note 24, Valeo, *supra* note 71, and Peugeot, *supra* note 71.

that certain technological innovations were "innovative at European level" and represented "a new standard for .. production at EEA level" of the product concerned.[176]

Aid for *rationalization* can be compatible with the common market if it brings about a necessary radical change in the structure and organization of the company's activities and if the financing goes beyond that which companies should normally be expected to finance from own resources. Activities which represent a "reasonably common activity in the industry" do not qualify as such.[177]

Aid to normal modernization and replacement investments can under no circumstances be allowed.[178] With regard to aid to product development, the Commission has pointed out that as product development is at the very heart of competition in the car industry, it will only contemplate authorizing aid for such investment to the extent, that it relates to the introduction of genuinely innovative products or processes at Community level.[179]

8.3.6.5 Aid for Research and Development

(i) Guidelines

The Commission has a positive attitude towards aid for so-called pre-competitive research and development. In keeping with the Commission's Framework on state aid for research and development, the Commission will ensure that a clear

---

[176] Sevel, *supra* note 160. See also State Aid N 538/93 Spain (Ford Espana), OJ 1996, C94/7; XXIInd Report on Competition Policy, par. 407, at 233 (Volvo Ghent), and par. 410, at 234 (Iveco-Elena); State aid N 136/95 and N 137/95 (Austria/SFT), OJ 1996, C201/4, and France/Smart, *supra* note 135. In Austria-BMW Steyr, *supra* note 161, the Commission asked independent experts to assess the technical aspects of the project concerned and to compare them with the current state of the art in the European motor industry.

[177] In VW Brussels, *supra* note 128, the Commission qualified as such common activity in the industry "projects .. largely designed to rearrange and make more efficient use of the existing site and to subsidize the purchase of machinery for production, thereby improving profitability".

[178] See, *inter alia*, VW I, *supra* note 48, L385/13. The Commission has initiated studies on the manner in which innovation can be distinguished from modernization in the automobile industry. See, *inter alia*, Bhaskar, *supra* note 70.

[179] Mezzogiorno II, *supra* note 5.

distinction is established between genuine research and development, on the one hand, and the introduction of new technologies inherent to production investment (modernization), on the other hand.

(ii) Comments

The Commission recognizes the potential beneficial effects of R&D activity on economic development and takes a favourable view of aid to such activity, provided that it is not likely to adversely affect trading conditions to an extent contrary to the EC Treaty.[180] The assessment of aid for R&D in the automobile industry takes place under the Framework and the Framework on state aid for research and development.[181]

The assessment of the aid takes into account several factors such as the nature of the project, whether it really relates to genuinely innovative products or processes, the technical and financial risk involved and the risk of distortion of competition. Processes and operations can be considered as genuinely innovative by reference to the current state of technology in the Community automobile industry.[182] In addition, the Commission will try to determine whether the project includes sufficient elements of pre-competitive research which can be classified as either basic or applied research, to justify the level of state aid.[183] Research is probably not at a pre-competitive stage if the projects "come on stream within a

[180] It is interesting to note that in Ford Espana, *supra* note 176, the Commission took a positive attitude towards Spanish aid to Ford Espana for R&D which was to take place *outside* Spain. Ford Espana would pay for the R&D and become the owner of the results of the aided R&D expenditure. Furthermore, Ford Espana guaranteed that no other aid would be claimed for the R&D.

[181] The Commission emphasized in State Aid N 704/91 France (VSR), OJ 1993, C214/5, that the Framework does not intent to submit the car industry to a stricter discipline than other sectors, with regard to basic and applied research. See also XXIIIrd Report on Competition Policy, par. 514, at 297.

[182] See State Aid N 135/95 (Opel Austria), OJ 1995, C310/5, and Ford Espana, *supra* note 176.

[183] Daf Netherlands, *supra* note 129, L15/43. On 14 March 1996, the Commission published a summary of its Decision State Aid N 657/94 Netherlands, OJ 1996, C74/8, not to oppose aid by the Dutch authorities to Daf for research and development in the (new) Volem project. The Commission considered the aid to be in conformity with the framework for state aid for research and development *and* the Framework *and* emphasized in addition that the project was in the common interest as it focused on the development of engines that will produce less polluting emissions in advance of the adoption of new emission standards.

couple of years".[184] For basic industrial research, the level of aid should, as a general rule, not exceed 50% of the eligible cost. As the activity gets nearer to the market (given the current state of the automobile industry in Europe) involving the areas of product and process development, the Commission looks for progressively lower levels of aid.[185] There are cases in which the Commission concluded that aid was acceptable since various elements in both the product and process development were to be considered genuinely innovative on a European level.[186]

State aid for R&D should serve as an incentive and must have as its effect the encouragement of additional effort in this field, over and above the normal operations which firms carry out in any case, in their day-to-day operations, or to respond to exceptional conditions for which their own resources are too limited. The objective of the aid should be to serve as an incentive and to compensate for special risks and costs.[187]

8.3.6.6 Aid for Environmental and Energy Saving

(i) Guidelines

The Commission takes a critical attitude towards this type of aid as the development of less polluting and energy saving vehicles is considered to be a standard requirement for the industry, partly imposed by Community legislation, and should therefore be financed from the company's own resources. Aid for general pollution control (e.g. granted under the terms of the environmental aid framework) may still be acceptable under the existing aid schemes and will have to be examined individually by the Commission.

(ii) Comments

The assessment of aid for environmental and energy saving in the automobile industry takes place under the Framework in line with the Community guidelines

---

[184] Mezzogiorno II, *supra* note 5.

[185] See Ford Espana, *supra* note 176; Opel Austria, *supra* note 182, and Austria/SFT, *supra* note 176.

[186] Opel Austria, *supra* note 182.

[187] See, *inter alia*, Opel Austria, *supra* note 182, and State Aid N 680/96 (Germany/ADA), OJ 1997, C311/6.

on state aid for environmental protection.[188]

The Commission considers the development of new models, which are less polluting and more fuel efficient than their predecessors, to be a standard requirement for companies in the automobile industry in order to remain competitive on the market concerned. Such development should therefore not be granted state aid.[189] However, the Commission takes a positive attitude towards aid for the application of new environmental friendly techniques that will result in a level of pollution control that exceeds largely existing or foreseen national and European emission standards.[190]

In principle, aid for energy-saving in favour of new establishments will not be authorized as the investor is considered normally to choose the best technology available, also in terms of energy efficiency. However, the Community guidelines on state aid for environmental protection admit that investments in fields where there are no mandatory standards or other legal obligations on firms to protect the environment may be granted aid in those cases where the firms' investment will significantly improve their environmental

---

[188] See Ford Genk, *supra* note 164; Austria/SFT, *supra* note 176; UK/Jaguar X 200, *supra* note 165, and Austria-BMW Steyr, *supra* note 161.

[189] Decision Daf Netherlands, *supra* note 129. In VW II, *supra* note 48, the Commission noted that all car manufacturers in the Community strive to achieve high levels of environmental protection in their new plants throughout the Community, even in the continuing absence of appropriate regulations in some Member States.

[190] See Opel Eisenach, *supra* note 63; Sevel, *supra* note 160; Opel Austria, *supra* note 182; Ford Genk, *supra* note 164; Ford Espana, *supra* note 176, and XXIInd Report on Competition Policy, par. 407, at 233 (Volvo Ghent), and France/Smart, *supra* note 135.

performance if the aid is granted at the same levels and subject to the same conditions of proportionality as for exceeding existing standards.[191]

8.3.6.7 Aid for Vocational Training linked to Investments

(i) Guidelines

Notwithstanding the fact that the Commission has a generally positive attitude towards training, retraining and reconversion programmes, it will ensure that an aid to one of these programmes does not simply alleviate the cost burden which companies would normally have to bear, in particular that they do not undermine the guidelines. Therefore, the Commission will carefully examine aid for company specific vocational training measures which are prompted by, and thus directly linked, to investments.

The Commission will ensure that (i) such aid does not exceed a reasonable intensity, whenever linked with production investments, and (ii) the vocational training measures involved in the project correspond to genuinely qualitative changes in the required qualifications of the labour force and relate to a significant proportion of the workers, so that it can be assumed that these measures are intended to safeguard employment and develop new employment possibilities for persons at risk of unemployment. The Commission will consider vocational training measures prompted by investments which do not fulfil these criteria, as part of the investment, and submitted to the criteria regarding the different forms of investment aids set out in the Framework.

Vocational training measures which are related to workers being retrained for continued employment in the company which are not linked to investment and which are intended to safeguard employment and develop new employment possibilities for persons at risk of unemployment in the framework of restructuring, can be considered compatible.

---

[191] Ford Espana, *supra* note 176. The Commission noted that without the incentive of state aid, private companies will not invest in the generation of their own energy requirements considering the extra long pay-back period of such investments which also depend heavily on the assumptions of future energy prices.

(ii) Comments

The Commission takes a positive attitude towards aid for vocational training linked to investments if the project concerned has an innovative nature and includes the development of new products and production processes (and possibly the introduction of a new assembly work structure). In principle, trainee's wages should be excluded and a distinction has to be made between basic and on-the-job training. The vocational training measures have to correspond to genuinely qualitative changes in the required skills of the workforce.[192] In addition, the basic training elements should *not* be company specific; the public utility of the education should be acknowledged.[193]

8.3.6.8 Operating Aid

(i) Guidelines

The text of the Framework with regard to operating aid is very clear indeed. As operating aid has a direct and ongoing distortive effect a sensitive sector such as the motor vehicle industry, the Commission will not authorize any new operating aid even in disadvantaged regions.[194] The progressive disappearance of existing

---

[192] See Portugal/GM-Opel, *supra* note 172; UK/Vauxhall, *supra* note 165, and Austria-BMW Steyr, *supra* note 161.

[193] Opel Austria, *supra* note 182. See also AutoEuropa, *supra* note 35; Ford Espana, *supra* note 176, and UK/Jaguar X 200, *supra* note 165. In Ford Espana, the Commission did not raise objections against aid for the generic training programmes carried out by Ford Espana in conformity with the professional training school system in Spain (i.e. the courses are also open to workers and students not linked to Ford). According to the Commission, it was a general measure whose beneficiary was not necessarily Ford. In UK/Vauxhall, *supra* note 165, the Commission did not consider training support to be state aid as it was for generic courses providing general vocational knowledge to new recruits which could be utilized in the labour market and led to a certification/qualification recognized by other companies and sectors in the economy.

[194] The Guidelines for the examination of State aids in the fisheries and aquaculture sector (OJ 1992, C152/2), define operating aid as "[s]tate aids which are granted without imposing any obligation on the part of recipients and which are intended to improve the liquidity situation of their undertakings, the amount of which depends on the quantity produced or marketed, the prices of products, the unit of production or the factors of production and the result of which would be a reduction in the recipient's production costs or an improvement in the recipients's income".

operating aid will be pursued by the Commission on the basis of Article 93(1) EC.[195]

(ii) Comments

Operating aid means aid which relieves a company of part of its normal operational costs.[196] It has been confirmed several times that operating aid will not be authorized in the automobile industry under any circumstances. For instance, the Commission noted in *VW I* that "the proposed compensation of ... losses ... would be out of proportion to the restructuring costs and would have no regional justification" and would be "in the nature of an operating aid which, under the rules of the Community framework, can under no circumstances be allowed".[197]

8.4 1998 Framework for State Aid to the Motor Vehicle Industry

8.4.1 Introductory Remarks

In 1996, the Commission carried out an in-depth study of the Framework which led to the conclusion that although it was generally effective,[198] the Framework could be improved on the point of the notification thresholds, the definition of the sector and the methods of carrying out the cost-benefit analysis. The Commission presented a draft for a new Framework which was discussed with the Member

[195] See "Motor cars: Vice-Presidents Brittan and Bangemann recall that priority should go to restructuring on the Community market", *Agence Europe*, 14 March 1990, at 7, in which it was confirmed that "The Commission has decided that, since production aid has direct distortion effect in this sector, it will no longer be allowed, even in the less favoured regions. The Commission will no longer autorise aid for production and will try to ensure that this aid which already exists, disappears".

[196] Sweden/Volvo Umea, *supra* note 133.

[197] VW I, *supra* note 48. See Daf Flanders, *supra* note 129; Mercedes-Benz/Ludwigsfelde, *supra* note 48, and Sweden/Volvo Umea, *supra* note 133. See also "Volvo Truck must not benefit from the Swedish scheme of aid to transport for the norther regions beyond 2002", *Agence Europe*, 27 March 1998, at 13.

[198] For instance, it was reported in Community framework for state aid to the motor vehicle industry, OJ 1997, C279/1, footnote 1, that whereas in 1977 to 1987, state aid to the motor vehicle industry is estimated at ECU 26 billion, the Commission approved between 1989 (when the framework entered into force) and July 1996, the amount of ECU 5,4 billion of aid to the industry.

States at two multilateral meetings. On 6 August 1997, the Commission provided the Member States with an amended proposal that was accepted by no less than fourteen Member States. Initially, Sweden refused to accept the new Framework and the Commission decided to initiate the procedure under Article 93(2) EC in respect of all approved schemes in force in Sweden which could potentially benefit the motor vehicle industry.[199] In January 1998, Sweden informed the Commission that it accepted the Framework after all.[200]

On 15 September 1997, the Community Framework for state aid to the motor vehicle industry was published.[201] The Framework entered into force on 1 January 1998 and will apply for a period of three years covering the period 1998, 1999 and 2000. The preceeding Framework continues to serve as a basis for the assessment of aid proposals which were notified before 1 November 1997 but which have not yet been declared compatible by the Commission or are the subject of proceedings under Article 93(2) EC initiated before that date.

The amendments to the guidelines introduced by the Framework should be seen in the context of the Commission's intention to bring the Framework "into line with the new economic situation" which is characterized by a faster globalization of the car market and overcapacity (since 1993, a production capacity utilization rate of below 80%). According to the Commission, this adjustment to the new economic situation is consistent with efforts to catch up with the U.S.A. or Japan which entail "targets" such as "a stronger emphasis on intangible investments, especially in R&D and training, the development of industrial cooperation, modernization of the role of public authorities, creation of a stable and favourable economic climate and a guarantee of effective competition".[202]

---

[199] State Aid C 66/97 (Sweden), OJ 1997, C326/3.

[200] See State Aid C66/97 (Sweden), OJ 1998, C122/4. See also *Agence Europe*, "Commission takes note of the fact that Sweden has agreed unconditionally to new aid code in the car sector", 22 January 1998, at 8.

[201] OJ 1997, C279/1.

[202] Point 1(b), par. 3 of the 1998 Framework.

8.4.2 Extended Scope

The extended scope of the Framework seems to reflect the development towards lean and virtual production as it recognizes the growing role of suppliers in the manufacturing process. The 1998 Framework defines the term *motor vehicle industry* as the development, manufacture and assembly of "motor vehicles", "engines" for motor vehicles and "modules or sub-systems" for such vehicles or engines, either direct by a manufacturer or by a "first-tier component supplier" and, in the latter case, only in the context of an "overall project". The Commission explained that "first-tier component suppliers" are not included in the definition and that only projects carried out by first-tier component suppliers providing modules or sub-systems as part of an overall project are covered.[203] The definition of *motor vehicle* remains the same.[204] The definition of *motor vehicle engine*, however, has been widened to include compression and spark ignition engines as well as electric motors and turbine, gas, hybrid or other engines for motor vehicles.

The new term *module* or *sub-system* means a set of primary components intended for a vehicle or engine which is produced, assembled or fitted by a first-tier component supplier and supplied through a computerized ordering system or on a just-in-time basis. In addition, logistical supply and storage systems and subcontracted complete operations which form part of the production chain, such as the painting of sub-assemblies, should likewise be classified among these modules and sub-systems.

The term *first-tier component supplier* is described as a supplier, whether independent or not, supplying a manufacturer, sharing responsibility for design and development (these two often take place on the manufacturer's project site),

---

[203] See State Aid C 66/97 (Sweden), OJ 1997, C326/3, par. 2. The Commission's initial proposal contained an even broader definition which included all first-tier component suppliers involved in developing, manufacturing or assembling modules or sub-systems, irrespective of whether they were part of an overall project.

[204] The term "motor vehicles" means passenger cars, vans, trucks, road tractors, buses, coaches and other commercial vehicles. It does not include racing cars, vehicles intended for off-road use (for example, vehicles designed for use on snow or for carrying persons on golf courses), motorcycles, trailers, agricultural and forestry tractors, caravans, special purpose vehicles (for example, firefighting vehicles, mobile workshops), dump trucks, works' trucks (for example, fork lift trucks, straddle carrier trucks and platform trucks) and military vehicles intended for armies.

and manufacturing, assembling or supplying a vehicle manufacturer during the manufacturing or assembly stage with sub-assemblies or modules. It is recognized that as industrial partners, such suppliers are often linked to a manufacturer by a contract of approximately the same duration as the life of the model (for example, until the model is restyled). A first-tier component supplier may also supply services, especially logistical services, such as the management of a supply centre.

The 1998 Framework recognizes that a manufacturer may, on the actual site of the investment or in one or several industrial parks in fairly close geographical proximity (including the form of a fixed link allowing the delivery of modules directly into the car factory), integrate one or more projects of first-tier component suppliers for the supply of modules or sub-systems for the vehicle or engines being produced. Under the 1998 Framework, an *overall project* means one which groups together such projects and lasts for the life of the vehicle manufacturer's investment project. It is specified that an investment of one first-tier component supplier is integrated within the definition of a global project if at least half the output resulting from that investment is delivered to the manufacturer concerned at the plant in question. According to the Commission, the concept of "overall project" places significant restrictions on the projects of component suppliers subject to the notification requirement in so far as the investment must be made on the manufacturer's actual site or in one or more industrial parks in fairly close geographical proximity and in so far as at least half the output resulting from that investment is delivered to the manufacturer concerned at the plant in question.[205]

8.4.3 Notification and Annual Report

The Framework specifies that all aid which the public authorities plan to grant to an individual project or an overall project *under* authorized aid schemes for a firm or firms operating in the motor vehicle industry must, in accordance with Article 93(3) EC, be notified to the Commission before being granted if either of the

[205] State Aid C 66/97 (Sweden), OJ 1997, C326/3.

following thresholds is reached (i) nominal amount of the investment project[206] (total cost of the project[207]): ECU 50 million, or (ii) total gross aid for the project,[208] whether state aid or aid from Community instruments (Structural Funds and framework programmes), irrespective of the form and objectives of the measure: ECU 5 million.[209] Any aid which the public authorities intend to grant *outside* an approved scheme to one (or several) undertaking(s) operating in the motor vehicle industry[210] must be notified in advance under Article 93(3) EC, unless it complies with the thresholds and rules of the *de minimis* notice. The Framework explicitly confirms that these notification requirements also apply to rescue and restructuring aid.

In addition, the Commission requests the Member States to provide it with an annual report by 1 April of the year following the reference year, giving data on *all* aid, whatever its form, granted in the past year to undertakings in the motor vehicle industry. The Framework specifies that the annual report must also mention aid which does not have to be notified to the Commission.

The Framework provides for a notification form which has to be supplemented by an appropriate form to be obtained from the Commission.

---

[206] According to the 1998 Framework, an investment project is usually defined as an investment by an undertaking in new assets that are necessary to set up, expand, modernize or rationalize production facilities on a specific industrial site. In addition, an investment project should not be artificially broken down into several sub-projects and/or over several financial years in order to avoid the obligation to notify.

[207] The 1998 Framework defines the total cost of a project as the total expenditure by an undertaking on the acquisition of new tangible and intangible fixed assets which are part of an investment project and will be depreciated (or leased) during their lifetime; consequently, the cost is equal to the amount of capital invested in a project. It is emphasized that the cost of the project may be different from the cost that is eligible for state aid.

[208] The 1998 Framework specifies that the gross aid is obtained by adding the grants and grant equivalents of the aid envisaged; if aid is granted net of tax, it should be changed into gross equivalent aid by taking account of the tax effect wherever possible.

[209] The Commission pointed out in State Aid C 66/97 (Sweden), OJ 1997, C326/3, par. 3, that the chosen notification thresholds reflect the fact that very substantial investments (sometimes amounting to several hundred million ecus) may receive nominal amounts of aid which could distort competition in this sensitive industry by favouring certain undertakings or the production of certain goods even where aid intensity is low.

[210] The 1998 Framework uses the words "operating in the motor vehicle sector defined above". This is probably a mistake in view of the fact that the 1998 Framework defines the term motor vehicle *industry* instead of motor vehicle *sector*. The latter term was used in the (old) Framework.

8.4.4 Monitoring

The Framework confirms that in its decision on aid measures, the Commission may require *ex post* monitoring and assessment of aid already granted, the amount of detail varying according to the case and the potential distortion of competition. A copy of the final aid contract between the Member State and the aid recipient must be sent to the Commission immediately after signing by the parties. In addition, an interim report on the aid payments or a copy of the interim report on performance of the aid contract must be submitted followed by a final report on the objectives, in terms of timetable, investments and compliance with the specific conditions imposed by the Member State, and the actual achievements at the end.

Furthermore, the Commission has a duty to monitor all aid applications and authorizations under Community instruments and ensure that they are consistent with these guidelines. More specifically, the Commission has to ensure that measures financed by the Structural Funds or benefiting from aid from the European Investment Bank or other financial instruments comply with Articles 92 to 94 EC.

8.4.5 Categories of Aid

8.4.5.1 Introduction

The Framework emphasizes that although the assessment of aid must take account of general economic and industrial factors, sectoral considerations and regional, environmental and social factors, the Commission does not intend to impose an industrial strategy on the sector since it considers it to be preferable for a strategy to be defined within the sector and the market. The Commission's aim is described as to make sure that motor vehicle manufacturers in the Community operate in a climate of fair competition by limiting distortions of competition caused by certain aid measures and to maintain a competitive environment which boosts competitiveness and productivity in the automobile industry. The 1998 Framework confirms that although the criteria which the Commission uses to assess aid vary according to the objectives of the aid in question, it checks in every instance whether the aid granted is both *proportional* to the gravity of the problems to be resolved and *necessary* for the realization of the project. The Commission will only authorize state aid in the motor vehicle industry if both tests, proportionality and necessity, are satisfied.

The 1998 Framework distinguishes eight instead of seven separate categories of state aid. The 1998 guidelines are more detailed and structured. In view of the lack of decisions under the 1998 guidelines, only a description can be given.

8.4.5.2 Rescue and Restructuring Aid for Firms in Difficulty

The 1998 Framework specifies that rescue and restructuring aid is assessed under the Community Guidelines on state aid for rescuing and restructuring firms in difficulty, and that the Commission ensures in particular that restructuring aid, like rescue aid, is in principle a one-off operation. As structural overcapacity in the motor vehicle industry is set to continue until the end of the decade, the Commission will prohibit state aid which is aimed at a net increase in production capacity. In addition, the Commission will usually require a reduction in installed capacity. The Commission also considers it necessary for the reduction in production capacity to be proportional to the intensity of the aid, being the amount of the aid divided by the cost of restructuring.

8.4.5.3 Regional Aid

The 1998 Framework recognizes that the motor vehicle industry may benefit from regional aid to assist new plants and the extension of existing ones in the assisted areas of the Community, thereby making a valuable contribution to regional development by creating or safeguarding often highly skilled jobs and through significant indirect effects. However, plans for regional aid have to be notified in order to allow the Commission to compare in the form of a cost-benefit analysis, the advantages for regional development with any unfavourable consequences for the industry as a whole. The 1998 Framework specifies that this cost-benefit analysis is not to deny the essential contribution made by regional aid to cohesion at Community level but to ensure that other factors affecting the Community, such as development and the general competitiveness of the industry in Europe, as well as respect for fair competition, are also taken into consideration.

Subsequently, the 1998 Framework elaborates on how to determine the necessity of regional aid, the eligibility of costs relating to the mobile aspects of a project, the proportionality of aid and aid intensity. Furthermore, the (impact of the) analysis of the effects on the industry and on competition are elaborated upon. The considerations on these topics will be summarized.

(i) Necessity

The aid recipient must prove that he has an economically viable alternative location for his project or sub-part(s) of a project; this defines the *mobility* of a project.[211] To authorize regional aid, the Commission checks the region's eligibility for aid under Community law and studies the geographical mobility of the notified project.[212] No regional aid may be authorized for (parts of) projects that are not geographically mobile.[213] In demonstrating the mobility of a project, where the alternative location is not in the EEA or in one of the countries of Central and Eastern Europe (CEEC), an investor must prove, notably by means of a location study, that at least one commercially viable alternative to the location chosen has been considered in the EEA or in one of the CEEC-countries. Otherwise, the location chosen will simply be considered to be the best one. Regional aid intended for modernization and rationalization, which is generally not mobile, is not authorized in the motor vehicle industry. But a radical change in production structures on the existing site, a so-called "transformation", may be

[211] It is noted in the 1998 Framework that mobility alone is not always sufficient to establish the necessity for aid. For instance, the site chosen may have net competitive advantages in comparison with the alternative proposed by the investor.

[212] The 1998 Framework specifies that a project put forward by first-tier module or sub-system suppliers that is directly linked to a mobile investment by a motor vehicle manufacturer will by definition be considered mobile itself. A supplier's project may be mobile even if the manufacturer's project is not; the supplier would have to be able to satisfy the Commission on this point.

[213] The 1998 Framework specifies that if there were no other industrial site, whether new or in existence, capable of receiving the investment in question within the group, the undertaking would be compelled to carry out its project in the sole plant available, even in the absence of aid.

eligible for regional aid.[214] Such a transformation is not the same as "restructuring" which is applicable to firms in financial difficulties.

(ii) Eligibility of Costs

The Commission will determine whether or not costs relating to the mobile aspects of a project are eligible. The latter is defined by the regional scheme applicable in the assisted region concerned.

(iii) Proportionality of Aid

When considering the mobile aspects of a project, the Commission will satisfy itself by means of the *cost-benefit analysis* method that the planned aid is in proportion to the regional problems it is intended to help resolve.[215] In view of the fact that a mobile project located in an assisted region always suffers from minimum disadvantages, a cost-benefit analysis is considered not to be required if the intensity of the planned regional aid is 10%[216] or less of the regional ceiling.[217]

The 1998 Framework specifies that the cost-benefit analysis compares, with regard to the mobile elements, the costs which an investor would bear in order to carry out its project in the region in question with those it would bear for an identical project in a different location, which makes it possible to determine

---

[214] According to the 1998 Framework, entire production lines that are obsolete are sometimes dismantled in the motor vehicle industry, which may involve an element of mobility inasmuch as a firm is often faced with the choice of adapting the existing plant or closing it and setting up a new plant elsewhere, either in the form of an extension or on a greenfield site. Such a transformation is defined as the complete dismantling of bodywork lines (motor vehicles) or power plant lines (engines) and, simultaneously, of the final assembly lines of the plant in question and the setting-up of new bodywork lines, power plant lines and final assembly lines in an overall production structure that is clearly different from the previous one.

[215] It is somewhat curious that none of the guidelines makes an explicit reference to the rather extensive *Annex I* (entitled "Cost-benefit analysis in the context of the EC Framework on state aid to the automotive industry") of the 1998 Framework. The Commission pointed out in State Aid C 66/97 (Sweden), OJ 1997, C326/3, par. 5, that this explanatory annex describes the methodology of cost-benefit analysis in order to make the objectives and the procedures for assessing practical cases of aid even clearer and more transparent.

[216] Reference is made to State Aid N 781/96 (Ford Bridgend), OJ 1997, C139/4.

[217] The 1998 Framework specifies that this will be the case until the Commission has approved the regional maps in accordance with the new regional guidelines, which it should do by 1 January 2000. After that date, and in so far as the new regional maps have lower ceilings, the minimum intensity triggering a cost-benefit analysis will be 20% of the new regional ceiling.

the specific handicaps of the assisted region concerned. The comparator plant must be located in the EEA or a CEEC-country if the purpose of the investment is the manufacture of vehicles and parts of vehicles intended largely for the European markets.[218] If the comparator plant is located in another assisted area within the meaning of Article 92(3) EC or Article 61(3) EEA, any difference in regional aid rate is regarded as neutral by definition. The 1998 Framework prescribes that operational handicaps are assessed over three years in the case of expansion of projects and five years in the case of new plants on greenfield sites;[219] these periods are considered to be consistent with the time needed to overcome start-up difficulties and reach target operational levels in each case. The 1998 Framework leaves no doubt that the Commission authorizes regional aid within the limit of the regional handicaps resulting from the investment in the comparator plant.

In the case of an overall project, the first-tier component suppliers concerned may each benefit from the same regional handicap percentage as the vehicle manufacturer, as calculated by the cost-benefit analysis, no individual cost-benefit analysis being applied to them. However, if a first-tier component supplier taking part in an overall project considers it has the specific regional handicaps that would give it a higher aid intensity, it may request a separate cost-benefit analysis the results of which will be applied irrespective of the outcome.

The 1998 Framework provides in *Annex II* a copy of the standard notification forms for a cost-benefit analysis.

(iv) Analysis of the Effects on the Industry and on Competition

According to the 1998 Framework, the Commission proposes (in view of the sensitive character of the motor vehicle industry) to study the effects on competition of every investment project, looking in particular at variations in

---

[218] The 1998 Framework confirms that the study of the mobility of the investment and the cost-benefit analysis may be carried out using different alternative locations.

[219] Under the 1998 Framework, new plant means new plant on a new site which has not yet been developed. In such cases, compared with plant expansion, undertakings are faced with a lack of (i) adequate infrastructure, (ii) organized logistics, (iii) a workforce specifically trained for the needs of the undertaking and (iv) sub-contracting structure. If, however, such services can be provided by a unit of the same group located in close proximity, the project is regarded, in accordance with VW II, *supra* note 48, L308/46, as an expansion, even if it is actually built on a greenfield site.

production capacity on the relevant market in the group concerned.[220] Depending upon the impact on competitors, an adjustment will be made in the form of a particular "top-up" which consists of the percentage points listed hereunder, which will be added to or subtracted from the intensity allowable according to the cost-benefit analysis.

Impact on competitors		**Article 92(3)(a) EC-regions**	**Article 92(3)(c) EC-regions**
Negligible[221]	top-up:	+4	+2
Moderate[222]	top-up:	+2	+1
High[223]	top-up:	-1	-2

The 1998 Framework indicates that the distinction between Article 92(3)(a) regions and Article 92(3)(c) regions is needed in order to take better account of the difficulties encountered in each region and to increase the incentive effect of regional aid on investors.

(v) Determination of Aid Intensity

The 1998 Framework specifies that the authorized aid, expressed as a gross grant equivalent, may not exceed the total of the amounts calculated in stages (i) to (v) and usually discounted and expressed as a percentage of eligible investment so that they can be compared with the gross grant equivalent of the assisted region. The aid may not exceed the regional ceiling applicable to the type of undertaking concerned.

---

[220] The 1998 Framework specifies that the relevant product market covers the products (and possibly the services) referred to in the investment project and their possible substitutes from the consumer's standpoint (on the basis of product characteristics, prices and intended use) and that of the product (plant flexibility). The relevant geographic market in principle covers the EEA and the CEEC-countries.

[221] The 1998 Framework specifies that the impact is negligible where $C(f)/C(i) \leq 0{,}99$.

[222] The 1998 Framework specifies that the impact is moderate where $0{,}99 < C(f) / C(i) < 1{,}01$ or where a new segment is created on the relevant market.

[223] The 1998 Framework specifies that the impact on the industry is high where the ratio between the capacity of the group after the investment (C(f)) and the capacity of the group before the investment (C(i)) is 1,01 or over.

8.4.5.4 Research and Development Aid

The 1998 Framework specifies that research and development aid will be assessed under the Community framework for state aid for research and development. In addition, it emphasized that the Commission shall carry out a thorough analysis of the breakdown of costs keeping in mind the distinction between industrial research and genuine precompetitive development, on the one hand, and the introduction of new technology in the form of productive investment or competitive development, on the other.

8.4.5.5 Investment Aid for Innovation

The 1998 Framework recognizes that as the European motor vehicle industry has to improve its competitiveness as compared with its American, Japanese and Korean competitors, it will have to improve its ability to innovate in order to further reduce the technological and industrial gap. Innovation is defined as the development and industrialization in Europe, the EEA and the CEEC-countries of genuinely or substantially new products or processes, that is products or processes which have not yet been used or marketed by other parties operating in the industry.

A genuine innovation carries a risk of failure; the Commission will take account of the scale of this risk when it assesses the intensity of the aid envisaged. The 1998 Framework specifies that investment aid for innovation will only be authorized in duly justified cases, as an incentive to industrial or technological risk-taking. The maximum intensity of such aid is set at 10% of all eligible costs, corresponding to engineering activities and investments of direct and exclusive relevance to the innovative part of the project. An innovative project must concern only one plant location[224] within the same group in the motor vehicle industry. No aid will be granted for parts of the project carried out in other branches of a group.

[224] According to the 1998 Framework, this can also be a small number of sites if different complementary sub-projects take place on a small number of sites.

8.4.5.6 Aid for Environmental Protection and Energy Saving

The 1998 Framework confirms that aid to combat pollution in general, that is aid granted under the Community guidelines on State aid for environmental protection, may be regarded as compatible. These Community guidelines involve complex technical evaluations of such things as the "ecological" costs incurred by the investor. Moreover, when it assesses the compatibility of aid, the Commission makes a thorough study of the cost savings on energy, raw materials and so on which the investor has secured as a result of the environmental protection component in the project.

8.4.5.7 Aid to Vocational Training

The Commission has a generally positive attitude towards training, retraining and reconversion programmes.[225] State aid for such purposes will be scrutinized to ensure that it is not used solely to reduce the costs a firm would normally bear. The 1998 Framework announces a Community framework for training aid which will also apply to the motor vehicle industry.

8.4.5.8 Aid for Modernization and Rationalization

The 1998 Framework announces that no aid for modernization or rationalization may be granted to undertakings in the motor vehicle industry. Modernization and rationalization are essential if an undertaking is to remain competitive on a world market and should normally be financed from a company's own funds; they present a very high risk of distortion of competition. If an undertaking competing on an international market is unable to finance its own modernization and restructuring, its ability to compete and its viability will eventually disappear.

8.4.5.9 Operating Aid

---

[225] IP/98/120, and *Agence Europe*, "The Commission approves training aid to Opel Belgium", 5 February 1998, at 13, reported that on 4 February 1998, the Commission approved Belgian aid to Opel Belgium, in support of a training project that will help to adapt the plants workforce to new production methods which set new demands for the flexibility and the skills of the employees entailing new working methods and a whole new organisation culture.

Again, the 1998 Framework leaves no doubt about the fact that no new operating aid will be authorized by the Commission even in assisted areas. Operating aid creates lasting distortions of competition in sectors such as the motor vehicle industry. On the basis of Article 93(1) EC, the Commission will suggest that Member States currently granting operating aid under existing schemes should gradually abolish operating aid benefiting one or several undertakings in the motor vehicle industry.

8.5 Concluding Remarks

The Community is aware of the fact that for strategic, technical and socio-economic reasons, a number of Member States is quite readily prepared to grant state aid to their domestic automobile industry. In view of the structural overcapacity and fierce competition within this sector, any state aid is liable to affect intra-Community trade and impair competition. As such, state aid to undertakings active in the automobile industry constitutes a serious threat of distortion of competition in this highly competitive industry. State aid is an important obstacle to an efficient allocation of production factors within the Community. Therefore, the Community has a considerable interest in controlling and eventually reducing the influx of state aid into the automobile industry through the application of Articles 92 to 94 EC.

The Commission has developped policies on the manner in which the different categories of state aid are evaluated. In an effort to increase legal certainty, the Commission has published a number of horizontal and sectoral guidelines on the manner in which it will go about evaluating these categories of aid under Articles 92 to 94 EC. Unfortunately, transparency still leaves much to be desired as the Commission is still reluctant to publicly motivate its decisions on politically sensitive state aids. The 1989 Framework on state aid to the motor vehicle industry formulated concise guidelines on the manner in which the Community would evaluate the different categories of state aid in the automobile industry. The Commission confirmed its intention to examine the implications of aid measures in great detail. The 1989 Framework was replaced by a more detailed and elaborate 1998 Framework for State Aid to the Motor Vehicle Industry.

The Commission is competent to make its final decision conditional upon full compliance with certain conditions. For instance, with an eye on the structural overcapacity of the automobile industry, the Commission approved German aid to Volkswagen on the condition that for a certain period, Volkswagen's output would not increase. There is no doubt that the manner in which aid measures are evaluated by the Commission, is strongly influenced by its efforts to strengthen the competitiveness of Community industry.

9. CONCENTRATION AND COOPERATION IN THE AUTOMOBILE INDUSTRY

9.1 Introduction

The removal of barriers to intra-Community trade triggered concentrations and stimulated cooperations in the Community in most sectors of industry including the automobile industry. These concentrations and cooperations are scrutinized by the Community within the context of its competition policy[1] on the basis of Articles 85 and 86 EC and, since 21 September 1990, the Merger Regulation.[2] The socio-economic importance of the automobile industry makes the control of concentrations and cooperations, politically speaking, a highly sensitive topic. Member States identify and are identified with their national industries.[3] Member States regard their domestic automobile industry as a strategic industry that is closely related with national sovereignty.[4] The fact that nationality still matters was illustrated by the planned merger between Renault and Volvo which was called off at the very last minute because of cultural differences and Swedish fears that a "national champion" would eventually be taken over by a French company.[5] Another example of "playing the nationalist card" was the threat by Renault and Peugeot that if the "French" car components group Valeo

---

[1] The Council pointed out in Press release 11172/95 (Presse 307-G), at 31, following the 1880th Council meeting on 6 and 7 November 1995, that it is necessary to ensure a particularly close examination on how competition and competitiveness of European industry may be influenced by agreements, alliances, mergers and other forms of cooperation that are growing in number and scope, at both Community and international level; such a close and permanent examination being one of the crucial pre-conditions for any responsible competition policy of the Community dealing with concentrations and cooperations.

[2] Council Regulation 4064/89 of 21 December 1989 on the control of concentrations between undertakings, OJ 1989, L395/1. The corrected text was published in OJ 1990, L257/13. Most recently amended by Council Regulation 1310/97 of 30 June 1997, OJ 1997, L180/1.

[3] For instance, in what must have been a slip of the pen, the Commission noted in *European Economy - Competition and Integration - Community Merger Control Policy*, 1994, Number 57 ("*European Economy 1994*"), at 16, that the lowering of trade barriers resulted in fiercer competition amongst European *nations*; the term "undertakings" would have been more appropriate.

[4] See Chapter 2. According to *FT*, "Reshaping the car industry", 15 April 1996, at 16, states tend to wrap their domestic automobile industry in national flags.

[5] See *FT*, "Nationality still matters", 27 April 1994, and "Renault ends link with Volvo", 29 August 1997, at 18. See also *FT*, "Volvo plans growth drive" and "Volvo's lights burn brighter", 9 December 1997, at 17 and 19. *FT*, "Renault cost-cutting on target", 19 September 1996, reported that Renault's chairman, Schweitzer, noted that it was important to "have a national car, a national identity".

were to be sold to a rival car manufacturer or to a foreign component supplier, they might take their business elsewhere.[6] These nationalistic considerations still form an important barrier to the rationalization and reorganization of the automobile industry within the Community notwithstanding structural over-capacity and the entrance of new, mostly Asian competitors on the already highly competitive car market.[7] Already for some time, commentators expect the automobile industry to be on the eve of important mergers and joint ventures

---

[6] See, *inter alia*, *FT*, "Playing the nationalist card", 12 March 1996, at 24, and "Peugeot chief toughens stance on Valeo sale", 14 May 1996, at 17. As the controlling 27,7% stake in Valeo in question, is in the hands of the *Italian* C. De Benedetti, it is somewhat ironic to note that Mr J. Calvet, President of Peugeot, announced that he "will do everything to ensure that Valeo stays French". See *FT*, "French outburst over company sales to foreigners", 26-27 October 1996, at 1; "CGIP poised to buy Valeo stake", 5 November 1996, at 17, and "Valeo future secured by sale of 27% stake" and "Valeo deal hailed as happy coincidence", 6 November 1996, at 15 and 16, in which it was reported that CGIP's chairman, Seillière, conceded that the plan to purchase the stake was inspired partly by the desire to keep the company in French hands.

[7] For instance, *FT*, "Vickers appeals to Brussels over Rolls-Royce veto right", 7 January 1998, at 15, reported that under the licensing agreement between Rolls-Royce Motor Cars and Rolls-Royce Aircraft, the latter can terminate the licence if the former falls into "foreign control". This right to terminate gives Rolls-Royce Aircraft in effect a veto over a future sale of Rolls-Royce Motor Cars which is presently owned by Vickers but put up for sale to mostly "foreign" interested parties. The *FT*, "Rolls-Royce enthusiasts plan $1bn bid", 9 January 1998, at 24, reported that according to the Rolls-Royce Action group "[t]here is tremendous concern among our members about the loss of a famous British company and loss of national prestige". See also *Agence Europe*, "Difference between Rolls-Royce (Aircraft engines) and Vickers over the possible sale of Rolls-Royce cars to a foreign buyer", 8 January 1998, at 12, and *FT*, "Selling off the silver", 11-13 April 1998, at 7; "Patriotism is out of place in sale of Rolls-Royce", 15 May 1998, at 21, and "Shareholder anger at R-R Motors deal", 30 May 1998, at 1.

that will lead to further rationalization and reorganization.[8] This process is already taking place in the parts industry. It has been reported that "[i]n the biggest change in its history, the once-diversified components business is being rationalised as large specialists gobble up the minnows".[9]

This chapter examines the manner in which the Community deals with concentrations and certain forms of cooperations in the automobile industry.

---

[8] H. Simonian emphasized in *FT*, "Engine of demand sputters", 15 February 1996, at 13, that mergers and joint ventures should top European carmakers' agendas as they face overcapacity and declining profits. *FT*, "Motor industry capacity fears", 20 February 1996, at 2, reported that the chief executive of Lucas Industries warned that overcapacity of up to a third will drive Europe's motor industry into big restructuring and mergers which will "dramatically affect" European component suppliers. Furthermore, *FT*, "Motor industry set to contract", 27 March 1996, at 4, noted that the chairman of Ford emphasized that the world motor industry is set for further rationalisation, cuts and mergers. See in this context *FT*, "Daewoo wins better terms on Ssangyong deal", 12 January 1998, at 19; "Daewoo in talks with General Motors", 2 February 1998, at 19; "Crisis leaves carmakers running on empty", 4 February 1998, at 18; "Daewoo, GM to discuss fresh link-up", 3 February 1998, at 16; "Samsung car company seeks alliance with foreign partners", 12 February 1998, at 13; "Samsung's Ford talks feed Kia bid rumour", 13 February 1998, at 25; "Hyundai may bid for Kia" 23 March 1998, at 22; "Kia Motors says Ford is against Hyundai bid", 26 March 1998, at 14; "Rivals set to battle for Kia", 27 March 1998, at 17; "Vickers in talks with Ford over engines group", 4 May 1998, at 17; "Wheels set in motion", 8 May 1998, at 19; "Motor merger talks set to gather pace", 11 May 1998, at 17; "Samsung, Ford talks collapse", 26 May 1998, at 18; "VW takes over Lamborghini", 25-26 July 1998, at 23; "Proton lifts stake in Lotus", 29 May 1998, at 21; "Mazda may join Ford in bid for Kia", 3 June 1998, at 19; "Mitsubishi Motors-Merger with Volvo ruled out", 9 June 1998, at 5; "Fresco rejects Fiat, BMW talks rumours", 17 July 1998, at 18; "GM challenges Ford by joining bidders for Kia", 27 July 1998, at 13, and "General Motors pulls out of bidding for Kia", 24 August 1998, at 16. See also "Bargains galore", *The Economist*, 7 February 1998, at 79, and "Autoconcern Toyota neemt Daihatsu over", *Het Financieele Dagblad*, 29-31 August 1998, at 4. According to BMW's chairman, Mr. Pischetsrieder, in *FT*, "Cruising the autobahn", 31 July 1998, at 12, the automobile industry is in the grip of merger mania.

[9] See *FT*, "Star parts for bit players", 28 October 1996, at 17, which provides an overview of nine major international concentrations in the components sector in 1996. It is reported that in products like car seats, the braking business, exhaust systems, shock absorbers, airbags and seatbelts, the biggest rationalizations have already taken place. See also *FT*, "Lucas Varity has 1bn for acquisitions", 1 April 1998, at 23; "Lucas Varity in line for large acquisition", 5 June 1998, at 24, and "Valéo to buy ITT electricals", 26 June 1998, at 17. See also *Agence Europe*, "Magneti Marelli (FIAT group) may acquire joint control (with telespazio) of COMNET (infomobility sector)", 9 July 1998, at 10; "Dana and Echlin, American automotive components manufacturers, are authorized to merge because their activities are complementary in nature", 10 July 1998, at 11, and "Commission authorises Valéo to become first supplier of certain auto components (through acquisition of ITT industries division) as there is still considerable competition", 1 August 1998, at 6.

First, the control of concentrations with a Community dimension in the automobile industry will be dealt with (**9.2**). Then, the control of concentrations without a Community dimension (**9.3**) and the relevance of Articles 85 and 86 EC for horizontal and vertical cooperation (**9.4**) in the automobile industry will be examined. This chapter comes to an end with some concluding remarks (**9.5**).

9.2 Control of Concentrations with a Community dimension in the Automobile Industry

9.2.1 General Remarks

The Merger Regulation introduced a new regime for Community control of concentrations with a Community dimension.[10] In the preamble to the Merger Regulation, the Council recognized that the dismantling of internal frontiers for the achievement of the internal market leads to major reorganisations in the Community particularly in the form of concentrations.[11] The Council welcomed this development as being in line with the requirements of dynamic competition and capable of increasing the competitiveness of European industry, improving the conditions of growth and raising the standard of living in the Community.[12] Nevertheless, the Council emphasized that it must be ensured that the process of

---

[10] See on the Merger Regulation, *inter alia*, Bellamy and Child, *Common market law of competition* (V. Rose ed.), 1993, Sweet & Maxwell, London, at 306-385; I. Van Bael and J.-F. Bellis, *Competition Law of the European Community*, 3rd edition, 1994, CCH Europe, at 363-512; C.J. Cook and C.S. Kerse, *E.C. Merger Control* (2nd edition), 1996, Sweet & Maxwell, London; B.E. Hawk and H.L. Huser, *European Community Merger Control: A Practitioner's Guide*, 1996, Kluwer Law International, The Hague, and W. van Gerven, L. Gyselen, M. Maresceau and J. Stuyck, *Kartelrecht II*, 1997, W.E.J. Tjeenk Willink, at 731-901.

[11] 3rd Whereas, *supra* note 1. The Commission reported in *European Economy 1994*, *supra* note 3, at 16, that "[t]he first recorded European merger wave took place between 1958 and 1970, when trade barriers were lowered significantly following the establishment of the EEC". According to the Commission, a second European merger wave seems to have taken place between 1986 and 1992, which coincided with the single market programme. The Commission reported in *European Economy - Mergers and acquisitions*, Supplement A (Economic trends), Number 3, March 1995 ("*European Economy 1995*"), at 8, that after a period of stabilisation, the merger activity increased in 1994.

[12] 4th Whereas, *supra* note 1.

reorganisation does not result in lasting damage to competition and that Community law must therefore include provisions governing those concentrations which may significantly impede effective competition in the common market or in a substantial part of it.[13] As Articles 85 and 86 EC are not sufficient for this purpose, a new legal instrument was created in the form of the Merger Regulation to permit effective control of all concentrations from the point of view of their effect on the structure of competition in the Community and to be the only instrument applicable to such concentrations.[14] The preamble specifies that in establishing whether concentrations with a Community dimension are compatible or not with the common market from the point of view of the need to maintain and develop effective competition in the common market, the Commission must place its appraisal within the general framework of the achievement of the fundamental objectives referred to in Article 2 of the Treaty, including that of strengthening the Community's economic and social cohesion.[15] The Community's merger control is part of its competition policy and "[d]evised to serve the Community's objective, ..., of ensuring that competition in the common market is not distorted, it is also an instrument to facilitate integration and the further development of the internal market".[16] This confirms that Community policies other than competition policy can play a role in the application of the Merger Regulation.

9.2.2 The Scope of the Merger Regulation

The scope of the Merger Regulation is limited to concentrations with a Community dimension. The Merger Regulation also covers restrictions directly

---

[13] 5th Whereas. In IP/96/628, the Commission noted that "[a]n increasing number of firms operating in Europe regard the new opportunities offered by the single market and the European Economic Area as their cue to embark on mergers and concentrations, which the Commission must monitor in order to ensure compliance with the EU's competition rules".

[14] 7th Whereas.

[15] 13th Whereas, *supra* note 1.

[16] See, *inter alia*, *European Economy 1994*, *supra* note 3, at 7.

related and necessary to the implementation of the concentration.[17] Other restrictions are subject to the Commission's assessment under Articles 85 and 86 EC.

Article 3(1) of the Merger Regulation provides that a *concentration* shall be deemed to arise where:

> (a) two or more previously independent undertakings merge, or
> (b) one or more persons already controlling at least one undertaking, or one or more undertakings acquire, whether by purchase of securities or assets, by contract or by any other means, direct or indirect control of the whole or parts of one or more other undertakings.[18]

Pursuant to Article 3(2), a concentration also arises where a joint venture is created that performs on a lasting basis all the functions of an autonomous economic entity (a so-called "full-function" joint venture).[19] Article 3(5) of the Merger Regulation specifies, in short, that a concentration shall not be deemed to arise in case of (a) temporary acquisitions of securities holdings, (b) acquisitions of control by (insolvency) liquidators, or (c) acquisitions by

---

[17] Article 6(1)(b) of the Merger Regulation specifies that the Commission's decision declaring the concentration compatible with the common market also covers restrictions directly related and necessary to the implementation of the concentration. See in this context Commission Notice regarding restrictions ancillary to concentrations, OJ 1990, C203/5.

[18] Article 3(3) provides that *control* shall be constituted by "rights, contracts or any other means which, either separately or in combination and having regard to the considerations of fact or law involved, confer the possibility of exercising decisive influence on an undertaking, in particular by: (a) ownership or the right to use all or part of the assets of an undertaking; (b) rights or contracts which confer decisive influence on the composition, voting or decisions of the organs of an undertaking". Article 3(4) specifies that *control* is *acquired* by persons or undertakings which "(a) are holders of the rights or entitled to rights under the contracts concerned; or (b) while not being holders of such rights or entitled to rights under such contracts, have the power to exercise the rights deriving therefrom". As illustrated by Commission Decision of 7 March 1994 (Ford/Hertz), Case IV/M397 (OJ 1994, C121/4), operations which do not imply a change in the quality and degree of control do not satisfy the conditions of Article 3(1) of the Merger Regulation.

[19] See Commission Merger Control Notice ("Full-Function Joint Ventures"), OJ 1998, C66/1; Commission Merger Control Notice ("Concentration"), OJ 1998, C66/5, and Commission Merger Control Notice ("Information on Assessment of Full-Function Joint Ventures"), OJ 1998, C66/38. See also Written Question 1911/97 (Amadeo), OJ 1998, C60/66.

financial holding companies.

The Merger Regulation only covers concentrations with a *Community dimension*. Article 1(2) provides that a concentration has a Community dimension where:

> (a) the combined aggregate worldwide turnover of all the undertakings concerned is more than ECU 5000 million; and
> (b) the aggregate Community-wide turnover of each of at least two of the undertakings concerned is more than ECU 250 million, unless each of the undertakings concerned achieves more than two-thirds of its aggregate Community-wide turnover within one and the same Member State.[20]

In 1995, the Commission estimated that the number of mergers notified under the Merger Regulation, represented less than 4% of the total number of mergers in the period 1991-1994.[21] Due to the high level of the thresholds set out in Article 1(2), the number of mergers falling within the scope of the Merger Regulation is relatively small.[22] Article 1(3) of the Merger Regulation brings a special category of concentrations which do not meet the thresholds of Article 1(2), within the scope of the Regulation. Article 1(3) provides that a concentration also has a Community dimension where:

> (a) the combined aggregate worldwide turnover of all the undertakings concerned is more than ECU 2500 million;
> (b) in each of at least three Member States, the combined aggregate turnover of all the undertakings concerned is more than ECU 100 million;

---

[20] Article 5 of the Merger Regulation specifies the manner in which the turnover of the relevant undertakings has to be calculated. See in this context also Commission Merger Control Notice ("Undertakings concerned"), OJ 1998, C66/14, and Commission Merger Control Notice ("Calculation of Turnover"), OJ 1998, C66/25.

[21] *European Economy 1995*, *supra* note 11, at 12.

[22] The thresholds were the result of a political compromise between the Member States. See in this context the 1996 Community Merger Control Green Paper on the Review of the Merger Regulation, COM(96)19 final, 31 January 1996 ("*Green Paper on Merger Control*").

(c) in each of at least three Member States included for the purpose of (b), the aggregate turnover of each of at least two of the undertakings concerned is more than ECU 25 million; and

(d) the aggregate Community-wide turnover of each of at least two of the undertakings concerned is more than ECU 100 million,

unless each of the undertakings concerned achieves more than two-thirds of its aggregate Community-wide turnover within one and the same Member State.

Following a Commission report to the Council on the operation of the thresholds and criteria establishing Community dimension, the thresholds of Article 1(3) may be revised. This Commission report has to be made before 1 July 2000.

As car manufacturers tend to be very large, they are strongly represented amongst the cases notified under the Merger Regulation.[23] However, the Commission found that important mergers in the components sector often fall below the thresholds set by the Merger Regulation notwithstanding the fact that these concentrations have significant cross-border effects. According to the Commission, this is mainly due to the fact that despite the presence of some large manufacturers, there is a considerable degree of fragmentation due to a large number of small to medium-sized specialized manufacturers. As a result, acquisitions of specialized undertakings with significant market presence or transfers of divisions of larger groups can fall below the thresholds and thus be excluded from the scope of the Merger Regulation.[24]

9.2.3 One-Stop Shop

Concentrations with a Community dimension that fall within the scope of the Merger Regulation only have to be scrutinized by *one* public authority under *one* set of rules on Community level instead of having to deal with different

[23] *Ibidem*, at 14. See also *European Economy 1994, supra* note 3, at 45.

[24] *Green Paper on Merger Control*, *supra* note 22, at 12-13. See also IP/96/97 and *FT*, "Fresh look at thresholds", 20 March 1996, at 10.

national competition authorities and different national competition laws. The Merger Regulation is based on the "one-stop shop" principle which, according to the Commission, simplifies administrative procedures, enables businesses to minimize restructuring costs and creates a level playing field by ensuring that the same notification requirements, procedure and legal standard apply to all concentrations with significant cross-border effects.[25] Concentrations falling within the scope of the Merger Regulation have to be notified to the Commission by means of Form CO.[26] After an initial period of only one month ("phase 1"), the Commission must decide whether or not the notified case raises serious doubt as to its compatibility with the common market and, in the affirmative, initiate an in-depth investigation ("phase 2"). The Commission must take the final decision on the concentration within a period of four months after the initiation of the in-depth investigation.[27]

Article 21 of the Merger Regulation provides that the Commission has *sole* jurisdiction to take the decisions under the Merger Regulation and specifies that no Member State shall apply its national legislation on competition to any consideration that has a Community dimension.[28] However, under certain conditions, Member States may take appropriate measures to protect legitimate interests other than those taken into consideration by the Merger Regulation and compatible with the general principles and other provisions of Community law.[29] The Commission has to operate in close and constant liason with the competent authorities of the Member States and has to consult the Advisory

---

[25] *Green Paper on Merger Control*, *supra* note 22, at 10-11.

[26] See Annex to Commission Regulation 447/98 of 1 March 1998 on the notifications, time limits and hearings provided for in Council Regulation 4064/89 on the control of concentrations between undertakings, OJ 1998, L61/1.

[27] See Articles 6, 8 and 10 of the Merger Regulation.

[28] See Van Bael and Bellis, *supra* note 10, at 430-431, for a concise discussion of the residual application of Articles 85 and 86 EC to concentrations by national competition authorities or national courts.

[29] Article 21(3) of the Merger Regulation. See for an example IP/95/316 and IP/95/1469 on the concentration Lyonnaise des Eaux/Northumbrian Water.

Committee on Concentrations before any decision is taken.[30] Pursuant to Article 9 of the Merger Regulation, the Commission may decide upon the compatibility of the concentration with the common market itself or refer the notified concentration under certain circumstances, to the competent authorities of the Member State concerned in order to have them apply their national competition law to the concentration (the so-called "German Clause").[31]

9.2.4 Compatibility with the Common Market

9.2.4.1 Appraisal

The Commission has to establish whether notified concentrations falling within the scope of the Merger Regulation, are *compatible with the common market*. Article 2(1) of the Merger Regulation specifies that in making this appraisal, the Commission shall take account of:

> (a) the need to maintain and develop effective competition within the common market in view of, among other things, the structure of all the markets concerned and the actual or potential competition from undertakings located either within or outwith the Community; and
> (b) the market position of the undertakings concerned and their economic and financial power, the alternatives available to suppliers and users, their access to supplies or markets, any legal or other barriers to entry, supply and demand trends for the relevant goods and services, the interests of the intermediate and ultimate consumers, and the development of technical and economic progress provided that it is to consumers' advantage and does not form an obstacle to competition.

[30] Article 19 of the Merger Regulation. The advice of the Advisory Committee on Concentrations does not bind the Commission in any way which is illustrated by Commission Decision 91/595 of 31 July 1991 (Varta/Bosch), Case IV/M012, OJ 1991, L320/26, in which the Commission gave clearance to a merger against the advice of the Advisory Committee on Concentrations.

[31] Article 9 of the Merger Regulation (the so-called "German clause"). See, for instance, Decision Varta/Bosch, *ibidem*, in which the Commission denied the German Article 9-request to have the case referred.

Article 2(2) and (3) provide that the Commission will examine whether a concentration creates or strengthens a dominant position as a result of which effective competition would be significantly impeded in the common market or in a substantial part thereof. If so, the concentration will be declared incompatible with the common market. If not, the concentration will be declared compatible with the common market. Under the Merger Regulation, the creation or strengthening of a dominant position as such can be held incompatible with the common market, without abusive behaviour being necessary. The primary objective of the Merger Regulation is to safeguard a competitive structure of the market. The Commission has qualified the automobile industry as an industry "sensitive to mergers" since this sector is already highly concentrated at the Community level. The Commission confirmed that concentrations in this industry would require particular attention.[32]

It should be emphasized that *cooperative* aspects of the so-called "full-function" joint ventures are subjected to a special regime under the Merger Regulation. Before the Merger Regulation was amended by Regulation 1310/97, concentrative joint ventures fell within and cooperative joint ventures outside the scope of the Merger Regulation.[33] The Commission proposed to eliminate this discrepancy since these two types of joint venture essentially have "the same structural effect". The Commission suggested to examine "them all under the merger and concentration rules, applying Article 85 only to any cooperative aspects" so as to "enable businesses involved in both types of joint venture to know where they stand legally within a month of notification".[34] The amended text of Article 2(4) now provides that to the extent that the creation of a joint venture constituting a concentration within the meaning of Article 3, has as its object or effect the coordination of the competitive behaviour of undertakings

---

[32] See *European Economy 1994*, *supra* note 3, at 36.

[33] Decision Varta/Bosch, *supra* note 30, and Commission Decision of 14 January 1992 (Volvo/Atlas), Case IV/M152, OJ 1992, C17/10, are good examples of the manner in which the Commission checked the elements (i) joint control, (ii) full function undertaking/autonomous economic entity and (iii) absence of (risk of) coordination of competitive behaviour, before qualifying a joint venture as being concentrative. See also A. Brown, "Distinguishing between concentrative and co-operative joint ventures: Is it getting any easier?", [1996] 4 ECLR, at 240-249.

[34] IP/96/628. See also IP/96/97.

that remain independent, such coordination has to be appraised in accordance with the criteria of Article 85(1) and (3) EC, with a view to establishing whether or not the operation is compatible with the common market. Article 2(4) specifies that in making this appraisal, the Commission shall take into account in particular:

- whether two or more parent companies retain to a significant extent activities in the same market as the joint venture or in a market which is downstream or upstream from that of the joint venture or in a neighbouring market closely related to this market;
- whether the coordination which is the direct consequence of the creation of the joint venture affords the undertakings concerned the possibility of eliminating competition in respect of a substantial part of the products or services in question.

In short, cooperative aspects of "full-function" joint ventures have to be appraised under the Merger Regulation but in accordance with the criteria of Article 85(1) and (3) EC.

In appraising concentrations with a Community dimension, the Commission has to identify the relevant market (**9.2.4.2**) before it can examine whether the notified concentration creates or strengthens a dominant position as a result of which effective competition would be significantly impeded in the common market or in a substantial part thereof (**9.2.4.3**).

9.2.4.2 Relevant Market

The Commission identifies the relevant market by defining the product market and the geographical market.[35]

(i) Product Market

---

[35] See Commission Notice on the definition of relevant market for the purposes of Community competition law, OJ 1997, C372/5, which intends to provide guidance as to how the Commission applies the concept of relevant product and geographic market in its ongoing enforcement of Community competition law, in particular the application of Regulations 17/62 and 4064/89. See also L. Sleuwaegen, "The relevant antitrust market", *European Economy 1994*, *supra* note 3, at 109-129.

Form CO specifies that the product market comprises all those products and/or services which are regarded as interchangeable or substitutable by the consumer, by reason of the products' characteristics, their prices and their intended use.[36]

- Cars

With regard to the *manufacture* of cars, a distinction is often made between the generalist manufacturers like GM and Ford which compete on a full range of cars, and specialist manufacturers like BMW, Mercedes-Benz and Porsche which focus on a particular market segment. There is a tendency, however, for specialist manufacturers to expand into other ranges of cars and become more generalist. For instance, BMW did so by acquiring Rover[37] and will further do so through diversification,[38] Volkswagen entered the luxury market,[39] and Mercedes-Benz merged with Chrysler and puts its own small A-Class and

---

[36] Section 6 of Form CO, *supra* note 26.

[37] Commission Decision of 14 March 1994 (BMW/Rover), Case IV/M416, OJ 1994, C93/23, par. 6, illustrates that from BMW's point of view, the merger with Rover would change BMW from a specialist to a generalist producer competing with a full range of cars. See also *FT*, "Polishing up Rover's act", 2 May 1996, at 14; "BMW's motorcycle chief to head Rover", 5 July 1996, at 21; "The shock of absorption", 11 October 1996, at 13, and "Shift of pace as Rover changes gear to manoeuvre around challenges", 4 May 1998, at 18.

[38] For instance, *FT*, "BMW to build sports utility vehicle", 7 January 1998, at 18, reported that BMW will build a new vehicle in order to become a stronger player on the "sports utility" market. BMW failed in its effort to enter the "super-luxury" market through the take over of Rolls-Royce. See, *inter alia*, *FT*, "Rolls-Royce Motors auction hots up as BMW joins bidders" and "BMW puts in bid for Rolls-Royce", 27 March 1998, at 1 and 22; "BMW wins Rolls-Royce auction with £300m bid", 30 March 1998, at 1; "BMW to promote identity of R-R Motors" and "BMW embarks on its route to the top", 31 March 1998, at 19 and 20.

[39] See *FT*, "VW to challenge Mercedes' lead", 23 October 1997, at 20; "VW plans limo and upmarket Passat", 4 March 1998, at 15; "VW opens battle for Rolls-Royce Motors", 26 March 1998, at 1; "VW saw Rolls as best way to move up", 31 March 1998, at 20; "VW trumps BMW over R-R Motors" and "Agreement sealed as VW drops earlier demands", 8 May 1998, at 1 and 26; "VW sets sights on two more luxury carmakers", 26 May 1998, at 1; "Consortium to table bid for Rolls-Royce Motors", 2 June 1998, at 22; "VW wins R-R Motors vote" and "Rolls-Royce Motors/VW", 6-7 June 1998, at 1 and 24; "VW strategy in Europe pays off", 17 June 1998, at 3, and "BMW to make Rolls-Royce cars", 29 July 1998, at 1.

SMART-cars on the market[40] and intends to enter the "super-luxury" market with the Maybach limousine.[41]

Traditionally, the car market has been segmented through a number of objective criteria like engine size and the length of the car. In its assessment of the BMW-Rover merger, the Commission made the following segmentation:

- Mini (e.g. Nissan Micra, Seat Marbella)
- Small (e.g. Fiat Uno, Opel Corsa, VW Polo, Rover Metro)
- Medium (e.g. Fiat Tipo, VW Golf, Rover 200)
- Large (e.g. BMW 3 series, VW Passat, Honda Accord, Rover 400)

---

[40] See on small cars: *FT*, "Car trip into the unknown", 9 August 1996, at 11; "Smart car forecasts queried by report", 14 October 1996, at 19; "Mercedes considers Smart moves", 11 September 1997, at 18, and "Smart plans from Mercedes-Benz", 6 October 1997, at 19; "Smart plant opens amid doubts", 27 October 1997, at 20; "Daimler acts to ease fears over new car", 29 October 1997, at 18; "Small car creates a big problem", 13 November 1997, at 22; "Daimler-Benz delays second new car over safety fears", 19 December 1997, at 1; "Mercedes to resume making A-Class model", 4 February 1998, at 17; "Daimler ready with Smart car", 9 February 1998, at 17, and "Daimler-Benz aims small", 17 July 1998, at 17. The *FT*, "Smart car venture running on schedule", 19 September 1996, at 16, qualified the Smart venture between Mercedes-Benz and SMH "Europe's riskiest new car project". See on the merger with Chrysler: *FT*, "Daimler and Chrysler near merger", "Chrysler-Benz offers ideal motor marriage", "Buy me a Chrysler-Benz" and "The new model Chrysler-Benz", 7 May 1998, at 1, 23, 16 and 15; "Daimler and Chrysler agree $92 bn merger", "Deal finds favour across the industry", "Culture crucial to synergy equation", 8 May 1998, at 1, 22 and 22; "Unlikely fellow travellers", 9-10 May 1998, at 6; "Four months of fortune that favoured the brave", 14 May 1998, at 19; "Daimler-Chrysler jobs pledge", 28 May 1998, at 15, and *Agence Europe*, "Daimler-Benz/Chrysler merger raises no problems", 11-12 May 1998, at 9, and "Commission has no reservation about Chrysler/Daimler-Benz merger", 24 July 1998, at 12. See also Commission Decision Non-opposition to a notified concentration, Case IV/M.1204-Daimler Benz/Chrysler, OJ 1998, C252/8.

[41] See *FT*, "VW to challenge Mercedes' lead", 23 October 1997, at 20; "On your marques", FT How to spend it (February 1998, Issue 22), at 22-25, and "Rolls-Royce attracts third German group", 23 March 1998, at 20. *FT*, "Lincoln to challenge overseas rivals", 9-10 April 1998, at 20, reported that Ford will enter the luxury segment by the introduction of a new Lincoln-model.

- Executive (e.g. BMW 5 series, Opel Omega, Audi 100, Rover 800)
- Luxury (e.g. BMW 7 series, Mercedes-Benz S Class, Jaguar)
- Multi purpose/sports vehicles (e.g. Land Rover, Porsche).[42]

Although this traditional segmentation is blurred by factors like price, image and accessories, it is generally used by the car industry and is regarded as an important indicator for the positioning of a car in the market place. According to the Commission, important differences in price, technology and engineering requirements still exist between the top and bottom end of the car market.[43]

With regard to the *distribution* of cars, the Commission seems to consider the traditional segmentation of the car market of less importance. In its *Inchcape/IEP* decision, the Commission recognized, on the one hand, that it is common to divide cars into a number of different market segments according to the size and other characteristics of particular models reflecting differing consumer needs. The Commission emphasized, on the other hand, that most major car manufacturers offer a range of models that covers not only those market segments which are economically most important but also more specialized market segments like multi purpose/sports vehicles. The Commission argued that since for a given trade mark, a model range that covers different market segments is normally distributed through the same distribution channel, it is not necessary to analyse distribution channels by product market segment of the passenger car distributed.[44]

---

[42] Decision BMW/Rover, *supra* note 37, par. 10. In Commission Decision of 21 January 1992 (Inchcape/IEP), Case IV/M182, par. 9 (OJ 1992, C21/27), the Commission recognized that the different segments are important in terms of establishing product substitutability and noted that the small, medium and large product market segments cover over 80% of new passenger car registrations.

[43] Decision BMW/Rover, *supra* note 37, paras. 12-13. The Commission left open the question whether, for the purposes of the competitive analysis, the car market could be considered as one product market since even on the basis of the narrowest market definition, the concentration concerned would not lead to the creation or strengthening of a dominant position.

[44] Decision Inchcape/IEP, *supra* note 42, par. 9. See also Commission Decision of 21 May 1992 (Volvo/Lex UK), Case IV/M224, par. 7 (OJ 1992, C142/18); Commission Decision of 28 June 1991 (Nissan/R. Nissan), Case IV/M099 (OJ 1991, C181/21); Commission Decision of 1 July 1993 (Toyota Motor Corp./Walter Frey/Toyota France), Case IV/M326, paras. 9-11 (OJ 1993, C187/4), and Commission Decision of 4 February 1993 (Volkswagen/VAG UK), Case IV/M304, par. 7 (OJ 1993, C38/12).

- **Spare Parts**

Spare parts differ from cars in terms of product characteristics, price and intended use. The *product* market for spare parts can be separated from that of cars. The Commission does not consider cars and spare parts to form an "integral package". Spare parts are sold, at least to a significant extent, by independent suppliers through their own distribution networks to the independent aftermarket. As a result, original spare parts compete with parts from independent producers. However, cars and their spare parts can be part of one and the same *service* market. For instance, in its decision on Volvo's acquisition of the independent importer and distributor of Volvo cars in the United Kingdom, the Commission defined the relevant market as the distribution of cars and related accessories and spare parts.[45]

One "sector" of spare parts can be subdivided in several separate product markets taking into account differences in technology, use and customers.[46] The lead battery sector, for instance, can be divided into the traction battery market, the stationary battery market and the starter battery market. The latter can be further subdivided in the original equipment market for starter batteries and the replacement market for starter batteries.[47] For certain components, the different characteristics of the original equipment market ("OE-market") and the independent aftermarket ("AM-market") lead to the conclusion that one and the same component can form two separate product markets. This is in particular the result of the important differences in demand structure between, on the one hand, the market of the supply of components to car manufacturers for incorporation in new cars ("OEM-market") and distribution of components as spare parts through the manufacturers' authorized

---

[45] See in this context Decision BMW/Rover, *supra* note 37, par. 14; Decision Volvo/Lex UK, *supra* note 44, par. 7, and Commission Decision of 3 September 1992 (Volvo/Lex Ir), Case IV/M261, par. 7.

[46] See Commission Notice on the definition of relevant market for the purposes of Community competition law, OJ 1997, C372/5, at nr. 36 and 56.

[47] Commission Decision 91/403 of 24 May 1991 (Magneti Marelli/CEAc), Case IV/M043, paras. 8-10 (OJ 1991, L222/38). See for other examples of detailed assessments of various product markets, *inter alia*, Commission Decision of 9 December 1991 (Lucas/Eaton), Case IV/M149, paras. 20-34 (OJ 1991, C328/15) and Commission Decision of 21 December 1993 (Pilkington Techint/SIV), Case IV/M358, and Commission Decision of 11 July 1996 (Lucas/Varity), Case IV/M768, paras. 9-11.

distribution system ("OES-market"), and, on the other hand, the AM-market being the market of the supply of components to a large number of resellers outside the car manufacturers' authorized dealer network via which the components end up in the independent repair market.

The conditions of competition in the AM-market differ significantly from those in the OE-market. On the AM-market, part producers usually meet, through sophisticated distribution systems, a large number of relatively small resellers such as purchase organizations, wholesalers and dealers. This large number of relatively small and divers customers needs a great variety of component types for the different models and types of cars in order to meet the demand by consumers. Supply to the OE-market, on the other hand, requires high technical capacity, intense research and development, 100% reliability of the products, mostly "just-in-time" delivery and supply certification granted by the car manufacturers. Suppliers to the OE-market face a relatively small number of very large car manufacturers with a steady demand of a reduced number of component types that usually have to correspond to specifications set by the car manufacturer in question. Moreover, there is often a close cooperation between the supplier and the car manufacturer that is aimed at improving quality and efficiency, developping new products and a reduction of costs.[48] As a result of these differences, prices of components on the AM-market tend to be higher than on the OE-market.[49]

It is interesting to note that the Commission recognized in its decision *Mannesmann/Boge* that "[a]nother way to define the relevant product market would be to group the OES and AM-products together as one single product market" in view of the fact that both the OES and AM-products are designed as replacement parts. Unfortunately, the Commission did not further elaborate

[48] See, for instance, *FT*, "International rescue for car components", 18 September 1996, at 11, and "Components sector "declining" - Volkswagen chief hits at standards", 24 September 1996, at 10.

[49] See, *inter alia*, Decision Magneti Marelli/CEAc, *supra* note 47, par. 10; Decision Varta/Bosch, *supra* note 30, paras. 12-16 and 37; Commission Decision of 23 September 1991 (Mannesmann/Boge), Case IV/M134, paras. 9-11 (OJ 1991, C265/8); Commission Decision of 23 September 1993 (Arvin/Sogefi), Case IV/M360, par. 15 (OJ 1993, C305/11); Commission Decision of 15 October 1993 (Knorr-Bremse/Allied Signal), Case IV/337, paras. 25-27 (OJ 1993, C298/6); Decision Pilkington-Techint/SIV, *supra* note 47, par. 19; Commission Decision of 17 August 1992 (BTR/Pirelli), Case IV/M253, paras. 7-8, 18 and 24 (OJ 1992, C265/5). See also Case C-322/81, *Michelin* v *Commission* [1983] ECR 3461.

upon this possibility as it would not change the assessment of the concentration in question.[50]

(ii) Geographical Market

In Form CO, the geographical market is described as the area in which the undertakings concerned are involved in the supply and demand of relevant products or services, in which the conditions of competition are sufficiently homogeneous and which can be distinguished from neighbouring geographic areas because, in particular, conditions of competition are appreciably different in those areas. In determining the relevant geographical market, the following factors are to be taken into account: (i) the nature and characteristics of the products or services concerned; (ii) the existence of entry barriers; (iii) consumer preferences; (iv) appreciable differences in the undertakings' market shares between neighbouring geographic areas; or (v) substantial price differences.[51] In practice, the Commission tends to avoid a definition of the geographical market if it is of the opinion that the result of its assessment concerning the creation or strengthening of a dominant position would not be affected nor altered by such definition.[52]

- Cars

With respect to cars, the Commission has pointed out that whereas from a supply side perspective, production is international or even global in its outlook and the producers usually have an international presence, certain differences existing in the different Member States in respect of a number of factors including price, car taxation, or national distribution systems *might* indicate that individual countries could still be considered as different geographical

---

[50] Decision Mannesmann/Boge, *supra* note 49, par. 12.

[51] Section 6 of Form CO, *supra* note 26.

[52] See, *inter alia*, Decision Inchcape/IEP, *supra* note 42, par. 11, in which the Commission specified that it was not necessary to decide whether there existed a Community or national market for the wholesale distribution services for cars since, even in the latter alternative the operation did not raise serious doubts as to its compatibility with the common market. See for a similar reasoning Decision Volvo/Lex UK, *supra* note 44, par. 8; Decision Nissan/R. Nissan, *supra* note 44; Decision Volkswagen/VAG UK, *supra* note 44, par. 7, and Decision Volvo/Lex Ir, *supra* note 46, par. 8.

markets.[53] The future will tell under precisely what circumstances the Commission is prepared to conclude that the territory of one Member State constitutes a geographical market.

- **Spare Parts**

With respect to spare parts, the Commission made a similar argument when it specified in its *Mannesmann/VDO* decision:

> In the supply markets for the automobile industry differences in the respective national market shares will not usually be considered as a strong indicator for the existence of national markets. Although vehicle producers tend to purchase from more closely located suppliers, where possible and competitive, they are normally prepared to purchase from elsewhere in Europe. However, where these differences in national market shares are extreme and even large suppliers are not active on important national markets it seems at least doubtful if the general assumption of a Community-wide market can be upheld. Consequently, where there is a lack of Community-wide sourcing for a particular component as reflected in a significant lack of intra-Community trading for that product, it is considered as appropriate to assess the effect of a proposed concentration on an intra-Community market, e.g. the market within a given Member State. However, in assessing possible dominance within that smaller market, the Commission will, as in other cases, have regard to competition from outside suppliers.[54]

But even if the Commission finds indications for the possible existence of a national market, it tends to avoid going into the matter further, if it is of the

---

[53] See Decision BMW/Rover, *supra* note 37, par. 16. According to the Commission, the exact definition of the relevant geographic market in this particular case could be left open because even on the basis of the narrowest market definition, the concentration would not lead to the creation or strengthening of a dominant position. Nevertheless, the Commission concluded in par. 22 of the decision that the concentration would not lead to the creation or strengthening of a dominant position for BMW/Rover in the passenger car markets in the EEA.

[54] Commission Decision of 13 December 1991 (Mannesmann/VDO), Case IV/M164, par. 17 (OJ 1992, C88/13).

opinion that the result of its assessment on the creation or strengthening of a dominant position would not be affected nor altered.[55]

The following decisions regarding the markets for starter batteries and shock absorbers, illustrate the manner in which the Commission goes about defining the geographical market. In its *Magneti Marelli/CEAs* decision, the Commission argued that there were sufficiently homogeneous conditions of competition on the AM-market for starter batteries in *France*, which differed appreciably from the conditions existing in the other Member States. The Commission pointed at the fact that manufacturers in France were able to charge, for the same types of batteries, different prices than those which they charged in other Member States, and highlighted the very different market shares of manufacturers in each Member State. The Commission noted that these differences continued to exist despite the absence of any specific legal barriers. According to the Commission, the possible causes for these differences were: (i) the different make-up of car fleets and differences in level of service required in the Member States; (ii) consumer preferences for well-known brands; (iii) differences in the range of distribution channels; and (iv) the concentration of supply which varied considerably from one Member State to another.[56] In its *Mannesmann/Boge* decision, the Commission considered both the OEM/OES market and the AM-market for shock absorbers to be *Community-wide*. The Commission argued that both sides of the market had to take into account demand from all over Europe and noted with regard to the OEM/OES market, that if suppliers could not meet the market requirements on quality, price or other criteria, the automobile industry would shift its demand. With regard to the AM-market, the Commission pointed at the uniform distribution of market shares both in the Community and the Member States. According to the Commission, almost all competitors had a presence in all

---

[55] See, *inter alia*, Decision Mannesmann/VDO, *supra* note 54, par. 20; Decision Arvin/Sogefi, *supra* note 49, par. 17, and Decision Pilkington-Techint/SIV, *supra* note 47, par. 23.

[56] Decision Magneti Marelli/CEAc, *supra* note 47, par. 16. In Decision Varta/Bosch, *supra* note 30, paras. 17-31, the Commission gave a similar and rather extensive reasoning of its conclusion that a separate German and Spanish market existed.

Member States and there were no significant price differences between the Member States.[57]

9.2.4.3 Compatibility of the Creation or Strengthening of the Dominant Position with the Common Market

After defining the relevant market, the Commission will turn its attention to a great number of factors in an effort to assess whether the concentration in question creates or strengthens a single *or* collective dominant position on the relevant market as a result of which effective competition would be significantly impeded in the common market or in a substantial part of it. In its assessment, the Commission will examine both the horizontal and vertical effects of the concentration on competition on the relevant market. As already discussed, Article 2(1) of the Merger Regulation specifies that the Commission shall take the following factors into account while assessing whether a concentration is compatible with the common market:

> (a) the need to maintain and develop effective competition within the common market in view of, among other things, the structure of all the markets concerned and the actual or potential competition from undertakings located either within or without the Community;
> (b) the market position of the undertakings concerned and their economic and financial power, the alternatives available to suppliers and users, their access to supplies or markets, any legal or other barriers to entry, supply and demand trends for the relevant goods and services, the interests of the intermediate and ultimate consumers, and the development of technical and economic progress provided that it is to consumers' advantage and does not form an obstacle to competition.

It is evident that the Commission has to be fully aware of the factual situation on the relevant market before it can take a decision.

---

[57] Decision Mannesmann/Boge, *supra* note 49, paras. 14-16. See also Decision Lucas/ Eaton, *supra* note 47, par. 35; Decision Knorr-Bremse/Allied Signal, *supra* note 49, paras. 30-31; Decision BTR/Pirelli, *supra* note 49, paras. 9, 19, 25, and Decision Lucas/Varity, *supra* note 47, par. 12.

(i) Single Dominant Position

The Commission will try to determine whether the concentration in question will be able to act to an appreciable extent independently of its competitors, customers and consumers. In doing so, the Commission will look at market share and various other factors.[58] These factors include, on the *supply* side, the continued existence of comparable supply alternatives, the market share of competitors, their financial strength, technical know how, production capacity, access to the up- or downstream market, and, on the *demand* side, buying power in view of the strong competitive pressures in the market, suppliers' objective to build up and maintain a long term relationship with car manufacturer(s) and the trend in the automobile industry towards central purchasing or common purchasing structures, reduction of the number of suppliers, enhancement of outsourcing and a reduction of internal production depth.[59] Some of these factors can even be of a speculative nature.[60] The fact that market share is only one of the factors to be taken into account is illustrated by the Commission's decision in *Mannesmann/VDO* that on the basis of all the relevant factors, the concentration with about 70% of the market for instrument

---

[58] See for a thorough analysis of the application of the Merger Regulation on this point: Hawk and Huser, *supra* note 10, at 169-214.

[59] See, *inter alia*, Decision Magneti Marelli/CEAc, *supra* note 47, par. 16; Decision Varta/Bosch, *supra* note 30, par. 32; Decision Mannesmann/Boge, *supra* note 49, paras. 17-38; Decision Arvin/Sogefi, *supra* note 49, par. 22; Commission Decision of 14 October 1991 (Metallgesellschaft/Feldmuhle), Case IV/M119, par. 23 (OJ 1991, C276/4); Decision BTR/Pirelli, *supra* note 49, paras. 11-14, 20-22, 26-27; Commission Decision of 28 July 1992 (Elf Atochem/Rohm and Haas), Case IV/M160, par. 17 (OJ 1992, C201/27); Commission Decision of 29 November 1993 (Continental/Kaliko/DG Bank/Benecke), Case IV/M363, paras. 23-28 (OJ 1994, C3/5), and Decision Lucas/Varity, *supra* note 47, paras. 13-18.

[60] See, for instance, Decision Varta/Bosch, *supra* note 30, paras. 44-64, in which the Commission withdrew its objections against the concentration mainly on the basis of nothing more but an *expectation* that both Fiat's acquisition of CEAc and Sonnenschein, and the ending of the cooperation between Varta and Deta/Mareg, would lead to a situation on the German market that the concentration would not have an appreciable scope of action uncontrolled by its competitors. Another example is Decision Mannesmann/Boge, *supra* note 49, par. 27, in which the Commission noted that in view of the fact that motor vehicle manufacturers tend to have at least two sources of supply, it was uncertain whether the concentration would be able to preserve its high supply volume, especially with German and Scandinavian car manufacturers. The Commission expected that the concentration might permit competitors to increase their volume and market shares.

panels was compatible with the common market.[61] On the other hand, in the *Varta/Bosch* decision, the Commission found that in view of all the relevant factors, the concentration with 44,3% of the replacement market for starter batteries in Germany, and 44,5% in Spain, was not compatible with the common market.[62] In its *BMW/Rover* decision, the Commission argued that the concentration had a limited effect on the car market in terms of industry concentration since the Rover and BMW-product lines only overlapped in the executive car segment and the large car segment. In short, the Commission found that the aggregate market shares of the new concentration did not exceed 25% and expected that the concentration would have *pro*-competitive effects on the car market as it would enable BMW to compete with the large automobile producers on the full range of cars.[63]

(ii) Collective Dominant Position

In its decision *Nestlé/Perrier*, the Commission took the position that Article 2(3) of the Merger Regulation also covers market situations where effective competition is significantly impeded by more than one undertaking which together have the power to behave to an appreciable extent independently of the

---

[61] See, *inter alia*, Decision Mannesmann/VDO, *supra* note 54, paras. 27-28.

[62] Decision Varta/Bosch, *supra* note 30, par. 32. After certain factual changes and agreement on commitments entered into by Varta, the Commission concluded that the concentration did not have an appreciable scope of action uncontrolled by its competitors. As a result, the concentration was considered to be compatible with the common market. It is remarkable, however, that without giving a proper reasoning the Commission announced in par. 33 that as a result of an oral hearing it *only* "maintained its objections as to the German market". See also Decision Magneti Marelli/CEAc, *supra* note 47, paras. 15-16, in which the Commission concluded that a 60% market share in France established a dominant position. The Commission dropped its objections, however, after amendments were made to the proposed concentration resulting, *inter alia*, in a reduction of the market share with 18,4%. The Commission withdrew its objections relating to the AM-market in Italy after it established that the concentration only entailed a small increase in market share and significant competitors were present on the market.

[63] Decision BMW/Rover, *supra* note 37, paras. 17-23. It is interesting to note that *Agence Europe*, "Daimler-Benz/Chrysler merger raises no problems, Kirch-Bertelsmann alliance to be rejected if no modifications", 11-12 May 1998, at 9, reported that according to Commissioner Van Miert "at first sight the Daimler-Benz and Chrysler merger raised no problems, as the competition will anyway remain keen on the EU automobile market" but that "[t]he situation could be different for other possible mergers in the same sector".

remaining competitors, of customers and ultimately of consumers.[64] The Commission argued that collective dominant positions may significantly impede effective competition under certain market conditions and specified that "[t]his is in particular the case if there is already before the merger weakened competition between the oligopolists which is likely to be further weakened by a significant increase in concentration and if there is no sufficient price-constraining competition from actual or potential competition coming from outside the oligopoly".[65] Therefore, if a notified concentration does not lead to the creation or strengthening of a single dominant position, the Commission will examine whether it gives rise to the creation or strengthening of a collective dominant position.[66] In doing so, the Commission will look at a great variety of factors. The following headings used by the Commission in its decision *Pilkington-Techint/SIV* give an impression of several of these factors:

(i) Market shares,
  - small number of players with high degree of concentration,
  - asymmetrical market shares;

(ii) Production and market characteristics,
  - structural interdependence,
  - mature market with increasing overcapacity,
  - low elasticity of demand,
  - prior cartel behaviour,
  - prices and profitability;

---

[64] Commission Decision 92/553 of 22 July 1992 (Nestlé/Perrier), Case IV/M190, OJ 1992, L356/24, paras. 110-115. Confirmed in Case T-96/92, *Comité central d'entreprise de la Sociéte générale des grandes sources and others* v *Commission* [1995] ECR II-1213, and Case T-12/93, *Comité central d'entreprise de la société anonyme Vittel and others* v *Commission* [1995] ECR II-1247. As illustrated by L. Cohen-Tanugi and others, *La pratique communautaire du contrôle des concentrations*, 1995, De Boeck Université, at 86-90, the Commission has been criticized for taking this position.

[65] Decision Nestlé/Perrier, *ibidem*, par. 112.

[66] See in this context Decision Pilkington-Techint/SIV, *supra* note 47, par. 24. See for an interesting study of oligopolistic dominance: P.J. Williamson, "Oligopolistic dominance and EC merger policy", *European Economy 1994*, *supra* note 3, at 131-185. See Hawk and Huser, *supra* note 10, at 215-264, for an analysis of the application of the Merger Regulation on this point.

(iii) Market transparency,
- price transparency,
- producer links,
- technological links,
- cross-supply links,
- joint venture links;

(iv) Production costs and product heterogeneity;

(v) Actual and potential competition, and market entry barriers like import tariffs;

(vi) Stability of possible anti-competitive parallel behaviour,
- incentive to renege on tacit parallel behaviour,
- asymmetrical vertical integration,
- effects of new capacity.[67]

These headings illustrate that the Commission has to be fully aware of the factual situation on the relevant market before it can take a decision.

There are several examples of cases in the *spare parts sector* in which the Commission had to examine whether a concentration created or strengthened a collective dominant position between competitors resulting in a situation of oligopolistic dominance.[68] These cases indicate that the considerable demand side purchasing power of car manufacturers on the *OE-market* makes it difficult for the Commission to establish a collective dominant position. The purchasing power on the demand side is further strengthened by the shift from multiple towards single sourcing, which puts suppliers under an increasing competitive pressure to win or loose the full order. The fact that car manufacturers can often easily switch supplier makes the competition between suppliers even greater. The Commission found that the bargaining strength of car manufacturers is such that they can oblige their suppliers to make the necessary intellectual property rights on parts available to a possible new supplier. In addition, the Commission noted that the sophistication of the purchasing departments of car manufacturers

---

[67] See Decision Pilkington-Techint/SIV, *supra* note 47, paras. 25-49. See also Joined Cases C-68/94 and C-30/95, *SCPA and others* v *Commission*, judgment of 31 March 1998, not yet reported, paras. 179-250.

[68] See, *inter alia*, Decision Arvin/Sogefi, *supra* note 49, par. 22; Decision Knorr-Bremse/Allied Signal, *supra* note 49, paras. 45-46, and Decision Pilkington-Techint/SIV, *supra* note 47, paras. 24-63.

makes it possible for them to closely monitor both production costs and prices. In view of the decline in car sales in the Community, car manufacturers have been able to re-negotiate existing contracts with suppliers and establish new long-term contracts with price-down pressure. According to the Commission it is "becoming commonplace" that supply prices decrease in nominal terms during the course of the contract.[69] With regard to the *AM-market*, the Commission has recognized that there are a large number of independent suppliers in addition to the authorized suppliers on the OES-market, which will maintain effective competition. In practice, the demand side purchasing power of independent suppliers is increasing but cannot be compared to that of car manufacturers.

9.3 Control of Concentrations without a Community Dimension in the Automobile Industry

9.3.1 General Remarks

Article 22 of the Merger Regulation provides that the Merger Regulation *alone* shall apply to concentrations as defined in Article 3, and that Regulations 17/62,[70] 1017/68,[71] 4056/86[72] and 3975/87[73] shall not apply. Article 22 covers all "full-function" joint ventures with a Community dimension that have as their object or effect the coordination of the competitive behaviour of undertakings that remain independent. Article 22 does *not* cover those "full-function" joint ventures that do not have a Community dimension and which have as their object or effect the coordination of the competitive behaviour of undertakings that remain independent, and non-full-function joint ventures.[74] As Article 1 of

---

[69] Decision Pilkington-Techint/SIV, *supra* note 47, par. 56.

[70] OJ Special English Edition, 1962 at 204/62.

[71] OJ 1968, L175/1.

[72] OJ 1986, L378/4.

[73] OJ 1987, L374/1.

[74] See Commission Merger Control Notice ("Information on Assessment of Full-Function Joint Ventures"), OJ 1998, C66/38.

the Merger Regulation provides that without prejudice to Article 22, the Merger Regulation only applies to concentration *with* a Community dimension, the control of concentrations without a Community dimension is left to the national merger control systems of Member States (**9.3.2**). However, the Commission can, on request of the Member State concerned, apply the Merger Regulation to concentrations without a Community dimension (the so-called "Dutch clause") (**9.3.3**). Furthermore, it can be argued that notwithstanding the implications of Article 22 of the Merger Regulation, the Commission remains competent on the basis of Article 89 EC, to scrutinize these concentrations without Community dimension under the principles of Articles 85 and 86 EC (**9.3.4**). It is evident that due to the direct effect of Articles 85(1) and 86 EC, national courts are competent to do so as well.

9.3.2 National Control

A concentration without a Community dimension and with effects in only one Member State will in principle only be scrutinized under the national merger control system of the Member State concerned. On the other hand, a concentration without a Community dimension but with effects in more than one Member State can become the subject of more than one national system and may have to follow different national procedures in order to obtain approval of the various national competition authorities concerned. This is inconvenient for the parties concerned in view of the fact that there is a great variety between the Member States in notification requirements, procedures used and legal standards applied.[75] As a result, multiple national filings can lead to complications such as long delays, high costs and possibly conflicting decisions. Although these complications are contrary to the idea of a "level playing field" and therefore detrimental to all parties involved,[76] the formal cooperation and communication

---

[75] *Green Paper on Merger Control*, *supra* note 22, at 8-9. The *Green Paper on Merger Control* includes in Annex 2 a table setting out the main features of the existing national systems and the (at the time proposed) Dutch system. See Cohen-Tanugi and others, *supra* note 64, for a more elaborate description of the merger control systems of Germany, the United Kingdom and Italy.

[76] *Green Paper on Merger Control*, *supra* note 22, at 15-16, 19-22 and 34. In order to address the problem of multiple national filings, the Commission suggested to bring within the exclusive competence of the Commission cases of multiple notification below the current thresholds. This led eventually to the

between the competition authorities in the Member States is mostly restricted to information purposes only.[77]

9.3.3 Dutch Clause

Under Article 22(3) of the Merger Regulation, the Commission can, at the request of a Member State or at the joint request of two or more Member States and insofar as it affects trade between Member States, deal with a concentration that has no Community dimension but creates or strengthens a dominant position as a result of which effective competition would be significantly impeded within the territory of the Member State or States making the joint request. The Commission shall only take the measures strictly necessary to maintain or restore effective competition within the territory of the Member State or States at the request of which it intervenes. As most, if not all, Member States with a domestic automobile industry have a more or less sophisticated national system of concentration control, it appears unlikely that the scrutiny of a concentration without a Community dimension in the automobile industry, will be referred to the Commission. The reverse is the more likely situation.[78]

---

amended text of Article 1(3) of the Merger Regulation which brings mergers involving the competition authorities of at least three Member States and meet certain thresholds, within the scope of the Merger Regulation.

[77] *Green Paper on Merger Control*, *supra* note 22, at 8-9. It was reported in *FT*, "Mergers within EU made simpler", 30 September 1997, at 2, that "[c]ompetition authorities in the U.K., Germany and France have joined forces to simplify procedures for companies involved in multinational mergers in the European Union" and "will allow European businesses to submit the same information to the three authorities for mergers which have to be examined in more than one of the three countries". See in this context the "Common Form for mergers in the United Kingdom, in France and in Germany", published by the Office of Fair Trading (UK), DGCCRF (Fr) and Bundeskartellamt (Ge). Practice will show how (un)usefull this "Common Form" will be.

[78] Germany has made several requests on the basis of Article 9 of the Merger Regulation. See for instance, Decision Varta/Bosch, *supra* note 30, in which the Commission denied the German Article 9-request to have the case referred.

9.3.4 Application of the Principles of Articles 85 and 86 EC on the basis of Article 89 EC to Concentrations

9.3.4.1 Article 89 EC

Article 89(1) EC provides that the Commission can on its own initiative and in cooperation with the competent authorities in the Member States, who shall give it their assistance, investigate cases of suspected infringement of these principles. If the Commission finds that there has been an infringement, it shall propose appropriate measures to bring it to an end. Article 89(2) EC provides that if the infringement is not brought to an end, the Commission shall record such infringement of the principles in a reasoned decision which may be published. The Commission may authorise Member States to take the measures, the conditions and details of which it shall determine, needed to remedy the situation.[79] Article 89 EC seems to imply that *in theory*, one and the same concentration can be scrutinized by the competent national competition authority under its national merger control system and by the Commission on the basis of Article 89 EC. However, *in practice*, the Commission has been reluctant to use its powers under Article 89 EC. Sir Leon Brittan has confirmed that although the Commission has a residual power to apply Article(s) 86 (and 85) EC by using the procedure set out in Article 89 EC, "it will only do so where a very clear case of dominance is established that is not able to be dealt with by national competition authorities" since "[t]his policy enables the one-stop shop principle to function effectively, and ensures that all concentrations are subject to effective regulatory control in the Community".[80] There is little doubt that only overriding reasons such as the identification of new facts which were not taken into account by the national competition authorities, could lead the Commission to re-open a case which has already been dealt with under the national merger control system.

[79] See C. Kerse, "Enforcing Community competition policy under Articles 88 and 89 of the E.C. Treaty - New powers for U.K. competition authorities", [1997] 1 ECLR, at 17-23.

[80] IP/92/1048.

9.3.4.2 Principles laid down in Articles 85 and 86 EC

The principles laid down in Articles 85 and 86 EC, as referred to in Article 89(1) EC, have mainly been developped in the ECJ's case law. Which principles under Articles 85 and 86 EC are relevant to concentrations without a Community dimension?

(i) Article 85 EC

In *BAT and Reynolds*, the ECJ indicates that not only the acquisition of a minority shareholding in a company falls under the scope of Article 85 EC but a concentration as well. In view of the importance of this case, the most relevant paragraphs of the ECJ's judgment are quoted in full. In the context of Article 85 EC, the ECJ held:

> Although the acquisition by one company of an equity interest in a competitor does not in itself constitute conduct restricting competition, such an acquisition may nevertheless serve as an instrument for influencing the commercial conduct of the companies in question so as to restrict or distort competition on the market on which they carry on business.
>
> That will be true in particular where, by the acquisition of a shareholding or through subsidiary clauses in the agreement, the investing company obtains legal or *de facto* control of the commercial conduct of the other company or where the agreement provides for commercial cooperation between the companies or creates a structure likely to be used for such cooperation.
>
> That may also be the case where the agreement gives the investing company the possibility of reinforcing its position at a later stage and taking effective control of the other company. Account must be taken not only of the immediate effects of the agreement but also of its potential effects and of the possibility that the agreement may be part of a long-term plan.
>
> Finally, every agreement must be assessed in its economic context and

> in particular in the light of the situation on the relevant market. Moreover, where the companies concerned are multinational corporations which carry on business on a world-wide scale, their relationships outside the Community cannot be ignored. It is necessary in particular to consider the possibility that the agreement in question may be part of a policy of global cooperation between the companies which are party to it.[81]

The ECJ clearly qualifies the taking of legal or *de facto* control of the commercial conduct of another company through the acquisition of a shareholding, as an example of an instrument to influence the commercial conduct of the companies in question so as to restrict or distort competition on the market on which they carry on business. Notwithstanding the fact that this seems to indicate that the Commission can scrutinize a concentration under Article 85 EC,[82] commentators have reached a "nearly universal consensus"[83] that Article 85 EC does not cover concentrations.[84]

(ii) Article 86 EC

The ECJ held in *Continental Can* that Article 86 EC is not only directed at practices which may cause damage to consumers directly, but also at those which are detrimental through their impact on an effective competition structure, as referred to in Article 3(g) EC. The ECJ held that:

> [a]buse may therefore occur if an undertaking in a dominant position strengthens such position in such a way that the degree of dominance reached substantially fetters competition, i.e. that only undertakings

---

[81] Joined Cases 142 and 156/84, *British American Tobacco and Reynolds Industries* v *Commission (BAT and Reynolds)* [1987] ECR 4577, paras. 37-40.

[82] See L. Ritter, W.D. Braun and F. Rawlinson, *EEC Competition Law - A Practitioner's Guide*, 1993, Kluwer Law and Taxation Publishers, Deventer, at 333, footnote 5.

[83] Hawk and Huser, *supra* note 10, at 350.

[84] See, *inter alia*, Hawk and Huser, *supra* note 10, at 350-351; Van Bael and Bellis, *supra* note 10, at 368, and Bellamy and Child, *supra* note 10, at 379, footnote 62. See in this context XXth Report on Competition Policy, paras. 118-119.

remain in the market whose behaviour depends on the dominant one.[85]

The ECJ specified in *BAT and Reynolds* that an abuse of a dominant position can only arise where the acquisition of the shareholding in question results in effective control of the other company or at least in some influence on its commercial policy.[86] The Commission's competence under Article 86 EC with regard to concentrations is limited to the scrutiny of concentrations that strengthen the position of undertakings which were already in a dominant position. A merger between two undertakings without dominant position resulting in a concentration with a dominant position is not covered by Article 86 EC.

9.4 Application of Articles 85 and 86 EC to Certain Cooperations in the Automobile Industry

9.4.1 General Remarks

Several public[87] and private[88] organizations have made a serious effort to compile an overview of the various forms of cooperation in the automobile industry. These overviews in combination with press reports confirm that there are at present many forms of cooperation on different levels in the automobile

[85] Case 6/72 *Europemballage and Continental Can* v *Commission* [1973] ECR 245, par. 26. See in this context, *inter alia*, *Het vraagstuk van de concentraties in de Gemeenschappelijke markt*, *Serie concurrentie No.3*, Brussel 1966, at 21-27 (no English translation available).

[86] *BAT and Reynolds*, *supra* note 81, par. 65.

[87] For instance, until 1993, the German competition authority ("Bundeskartellamt") published an annual report on cooperation in the automobile industry entitled "*Strategische Allianzen in der Automobilindustrie*". This report was based on information from its proceedings and various publications including "Wards Automotive International" and press articles.

[88] See in this context *FT* (Survey - The Motor Industry), "Financial Times Motor Industry Survey", 20 October 1988, at IX, which gives an overview of the capital and operational relationships between the major automobile manufacturers in June 1988. The Economist Intelligence Unit offers for sale a Research Report No R336 which includes a sketch, entitled "Global Vehicle Production Trends - 1996 Edition", of the major international affiliations of the following 15 car manufacturers: Chrysler, Ford, GM, BMW, PSA, Renault, Fiat, VW, Mercedes-Benz, Toyota, Suzuki, Mitsubishi, Nissan, Honda and Mazda.

industry. Although cooperation is mostly initiated by the undertakings themselves, there are circumstances in which public authorities in pursuit of certain public interests such as the protection of the environment, will stimulate or even take the initiative to have undertakings cooperate.[89] Unfortunately, there is very little information on the manner in which the Community applies Articles 85 and 86 EC to these forms of cooperation in the automobile industry. There are very few official decisions and judgments available and Commission press releases and reports in documents like the annual Reports on Competition Policy are short and vague.[90] Nevertheless, an effort will be made on the basis of those documents and reports that are available, to examine the manner in which the Community deals with the forms of cooperation in question on the basis of Article 85 EC (**9.4.2**) and Article 86 EC (**9.4.3**).

9.4.2 Article 85 EC

9.4.2.1 Introductory Remarks

Cooperation in the automobile industry takes place between undertakings on a horizontal level (for instance between manufacturers) and on a vertical level (for instance between manufacturers and suppliers). There is a great variety of possible forms of cooperation between independent undertakings which may fall within the scope of Article 85(1) EC. These forms of cooperation vary from

---

[89] For instance, it was reported in the Dutch press ("Een zeepkist van één op dertig", *NRC Handelsblad*, 31 August 1996, Katern Wetenschap & Onderwijs, at 6) that VW, BMW, Mercedes-Benz and Porsche have agreed with the German state to each develop and market around the year 2000 a car which can drive 30 km on 1 liter. See also State Aid N 680/96 (Germany/ADA), OJ 1997, C311/6, on "Abgaszentrum der Automobilindustrie (Exhaust gas centre for the motor industry - ADA) which was set up by five German motor manufacturers to conduct a research and development programme consisting of industrial research and precompetitive development activity aimed at reducing pollutant emissions from petrol and diesel engines for motor vehicles. The Commission reported that the Bundeskartellamt gave conditional authorization for the project. See also *FT*, "Germany combines forces on green car", 12 May 1998, at 3.

[90] For instance, the Commission noted in its Decision of 7 November 1990 (Renault/Volvo), Case IV/M004, OJ 1990, C281/3, par. 1, that the cooperation between Volvo and Renault did not constitute a concentration but had to be dealt with under Articles 85 and 86 EC instead. In IP/90/895, the Commission noted with regard to the cooperation between Renault and Volvo on cars, that there were "no grounds for concern under general EC competition law".

joint ventures to cooperations with a somewhat lesser degree of commitment that may or may not be cemented by shareholdings.[91] Some forms of cooperation in the automobile industry will fall under a block exemption like Regulation 417/85 on specialisation agreements,[92] Regulation 418/85 on research and development agreements[93] or Regulation 1475/95 on motor vehicle distribution and servicing agreements.[94] Other forms of cooperation in the automobile industry will be notified to the Commission under Regulation 17/62 in an effort to obtain a negative clearance or an individual exemption under Article 85(3) EC.

Although reports in the press indicate that there are a number of joint ventures between car manufacturers at work in the automobile industry, the joint venture AutoEuropa seems to be the only example of a notification that actually led to an official Commission decision under Article 85(3) EC. The decisions and judgments with regard to AutoEuropa are the only public documents that shed some light on the manner in which Article 85 EC is applied to this kind of horizontal cooperation in the automobile industry (**9.4.2.2**). Furthermore, studies confirm that as a result of the implementation of lean production techniques and the shift towards virtual production, there is a growing need for vertical cooperation between car manufacturers and suppliers of components. Although press reports suggest that car manufacturers and suppliers closely cooperate, there are no public documents available on the manner in which Article 85 EC is applied to this specific kind of cooperation. Publications on the ACEA-CLEPA "European Guidelines for Cooperation

---

[91] IP/90/895 reported that the cooperation between Renault and Volvo on the car market involved 25% cross-shareholdings. The ECJ held in *BAT and Reynolds*, *supra* note 81, par. 37, that the acquisition of shareholdings by an undertaking in the capital of a competitor falls within the scope of Article 85 EC if the acquisition is an instrument for influencing the commercial conduct of the undertaking in question so as to restrict or distort competition on the market on which they carry on business. Commission Decision 93/252 of 10 November 1992 (Gillette), Cases IV/33.440 and IV/33.486, OJ 1993, L116/29, par. 34, illustrated that even if the acquisition of the shareholding itself cannot be considered to provide the acquiring undertaking with influence in the commercial conduct of its competitor, provisions in agreements which accompany the acquisition often will.

[92] OJ 1985, L53/1. Amended by Commission Regulation 151/93 of 23 December 1992, OJ 1992, L21/8.

[93] OJ 1985, L53/51. Amended by Commission Regulation 151/93 of 23 December 1992, OJ 1992, L21/8.

[94] See Chapter 7 *supra*.

between Automobile Manufacturers and their Suppliers" only give an impression of the manner in which car manufacturers and suppliers cooperate (**9.4.2.3**).

9.4.2.2 Horizontal Cooperation: Joint Venture "AutoEuropa"

AutoEuropa is a joint venture between Volkswagen ("VW"), the leading Community car manufacturer, and Ford, rated fifth in the Community passenger car market, and was set up for the development and production of the "VX62", a so-called multi-purpose vehicle ("MPV"), in Setúbal, Portugal. AutoEuropa would be jointly controlled and owned in equal shares. It would become operational in 1995[95] and would last for at least the MPV's projected life cycle of about 10 years. Product development would be carried out by VW whereas Ford was responsible for the manufacturing and plant engineering. Both parties would supply engines and transmissions and most of the remaining parts would be purchased from external suppliers. All costs relating to the MPV's development, engineering and manufacture would be shared equally. The two parties would each purchase about 50% of the production. The distribution of the MPV's and related parts, however, would take place independently of each other through separate authorized dealer networks in Europe. The MPV's would be distributed in different formats in order to preserve the parties brand image and because of vehicle servicing reasons.

In February 1991, Ford and VW *notified* the foundation agreement of AutoEuropa in order to obtain negative clearance or an individual exemption under Article 85(3) EC. In March and April 1991, the Portuguese authorities notified to the Commission under Article 93(3) EC a plan to grant a substantial state aid to AutoEuropa. About two months later, Matra lodged a *complaint* with the Commission under Articles 85, 92, 93 and 175 EC. Matra had an interest in taking legal action against AutoEuropa as it assembles and distributes through the distribution network of Renault the (at that time) only Community-produced MPV, named Renault Espace. Since the mid-1980's when the Renault Espace was introduced and the market for MPV's developed, Matra has held a

[95] See *FT*, "Espace - the final frontier", 12 April 1995, at 14, which reported that volume production began in March 1995.

strong leading position with an average share of above 50% of the MPV market.[96] One day after Matra's complaint was lodged, the Director-General of D.G. IV explained to Matra his refusal to initiate a procedure under Article 93(2) EC and expressed his intention to grant an exemption.

On 13 July 1991, the Commission published a *notice* in which it defined the product MPV and concluded that MPV's could be considered as a distinct market segment, only partly substitutable for vehicles in other segments. The Commission gave the following shares of the Community market in 1989:

- Renault Espace	: 58 %
- Mitsubishi Space Wagon	: 13 %
- Chrysler Voyager	: 11 %
- Nissan Prairie	: 9 %
- Toyota Space Cruiser	: 7 %

The Commission concluded with regard to the market-structure that the MPV market in the Community was dominanted by the Renault Espace and emphasized that the entry to the MPV market was "relatively difficult" in view of the considerable investment necessary for both development and production as well as the relatively small market volume. The parties involved estimated the minimum capacity for a production unit to be economically viable to be in excess of 110 000 units per year. In its notice, the Commission announced that it intended to take a favourable decision under Article 85(3) EC. But, in view of the important position of the parties in the market, the decision would be subject to certain conditions. Interested parties were invited to send in their comments.[97] Matra submitted its written observations on 9 August 1991. In the meantime, on 16 July 1991, the Commission had informed the Portuguese authorities that it considered under Article 93(3) EC that the notified state aid

[96] See Commission Decision 93/49 of 23 December 1992 (IV/33.814-Ford/Volkswagen), OJ 1993 L20/14, paras. 13 and 33.

[97] Notice pursuant to Article 19(3) of Council Regulation 17/62 concerning notification IV/33.814 - Ford/Volkswagen, OJ 1991 C 182/8.

was in conformity with Article 92 EC.[98] On 4 December 1991, the President of the ECJ dismissed Matra's application for the suspension of the operation of the Commission's decision to approve the Portuguese state aid.[99] Subsequently, Matra sought annulment of the decision. However, the ECJ confirmed the Commission's decision on the state aid in its judgment of 15 June 1993.[100]

In the end, the Commission rejected Matra's complaint and took the *decision* on 23 December 1992 to grant an exemption under Article 85(3) EC.[101] In its decision, the Commission first looked at the *factual context* of the joint venture and qualified the MPV market as a "relatively new and distinctive market segment by virtue of its specific product features although a certain interchangeability with cars from neighbouring segments exists".[102] The Commission listed the following shares on the MPV market in the Community for 1990:

- Renault Espace	: 54,7 %
- Chrysler Voyager	: 15,6 %
- Mitsubishi Space Wagon	: 12 %
- Nissan Prairie	: 7,6 %
- Toyota Previa	: 3,9 %
- Toyota Space Cruiser	: 2,9 %

The Commission noted that Ford already offered for sale a "comparatively old model" MPV named Aerostar which was successfully sold on the U.S.A. market but sales in Europe remained negligible (less than 1% market share in 1990). It also mentioned that Ford cooperated with Nissan in developing a successor for the Aerostar. Furthermore, the Commission pointed at Ford's

98 See Summary of the Commission Decision not to raise objections to the aid which the Portuguese Government plans to grant to the joint venture of Ford and Volkswagen to establish a multi-purpose vehicle plant in the Setubal peninsula (AutoEuropa), OJ 1991, C257/5.

99 Case C-225/91 R, *Matra* v *Commission* [1991] ECR 5823.

100 Case C-225/91, *Matra* v *Commission (Matra I)* [1993] ECR I-3250.

101 Decision Ford/Volkswagen, *supra* note 96. Confirmed in Case T-17/93, *Matra* v *Commission (Matra II)* [1994] ECR II-595.

102 Decision Ford/Volkswagen, *supra* note 96, par. 11.

minority shareholding in Mazda, the latter being involved in the manufacturing of MPV's which were not brought on the market in the Community. The Commission emphasized that it was likely that the MPV market would expand significantly in Europe and that several MPV projects were under consideration and further entries into the MPV market were expected before the end of the century.

With regard to *Article 85(1) EC*, the Commission noted that "[t]he development of new models is one of the key elements of competition in the car sector and a determining factor for the success of a manufacturer in the market". After specifying that any agreement between competitors likely to restrict this activity have to be regarded as serious restrictions of competition, the Commission focused on the specifics of the joint venture and acknowledged that in view of the financial, technical and research capacities of Ford and VW, either party was, in principle, capable of producing a MPV on its own. According to the Commission, the joint venture would mean that Ford nor VW would have any economic interest in independent activities in developing and producing an MPV in view of the "enormous investment of the parent companies and .. the obligation to buy fixed quantities of MPV's" from the joint venture. In addition, the joint venture would lead to "an extensive exchange and sharing of, *inter alia*, technical know-how which could affect the competitive behaviour of the two partners in neighbouring market segments like those of estate cars or light vans". As the joint venture would appreciably affect trade between Member States, the Commission concluded that the underlying agreement was contrary to Article 85(1) EC.

Subsequently, the Commission turned its attention to *Article 85(3) EC* and noted that the joint venture was characterized by the following elements:

- the MPV market segment has relatively low volume and will, at least in the medium term, stay that way despite positive forecasts,
- neither Ford nor VW have until now been a supplier in the MPV market worth mentioning,
- the structure of the MPV market is characterized by the clearly leading position of one supplier not exposed to any considerable competition from (other) European suppliers,
- the vehicle will be produced in a new and modern plant,

- the joint venture will have extremely positive effects on the infrastructure and employment in one of the poorest regions in the Community.

According to the Commission, the joint venture fulfilled the four conditions of Article 85(3) EC "[t]aking into account the exeptional circumstances of the case". In its decision, the Commission addressed each of the four conditions of Article 85(3) EC separately. The CFI confirmed the decision and underlined the Commission's discretionary power under Article 85(3) EC by stating that "where complex economic facts are involved, judicial review of the legal characterization of the facts is limited to the possibility of the Commission having committed a manifest error of assessment".[103]

With regard to the *first condition* of Article 85(3) EC ("improvement of production of goods or promotion of technical or economic progress"), the Commission noted that the cooperation would not only make available "an advanced vehicle designed to meet the requirements of European consumers", it would also improve production of goods "through a rationalization of product development and manufacturing", and promote technical progress "due to a pooling of the existing technical knowledge and its conversion into a significantly improved, and in several aspects, innovative MPV". The Commission emphasized that the joint venture would improve the production of MPV's in the Community "by the establishment of an entirely new and most modern manufacturing plant using the latest production technology" including a concept which was to become "the most efficient "Just-in-time" component logistic system in the world, producing better results than the Japanese invented "Kanban" component delivery system". According to the Commission, the MPV produced by the joint venture would constitute "a continuous development of technical progress of production in the Community" as it would "set new standards in the MPV segment in several respects compared to its competitors". The Commission pointed at newly developed systems to be used in the MPV and noted the improvement with respect to environmental requirements.

In its judgment, the CFI held that the Commission's assessment did not contain any manifest error. First of all, the CFI noted that "the manufacturing

[103] See *Matra II*, *supra* note 101, par. 104.

process to be used at Setúbal constitutes the first application by a European car manufacturer of the enhanced form of the manufacturing process recommended in 1990 by the most authoritative researchers in the field of technological development". According to the CFI, "an optimization of the manufacturing process of that kind" was in conformity with the first condition of Article 85(3) EC. Secondly, as regards the technical improvements made to the *product*, the CFI emphasized that "they must be assessed in relation to the state of development of car construction techniques in Europe when the Decision was adopted", after which it noted that "[a]dopting that approach", the technical improvements made to the MPV fall within the scope of Article 85(3) EC since "they bring together in a single product techniques which, where they exist, are at present used in isolation, on different models".[104]

The Commission concluded that the *second condition* of Article 85(3) EC ("fair share to consumers"), was met as the European consumer could be expected to benefit directly from the joint venture as "two versions of a high-quality and reasonable priced MPV" would be offered for sale through "the extensive networks" of the parties. Furthermore, in view of the parties' entry "along with that of other manufacturers into the expanding MPV segment", the Commission expected "increased competitive pressure on all suppliers leading to a more balanced segment" forcing Ford and VW to pass on the benefits to the consumer. The Commission emphasized that "[m]oreover, with VW and Ford further competitive European car manufacturers will be present in this market segement". In its judgment the CFI noted that the Commission's statement that the exempted project would "enable economies of scale to be achieved and promote intensified competition in the market, to the benefit of the European consumer", had not been seriously contested and concluded that "therefore the Decision cannot be regarded as vitiated by a manifest error or assessment on that point".[105]

In accordance with the *third condition* of Article 85(3) EC ("indispensability of restrictions"), the Commission had to assess whether the restrictions emanating from the joint venture were indispensable. In doing so, the Commission emphasized that the cooperation enabled Ford and VW "to

[104] See *Matra II*, *supra* note 101, paras. 109-111.

[105] See *Matra II*, *supra* note 101, paras. 120-125.

competitively offer a high-quality product, designed for the specific needs of European consumers, in the relatively new and low volume MPV market segment in a comparatively short time". According to the Commission, this could not have been done by simply adapting the parties' already existing models. In addition, the Commission noted that its assessment was not affected by the fact that Matra and certain Japanese producers were able to penetrate the MPV individually since their situation was not comparable to those of Ford and VW. The Commission pointed at Matra's strong leading position since the mid-1980s, "exposed only to limited competition from non-European suppliers and always far ahead of its next closest competitor" which enabled it to be profitable with a comparatively low annual production. The Commission noted that "[m]oreover, Matra had to enter into cooperation with Renault to distribute its vehicles" which is also "a supplier of key components for the "Espace"". Pursuant to the Commission, Japanese suppliers could "profit from considerable economies of scale due to a strong and largely closed national market". The Commission qualified the Japanese MPVs as "a compromise between the different requirements of the European and the US market" and noted that, "due to their competitive pricing strategies, the Japanese sell a certain amount of MPVs in Europe" and far more in the U.S.A. Although the Commission took the position that the restrictions of competition were limited to what was indispensable for the functioning of the joint venture, it imposed certain conditions and obligations on Ford and VW in order "to achieve and secure the minimum effects on competition, to maintain a certain level of product differentiation, and to limit potential spill-over effects of the cooperation". The Commission noted in the context of the MPV cooperation between Ford and Nissan, that both Ford and Nissan intended to individually market some of these MPVs in the Community. Furthermore, the Commission noted that Ford's cooperation with Mazda did not exclude competition between them in the MPV sector. Last but not least, the Commission acknowledged that in the assessment of the case, it had taken note of the fact that the project constituted the largest ever single foreign investment in Portugal, contributing "to the promotion of the harmonious development of the Community and the reduction of regional disparities which is one of the basic aims of the Treaty" and furthering "European market integration by linking Portugal more closely to the Community through one of its important industries". The Commission admitted that this would not be enough to make an exemption possible unless the conditions of Article 85(3) EC were fulfilled, but it stressed that it was an element which the Commission had taken into account.

The CFI started its review of the Commission's assessment with regard to the third condition of Article 85(3) EC by emphasizing that it was its task "to verify whether, ..., any adverse effects on competition deriving from the project in question are indispensable in order to attain the objectives of achieving economic and technical progress". According to the CFI, the answer to the crucial question whether "the joint venture is strictly indispensable to enable the founders to penetrate the market in question", was affirmative as it was not "contradicted in any serious way" that "if each of the founders actually was technically and financially capable of penetrating the market individually, such penetration could be achieved only at a loss, in view of the particularly high level of the joint venture's "break-even point" and of the information available concerning forecasts and market shares". According to the CFI, the "exceptional circumstances" referred to by the Commission in its Decision, "were taken into consideration by the Commission only superogatorily".[106] The CFI concluded that it was not established that the Commission's assessment with regard to the third condition of Article 85(3) EC was manifestly incorrect.

Last but not least, the Commission noted in the context of the *fourth condition* of Article 85(3) EC ("no elimination of competition") that the cooperation would not lead to an elimination of competition in the MPV segment. According to the Commission, it would stimulate competition through the creation of an additional choice and would lead to a more balanced structure in the MPV market segment. The Commission emphasized that there would also be increased competition concerning price and quality "over the next five to ten years with the further penetration of the segment by Japanese producers as well as other new entrants". The Commission was of the opinion that the product differentiation and profit margins in the MPV segment left sufficient scope for competition between Ford and VW on the distribution level, despite the fact that they will purchase their versions of the MPVs from the joint venture, in principle, at the same price. The Commission expected Ford and VW to compete with each other in the MPV segment in view of incremental sales

[106] See *Matra II*, *supra* note 101, paras. 135-140.

profits through increased individual sales. In addition, the Commission pointed out that "the mass producers strategy in the car sector is to offer their customers the whole range of products in order to establish or reinforce a brand loyalty and not just a model loyalty".

Matra challenged the Commission's assessment with regard to the fourth condition, arguing, *inter alia*, that the joint venture would give rise to excess production capacity in the market concerned. The CFI, however, rejected Matra's argument that the Commission's decision was incorrect in that respect. It stressed that in *Matra I*, the ECJ held that "as regards the evaluation of the risk of excess production capacity, ... the Commission carried out a comprehensive and detailed examination of this question before concluding that no such risk exists ... . In those circumstances, the arguments put forward by Matra ... are not such as to establish that the Commission based its decision on a manifestly incorrect assessment of the economic data".[107] According to the CFI, Matra had not established either that the joint venture would have the effect of limiting, to a sufficiently substantial extent, competition between Ford and VW, at the stage of product distribution, or, in any event, that the obligations and requirements laid down in the Commission's decision, were not adequate. Matra's argument that the differentiation of the products would not have any positive impact on competition between the founders at the stage of distribution, was therefore rejected.[108]

The Commission granted the exemption under Article 85(3) EC under a few *conditions*. Ford and VW each had to (i) maintain certain differences between the MPVs produced by the joint venture, (ii) establish appropriate procedures and safeguards to keep competitively sensitive information apart, and (iii) obtain the Commission's prior approval for a possible decision not to market its MPV in any Member State. In addition, if the joint venture agreement was terminated, each party had to grant or procure the granting of all technology licences necessary to enable the other party to continue to make MPVs separately. Last but not least, the parties could not expand the range of products to be produced by the joint venture without prior approval of the Commission, from MPV to other categories of vehicles. Furthermore, the

---

[107] See *Matra II*, *supra* note 101, par. 152.

[108] See *Matra II*, *supra* note 101, paras. 150-158.

Commission *obliged* the parties to submit certain reports and to provide it with particular information.

9.4.2.3 Vertical Cooperation: ACEA-CLEPA Guidelines

As a result of the implementation of lean production techniques and the shift towards virtual production, car manufacturers further reduce in-house production of parts, increase out-sourcing and expect suppliers to take a more pro-active role in the production process.[109] In addition, car manufacturers reduce the number of suppliers, demand better quality, request lower prices and expect suppliers to participate in the early stages of the research and development of new car models and become involved in car manufacturing.[110] In short, car manufacturers try to use their suppliers' skills and knowledge to ensure efficiency and quality. In doing so, car manufacturers and suppliers have become more interdependent[111] which can result in car manufacturers cementing relationships by taking a shareholding in a supplier.[112]

Rival car manufacturers Honda, Nissan, Toyota, Volkswagen and General Motors have joined forces to raise standards in the British components sector in an effort to improve their British manufacturing presence. According to studies, British productivity is less than half that of the best Japanese

---

[109] For instance, W.H. Davidow, M.S. Malone, *The virtual corporation*, 1992, Harper Business, New York, at 150, report that more than 90% of Chrysler's Viper sportscar and 70% of the parts of the typical Chrysler vehicle comes from suppliers. In IP/96/797, the Commission recognized in the context of the formation of the joint venture between Siemens and Sommer Allibert Industrie for the development, production, installation and sales of integrated cockpits for cars, that "[t]he joint venture is part of a general trend in the car manufacturing industry to reduce the scope of inhouse production by purchasing fully-assembled subsystems from outside suppliers".

[110] For instance, Davidow and Malone, *supra* note 109, at 148, report that GM's paint supplier runs GM's factory paint shop at the Buick Reatta plant. *FT*, "Smart car forecasts queried by report", 14 October 1996, at 19, reported that "suppliers for the Smart will build and partly assemble parts for the Smart on the production line at the new factory". *FT*, "Alliances forged in the factory", 4 November 1996, at 10, reported on the manner in which manufacturers and suppliers are pioneering techniques for working side by side.

[111] *FT*, "Star parts for bit players", 28 October 1996, at 17, reported that instead of inviting suppliers to annual bidding contests, manufacturers are forging longer-term bonds with suppliers by global supply deals and outsourcing.

[112] See *FT*, "Peugeot buys Faure stake", 10 October 1996, at 20.

suppliers and product defect rates are 100 times worse than the best plants in Japan.[113] Davidow and Malone describe the advantages to car manufacturers of this new "virtualized supplier relationship" as follows:

> fewer and more skillful suppliers, higher-quality, lower-cost components arriving in a more timely manner, even a staff of design engineers to help out when needed. Add to this the less obvious advantage of being able, through greater outsourcing, to share the capital investment required to build a new product ...[114]

Davidow and Malone identify the following advantages to the suppliers:

> Enlightened suppliers realize that by reducing cycle times, improving deliveries, and building high-quality products they reduce their own costs and make themselves more valuable to their customers. They know that when customers invest in linking computers so they can share information, and when they become dependent on suppliers to develop products for them, they are being guaranteed a long-term source of revenue. ... Some companies, such as BMW, sweeten the deal by rewarding their best performing suppliers with higher margins. Others pay for their suppliers' training. And some even go so far as to invest in their key suppliers - as Ford did with windshield maker Excel ... . The result, as one .. supplier that survived the cut explained, is that now "we get to think long-term" and "make investments that will boost quality and productivity".[115]

In order to facilitate cooperation between car manufacturers and suppliers, ACEA and CLEPA signed on 12 April 1994, the "European Guidelines for Cooperation between Automobile Manufacturers and their Suppliers". It was

---

[113] *FT*, "International rescue for car components", 18 September 1996, at 11. See also *FT*, "Components sector "declining" - Volkswagen chief hits at standards", 24 September 1996, at 10. See for a different opinion: *FT*, "Car parts claims cause surprise", 7 November 1996, at 11.

[114] Davidow and Malone, *supra* note 109, at 150.

[115] Davidow and Malone, *supra* note 109, at 151.

reported in the press that according to Mr. Garuzzo, at that time president of ACEA, the Guidelines constitute a European framework to improve relations between the two sides. Garuzzo told reporters that this was necessary as cooperation between the two sectors would have immediate repercussions on the competitiveness of the entire European automobile industry, because over 50% of components were produced by external suppliers. Garuzzo added that even if the joint declaration is not legally binding for the two parties, it defines the "spirit" of the future cooperation and will enable the European automobile industry to make "considerable" savings on production costs, thus helping strengthen its competitiveness. Furthermore, he confirmed that car manufacturers "are going to continue pressuring equipment suppliers as long as our customers and market trends continue to pressure us". Mr. Planchon, president of CLEPA, emphasized that it is important to find a middle ground between a reduction in production costs for car manufacturers and a reduction in prices of equipment suppliers.[116]

The following description of the context of the Guidelines was given in the preamble:

> In the face of globalisation within the automotive industry and increasing world-wide competition, the European Automotive Industry must continue improvement in many key areas. The automobile manufacturers and their suppliers recognise the need to achieve adequate profitability in order to invest in new technology and innovation to maintain World Class positions.
>
> They recognise the mutual benefit derived from a close partnership between a manufacturer and a certain number of system suppliers. This equally requires a balanced structure, at the supplier level, between system suppliers and their sub-system suppliers.
>
> This new partnership relationship between the automobile manufacturers and their suppliers is based upon an open dialogue and

---

[116] See also *Agence Europe* of 13 April 1994, at 15 ("Framework agreement between car makers and suppliers of parts aimed at cost reduction, cooperation and technological progress").

exchange of information throughout the supply chain, to enable all partners to strive towards continuous improvement of products and processes, in a spirit of mutual agreement.

Although the Guidelines, according to the preamble, do not cover the independent aftermarket and "do not aspire to establish a legal or contractual definition of the relationship between automobile manufacturers and their supliers", they do "determine the fundamental principles and set a recommended framework for cooperation within the European Automotive Industry". The Guidelines provide for some basic rules on cooperation in design and manufacturing planning, price/cost relationship, effective adoption of modern manufacturing processes, quality, logistics and include some "legal rules" on re-negotiation clauses, changes in prices and conditions, confidentiality of information, respect for intellectual property rights and the use of "brand marks".

It is not at all clear whether these Guidelines have been scrutinized by the Commission under Article 85 EC. This is remarkable since the Guidelines regard the vertical relationship between car manufacturers and suppliers. Moreover, the last paragraph of the preamble to the Guidelines provides that the Guidelines do not cover the independent aftermarket "where partners may operate separately". A suspicious mind could argue that *a contrario* the parties are not free on the OE-market. Furthermore, one could question the non-binding nature of the Guidelines as they seem to embody not only an agreement between ACEA and CLEPA but between the members of the two associations as well. The Guidelines have the potential of restricting competition between ACEA's members in negotiating terms and conditions with suppliers and *vice versa*. The Guidelines seem to reflect a basic agreement on certain crucial issues which allows parties on both sides to form one united front in their negotiations with each other.

9.4.3 Article 86 EC

9.4.3.1 Cooperation between Undertakings without a Dominant Position

In principle, Article 86 EC is not relevant for cooperation between undertakings without a dominant position. However, Article 86 EC can become relevant as soon as undertakings without a dominant position form such economic links that they create a collective dominant position on a particular market. This could be the case, for instance, where two or more independent undertakings jointly have, through agreements or licences, a technological lead affording them the power to behave to an appreciable extent independently of their competitors, their customers and ultimately of their consumers.[117] In order for such a dominant position to exist, the undertakings in the group must be linked in such a way that they adopt the same conduct on the market.[118] A collective dominant position can just as easily be abused as a single one. However, since a finding of a dominant position, single or collective, is not in itself a matter of reproach,[119] it seems very unlikely that if none of the participating undertakings is in a dominant position, the *creation* of a collective dominant position in itself, by bringing about the necessary economic links, can violate Article 86 EC.[120] Not the mere creation of a collective dominant position but its abuse can violate Article 86 EC.[121] *Extending* a collective dominant position, on the other hand,

---

[117] See Joined Cases T-68/89, T-77/89 and T-78/89, *Società Italiana Vetro and others* v *Commission (Vetro)* [1992] ECR II-1548, par. 358. In its Decision Ford/Volkswagen, *supra* note 96, par. 39, the Commission noted that "[i]n the light of the conditions of competition in the MPV segment it is not likely that the cooperation, ..., will create such competitive advantages as to enable Ford and VW to prevent effective competition being maintained by giving them the power to behave to an appreciable extent independently of competitors in the MPV segment".

[118] Case C-393/92, *Gemeente Almelo and Others and Energiebedrijf IJsselmij* [1994] ECR I-1520, par. 42.

[119] See *Vetro*, *supra* note 117, par. 360.

[120] It is therefore doubtful whether Hask and Huser, *supra* note 10, at 359, are right in stating for a fact that the CFI in *Vetro* held that competitors may abuse a collective dominant position under Article 86 EC if they *create* sufficient structural links between themselves in a highly oligopolistic industry. Is in principle not the existence of a collective dominance needed before it can actually be abused?

[121] See, for instance, *Matra II*, *supra* note 101, par. 170, in which the CFI rejected the plea as to an error of law committed by the Commission concerning the applicability of Article 86 EC "since the conditions laid down by that provision concerning the existence, actually ascertained, of an abuse by one or more

by further strengthening the existing links or including a new participant in the collectivity, can probably violate Article 86 EC as it changes the structure of the market and is likely to have an adverse effect on competition in that market.

9.4.3.2 Cooperation with an Undertaking in a Dominant Position

An undertaking can abuse its dominant position by acquiring a shareholding in a competitor.[122] The ECJ held in *Hoffmann-La Roche*:

> The concept of abuse is an objective concept relating to the behaviour of an undertaking in a dominant position which is such as to influence the structure of a market where, as a result of the very presence of the undertaking in question, the degree of competition is weakened and which, through recourse to methods different from those which condition normal competition in products or services on the basis of the transactions of commercial operators, has the effect of hindering the maintenance of the degree of competition still existing in the market or the growth of that competition.[123]

The mere change in the structure of the market brought about by the acquisition of a shareholding may have an adverse effect on competition in that market in the Community and can therefore amount to an abuse of dominant position.[124] But, as pointed out by the ECJ in *BAT and Reynolds*, the acquisition of a shareholding can only amount to an abuse of dominant position if it results in effective control of the company in question or at least in some influence on its commercial policy.[125] The Commission will look at the particular facts of the case in order to decide whether the latter is the case. For instance, in its decision *Gillette*, the Commission noted that Gillette had not only become a

---

undertakings acting collectively are certainly not fulfilled".

[122] See Case 322/81, *Michelin* v *Commission* [1983] ECR 3511, par. 57, and Decision Gillette, *supra* note 91, par. 23.

[123] Case 85/76, *Hoffmann-La Roche* v *Commission* [1979] ECR 541, par. 91.

[124] See, *inter alia*, Decision Gillette, *supra* note 91, par. 23.

[125] See *BAT and Reynolds*, *supra* note 81, par. 65.

major shareholder but had also become its largest creditor and had acquired important pre-emption and conversion rights and options in the company in question. According to the Commission, "[t]he position of Gillette is a matter which the management of Eemland will be obliged to take into account and consequently it is a factor which will influence the commercial conduct of Eemland. It follows that Gillette will have at least some influence on Eemland's commercial policy".[126] The Commission noted that "[b]y weakening the competitive position of Eemland, Gillette as the dominant player on this market will benefit from this lessening of competition"[127] and concluded that "Gillette's participation in this operation involving one of its principal competitors on the wet-shaving market in the Community constitutes an infringement of Article 86".[128]

9.5 Concluding Remarks

The removal of barriers to intra-Community trade and the further globalisation of the economy stimulate concentrations and in particular various forms of cooperation in the automobile industry. The fact that Member States consider their domestic car manufacturers of strategic importance and directly related to national prestige, acted (and at times still acts) as an important barrier to the further rationalization and restructuring of the automobile industry in the Community. Nevertheless, experts believe in view of the structural overcapacity, that the car sector is on the eve of important concentrations. In fact, the process of concentration has already taken place in the component sector and seems to have started in the car sector. The Chrysler/Daimler Benz merger may serve as a catalyst. The further introduction of lean production techniques and the shift towards virtual production stimulates the need for horizontal and especially vertical forms of cooperation between the various actors in the automobile industry. There seems to be a tendency among manufacturers, suppliers and distributors to strengthen various forms of cooperation in an effort to cut costs, improve efficiency and thereby strengthen

---

[126] Decision Gillette, *supra* note 91, par. 24.

[127] *Ibidem*, par. 30.

[128] *Ibidem*, par. 32.

competitiveness. This changes the relationship between the various actors within the automobile industry.

The Community can have an important impact on certain concentrations and cooperations in the automobile industry, within the context of its competition policy on the basis of Articles 85 and 86 EC and the Merger Control Regulation. However, various conflicting interests complicate the Community's scrutiny of concentrations and cooperations in the automobile industry. For instance, the automobile industry is dominated by a relatively small number of very large car manufacturers. As a result, concentrations and cooperations between these manufacturers can have a considerable impact on competition within the Community. It is up to the Community to guarantee effective competition. On the other hand, car manufacturers have to compete on a global and highly competitive market. Experts believe that in order to thrive or survive on the global market, the relatively few large Community car manufacturers will have to merge and cooperate. In addition, there is a tendency amongst car manufacturers to become generalist manufacturers. The Chrysler/Daimler Benz merger and the Ford/Volkswagen joint-venture "AutoEuropa" indicate that even the major manufacturers are willing to merge and cooperate in order to be able to compete on the global market. This can be detrimental to competition within the Community. At the same time, however, it is a manner to strengthen competitiveness in order to survive on the global market.

There is very little information on the concentrations and various forms of cooperation within the automobile industry. There seems to be no complete overview of the various links between the actors in the automobile industry. In addition, there is little information available on the so-called ins and outs of the concentrations and forms of cooperation that are known to the public. In view of this remarkable lack of information, one wonders how the Community can come up with a proper evaluation of a concentration or form of cooperation under Articles 85 and 86 EC or the Merger Regulation. In addition, there is relatively little information available on the manner in which the Community scrutinizes the concentrations and forms of cooperations. It is evident that this lack of information complicates a thorough analysis of this important topic. A lack of information can also undermine the credibility of the Community's decisions on these concentrations and forms of cooperations.

Nevertheless, looking at the information available to the public, one gets the impression that the Community tries to facilitate concentrations and various forms of cooperation in an effort to strengthen the competitiveness of the automobile industry within the Community. In other words, considerations that are directly related to the need to strengthen the competitiveness of the automobile industry within the Community play a role within the Community's competition policy dealing with concentrations and cooperations within the automobile industry.

10. STRENGTHENING OF THE COMPETITIVENESS OF COMMUNITY INDUSTRY AND THE AUTOMOBILE INDUSTRY

10.1 Introduction

Article 3(l) EC prescribes that, for the purposes set out in Article 2 EC, the activities of the EC shall include the strengthening of the competitiveness of Community industry. Article 3(l) EC is further amplified in Article 130 EC.[1] The Community policy with regard to the industry is based on Articles 3(l) and 130 EC and the explicit reference to "the strengthening of the competitiveness of Community industry" in Article 3(1) EC, seems to express the specific objective which the EC Treaty assigns to this particular policy. In this chapter, Article 130 EC will first be looked at (**10.2**). A concise summary will then be given of a string of Community publications on the manner in which the Community tries to contribute to the strengthening of the competitiveness of Community industry in general, and the automobile industry in particular (**10.3**). In the end, some concluding remarks will be made (**10.4**).

10.2 Article 130 EC

Article 130(1) EC provides that *both* the Community and the Member States shall ensure that the conditions necessary for the competitiveness of the Community's industry exist. For that purpose, the action by the Community and the Member States shall be aimed at:

> (a) speeding up the adjustment of industry to structural changes;
> (b) encouraging an environment favourable to initiative and to the development of undertakings throughout the Community, particularly small and medium-sized undertakings;
> (c) encouraging an environment favourable to cooperation between undertakings, and
> (d) fostering better exploitation of the industrial potential of policies of innovation, research and technological development.

---

[1] See Article G(38) TEU. See on Title XIII EC: W. Sauter, *Competition law and industrial policy in the EU*, 1997, Clarendon Press, Oxford, at 93-105.

Article 130(1) EC prescribes that all this has to take place in accordance with a system of open and competitive markets.

The wording of Article 130(1) EC indicates that both the Community and the Member States have to take an active stand in order to ensure the existence of conditions necessary for the competitiveness of the Community's industry. Article 130(2) EC obliges the Member States to consult each other in liaison with the Commission and, where necessary, coordinate their action. The Commission may take any useful initiative to promote such coordination.

Article 130(3) EC provides that the Community shall contribute to the achievement of the objectives set out in Article 130(1) EC through the policies and activities it pursues under other provisions of the EC Treaty. This makes it legitimate for the Community to use its other policies and activities for the benefit of the competitiveness of the Community industry. In addition, Article 130(3) EC provides that the Council, acting unanimously on a proposal from the Commission, after consulting the European Parliament and the Economic and Social Committee, may decide on specific measures in support of action taken in the Member States to achieve the objectives set out in Article 130(1) EC.

The very last paragraph of Article 130(3) EC confirms that Article 130 EC shall *not* provide a basis for the introduction by the Community of any measure which could lead to a distortion of competition. The possible impact of this provision, however, is not at all clear. The term "distortion of competition" is vague and the implications of this provision in a situation in which the Community contributes to the achievement of the objectives set out in Article 130(1) EC through the implementation of one of its *other* policies and activities under the EC Treaty are not evident.

The Commission's use of its other policies and activities to strengthen the competitiveness of the industry often has an impact on competition and it is not clear when and under what conditions such implications lead to a distortion of competition within the meaning of Article 130(3) EC. For instance, there are indications that Community competition policy has made broad allowances for new forms of cooperation between undertakings in view of the importance of the ability to cooperate and share risks for the strengthening of competitiveness of Community industry.[2] Another example is the fact that the Community seems to further move its policy with regard to research and development away from pure scientific and pre-competitive research towards initiatives closer to the market that will help strengthen the competitiveness of its industry.[3] This move has important implications for competition as research and development close to the market tends to be an area of fierce competition within the industry. A last example is the discussion on design rights on parts which seems to be influenced by the need to protect or strengthen the competitiveness of the Community industry. Commissioner Bangemann has publicly qualified design rights as an instrument to protect the competitiveness of the Community industry.[4]

10.3 Strengthening of the Competitiveness of the Automobile Industry

Although the Community recognizes that the competitiveness of Community industry is first and foremost a matter for the industry itself, the Commission took the position in its 1990 communication *Industrial policy in an open and competitive environment*, that the Community has an important role to play "as a catalyst and pathbreaker for innovation" and in identifying and providing

---

[2] Commission White Paper "Growth, competitiveness, employment - The challenges and ways forward into the 21st century", COM(93)700 final, 5 December 1993 ("White Paper on Growth, competitiveness, employment"), at 10. It was pointed out in Communication from the Commission to the Council, the European Parliament, the Economic and Social Committee and the Committee of the Regions "Action programme and timetable for implementation of the action announced in the communication on an industrial competitiveness policy for the European Union", COM(95)87 final, 22 March 1995, at 6, that "[t]he completion of the internal market is being accompanied by closer industrial co-operation within the European Union, for which the public authorities must create the right climate, in conformity with competition rules". See also COM(95)87 final/2, 30 March 1995. See Sauter, *supra* note 1, at 109-161, for an analysis of the competition policy of the Community and the competitiveness of European industry.

[3] *FT*, "Brussels points research in new direction", 31 July 1997, at 2, reported that researchers have criticised "the Commission's research directorate, under the stewardship of Mrs Cresson, a former French prime minister, for pushing research efforts closer and closer to the market, to the point where the EU is funding industrial as opposed to scientific research". J. Peterson, "Research and development policy" in *The European Union and national industrial policy* (H. Kassim and A. Menon eds.), 1996, Routledge, London, at 243, footnote 4, reports that a senior official in Ireland's public R&D agency echoes the widely held view that "[i]t is now assumed that the 4th EC Framework programme [on R&D] will move nearer to the market".

[4] See Chapter 4, section 4.5.

conditions which "strengthen the optimal allocation of resources by market forces, towards accelerating structural adjustment and towards improving industrial competitiveness and the industrial and particularly technological long term framework" since "only a competitive industry will allow the Community to maintain its position in the world economy, which constitutes the essence of the Community interest".[5] In its communication, the Commission set out the principles and objectives for a modern industrial policy for the Community. It is interesting to note that the Commission recognized that sectoral approaches to industrial policy entail inevitably the risk of delaying structural adjustments and that by experience, a competitive environment applied to all on the same basis is the best guarantee for a strong and competitive industry.[6] Nevertheless, discussions were held within the Commission on a Community strategy for the automobile industry.[7]

In 1990, the Commission published its *first* communication on the automobile industry summarizing the discussions on the conditions for completing the single market in the automobile industry.[8] In its communication, the Commission concluded, looking at the position on overseas markets,

---

[5] Communication of the Commission to the Council and to the European Parliament "Industrial policy in an open and competitive environment - Guidelines for a Community approach", COM(90)556 final, 16 November 1990, at 1-2. See also Council Conclusions of 26 November 1990, 10159/90(Presse 198).

[6] *Ibidem*, at 5-6. The Commission further recognized that most "sectoral" policies in practice have been directed more towards social objectives than the achievement of adjustment. The Commission noted that the Community's industrial approach should be based on the active promotion of positive adjustment and that sectoral policies must promote structural adjustment and not retard it. Sector specific policies have to be carefully examined and possibly adapted.

[7] See *Agence Europe*, "Premier débat de la Commission sur la stratégie CEE", 1 June 1989, at 6, and "Industrie automobile: Positif sur les orientations génerales de la stratégie propose par M. Bangemann, les constructeurs Europeens restent cependant sceptiques quant à certaines modalités d'application", 5-6 June 1989, at 11. *Agence Europe*, "According to Sir Leon Brittan, the transition period for Japanese car imports should not go beyond 1996-For vigorous EEC action in support of the European industry", 14 February 1990, at 12, reported that during a speech, Sir Leon Brittan made reference to a "special policy" benefitting the car sector and described what the Commission could do to aid the automobile industry.

[8] Commission Communication "A single Community motor-vehicle market" SEC(89)2118 final, 18 January 1990 ("1990 Communication"). See also *Agence Europe*, "Motor cars: Vice-Presidents Brittan and Bangemann recall that priority should go to restructuring on the Community market", 14 March 1990, at 7. See in this context also Report of the European Parliament Committee on Economic and Monetary Affairs and Industrial Policy (Rapporteur C. Tongue), A3-140/91 (PE 146.412/fin.), 23 May 1991.

financial resources, the position of part suppliers and competition from new transplants, that there was cause for concern about the automobile industry's competitiveness. According to the Commission, the industry had to increase its logistical planning, its productivity, quality, and diversify its sources of supply and encourage innovation, if it wanted to counter the global strategies of non-Community producers. The Commission stressed that the automobile industry had to seize the opportunity presented by the existence of a large internal market in order to maintain a major role on the world market and take into account transplants when working out a strategy. The Commission pointed out that the necessary process of radical restructuring and technical adjustment would be accelerated and facilitated by the completion of the single market and more in particular by (i) technical harmonisation, (ii) approximating indirect taxation, (iii) managing state intervention (state aid), (iv) research and technology policy, (v) training and retraining, and (vi) dismantling internal quantitative restrictions.

A *second* Commission communication on the automobile industry was published in 1992.[9] With reference to the concept of industrial policy as reflected in Article 130 EC, the Commission called for a structured Community-wide approach in support of the adjustment of the automobile industry since: (i) the high level of intra-Community car trade made Community coordination necessary to avoid distorting national policy measures, and (ii) the Community's responsibility for external trade policy which could have an impact on the Community's automobile industry as a whole. The Commission announced that it would apply Community instruments to facilitate the adjustment of the automobile industry's structures with the aim of supporting its competitiveness in order to make it fit for increased competition in the years ahead, by contributing "to the examination of the industrial and technological conditions for the success of the Community's car and car component industry", and by explaining "how the motor vehicle industry can benefit from the range of horizontal measures which exist, or have been proposed, to support the

---

[9] Communication from the Commission to the Council, the European Parliament and the Economic and Social Committee on "The European motor vehicle industry: Situation, issues at state, and proposals for action", COM(92)166 final, 8 May 1992 ("1992 Communication"). See in this context also Report of the European Parliament Committee on Economic and Monetary Affairs and Industrial Policy (Rapporteur C. Tongue), A3-266/93 (PE 204.819/fin.), 27 September 1993.

industry in its efforts to become more competitive".[10] The Commission repeated, however, that the Community could only intervene through measures subsidiary to the industry's own strategies and specified that it had contacted ACEA and CLEPA to discuss questions and options.[11] In its communication, the Commission elaborated *in extenso* upon (i) the impact of the single market on competitiveness, (ii) research and development policy, (iii) training and retraining, (iv) activities upstream and downstream of motor vehicle assembly, (v) improving the Community industry's access to third markets, and (vi) the responsibility of the social partners. Following these two Commission communications on the automobile industry, the Council adopted in 1992 a resolution in which it recognized that there were considerable weaknesses in the organizational and productivity sphere to be overcome by the automobile industry. The Council emphasized that the main role in developing the necessary strategies was to be played by undertakings "it being for the public authorities to create an efficient working environment favourable to moves by undertakings to adjust, with due regard for the principle of subsidiarity",[12] and called on the Commission to follow progress achieved in implementing the aims established in the Council's resolution, including developments in the area of competitiveness, and to report regularly, and at least once a year, on progress achieved.

[10] *Ibidem*, at 1. The Commission emphasized on p. 9, that the Commission's approach towards cooperation in the motor vehicle sector is continuing to take account of certain specific aspects of the sector. According to the Commission, certain types of cooperation, carried out within the framework of the rules referred to in Annex "General acts taken under competition law and with a bearing on the motor vehicle industry", listing Community instruments such as the block exemption on cooperation on R&D (Reg. 418/85), specialization (Reg. 417/85), patents and know-how licensing (Reg. 2349/84 and 556/89) and motor vehicle distribution and servicing (Reg. 123/85), would be viewed positively, even at the assembly stage, if this widens the choice.

[11] *Ibidem*, at 1. This simple recognition probably brought *Agence Europe*, "European Commission guidelines relating to the car industry" (Europe Documents), 12 June 1992, at 1, to the conclusion that the Commission prepared the Communication while respecting the doctrine according to which Community "industrial policy" should not be interventionist. It is interesting to note that *Agence Europe*, "On Wednesday, the Commission is to publish the 1994 edition of the panorama of European industry and is preparing a new document on industrial policy", 24 August 1994, at 4, reported that "[t]he old polemic on the very term "industrial policy" is now over and there is no more dispute about the significance and extent of Community action (which neither does nor will comprise in any case sectoral measures of an interventionist or protectionist nature, ...).

[12] Council Resolution of 17 June 1992 on the European motor vehicle industry, OJ 1992, C178/6.

In the 1993 White Paper on *Growth, competitiveness and employment*, the Commission put the importance of competitiveness in a wider socio-economic context and stressed the link between competitiveness and the (lack of) creation of jobs. In the White Paper, the Commission elaborated extensively on: (i) the conditions for growth and enhanced competitiveness, (ii) trans-European networks, (iii) research and technological development, (iv) the changing society and new technologies, and (v) the Community as an open and reliable partner.[13] In doing so, the Commission confirmed the Community's active role in the strengthening of the competitiveness of the industry as "no-one is in any doubt as to the responsibility of governments and of the Community to create as favourable an environment as possible for company competitiveness".[14] The Commission repeated that it is the responsibility of the national and Community authorities to provide industry with a favourable environment, to open up clear and reliable prospects for it and to promote its international competitiveness.[15]

In February 1994, the Commission published an extensive *third* communication on the automobile industry in which it responded to the Council's request to report on progress achieved in implementing the aims established in the Council's 1992 resolution and on developments in the competitiveness of the industry. The Commission gave a detailed overview of the development of markets and production, the reaction of industry to past and future challenges and the Community's role in improving the business environment. Special attention was paid to the Community's role with regard to

---

[13] White Paper on Growth, competitiveness and employment, *supra* note 2, Part B-II "Competitiveness".

[14] *Ibidem*, at 9.

[15] *Ibidem*, at 60. See also Council Conclusions of 22 April 1994, 6442/94(Presse 76).

the completion of the internal market, structural interventions and human resources, research and technological development and external trade policy.[16] In May 1994, the Council adopted a resolution in which it invited the Commission to encourage, within the horizontal industrial policy framework adopted by the Community, the structural adjustment process of the industry. The Council invited the Commission to pay particular attention to certain issues which are part of various Community policies such as that on research and technological development, competition and commercial policy. The Council requested the Commission to present a progress report by the end of 1995.[17]

In the fall of 1994, the Commission published its 1994 communication *An industrial competitiveness policy for the European Union* which was based on principles set out in the 1990 communication *Industrial policy in an open and competitive environment* and included an action programme for the implementation of the objectives identified in the White Paper *Growth, competitiveness and employment*. The action programme focused on the need to (i) promote intangible investment, (ii) develop industrial cooperation, (iii) ensure fair competition, and (iv) modernise the role of the public authorities.[18] The Commission repeated that the Treaty on European Union calls on the Community and the Member States to ensure that the conditions necessary for the competitiveness of the Community's industry exist and stressed that this

---

[16] Communication from the European Commission to the Council and to the European Parliament on the European Union automobile industry, COM(94)49 final, 23 February 1994. See also the Written proceedings of the Forum on the European automobile industry (1 March 1994), European Commission and European Parliament, Brussels. See also *Agence Europe*, "Presenting the Commission's communication, Mr. Bangemann sets out the guidelines which will enable the European industry to be competitive - Community support measures", 24 February 1994, at 5; *Agence Europe*, "The EP rapporteur calls for a motor car programme similar to the RECHAR (coal) or CONVER (military industry) programmes", 28 February 1994, at 9, reported that C. Tongue called on the Commission to develop an action programme for the automobile sector which would include the establishment of a coordination committee.

[17] Council Resolution of 16 May 1994 on the automobile industry, OJ 1994, C149/1. See also *Agence Europe*, "Industry Council guidelines for the automobile industry", 25-26 April 1994, at 8.

[18] See also *Agence Europe*, "Commission document on industrial competitiveness defines four action priorities including modernisation of public authorities", 15 September 1994, at 4. According to Commissioner Bangemann, the automobile sector had been able to considerably improve its international competitiveness since 1990.

objective had to be pursued "vigorously and dynamically" in order to create and attract new jobs. Again, the Commission specified that although it is primarily up to businesses to ensure that they are competitive on the market, "the public authorities in turn must ensure the consistency of all the measures which could enhance industrial efficiency".[19] According to the Commission, the Treaty on European Union introduced:

> the legal bases for implementing the industrial policy which, in line with the subsidiarity principle, is defined as a general obligation shared between the Community and the Member States for "the strengthening of the competitiveness of Community industry" (Article 3 of the Treaty) and to "ensure that the conditions necessary for the competitiveness of the Community's industry exist" (Article 130(1)).[20]

The Commission gave the following interpretation of the Community's role in strengthening industrial competitiveness:

> It is primarily up to the Member States and the decentralised authorities to foster industrial competitiveness with the aid of a system of open and competitive markets.
> However, Article 130(2) adds that in order to attain these objectives the Member States "shall consult each other in liaison with the Commission and, where necessary, shall co-ordinate their action". The Commission is assigned the specific duty to "take any useful initiative to promote such coordination".
> To support this national action, the Community will generally help to achieve this objective of improving competitiveness by taking horizontal measures under a series of common policies (on research, cohesion, vocational training, networks and foreign trade), implemented

[19] Communication from the Commission to the Council, to the European Parliament, Economic and Social Committee and the Committee of the Regions "An industrial competitiveness policy for the European Union", COM(94)319 final, 14 September 1994, at 1.

[20] *Ibidem*, at 10-11.

> by qualified majority vote in most cases, and by implementing the competition policy.
>
> The Council may also, ruling unanimously on a proposal from the Commission "decide specific measures destined to support actions taken by Member States in order to attain stated objectives" according to Article 130, paragraph 1 of the Treaty.
>
> Accordingly, a policy for industrial competitiveness has a coherent legal basis in Title XIII ("Industry") of the Treaty on European Union, Title XV (Articles 130f *et seq.*) on research and technological development, Title VIII (Article 123) on social policy and industrial changes, Title XIV on economic and social cohesion (Articles 130a and 130b) and Title XII on trans-European networks.[21]

The above confirms that the Commission sees an important role for the Community on the basis of Article 130 EC, in strengthening the competitiveness of Community industry.[22]

In a resolution of 21 November 1994, the Council noted that the principles embodied in the 1990 communication *Industrial policy in an open and competitive environment* had been reflected in various Council resolutions and conclusions, and in several Commission communications concerning specific sectors such as the automobile industry.[23] The Council welcomed the communication and emphasized that an industrial policy for the European Community should be market-driven but added at the same time, that it should

---

[21] *Ibidem*, at 10-11.

[22] The important role attributed to public authorities, in strengthening industrial competitiveness has been criticized. For instance, *Agence Europe*, "Representatives of industry disagree on the causes of Europe's lack of international competitiveness", 21 September 1994, at 12, reported that at a Conference on "A strategy for Europe's competitiveness", Prof. S. Garelli of the University of Lausanne, took the position that public authorities are simply incapable of reacting with the necessary flexibility and speed. Garelli recommended that public authorities be excluded from the effort (to strenghten competitiveness) and suggested to proceed with the privatisation and deregulation of markets to enable industry itself to take the necessary measures at the earliest opportunity. *FT*, "Europe urged to copy US business approach", 7 April 1997, at 2, reported on a Eurostudy/Fortune survey of European business leaders which is in favour of reducing the state's role in regulating industry.

[23] Council resolution of 21 November 1994 on the strengthening of the competitiveness of Community industry, OJ 1994, C343/1.

respond to the global challenges with the aim of a substantial improvement of the competitive position of the European industry in global markets. The Council identified a number of "spheres" in which action by the Community and the Member States within the framework of their respective powers was considered urgent.[24] The Council invited the Commission to come up with an action programme and timetable and repeated its request to receive an annual report on the development of the competitiveness of European industry. On 22 March 1995, the Commission finalized the requested report on the implementation of the Council resolutions and conclusions on industrial policy[25] and published a communication with annexed the requested action programme and timetable.[26] The Commission specified that it considered the following four objectives of particular importance in industrial competitiveness policy: (i) development of the internal market, (ii) better taking industry's needs into account in research policy, (iii) establishment of the information society, and (iv) promotion of industrial co-operation.[27] The Commission announced a number of initiatives including action to modernise the role played by the public authorities in industry and the establishment of Task Forces to start joint projects in the interest of industry. The Commission confirmed that it would take account of the approach in its action programme when drafting communications on specific sectors of industry. On 25 June 1996, the Council decided on the basis of Article 130(3) EC, to accept the proposed initiatives in

---

[24] The list includes (i) creation of stable, economically-viable framework conditions, (ii) elimination of unnecessary bureaucratic burdens for enterprises, (iii) ensuring undistorted internal and external competition, (iv) strengthening of industrial cooperation with third countries, and (v) promotion of intangible competitive factors, with respect to the increasing complementarity of physical and non-physical investments.

[25] Commission working paper "Report on implementation of the Council resolutions and conclusions on industrial policy, SEC(95)437 final, 22 March 1995.

[26] Communication from the Commission to the Council, the European Parliament, the Economic and Social Committee and the Committee of the Regions "Action programme and timetable for implementation of the action announced in the communication on an industrial competitiveness policy for the European Union", COM(95)87 final, 22 March 1995. See also COM(95)87 final/2, 30 March 1995. See in this context also Council Conclusions of 7 April 1995, 6317/94(Presse 112); Council Conclusions of 6-7 November 1995, 11172/95(Presse 307); Written Question 725/95 (Alonso), OJ 1995, C222/13, and Written Question 1244-1248/96 (Amadeo), OJ 1996, C356/19.

[27] *Ibidem*, at 2-7.

an effort to modernize the industrial role of public authorities, to ensure undisturbed competition both internal and external to the Community, to strengthen industrial cooperation, and to promote intangible competitiveness factors. The Council requested the Commission to prepare an annual report evaluating the results obtained together with, where necessary, appropriate proposals.[28]

In July 1996, the Commission published its *fourth* communication on the European Automobile Industry.[29] The Commission announced that it would support an initiative advocated by the Economic and Social Committee and taken up by the European Parliament, to create a high-level panel of representatives of the various actors in the automobile industry (including manufacturers, suppliers and the unions) to advise the Commission on questions concerning the automobile industry and the use of the automobile as a means of transport. The Commission suggested to model the panel after the one already existing in the maritime industry. A second panel was to advise the Commission on research priorities and strategies. The Commission suggested to merge these two panels.[30]

In the fall of 1996, the Commission published the communication *Benchmarking the competitiveness of European industry* and presented benchmarking as a tool to monitor and promote on an ongoing basis better implementation of measures in key areas for competitiveness and assess the

---

[28] Council decision 96/413 of 25 June 1996 on the implementation of a Community action programme to strengthen the competitiveness of European industry, OJ 1996, L167/55.

[29] Communication from the Commission to the Council, the European Parliament, the Economic and Social Committee and the Committee of the Regions "European automobile industry - 1996", COM(96)327 final, 10 July 1996. See also Council conclusions 14 November 1996, 11221/96(Presse 303).

[30] Communication from the Commission to the Council, the European Parliament, the Economic and Social Committee and the Committee of the Regions on the "European Automobile Industry", 10 July 1996, COM(96) 327 final, at 21. See also "Mr Bangemann is willing to agree to Mr Donnelly's proposal for creation of a high-level panel of representatives of car makers and unions - The Renault case", *Agence Europe*, 12 March 1997, at 9. The Commission noted in Written Question 1167/97 (Arias), OJ 1997, C391/46, that it had created a "permanent high-level group" in order "to review the impact of the range of European policies as they affect the automobile industry". The first meeting was to take place on 24 June 1997.

situation against continuously improving best practice worldwide.[31] The Commission had already underlined the significance of benchmarking for sectors in its communication on the autombile industry, and confirmed that it had begun to benchmark the competitiveness of European manufacturing locations for the automobile industry. The Council's 1994 request for an annual report on the development of the competitiveness of European industry was met with the publication of the 1997 Commission communication *The competitiveness of European industry*.[32] In addition, the Commission published a second communication on benchmarking in which it was announced that benchmarking pilot programmes for component suppliers would be started and other initiatives would be launched by the automobile industry.[33]

---

[31] Commission Communication "Benchmarking the competitiveness of European industry", COM(96)463, 9 October 1996. The Commission confirmed that the primary responsibility for ensuring that enterprises remain competitive lies with firms themselves. However, the Commission emphasized that public authorities sustain competitiveness by putting in place the appropriate framework conditions under which enterprises operate, and specified that this takes the form of providing necessary infrastucture, putting in place an appropriate regulatory invironment and specific initiatives. According to the Commission, there is a necessity to develop a coherent approach concentrating on those factors in the business environment which are determining for enterprises. See also IP/96/903, and Fourth "Barnevik"-Report to the President of the European Commission, the Prime Ministers and Heads of State "Enhancing European competitiveness", Competitiveness advisory group, December 1996. See also Written Question 2619/97 (Gallagher), OJ 1998, C76/131, and *Agence Europe*, "Work of high-level group on benchmarking gets under way", 11-12 May 1998, at 14.

[32] The competitiveness of European Industry (based on the working document of Commission services), 1997, EUR-OP, Luxembourg. *Agence Europe*, "UNICE awaits European Commission analysis on industrial competitiveness and approves ECOFIN Council's position on networks", 25 October 1996, at 14, reported that the President of UNICE was impatient, if not concerned, by the delay in the publication of the global report on the competitiveness of European industry, as "[e]arly publication of the Commission's report will stimulate the implementation of any actions". See also *FT*, "Minister pledges EU competitiveness drive", 12 November 1997, at 7, and *Agence Europe*, "Council approves work programme allowing its attention to be focused on competitiveness of European industry - First discussions", 15 November 1997, at 8, and "Jacques Santer rejects UNICE's criticisms over on-going action in favour of competitiveness of European industry and points to progress achieved", 20 February 1998, at 14. See "Benchmarking Europe's competitiveness: from analysis to action", Unice, December 1997.

[33] Communication from the Commission to the Council, the European Parliament, the Economic and Social Committee and the Committee of the Regions "Benchmarking - Implementation of an instrument available to economic actors and public authorities", COM(97)153 final, 16 April 1997, at 5. See for an evaluation of benchmarking under Community competition law: J. Carle and M. Johnsson, "Benchmarking and E.C. competition law", [1998] E.C.L.R. at 74-84. See also Written Question 3870/97 (Amadeo), OJ 1998,

10.4 Concluding Remarks

Since 1990, the Community has developped an active industrial policy with a strong focus on the strengthening of the competitiveness of Community industry. This policy on competitiveness on the basis of Articles 3(l) and 130 EC has an important impact on other Community activities and policies. One only has to look at the contents of the various communications on the automobile industry to find confirmation of the fact that the Commission is determined to contribute to a favourable framework for the automobile industry through the implementation of various Community policies and activities. The Community's strategy is focused on promoting intangible investment, ensuring strong and fair competition, developing industrial co-operation, and modernising the role of public authorities and creating a stable and beneficial business environment. The communications on the automobile industry specify that a wide range of Community policies and activities are *instrumental* to the strengthening of the competitiveness of Community industry. They illustrate that these policies and activities are at times implemented with the improvement of competitiveness in mind. A good example is the manner in which the Community deals with both the importation of Japanese cars and the block exemption on the distribution and servicing of automobiles which are heavily influenced if not determined, by competitiveness considerations.

In view of the globalization of the economy, the Community seems to have the intention to keep up with the U.S.A. and Japan in supporting and improving the competitiveness of its automobile industry as only a competitive industry will enable the Community to keep its position in the world economy which, according to the Commission, constitutes the essence of the Community interest. The extensive and detailed communications on the automobile industry show that the Community keeps a close eye on its automobile industry and that it is up to the Commission to encourage the structural adjustment process of the industry. There is no doubt that the Community has become more interventionist in order to strengthen the competitiveness of its industry. The reorganisation of the automobile industry within the Community is not in its

C196/25, and Written Question 3871/97 (Amadeo), OJ 1998, C187/74.

entirety left up to the industry itself. The creation of several Task Forces and a so-called "high-level panel" of representatives of the various actors in the automobile industry to advise the Commission on questions concerning the automobile industry, should be seen in this context. Information on the workings of the several Task Forces is readily available. It is unfortunate that detailed information on the workings of the "high-level panel" is difficult, if not impossible, to obtain.

11. PROMOTION OF RESEARCH AND TECHNOLOGICAL DEVELOPMENT AND THE AUTOMOBILE INDUSTRY

11.1 Introduction

Article 3(m) EC prescribes that, for the purposes set out in Article 2 EC, the activities of the EC shall include the promotion of research and technological development. This is further elaborated upon in Articles 130f to 130p EC.[1] Although experts disagree on the question whether Community programmes on research and technological development, have effectively overshadowed national programmes of high technology support, there is little doubt that the role of the Community in this area has grown considerably and extends to almost every possible technological sector.[2] The automobile industry is one of the main beneficiaries of the Community's effort in the area of research and technological development. In this chapter, Articles 130f to 130p EC will first be elaborated upon (**11.2**) after which a concise description will be given of the Community measures promoting research and technological development in the automobile industry (**11.3**). Some concluding remarks will then be made (**11.4**).

11.2 Articles 130f to 130p EC

11.2.1 Objectives

Article 130f(1) EC provides that the Community shall have the objective of strengthening the scientific and technological bases of Community industry and encouraging it to become more competitive at international level, while promoting all the research activities deemed necessary by virtue of other Chapters of the EC Treaty. These objectives are formulated in broad terms and the wording indicates that this provision can serve as the legal basis for a wide variety of Community activities pursuing the Community's objectives set out in Article 130f(1) EC.

There is no doubt that the strengthening of the scientific and technological bases of Community industry is a means to encourage the competitiveness of Community industry at international level. However, the

---

[1] See Article G(38) TEU.

[2] See in this sense J. Peterson, "Research and development policy" in *The European Union and national industrial policy* (H. Kassim and A. Menon eds.), 1996, Routledge, London, at 226-227.

wording of Article 130f(1) EC, indicates that these two objectives are cumulative but distinct. One could therefore argue that Article 130f(1) EC may very well constitute the legal basis for Community activities other than those strictly related to the strengthening of the scientific and technological bases of Community industry but necessary for the encouragement of the competitiveness of Community industry at international level. Article 130f(1) EC complements Articles 3(l) and 130 EC.

The fact that the objective of strengthening the scientific and technological bases of Community industry and encouraging it to become more competitive at international level, has to be pursued "while promoting all the research activities deemed necessary by virtue of other Chapters of the EC Treaty" indicates that the Community's policy on research and technological development is first and foremost *instrumental* to the various other Community policies and activities including the strengthening of the competitiveness of its industry on the basis of Articles 3(l) and 130 EC. Article 130f(1) EC provides a legal basis for research activities "deemed necessary" in support of Community policies or activities set out in other Chapters of the EC Treaty.

11.2.2 Means

Article 130f(3) EC specifies that *all* Community activities under the EC Treaty in the area of research and technological development, including demonstration projects, shall be decided on and implemented in accordance with the provisions of Article 130f to 130p EC. This implies that activities in the area of research and technological development cannot be based on other provisions such as Articles 3(l) and 130 EC dealing with the strengthening of the competitiveness of Community industry.

Article 130f(2) EC provides that for the purpose set out in Article 130f(1) EC, the Community shall, throughout the Community, encourage undertakings, including small and medium-sized undertakings, research centres and universities in their research and technological development activities of high quality. In addition, the Community shall support their efforts to cooperate with one another, aiming, notably, at enabling undertakings to exploit the internal market potential to the full, in particular through the opening up of national public contracts, the definition of common standards and the removal of legal and fiscal obstacles to that cooperation.

Article 130g EC provides that, in pursuing these objectives, the Community shall carry out the following activities, complementing the activities carried out in the Member States:

(a) implementation of research, technological development and demonstration programmes, by promoting cooperation with and between undertakings, research centres and universities;
(b) promotion of cooperation in the field of Community research, technological development and demonstration with third countries and international organisations;
(c) the dissemination and optimisation of the results of activities in Community research, technological development and demonstration;
(d) stimulation of the training and mobility of researchers in the Community.

The word "complementing" confirms that the Member States still have the lead in the area of research and technological development.[3]

In order to ensure that national and Community policies are mutually consistent, Article 130h(1) EC prescribes that the Community and the Member States shall coordinate their research and technological development activities. Pursuant to Article 130h(2) EC, the Commission may take any useful initiative to promote such coordination.

Article 130i(1) EC obliges the Council to adopt a *multi-annual framework programme* which shall:

- establish the scientific and technological objectives to be achieved by the activities provided for in Article 130g EC and fix the relevant priorities;
- indicate the broad lines of such activities;

[3] This, notwithstanding the fact that one could argue that the words "the activities carried out in the Member States" do not necessarily imply that these activities are carried out or initiated *by* the Member States themselves. It could well be that the activities concerned are initiated by the Community and subsequently carried out in the Member States.

- fix the maximum overall amount and the detailed rules for Community financial participation in the framework programme and the respective shares in each of the activities provided for.

This framework programme shall be adopted by the Council, acting unanimously throughout the procedure referred to in Article 189b EC, after consulting the Economic and Social Committee. Article 130(i)(2) EC prescribes that the framework programme shall be adapted or supplemented as the situation changes.

Pursuant to Article 130i(3) EC, the framework programme shall be implemented through *specific programmes* developed within each activity. Each specific programme shall define the detailed rules for implementing it, fix its duration and provide for the means deemed necessary. The sum of the amounts deemed necessary, fixed in the specific programmes, may not exceed the overall maximum amount fixed for the framework programme and each activity. Article 130i(4) EC provides that these specific programmes shall be adopted by the Council, acting by a qualified majority on a proposal from the Commission and after consulting the European Parliament and the Economic and Social Committee. Article 130j EC specifies that for the implementation of the multi-annual framework programme, the Council shall (i) determine the rules for the participation of undertakings, research centres and universities, and (ii) lay down the rules governing the dissemination of research results.[4]

In implementing the multi-annual framework programme, the Community can take various *initiatives*. First of all, Article 130k EC provides that supplementary programmes may be decided on involving the participation of certain Member States only, which shall finance them subject to possible Community participation. The Council shall adopt the rules applicable to supplementary programmes, particularly as regards the dissemination of knowledge and access by other Member States.[5] Secondly, pursuant to Article

[4] Article 130o(2) EC provides that these provisions shall be adopted by the Council, acting in accordance with the procedure referred to in Article 189c EC and after consulting the Economic and Social Committee.

[5] Article 130o EC provides that these provisions shall be adopted by the Counci, acting in accordance with the procedure referred to in Article 189c EC and after consulting the Economic and Social Committee. Adoption of the supplementary programmes shall require the agreement of the Member States concerned.

130l EC, the Community may make provision, in agreement with the Member States concerned, for participation in research and development programmes undertaken by several Member States, including participation in the structures created for the execution of those programmes.[6] Thirdly, Article 130m EC specifies that the Community may make provision for cooperation in Community research, technological development and demonstration with third countries or international organisations. The detailed arrangements for such cooperation may be the subject of agreements between the Community and the third parties concerned, which shall be negotiated and concluded in accordance with Article 228 EC. Last but not least, under Article 130n EC, the Community may set up joint undertakings or any other structure necessary for the efficient execution of Community research, technological development and demonstration programmes.[7]

11.2.3 Report

Article 130p EC obliges the Commission, at the beginning of each year, to send to the European Parliament and the Council, a report with information on research and technological development activities and the dissemination of results during the previous year, and the work programme for the current year.[8]

11.3 Promotion of Research and Technological Development in the Automobile Industry

The policy of the Community on research and technological development has long been thwarted by certain Member States which were fiercely opposed to a Community policy in this area. As a result, the Commission initially tried to take advantage of crises in particular sectors, or argued public interest in

---

[6] Article 130o EC provides that these provisions shall be adopted by the Council in accordance with the procedure referred to in Article 189c EC and after consulting the Economic and Social Committee.

[7] Article 130o(1) EC provides that the provisions referred to in Article 130n EC, shall be adopted by the Council, acting unanimously on a proposal from the Commission and after consulting the European Parliament and the Economic and Social Committee.

[8] There is an annual report on research and technological development activities of the European Union on 1995 (COM(95)443 final), 1996 (COM(96)437 final) and 1997 (COM(97)373 final).

particular fields of research, in order to have certain Community initiatives in the field of research and technological development accepted by the Member States.[9] Between 1982 and 1983, the Commission made efforts to reorganise this policy of bits and pieces and came up with the more comprehensive *First Framework Programme* (1984-1987) which has been qualified as "a considerable step forward in the rationalisation of programmes already underway and in planning for the medium term, both in terms of identifying scientific and technological priorities and in planning future financial involvement".[10] The First Framework Programme had resources shifted towards research into industrial competitiveness.[11] Under the *Second Framework Programme* (1987-1991), resources were further shifted towards research into industrial innovation.[12] The Community measures on research and technological development which were to have a positive impact on the automobile industry, are reported on in the Commission communications on the automobile industry. For instance, in 1990, the Commission stressed the need for the Community's automobile industry to become more competitive and underlined that a major campaign to boost research and technological development in the automobile industry was needed at Community level. The Commission reported that it had embarked on the following cooperative research of interest to the automobile industry: BRITE/EURAM (generic manufacturing and materials technology), BCR (reference materials and methods), ESPRIT (computer assisted design and manufacture), JOULE (combustion), and DRIVE in combination with the EUREKA-project "Prometheus" (covering computer applications in road traffic management and road safety).[13]

The Commission announced that this work was to be continued and

---

[9] See in this sense L. Guzzetti, *A brief history of European Union research policy* (European Commission, Science research development - Studies 5), October 1995, EUR-OP, Brussels.

[10] *Ibidem*, at 84.

[11] Guzzetti, *supra* note 9, at 84, reported that between 1982 and 1985, the spending on research into industrial competitiveness rose from 17% to 32%.

[12] Guzzetti, *supra* note 9, at 123, reported that the Community invested by that time more than 60% of its research budget in research into industrial innovation.

[13] Communication from the Commission "A Single Community Motor-vehicle market", SEC(89)2118 final, 18 January 1990 ("1990 Communication"), at 7-9.

extended in the context of the *Third Framework Programme* (1990-1994) which provided for the continued promotion of generic technologies and for major integrated projects designed to incorporate new technologies into design and production processes. The latter were to enable users and suppliers to (i) agree on common objectives such as "clean cars", (ii) define necessary technologies and (iii) agree on the precise roles to be played by industry, governments and the Community.[14] About 10% of the amounts expended under the Third Framework Programme were of direct or indirect interest to the automobile industry. The automobile industry was a particularly active user of the BRITE/EURAM, ESPRIT, DRIVE and JOULE programmes.[15]

In 1992, the Commission stressed the instrumental use of the Community's policy on research and technological development when it announced that the Community needed to *reorient* its policy on research and technological development with a view to making Community industry more competitive. According to the Commission, the main problem was not the level of expenditure but the lack of ability to translate research and technological development activities into innovative products and processes and market share. The Commission announced that its conventional programmes would have to take greater account of market expectations and would be focused on certain topics corresponding to clearly identified industrial objectives, and that it would introduce a number of technological priority projects ("TP projects") focused on developing key technologies and achieving a better return on research and technological development investment in terms of industrial competitiveness. These TP projects were to rest on increased cooperation between businesses on the precompetitive level being all those research and technological development activities which businesses can carry out together before developing and marketing their own individual products. According to the Commission, this type of cooperation can be compatible with competition rules. The Commission noted that block exemption Regulation 418/85 on research and development

[14] *Ibidem*, at 7-9.

[15] Communication from the European Commission to the Council and to the European Parliament on the European Union automobile industry, COM(94)49 final, 23 February 1994 ("1994 Communication"), at 22.

agreements, favours under certain conditions, cooperation on research and technological development, and joint exploitation of research findings.[16]

Under the *Fourth Framework Programme* (1994-1998), the focus would remain on generic, precompetitive research with a multi-sectoral impact and would include improved access to programmes for small and medium-size enterprises.[17] The latter was of particular importance to the automobile industry as component suppliers were increasingly required to assume greater technological competences in the light of the restructuring of the value chain. The Commission identified several research activities under the Fourth Framework Programme which would be of major interest to the automobile industry. These activities included a variety of areas such as (i) information technologies (*e.g.* MICROMOBILE and Telematics), (ii) industrial technologies (*e.g.* Targeted Research Actions on Environmentally Friendly Vehicle Technologies, CRAFT and Technologies for Transport Means), (iii) clean and efficient energy technologies (coordinated with EPEFE (Auto-Oil) industry project),[18] (iv) environment and (v) education and training.[19]

In 1995, the Commission set up a number of Task Forces for industrial

---

[16] Communication from the Commission to the Council, the European Parliament and the Economic and Social Committee "The European motor vehicle industry: Situation, issues at stake, and proposals for action", COM(92)166 final, 8 May 1992, at 10-13. Council resolution of 17 June 1992 on the European motor vehicle industry, OJ 1992, C178/6, par. I-8, recognized the need for the Community and the Member States to optimize research efforts and intensify synergy under Community research programmes and Eureka projects.

[17] See in this context "EC research funding - A guide for applicants" on the Fourth Framework Programme 1994-1998, 4th edition, 1996, EUR-OP, Brussels.

[18] See Commission Communication to the European Parliament and the Council on a future strategy for the control of atmospheric emissions from road transport taking into account the results of the Auto/Oil Programme, COM(96)248, 18 June 1996. See also Written Question 607/97 (Bolea), OJ 1997, C319/131; Written Question 608/97 (Bolea), OJ 1997, C319/132; Written Question 609/97 (Bolea), OJ 1997, C319/132; Written Question 610/97 (Bolea), OJ 1997, C319/133; Written Question 611/97 (Bolea), OJ 1997, C319/133, and Written Question 612/97 (Bolea), OJ 1997, C319/134. *FT*, "GM and Amoco unveil fuels link-up", 5 February 1998, at 23, confirms the fact that car manufacturers and oil companies are stepping up efforts to co-operate on cleaner fuels.

[19] 1994 Communication, *supra* note 15, at 22-25. See "Research and technological development activities of the European Union - Annual report 1995", COM(95)443 final, 28 September 1995. See also Council resolution of 16 May 1994 on the automobile industry, OJ 1994, C149/1; Written Question 3453/93 (Piquer), OJ 1994, C279/57, and Written Question 629/94 (Denys), OJ 1994, C306/40.

research which includes a Task Force "*The car of the Future*".[20] These Task Forces were set up in an effort to help research to translate its achievements into practical results, and to match the Community's technological competitors.[21] According to the Commission, the initiative to set up a Task Force "The car of the Future" was designed to better coordinate and focus research activities in the area of the ultra low and zero emission cars of the future and the associated infrastructure for road telematics, refuelling and recharging, and served to assure regulatory stability and coherence through better coordination and planning of research activities with regulatory policy. The Commission leaves it up to the automobile industry to come up with joint research proposals. In addition, the Commission supports the needs of the automobile industry as set out in the EUCAR Master Plan for research and technological development.[22]

---

[20] See *Agence Europe*, "Mrs Cresson and Mr Bangemann coordinate industrial and research initiatives for the Car of Tomorrow, the New Generation Aircraft, the Train of the Future, Multimedia, certain vaccines", 13-14 March 1995, at 8. See also "Research-Industry Task Forces - An overview" (European Commission - D.G. XII Science Research Development), 1997, EUR-OP, Brussels, at 24-28.

[21] Guzzetti, *supra* note 9, at 177. The initiative to set up a Task Force "The car of the Future" is similar to the American industry-led sectoral initiative to build a prototype of a New Generation Vehicle. See 1994 Communication, *supra* note 15, at 21.

[22] Communication from the Commission to the Council, the European Parliament, the Economic and Social Committee and the Committee of the Regions "European automobile industry 1996", COM(96)327 final, at 10-11. See "Car of Tomorrow - Plan of action" (European Commission - Task Force "Car of Tomorrow"), December 1995, and the newsletters published by the Task Force, for more information on the Task Force "Car of Tomorrow".

The activities of the Task force contributed to the setting of priorities for research under the *Fifth Framework Programme* (1998-2002).[23]

11.4 Concluding Remarks

The Community policy on research and technological development is to a large extent used for the strengthening of the competitiveness of Community industry. According to experts, the Commission is pushing research efforts closer and closer to the market, to the point where the Community is funding industrial as opposed to scientific research. In theory, the Community's policy on research and technological development is a horizontal policy. In practice, however, the policy has sectoral characteristics. For instance, the Task Force "The Car of Tomorrow" is to improve the Community's ability to meet the needs of the automobile industry, to help translate research achievements into practical results and to match the Community's technological competitors. Again, in what seems to be an effort to keep up with the U.S.A. and Japan, the Community tries to strengthen the competitiveness of the automobile industry by actively assisting the automobile industry within the Community in identifying and finding solutions for the shortcomings of its research and technological development policy, and by providing assistance in anticipating new

[23] See Second amended Proposal for a European Parliament and Council Decision concerning the fifth framework programme of the European Community for research, technological development and demonstration activities (1998 to 2002), COM(98)8 final, OJ 1998, C106/1. See also *Agence Europe*, "ECU 233 million for research in field of transport and basic industrial research (BRITE-EURAM III Programme) - Conference on 5th Framework Programme", 15 October 1997, at 14; "Commission provides details on scientific content of specific programmes for the period 1999-2002", 6 November 1997, at 6; "Ministers progress in preparing 5th Framework Programme - First exchange of views on budget", 10-11 November 1997; "Mrs Cresson expresses concern about the link maintained by Spain between new Framework Programme and future EU financing - Agreements on several guidelines, interim conclusions on management", 14 November 1997, at 8; "Commission publishes its proposal on rules for participation in the new Framework Programme and diffusion of results", 10 January 1998, at 10; "Spain agrees global allocation should be fixed for 5th Framework Programme, it being agreed that the amount for 2000 and 2002 could be renegotiated", 14 February 1998, at 4, and *FT*, "The fifth element", 15 January 1998, at 21.

technological developments. The need for the Community's automobile industry to strengthen its competitiveness is of overriding importance within the context of the promotion of research and technological development in the automobile industry.

12. EDUCATION AND VOCATIONAL TRAINING AND THE AUTOMOBILE INDUSTRY

12.1 Introduction

Article 3(p) EC prescribes that, for the purposes set out in Article 2 EC, the activities of the Community shall include a contribution to education and training of quality and to the so-called "flowering" of the cultures of the Member States. This is further elaborated upon with regard to education and vocational training, in Articles 123 to 125 EC on the European Social Fund, and Articles 126 and 127 EC on education, vocational training and youth.[1] Community measures based on these provisions have been relevant to the automobile industry in view of the radical shift towards lean production which requires different and often more advanced skills of workers. In this chapter, Articles 123 to 127 EC will first be elaborated upon (**12.2**). Subsequently, the significance of Community measures on education and vocational training for the automobile industry, will be looked at (**12.3**). This chapter will come to an end with a number of concluding remarks (**12.4**).

12.2 Articles 123 to 127 EC

12.2.1 The European Social Fund

Article 123 EC specifies that the European Social Fund is established in order to improve employment opportunities for workers in the internal market and to contribute thereby to raising the standard of living. Furthermore, the European Social Fund shall aim to render the employment of workers easier and to increase their geographical and occupational mobility within the Community, and to facilitate their adaptation to industrial changes and to changes in production systems, in particular through vocational training and retraining.[2] In addition, Article 124 EC provides that the European Social Fund shall be administered by the Commission, assisted by a Committee presided over by a member of the Commission and composed of representatives of Governments,

---

[1] See Article G(36) TEU.

[2] The European Social Fund is one of the Structural Funds. See in this context Articles 130a to 130e EC. See also Regulation 2084/93, OJ 1993, L193/39; Regulation 2082/93, OJ 1993, L193/20, and Regulation 2081/93, OJ 1993, L193/5.

trade unions and employers' organisations. According to Article 125 EC, the Council shall adopt implementing decisions relating to the European Social Fund.[3]

12.2.2 Quality Education and Vocational Training

Article 126(1) EC provides that the Community shall contribute to the development of *quality education* by encouraging cooperation between Member States and, if necessary, by supporting and supplementing their action, while fully respecting the responsibility of the Member States for the content of teaching and the organisation of educational systems and their cultural and linguistic diversity. The wording of Article 126(1) EC indicates that the prime responsibility for the development of quality education is left in the hands of the Member States. The Community has a supporting role only. The Community's role is further defined in Article 126(2) EC which provides that Community action shall be aimed at (i) developing the European dimension in education, particularly through the teaching and dissemination of the languages of the Member States, (ii) encouraging mobility of students and teachers, *inter alia* by encouraging the academic recognition of diplomas and periods of study, (iii) promoting cooperation between educational establishments, (iv) developing exchanges of information and experience on issues common to the education systems of the Member States, (v) encouraging the development of youth exchanges and of exchanges of socio-educational instructors, and (vi) encouraging the development of distance education. In addition, Article 126(3) EC specifies that the Community and the Member States shall foster co-operation with third countries and the competent international organisations in the field of education, in particular the Council of Europe. Article 126(4) EC provides that in order to contribute to the achievement of these objectives, the

---

[3] Pursuant to Article 124 EC, the Council can do so acting in accordance with the procedure referred to in Article 189c EC and after consulting the Economic and Social Committee.

Council shall adopt incentive measures,[4] excluding any harmonisation of the laws and regulations of the Member States, and adopt recommendations.[5]

Pursuant to Article 127(1) EC, the Community shall implement a *vocational training* policy which shall support and supplement the action of the Member States, while fully respecting the responsibility of the Member States for the content and origination of vocational training. The wording clearly indicates that the prime responsibility for vocational training remains in the hands of the Member States. Although the Community is in a supporting role, it is competent to implement a vocational training policy as such in order to "support and supplement the action of the Member States". The Community's competence to act on the basis of Article 127 EC seems somewhat wider than its competence to take action on the basis of Article 126 EC.[6] Pursuant to Article 127(2) EC, Community action shall aim to (i) facilitate adaptation to industrial changes, in particular through vocational training and retraining, (ii) improve initial and continuing vocational training in order to facilitate vocational integration and reintegration into the labour market, (iii) facilitate access to vocational training and encourage mobility of instructors and trainees and particularly young people, (iv) stimulate cooperation on training between educational or training establishments and firms, and (v) develop exchanges of information and experience on issues common to the training systems of the Member States. In addition, Article 127(3) EC specifies that the Community and the Member States shall foster cooperation with third countries and the competent international organisations in the sphere of vocational training. Article 127(4) EC provides that the Council shall adopt measures to contribute to the achievement of the objectives referred to in Article 127 EC, excluding

[4] Pursuant to Article 126(4) EC, the Council can do so acting in accordance with the procedure referred to in Article 189b, after consulting the Economic and Social Committee and the Committee of the Regions.

[5] Pursuant to Article 126(4) EC, the Council can do so acting by a qualified majority on a proposal from the Commission.

[6] See in a similar sense L.A. Geelhoed in P.J.G. Kapteyn and P. VerLoren van Themaat, *Inleiding tot het recht van de Europese Gemeenschappen - Na Maastricht*, 5th edition, 1995, Kluwer, Deventer, at 631.

any harmonisation of the laws and regulations of the Member States.[7]

12.3 Community Measures on Education and Vocational Training and the Automobile Industry

In 1990, the Commission recognized that as the automobile industry within the Community had to become more competitive in order to be able to face up to international competition, major quantitative, qualitative and structural changes were to be expected on the employment front. The Commission noted that employment in the automobile industry was going down and new lean production methods were introduced leading to an important change in the structure of the qualifications required.[8] In fact, the shift from mass production to lean production was a crucial step in the process of improving the competitiveness of the automobile industry within the Community. However, this shift was only to be possible if there were sufficient workers available with the skills to participate in the lean production process. Workers had to be educated and (re)trained in order to make it possible for them to participate in the lean production process.

The Community measures on education and vocational training which were to have a positive impact on the automobile industry within the Community, are reported on in the Commission communications on the automobile industry. For instance, in 1992, the Commission noted that Article

[7] Article 127(4) EC provides that the Council can do so acting in accordance with the procedure referred to in Article 189c EC and after consulting the Economic and Social Committee.

[8] Communication from the Commission "A Single Community Motor-vehicle market", SEC(89)2118 final, 18 January 1990, at 10-11. According to the Commission, in view of the essential tasks to be performed as regards quality and productivity, measures adopted in the field of training and employment in close cooperation with both sides of industry, had to concentrate on (i) adaptation of professional profiles, (ii) expansion of new forms of in-service training or redeployment as part of the COMETT II/EUROTECNET programmes and the draft FORCE programme after this has been adopted by the Council, (iii) dissemination and exchange of information on social innovations in contract policy for the most effective management of future personnel and job requirements, (iv) feasibility of a programme for the transfer of new know-how acquired in the installation of flexible production systems, and (v) development of new openings for skilled jobs in the context of the flanking policies and missions to be affected by the structural Funds.

123 EC constitutes very wide terms of reference for a *human resources policy* which includes the possibility of using the European Social Fund to make it easier for workers to adapt to industrial changes and to changes in production systems, in particular through vocational training and retraining. The Commission announced that it would redefine Objectives 3 and 4 of the Structural Funds so that a major effort could be devoted throughout the Community to vocational training and retraining in anticipation of industrial and technological changes, and would permit "action of the kind desired by the motor industry even outside the regions which have priority in the context of Community regional policy".[9] Although the Commission announced a general and *horizontal* approach to be applied to industry as a whole which precluded specific Community assistance for training and retraining limited to the automobile industry, the Commission made it very clear that in view of the changes taking place in the automobile industry, it expected the latter to benefit from Community action to (i) anticipate the effects on employment caused by these changes and the resulting adaptation problems, (ii) make changes economically efficient and socially acceptable, and (iii) help in retraining and redeployment. The Commission confirmed that it examined ways to improve its vocational training programmes FORCE, COMETT, EUROTECNET and PETRA, and to increase their effect on policies and activities at national level.[10]

In 1994, the Commission reported that the automobile industry had been a beneficiary of loans granted by the European Investment Bank and the actions taken by the European Regional Development Fund and the European Social Fund in support of productive investments and vocational training to various degrees in industries concentrated in the regions eligible for such support. The Commission took the position that a particular emphasis, regardless of region, had to be given to the development of human resources and qualified the latter as a key area of industrial policy. The Commission took this position in view of the fact that measures in the field of (re)training to adapt to industrial change and progress in production systems, enhance

[9] Communication from the Commission to the Council, the European Parliament and the Economic and Social Committee "The European motor vehicle industry: Situation, issues at stake, and proposals for action", COM(92)166 final, 8 May 1992, at 13-14.

[10] *Ibidem*.

competitiveness of firms and avoid unemployment at the same time. The Commission reported in detail on the relevance for the automobile industry of the activities of the Task Force Human Resources, the Community initiatives ADAPT and PME,[11] and the new Objective 4 of the Structural Funds on the facilitation of the adaptation of workers to industrial change and to changes in production systems. In addition, the Commission announced certain initiatives such as the creation of a transnational training network for the automobile industry within the framework of the FORCE-programme. Although the Commission stressed that Objective 4 is based on a *horizontal* approach and is not limited to particular sectors or regions, the Commission expected the automobile industry to benefit and specified that it had already organised meetings in order to obtain precise information about the automobile's restructuring and training needs.[12]

The Commission reported in 1996 that the new Leonardo da Vinci vocational training programme (1995-1999), which was set up as a "European laboratory of innovation" in the field of vocational training, had entered into force, and that the transnational training network for the automobile industry within the context of FORCE resulted in 53 model projects under the headings "Training for new work structures", "Training for co-makership (Manufacturer/Supplier relations)", and "Learning while working/on-the-job training".[13] The Commission pointed at the growing need for the exchange of information, experience, and training material and expressed the hope that the European network of training projects as developopped by ACEA and CLEPA, as a follow-up to the FORCE-network can serve as a clearing house for the

[11] See in this context Article 12(5) of Regulation 2081/93, *supra* note 2, and Article 11(1) and (2) of Regulation 2082/93, *supra* note 2, on Community initiatives. See also "The future of Community initiatives under the Structural Funds", COM(94)46 final/2, 25 March 1994.

[12] Communication from the European Commission to the Council and to the European Parliament on the "European Union automobile industry", COM(94)49 final, 23 February 1994, at 16-20. See also Council Resolution of 16 May 1994 on the automobile industry, OJ 1994, C149/1.

[13] Upon request, the Technical Assistance Office to the European Commission for the Leonardo da Vinci-program provides interested parties with information on the various projects in the sector of the automobile industry which were selected under the Leonarda da Vinci-program.

exchange of information and as the starting point for common training approaches of the industry.[14]

12.4 Concluding Remarks

The Community's policy on education and training is an instrument to strengthen the competitiveness of Community industry. Although this policy is a horizontal policy, the Commission's communications on the automobile industry confirm that specific Community measures were taken to facilitate the adaptation of this industry to the important shift from mass production to lean production. The introduction of lean production techniques requires more advanced skills of workers. In order to strengthen the competitiveness of its automobile industry and avoid unemployment, the Community has taken an active role in facilitating the (re)training of workers in order to have them adapt to the new manufacturing techniques.

[14] Communication from the Commission to the Council, the European Parliament, the Economic and Social Committee and the Committee of the Regions "European automobile industry - 1996", COM(96)327 final, 10 July 1996, at 11-12.

PART III - CONCLUSIONS

13. GENERAL CONCLUSIONS: EUROPEAN COMMUNITY LAW AND THE AUTOMOBILE INDUSTRY

The following general conclusions can be drawn from this study on European Community law and the automobile industry.

I. First of all, the study shows that the Community and the Commission in particular, is increasingly making use of the various competences set out in the EC Treaty, to intervene in the automobile industry.

The EC Treaty provides for a Community based upon a mixed economy that combines a free market economy with a great variety of Community interventions. According to the EC Treaty, the forces of the market mechanism have to play a central role in the economic process yet, at the same time, the Community has ample competence to intervene in the workings of the market mechanism within the context of the policies and activities listed in Articles 3 and 3a EC. This study confirms that legal measures are important instruments for such intervention. At times, the Commission even resorts to disputed means such as the so-called "Elements of Consensus" between the Community and Japan on trade in cars.

After a period of Community intervention with an emphasis on market integration, policy integration has become much more prominent within the Community. Whereas in the context of market integration, the Community focused first and foremost on the creation and implementation of a Community legal framework that enables and guarantees the free movement of goods, services and capital, the freedom of establishment and the maintenance of undistorted competition, efforts to achieve policy integration led to the development and implementation of Community policies that directly intervene in the workings of the market mechanism in the automobile industry. Market integration is aimed at removing barriers to an efficient allocation of resources. It leaves it up to industry itself to develop strategies to survive and profit from the possibility to operate on a market that comes close(r) to being one single market instead of having to confront a number of domestic markets separated by trade barriers. Policy integration, on the other hand, is aimed at facilitating, coordinating, stimulating and even initiating particular strategies. Since the entry into force of the EU Treaty, the Community is in a legal position to step up initiatives for the development and implementation of Community policies such as those on the strengthening of the competitiveness of Community industry, the promotion of research and technological development, education and vocational training. In fact, the Community keeps a close eye on developments in industry and publishes detailed bi-annual Commission reports on the automobile industry that describe market and production developments, provide an evaluation of competitiveness and elaborate on the Community's policy on the automobile industry with regard to the promotion of intangible investment, ensurance of strong and fair competition, development of industrial co-operation and modernisation of the role of public authorities, and the creation of a stable and beneficial business environment.

A process has been set in motion which makes the "visible hand" of the Community ever more prominent next to the "invisible hand" of the market mechanism. This process reinforces the role of public authorities like the Commission and contributes to the further politisation of the workings of the automobile industry. It seems that the long-term benefits of letting the "invisible hand" of the market mechanism take its course is impeded upon by the Community's inclination to intervene through the "visible hand" in the economic process in pursuit of what can often be considered mostly short-term political interests. In particular, the study indicates that the Commission is increasingly intervening in an effort to strengthen the competitiveness of the Community's automobile industry. This is alarming since it is at least doubtful whether a public authority is able, let alone capable, of doing a better job at initiating and stimulating the measures and strategies necessary to improve competitiveness, than the automobile industry itself. On the contrary, it is submitted that past experiences have shown that public intervention through means such as import tariffs, quota's, voluntary export restraints and state aid measures, have in fact impeded upon the competitiveness of the Community's automobile industry. In simple terms, the automobile industry grew too comfortable and complacent behind the walls of the national fortress that provided protection against international competition.

It should be kept in mind, however, that the Community does not "regulate" the automobile industry. There is no "regulatory" Community regime for the automobile industry such as there is for agriculture. Nevertheless, the study confirms that the Community in general, and the Commission in particular, has an important impact on the automobile industry through the implementation of Community legal measures within the context of the policies and activities set out in Articles 3 and 3a EC. Over the years, the Community has created a formidable body of general and industry-specific legal measures including the highly technical Community type-approval procedure, the block exemption Regulation 1475/95 for the distribution and servicing of cars, and the 1998 Framework for state aid to the motor vehicle industry. This body of legal measures constitutes an important part of the Community legal framework in which the automobile industry has to operate. It not only facilitates but also re-directs or even restricts the workings of the market mechanism in the automobile industry.

At times, the Community engages in re-directing the market mechanism in pursuit of certain public interests. For instance, the Community partly develops and implements a policy on the protection of the environment and consumer safety, through the introduction of, and amendments to, the technical Community directives within the context of the Community type-approval procedure. The introduction and amendments to these technical directives is politically very sensitive. In view of the seemingly ever increasing number and use of cars within the Community, it is to be expected that the Community will further intervene in order to protect the environment. Notwithstanding the industry's initiative to come up with a voluntary undertaking regarding a reduction of carbon dioxide emissions, it is highly unlikely that the Community can leave it up to the automobile industry itself to take the costly measures that are necessary to reduce the various polluting effects of the use of cars. It is also up to the Community to contribute to negotiations with third countries such as the U.S.A. and Japan, in an effort to agree on effective measures that will protect the environment and harmonize the different environmental requirements that constitute barriers to trade and distort competition within the automobile industry. The Community has become more interventionist as a result of the fact that, in certain respects, it has taken over this role from the Member States. For instance, some Member States took measures against the import of Japanese cars; now the Community is doing so within the context of its common commercial policy in which it has exclusive competence. Policy integration also stimulated Community intervention. The Community, and the Commission in particular, is well aware of the fact that it is taking on a more interventionist role. In its 1996 Communication on the European Automobile Industry, the Commission pointed out that although the achievement of competitiveness on a global scale is primarily the responsibility of industry itself, public authorities have a key role to play in creating a favourable business environment within which industry can prosper, since high value added employment in the long run can only be sustained by a competitive industry. The Commission recognized that "regulatory pressure" on industry has become more intense as public authorities have been obliged to react to public pressure demanding the "further regulation and control of the industry" and noted that all these (initiatives for) measures collectively amount to "a quite formidable system of regulation or potential regulation on the industry" which, taken as a whole, profoundly affects the business environment in which the automobile industry functions in Europe and, indirectly, in third markets.[1] Following the American example and trying to improve both the credibility and effectiveness of Community intervention, a so-called "high-level panel" of the Commission and various actors in the automobile industry has been set up in order to discuss and coordinate initiatives by the Community and the automobile industry. Is there any better indication of an intervening Community in the automobile industry?

II. Secondly, the study indicates that this development towards an increasingly interventionist Community is further stimulated by the process of internationalisation or even globalisation of the world economy.

The process of internationalisation or even globalisation, diminishes the role of national economic law. States have lost some of their grip on multi-national manufacturers which are now in a position to shop around for the best conditions. States compete for direct investment as manufacturers will locate new production sites in the state that offers the most attractive socio-economic conditions such as low wages and flexible workers. A considerable part of the production of cars is already taking place in areas with cheap labour such as Eastern Europe and Mexico. This development evidently constitutes a threat to employment at production sites within the Community. The process of internationalisation or even globalisation, highlighted the urgent need for a

[1] Communication from the Commission to the Council, the European Parliament, the Economic and Social Committee and the Committee of the Regions on the "European Automobile Industry", 10 July 1996, COM(96) 327 final, at 20.

dramatic improvement in the competitiveness of the Community's automobile industry. A shift had to be made from mass production to lean production techniques in an effort to keep up with the Japanese and American automobile industry. Costs had to be brought down and quality and efficiency had to be improved. The manufacturing process has become truly international; products are assembled from parts that come from the best, and cheapest, suppliers all over the world. This shift towards lean and, according to some experts, virtual production has important socio-economic consequences such as lay-offs and the need for workers with better skills. The fact that studies indicate that competitiveness is crucial for the overall socio-economic well-being of the Community, further stimulates the Community to actively intervene in the industry.

Member States have lost some of the grip on their national economies. This leads to the question as to whether this lost control should, and indeed can, be regained by the Community within the legal system of the EC Treaty. The actions taken by the Community within the context of policies such as those on the strengthening of competitiveness of the Community's industry, the promotion of research and technological development, and education and vocational training, indicate that the Community is presently making an effort to regain some degree of control within the context of the EC Treaty in order to strengthen its automobile industry and thereby its economy. It should be added that, at times, the Community seems to intervene on the side of its automobile industry in order to meet the challenge of the American and Japanese authorities assisting their respective industries. It is probable that in view of the internationalisation or even globalisation of the world economy, the role of Community law will also change and diminish in the long term. International economic law will become even more important.

III. Thirdly, the study shows that there is a need for a much more unambiguous, coherent and transparent legal framework in which the automobile industry has to operate.

Community intervention does not necessarily lead to an unambiguous legal framework since Member States have their own national policies and do not always agree with, nor support, Community intervention in the automobile industry. Community intervention could very well be to the detriment of their domestic industry. In addition, there is a great variety of conflicting interests in the automobile industry itself.

Many, if not all, legal measures taken by the Community within the context of the policies and activities referred to in Articles 3 and 3a EC specifically dealing with the automobile industry, are the outcome of conflicts of interest between the various actors and interested parties in this industry and tend to be the result of political compromises. There are even examples of public conflicts between and within Community institutions themselves, during decision-making processes. The discussion on Community measures to decrease the substantial differences in price for the same model in different Member States, and the fierce debate on the harmonisation of design rights, are good examples. These conflicts of interest often lead to ambiguous texts and a lack of transparency in the decision-making process. At times, one can even doubt whether ambiguous compromises like the "Elements of Consensus" between the Community and Japan, remain within the legal boundaries set by the EC Treaty and GATT. The lack of transparency in areas such as state aid and the control of concentrations and the different forms of cooperation in the automobile industry, is a serious problem that impedes upon the credibility of the Community's decision-making process and obstructs public scrutiny of Community measures. In particular in the areas mentioned above, in which the Commission has a wide margin of discretion, transparency should be improved.

According to Buigues, Jacquemin and Sapir, "all public authorities must be concerned by the problem of coherence among their policies, be they micro or macroeconomic" in view of the fact that "[c]ontradictions between them lead to inefficiencies of each instrument, put into question their credibility and create a climate of insecurity for private as well as public actors" and "[c]onversely, exploiting the possible complementarity between the various public policies can correct each others' specific deficiencies, facilitate their enforcement and increase institutional credibility".[2] On several occasions, the Commission has recognized that there is a need for some kind of coordination of both the development and implementation of its policies and activities with

[2] P. Buigues, A. Jacquemin and A. Sapir, "Introduction: Complementarities and conflicts in EC microeconomic policies", in *European policies on competition, trade and industry* (P. Buigues, A. Jacquemin and A. Sapir eds.), 1995, Edward Elgar, Aldershot, at xi.

regard to the automobile industry. For instance, while preparing the text of block exemption Regulation 1475/95, the Commission noted that it would take into account the contribution of the selective and exclusive distribution system (competition policy) to the efficient management of the implementation of the "Elements of Consensus" between Japan and the Community (common commercial policy). It should be emphasized, however, that there is a tension between the need to coordinate policies and activities in order to achieve a coherent legal framework, and the legal possibilities to do so within the context of a particular policy or activity. For instance, it is highly doubtful whether the implementation of the "Elements of Consensus" between Japan and the Community can play a role within the context of the Community's competition policy. Admittedly, it must be tempting for the Commission to take the implementation of the Community's arrangement with Japan into consideration while applying the competition rules. However, as elaborated upon in this study, the legality of such a form of coordination between different policies is doubtful.

Furthermore, the detailed bi-annual Commission reports on the automobile industry confirm that in particular the Community's policy on the strengthening of the competitiveness of Community industry has important implications for various other Community policies. For instance, the Community's common commercial policy is used as an instrument to strengthen the competitiveness of the automobile industry by limiting imports of Japanese cars, and by enhancing possibilities for exports and facilitating access to markets in third countries. Another example is the Community's competition policy which is not only geared towards the maintenance of undistorted competition but also towards other Community interests such as the removal of trade barriers and the strengthening of the competitiveness of Community industry.

The study confirms that the automobile industry within the Community is going through a difficult period. There is a structural over-capacity, new manufacturers are still trying to enter the market, employment goes down, and more concentrations and cooperations can be expected. In view of its importance for the socio-economic well-being of the Community and the Member States, it is understandable that the Community wants to contribute to the process of adaptation of its automobile industry to the quickly changing market conditions. Nevertheless, it is first and foremost up to the automobile industry itself, to develop and implement strategies that will allow its survival on an increasingly competitive global market. Past experiences justify the expectation that increasing Community intervention in the automobile industry will only further politicise and thereby complicate the workings of the automobile industry. On the long term, this is not in the interest of the automobile industry, nor of the Community itself.

SELECTIVE BIBLIOGRAPHY

Abbamonte G.B., "Market economy investor principle: A legal analysis of an economic problem", [1996] 3 ECLR, at 258-268

Abo T., "The Japanese production system" in *States against markets* (R. Boyer and D. Drache eds.), 1996, Routledge, London

ACEA, "The machine is getting leaner", *ACEA - The European Automakers*, January 1997

* "End of life vehicles: Commission proposal weakens Government/Industry consensus", Newsletter, September 1997, no. 45

* "Is the climate changing as Kyoto approaches?", Newsletter, October 1997, no. 46, at 1-3.

* "ACEA calls for limits on sulphur in fuels", Newsletter, November 1997, no. 47, at 11

* "The European automobile manufacturers commit to substantial CO2 emission reductions from new passenger cars", Press Release, 29 July 1998

Allen, R.E. (ed.), *The Concise Oxford Dictionary of Current English*, 8th edition, 1990, Clarendon Press, Oxford

Audretsch D.B., *The market and the state*, 1989, Harvester Wheatsheaf, New York

Barents R. in P.J.G. Kapteyn and P. VerLoren van Themaat, *Inleiding tot het recht van de Europese Gemeenschappen - Na Maastricht*, 5th edition, 1995, Kluwer, Deventer

* "Milieu en interne markt", SEW 1 (1993) at 20-21

Barber B.R., *Jihad vs. McWorld*, 1995, Times Books, New York

Barnet R.J. and Cavanagh J., *Global dreams: Imperial corporations and the new world order*, 1994, Simon & Schuster, New York

Barnevik-Report to the President of the European Commission, the Prime Ministers and Heads of State "Enhancing European competitiveness", Competitiveness advisory group, December 1996

Bellamy C. and Child G., *Common Market Law of Competition* (V. Rose ed.), 4th edition, 1993, Sweet & Maxwell, London

Berg H., "Motorcars: Between growth and protectionism" in *The structure of European industry* (H.W. de Jong ed.), 3rd revised edition, 1993, Kluwer, Dordrecht

Bernard N., "The future of European economic law in the light of the principle of subsidiarity", 33 CML Rev. at 633-666.

Berrisch G., *Der völkerrechtliche Status der Europäischen Wirtschaftsgemeinschaft im GATT*, 1992, Florentz

Bhaskar K., *Innovation in the EC automotive industry - An analysis from the perspective of state aid policy*, April 1988, Luxembourg, EUR-OP

* and the Motor industry research unit, *The effect of different state aid measures on intra-Community*

competition - Exemplified by the case of the automotive industry, March 1990, Luxembourg, EUR-OP

Bleckmann A., "Art. 5 EWG-Vertrag und die Gemeinschaftstreue", DVBl. 1 July 1976, at 483-487

Blokker N.M., *International regulation of world trade in textiles*, 1989, Martinus Nijhoff Publishers, Dordrecht

* "GATT en vrijwillige exportbeperkingen; het panelrapport over Japanse halfgeleiders", SEW 2 (1989) February, at 90-104

Bongardt A., "The automotive industry: Supply relations in context" in *The structure of European industry* (H.W. de Jong ed.), 3rd revised edition, 1993, Kluwer, Dordrecht

Boot R. and Schmeits A., "Overheidsingrijpen in de industriefinanciering", ESB 13-11-1996, at 928

Bourgeois J.H.J. and Demaret P., "The working of EC policies on competition, industry and trade: a legal analysis" in *European policies on competition, trade and industry* (P. Buigues, A. Jacquemin and A. Sapir eds.), 1995, Edward Elgar, Aldershot

* "The Uruguay Round of GATT: Some general comments from an EC standpoint" in *The European Union and world trade law: After the GATT Uruguay Round* (N. Emiliou and D. O'Keeffe eds.), 1996, Wiley, Chicester

Bouterse R.B., *Competition and Integration - What Goals Count?* (European Monographs No. 8), 1994, Kluwer, Deventer

Bos D.I., *Marktwerking en regulering*, 1995, Onderzoeksreeks Directie Marktwerking, Ministerie van Economische Zaken

Boyer R., "State and market - A new engagement for the twenty-first century?" in *States against markets* (R. Boyer and D. Drache eds.), 1996, Routledge, London

* and Drache D., "Introduction" in *States against markets* (R. Boyer and D. Drache eds.), 1996, Routledge, London

Brittan L. (Guest Editorial), 31 CML Rev. at 229

Brogan H., *The Penguin History of the United States of America*, 1990, Penguin Books, London

Brown A., "Distinguishing between concentrative and co-operative joint ventures: Is it getting any easier?", [1996] 4 ECLR, at 240-249

Brown L.R., Flavin C. and Norman C., *Running on Empty - The Future of the Automobile in an Oil Short World*, 1979, W.W. Norton & Company, New York

Bronckers M.C.E.J., "A legal analysis of protectionist measures affecting Japanese imports into the European Community - Revisited" in *Protectionism and the European Community* (E.L.M. Völker ed.), 2nd edition, 1986, Kluwer, Deventer

Buigues P., Jacquemin A. and Sapir A., "Introduction: Complementarities and conflicts in EC microeconomic policies", in *European policies on competition, trade and industry* (P. Buigues, A. Jacquemin and A. Sapir eds.), 1995, Edward Elgar, Aldershot

SELECTIVE BIBLIOGRAPHY

Carle J. and Johnsson M., "Benchmarking and E.C. competition law", [1998] E.C.L.R. at 74-84

Carlin F.M., "Vertical restraints: Time for change?", [1996] 5 ECLR, at 283-288

Carreau D., Flory T. and Juillard P., *Manuel-Droit International Economique*, 3rd edition, 1990, Librairie Generale de droit et de jurisprudence Paris

Carreras A.C., *La Distribucion de Automoviles en la Comunidad Europea*, 1997, Tirant lo Blanch, Valencia

Castillo de la Torre F., "The Status of GATT in EC Law, Revisited - The consequences of the judgment on the banana import regime for the enforcement of the Uruguay Round Agreements", 29 J.W.T. 1 at 53-68

Chandler Jr. A.D., *Giant enterprise*, 1964, Harcourt, Brace & World Inc., New York

Clark J.M., *Toward a Concept of Workable Competition*, 30 American Economic Review, 1940

Cohen-Tanugi L. and others, *La pratique communautaire du contrôle des concentrations*, 1995, De Boeck Université

Constantinesco V., "L'article 5 CEE, de la bonne foi à la loyauté communautaire" in *Du droit international au droit de l'intégration*, Liber Amicorum Pierre Pescatore (Capotorti and others eds.), 1987, Nomos Verlagsgesellschaft, Baden Baden

Cook C.J. and Kerse C.S., *E.C. Merger Control* (2nd edition), 1996, Sweet & Maxwell, London

Cottier T., "Dispute settlement in the World Trade Organization: Characteristics and structural implications for the European Union", 35 CML Rev. at 325-378

Crandall R.W., Gruenspecht H.K., Keeler T.E. and Lave L.B., *Regulating the automobile*, 1986, The Brookings Institution, Washington, D.C.

Creutzig J., "Die neue Gruppenfreistellungsverordnung für Vertriebs- und Kundendienstvereinbarungen im Kfz-Bereich", 21/1995 EuZW, at 723

* "Vertrieb von Kraftfahrzeugen - Zum Leitfaden der Kommission vom Oktober 1995", 7/1996 EuZW, at 197-201

Cusumano M.A., *The Japanese automobile industry*, 1985, The Harvard University Press, Cambridge Mass.

Daintith T., "Law as a policy instrument: comparative perspective" in *Law as an instrument of economic policy: Comparative and critical approaches* (T. Daintith ed.), 1988, Walter de Gruyter, Berlin

Davey W.J., "An overview of the General Agreement on Tariffs and Trade" in *Handbook of GATT Dispute Settlement* (P. Pescatore, W.J. Davey and A. Lowenfeld eds.), 1991, Transnational Juris Publications, Kluwer, Deventer

Davidow W.H. and Malone M.S., *The virtual corporation*, 1992, Harper Business, New York

De Gaay Fortman B., *Theory of Competition Policy*, 1966, North-Holland Publishing Company,

Amsterdam

De Jong H.W., "European competition policy: Goals and achievements" in *The structure of European industry* (H.W. de Jong ed.), 3rd revised edition, 1993, Kluwer, Dordrecht

* "Competition and combination in the European market economy" in *Competition in Europe*, Essays in honour of Henk W. de Jong (P. de Wolf ed.), 1991, Kluwer, Dordrecht

* and de Boer C.J.P., *Competition and concentration in the passenger carmarket of the Netherlands*, Nr. 33, Evolution of concentration and competition series: Working papers, EUR-OP, IV/458/81-EN

De Man A.P., "Nieuwe organisatievormen en het industriebeleid", ESB 12 March 1997, at 214

De Sitter L.U., *Synergetisch produceren*, 1994, Van Gorcum, Assen

Delors Committee, Committee for the Study of Economic and Monetary Union, *Report on Economic and Monetary Union in Europe*, 1989

Demaret P., "Le régime des échanges internes et externes de la Communauté à la lumière des notions d'union douanière et de zône de libre-échange" in *Du droit international au droit de l'intégration*, Liber Amicorum Pierre Pescatore (Capotorti and others eds.), 1987, Nomos Verlagsgesellschaft, Baden Baden

* and Bellis J.-F. and Jimenez G.G., *Regionalism and multilateralism after the Uruguay Round*, 1997, EIP, Brussels

Devroe W., "Privatizations and Community law: Neutrality versus policy", 34 CML Rev. at 299-300

Dicken P., *Global shift*, 2nd edition, 1992, PCP, London

* "Europe 1992 and strategic change in the international automobile industry", *Environment and Planning A*, 1992, Volume 24, at 27-30

Dimock M.E., *The new American political economy; a synthesis of politics and economics*, 1962, New York

Dony M., "L'affaire des bananes", 1995 CDE XXXI (no 3-4), at 461-496

Drache D., "New work and employment relations" in *States against markets* (R. Boyer and D. Drache eds.), 1996, Routledge, London

Drucker P., *Concept of the corporation*, 1946, The John Day Company, New York

Due O., "Artikel 5 van het EEG- Verdrag - Een bepaling met een federaal karakter?, SEW 1992, at 355-366

Dunnett P.J.S., *The decline of the British Motor Industry*, 1980, Croom Helm, London

Ebenroth C.T., Lange K.W., Mersch S.A., *Die EG-Gruppenfreistellungs-verordnung für Vertriebs- und Kundendienstvereinbarungen über Kraftfahrzeuge*, 1995, Verlag Recht und Wirtschaft, Heidelberg

Eccles R., "When is a British car not a British car? - Issues raised by Nissan", 10 ECLR (1989), at 1-3

Economist Intelligence Unit, "The Japanese in Western Europe", *Japanese Motor Business*, June 1989

* "Global vehicle production trends - 1996 edition" in Research Report No R336

SELECTIVE BIBLIOGRAPHY

Eeckhout P., *The European internal market and international trade: A legal analysis*, 1994, Clarendon Press, Oxford

* "The domestic legal status of the WTO agreement: Interconnecting legal systems", 34 CML Rev. at 11-58

* annotation of Case C-61/94, *Commission* v *Germany*, 35 CML Rev. at 557-566

Ehlermann C.-D., "The contribution of EC Competition Policy to the Single Market", 29 CML Rev., at 257-282

Ellman M., *Socialist planning*, 2nd edition, 1989, Cambridge University Press, Cambridge

Emiliou N., "The death of exclusive competence?", (1996) 21 E.L.Rev., at 294-311

* and O'Keeffe D. (eds.), *The European Union and world trade law - After the GATT Uruguay Round*, 1996, Wiley, Chichester

Eucken W., *Die Grundlagen der Nationalökonomie*, 1950, Springer, Berlin

* *Grundsätze der Wirtschaftspolitik*, 1952, A. Francke A.G. Verlag, Bern

Evans A., *European Community law of state aid*, 1997, Clarendon Press, Oxford

Firth A., "Aspects of design protection in Europe", [1993] 2 EIPR, at 42-47

Footer M.E., "Participation of the European Communities in the World Trade Organization" in *The legal regulation of the European Community's external relations after the completion of the internal market* (S.V. Konstadinidis ed.), 1996, Dartmouth, Aldershot

Franzosi M., Conference paper on "The vehicle manufacturer's case for design protection of spare parts" (Legal view), IBC Legal Studies-Conference on "The Commission's amended proposal for a Directive on the legal protection of designs - The implications for the Automotive Industries and the Automotive After Market", 18 June 1996, Munich, Germany

Furse M., "The role of competition policy: A survey", [1996] 4 ECLR, at 250-258

GATT, *Analytical Index: Guide to GATT Law and Practice*, 6th Edition, 1994

Geelhoed L.A. in P.J.G. Kapteyn and P. VerLoren van Themaat, *Inleiding tot het recht van de Europese Gemeenschappen - Na Maastricht*, 5th edition, 1995, Kluwer, Deventer

George K., "Public ownership versus privatisation" in *Competition in Europe* (P. de Wolf ed.), Essays in honour of H.W. de Jong, 1991, Kluwer, Dordrecht

Gilpin R., *U.S. power and the multinational corporation*, 1975, Basic Books Inc., London

Govaere I., *The use and abuse of intellectual property rights in E.C. law*, 1996, Sweet & Maxwell, London

Goyder D.G., *EC Competition Law*, 2nd edition, 1993, Clarendon Press, Oxford

Graham E.M., *Global corporations and national governments*, 1996, Institute for International Economics, Washington DC

Greenaway D. and Hindley B., *What Britain pays for voluntary export restraints*, Thames Essay No.

43, 1985, Trade Policy Research Centre, London

Greenpeace, "The SmILE Concept - The technology", August 1996, Hamburg

* "The dirty track of the car industry - A Greenpeace Report", July 1996, Amsterdam

* "The first step towards a fossil fuel free future", August 1996

Groves P.J., "Motor Vehicle Distribution: The Block Exemption", [1987] ECLR at 86

* "Intermediaries: Last chance saloon for selective distribution in the automobile sector?", [1993] 1 ECLR 21-25

Guzzetti L., *A brief history of European Union research policy* (European Commission, Science research development - Studies 5), October 1995, EUR-OP, Brussels

Hahn H., "The Stability Pact for European Monetary Union: Compliance with deficit limit as a constant legal duty", 35 CML Rev. at 77-100

Hall G., "Introduction" in *European industrial policy*, 1986, Croom Helm, London

Hamilton W.H., *Price and Price Policies*, 1938, McGraw-Hill, New York

Hancher L. and Sevenster H., annotation of Case C-2/90, *Commission* v *Belgium*, CML Rev. at 360

Hancher L., Ottervanger T. and Slot P.J., *EC State Aids*, 1993, Chancery Law Publishing, London

Harden I. (ed.), *State aid: Community law and policy*, 1993, Bundesanzeiger, Koln

* "The European Central Bank and the Role of National Central Banks in Economic and Monetary Union", in *Economic and Monetary Union: Implications for National Policy-Makers*, (K. Gretschmann ed.), 1993, Martinus Nijhoff Publishers, Dordrecht

Hartley T.C., *The foundations of European Community law*, 3th edition, 1994, Clarendon Press, London

Hawk B.E. and Huser H.L., *European Community Merger Control: A Practitioner's Guide*, 1996, Kluwer, The Hague

Hayek F.A., *The road to serfdom*, 1944, University of Chicago Press, Chicago

Hellingman K. and Mortelmans K.J.M., *Economisch publiekrecht*, 1989, Kluwer, Deventer

Hennipman P., "Doeleinden en criteria der economische politiek", in *Theorie van de Economische Politiek*, 1962, H.E. Stenfert Kroese N.V., Leiden

* *De taak van de mededingingspolitiek*, 1966, De Erven F. Bohn, Haarlem

Herdegen M., "Price stability and budgetary restraints in the Economic and Monetary Union: The law as guardian of economic wisdom", 35 CML Rev. at 9-32

Holmes P. and Smith A., "Automobile industry" in *European Policies on Competition, Trade and Industry* (P. Buigues, A. Jacquemin and A. Sapir eds.), 1995, Edward Elgar, Aldershot

Hudec R.E., *The GATT Legal System and World Trade Diplomacy*, 2nd edition, 1990, Buttersworth Legal Publishers, Salem

* *Enforcing International Trade Law - The Evolution of the Modern GATT Legal System*, 1993,

Buttersworth Legal Publishers, Salem

Hufbauer, G.C., "An overview" in *Europe 1992 - An American perspective* (G.C. Hufbauer ed.), 1990, The Brookings Institution, Washington D.C.

Hughes R., Conference paper on "The after market case against design protection of spare parts" (Public and legal policy-legislator's opinions), IBC Legal Studies-Conference on "The Commission's amended proposal for a Directive on the legal protection of designs - The implications for the Automotive Industries and the Automotive After Market", 18 June 1996, Munich, Germany

Ingrassia P. and White J.B., *Comeback - The fall and rise of the American automobile industry*, 1994, Simon & Schuster, New York

Italianer A., "Mastering Maastricht: EMU Issues and How They Were Settled", in *Economic and Monetary Union: Implications for National Policy-Makers*, (K. Gretschmann ed.), 1993, Martinus Nijhoff Publishers, Dordrecht

Jackson J.H., *World Trade and the law of GATT*, 1969, The Michie Company Law Publishers, Charlottesville

* *The world trading system*, 2nd edition, 1997, The MIT Press, Cambridge Massachusetts

Jacobs, F.G., "The completion of the internal market v the incomplete common commercial policy" in *The legal regulation of the European Community's external relations after the completion of the internal market* (S.V. Konstadinidis ed.), 1996, Dartmouth, Aldershot

Jarass H.D., "Regulation as an instrument of economic policy" in *Law as an instrument of economic policy: Comparative and critical approaches* (T. Daintith ed.), 1988, Walter de Gruyter, Berlin

Joerges Ch., "European economic law, the nation-state and the Maastricht Treaty" in *Europe after Maastricht - An ever closer Union?* (R. Dehousse ed.), 1994, LBE, München

* and Hiller E., Holzscheck K. and icklitz H.-W., *Vertriebspraktiken im automobilersatzteilsektor - Ihre Auswirkungen auf die Interessen der Verbraucher*, 1985, Verlag Peter Lang, Frankfurt am Main

Joris T., *Nationale steunmaatregelen en het Europees gemeenschapsrecht*, 1994, MAKLU, Antwerpen

Jovanovic M.N., *European economic integration - Limits and prospects*, 1997, Routledge, London

Kahn A.E., *The economics of regulation: Principles and institutions*, 1970, John Wiley & Sons, New York, Volume I

Kapteyn P.J.G., "Outgrowing the Treaty of Rome: From market integration to policy integration" in *Mélanges Fernand Dehousse*, Volume 2, 1979, Fernand Nathan, Paris

* and VerLoren van Themaat P., *Introduction to the law of the European Communities* (L.W. Gormley ed.), 2nd edition, 1989, Kluwer, Deventer

Kassim H. and Menon A. (eds.), *The European Union and national industrial policy* , 1996, Routledge, London

Kelley P.L. and Onkelinx I., *EEC Customs Law*, 3rd Supplement, 1990 ECS Publishing Limited,

Oxford, Part 1

Kerse C., "Enforcing Community competition policy under Articles 88 and 89 of the E.C. Treaty - New powers for U.K. competition authorities", [1997] 1 ECLR, at 17-23

Keynes J.M., *The general theory of employment, interest and money*, 1936, Macmillan, London

Kingston E.I., "The economics of rules of origin" in *Rules of origin in international trade* (E. Vermulst, P. Waer and J. Bourgeois eds.), 1994, The University of Michigan Press, Michigan

Kirschen E.S. and others, *Economic Policy in Our Time*, 1964, North-Holland Publishing Company, Amsterdam

* and Blackaby F., Csapo L., Kamecki Z. and Kestens P., *Economic policies compared - West and East*, 1974, North-Holland Publishing Company, Amsterdam

Kleinknecht A. and Ter Wengel J., "Feiten over globalisering", ESB, 9 October 1996, at 831-833

Kojima T., *Die zweite Lean Revolution: was kommt nach lean production?*, 1995, Verlag Moderne Industrie, Landsberg

Koninklijke Vereniging voor de Staatshuishoudkunde, *Marktwerking versus coördinatie*, Preadviezen 1996 (A. Nentjes ed.), 1996, Lemma, Utrecht

Konstadinidis S.V., "The new face of the Community's external relations: Recent developments on certain controversial issues" in *The legal regulation of the European Community's external relations after the completion of the internal market* (S.V. Konstadinidis ed.), 1996, Dartmouth, Aldershot

Kroher J., Conference paper on "The vehicle manufacturer's case for design protection of spare parts" (Economic and public policy), IBC Legal Studies-Conference on "The Commission's amended proposal for a Directive on the legal protection of designs - The implications for the Automotive Industries and the Automotive After Market", 18 June 1996, Munich, Germany

Krugman P., *Pop internationalism*, 1996, MIT Press, Cambridge

* and Obstfeld M., *International Economics - Theory and Policy*, 3rd edition, 1994, Harper Collins College Publishers, New York

Kuyper P.J., "Booze and fast cars: Tax discrimination under GATT and the EC" in Legal Issues of European Integration 1996/1 (Special edition dedicated to R.H. Lauwaars), Kluwer, at 129-144

LaNasa III J.A., "Rules of origin and the Uruguay Round's effectiveness in harmonizing and regulating them", 90 AJIL (1996), at 636-637

Lane R., "New Community competences under the Maastricht Treaty", 30 CML Rev. at 943-944, 966

Lasok D. and Cairns W., *The Customs Law of the European Economic Community*, 1983, Kluwer, Deventer

Lazonick W., *Business organization and the myth of the market economy*, 1991, Cambridge University Press, Cambridge

Leefmans P.J., *Externe milieubevoegdheden*, 1997, Kluwer, Deventer

SELECTIVE BIBLIOGRAPHY

Lenaerts K. and Van Nuffel P., *Europees Recht in Hoofdlijnen*, 1995, MAKLU Uitgevers, Antwerpen

Lever J., annotation of Case 81/87, *The Queen* v *Daily Mail*, 26 CML Rev. at 334

Lewchuk W., *American technology and the British vehicle industry*, 1987, Cambridge University Press, Cambridge

Linda R., "Industrial and market concentration in Europe" in *Competition in Europe*, Essays in honour of Henk W. de Jong (P. de Wolf ed.), 1991, Kluwer, Dordrecht

Locke S., Conference paper on "The consumer interest in a free market in spare parts", IBC Legal Studies-Conference on "The Commission's amended proposal for a Directive on the legal protection of designs - The implications for the Automotive Industries and the Automotive After Market", 18 June 1996, Munich, Germany

Louis J.-V., "L'Union Economique et Monetaire", 1992 CDE XXVIII (no 3-4), at 252-255

* "A legal and institutional approach for building a Monetary Union", 35 CML Rev. at 33-76

Lubbers R.F.M., "Globalisering is meer dan handel", ESB, 6 November 1996, at 917

Ludvigsen Associates, *Research on the "cost of non-Europe", Basic findings - The EC 92 automobile sector*, Volume 11, 1988, EUR-OP

Lugard H.H.P., "Vertical restraints under EC competition law: A horizontal approach?", [1996] 3 ECLR, at 166-177

Lukoff F.L., "European Competition Law And Distribution In The Motor Vehicle Sector: Commission Regulation 123/85 of 12 December 1984", 23 CML Rev. 1986, at 865

Macleod I., Hendry I.D. and Hyett S., *The external relations of the European Communities*, 1996, Clarendon Press, Oxford

Majone G., "The European Community as a regulatory state" in *Collected courses of the Academy of European Law*, Volume V, Book I, 1994, Martinus Nijhoff Publishers, The Hague

* and others, *Regulating Europe*, 1996, Routledge, London

Manin P., "A propos de l'accord instituant l'Organisation mondiale du commerce et de l'accord sur les marchés publics: la question de l'invocabilité des accords internationaux conclus par la Communauté européenne", RTD Eur. 33(3) 1997, at 399-428

Martin S. (ed.), *Competition policies in Europe*, 1998, North-Holland, Amsterdam

Matteucci M., *History of the Motor Car*, 1970, New English Library, Turin

Mayntz R., "Political intentions and legal measures: The determinants of policy decisions" in *Law as an instrument of economic policy: Comparative and critical approaches* (T. Daintith ed.), 1988, Walter de Gruyter, Berlin

McCahery J., Bratton W.W., Picciotto S. and Scott C. (eds.), *International regulatory competition and coordination*, 1996, Clarendon Press, Oxford

Mensink N. and Van Bergeijk P., "Globlablablah", ESB, 6 November 1996, at 914-916

Mercer G.A., "Don't just optimize - unbundle", *The McKinsey Quarterly* 1994, No 3, at 103-116

Mertens de Wilmars J., "De economische opvattingen in de rechtspraak van het Hof van Justitie van de Europese Gemeenschappen" in *Miscellanea W.J. Ganshof van der Meersch*, Volume II, 1972, Bruylant, Brussels

Mestmäcker E.-J., *Die sichtbare Hand des Rechts*, 1978, Nomos Verlagsgesellschaft, Baden-Baden

Molle W., *The Economics of European Integration-Theory, Practice, Policy*, 2nd edition, 1994, Dartmouth, Aldershot

Mortelmans K.J.M., *Ordenend en sturend beleid en economisch publiekrecht*, 1985, Kluwer, Deventer

* "Short and long-term policy objectives and the choice of instruments and measures" in *Law as an instrument of economic policy: Comparative and critical approaches* (T. Daintith ed.), 1988, Walter de Gruyter, Berlin

* "The common market, the internal market and the single market, what's in a market?", 35 CML Rev. at 101-136

Murfin A., "Price discrimination and tax differences in the European motor industry" in *Tax coordination in the European Community* (S. Cnossen ed.), 1987, Kluwer, Deventer

Musgrave R.A. and Musgrave P.B., *Public finance in theory and practice*, 5th edition, 1973, McGraw-Hill, New York

Neuwahl N.A.E.M., "Individuals and the GATT: Direct effect and indirect effects of the General Agreement of Tariffs and Trade in Community Law", both in *The European Union and world trade law: After the GATT Uruguay Round* (N. Emiliou and D. O'Keeffe eds.), 1996, Wiley, Chicester

Nevin E., *The economics of Europe*, 1990, St. Martin's Press, New York

Nevins A. and Hill F.E., *Ford - Decline and rebirth*, 1962, Charles Scribner's Sons, New York

Nicolaides P. (ed.), *Industrial policy in the European Community: A necessary response to economic integration?*, 1993, Martinus Nijhoff Publishers, Dordrecht

* "The role of competition policy in economic integration" in *The competition policy of the European Community* (P. Nicolaides and A. van der Klugt eds.), 1994, EIPA, Maastricht

Nilsson J.-E., Dicken P. and Peck. J., *The internationalization process*, 1996, PCP, London

Nooteboom B., "Innoveren, globaliseren", ESB, 9 October 1996, at 828-830

* "Makeling van clusters is een klus voor bedrijven", ESB, 10-12-1997, at 947

Ogus A.I., *Regulation - Legal form and economic theory*, 1994, Clarendon Press, Oxford

Oliver P., *Free movement of goods in the European Community*, 1996, Sweet & Maxwell, London

Padoa-Schioppa T. and others, *Efficiency, stability, and equity*, 1987, Oxford University Press, Oxford

Pelkmans J., *European integration - Methods and economic analysis*, 1997, Longman (Netherlands

Open University), Heerlen

* and Winters L.A., *Europe's domestic market* (Chatham House Papers - 43), 1988, Routledge, London

Perry B., "State aids to the former East Germany: A note on the VW/Saxony case", (1997) 22 E.L.Rev. Feb., at 86-88

Petersmann E.U., "Participation of the European Communities in the GATT: International Law and Community Law Aspects" in *Mixed Agreements* (D. O'Keeffe and H.G. Schermers eds.), 1983, Kluwer, Deventer

* "The EEC as a GATT Member - Legal conflicts between GATT law and European Community law" in *The European Community and GATT*, Studies in transnational economic law, Volume 4 (M. Hilf, F.G. Jacobs and E.U. Petersmann eds.), 1986, Kluwer, Deventer

* "Application of GATT by the Court of Justice of the European Communities", 20 CML Rev. at 401

* "Darf die EG das Völkerrecht ignorieren?", 11/1997 EuZW, at 325-331

* *The GATT/WTO dispute settlement system*, 1997, Kluwer, London

* "The GATT dispute settlement system as an instrument of the foreign trade policy of the EC" in *The European Union and world trade law: After the GATT Uruguay Round* (N. Emiliou and D. O'Keeffe eds.), 1996, Wiley, Chicester

Peterson J., "Research and development policy" in *The European Union and national industrial policy* (H. Kassim and A. Menon eds.), 1996, Routledge, London

Philip A.B., "Europe's industrial policies", in *European industrial policy*, 1986, Croom Helm, London

Pipkorn J., "Legal Arrangements in the Treaty of Maastricht for the Effectiveness of the Economic and Monetary Union", 31 CML Rev. at 263

Posner B., "The Community design. Purpose and scope of the Green Paper on the legal protection of industrial design" in *The Green Paper on the legal protection of industrial design* (F. Gotzen ed.), 1992, E. Story-Scientia, Brussels

* "Proposal for a Directive on the legal protection of designs", International Business Lawyer, February 1998, at 80-82

Priess H.-J. and Pethke R., "The pan-European rules of origin: The beginning of a new era in European free trade", 34 CML Rev. at 773-809

RDC-dossier Nr. 3, *La distribution dans le secteur automobile*, 1996, E. Story-Scientia, Diegem

Reich S., "Roads to follow: Regulating direct foreign investment", *International Organization* 43, 4, Autumn 1989, at 553-568

Reich R.B., *The work of nations*, 1991, Alfred A. Knopf, New York

Rhys D.G., *The motor industry: An economic survey*, 1972, Butterworths, London

Riehle G., Conference paper on "The after market case against design protection of spare parts" (Legal view), IBC Legal Studies-Conference on "The Commission's amended proposal for a Directive on the legal protection of designs - The implications for the Automotive Industries and the Automotive After Market", 18 June 1996, Munich, Germany

Ritter L., Braun D. and Rawlinson R., *EEC Competition Law*, Compact Edition, 1993, Kluwer, Deventer

Rocca G., "La politique communautaire de concurrence en matière de distribution" in "Proceedings of the Second Seminar on European Union/Japan Competition Policy", Brussel, 16 September 1994

Roediger W., *Hundert Jahre Automobil*, 3rd edition, 1990, Urania Verlag, Leipzig

Rosecrance R., "The rise of the virtual state", Foreign Affairs, July/August 1996, at 45-61

Röpke W., "Economic order and international law", R.d.C. 1954-II, at 224, 227, 233 and 236-237

Rosenthal D.E., "Competition policy" in *Europe 1992 - An American perspective* (G.C. Hufbauer ed.), 1990, The Brookings Institution, Washington D.C.

Roseren P., "The application of Community law by French courts from 1982 to 1993", 31 CML Rev. at 361

Samuelson P.A. and Nordhaus W.D., *Economics*, 12th edition, 1985, McGraw-Hill, Singapore

Sauter W., *Competition law and industrial policy in the EU*, 1997, Clarendon Press Oxford

Schermers H.G. and Waelbroeck D., *Judicial Protection in the European Communities*, 5th edition, 1992, Kluwer, Deventer

Schilling T., "The autonomy of the Community legal order: An analysis of possible foundations", 37 HILJ 1996, at 389-409

Schrans G., "The instrumentality and the morality of European economic law" in *Miscellanea W.J. Ganshof van der Meersch*, Volume II, 1972, Bruylant, Brussels

Schrauwen A.M.M., "De interne markt na Maastricht", SEW 10 (1992) at 771-778

Schwemer R.-O., *Die Binding des Gemeinschaftsgesetzgebers an die Grundfreiheiten* (Schriften zum internationalen und zum öffentlichen Recht), 1995, Peter Lang, Frankfurt am Main

Schumpeter J.A., *Capitalism, Socialism and Democracy*, 2nd edition, 1947, Harper, New York

Seidl-Hohenveldern I., *International economic law*, 1989, Martinus Nijhoff Publishers, Dordrecht

Servan-Schreiber J.-J., *The American Challenge*, 1969, Pelican Books, Middlesex

Sevenster H.G., *Milieubeleid en gemeenschapsrecht*, 1992, Kluwer, Deventer

Shepherd W.G. and Wilcox C., *Public policies towards business*, 6th edition, 1979, Richard D. Irwin, Homewood

Shimokawa K., *The Japanese Automobile Industry - A Business History*, 1994, The Athlone Press, London

Sleuwaegen L., "The relevant antitrust market" in European Economy - Competition and Integration - Community Merger Control Policy, 1994, Number 57

Slot P.J., *Technical and administrative obstacles to trade in the EEC*, 1975, A.W. Sijthoff, Leiden

* "Sturing en Economisch Recht" in *Het Schip van Staat* (M.A.P. Bovens/W.J. Witteveen), 1985, W.E.J. Tjeenk Willink, Zwolle

* "The Institutional Provisions of the EMU", in *Institutional Dynamics of European Integration*, Essays in Honour of Henry G. Schermers - Volume II (D. Curtin and T. Heukels eds.) 1994, Martinus Nijhoff Publishers, Dordrecht

* "Harmonisation", E.L.Rev. 1996, at 380

Slotboom M.M., "State Aid in Community Law: A Broad or a Narrow Definition?", (1995) 20 E.L.Rev, at 289-301

Smith A. and Venables A.J., "Automobiles" in *Europe 1992 - An American perspective* (G.C. Hufbauer ed.), 1990, The Brookings Institution, Washington D.C.

Smith R.S., "Motor vehicle tax harmonization" in *Tax coordination in the European Community* (S. Cnossen ed.), 1987, Kluwer, Deventer

Smits R., "De Monetaire Unie van Maastricht", SEW 8/9 (1992) at 710

Sosnick S.H., "A critique of concepts of workable competition", 72 (1958) QJE at 383

Speyart H.M.H., "The Grand Design: An update on the EC design proposals", [1997] 10 EIPR, at 603-612

Steinberger H., *GATT und regionale Wirtschaftszusammenschlüsse*, Max-Planck-Institut für Ausländisches Öffentliches Recht Und Völkerrecht, 1963, Carl Heymanns Verlag, Köln

Stewart R.B., "Regulation and the crisis of legalisation in the United States" in *Law as an instrument of economic policy: Comparative and critical approaches* (T. Daintith ed.), 1988, Walter de Gruyter, Berlin

Stopford J.M. and Turner L., *Britain and the multinationals*, 1985, John Wiley, Chichester

Stopford J.M., Strange S. and Henley J.S., *Rival states, rival firms*, 1991, Cambridge University Press, Cambridge

Stöver K., *The EC Block Exemption Regulation for Motor Vehicule Distribution Agreements (EEC/123/85)*, a compilation of statements by Stöver until mid 1992, C.E.C.R.A.

Streeck W. in "Public power beyond the nation-state - The case of the European Community" in *States against markets* (R. Boyer and D. Drache eds.), 1996, Routledge, London

Stuart E.G., "Recent developments in EU law and policy on state aids", [1996] 4 ECLR, at 229-231

Temple Lang J., "Community Constitutional Law: Article 5 EEC Treaty", 27 CML Rev. at 645-681

Tinbergen J., *Economic policy: Principles and design*, 1966, North-Holland Publishing Company, Amsterdam

* *International economic integration*, 2nd revised edition, 1965, Elsevier Publishing Company, Amsterdam

Travers N., "Retroactivity and the Commission's powers to implement state aid rules", (1998) 23

E.L.Rev., at 264-271

Treacy R. and Feaster T., "When two into one will go: Intra-group agreements and Article 85(1)", (1997) 22 E.L.Rev., at 573-578

Uitermark P.J., *Economische mededinging en algemeen belang*, 1990, Wolters-Noordhoff, Groningen

* "Industriepolitiek in Europa" SEW 6 (1992) June, at 504-508

UNCTAD, *World Investment Report 1994 - Transnational corporations, employment and the workplace*, 1994, UN, New York

UNICE Position Paper, "Greater transparency and improved enforcement of state aid rules", 28 June 1996

* "Benchmarking Europe's competitiveness: from analysis to action", December 1997

Usher J., "Consequences of the Customs Union" in *The European Union and world trade law - After the Uruguay Round* (N. Emiliou and D. O'Keeffe eds.), 1996, Wiley, Chicester

Van Bael I., "Discretionary powers of the Commission and their legal control in trade and antitrust matters" in *Discretionary powers of the Member States in the field of economic policies and their limits under the EEC Treaty* (J. Schwarze ed.), European University Institute in Florence, 1988, Nomos Verlagsgesellschaft, Baden-Baden

* and Bellis J.-F., *Anti-dumping and other trade protection laws of the EC*, 3rd edition, 1996, CCH Europe, Bicester

* and Bellis J.-F., *Competition Law of the European Community*, 3rd edition, 1994, CCH Europe

Van Damme E.E.C., "Marktwerking en herregulering" in *Markt en wet* (R.A.J. van Gestel and Ph. Eijlander and others eds.), 1996, W.E.J. Tjeenk Willink, Deventer

Van den Bergh R., *Economische analyse van het mededingingsrecht*, 1993 Gouda Quint, Arnhem

Van den Bossche P.L.H., "The European Community and the Uruguay Round Agreements" in *Implementing the Uruguay Round* (J.H. Jackson and A. Sykes eds.), 1997, Clarendon Press, Oxford

Van der Esch B., "EC rules on undistorted competition and U.S. antitrust laws: The limits of comparability" in *European/American Antitrust and Trade Law*, 1988 Fordham Corp. L. Inst. (B. Hawk ed.)

Van Gerven W. and Gilliams H., "Gemeenschapstrouw: goede trouw in EG-verband", Rechtskundig Weekblad 1989-1990, nr 33, at 1158-1169

Van Gerven W., Gyselen L., Maresceau M. and Stuyck J., *Kartelrecht II-Europese Gemeenschap*, 1997, W.E.J. Tjeenk Willink

Van Mourik A., "The role of competition policy in a market economy" in *The competition policy of the European Community* (P. Nicolaides and A. vander Klugt eds.), 1994, EIPA, Maastricht

Van den Bossche P.L.H., "The European Community and the Uruguay Round Agreements" in *Implementing the Uruguay Round* (J.H. Jackson and A. Sykes eds.), 1997, Clarendon Press, Oxford

SELECTIVE BIBLIOGRAPHY

Van Overbeek W.B.J., *Contacten & contracten* (RAI Vereniging, Afdeling Auto's), 1996, SPR Producties, Eemnes

Van der Schueren P., "Customs Classification: One of the cornerstones of the single European market, but one which cannot be exhaustively regulated", 28 CML Rev. at 856

Vaulont N., *De douane-unie van de Europese Economische Gemeenschap*, 2nd edition, Bureau voor officiële publikaties der Europese Gemeenschappen, 1986

VerLoren van Themaat P. in P.J.G. Kapteyn and P. VerLoren van Themaat, *Inleiding tot het recht van de Europese Gemeenschappen - Na Maastricht*, 5th edition, 1995, Kluwer, Deventer

* bookreview of R.-O. Schwemer, *Die Binding des Gemeinschaftsgesetzgebers an die Grundfreiheiten* (Schriften zum internationalen und zum öffentlichen Recht), 1995, Peter Lang, Frankfurt am Main, in 33 CML Rev. at 1089-1094

Vermulst E.A., "Rules of origin as commercial policy instruments? - Revisited" in *Rules of origin in international trade* (E. Vermulst, P. Waer and J. Bourgeois eds.), 1994, The University of Michigan Press, Michigan

* and Waer P., "European Community rules of origin as commercial policy instruments", 24 JWT (1990), at 55-99

Vernon R. (ed.), *Big business and the state*, 1974, MacMillan, London

Vigier P., "La politique communautaire de l'automobile", 1992 Revue du Marché Unique Européen, Nr. 2, at 108-111 and Nr. 4, at 89

Völker E.L.M., "The Direct Effect of International Agreements in the Community's Legal Order", LIEI 1983/1, at 143

* *Barriers to External and Internal Community Trade*, Ph.D. thesis (Amsterdam - 1993)

Waer P., "European Community rules of origin" in *Rules of origin in international trade* (E. Vermulst, P. Waer and J. Bourgeois eds.), 1994, The University of Michigan Press, Michigan

Wagener H.-J., *Elementen van economische orde*, 1988, Wolters-Noordhoff, Groningen

Weatherill S., "After *Keck*: Some thoughts on how to clarify the clarification", 33 CML Rev. at 885-906

* "Compulsory notification of draft technical regulations: The contribution of Directive 83/189 to the management of the internal market", (1996) 16 Yearbook of European Law

Weiler J.H.H. and Haltern U.R., "The autonomy of the Community legal order: Through the Looking Glass", 37 HILJ 1996, at 411-448

Wells Jr. L.T., "Automobiles" in *Big business and the state* (R. Vernon ed.), 1974, MacMillan, London

Wesseling R., "Subsidiarity in Community antitrust law: Setting the right agenda", (1997) 22 E.L.Rev (Feb), at 38-39 and 43-47

Whish R., *Competition Law*, 3rd edition, 1993, Buttersworth, London

Wijers G.J., *Industriepolitiek*, 1982, H.E. Stenfert Kroese, Leiden

Wijckmans F. and Vanderelst A., "The EC Commission's draft regulation on motor vehicle distribution: Alea lacta est?", [1995] 3 ECLR, at 225-236

Wilkins M. and Hill F.E., *American business abroad - Ford on six continents*, 1964, Wayne State University Press, Detroit

Wilks S., *Industrial policy and the motor industry*, 1984, Manchester University Press, Manchester

Williamson P.J., "Oligopolistic dominance and EC merger policy" in European Economy - Competition and Integration - Community Merger Control Policy, 1994, Number 57

Womack J.P., Jones D.T. and Roos D., *The machine that changed the world*, 1991, Harper Perennial, New York

Womack J.P. and Jones D.T., *Lean Thinking*, 1996, Simon & Schuster, New York

Wyatt D. and Dashwood A., *European Community Law*, 3rd edition, 1993, Sweet & Maxwell, London

Yamane H., "Grey area measures, the Uruguay Round, and the EC/Japan commercial census on cars" in *The European Union and world trade law - After the GATT Uruguay Round* (N. Emiliou and D. O'Keeffe eds.), 1996, Wiley, Chichester

Zuleeg M., in H. Von der Groeben, J. Thiesing and C.-D. Ehlermann, *Kommentar zum EWG-Vertrag*, 4th edition, 1991, Nomos Verlagsgesellschaft, Baden-Baden

TABLE OF CASES

Court of Justice

- Case 30/59, *GSL* v *High Authority*, [1961] ECR 19
- Case 10/61, *Commission* v *Italy* [1962] ECR 1
- Joined Cases 2 and 3/62, *Commission* v *Luxembourg and Belgium*, [1962] ECR 432
- Case 26/62, *Van Gend en Loos* v *Nederlandse Administratie der belastingen*, [1963] ECR 12, 13
- Case 6/64, *Costa* v *ENEL*, [1964] ECR 593
- Joined Cases 56 and 58/64, *Consten and Grundig* v *Commission*, [1966] ECR 340
- Case 32/65, *Italy* v *Council and Commission*, [1966] ECR 405
- Joined Cases 52 and 55/65, *Germany* v *Commission*, [1966] ECR 169
- Case 57/65, *Lütticke* v *Hauptzollamt Saarlouis*, [1966] ECR 211
- Case 24/67, *Parke, Davis* v *Centrafarm*, [1968] ECR 71
- Case 7/68, *Commission* v *Italy*, [1968] ECR 423
- Joined Cases 2 and 3/69, *Sociaal Fonds voor de Diamantarbeiders* v *Brachfeld and Chougol Diamond*, [1969] ECR 222
- Case 5/69, *Völk* v *Vervaecke*, [1969] ECR 302
- Joined Cases 6 and 11/69, *Commission* v *France*, [1969] ECR 540
- Case 40/69, *Hauptzollamt Hamburg* v *Bollman* [1970] ECR 69
- Case 48/69, *ICI* v *Commission*, [1972] ECR 619
- Case 74/69, *Hauptzollamt Bremen* v *Krohn* [1970] ECR 451
- Case 33/70, *SACE* v *Italian Ministry for Finance*, [1970] ECR 1222
- Case 78/70, *Deutsche Grammophon* v *Metro*, [1971] ECR 499
- Case 18/71, *Eunomia di Porro* v *Italian Ministry of Education*, [1971] ECR 816
- Case 92/71, *Interfood* v *Hauptzollamt Hamburg*, [1972] ECR 231
- Case 6/72, *Continental Can* v *Commission*, [1973] ECR 244
- Joined Cases 21 to 24/72, *International Fruit Co.* v *Produktschap voor Groenten en Fruit* [1972] ECR 1219 and 1226-1228
- Case 70/72, *Commission* v *Germany*, [1973] ECR 829
- Case 77/72, *Capolongo* v *Azienda Agricola Maya*, [1973] ECR 623
- Case 9/73, *Schlüter* v *Hauptzollamt Lörrach*, [1973] ECR 1160
- Joined Cases 37 and 38/73, *Sociaal Fonds voor de Diamantarbeiders* v *Indiamex en De Belder*, [1973] ECR 1622-1625
- Case 120/73, *Lorenz* v *Germany*, [1973] ECR 1471
- Case 130/73, *Vandeweghe* v *Berufsgenossenschaft für die chemische Industrie* [1973] ECR 1333
- Case 173/73, *Italy* v *Commission*, [1974] ECR 709
- Case 181/73, *Haegeman* v *Belgium* [1974] ECR 459-460

TABLE OF CASES

- Case 2/74, *Reyners* v *Belgium*, [1974] ECR 650
- Opinion 1/75, [1975] ECR 1363
- Case 26/75, *General Motors Continental* v *Commission*, [1975] ECR 1367
- Case 38/75, *Nederlandse Spoorwegen* v *Inspecteur der invoerrechten en accijnzen*, [1975] ECR 1439 and 1450
- Case 119/75, *Terrapin* v *Terranova*, [1976] ECR 1061
- Case 127/75, *Bobie* v *Hauptzollamt Aachen-Nord*, [1976] ECR 1087, par. 9
- Case 26/76, *Metro SB-Grossmärkte* v *Commission*, [1977] ECR 1905
- Case 41/76, *Donckerwolcke* v *Procureur de la République*, [1976] ECR 1936
- Case 74/76, *Iannelli & Volpi* v *Meroni*, [1977) ECR 575
- Case 78/76, *Firma Steinike und Weinlig* v *Germany*, [1977] ECR 609
- Case 85/76, *Hoffmann-La Roche* v *Commission*, [1979] 553
- Opinion 1/78, [1979] ECR 2913
- Joined Cases 32/78 and 36 to 82/78, *BMW Belgium and others* v *Commission*, [1979] ECR 2435
- Case 34/78, *Yoshida*, [1979] ECR 115
- Case 114/78, *Yoshida*, [1979] ECR 151
- Case 141/78, *France* v *United Kingdom*, [1979] ECR 2942
- Case 120/78, *Rewe-Zentrale* v *Bundesmonopolverwaltung für Branntwein*, [1979] ECR 649
- Case 32/79, *Commission* v *United Kingdom*, [1980] ECR 2432
- Case 61/79, *Amministrazione delle Finanze dello Stato* v *Denkavit*, [1980] ECR 1228
- Case 136/79, *National Panasonic* v *Commission*, [1980] ECR 2057
- Case 730/79, *Philip Morris Holland* v *Commission*, [1980] ECR 2690
- Case 804/79, *Commission* v *United Kingdom*, [1981] ECR 1075
- Case 812/79, *Attorney General* v *Burgoa* [1980] ECR 2802
- Case 112/80, *Dürbeck* v *Hauptzollamt Frankfurt* [1981] ECR 1095
- Case 270/80, *Polydor* v *Harlequin Record Shops*, [1982] ECR 348
- Case 15/81, *Schul* v *Inspecteur der Invoerrechten en Accijnzen*, [1982] ECR 1431-1432
- Case 104/81, *Hauptzollamt Mainz* v *Kupferberg* [1982] ECR 3662
- Case 266/81, *S.I.O.T.* v *Ministerio delle Finanze and Others* [1983] ECR 731 and 780
- Joined Cases 267 to 269/81, *Amministrazione delle Finanze dello Stato* v *SPI and SAMI*, [1983] ECR 801
- Joined Cases 290 and 291/81, *Singer and Geigy* v *Amministrazione delle Finanze dello Stato* [1983] ECR 801 and 847
- Case C-322/81, *Michelin* v *Commission* [1983] ECR 3461
- Case 84/82, *Germany* v *Commission*, [1984] ECR 1488

TABLE OF CASES

- Case 203/82, *Commission* v *Italy*, [1983] ECR 2525
- Joined Cases 228 and 229/82 R, *Ford* v *Commission*, [1982] ECR 3091
- Joined Cases 228 and 229/82, *Ford* v *Commission*, [1984] ECR 1129
- Joined Cases 296 and 318/82, *The Netherlands and Leeuwarder Papierwarenfabriek* v *Commission*, [1985] ECR 824-826
- Case 323/82, *Intermills* v *Commission*, [1984] ECR 3826
- Case 324/82, *Commission* v *Belgium*, [1984] ECR 1861
- Case 50/83, *Commission* v *Italy*, [1984] ECR 1642-1643
- Case 134/83, *Abbink*, [1984] ECR 4097
- Case 170/83, *Hydrotherm Geratebau* v *Compact*, [1984] ECR 3018-3019
- Case 240/83, *Procureur de la République* v *Association de défense des brûleurs d'huiles usagées*, [1985] ECR 531
- Case 229/83, *Association des Centres distributeurs E. Leclerc and others/Sàrl 'Au blé vert' and others*, [1985] ECR 1
- Case 294/83, *Les Verts* v *European Parliament*, [1986] ECR 1365
- Joined Cases 25 and 26/84, *Ford* v *Commission*, [1985] ECR 2725
- Case 44/84, *Hurd* v *Jones*, [1986] ECR 81
- Case 47/84, *Schul* v *Inspecteur der Invoerrechten en Accijnzen*, [1985] ECR 1491
- Case 52/84, *Commission* v *Belgium*, [1986] ECR 105
- Case 75/84, *Metro SB-Grossmärkte* v *Commission*, [1986] ECR 3085
- Case 112/84, *Humblot* v *Directeur des services fiscaux*, [1985] ECR 1378-1379
- Joined Cases 142 and 156/84, *British American Tobacco and Reynolds Industries* v *Commission* [1987] ECR 4577
- Case 226/84, *British Leyland* v *Commission*, [1986] ECR 3301
- Case 248/84, *Germany* v *Commission*, [1987] ECR 4041
- Case 50/85, *Schloh* v *Auto controle technique*, [1986] ECR 1867
- Case 154/85, *Commission* v *Italy*, [1987] ECR 2717
- Case 186/85, *Commission* v *Belgium*, [1987] ECR 2057
- Case 193/85, *Co-Frutta* v *Amministrazione delle Finanze dello Stato*, [1987] ECR 2108, par. 10
- Case 248/85, *Germany* v *Commission*, [1987] ECR 4042
- Case 310/85, *Deufil* v *Commission*, [1987] ECR 926
- Case 391/85, *Commission* v *Belgium*, [1988] ECR 579
- Case 406/85, *Procureur de la Republique* v *Gofette and Gilliard*, [1987] ECR 2542
- Case 433/85, *Feldain* v *Directeur des services fiscaux*, [1987] ECR 3540-3541
- Case 10/86, *VAG* v *Magne*, [1986] ECR 4088

- Case 60/86, *Commission* v *U.K. and Northern Ireland*, [1988] ECR 3934
- Case 252/86, *Bergandi* v *Directeur général des impôts*, [1988] ECR 1374, par. 24
- Case 267/86, *Van Eycke* v *ASPA*, [1988] ECR 4791
- Case 299/86, *Rainer Drexl*, [1988] ECR 1235
- Case 53/87, *Maxicar* v *Renault*, [1988] ECR 6069
- Case 70/87, *Fediol* v *Commission*, [1989] ECR 1781
- Joined Cases 76, 86 to 89 and 149/87, *Seguela and Lachkar and others* v *Administration des impôts*, [1988] ECR 2397
- Case 81/87, *The Queen* v *Daily Mail*, [1988] ECR 5511
- Case 82/87R, *Autexpo* v *Commission*, [1987] ECR 2131
- Case 94/87, *Commission* v *Germany*, [1989] ECR 192
- Case 102/87, *France* v *Commission*, [1988] ECR 4087
- Case 165/87, *Commission* v *Council*, [1988] ECR 5560
- Case C-175/87, *Matsushita* v *Council*, [1992] ECR I-1409
- Case 235/87, *Matteucci*, [1988] ECR 5611
- Case 238/87, *Volvo* v *Veng*, [1987] ECR 6233
- Case 240/87, *Deville* v *Administration des impôts*, [1988] ECR 3513
- Case C-301/87, *France* v *Commission*, [1990] ECR I-354
- Case C-47/88, *Commission* v *Denmark*, [1990] ECR I-4533
- Joined Cases 93/88 and 94/88, *Wisselink and others* v *Staatssecretaris van Financiën*, [1989] ECR 2705
- Case C-132/88, *Commission* v *Greece*, [1990] ECR I-1588
- Case 170/88, *Ford Espana* v *Spain*, [1989] ECR 2305-2308
- Case C-188/88, *NMB* v *Commission*, [1992] ECR I-1689
- Case C-69/89, *Nakajima* v *Council*, [1991] ECR I-2069
- Case C-79/89, *Brown Boveri*, [1991] ECR I-1853
- Case C-228/89, *Farfalla Flemming und Partner* v *Hauptzollamt München* [1990] ECR 3406
- Case 246/89, *Commission* v *United Kingdom*, [1991] ECR I-4615
- Case C-300/89, *Commission* v *Council*, [1991] ECR I-2869
- Case C-305/89, *Italy* v *Commission*, [1991] ECR I-1640
- Case C-339/89, *Alsthom Atlantique* v *Sulzer*, [1991] ECR I-123
- Case C-384/89, *Ministère public* v *Tomatis and Fulchiron*, [1991] ECR 1127-131
- Case C-2/90, *Commission* v *Belgium*, [1992] ECR I-4478
- Case C-72/90, *Asia Motor France* v *Commission*, [1990] ECR I-2181
- Case C-105/90, *Goldstar* v *Council*, [1992] ECR I-677

TABLE OF CASES

- Case C-294/90, *British Aerospace and Rover* v *Commission*, [1992] ECR I-493
- Case C-313/90, *CIRFS and others* v *Commission*, [1993] ECR I-1186
- Case C-327/90, *Commission* v *Greece*, [1992] ECR I-3058
- Case C-343/90, *Dias* v *Director da Alfandega do Porto*, [1992] ECR I-4717, paras. 53-55
- Case C-354/90, *Fédération nationale du commerce extérieur des produits alimentaires and Syndicat national des négociants et transformateurs de saumon* v *France*, [1991] ECR I-5527
- Case C-373/90, *Criminal Proceedings against X*, [1992] ECR I-149
- Opinion 1/91, [1991] ECR I-6102
- Cases C-72/91 and C-73/91, *Sloman Neptun*, [1993] ECR I-887
- Case C-158/91, *Levy* [1993] ECR I-4300
- Case C-225/91 R, *Matra* v *Commission*, [1991] ECR 5823
- Case C-225/91, *Matra* v *Commission*, [1993] ECR I-3250
- Joined Cases C-241/91P and C-242/91P, *RTE and ITP* v *Commission*, [1995] ECR I-743
- Joined Cases C-267/91 and C-268/91, *Keck and Mithouard*, [1993] ECR I-6131
- Case C-9/92, *Commission* v *Greece*, [1993] ECR I-4494
- Case 17/92, *Fedicine* v *Spain*, [1993] ECR I-2272
- Case C-29/92, *Asia Motor France* v *Commission*, [1992] ECR I-3936
- Joined Cases C-92/92 and C-326/92, *Phil Collins*, [1993] ECR I-5179
- Case C-386/92, *Monin Automobiles - Maison du Deux-Roues*, [1993] ECR I-2049
- Case C-387/92, *Banco Exterior de España*, [1994] ECR I-909
- Case C-393/92, *Gemeente Almelo and Others and Energiebedrijf IJsselmij* [1994] ECR I-1520
- Case C-55/93, *Van Schaik*, [1994] ECR I-4857
- Case C-70/93, *BMW* v *ALD Auto-Leasing*, [1995] ECR I-3473
- Case C-135/93, *Spain* v *Commission*, [1995] ECR I-1683
- Case C-266/93, *Bundeskartellamt* v *Volkswagen*, [1995] ECR I-3520
- Case C-280/93, *Germany* v *Council*, [1994] ECR I-4973
- Joined Cases C-319/93, C-40/94 and C-224/94, *Dijkstra*, [1995] ECR I-4506
- Case C-322/93 P, *Peugeot* v *Commission*, [1994] ECR I-2727
- Case C-345/93, *Fazenda Pùblica* v *Nunes Tadeu*, [1995] ECR I-494
- Case C-348/93, *Commission* v *Italy*, [1995] ECR I-673
- Case C-428/93, *Monin Automobiles - Maison du Deux-Roues*, [1994] ECR I-1707
- Case C-469/93, *Amministrazione delle Finanze dello Stato* v *Chiquita Italia*, [1995] ECR I-4565
- Opinion 1/94, [1994] ECR I-5267
- Case C-61/94, *Commission* v *Germany*, [1996] ECR I-3989
- Joined Cases C-68/94 and C-30/95, *SCPA and others* v *Commission*, judgment of 31 March 1998, not

yet reported

- Case C-70/94, *Werner* v *Germany*, [1995] ECR I-3189
- Case C-83/94, *Leifer*, [1995] ECR I-3231
- Case C-113/94, *Jacquier* v *Directeur Général des Impôts*, [1995] ECR I-4220-4221
- Case C-194/94, *CIA Security International* v *Signalson and Securitel*, [1996] ECR I-2201
- Case C-226/94, *Grand Garage Albigeois and others* v *Garage Massol*, [1996] ECR I-651
- Case C-309/94, *Nissan France and others* v *Dupasquier and others*, [1996] ECR 677
- Case C-311/94, *IJssel-Vliet Combinatie* v *Minister van Economische Zaken*, [1996] ECR I-5056
- Case C-73/95P, *Viho Europe* v *Commission*, [1996] ECR I-5457
- Case C-128/95, *Fontaine and others* v *Acqueducs Automobiles*, [1997] ECR I-967
- Case C-240/95, *Rémy Schmit*, [1996] ECR I-3179
- Case C-282/95P, *Guérin* v *Commission*, [1997] ECR I-1531
- Case C-292/95, *Spain* v *Commission*, [1997] ECR I-1957
- Case C-329/95, *VAG Sverige*, [1997] ECR I-2675
- Joined Cases C-364/95 and C-365/95, *T. Port*, judgment of 10 March 1998, not yet reported
- Case C-375/95, *Commission* v *Greece*, [1997] ECR I-5981
- Case C-389/95, *Klattner* v *Greece*, [1997] ECR I-2719
- Case C-410/95, *Société des Grands Garages Méditerranéens and Nissan France* v *Société Nice Ouest*, OJ 1996, C46/12 (see also OJ 1997, C40/14)
- Case C-13/96, *Bic Benelux* v *Belgium*, [1997] ECR I-1776
- Case C-41/96, *VAG-Händlerbeirat* v *SYD-Consult*, [1997] ECR I-3123
- Case C-53/96, *Hermès International* v *FHT Marketing Choice*, judgment of 16 June 1998, not yet reported
- Case C-162/96, *Racke*, judgment of 16 June 1998, not yet reported
- Case C-230/96, *Cabour and others* v *Arnor "Soco"*, judgment of 30 April 1998, not yet reported
- Case C-284/96, *Tabouillot* v *Directeur des Services Fiscaux*, [1997] ECR I-7471
- Case C-301/96, *Germany* v *Commission*, OJ 1996, C336/18
- Case C-302/96, *Commission* v *Germany*, OJ 1996, C336/19
- Case C-401/96P, *Somaco*, OJ 1997, C54/15
- Case C-226/97, *Lemmens*, judgment of 16 June 1998, not yet reported
- Case C-421/97, *Tarantik*, OJ 1998, C41/15
- Cases C-28/98 and C-29/98, *Charreire and Hirtsmann*, OJ 1998, C94/13
- Case C-38/98, *Renault* v *Maxicar and Orazio Formento*, OJ 1998, C113/8
- Case C-153/98 P, *Guérin* v *Commission*, OJ 1998, C234/12
- Case C-154/98 P, *Guérin* v *Commission*, OJ 1998, C258/13

TABLE OF CASES

Court of First Instance

- Case T-64/89, *Automec S.r.l.* v *Commission*, [1990] ECR II-367
- Joined Cases T-68/89, T-77/89 and T-78/89, *Società Italiana Vetro and others* v *Commission*, [1992] ECR II-1548
- Case T-23/90R, *Peugeot* v *Commission*, [1990] ECR II-195
- Case T-23/90, *Peugeot* v *Commission*, [1991] ECR II-653
- Cases T-23/90 (92) and T-9/92 (92), *Peugeot* v *Commission*, [1995] ECR II-2068
- Case T-24/90, *Automec S.r.l.* v *Commission*, [1992] ECR II-2223
- Case T-28/90, *Asia Motor France* v *Commission*, [1992] ECR II-2285
- Case T-32/90, *OEC Nederland* v *Commission*, OJ 1990, C288/10 (see OJ 1991, C67/7)
- Case T-7/92, *Asia Motor France and others* v *Commission*, [1993] ECR II-669
- Case T-9/92, *Peugeot* v *Commission*, [1993] ECR II-509
- Case T-37/92, *BEUC* v *Commission*, [1994] ECR II-285
- Case T-96/92, *Comité central d'entreprise de la Sociéte générale des grandes sources and others* v *Commission* [1995] ECR II-1213
- Case T-102/92, *Viho Europe* v *Commission*, [1995] ECR II-17
- Case T-12/93, *Comité central d'entreprise de la société anonyme Vittel and others* v *Commission* [1995] ECR II-1247
- Case T-17/93, *Matra* v *Commission*, [1994] ECR II-595
- Case T-504/93, *Tiercé Ladbroke* v *Commission*, [1997] ECR II-923
- Case T-574/93, *Nouveau Garage and Max Labat* v *Commission*, OJ 1994, C43/12 (see OJ 1994, C161/15)
- Case T-115/94, *Opel Austria* v *Council*, [1997] ECR II-39
- Case T-162/94, *NMB* v *Commission*, [1996] ECR II-427
- Joined Cases T-163/94 and T-165/94, *NTN Corporation and Koyo Seiko* v *Council*, [1995] ECR II-1381
- Case T-186/94, *Guérin* v *Commission*, [1995] ECR II-1753
- Case T-387/94, *Asia Motor France and others* v *Commission*, [1996] ECR II-965
- Case T-195/95, *Guérin* v *Commission*, [1996] ECR II-171
- Case T-195/95, *Guérin* v *Commission*, [1997] ECR II-679
- Case T-9/96, *Européenne Automobiles* v *Commission*, OJ 1996, C95/16
- Case T-38/96, *Guérin* v *Commission*, [1997] ECR II-1223
- Case T-77/96, *Garage Massol* v *Commission*, OJ 1996, C210/23
- Case T-123/96, *SGA* v *Commission*, OJ 1996, C318/13
- Case T-132/96, *Sachsen* v *Commission*, OJ 1996, C336/29

TABLE OF CASES

- Case T-143/96, *Volkswagen* v *Commission*, OJ 1996, C336/30
- Case T-185/96, *Max Labat and others* v *Commission*, OJ 1997, C54/24
- Case T-189/96, *Garage des Quatre Vallées and others* v *Commission*, OJ 1997, C54/25
- Case T-190/96, *Palma and others* v *Commission*, OJ 1997, C54/25
- Case T-211/96, *Européenne Automobiles* v *Commission*, OJ 1997, C54/33
- Case T-225/97, *Asia Motor France and others* v *Commission*, OJ 1997, C318/28 and OJ 1998, C41/24
- Case T-226/97, *Guérin* v *Commission*, OJ 1997, C318/28 (see OJ 1998, C7/29)
- Case T-275/97, *Guérin* v *Commission*, OJ 1998, C7/21 (see OJ 1998, C113/15)
- Case T-276/97, *Guérin* v *Commission*, judgment of 13 februari 1998, not yet reported

INDEX

(This index of chapters 1 to 12 complements the detailed table of contents)

Abuse of dominant position 212,273-275
Access to third countries 181-187
Acquisition of domestic securities (see Capital)
After-sales market (see Car parts)
Agency (see Establishment)
Agreement on the European Economic Area 176
Allocation of resources 3,4,5,7
AM-market (see Merger Regulation)
Anti-dumping (see Dumping)
Anti-subsidy (see Subsidy)
Auto/Oil Programma 130,418
Automobile industry 29-64
-definition 20
-effect of single market programme 96
-global market 45-52
-role of the state 55-63
-overcapacity 24,40,344
-restructuring 22,24,344
-socio-economic significance 21,52-54

Benchmarking 406,407
Block exemption (see Distribution system for automobiles)
Branche (see Establishment)

Capital, free movement of 167-170
Captive market (see Car parts)
Car parts 156
-exercise of design and copyrights 156-158
-harmonisation of (industrial) design rights 158-165
-interconnection clause 160
-must-fit & must-match 160
-repair clause 160
-see Merger Regulation

Car tax (see Taxation-internal taxation)
CDK sets 192
Collectivist system 2,5,6
Combined tariff nomenclature 105
Common commercial policy 16,105,173-204
Common Customs Tariff 104-109
Common market 70,71,72,95,164,174,217
Community Customs Code 98,107,108
Competition policy (objectives) 7,16,191,197,205-210
Competition rules 205,210-214
Competitiveness (Policy on -) 16,18,19,191,395-409,426
Concentration and cooperation 343-394
Consumption tax (see Taxation-internal taxation)
Copyright (see Car parts)
Corporate Average Fuel Economy requirements (U.S.A.) 182
Craft production 24,29-31,45
Customs classification 107
Customs duties and charges having equivalent effect 102-104
Customs union 97-109
Customs union agreements 176

De minimis-rule 210-211 (see also State aid)
Design rights (see Car parts)
Direct investment (see Capital)
Distribution system for automobiles 199,200
-abuse of dominant position 270-275
-common marketing philosophy 215,216
-control by manufacturers 216
-costs 217
-early days 217-226
-pyramidal structure 215
-regulation 19/65 227,228
-regulation 123/85 (see Regulation 123/85)
-regulation 1475/95 (see Regulation 1475/95)
Dumping 175,184

INDEX

EC Treaty
-basic constitutional charter 65
-legal significance of preamble 67
-motives and ideals 65-66
Economic and monetary union 70,72-74
Economic integration
-regional 10
Economic law
-national 9,13
-international 9,10,13
Economic policy 1,3,6-8,12
-instrument 8-9
-measure 9
-ordering policy 8
-process policy 8
Economic value-added test (see Local content rule)
Education and vocational training of quality (Policy on -) 16,423-429
-ADAPT 428
-COMETT 427
-European Investment Bank 427
-European Regional Development Fund 427
-European Social Fund (see European Social Fund)
-EUROTECNET 427
-FORCE 427,428
-human resources policy 427
-Leonardo da Vinci program 428
-PETRA 427
-PME 428
-Task Force Human Resources 428
Effective competition 209,210
Elements of consensus (see Voluntary export restraints)
Environment
-policy 16
-various technical requirements 128-133
Establishment, right of 164-167,169,170

EU Treaty
-legal significance of preamble 66-68
-motives and ideals 65,66
European Community
-mixed economy 14,15,17
-policies and activities 15-17,20,21,24,75-78
-task 14,15,68-70
-means 70-71
European Programme on Engines, Fuels and Emissions 130
European Social Fund 423-427
Excise duty (see Taxation-internal taxation)
Export 175
-common rules 177-183
-access to third countries 178-183

Fordism (see Mass production)
Foreign direct investment 11
Fortress Europe 108
Framework directive (see Type-approval)
Free market economy 1-5
Free Trade Agreements 176

Gas Guzzler tax (U.S.A.) 182
GATT (see WTO Agreement)
GATT 1994 86,89
GATTs 86,88
Gemeinschaftstreue 78,79
Generalized System of Preferences (GSP) 108
Globalisation 12
-automobile industry 49-51
Great depression 2

High-level panel 406

Import

-common rules 183-202
-quota 56,57,184
-tariffs 56,57
Industrial design (see Car parts)
Industrial policy 7,12,18,19,395-409
Industrial revolution 1
Integration
-negative or market 17
-positive or policy 17
Interim Agreements 178
Intermediaries 200
Intellectual property rights
-abuse of dominant position 273-275
-car parts 154-164
Internal market 72
Internationalisation 12,13
-automobile industry 49-51
Intra-EU investment 167,168
Invisible hand 2,6

Japan (see also Lean production)
-trade imbalances 46
Just-in-time system (see Lean production)

Kanban system (see Lean production)
Keck-formula 110,111

Laissez-faire 1
Lean production 24,36-42,423,426
Liberal market (see Free market economy)
Local content rule 47,57,58,98-101,182(Brazil),192
Luxury tax (U.S.A.) 182

Mandatory technical requirements (see Type-approval)
Mass production 24,32-36,45

Merger Control 213,214,343-345
Merger Regulation 346-368
-AM-market 358-362,368
-application of Articles 85 and 86 EC 371-392
-concentration with Community dimension 346-350,369
-concentrations without Community dimenstion 369-374
-dominant position 352,353,363-368
-Dutch Clause 370
-internal market 346
-Form CO 351,355,360
-full-function joint venture 348,353,354,368
-national authorities 351,370
-number of mergers notified 349,350
-OE-market 358-362,367
-one-stop shop 350-352
-relevant geographical market 360-363
-relevant product market 354-360
Minimal state 1
Mixed economy 2,6,10
-European Community 14,15,17
-France 11,18
-Germany 12,18
-Spain 12
Model T or 'Thin Lizzie' (see Mass production-Ford)
Model year dates 112,113
Multi-nationals 11,22

Normal residence (see Registration of automobiles)

OE-market (see Merger Regulation)
On-board diagnostic 130

Package-theory 161,215
Permanent car importation 153
Protectionism 9,10,45,46,48,57

Public intervention 3,11

Quantitative restrictions and measures having equivalent effect 109-139

Regionalization 49
Registration duty (see Taxation-internal taxation)
Registration of automobiles 133-135
Regulation 2,5
Regulation 123/85 227-251
-activities outside contract territory 237
-agricultural machinery 233
-background 227-229
-category of agreements 231,234
-competing products 236,239
-concluding other agreements 236,237
-connected undertakings 233
-dealer 233
-demonstration models 240
-discounts 242
-effect 234,243,245-248
-exclusivity 231,232,242,243,247
-guarantee, free servicing and recall 240,241
-independent dealer 235
-intermediary 235,237,238
-leasing 233,238,239
-legal basis 227-231
-minimum standards dealer 239
-modification 235
-motorcycles 233
-new motor vehicles 232
-no application 244,245
-no-competition 234
-optional 234-236,243
-ordering dates 239
-parallel imports 235,237,248

-possible obligations on dealer 235-240
-preamble 229-231
-price differences 247,248
-review of Regulation 123/85 249-251
-role of national court 234
-sales target 240
-spare parts 232,233,240
-stock 240
-supplier 233
-supply model in contract programme 242
-supply to authorized reseller 237
-withdrawal 246-248
Regulation 1475/95 251-270
-activities outside contract territory 261
-background 251-258
-black clauses 267
-black list 264-268
-black practices 268
-category of agreements 259
-comparison with Regulation 123/85 257,258
-competing products 260-262
-concluding other agreements 261
-critical economist 255,256
-discriminatory prices and conditions 269
-effect 268
-EFTA Surveillance Authority 255
-evaluation 269
-expert third party 262
-Explanatory Brochure 258
-franchising 257,265
-guarantee, free service and recall 263
-intermediary 261,265
-lack of transparency 252,253
-leasing 262
-modification 260

-multi-brand 260,261
-new automobiles and spare parts therefor 259
-parallel import 266
-preamble 258,259
-price differences 269
-reinforced position of dealer 260-262
-resale 262
-role of national courts 258
-supply to authorized reseller 261
-termination 263,264
-withdrawal 268
Research and technological development (Policy on -) 16,411-421
-BCR 416
-BRITE/EURAM 416
-CRAFT 418
-DRIVE 416
-EPEFE (Auto/Oil) 418
-ESPRIT 417
-EUCAR Master Plan for R & D 419
-EUREKA 416
-initiatives 414,415
-JOULE 417
-MICROMOBILE 418
-multi-annual framework programme 413,414,416-420
-report 415
-role of the Member States 416
-specific programmes 414
-Targeted Research Actions on Environmentally Friendly Vehicle Technologies 418
-Task Force "The car of the Future" (see Task Force Car of Tomorrow)
-Technologies for Transport Means 418
-Telematics 418
-TP projects 417
Restrictive administrative practices 58,184
Restrictive agreements, decisions and practices 210-212

Road tax (see Taxation-internal taxation)
Roadworthiness tests 135-139
Rules of origin 98-102

Safeguard measures 175
Screw-driver plant (see Local content rule)
Single product theory (see Package theory)
State aid 212,213,277-341
-block exemption 301
-compatibility with common market 285-298
-concept 282-285
-*de minimis* 287,288
-distortion of competition 280
-environmental aid 295,323-325,339
-existing aid 299
-for domestic automobile industry 59,278-282
-frameworks 296-298
-1989 Framework on State Aid to the Motor Vehicle Industry 302-327
-1998 Framework for State Aid to the Motor Vehicle Industry 327-340
-guidelines 296-298
-infrastructure 286
-innovation, modernization or rationalization aid 295,320-321,338,339
-lack of transparency 277,278
-market economy investor principle 284,285
-new aid 299
-notification 299,311,312,330,331
-operating aid 326,327,339
-procedure 298-301
-project 294 -
-regional aid 292,293,316-319,333
-remedy of serious disturbance in the economy 294
-rescue or restructuring aid 294,313-316,333
-research and development aid 321-323,338
-review 298-301
-subsidy race 61

-to attract direct foreign investment 61
-variety 283,284
-vocational training aid 325,326,339
Structural Funds (see European Social Fund)
Subsidiary (see Establishment)
Subsidies (see State aid)

Taric 105
Tariff and trade agreements 101,108,176
Tariff classification 106,107
Tariff preferences 108,109
Task Force "The car of the Future" (see Task Force Car of Tomorrow)
Task Force Car of Tomorrow 130,419
Task Forces 405
Tax competition 141
Taxation
-incentives for domestic market 60
-internal taxation 139-154
-obstruction of imports 58
Technical barriers to trade 113-116
Technical requirements directives (see Type-approval)
Technical standards and regulations
- notification 114,115
- exchange of information 115
Temporary car importation 152
Toyota production system (see Lean production)
Trade Barriers Regulation 175,181
Trade protection measures 175
Transparency (lack of) 22
Transplants (see Local content rule)
TRIPs 86,88
Type-approval 57,116-133
-UN/ECE Agreement 178,179
-abuse of dominant position 271-273

Value-added test (see Local content rule)
VAT (see Taxation-internal taxation)
Virtual production 24,42-45
Visible hand 6
Voluntary export restraints
-Community/Japan 48,58,185-202
-SMMT/JAMA 58,186,195,200

Workable competition 207-209
WTO Agreement and GATT 24
-European Community and GATT 79-85
-European Community and WTO Agreement 86,87
-Impact within legal order of European Community 88-91
-Use of WTO dispute settlement system 181-183
-Voluntary export restraint Community/Japan 202

TABLES OF EQUIVALENCES REFERRED TO IN ARTICLE 12 OF THE TREATY OF AMSTERDAM

A. Treaty on European Union

Previous numbering	New numbering
Title I	Title I
Article A	Article 1
Article B	Article 2
Article C	Article 3
Article D	Article 4
Article E	Article 5
Article F	Article 6
Article F.1 ()	Article 7
Title II	Title II
Article G	Article 8
Title III	Title III
Article H	Article 9
Title IV	Title IV
Article I	Article 10
Title V (***)	Title V
Article J.1	Article 11
Article J.2	Article 12
Article J.3	Article 13
Article J.4	Article 14
Article J.5	Article 15
Article J.6	Article 16
Article J.7	Article 17
Article J.8	Article 18
Article J.9	Article 19
Article J.10	Article 20
Article J.11	Article 21
Article J.12	Article 22
Article J.13	Article 23
Article J.14	Article 24
Article J.15	Article 25
Article J.16	Article 26
Article J.17	Article 27
Article J.18	Article 28

(*) New Article introduced by the Treaty of Amsterdam
(***) Title restructured by the Treaty of Amsterdam

Previous numbering	New numbering
Title VI (***)	Title VI
Article K.1	Article 29
Article K.2	Article 30
Article K.3	Article 31
Article K.4	Article 32
Article K.5	Article 33
Article K.6	Article 34
Article K.7	Article 35
Article K.8	Article 36
Article K.9	Article 37
Article K.10	Article 38
Article K.11	Article 39
Article K.12	Article 40
Article K.13	Article 41
Article K.14	Article 42
Title VIa (**)	Title VII
Article K.15 ()	Article 43
Article K.16 (*)	Article 44
Article K.17 (*)	Article 45
Title VII	Title VIII
Article L	Article 46
Article M	Article 47
Article N	Article 48
Article O	Article 49
Article P	Article 50
Article Q	Article 51
Article R	Article 52
Article S	Article 53

B. Treaty Establishing the European Community

Previous numbering	New numbering
Part One	Part One
Article 1	Article 1
Article 2	Article 2
Article 3	Article 3
Article 3a	Article 4
Article 3b	Article 5
Article 3c ()	Article 6
Article 4	Article 7
Article 4a	Article 8
Article 4b	Article 9
Article 5	Article 10

(*) New Article introduced by the Treaty of Amsterdam
(**) New Title introduced by the Treaty of Amsterdam
(***) Title restructured by the Treaty of Amsterdam

Previous numbering	New numbering
Article 5a (*)	Article 11
Article 6	Article 12
Article 6a (*)	Article 13
Article 7 (repealed)	–
Article 7a	Article 14
Article 7b (repealed)	–
Article 7c	Article 15
Article 7d (*)	Article 16
Part Two	Part Two
Article 8	Article 17
Article 8a	Article 18
Article 8b	Article 19
Article 8c	Article 20
Article 8d	Article 21
Article 8e	Article 22
Part Three	Part Three
Title I	Title I
Article 9	Article 23
Article 10	Article 24
Article 11 (repealed)	–
Chapter 1	Chapter 1
Section 1 (deleted)	–
Article 12	Article 25
Article 13 (repealed)	–
Article 14 (repealed)	–
Article 15 (repealed)	–
Article 16 (repealed	–
Article 17 (repealed)	
Section 2 (deleted)	–
Article 18 (repealed)	–
Article 19 (repealed)	–
Article 20 (repealed)	–
Article 21 (repealed)	–
Article 22 (repealed)	–
Article 23 (repealed)	–
Article 24 (repealed)	–
Article 25 (repealed)	–
Article 26 (repealed)	–
Article 27 (repealed)	–
Article 28	Article 26
Article 29	Article 27
Chapter 2	Chapter 2
Article 30	Article 28
Article 31 (repealed)	–
Article 32 (repealed)	–

(*) New Article introduced by the Treaty of Amsterdam

Previous numbering	New numbering
Article 33 (repealed)	–
Article 34	Article 29
Article 35 (repealed)	–
Article 36	Article 30
Article 37	Article 31
Title II	Title II
Article 38	Article 32
Article 39	Article 33
Article 40	Article 34
Article 41	Article 35
Article 42	Article 36
Article 43	Article 37
Article 44 (repealed)	–
Article 45 (repealed)	–
Article 46	Article 38
Article 47 (repealed)	
Title III	Title III
Chapter 1	Chapter 1
Article 48	Article 39
Article 49	Article 40
Article 50	Article 41
Article 51	Article 42
Chapter 2	Chapter 2
Article 52	Article 43
Article 53 (repealed)	–
Article 54	Article 44
Article 55	Article 45
Article 56	Article 46
Article 57	Article 47
Article 58	Article 48
Chapter 3	Chapter 3
Article 59	Article 49
Article 60	Article 50
Article 61	Article 51
Article 62 (repealed)	–
Article 63	Article 52
Article 64	Article 53
Article 65	Article 54
Article 66	Article 55
Chapter 4	Chapter 4
Article 67 (repealed)	–
Article 68 (repealed)	–
Article 69 (repealed)	–
Article 70 (repealed)	–
Article 71 (repealed)	–
Article 72 (repealed)	–

Previous numbering	New numbering
Article 73 (repealed)	–
Article 73a (repealed)	–
Article 73b	Article 56
Article 73c	Article 57
Article 73d	Article 58
Article 73e (repealed)	–
Article 73f	Article 59
Article 73g	Article 60
Article 73h (repealed)	–
Title IIIa (**)	Title IV
Article 73i (*)	Article 61
Article 73j (*)	Article 62
Article 73k (*)	Article 63
Article 73l (*)	Article 64
Article 73m (*)	Article 65
Article 73n (*)	Article 66
Article 73o (*)	Article 67
Article 73p (*)	Article 68
Article 73q (*)	Article 69
Title IV	Title V
Article 74	Article 70
Article 75	Article 71
Article 76	Article 72
Article 77	Article 73
Article 78	Article 74
Article 79	Article 75
Article 80	Article 76
Article 81	Article 77
Article 82	Article 78
Article 83	Article 79
Article 84	Article 80
Title V	Title VI
Chapter 1	Chapter 1
Section 1	Section 1
Article 85	Article 81
Article 86	Article 82
Article 87	Article 83
Article 88	Article 84
Article 89	Article 85
Article 90	Article 86
Section 2 (deleted)	–
Article 91 (repealed)	–
Section 3	Section 2
Article 92	Article 87
Article 93	Article 88

(*) New Article introduced by the Treaty of Amsterdam
(**) New Title introduced by the Treaty of Amsterdam

Previous numbering	New numbering
Article 94	Article 89
Chapter 2	Chapter 2
Article 95	Article 90
Article 96	Article 91
Article 97 (repealed)	–
Article 98	Article 92
Article 99	Article 93
Chapter 3	Chapter 3
Article 100	Article 94
Article 100a	Article 95
Article 100b (repealed)	–
Article 100c (repealed)	–
Article 100d (repealed)	–
Article 101	Article 96
Article 102	Article 97
Title VI	Title VII
Chapter 1	Chapter 1
Article 102a	Article 98
Article 103	Article 99
Article 103a	Article 100
Article 104	Article 101
Article 104a	Article 102
Article 104b	Article 103
Article 104c	Article 104
Chapter 2	Chapter 2
Article 105	Article 105
Article 105a	Article 106
Article 106	Article 107
Article 107	Article 108
Article 108	Article 109
Article 108a	Article 110
Article 109	Article 111
Chapter 3	Chapter 3
Article 109a	Article 112
Article 109b	Article 113
Article 109c	Article 114
Article 109d	Article 115
Chapter 4	Chapter 4
Article 109e	Article 116
Article 109f	Article 117
Article 109g	Article 118
Article 109h	Article 119
Article 109i	Article 120
Article 109j	Article 121
Article 109k	Article 122

Previous numbering	New numbering
Article 109l	Article 123
Article 109m	Article 124
Title VIa (**)	Title VIII
Article 109n (*)	Article 125
Article 109o (*)	Article 126
Article 109p (*)	Article 127
Article 109q (*)	Article 128
Article 109r (*)	Article 129
Article 109s (*)	Article 130
Title VII	Title IX
Article 110	Article 131
Article 111 (repealed)	–
Article 112	Article 132
Article 113	Article 133
Article 114 (repealed)	–
Article 115	Article 134
Article 116 (repealed)	–
Title VIIa (**)	Title X
Article 116 ()	Article 135
Title VIII Chapter 1 (***)	Title XI Chapter 1
Article 117	Article 136
Article 118	Article 137
Article 118a	Article 138
Article 118b	Article 139
Article 118c	Article 140
Article 119	Article 141
Article 119a	Article 142
Article 120	Article 143
Article 121	Article 144
Article 122	Article 145
Chapter 2	Chapter 2
Article 123	Article 146
Article 124	Article 147
Article 125	Article 148
Chapter 3	Chapter 3
Article 126	Article 149
Article 127	Article 150
Title IX	Title XII
Article 128	Article 151

(*) New Article introduced by the Treaty of Amsterdam
(**) New Title introduced by the Treaty of Amsterdam
(***) Title restructured by the Treaty of Amsterdam

Previous numbering	New numbering
Title X	Title XIII
Article 129	Article 152
Title XI	Title XIV
Article 129a	Article 153
Title XII	Title XV
Article 129b	Article 154
Article 129c	Article 155
Article 129d	Article 156
Title XIII	Title XVI
Article 130	Article 157
Title XIV	Title XVII
Article 130a	Article 158
Article 130b	Article 159
Article 130c	Article 160
Article 130d	Article 161
Article 130e	Article 162
Title XV	Title XVIII
Article 130f	Article 163
Article 130g	Article 164
Article 130h	Article 165
Article 130i	Article 166
Article 130j	Article 167
Article 130k	Article 168
Article 130l	Article 169
Article 130m	Article 170
Article 130n	Article 171
Article 130o	Article 172
Article 130p	Article 173
Article 130q (repealed)	–
Title XVI	Title XIX
Article 130r	Article 174
Article 130s	Article 175
Article 130t	Article 176
Title XVII	Title XX
Article 130u	Article 177
Article 130v	Article 178
Article 130w	Article 179
Article 130x	Article 180
Article 130y	Article 181
Part Four	Part Four
Article 131	Article 182
Article 132	Article 183
Article 133	Article 184
Article 134	Article 185

Previous numbering	New numbering
Article 135	Article 186
Article 136	Article 187
Article 136a	Article 188
Part Five	Part Five
Title I	Title I
Chapter 1	Chapter 1
Section 1	Section 1
Article 137	Article 189
Article 138	Article 190
Article 138a	Article 191
Article 138b	Article 192
Article 138c	Article 193
Article 138d	Article 194
Article 138e	Article 195
Article 139	Article 196
Article 140	Article 197
Article 141	Article 198
Article 142	Article 199
Article 143	Article 200
Article 144	Article 201
Section 2	Section 2
Article 145	Article 202
Article 146	Article 203
Article 147	Article 204
Article 148	Article 205
Article 149 (repealed)	–
Article 150	Article 206
Article 151	Article 207
Article 152	Article 208
Article 153	Article 209
Article 154	Article 210
Section 3	Section 3
Article 155	Article 211
Article 156	Article 212
Article 157	Article 213
Article 158	Article 214
Article 159	Article 215
Article 160	Article 216
Article 161	Article 217
Article 162	Article 218
Article 163	Article 219
Section 4	Section 4
Article 164	Article 220
Article 165	Article 221
Article 166	Article 222
Article 167	Article 223

Previous numbering	New numbering
Article 168	Article 224
Article 168 a	Article 225
Article 169	Article 226
Article 170	Article 227
Article 171	Article 228
Article 172	Article 229
Article 173	Article 230
Article 174	Article 231
Article 175	Article 232
Article 176	Article 233
Article 177	Article 234
Article 178	Article 235
Article 179	Article 236
Article 180	Article 237
Article 181	Article 238
Article 182	Article 239
Article 183	Article 240
Article 184	Article 241
Article 185	Article 242
Article 186	Article 243
Article 187	Article 244
Article 188	Article 245
Section 5	Section 5
Article 188a	Article 246
Article 188b	Article 247
Article 188c	Article 248
Chapter 2	Chapter 2
Article 189	Article 249
Article 189a	Article 250
Article 189b	Article 251
Article 189c	Article 252
Article 190	Article 253
Article 191	Article 254
Article 191a (*)	Article 255
Article 192	Article 256
Chapter 3	Chapter 3
Article 193	Article 257
Article 194	Article 258
Article 195	Article 259
Article 196	Article 260
Article 197	Article 261
Article 198	Article 262
Chapter 4	Chapter 4
Article 198a	Article 263
Article 198b	Article 264
Article 198c	Article 265

(*) New Article introduced by the Treaty of Amsterdam

Previous numbering	New numbering
Chapter 5	Chapter 5
Article 198d	Article 266
Article 198e	Article 267
Title II	Title II
Article 199	Article 268
Article 200 (repealed)	–
Article 201	Article 269
Article 201a	Article 270
Article 202	Article 271
Article 203	Article 272
Article 204	Article 273
Article 205	Article 274
Article 205a	Article 275
Article 206	Article 276
Article 206a (repealed)	–
Article 207	Article 277
Article 208	Article 278
Article 209	Article 279
Article 209a	Article 280
Part Six	Part Six
Article 210	Article 281
Article 211	Article 282
Article 212 (*)	Article 283
Article 213	Article 284
Article 213a (*)	Article 285
Article 213b (*)	Article 286
Article 214	Article 287
Article 215	Article 288
Article 216	Article 289
Article 217	Article 290
Article 218 (*)	Article 291
Article 219	Article 292
Article 220	Article 293
Article 221	Article 294
Article 222	Article 295
Article 223	Article 296
Article 224	Article 297
Article 225	Article 298
Article 226 (repealed)	–
Article 227	Article 299
Article 228	Article 300
Article 228a	Article 301
Article 229	Article 302
Article 230	Article 303
Article 231	Article 304
Article 232	Article 305
Article 233	Article 306
Article 234	Article 307

(*) New Article introduced by the Treaty of Amsterdam

Previous numbering	New numbering
Article 235	Article 308
Article 236 (*)	Article 309
Article 237 (repealed)	–
Article 238	Article 310
Article 239	Article 311
Article 240	Article 312
Article 241 (repealed)	–
Article 242 (repealed)	–
Article 243 (repealed)	–
Article 244 (repealed)	–
Article 245 (repealed)	–
Article 246 (repealed)	–
Final Provisions	Final Provisions
Article 247	Article 313
Article 248	Article 314

(*) New Article introduced by the Treaty of Amsterdam